Russell, Idealism, and the Emergence
of Analytic Philosophy

£18

Russell, Idealism, and the Emergence of Analytic Philosophy

Peter Hylton

CLARENDON PRESS · OXFORD

Oxford University Press, Walton Street, Oxford OX2 6DP
Oxford New York
Athens Auckland Bangkok Bombay
Calcutta Cape Town Dar es Salaam Delhi
Florence Hong Kong Istanbul Karachi
Kuala Lumpur Madras Madrid Melbourne
Mexico City Nairobi Paris Singapore
Taipei Tokyo Toronto
and associated companies in
Berlin Ibadan

Oxford is a trade mark of Oxford University Press

Published in the United States by
Oxford University Press Inc., New York

British Library Cataloguing in Publication Data
Hylton, Peter
Russell, idealism, and the emergence of analytic
philosophy.
1. Analytic philosophy, history
I. Title
190'.9
ISBN 0-19-824018-X

Library of Congress Cataloging in Publication Data
Hylton, Peter.
Russell, idealism, and the emergence of analytic philosophy/
Peter Hylton.
Includes bibliographical references.
1. Russell, Bertrand 1872-1970—Contributions to emergence of
analytic philosophy. 2. Analysis (Philosophy)—History.
3. Idealism—History—20th century. I. Title.
B1649.R94H95 1990 146'.4—dc20 89-38213
ISBN 0-19-824018-X

3 5 7 9 10 8 6 4

Printed in Great Britain on acid-free paper by
Bookcraft (Bath) Ltd, Midsomer Norton, Avon

*To my mother, and
to the memory of my father*

Preface

This book arises out of an interest in the origins of analytic philosophy—that is, roughly, of the philosophical tradition which has been dominant in English-speaking countries for most of this century. My interest in the origins of this tradition arises, in turn, from the twofold reaction which I had to philosophy, beginning almost as early as my first serious study of the subject. On the one hand, it completely absorbed me. On the other hand, its inconclusiveness frustrated me: I was only too well aware of the vulnerability of any philosophical claim, and could not convince myself that my own views might somehow be exempt. During my second and third years of graduate study I began to work my way towards an escape from this intellectual *impasse*. I ceased to take the subject simply at (what seemed to me to be) its face value, as consisting of well-defined problems and attempts to solve them. I began, rather, to take seriously the fact that the formulation of a philosophical problem arises out of a particular historical context. So, gradually, I developed the idea of trying to understand analytic philosophy in this way, as an historically conditioned phenomenon. I hoped that such an approach might enable me to situate myself relative to the tradition. More ambitiously, I hoped that work of this sort might help the tradition to come to terms with its past, and thereby to achieve a new understanding of itself.

For one trained within the analytic tradition to study the history of that tradition might seem to be a small step. And so, in one sense, it is; certainly part of its attraction for me was precisely that the project did not involve a complete repudiation of what I had been taught. But in another sense it is a revolutionary move. Analytic philosophy has largely rejected historical modes of understanding. Attempts to apply that mode of understanding to analytic philosophy itself are so rare as to be almost non-existent. It struck me as strange that the period I write about, which was crucial to the formation of the analytic tradition, had been largely neglected. This neglect, however, is not accidental: it is the result of the general repudiation of the historical mode of understanding within analytic philosophy. In particular, analytic philosophy seems to think of itself as taking place within a single timeless moment. While this way of thinking may have its place, and may lead to interesting work, I want to insist that it is not the only way to think about philosophy. The experience of writing this book has reinforced me in my view that historical understanding need not be opposed to philosophical understanding, and that an historical approach to philosophy can bring a kind of insight, and a kind of self-knowledge, not otherwise available.

The book that follows is an attempt to illustrate and justify these ideas in what seems to me the only possible way—by carrying out a detailed historical study. The level of detail is crucial, for it is crucial that the reader should be able to understand unfamiliar ideas without simply assimilating them to the familiar. One point of the enterprise, after all, is to see how what is now familiar has developed out of something quite different. Only by achieving sufficient distance from current assumptions and methods can we begin to bring them into perspective. This is also one reason for beginning, as I do, with British Idealism, and going on to discuss in detail the Moore-Russell reaction against Idealism. (Another reason is simply that it is a fascinating story, which is almost unknown, except in broadest outline.) From there I discuss the development of Russell's thought in the period up to 1912, with some glimpses ahead. Even though the period is brief we do, I think, see many of the themes of later analytic philosophy being articulated, and many of its characteristic methods and problems being developed. (It should go without saying, but let me say it anyway: I do not think of myself as even attempting to give anything approaching a complete account of the origins of analytic philosophy.)

The material published here has been my primary intellectual concern for more than a dozen years. During that time I have greatly benefited from the advice and criticism that I received as I wrote and rewrote. Foremost among those to whom I am indebted is Burton Dreben. His powerful and perceptive criticism has influenced this work, for the good, beyond my power to measure; his belief in the project sustained me when my own was weak. I have also relied on the discussion, criticism, and support of four people who, like me, have benefited from Dreben's teaching: Michael Friedman, Warren Goldfarb, Bill Hart, and Thomas Ricketts. Stanley Cavell was a reader for the dissertation that was the seed from which this book grew; I thank him for his help, as well as for the inspiration of his writing. I had very useful correspondence with Leonard Linsky, especially about Russell's logic, and Thomas Baldwin, especially about G. E. Moore. At an early stage I had extensive and always fruitful conversations with Susan Neiman about the ideas now in the Introduction, and about Idealism. In addition, I am indebted to Frederick Beiser, Daniel Brudney, Francis Dauer, Noel Fleming, Christine Korsgaard, Hilary Putnam, John Rawls, David Sachs, Nathan Salmon, Hubert Schwyzer, and an anonymous reader for Oxford University Press. Here I have attempted to list only those who have read parts of the book in preparation and discussed in with me. Even so, I may well have omitted some people; I can only beg their forgiveness.

I have received excellent secretarial assistance from the staff of the Philosophy Department at the University of Californa, Santa Barbara, and I gratefully acknowledge it. In particular, I must mention Paula Ryan, who over the past few years has done all of the secretarial work on the book; her combination of cheerfulness and unfailing efficiency has made her a pleasure to work with. Bruce Johnsen did most of the work of compiling the bibliography and the index, and Jane Sessions assisted with proof-reading. I am particularly grateful to Lorna Clymer, who shared, and greatly lightened, my part of the burden of these tasks.

John and Muriel Ridland, and Dr Laurence Mamlet, kept me going through the difficult spring and summer during which the main text of the book was finally finished.

Those with whom I dealt at Oxford University Press were invariably courteous and tactful. In particular, I should like to thank Adam Hodgkin, who was the editor with whom I initially agreed upon publication; Jacqueline Pritchard, who was a meticulous copy-editor; and, especially, Angela Blackburn, who was the editor when the book was actually completed, and who played the largest role of seeing it safely through the Press.

I am indebted also to a number of institutions. Merton College, Oxford, the Mrs Giles Whiting Foundation, the American Council of Learned Societies, the Rockefeller Foundation, the National Endowment for the Humanities, and the Regents of the University of California, have all made it possible for me to take time away from teaching, time which was wholly or largely devoted to this work. The Academic Senate of the University of California Santa Barabara, and the Interdisciplinary Humanities Center of the same campus, made it possible to obtain assistance with the compilation of the bibliography and the index, and with the final proof-reading.

Portions of the first chapter of the book were published in the *History of Philosophy Quarterly*, under the title 'The Metaphysics of T. H. Green', and I am grateful to the editor for permission to use that material again. I am grateful also to the Russell Archives, at McMaster University for giving me access to, and permission to quote from, the unpublished work of Russell; and to the Syndics of Cambridge University Library for permission to quote from the unpublished work of G. E. Moore.

This book is dedicated to my parents, to whom I owe more than the usual unpayable filial debt. My father died while the book was at press; it is a particular sorrow to me that he did not see it in final form.

Preface to the Paperback Edition

I take this opportunity to correct a number of typographical errors. I should like to thank Stewart Candlish and Richard Creath, each of whom has drawn to my attention a number of such errors; I also thank Frances Morphy, my editor at Oxford.

P ETER H YLTON

April 1992

Contents

Abbreviations

A. & R.	F. H. Bradley, *Appearance and Reality* (Oxford: OUP, 1968; 1st edn. 1893).
CE	F. H. Bradley, *Collected Essays* (Oxford: OUP, 1969; 1st edn. 1935).
Critique of Pure Reason	I. Kant, *Critik der reinen Vernunft*, trans. as *Immanuel Kant's Critique of Pure Reason* by Norman Kemp Smith (London: Macmillan, 1968; 1st edn. of trans. 1929). I follow the usual practice of locating passages by the pagination of the 1st edn. of 1781 (A) or the 2nd edn. of 1787 (B) or both.
Dictionary	J. M. Baldwin (ed.), *Dictionary of Philosophy and Psychology* (New York: Macmillan, 1901–5).
E. & E.	G. E. Moore, 'Experience and Empiricism', *Proceedings of the Aristotelian Society* (1902–3), 80–95.
EIP	B. Russell, 'The Existential Import of Propositions', *Mind* (1905), repr. in Lackey, pp. 398–401.
Essay	J. Locke, *Essay concerning Human Understanding* (Oxford: OUP, 1975; 1st edn. 1690).
ETR	F. H. Bradley, *Essays on Truth and Reality* (Oxford: OUP, 1914).
FG	B. Russell, *An Essay on the Foundations of Geometry* (Cambridge: CUP, 1897).
Id.	G. E. Moore, 'Identity', *Proceedings of the Aristotelian Society* (1901–2), 103–27.
KAKD	B. Russell, 'Knowledge by Acquaintance and Knowledge by Description', *Proceedings of the Aristotelian Society*, NS 11 (1910–11), 108–28; repr. in *Mysticism and Logic* (New York: Longmans, Green & Co., 1918), pp. 209–32.
Lackey	B. Russell, *Essays in Analysis*, ed. D. Lackey (London: Allen & Unwin, 1973).

Leibniz	B. Russell, *The Philosophy of Leibniz* (Cambridge: CUP, 1897).
Marsh	B. Russell, *Logic and Knowledge*, ed. R. Marsh (London: Allen & Unwin, 1956).
ML	B. Russell, 'Mathematical Logic as Based on the Theory of Types', *American Journal of Mathematics*, 30 (1908), 222–62; repr. in Marsh, pp. 59–102, and van Heijenoort, pp. 152–82.
MPD	B. Russell, *My Philosophical Development* (London: Allen & Unwin, 1959).
MTCA	B. Russell, 'Meinong's Theory of Complexes and Assumptions', *Mind* (1904), 204–19, 336–54, 509–24; repr. in Lackey, pp. 21–76.
Nec.	G. E. Moore, 'Necessity', *Mind*, NS 9 (1900), 289–304.
NJ	G. E. Moore, 'The Nature of Judgment', *Mind* (1898), 176–93.
OD	B. Russell, 'On Denoting', *Mind*, NS 14 (1905), 479–93; repr. in Marsh, pp. 41–56, and Lackey, pp. 103–19.
OF	B. Russell, 'On Fundamentals' (unpublished), Russell Archives, McMaster University, Hamilton, Ontario.
OKEW	B. Russell, *Our Knowledge of the Exterior World as a Field for Scientific Method in Philosophy* (London: Allen & Unwin, 1914; rev. edn. 1926).
OM	B. Russell, 'On Matter' (unpublished), Russell Archives, McMaster University, Hamilton, Ontario.
OMD	B. Russell, 'On Meaning and Denotation' (unpublished), Russell Archives, McMaster University, Hamilton, Ontario.
PE	G. E. Moore, *Principia Ethica* (Cambridge: CUP, 1968; 1st edn. 1903).
PL	F. H. Bradley, *Principles of Logic* (Oxford: OUP, 1922; 1st edn. 1883).
PM	A. N. Whitehead and B. Russell, *Principia Mathematica* (Cambridge: CUP, 1910–13; 2nd edn. 1927).
Principles	B. Russell, *Principles of Mathematics* (London: Allen & Unwin, 1937; 1st edn. 1903).
Problems	B. Russell, *The Problems of Philosophy* (Oxford: OUP, 1952; 1st edn. 1912).

Prol. Eth.	T. H. Green, *Prolegomena to Ethics* (Oxford: OUP, 1883).
RSDP	B. Russell, 'The Relation of Sense-Data to Physics', *Scientia*, 4 (1914); repr. in *Mysticism and Logic* (New York: Longmans, Green & Co., 1918), pp. 145–79.
Studies	J. M. E. McTaggart, *Studies in the Hegelian Dialectic* (Cambridge: CUP, 1922; 1st edn. 1896).
ThK	B. Russell, *Theory of Knowledge*, vol. vii of *Russell's Collected Papers*, ed. Elizabeth Ramsden Eames with Kenneth Blackwell (London: Allen & Unwin, 1984).
Treatise	D. Hume, *Treatise of Human Nature* (Oxford: OUP 1968; 1st edn. 1739).
van Heijenoort	J. van Heijenoort (ed.), *From Frege to Gödel: A Source Book in Mathematical Logic* (Cambridge, Mass.: Harvard University Press, 1971; 1st edn. 1967).
Works	*The Works of Thomas Hill Green* (London: Longmans, Green & Co., 1911–18).

... we cannot learn philosophy; for where is it, who is in possession of it, and how shall we recognise it? We can only learn to philosophise, that is, to exercise the talent of reason, in accordance with its universal principles, on certain actually existing attempts at philosophy ...

(Kant, *Critique of Pure Reason*)

Introduction

It is, I think, a truism that one of the roots of twentieth-century analytic philosophy is the rejection of Idealism by Moore and Russell. The significance of this fact, however, is little examined. What can we learn about the early philosophy of Russell and Moore by placing it against its Idealist background? How exactly did the rejection occur? If we take this rejection as a more or less typical example of philosophical evolution or revolution, what can we infer? What, if anything, can we learn about analytic philosophy by taking seriously the fact that this is one of its points of origin? In so far as we are ourselves within the tradition of analytic philosophy, what can we learn about ourselves and our own philosophical instincts and practices? Such questions naturally suggest themselves on the basis of our initial truism. The rejection of Idealism by Russell and Moore would thus seem to be of evident interest to those who think of themselves as engaged in analytic philosophy. The period has none the less been the subject of relatively little sustained and careful examination; none, I think, which has in mind the sorts of questions that I have indicated. The primary aim of this book is to carry out such an examination. As my questions suggest, I think that such a study may be useful not merely as a means of understanding the relevant works of Russell and of Moore but also as a way of gaining perspective on the tradition of twentieth-century analytic philosophy, and thus of learning something about our own philosophical situation.

This book is a historical study of the influence of British Idealism on Bertrand Russell, of the rejection of Idealism by Moore and Russell, and of the subsequent development of Russell's thought to about 1913. In such a study, any stopping point is to some extent arbitrary. I have chosen 1913 because at this point the influence of Wittgenstein on Russell becomes important, which greatly complicates the story; and because after this point Russell ceases, for a time, to work on the issues which are, by his own account, philosophically most fundamental. My later discussions allude to Russell's 1918 lectures, 'The Philosophy of Logical Atomism', where he returns to such issues; but this work is not considered in detail. The book might be thought of as dealing with the background to Russell's Logical Atomism or, in part, to Wittgenstein's *Tractatus*. My concern is entirely with theoretical philosophy—metaphysics, logic, epistemology, and so on—and not at all with practical philosophy—ethics, political philosophy; there is a rather different historical story to be told about this latter subject. Within theoretical philosophy a particular interest of mine is in the incorporation into philosophy of the techniques of mathematical logic. These two points explain why it is the development of Russell's philosophy, rather than Moore's, that is my main subject.

Philosophy and Its History

I conceive of the primary task of this book as a historical and interpretative one. My subject is the development of certain views through time; my aim is to find the best interpretation that I can of the texts that I discuss, where the criteria for 'best interpretation' have to do with being true to the text, and to the context in which it was written. If this book were an essay in the history of biology, say, or of any one of a number of subjects other than philosophy, it would probably be completely otiose to make this point. History of philosophy, however, occupies a peculiar, and peculiarly uneasy, position. Works in the history of philosophy, perhaps especially in the analytic tradition, are frequently presented as being in the same genre as the texts which they discuss:[1] as having the discussion of philosophical problems, rather than historical understanding, as their main aim. This is, moreover, not simply a matter of self-presentation: in many cases it is natural for the reader to agree that the ostensibly historical work is also—or instead—philosophical. This is, or ought to be, quite puzzling. A physicist, say, would not, except under the most extraordinary circumstances, think of looking to the history of eighteenth-century physics for insight into the current problems of physics. Why is philosophy different? How can a piece of the history of philosophy also be a piece of philosophy? Connected with this: why is the past of philosophy still relevant to its present?

There is one kind of answer to the question, how the history of philosophy can be philosophical, which, I think, commands wide, though usually tacit, assent. According to this answer, much of the history of philosophy is philosophy because it is not really history— not, that is to say, really concerned with the unfolding of events in

---

[1] For an explicit statement to this effect, see Bernard Williams, *Descartes, The Project of Pure Enquiry* (London: Pelican Books, 1978), p. 9.

time, and the connections between those events. The practitioners of this subject will typically concede that there is also at least the possibility of a genuinely historical study; but this subject, so the story goes, is not of philosophical interest. Rorty has expressed this sort of distinction between types of history of philosophy as follows:[2]

There seems to be a dilemma: either we anachronistically impose enough of our own problems and vocabulary on the dead to make them conversational partners, or we confine our interpretive activity to making their falsehoods look less silly by placing them in the context of the benighted times in which they were written.

Those alternatives, however, do not constitute a dilemma. We should do both of these things, but do them separately.

Rorty's distinction is not one that I can accept. There are not two separate and theoretically distinct kinds of history of philosophy, but only different emphases and purposes. (The history of philosophy is in this way like the history of any other human activity.) Even the most ahistorical history presumably aims at understanding the texts that are its subject, and understanding requires that the works be interpreted by being read in context.[3] It is in one sense trivial that anything I can understand is intelligible to me in my terms, for how could I understand something phrased in terms that were not mine? A historical investigation worthy of the name, however, does not take those terms as fixed at the outset; on the contrary, much of the investigation consists precisely in making certain terms one's own. The alternative to imposing 'our own problems and vocabulary' is not the absurdity of using another vocabulary (which, by supposition, we do not understand).[4] It is, rather, letting one's own vocabulary, one's own assumptions and formulations, be modified, at least for the moment, by those

[2] Richard Rorty, 'The Historiography of Philosophy: Four Genres', in Richard Rorty, J. B. Schneewind, and Quentin Skinner (eds), *Philosophy in History* (Cambridge: CUP, 1984), p. 49. I discuss Rorty in this context because he seems to me to articulate ideas which are often presupposed.

[3] In a somewhat different context, Rorty cites Davidson in defence of the idea that understanding requires this sort of interpretation or reinterpretation. See ibid. p. 55 and n. 3; also *Philosophy and the Mirror of Nature* (Princeton: Princeton University Press, 1979), especially Ch. VI.

[4] In a footnote to the article cited, Rorty seems to concede that the idea of a purely antiquarian history of philosophy, which occupies one side of his dichotomy, is incoherent; he also suggests that the historical side of the dichotomy cannot exist without attention to context. It is in fact somewhat unclear what claim he is making that is *not* withdrawn by this footnote. See op. cit. n. 2 above, pp. 52–3, n. 1.

of the author one is reading.[5] To read a philosophical text from the past (or even from the present) is to attempt to learn how the author thinks of philosophy, of its problems, of the means available for solving those problems, and so on. Reading such a text is in some ways analogous to reading a work in a language which overlaps but also differs from one's own. (Compare reading Chaucer, or even Milton. Compare also teaching logic to the uninitiated: does one address them in their terms or attempt to impose an alien vocabulary upon them?—Of course one begins by talking in their terms, but one inducts them into the alien vocabulary.) To say that this is to be done by placing the words one reads within their context is, again, a triviality. There are serious questions as to how much of the context will be relevant, how far we may simply assume that it is the same as our own, and so on. It is characteristic of much history of philosophy written within the analytic tradition to presuppose that very little of the context is relevant, that the problems and assumptions of another age are to be assumed to be the same as ours except where this is manifestly impossible; and so on—in short, to make history as ahistorical as possible. This practice, however, cannot be defended by claiming that there is a quite different sort of history being practised. Its defence must rather appeal to the purposes the history is intended to serve—a matter to which we shall return.

What gives the history of philosophy a peculiar status is not the problem of understanding the text. Perhaps philosophy is particularly difficult in this regard, but the kind of understanding sought is akin to that of any other kind of history; there is no particular reason for the historian of philosophy, rather than the historian of physics, say, to be bullied by the question: do we understand them in our terms or in theirs? What makes the history of philosophy clearly different in kind from the history of physics is the use to which this understanding is put. Relative to the practice of physics, the history of physics (at least of physics before the twentieth century) is a disinterested activity. Whatever the historian learns about eighteenth-century physics will make no difference to physics as it is currently practised.[6] Philosophy, by contrast, typically looks to its past as a source both of intellectual inspiration and of intellectual competition. In studying Kant, say, or

[5] This point is, I think, connected with a feature of the history of science that Kuhn has emphasized. He claims that what is most philosophically significant about the history of science *cannot* be captured by narrative history, but can only be learnt by doing the sort of work that must be done by one who would write such a history. See the Preface to *The Essential Tension* (Chicago: University of Chicago Press, 1977), p. x; see also p. 16 of that work.

[6] Compare Kuhn, op. cit. n. 5 above, p. 120.

Aristotle or Hume, one may find a context which enables one to reconceive some current question. Or the past may threaten the current understanding of some problem; it may subvert our conception of what the real issues, and the real problems, are. This holds not only for the most recent history of philosophy but for almost any period: it thus marks a distinction between philosophy and the natural sciences.

I am assuming that there is a clear contrast between the way we think about the history of philosophy and the way we think about the history of science. I also assume that this is not simply a mistake on our part, but is based on differences between the subjects themselves. This latter claim seems to be denied by Rorty, who urges us to think about the histories of the subjects in the same way:

> We should treat the history of philosophy as we treat the history of science. In the latter field, we have no reluctance in saying that we know better than our ancestors what they were talking about. We do not think it anachronistic to say that Aristotle had a false model of the heavens.... We should be equally willing to say that Aristotle was unfortunately ignorant that there are no such things as real essences, or Leibniz that God does not exist, or Descartes that the mind is just the central nervous system under another description. We hesitate merely because we have colleagues who are themselves ignorant of such facts, and whom we courteously describe not as 'ignorant', but as 'holding different philosophical positions'. Historians of science have no colleagues who believe in crystalline spheres.... (loc. cit.)

Rorty's prescription for the study of the history of philosophy clearly depends upon the idea that the historian knows better than did the original author—knows the truth, indeed—about the issues which the texts discuss.[7] This assumption, however, seems questionable. Do we really hold our philosophical views with the same confidence with which we believe that the perceived motions of the sun, moon, planets, and stars have nothing to do with crystalline spheres?

---

[7] This view might be thought to come oddly from Rorty, whose *Philosophy and the Mirror of Nature* is usually understood as putting forward a sceptical historicist and even relativistic view of philosophy. The book seems to me, however, not relativistic about crucial points. Thus Rorty argues for, and claims to have shown, for example, that 'Unless we wish to revive the seventeenth century's somewhat awkward and inconsistent use of the Aristotelian notion of "substance" we shall not make sense of the notion of two ontological realms—the mental and the physical' (p. 125). Rorty does not present this conclusion as a relativistic one; and he argues for it in much the fashion that other contemporary philosophers argue for their conclusions. There is a relativistic air to the concession that we may, after all, *wish* to revive the 17th century's use of the Aristotelian notion of substance: he does not present himself as having *refuted* the 17th-century view. This air of relativism (and thus of being above the fray) strikes me, however, as spurious: if one has shown that a view is 'somewhat awkward and inconsistent', and shown, moreover, that we can manage perfectly well without it, this surely is a refutation in all but name.

The question, whether there is progress in philosophy, is notoriously controversial and difficult. What should not be controversial, however, is that philosophy is not progressive in the way that the natural sciences often are. One basis for this claim is the undeniable fact that philosophers disagree with one another, not occasionally, or when one party is incompetent, or when the discipline is at crisis point, but routinely. These disagreements, moreover, are not merely about the truth of a given question but also about such things as how the question is to be stated, what would count as a satisfactory answer, which questions are basic and which may comfortably be left unanswered, and so on. That there are such disagreements is not a fact of nature which exists independent of conscious human decisions. It exists because we continue to tolerate such divergent views in the graduate students whom we train, and in the colleagues whom we hire. This tolerance, again, is presumably not an adventitious fact, but stems from some recognition that a reasonable and well-trained philosopher may disagree with us over fundamental philosophical questions (whereas a reasonable and well-trained scientist may not disagree with his or her colleagues over the existence of crystalline spheres). Now it is of course open to someone to claim that the fact of disagreement is not intrinsic to the subject, that the subject has at last found, or is about to find, the sure path of a science. This is a claim that does not lack for precedent; in the nature of the case, however, the existence of precedents must be more discouraging than encouraging. Nothing that one can say will show that the moment has not arrived when the disagreements of the past are to be put behind us: induction is not deduction. Such a view, however, must rest in part on faith, or narrowing of vision.

Rorty's comparison of the history of science and the history of philosophy seems to me to ignore a crucial disanalogy. Philosophy cannot, as the natural sciences perhaps can, absorb what is correct in its past and conclusively refute what is incorrect, for the difference is unsettled. There is as little finality in our views as to what is correct in the philosophies of Plato or Hume or Kant or Russell as there is in our views on the most contemporary issue. (There would even be disagreement over whether the question, what is correct in the philosophy of Plato?, is a sensible or coherent one.) Philosophy thus always has the hope of learning neglected lessons from its past. It also, and perhaps more characteristically, is always in a state of potential rivalry with its past, defining itself against its past, and threatened by it. It is for this reason that the history of philosophy often has an evaluative and judgemental tone—precisely *not* the tone of one who has a secure understanding of the matters at issue, but the tone of one whose understanding is threatened. The deliberately ahistorical character of much history of philosophy seems to me not accidental, but a product of this insecure relationship between philosophy and its past. We approach the past ahistorically in order to refute it—as if the past of philosophy will not stay in the past, but constantly threatens to come back to life. Our uncertainty over the status of the history of philosophy—whether it is history, whether it is philosophy, whether it can be both—seems to correspond to the uneasiness of the relation between philosophy and its past, and to our unease about the status of the subject as a whole.

Reading Russell in Context

My purpose in this book is not one of those which I have mentioned as being the typical purposes of the history of philosophy. My aim is not to refute the views of Russell, or of the other authors whom I discuss. Neither is it to suggest that their way of understanding the problems of philosophy, or their way of solving them, may be in any direct way superior to those current today. My aim in the first instance is to advance an interpretation of the texts which I discuss—texts that seem to me for the most part unduly neglected. In doing this, as will emerge, I hope to suggest a certain view of philosophy, a view which emphasizes that a philosophical work is partly to be understood by understanding the philosophical context against which it was written. Since the texts that I discuss represent one of the points of departure of analytic philosophy, my discussion is intended also to contribute to this sort of historical understanding of our own philosophical position.

Since my primary aim is not refutation or appropriation, I attempt as far as possible to explain the point of view of the author under dis-cussion—to act as the author's advocate, so to speak. This does not mean that I suppress criticism of the works that I discuss, but it does mean that my primary interest in discussing potential weaknesses of various views is in seeing how they lead to changes of doctrine, in the given author or in his successors. Thus I discuss criticisms which various philosophers made of one another: Green of Kant, Bradley of Green, Moore and Russell of Idealism as a whole. And in discussing any given author I emphasize those which would have seemed press-ing to him. In the case of Russell, in particular, understanding such criticisms often leads to an understanding of the way in which his philosophy evolved. (Thus I do not give detailed criticisms of Bradley, say, because it seems to me that the reaction against his views by

Moore and Russell does not at all depend on detailed difficulties of his view, but is rather a wholesale rejection of its most general outline. This may of course be incorrect; here I am only concerned to indicate the task that I have set myself.) As any historian of philosophy must, I give much space and weight to argument: philosophy is enunciated in argument. But my concern is always with the context or the presuppositions of an argument, what makes it convincing to its author but not, very often, to others (and, especially in Russell's case, what makes it convincing to him at one moment and not at another).

Because criticism is not my primary aim, my interpretation is more self-consciously historical and contextual than is the case with most history of philosophy written from within the analytic tradition. In the second half of this book we discuss, at least in outline, many of the ideas for which Russell is best known: the attempt to reduce mathematics to logic; the theory of types; the theory of descriptions, and the associated idea of an incomplete symbol; the multiple relation theory of judgement; the attempt to define truth in terms of correspondence with fact; and the project of constructing our knowledge of the external world on the basis of our knowledge of sense-data (and of abstract objects). Although these ideas are well known, and still discussed, they are seldom put in context. There is a tendency among those interested in Russell's philosophy to study it as if it began in earnest in 1905, with a single idea (the theory of descriptions, contained in 'On Denoting'), and then was diverted into a concern with logic which is more or less irrelevant to philosophy, and then resumed with *The Problems of Philosophy* in 1912.[8] Russell's work before 1905 is largely ignored, and the influence of Idealism on Russell, though acknowledged, is in practice seldom taken into account. As I see the matter, however, Idealism, and the need to refute it, forms a crucial context of this period of Russell's work, and needs to be considered in some detail. A second sort of context is equally crucial, and also largely neglected by those concerned with Russell's philosophy. This context is provided by Russell's development of mathematical logic, and in particular by the project of reducing mathematics to logic.[9] From Au-

---

[8] Thus David Pears's *Bertrand Russell and the British Tradition in Philosophy* (London: Fontana, 1972; 1st edn. 1967) deals with Russell's philosophy 1905–19 (see p. 11). I think it is also fair to say that the works which it discusses in detail, apart from 'On Denoting', date from 1912 or later.

[9] There are commentators for whom Russell's logic is the main focus of interest; their concern in general has been to appropriate the achievement of *Principia Mathematica*, rather than to understand Russell's work in context.

gust 1900 until the completion of *Principia Mathematica* in 1910 Russell
was both a metaphysician and a working logician. The two are completely intertwined in his work: metaphysics was to provide the basis
for logic; logic and logicism were to be the basis for arguments for the
metaphysics. How far Russell succeeded in bringing the logic and the
metaphysics together into a coherent whole is of course open to question; the attempt, however, was central to Russell's thought in this
period.

Both Idealism and logic are, I think, unduly neglected as contexts
for Russell's work in the period which is my concern. Let us briefly
consider some examples which will indicate why I take it to be
important to read that work to its context. To begin with, the neglect of
the context has resulted in what I see as significant distortions of
Russell's thought. Perhaps the most striking distortion is that Russell is
taken to be centrally concerned with knowledge and with 'the challenge of scepticism'.[10] More particularly, Russell is interpreted both as
influenced by the British empiricist philosophers (especially Hume)
and as being himself an Empiricist. Thus Pears says that he devotes
considerable space to Hume's philosophy 'in order to show how Russell's developed out of it' (p. 11) and claims that '[c]ertainly the truest
single thing that can be said about Russell's philosophy is that it stands
in the direct line of descent from Hume' (p. 268). These claims are
misleading about Russell's thought of the period before the First World
War. Furthermore they threaten to distort our view of earlier British
Empiricism. In Russell's thought throughout this period abstract (non-
physical, non-mental) entities are freely postulated to explain the possibility of any sort of assertion or thought; such entities are also invoked
to explain the possibility of logic and mathematics; and these latter
subjects are crucial to his thought. To assimilate such a view to the
Empiricism of Hume or J. S. Mill must distort both of the views being
compared. Such distortion has an effect which is of particular interest
from our point of view. Over the period which is discussed in this
book, Russell's views shift, from a view which has nothing at all in
common with the tradition of British Empiricism to a view which
shares some important elements with that tradition, though still differing from it in crucial ways. Now if one simply begins by assimilating
Russell to the empiricist tradition, one loses the possibility of asking
the question: why, in response to what intellectual pressures, does

---

[10] This phrase is the title of the first and introductory chapter of A. J. Ayer's *Russell
and Moore: The Analytical Heritage* (London: Macmillan, 1973; 1st edn. 1971).

Russell's view change in this way? It is precisely this sort of develop-
mental question that I wish to leave room for.[11]

A second kind of example is more significant for my purposes. This
is not an example of a misreading of Russell but of a claim made or
assumed by Russell, a claim whose significance is easily overlooked or
underestimated by the modern reader. From the time of his rejection of
Idealism onwards he takes it that truth is an absolute concept: either a
thing is true or it is not, there can be no qualifications, and no degrees;
and also that there are entities, independently identifiable, each of
which has the property that it is either absolutely and unqualifiedly
true or equally absolutely false. These are philosophical claims, as
much as any others: they are not given immediately as soon as one
thinks, nor are they ineluctably presupposed in our ordinary thought
and speech (even analytic philosophers, when truth is not the subject,
are prone to speak of one thing being more true than another; we just
saw Pears call one claim about Russell 'the truest', and such language
is in fact perfectly normal). This claim or assumption is largely hidden
from the modern reader in the analytic tradition by the fact that such a
reader has been educated to make the same assumption—to see it,
indeed, as inevitable, and so not an assumption at all. The comparison
with Idealism forces the assumption into the open. More generally:
understanding the intellectual competition facing Russell gives one a
clearer sense of the depth, and the boldness, of his work. A moral
about logic can also be drawn. What I have called Russell's assumption
is required for ordinary truth-functional logic. For the modern reader
this may simply contribute to the idea that there is no alternative to the
assumption, but for Russell the assumption and modern logic were
part of a single controversial philosophical view. He held that we have
more reason to accept the assumption because it is required for logic.
We can see that it shows that logic, in Russell's hands, was not a
philosophically neutral tool, but a source of philosophical claims and of
reasons for those claims. Our example, finally, seems to show something about us, or at least about the reader I have postulated: that we
do tend to make the Russellian assumption; that we are not conscious
of it as an assumption; and that we do take logic as a philosophically
neutral tool.

A third kind of example will illustrate a different point. Let us briefly
consider some of the salient features of the dispute between Russell

---

[11] Another example of the same kind is the concern with language, in the sense of
symbolism. Such a concern is often read back into Russell's early thought, which not
only distorts it but also prevents the question: how does this concern evolve?

and Bradley over the reality of relations. One might be inclined to treat this dispute as if there were some quite definite proposition which Russell asserted and Bradley denied. But even the attempt to find a neutral form of words in which to state the issue begins to cast this in doubt. Suppose that we state that relations are real, and that some (irreducibly) relational propositions are true.[12] Russell would, of course, straightforwardly assent to these statements. Bradley, however, would not straightforwardly deny them. He would say that in some sense they are correct. Relational propositions may be true—true to some extent, that is. Bradley does not deny that I can correctly assert that my coffee-cup is on the desk (nor does he think, as Russell often suggests, that this assertion is reducible to non-relational assertions about my cup and my desk). He would deny only that such assertions are capable of ultimate or complete truth; they may be partially or relatively true, they are certainly useful, even indispensable, but their truth is relative only. Russell, of course, would dismiss the attempt to distinguish relative truth from absolute truth as mere sophistry. For him truth is truth, and does not come in degrees. The point here is that even in trying to say what is being disputed in the dispute over relations we are forced to use terms, such as 'true', or 'real', which are themselves the subjects of philosophical dispute. Nor can we happily say that relations are one thing and truth another, and that the two issues should be dealt with one by one. The two issues are too intimately bound up for that. If one attributes a Russellian view of truth to Bradley, his views on relations become absurd, as Bradley himself would acknowledge; it is equally absurd to suppose that we can discuss the dispute over relations while leaving the nature of truth as an open question, to be resolved later. An attempt to formulate the differences between Bradley and Russell over the nature of truth will encounter the same problems as the attempt to formulate the issue of relations: other doctrines of each philosopher are at once involved. Most obviously, perhaps, Bradley's views about truth are governed by a vision of what it would be to find the world perfectly intelligible, coherent, and consistent. In Russell's philosophy either there is no corresponding concern, or else it manifests itself in such a different way that the correspondence is far from apparent. Bradley's view of a perfectly coherent world also connects directly with his denial of relations. To acknowledge the ultimate reality of relations would, he

---

[12] This way of putting the matter has usually been adopted by those who approach it from a Russellian point of view, for it seems to put Bradley in the position of denying an obvious truth. See e.g. Sainsbury, *Russell* (London: Routledge & Kegan Paul, 1979), p. 236.

argues, be to admit an element which is not fully intelligible, and which is thus incompatible with the perfect coherence of the world. Bradley's views about relations are, again, informed by a concern with the nature of experience, in a sense of 'experience' in which the nature of experience and the nature of the world are not completely distinct issues. Russell, in the relevant period, would deny that there is any such sense of 'experience', and is not concerned with the nature of experience in any sense. Russell's views about relations and truth are, in turn, affected and supported by his reliance on mathematics as a paradigm of truth whose objectivity and consistency are beyond question. For Bradley, mathematics does not possess this paradigmatic status, but is simply one more branch of human knowledge, of no particular philosophical interest. For both Bradley and Russell the question of the reality of relations is connected with issues of the nature and possibility of unity—especially the unity of diverse elements in the proposition. Bradley finds this issue intractable, and this is, I think, essential to his denial of the reality of relations. Russell finds it no less intractable, but is content to leave it as an unsolved problem within his philosophy, without letting it affect his insistence on the reality of relations. Both Bradley and Russell, finally, are responding, in their views about relations, to other philosophers. Bradley is responding to the sort of neo-Hegelianism, or Hegelian version of Kantianism, which is found in T. H. Green. His denial of the ultimate reality of relations is to be understood as a reaction to what can be seen as an equivocation or incoherence in that philosophy. Russell, of course, is responding primarily to Bradley himself.

The above example indicates the complexity of what might appear to be a straightforward issue. For both Russell and Bradley, the question of the reality of relations is bound up with a philosophical view as a whole. This complexity gives Bradley's claim, and Russell's response, its philosophical point, and makes neither the claim nor the response trivial. It also begins to explain the peculiar intractability of this and other philosophical issues, and why philosophers so often seem to talk past one another, to speak to different issues or concerns even when they use the same words. What a 'philosophical view' is, and what it is to hold one, is not as simple a matter as might be thought. Bradley held one view about relations, and Russell held another. What makes these statements more than biographical remarks is the fact that in each case, as indicated, the 'view' is intimately connected with other doctrines of the philosopher, his historical position, and his general philosophical and intellectual outlook. Understanding a philosophical view is similarly bound up with understanding such factors.

Analytic Philosophy and Its History

I have said that my purpose in this book is neither to compete with the texts that I discuss nor to draw any direct philosophical lessons from them. It ought not to be controversial that the history of philosophy can be done without these aims. Philosophical problems, and the concepts in which they are formulated, and the assumptions on which they rest, have a history; and this history is surely a legitimate subject of study. What is likely to be controversial is the interest of such a study. It may be said that in so far as the study is genuinely historical it is of no particular *philosophical* interest. Such a remark seems to me to display an unjustifiable dogmatism about what philosophy is, and about one's own right to speak for it. (As the characteristic emphasis on the word 'philosophical' suggests, such dogmatism may overlie a deeper insecurity.) The nature of philosophy is, after all, itself a substantive philosophical issue on which there has been much disagreement. This fact argues that we should not be too quick to decide about what is and what is not of philosophical interest. It also indicates one of the ways in which the history of philosophy may be clearly relevant to philosophy.

Over the last thirty years the work of a number of historians and philosophers of science—Kuhn being perhaps the most notable—has made it all but undeniable that the history of science has much to teach us about science itself: that the history of science is relevant to the philosophy of science. Similarly, studying the history of philosophy at a given period has much to teach us about the nature of philosophy, at least as it was practised in that period: it may suggest a view of the nature of philosophy and of philosophical understanding. Such a view was suggested by the final example of the last section, with its emphasis on the need to see Russell's opinion about relations within the context both of his view as a whole and of his reaction to Bradley. This sort of view of philosophy cannot be be established by direct argument, but by the accumulated weight of instances in which it is shown that a given form of words conveys the philosophical view or problem that it does only because of the context within which and the background against which it is written. My concern is to articulate the conditions under which such words have significance, and to indicate the role that their context and their historical position has in constituting that significance.

Here, then, is a general way of thinking about how a study such as the present work could indeed be of philosophical interest. What the history of science has to teach us is unlikely to be relevant to science;

but what the history of philosophy has to teach us about philosophy will be relevant to philosophy. One way to put this is to say that philosophy of science is not science, but philosophy of philosophy *is* philosophy. At least since the meta-critical attack on Kant, philosophers have recognized the need to account for the status of their own work.[13] This is not only because of the generality of the subject. Because philosophy is not progressive in the way that the sciences are, it is a subject in which the meaningfulness of its terms and the correctness of its procedures is always at issue. There is no distinction between substantive questions and questions of method because there is no agreed framework within which problems can be addressed while leaving method to one side. The distinction between philosophy and meta-philosophy is not a useful one. No line has been drawn, and if one were drawn then we should find that the supposed meta-issues would constantly arise within the practice of the subject.[14]

Besides the general idea that the history of philosophy may have something to teach us about the nature of the subject, there is also a more particular point to be made in connection with twentieth-century analytic philosophy. In speaking of analytic philosophy here I have in mind that tradition which looks for inspiration to the works of Frege, of Russell, and of Carnap. Salient features of this tradition are its employment of mathematical logic as a tool, or method, of philosophy; its emphasis on language and meaning; its generally atomistic and empiricist assumptions; and the fact that many of its practitioners have viewed science, especially physics, as a paradigm of human knowledge (and, like many earlier philosophers, have taken knowledge rather than, say, art or human relations or politics to be the paradigmatic field for the exercise of human reason). Like other philosophical traditions, this one can be understood more or less narrowly. Taken broadly, as including both those who define themselves by opposition to the sorts of ideas mentioned above and those who see themselves as modifying such ideas, the tradition has been and continues to be dominant in the leading English-speaking universities. A distinctive characteristic of the tradition, more narrowly conceived, is the hope that the logic of Frege and Russell would enable us to find an agreed framework or method for philosophy, and that philosophy would thus achieve something

---

[13] For discussion of the meta-critical attack, see Frederick C. Beiser, *The Fate of Reason* (Cambridge, Mass.: Harvard University Press, 1987).

[14] Compare Cavell, *Must We Mean What We Say?* (New York: Charles Scribner's Sons, 1969), Foreword, p. xviii. In thinking about philosophy and its history I am generally indebted to Cavell's work, and especially to that piece of writing.

like the status of a science.[15] (The emergence of the idea of such a method is an important theme of the second half of this book; see especially Chapter 8, Section 2.) This hope has not been realized. Perhaps the correct method has been discovered, but there is no *agreed* method.

Among those who are clearly within the tradition of analytic philosophy, there are various reactions to the failure of the tradition to find an agreed method which would set the subject on the sure path of a science. One is perhaps a non-reaction or refusal to react: to focus on individual 'problems', taken more or less as given, and to attempt to 'solve' them by whatever means may seem appropriate, without general methodological reflection. There are also those who continue to look for a method; or, more often, to insist that the correct method has been found, and that those who fail to recognize this fact are simply mistaken. Another reaction is to say that analytic philosophy has ended, and will be replaced by a rather different sort of philosophical tradition which will evolve or is evolving.[16] Again there are those who accept that analytic philosophy has failed, and take this failure as the failure of philosophy *tout court*. Here it sometimes seems as if the role left to philosophy is that of proving that it does not exist.[17]

This book represents a different sort of reaction to the failure of analytic philosophy to achieve the goal which inspired it. It is intended neither as a repudiation of analytic philosophy nor as a work which straightforwardly draws its problems and assumptions and methods from that tradition. It is, rather, part of an attempt to come to terms with the tradition, and with our own relation to it, by understanding it historically.

During the relatively brief period discussed by this book one can see the development, within Russell's thought, of fundamental ideas about

---

[15] This view of analytic philosophy is, I think, consonant with that of Putnam, that analytic philosophy was driven by the ambitious programmes of Logical Atomism and Logical Positivism; see his *Philosophical Papers, vol. iii* (Cambridge: CUP, 1983), p. 303. Rorty's description of the distinctively post-Fregean subject of 'pure philosophy of language' uses a concept of systematization which depends entirely upon quantification theory; see op. cit. n. 3 above, p. 257.

[16] Rorty suggests just this in *Philosophy and the Mirror of Nature* (op. cit. n. 3 above); see Ch. VIII, especially p. 394. Rorty's tone here bespeaks a curiously detached attitude towards the evolution of new philosophical ideas, as if it were a process that proceeded quite independently of him and of his writing.

[17] The work of Quine requires special mention here. He argues that what is worth having of philosophy has the same status as natural science. Those who take a distinction between philosophy and science as axiomatic will see this argument as claiming that there is no philosophy; but clearly Quine would not agree. These issues come to the surface most explicitly in 'Epistemology Naturalised', repr. in *Ontological Relativity and Other Essays* (New York: Columbia University Press, 1969), pp. 69–90.

what philosophy is, in what terms it is to be carried on, and what its aims and problems are—ideas that are still alive. By saying this I do not, of course, mean that anyone today shares exactly Russell's views on these matters. What I do mean is that the fundamental assumptions of one important way of thinking about philosophy are recognizable as modifications or developments of Russellian assumptions; and that other ways of thinking about the subject can be seen as more or less drastic attempts to escape from Russellian assumptions and those directly related to them. The period studied in this book is a period in which many influential assumptions and methods and criteria for success can be seen in the process of being formed, although not yet fully present. A complete story of the origin of analytic philosophy would of course involve many other figures besides Russell. But it was Russell, as much as anyone, who set the tone and the agenda for later analytic philosophy. In studying the development of Russell's philosophy, therefore, we who are broadly within the analytic tradition are also studying the development of our own philosophical tradition.

The idea that we are studying the development of our own philosophical tradition holds out the hope of understanding our philosophical position. We may in this way come to a better understanding of the tradition within which or against which we think, and of our own position within that tradition. By seeing how the terms in which we do philosophy have developed, and what gives them their significance and their force, we shall be better able to understand what it is that we are doing in doing philosophy in the late twentieth century, and to articulate the presuppositions of our own thought. Philosophy is sometimes thought of as a discipline which examines, articulates, and criticizes the presuppositions of various forms of human activity. It is natural, at least since Kant, to think of turning this critical light upon philosophy itself. One might equally suppose that since Hegel it would be natural to think of the historical method as a way of doing this. Hegel, however, is largely seen, within the analytic tradition, as discredited; and Kant generally read in a one-sided fashion. Perhaps for these reasons, the idea of understanding our philosophical situation historically has been largely ignored within the analytic tradition. The idea that we understand ourselves, and our intellectual activity, through understanding our history does not, however, seem to depend upon any questionable Hegelian metaphysics. This book is an attempt to suggest, by example, that this idea can be profitably applied to analytic philosophy: we can write a history of our own philosophical tradition, and thereby attain a kind of self-knowledge.

The relation between philosophy and its history is always likely to be an uneasy one; a new philosophical movement almost invariably begins by repudiating the past. This critical relation between philosophy and its history is, I have suggested, not the only one. The past which is repudiated is not simply gone; it continues to influence the present, just as one's personal history influences, and may distort, the way one lives in the present. Our attitude towards the past need not simply be that of repudiation; we may seek to understand it, and to understand how it affects the present. Philosophy can hope to know itself, through knowing the history of its development.

PART I
The Idealist Background

1

T. H. Green

Thomas Hill Green was the most notable of the first generation of British Idealists. He was born in 1836 and spent almost the whole of his adult life at Oxford. He became Whyte's Professor of Moral Philosophy in 1878 and died in 1882; for the decade or so before his death he was the dominant philosophical figure at Oxford.[1] I begin my account of the background to the early works of Moore and Russell with a discussion of Green's metaphysical views and not, as is more common,[2] with a discussion of F. H. Bradley's philosophy. Bradley's form of Idealism is, as we shall see in the next chapter, quite eccentric. One consequence of this is that focusing on Bradley gives a misleading impression of British Idealism in general. Moore and Russell were, however, reacting to all forms of Idealism, not only to Bradley's variety. A second consequence, which I at least have found, is that Bradley's views are very difficult to understand, and to explain, unless they are themselves seen as modifications of, and reactions to, a more standard form of Idealism. I begin, therefore, with Green.

Green was the first major British philosopher to assimilate German Idealism, to incorporate it, critically and selectively, into his own system of thought.[3] More directly than his German predecessors, Green was confronted by the powerful empiricist tradition of Locke, of Hume, and of their nineteenth-century followers. His own views were first worked out in detail in his lengthy criticism of Locke and of Hume (Works, i. 1–371), and he later applied the same principles to J. S. Mill, Herbert Spencer, and others (Works, ii. 195–306; i. 373–541). This fact

---

[1] For biographical details, see R. L. Nettleship's 'memoir' in vol. iii of The Works of Thomas Hill Green, pp. xi–clxi.

[2] See e.g. J. O. Urmson, Philosophical Analysis (Oxford: OUP, 1956), pp. 1–4; D. F. Pears, Bertrand Russell and the British Tradition in Philosophy (London: Fontana, 1972), Ch. X.

[3] The origin of British Idealism is sometimes said to be the publication, in 1865, of H. Stirling's The Secret of Hegel. Other figures who might be mentioned in this connection include Coleridge, Carlyle, Ferrier, and Grote. See Jean Pucelle, L'Idéalisme en Angleterre (Neuchâtel: Éditions de la Baconnière, Boudry, 1955); J. Muirhead, The Platonic Tradition in Anglo-Saxon Philosophy (London: Allen & Unwin, 1931); and Ch. 3 of Passmore, A Hundred Years of Philosophy (Harmondsworth: Penguin Books, 1968; 1st edn. 1957).

is of particular interest from our point of view. Moore and Russell, in their early work, seem to assume that Empiricism is false—they do not take it seriously enough to argue against it in any detail. They both explicitly accept that the Idealists have refuted Empiricism. We need to understand the context which made this anti-empiricist assumption possible. My discussion, therefore, begins with Green's attack on Empiricism.

1. The Critique of Empiricism

An important characteristic of Green's philosophy is that it presents a picture of the history of philosophy, and presents itself, in part, by so doing. According to this picture, Empiricism forms a single school of thought, whose history is roughly as follows: it was first articulated by Locke, whose common sense, or lack of logical strictness, stopped him from thinking the view through to its ultimate, and absurd, conclusion. Berkeley produced an interesting variant of Empiricism without, however, changing matters fundamentally. Hume's great genius lay in the rigour with which he argued from Locke's fundamental principles, resolutely ignoring common sense, and arriving at absurdity. For empiricist philosophers after Hume, Green has very little respect, for he sees in their work a series of attempts to evade or disguise the bankruptcy of Empiricism which Hume had demonstrated (see *Works*, i. 1–5).

We can best begin our discussion of Green's attack on Empiricism by seeing how he understood that philosophy; in this paragraph and the next two I shall briefly present what I take to be Green's understanding of Empiricism. The problem that the Empiricists set themselves was that of 'the origin of "ideas" in the individual man, and their connection as constituting knowledge' (*Works*, i. 6). This enquiry into the origin of our ideas and knowledge is an enquiry into our capacities as knowers, i.e. into the question, what things are possible objects of knowledge for us. The enquiry is, therefore, fundamental, for all other putative branches of knowledge depend upon it:

'Tis evident that all the sciences have a relation, greater or less, to human nature and that however wide any of them may seem to run from it they still return back by one passage or another. Even Mathematics, Natural Philosophy and Natural Religion, are in some measure dependent on the science of MAN: since they lie under the cognizance of men and are judged of by their powers and faculties.[4]

[4] Hume, *A Treatise of Human Nature* ed. L. A. Selby-Bigge (Oxford: Clarendon Press, 1968; 1st edn. 1888), p. xix. Where references are to the Preface, I shall cite them by page number of this ed. Other references will be cited by Book, Part, and Section, using the relevant numbers standing alone.

Since the study of human nature is itself one that results in claims to knowledge, it follows that in this study we should use only those methods of 'observation and experience' which this study itself will show are the way to obtain knowledge in general. (In Hume this point is quite explicit; see *Treatise*, pp. xx–xxiii.) The object of observation, in the philosophical enquiry, is one's own mind; the method of the Empiricists is introspection (*Works*, i. 6). The mind is spoken of almost in spatial terms, as if it were a place in which certain kinds of objects, mental items, could be contained. To see what is in my mind I simply have to observe, to introspect. Thus Locke says: 'if we look immediately into ourselves, and reflect on what is observable there, we shall find our Ideas'.[5] Hume also constantly appeals to our knowledge of our own minds, and represents this knowledge as quasi-perceptual in character, as in this passage: 'Tis evident at first sight that the ideas of memory are much more strong and lively than those of the imagination' (*Treatise*, I. i. 3).

The ideas which introspection shows to be in our minds are either complex, i.e. made up of other ideas, or simple, i.e. non-composite. Simple ideas are discrete, in the sense that each one of them is independent of all others, and complex ideas are dependent only upon the simple ideas which compose them. In all cases the occurrence of any one idea is distinct from, and independent of, the occurrence of any other. Sensation, or sensory perception, is held to be a process in which the mind is wholly passive and receptive; the basic stock of ideas in the mind consists of those ideas which have been given to the mind in this way. This basic stock of ideas is augmented in two ways. First, the mind performs certain operations upon the ideas it has: it can recall any idea which it has once had—not, that is, the very same idea which it once had, but one which exactly resembles it except in vividness; the mind can decompose complex ideas into simple ones, and can compound simple ideas into complex ideas which may be unlike any complex ideas given to it in sensation; according to Locke (though not, as we shall see, to Hume) the mind can, by abstraction, form from several more or less resembling ideas a single idea which has those features which are common to the original ideas, but lacks those features which distinguish those ideas from one another. Second, the mind which performs these operations can perceive its own operations, and this perception, called 'reflection' (e.g. *Essay*, IV. i. 4), is a source of ideas which are not given in sensation—though reflection is often spoken of as if it were exactly parallel to ordinary sensation. The

---

[5] Locke, *An Essay Concerning Human Understanding* ed. Peter H. Nidditch (Oxford: OUP, 1975; 1st edn. 1690), B. II, Ch. vii, s. 9. Hereafter cited in this style, but using the relevant numbers standing alone.

whole process is self-perpetuating, in the sense that ideas obtained by operations of the mind, or by its reflections upon those operations, may themselves be the material of further operations of the mind, giving rise to new ideas to which the same applies.

There is a distinction between those ideas in relation to which the mind is purely passive and receptive—those which it passively receives, or which are given to it—and those which the mind recalls or actively creates by composition or abstraction. A point of empiricist doctrine which Green often focuses upon is the apparently common-sensical view that it is only those ideas which are given to the mind that can be taken to represent reality. The mind is, according to the Empiricists, wholly distinct from the (extra-mental) reality which it seeks to know; so the mind, in knowledge, is passive and receptive rather than active and creative. The importance of this point will emerge when we see how Green wishes to oppose this distinction, which he calls 'the antithesis between thought and reality'.

Green's criticism of Empiricism is both detailed and fundamental. His charge against it is not, as one might expect, that it fails to explain the possibility of some of our relatively sophisticated ideas or forms of knowledge, but rather that it can give no account of any kind of knowledge, even of the simplest form. He believes, indeed, that only an attack at this basic level can be completely successful:

The weakness of Hume's opponents . . . has lain primarily in their allowing that his doctrine would account for any significant predication whatsoever, as distinct from exclamations prompted by feelings as they occur. . . just as Locke's empiricism becomes invincible as soon as it is admitted that qualified things are 'found in nature' without any constitutive action of the mind. (*Works*, i. 185)

Following Kant, Green claims that certain 'formal conceptions' are presupposed by even the simplest kind of knowledge or claim to knowledge—and thus by all judgement and all (knowable) facts. These formal conceptions include subject and object, substance and quality, cause and effect, spatiality, and temporality. The notion of presupposition which is in play here is an important one. Note in particular that it is our (claims to) knowledge which are said to have presuppositions; Green does not contemplate, and would resist, the complete abstraction of the known fact from our knowledge. In this matter he confronts the Empiricists on their own ground. The Empiricists, after all, were concerned to explain our knowledge, or our possession of certain ideas. In particular, they attempted to explain how, on the basis of simpler, more directly sensory, knowledge, we could come to acquire what Green calls 'the formal conceptions', or the illusion of having them. Green argues that these explanations are useless, because the supposedly simpler kinds of knowledge which they assume as unproblematic in fact already presuppose the formal conceptions. In the case of cause and effect, for example, Locke claims that we acquire this idea on the basis of our knowledge of the circumstances under which things begin to exist (*Essay*, II. xxvi. 1; Hume's account is more complex but not, for our purposes, importantly different). Green argues that this account presupposes the idea of substance or external thing: a variation in our sensations gives us no basis upon which to form the idea of cause unless we take the sensations as signs of (or as 'referred to', as Green often says) outer things. But our only understanding of the notion of an outer thing, according to Locke himself, is as that which *causes* our sensations, and to see our sensations as signs of outer things is to see them as *caused* by outer things:

But the reference of a sensation to a sensible thing means its reference to a cause. In other words the invented relation of cause and effect must be grounded in the primary experience in order that it may be got from it. (*Works*, i. 57)

The knowledge from which we were supposed to derive our notion of cause and effect thus presupposes this notion. Such knowledge would be impossible for us unless we already had, at least implicitly, a grasp on the relation of cause and effect.

This tactic of offering definitions, or explanations, of notions in terms which in fact presuppose those notions is one that Green finds repeated throughout the works of Locke and Hume. It is hidden from the authors, and from most readers, Green claims, by a fundamental equivocation:

The essential question is whether 'simple idea', as the original of knowledge, is on the one hand a mere feeling, or on the other, a thing or a quality of a thing. This question is the crux of empirical psychology. (*Works*, i. 13)

According to Green, Empiricism is plausible only because of this equivocation. Taking a simple idea as the mere occurrence of a sensation or feeling makes it plausible that the occurrence of an idea has no presuppositions except passive receptivity to sensation. Taking a simple idea as knowledge of an external thing or of a quality of a thing enables us to show how more complex ideas and forms of knowledge grow out of this basic kind; it also makes it seem as if the occurrence of a simple idea could by itself amount to knowledge. Green's claim is thus that the equivocation is not accidental, nothing that a more careful statement of the empiricist programme could avoid; it is, rather, essential to that programme, and found in all statements of it. The passage I have just quoted comes from Green's discussion of Locke; he speaks in similar terms of Hume (*Works*, i. 206) and of 'the modern treatises of Logic'[6] (*Works*, i. 267).

It is not that Green wishes to deny that knowledge comes from experience. On the contrary, the two notions are as firmly linked for him as for any Empiricist: the formal conceptions which he sees as the presuppositions of knowledge he sees equally as the presuppositions of experience. The view of the Empiricists is that the crucial element in experience is the passive reception of ideas, which has no presuppositions beyond sensory receptivity. Green insists that 'in experience we already go beyond sense' (*Works*, i. 267). Green's claim, as we shall see in some detail, is that a succession of feelings or sensations can amount to experience, in the relevant sense, only if each feeling is present to a relatively permanent self-conscious mind, which distinguishes itself from those feelings. Only for such a mind can the transitory feelings be related to one another; since the formal conceptions—cause and effect, substance and quality, and so on—are all ultimately relational in character, they are constituted by the action upon the feelings of the self-conscious mind to which they are present.

A crucial preliminary to Green's argument for this line of thought is the notion of experience that he employs. Experience, in the sense relevant to an enquiry into the origin and presuppositions of knowledge, Green insists, is conscious experience. He explicitly discards experience 'in the sense in which, for instance, a plant might be said to experience a succession of atmospheric or chemical changes, or in which we ourselves pass through a definite physical experience during sleep or in respect of the numberless events which affect us but of which we are not aware' (*Prol. Eth.*, s. 15). The experience which is relevant to an explanation of knowledge is, rather, 'experience of matters of fact *recognized as such*' (emphasis in the original), or 'a consciousness of events as related or as a series of changes' (*Prol. Eth.*, s. 16). Green attempts to show that 'mere feeling' cannot amount to experience, in the relevant sense, unless we suppose it felt by a subject whose capacities go far beyond receptivity. He presents various interwoven considerations towards this conclusion. At the cost of some subtlety and complexity, I shall condense them into a two-step argument: first, that for the merely receptive consciousness there are no relations between feelings; secondly, that considered in themselves,

---

[6] It seems to be J. S. Mill whom Green has primarily in mind here. See *Works*, ii. 197–200, where Green charges Mill with being ambiguous in exactly this way in his *Logic*.

i.e. without relations, feelings cannot constitute knowledge or experience (for Green's own rather similar summaries of his argument, see *Works*, ii. 177; and i. 150). The emphasis on relations, generally accepted as a characteristic of Bradley's philosophy, is thus no less clear in Green's. And in this context it is, I think, recognizable as the same issue which Kant had called synthesis: the question is one of the basis of the unity of the diverse, how things come to be put together to form a whole. No less important is the emphasis on knowledge or experience. Here again, Green might be thought of as following Kant; with the difference, which we shall discuss in Section 2, that Kant opposes the knowable world to the world of things as they are in themselves, whereas Green rejects this distinction. Equally, Green is responding to the Empiricists, accepting their presupposition that all knowledge is relative to our cognitive powers. What are we to make of this presupposition? It is tautologous to say that we can only know what is knowable, and it is clearly useless to attempt to know what we cannot know; but complex issues are concealed here. One is the sense in which a thing is said to be knowable, or the basis for the claim that it is knowable: is it simply a matter of human psychology, or can we see it as somehow inherent in the nature of knowledge or experience itself? Here Green, like Kant, rejects the psychological approach which may be thought to characterize the Empiricists. Russell and Moore, as we shall see, attempt to cut through the issue by claiming that knowledge has no presuppositions; they appeal at this point to a direct intuition of, or acquaintance with, things outside us (things as they are in themselves, one might say).

There is a prima facie reason to think that a theory which attempts to account for knowledge in terms of passively received feelings will have trouble with the question of relations between feelings (or, in the light of the immediately preceding discussion, of our consciousness of such relations). In the first place a relation between feelings is not itself a feeling, nor is it felt (*Works*, i. 149). Again, feelings themselves are transient, each being over before the next comes into existence. If a relation were a feeling, when would it occur? At the time of the first relatum? or the second? or in the middle?—all of these possibilities seem absurd. The obvious answer is to say that one or both of the feelings is recalled, and a feeling and a recollection of a feeling may be contemporaneous. But to recall a feeling means to have an idea resembling it; and resemblance is itself a relation between feelings, subject to the same sorts of questions as all others.

Locke's view of relations is that they are the work of the mind and thus not an element in the reality that we try to know; relations, Locke says, are 'not contained in the real existence of Things, but something extraneous and superinduced'. (*Essay*, II. xxv. 8; cited by Green at *Works*, i. 55). Green claims, however, that Locke cannot consistently hold this view:

When it is said that the idea of identity, or of any other relation, is formed upon consideration of things as existing in a certain way, this is naturally understood to mean—indeed, otherwise it is unmeaning—that the things are first *known* as existing, and that afterwards the idea of the relation in question is formed. But according to Locke, as we have seen, the first and simplest act of knowledge possible is the perception of identity between ideas. (*Works*, i. 59; emphasis in the original)

In calling relations 'superinduced' Locke should presumably be understood to mean that we form an idea of relation on the basis of simpler, non-relational, kinds of knowledge: I know one thing and (independently) know another, and this is the basis upon which I form the idea of a relation between them. But according to Locke there is no non-relational knowledge, for he defines knowledge as 'the perception of the connexion and agreement or disagreement and repugnancy, of any of our Ideas' (*Essay*, IV. i. 2). Since all knowledge involves relations, we can only superinduce the idea of relation on the basis of knowledge which already presupposes it. Green's conclusion, accordingly, is that Lockean principles cannot explain how it is possible to come by any ideas of relation.

A more general way of understanding Green's claim that the Empiricists cannot, consistently with their own doctrine, give any account of relations, is to see Green as employing the very weapons which Hume had used in criticism of such notions as substance, causation, and the self. In attacking the notion of the self, Hume had said, 'It is from some one impression that every real idea is derived' (*Treatise*, I. iv. 6). 'What, then', writes Green, 'is the one impression from which the idea of relation is derived?' (*Works*, i. 174.) Again, speaking of substance, Hume had said, 'if it be conveyed to us by our sense, I ask which one of them and after what manner? If it be perceived by the eyes, it must be a colour; if by the ears a sound; if by the palate, a taste; and so on of the other senses'. If it is not an impression of the sense, it 'must therefore be derived from an impression of reflexion, if it really exists. But the impressions of reflection resolve themselves into our passions and emotions; none of which can possibly represent a substance' (*Treatise*, I. i. 7). Hume's conclusion, of course, is that we do not in fact have any idea of substance at all; Green's claim is that the same line of argument will show that on Hume's account we can have no idea of relation either. A relation cannot be an impression or a simple idea

because there is no sense by which it could be conveyed to the mind—
a relation is not a colour, or a sound or a taste. The idea of reflection
will not help, for it is no more plausible to suppose a relation to be a
passion or an emotion. Green thus uses Hume's own critical weapons
to argue that Hume's premisses make all ideas of relation impossible.
The argument is not put forward *ad hominem*, however. Green clearly
thinks that Hume's criticisms are a legitimate part of any consistent
Empiricism. He therefore takes himself to have shown that relations
cannot be accounted for on any empiricist principles.

The second step of the two-step argument I am attributing to Green
is that belief (and therefore knowledge) and even experience are relational in character. Without relations, therefore, there would be no
knowledge, no experience, and no (knowable) world. Let us begin
with judgement or belief. Green's claim looks least plausible if we
consider the beliefs which I have, at a given moment, concerning my
ideas at that moment, so this case will provide us with the best test of
this claim. Consider the minimal counter-claim, that without relations I
could at least have knowledge of the idea that I am currently having.
What form would this knowledge take? Presumably, it would be a
description of a present sensation, such as 'I'm now having a blue
visual sensation' or, more likely, 'This is blue'. How can we account for
this sort of minimal assertion along empiricist lines? A difficulty is most
likely to arise about the general term 'blue': what account can we give
of its meaning? Locke's answer is that blueness is an abstract idea,
formed from various particular blue ideas by ignoring those properties
not shared by all of them, and thus ending (presumably) with an idea
whose sole property is blueness. This account, however, makes general ideas depend upon relations among ideas, for the general idea
must, presumably, be thought of as formed in the way described.
Furthermore (and it is this objection that Green emphasizes), an idea
must have the property of being blue before we can use that idea to
form the idea of blueness. Green's challenge is this: is the simplest
form of experience to be that of an idea as qualified by the possession
of various properties, or that of an idea with no such qualification? (See
e.g. *Works*, i. 37–9.) If the former, then, Green says, the notion of a
property, which was to be explained by abstraction, has been assumed
as given. If the latter, however, the process of abstraction will simply
never be able to get under way. Locke maintains his position only by
switching back and forth between these two doctrines as his argument
requires (*Works*, i. 33).

Hume, following Berkeley, denied the existence of Lockean 'abstract
ideas' (Green, *Works*, i. 178–9). If each idea is a separate, datable
mental object, then each idea is particular—to speak of a general or

abstract idea is without sense. Thus 'blue' must indicate a particular blue idea. This particular idea, according to Hume, appears to be general because we are constantly ready to substitute other (particular) blue ideas for it. This readiness ensures that we do not assert that some idea is blue if the feature it has in common with the idea indicated by 'blue' is some feature other than being blue. But the replacement of Locke's answer by Hume's only reveals more clearly that the empiricist account of generality relies upon relations. In the case of Locke's answer, the abstract idea is related to the particular ideas from which it is formed, and essentially so, since abstract ideas can only be conceived as formed in some such way. In the case of Hume's answer, 'blue' indicates a particular idea; some ideas I am ready to substitute for this idea, and others I am not. But my being ready to substitute one idea for another is a relation between them, and this relation is quite essential to Hume's account of the generality of words such as 'blue'. So the conclusion is that without relations no account of properties or qualities is possible—not even if the properties are the simplest properties of current sensations.

Having reached this point, Green presses the attack even further. It might be thought that even though I cannot describe my sensation without implicitly relating it to other sensations, still I can know that I am having a sensation; or, if 'sensation' causes trouble, that I am having *something*, even if I cannot describe it at all. But this too Green denies. He argues that even words which seem merely to pick out what is immediately present—'this', 'now', 'here'—are in fact essentially general and thus relational in character.[7] Many different places can be (truly) called 'here', and a given use of the word can succeed in referring to a particular place only because other uses of the word, to refer to other places, are possible:

according to this doctrine [i.e. Locke's] the 'really existent' [i.e. feeling or sensation] is the unmeaning, and . . . any statement about it is impossible. We cannot judge of it without bringing it into relation, in which it ceases to be what in its mere singleness it is, and thus loses its reality. . . . Nay, if we say that it is the mere 'this' or 'that'—the simple 'here' and 'now'—the very 'this' in being mentioned or judged of, becomes related to other things which we have called 'this', and the 'now' to other 'nows'. Thus each acquires a generality and with it becomes fictitious. As Plato long ago taught . . . a consistent sensationalism must be speechless. (*Works*, i. 36; cf. ii. 168)

Green's claim is that all thought and language requires generality, and

---

[7] Compare Hegel, *Phänomenologie des Geistes*, Ch. I ('Sinnlich Gewißheit'). Green's thought at this point might also be compared with Wittgenstein's so-called 'private-language argument'.

generality is impossible without relations. The view that can give no account of relations can give no account of the possibility of thought or language.

It is easy to underestimate the depth of Green's argument at this point. One is perhaps inclined to think that an experience is what it is regardless of one's ability to describe it or conceptualize it. Now there certainly are cases in which one seems to know what one feels, yet words fail one in the attempt to describe it. One can, however, always say something about such an experience, even if only that it is hard to describe or that it is unlike any of one's previous experiences. In such a case, therefore, conceptualization remains at a vague or indeterminate level, but it does not fail completely. Green's argument, if successful, shows that without relations no conceptualization would be possible; no thought at all would be possible about the given experience or any other experience, so the failure of conceptualization would be total. This situation cannot be equated with the sorts of difficulties with which we may be familiar. Where no conceptualization at all is possible, one could not have the thought of oneself as having a given kind of experience, or of having an experience at all. Under such conditions there would be no experience, at least in the sense of experience with which Green is concerned (see p. 26, above). It is the very possibility of experience that Green takes to be at stake in his argument.

Thus Green takes himself to have shown both that the Empiricists can give no account of relations, and that a failure to account for relations is also a failure to account for the possibility of experience. Experience, according to Green, presupposes not merely the faculty of passively receiving ideas but also an agency which combines and relates these ideas; such an agency is to be understood as at least analogous to our own intelligence (see *Prol. Eth.*, ss. 28–9). Green thus accepts that thought or intellectual activity is not antithetical to, but is constitutive of, experience, and hence of any reality of which we could have experience. He takes this to be the essential principle of Kantianism and of post-Kantian Idealism, and the recognition of this principle to be the decisive advance that Kant made over Hume. The principle as I have stated it, however, is vague. How Green understood it will be the subject of the next section.

2. The Reinterpretation of Kant

The position from which Green criticizes the Empiricists may, as he says himself, 'be called broadly the Kantian view' (*Prol. Eth.*, s. 35). He emphasizes the Kantian question as to the conditions under which

experience is possible (e.g. *Prol. Eth.*, s. 8; *Works*, ii. 158). These conditions are certain formal conceptions, for which Green also uses the
Kantian term 'categories' (e.g. *Works*, i. 198, ii. 196, 207 ff.), which have
their source in the self-conscious subject of knowledge. Green explicitly
identifies his 'principle of consciousness which forms the bond of
relation between objects' with Kant's synthetic unity of apperception
(*Prol. Eth.*, ss. 32–3); and, like Kant, he holds this principle to be, at
least in part, constitutive of the world which is known.

Green is not, however, a thoroughgoing Kantian. His attitude towards Kant may be gathered from his laudatory review of Edward
Caird's *The Philosophy of Kant*.[8] Green says that Caird's book

is based on the principles which Kant himself was the first to assert. Its
objections are not to his idealism, but to that incomplete development of his
idealism which is shown by his partial retention ... of that antithesis between
the world of experience and the world of ideas which he inherited. (*Works*, iii.
137)

The attitude towards Kant which is attributed to Caird here is very
much Green's own. Green holds that Kant's real principles are fundamentally correct; that Kant himself was unable to free himself entirely of the views that he was attacking; that he therefore did not follow
out his own principles consistently;[9] and that if these principles are so
followed out they lead to a position which may, with a number of
qualifications and caveats, be called 'Hegelian' (for Green's rather cau-
tious use of this word in describing Caird, see *Works*, iii. 129).

At the end of the previous section I indicated the crucial issue for
Green's reinterpretation of Kant: the correct understanding of the
idealist principle that the mind, or intellectual activity, is constitutive of
reality. Now for Kant, there are two quite different notions of reality.[10]
On the one hand there is empirical reality, the world of phenomena or
of appearances. For this world Kant accepts the idealist principle: the
mind is (at least partially) constitutive of the phenomenal world. On
the other hand there are things as they are in themselves, and here
Kant rejects the idealist principle. Things-in-themselves are completely

---

[8] E. Caird, *Philosophy of Kant*; Green's review appeared in the *Academy* (22 Sept. 1877),
and is reprinted in *Works*, iii. 126–37.

[9] In his review of another book on Kant (J. Watson, *Kant and his English Critics*), Green
acknowledges that Kant is inconsistent. The question, he says, is 'whether we are to
understand [Kant] according to the letter of statements which he undoubtedly makes,
but which we may be inclined to regard as survivals of a way of thinking which it was
the true result of his philosophy to set aside, or according to what may seem to us to be
the spirit of his more pregnant passages' (*Works*, iii. 148).

[10] Here, as later, it is Green's understanding of Kant, rather than my own, which I
seek to convey.

antithetical to human thought, which plays no role in constituting them. We have seen Green argue that such an antithesis between thought and reality makes the real world inaccessible to knowledge and thought, makes it 'the unmeaning, the empty, of which nothing can be said' (*Works*, i. 41). Unlike the Empiricists, Kant, according to Green, accepts this consequence; the world of things-in-themselves is something of which we can say and know nothing—except that it exists.[11] What we know and talk about are the appearances to us of this real world. But these appearances cohere in such a way that we are able to speak of them as forming a world—the phenomenal world. Although this world is only the appearance to us of things-in-themselves, the distinction between appearance and reality, or the subjective and the objective, makes sense when construed as about this phenomenal world. Indeed it is only *within* the phenomenal world, i.e. as a distinction among appearances, that this distinction does make sense; we cannot contrast appearances with what is beyond all appearances, because this latter is inaccessible to us, and attempts to speak of it are empty. All our everyday and scientific discourse is about the phenomenal world. In this phenomenal world the antithesis between thought and reality is overcome, for this world is not formed of appearances as they are independently of us, or as they would be to a purely receptive mind; rather the phenomenal world is made up of appearances *to us*, i.e. to self-conscious subjects who impose structure and form upon the given. This structure-imposing activity is responsible for space, time, causality, substance, and other notions which Green calls 'formal conceptions'. These categories are the conditions of any possible experience, and are not derived from experience but imposed by the knowing subject upon what is not, in itself, experienceable.

Like earlier Absolute Idealists,[12] Green holds that the postulation of a world of things-in-themselves, defined by its role in the Kantian system as unknowable, is indefensible. A world which was completely antithetical to thought would be a world about which we could say or think nothing whatsoever—not even that it existed, or that it was antithetical to thought.[13] To say that this world is antithetical to

[11] Kant in fact seems to hold that we could think about things-in-themselves, and have reason to believe certain things about them, even though we could not *know* anything about them. As we shall soon see, Green finds this position untenable.

[12] Cf. e.g. ss. 40–52 of *Hegel's Logic, Being Part One of the Encyclopedia of the Philosophical Sciences (1830)*, trans. William Wallace (Oxford: Clarendon Press, 1975; 1st edn. 1873).

[13] Here as elsewhere I accept, for the purposes of exposition, Green's view that the Kantian noumenal world is wholly inaccessible to thought. But in fact it is far from clear that this is Kant's position. Kant does seem to hold that the noumenal is independent of (human) intuition, and thus also of the schematized categories. But his view at least

thought is, after all, to say that it is related to thought: but if relations are the work of the mind then the antithesis cannot, after all, be absolute. Green seems to think that Kant failed to see this point only because he was still influenced by earlier views which he had in fact rejected (see *Prol. Eth.*, s. 41). Once the idea of the world of things-in-themselves, or a world beyond all possible experience, is rejected, we are left with the phenomenal world as the only world. Thus for Green the antithesis between thought and reality is unambiguously overcome, and thought recognized as playing a role in the constitution of the real world.

The denial of the noumenal world, and the according of full reality to the phenomenal world, exacerbate two difficulties or tensions which are perhaps inherent in Kant's philosophy in any case. The first concerns the nature of the mind or intelligence which, by its acts of combination or synthesis, plays a role in constituting the phenomenal world. In the ordinary sense of mind there are at least as many minds as there are ordinarily competent human beings: you have one mind and I have another. But in this sense of mind it is implausible to say that the single phenomenal world which we all inhabit and investigate is constituted by the action of mind. For in this case, whose mind are we to suppose is responsible for constituting the world? Yours? Mine? All of our minds somehow jointly? The more the phenomenal world takes on the aspect of full reality and objectivity, rather than simply the appearances of things-in-themselves to us, the more pressing these questions become. It is this difficulty, Green claims, that makes us accept the antithesis between thought and reality—but only because 'we conceive of no intellectual action but that which this or that person exercises' (*Prol. Eth.*, s. 34). This latter assumption, according to Green, is false:

Nature is the system of related appearances, and related appearances are impossible apart from the action of an intelligence.... Does this imply the absurdity that nature comes into existence in the process by which this or that person begins to think? Not at all, unless it is necessary to suppose that intelligence first comes into existence when this or that person begins to understand—a supposition not only not necessary, but which, on examination, will be found to involve impossibilities. (*Prol. Eth.*, s. 36)

The intelligence which plays a role in constituting reality is, according to Green, not human intelligence but that of a single, eternal, self-

leaves room for the idea that the noumenal is not independent of the understanding (see *Critique of Pure Reason*, A253–4=B309–10), and hence also for the claim that we can *think* of things-in-themselves. Kant's view here clearly depends upon the distinction between sensibility and the understanding, which most of his idealist successors rejected.

conscious mind. Part of the 'vital truth' which Green says he accepts from Hegel is that 'there is a single spiritual or self-conscious being, of which all that is real is the activity or expression' (*Works*, iii. 146).

Now it would seem that the introduction of such a self-consciousness will not help to solve the problem of the possibility of our knowledge or our experience: presumably only *my* acts of synthesis could explain *my* awareness of relations. But for Green the eternal self-consciousness is not wholly distinct from my self-consciousness, or from that of other human minds: 'we are related to this being, not merely as parts of the world which is its expression, but as partakers in some inchoate measure of the self-consciousness through which it at once constitutes and distinguishes itself from the world' (*Works*, iii. 146). There is a single self-consciousness, which both has an eternal existence independent of human beings and manifests or realizes itself, imperfectly and incompletely, in human minds. In so far as we are self-conscious, we share in this eternal self-consciousness:

an animal organism, which has its history in time, gradually becomes the vehicle of an eternally complete consciousness. What we call our mental history is not a history of this consciousness, which in itself can have no history, but a history of the process by which the animal organism becomes its vehicle. (*Prol. Eth.*, s. 67)

It is at this point in our discussion that Green's theological concerns first arise in an obvious fashion. Green's doctrine of an eternal and world-constituting self-consciousness is one of the bases on which he attempts to give a rational defence of his own version of nineteenth-century evangelical Anglicanism.[14] The difficulty which there undoubtedly is in understanding Green's notion of an 'eternal self-consciousness' in which we somehow 'partake' might perhaps be approached through a discussion of theological attempts to deny the ultimate separateness of God and humanity. I shall undertake no such discussion; but it is worth pointing out that while Green's philosophy is consciously anti-materialistic, it is not crudely so. In particular, Green does not take his view to be incompatible with what he sees as the straightforwardly scientific aspects of Darwin's theory of evolution. It is, he says, possible 'that countless generations should have passed during which a transmitted organism was progressively modified ... by struggle for existence, or otherwise, till its functions became such that an eternal consciousness could realize or reproduce itself through them' (*Prol. Eth.*, s. 83). A scientific account may be

---

[14] For a discussion of Green's religious views, see M. Richter, *The Politics of Conscience* (Cambridge, Mass.: Harvard University Press, 1964), especially Ch. 4.

possible, Green admits, of 'the development of the human organism out of lower forms' (*Prol. Eth.*, s. 84), but this is not the same as an account of the development of consciousness. Of this, Green insists, no naturalistic explanation is possible, because it is due to the action of a principle which constitutes the order of nature but is distinct from it.

A second difficulty in Kant's philosophy arises from the fact that his picture of knowledge and experience is a dualistic one. The understanding performs acts of synthesis upon material given to it in intuition; experience requires both the synthesis and the given material.[15] One way in which Kant articulates this dualism is by thinking of the world of things-in-themselves as the source of the matter or content of experience, upon which the mind then imposes a form or structure (see *Prol. Eth.*, ss. 38–9 for this view of Kant). This way of articulating Kant's dualism is not available once the idea of a world of things-in-themselves has been rejected. From Green's point of view there are, moreover, independent considerations which make the dualistic view of experience seem untenable. Even if we remove the idea that it is the noumenal world which is the source of the matter of experience, the dualistic view looks like an attempt to make assertions about what is beyond the limits of human knowledge. We have already examined Green's arguments to the conclusion that if we abstract the work of the mind from human experience, to try to find a given which is independent of the mind, then we are left with nothing, or with something of which nothing can be said, not even that it is something of which nothing can be said, not even that there is such a thing. But an element in human knowledge which was independent of the understanding would have to be of this kind, so the attempt to say that there is such an element is an attempt to say something without meaning: 'to assume that there are . . . mere sensations, antecedently to any action of the intellect . . . is an abstraction which may be put into words, but to which no real meaning can be attached' (*Prol. Eth.*, s. 44). It is only as related that a sensation, or anything else, can be an object of possible experience, or that its existence can be a fact. But then to suppose that there is a content of experience which is independent of the relations created by the intellect is to suppose something which is not within the bounds of possible experience, and which is not a possible fact. We cannot suppose that the intellect constitutes the world by acting upon something given to it; the supposition of such a given is unintelligible.

---

[15] Kant says: 'there are two stems of human knowledge, sensibility and understanding, which perhaps spring from a single, but to us unknown, root' (first *Critique*, A15=B29). Many of Kant's idealist successors rejected this dualism, which they did not always distinguish sharply from the dualism of the phenomenal and noumenal worlds.

Green's alternative to Kant's dualism seems to be that the world is constituted by the activity of the intellect alone. There is an air of paradox about this view, to which we can give a precise form by recalling Green's emphasis on relations as the work of the intellect. If the intellect constitutes the world by creating relations, must not something—the objects among which the relations hold—be given to the intellect? As Green himself puts it:

We cannot reduce the world of experience to a web of relations in which nothing is related.... After all our protests against Dualism ... are we not at least left with an unaccountable residuum—an essential element of the real world of experience, which we cannot trace to what we regard as the organiz-ing principle of that world, but which is as necessary to make the world what it is as that principle itself? ... Does it not remain a thing-in-itself, alien and opposite to anything that we can explain as the construction of intelligence? (*Prol. Eth.*, s. 42)

Green's response to these difficulties is to say that they 'are due to the abstraction of the "matter" from the "form" of experience' (*Prol. Eth.*, s. 43); this answer, and in particular the notion of abstraction upon which it relies, require some explanation.

There is a distinction which we can express as the distinction be-tween the form of experience and its matter, or between thought and feeling (Green, as we shall see, also equates this distinction with that between subject and object). Green's view is based upon the insistence that this distinction, like any other intelligible distinction, is one that we draw, and draw *within* experience.[16] If this is correct, then the distinction is wrongly construed if we take it as a distinction between two unknowable factors which combine in some mysterious fashion to constitute our experience. It is, rather, a distinction that we draw within the realm of the knowable. This is what it means to say that thought and feeling are both abstractions from experience. We can only understand either of them, according to Green, by beginning with experience and thinking of it as made up of these two factors. This we can do; but our ability to do it should not fool us into supposing that we have, in thought and feeling, two separate and independent items. On the contrary, the fact that we can only think of either by first considering experience, then conceiving of experience as made up of two factors, and concentrating on one of the factors to the exclusion of the other—this fact shows that each of the notions of thought and feeling is dependent for its meaning on the other, and that both are

---

[16] Cf. *Works*, i. 449: 'the only valid idealism—that idealism which trusts, not to a guess about what is beyond experience, but to an analysis of what is within it'.

ultimately dependent upon experience. But then it is wrong to think of two separate elements as making up experience: the two elements are essentially correlative, not separate; experience is prior to them, and 'made up' from them only in a metaphorical sense:

undoubtedly there is something other than thought. Feeling is so; the whole system of nature, on which feeling depends, is so; its otherness to thought makes it what it is, but this is the same as saying that relation to thought makes it what it is, that but for thought it would not be. Conversely, 'other-ness' from nature makes thought what it is. The very idea of thought implies a ἕτερον, for thought = self-consciousness ... and thought cannot be conscious of itself except in distinction from an object.... Subject and object, thought and its correlative, are complementary factors in the whole of self-conscious-ness, or (which is the same) together constitute the reality of the world. Each is what it is only *in relation* to the other. (*Works*, ii. 181–2)

These considerations may help to make Green's alternative to Kant's dualism more intelligible; but they seem to do so at the cost of the complete surrender of the idea that the world is constituted by thought. If thought is correlative with feeling, and is an abstraction from experience, it surely cannot constitute experience. Green accepts this point. In the sense in which thought is an abstraction from experience—'mere thought', Green calls it—it does not constitute the world. Indeed, as abstractions, Green holds that neither 'mere thought' or 'mere feeling' is genuinely and independently real: 'we deny that there is really such a thing as "mere feeling" or "mere thought". We hold that these phrases represent abstractions to which no reality cor-responds' (*Prol. Eth.*, s. 51). The thought which constitutes the world is not the 'mere thought' which is an abstraction from experience, and which is what usually goes under the name 'thought':

If thought and reality are to be identified, if the statement that God is thought is to be more than a presumptuous paradox, thought must be other than the discursive activity exhibited in our inferences and analyses, other than a par-ticular mode of consciousness. (*Works*, iii. 142–3)

The thought which constitutes the world ('Thought', I shall call it) is thus contrasted with the 'mere thought' with which we are familiar. But if Thought is not to be identified with the thought we know, what is it? More importantly, perhaps, what is the justification for saying that it is Thought (or Mind or Intellect) which constitutes the world, if these words do not have the same meanings as their uncapitalized versions? Green acknowledges the force of questions of this sort (see *Works*, iii. 143). To the second his answer seems to be that the element which Thought and Mind have in common with our mundane thought and mind, the element which justifies the use of the same words, is self-consciousness (see *Works*, ii. 182). Since the unifying principle of the world must be self-conscious, we can best think of it by analogy with the loci of self-consciousness which are within our experience—our own minds. I think Green accepts, however, that our understanding of Thought remains partial and limited; this is part of the price that he is willing to pay for his metaphysics. Here again a comparison with the concerns of traditional theology may be helpful. We can only understand the mind of God by analogy with our own minds. To think the analogy perfect, however, would be as mistaken as to deny it entirely; it is only to be expected that the nature of God should remain for us an ultimate mystery.

3. Holism and Necessity

In this section I shall articulate some further aspects of Green's anti-dualist metaphysics, beginning with his view of thought and knowledge. The dualist view of thought, which Green contrasts with his own view, sees it as involving entities of two different kinds, intellectual and sensible. It thus distinguishes and contrasts universals and particulars, or attributes and substance; this view of thought has ontological consequences.[17] An intrinsic part of the dualist view is that sensible particulars are given with their properties or attributes (otherwise they would be, according to Green, completely indeterminate and unknowable); and that universals or attributes are first known by abstraction from particulars:

When philosophy speaks to [the scholar] . . . of the 'sensible thing', he thinks of it as the individual basis of definite properties, of which he believes himself to have a direct knowledge through the senses. . . . From this view of the office of sense, a certain view as to the action of thought and the generality represented by common nouns necessarily flows. If sense gives the knowledge of the thing, as a definite complex of attributes, nothing remains for thought but to detach these attributes from the sensible thing and from each other, and recombine them. The residuum of this process is the 'universal', whether regarded as an 'essence' in the real world, or as a property. (*Works*, iii. 48–9)

As the last sentence suggests, Green is here not only speaking of those who hold, with the Empiricists, that properties are the work of the mind and thus unreal. He takes his diagnosis to apply equally to those who suppose that universals form a genuine reality distinct from or

---

[17] Exactly what ontological consequences the view has depends, as we shall see, on how it is articulated. Since Green holds that the same error underlies all forms of dualism, however, these differences are not to this point.

superior to that of the sensible world.[18] Any version of the dualist view makes it seem as if thought had no role to play in knowledge:

If sense gives us a knowledge of properties, nothing remains for thought but to abstract and combine them.... Thought has abdicated its proper prerogatives. It has admitted that experience is something given to it from without, not that in which it comes to itself. It inevitably follows that in what it does for itself, when not simply receptive of experience, it is merely draining away in narrower and more remote channels the fullness of the real world. We cannot know by abstraction, for properties must be known before they can be abstracted. If thought, then, is a process of abstraction ... we think by other methods than we know. Thought, therefore, cannot give us knowledge, but only lead us away from it. (*Works*, iii. 61–2)

Green denies the fundamental dualism on which this picture of thought is based: 'the world is not composed of two opposite sets of things, the sensible and the intelligible. There is but one real world' (*Works*, iii. 84). We cannot, according to this view, contrast the sensible particular with the universal, because there is no particular, no 'real thing', without the universal activity of thought: nor is there any universal beyond this activity. The abstraction of the 'bare particular' and the 'abstract universal' from the real thing is just another manifestation of the abstraction of 'mere feeling' and 'mere thought' from experience:

The real thing of intelligent experience unites the two sides of individuality and universality.... It is a centre of relations, which constitute its properties. As differenced from all things else by the sum of these relations, it is an individual, but to be so differenced from them it must have an element in common with them.... If then the thing of experience turns out to be what 'thinking makes it', while, on the other hand, the motion of thought is no other than the correlative 'differentiation and integration', which constitutes the phenomenal world, where is the obstacle to the admission that the world of experience is a world of ideas, or things as thought of, that it is an order of thought? (*Works*, iii. 65)

Reality, on this view, is constituted by the act of thought upon sense, universalizing, relating, and comparing (cf. *Works*, i. 42). Thought thus neither gains us access to a super-sensible realm beyond the ordinary world, nor leads us away from reality to emptier and emptier abstractions. Because the world is constituted by intellectual activity, thought can be a genuine means of gaining knowledge of the world.

Green's view of thought thus involves what is sometimes known as 'the doctrine of the concrete universal'. Particulars are real only in so far as they are constituted and determined by their relations—i.e. by

---

[18] Realism of this sort, Green says, 'is virtually nominalism'; *Works*, iii. 60.

universals. Universals are real only in so far as they constitute and relate things. The real thing is particular or universal according as we concentrate on its differentiation from other things or on its relation to them: but as it is differentiated by its relations, and only related in so far as differentiated, these are two aspects of the same fact. Green attributes this doctrine, in embryonic form, to Aristotle, and denies that it implies the unreality of universals:

The assertion of Aristotle against Plato, that the universal is not to be found apart from 'sensible things', but attaches to them, has been strangely thought to be an abandonment of the doctrine of the reality of universals. It can only be so on the supposition that a thing is more real than its properties . . . if, on the other hand, the individual thing is what it is in virtue of its attributes, if these constitute its reality, then the Aristotelian doctrine, by treating the universal as a property or sum of properties, while it in no way modifies the reality which Plato ascribed to it, avoids the error of admitting a quasi-reality in distinction from it. (*Works*, iii. 67–8)

We tend, Green thinks, to oppose the particular to the universal, so that we assume that if only the particular is real then the universal is unreal. This is just the basic error, of opposing thought and reality, in a different guise. The true view, according to Green, is that the real thing is as much a universal as it is a particular. The universal made concrete, or the particular made universal by being brought into relation with other things, are just different aspects of the true individual which alone is real.

One consequence of this is that Green's view of the world is a holistic one. The world is not made up of separate and independent items. The relating activity of Thought, therefore, does not simply relate things which are already there; on the contrary: we are clearly to think of this activity as constituting the world and the 'things' in it. Since any two things stand in some relation or other, no two things can be completely independent. This claim is perhaps best thought of as an expression of the view that the world is constituted by a *single* eternal Mind: the world is unified by one mind that constitutes every part of it, and relates every part to every other. The claim has, however, consequences for Green's view of human knowledge. In our attempts at knowledge we try to retrace in our own thought the process by which the world is, timelessly, constituted. Knowledge, therefore, does not come piecemeal, by first knowing one thing, then proceeding to the next, and so on. It is, rather, a process of relating and comparing. Nothing can be fully known until we know all its relations, and all the things to which it is related. It follows that we cannot have fully adequate knowledge of anything short of the world as a whole.

Closely connected with this holistic view of knowledge is the dis-
appearance, within Green's philosophy, of any kind of distinction
between the necessary and the contingent, or the a priori and the a
posteriori. Because of their sensory atomism, and their view that the
mind is wholly passive in its perception of matters of fact, the Empiricists had denied that connections between matters of fact could be
necessary, or could be known a priori. Relations between ideas, by
contrast, had for them something of the character of necessary or a
priori truths: since they concerned only the contents of the mind, the
mind could know them without relying on the vagaries of sense-
experience. Kant's distinction between the analytic and the synthetic is
analogous to this distinction between relations of ideas and matters of
fact. Analytic judgements are known a priori, because they involve no
more than the analysis of the concepts we are using, and thus do not
add to our knowledge—in Kant's terms, they are explicative rather
than ampliative (see *Critique of Pure Reason*, A7=B11). Kant also distinguished, within the synthetic judgements, those which are a priori
from those which are a posteriori. This distinction corresponds to, and
is made possible by, the distinction between the work of thought,
which constitutes the form of experience, and the role of intuition,
which gives the content of experience. Judgements which are true in
virtue of the form of experience can be known a priori—since the form
of experience is, after all, the mind's own imposition. Thus synthetic a
priori judgements owe their truth to the work of the mind; yet they can
be true of the world, because of the role the mind plays in constituting
the (knowable) world.

The intuition which lies behind the distinctions drawn by the Empiricists and by Kant is that a truth can be necessary, or known a priori,
only if it is—in some sense—the work of the mind. (Kant differs
crucially from the Empiricists, as we have seen, because of his view
that some aspects of the work of the mind are constitutive of (knowable) reality, not opposed to it. But this divergence is not to the present
point.) What is totally independent of the mind cannot be known a
priori, and is not necessary in any sense that we can understand.
Green does not deny this basic intuition. What he does deny is that
there is any element in experience which is not, in some sense, the
work of the mind. This is the basis for his claim that all propositions
are necessary.

Green does not claim that we can know all truths by a priori means,
or that we can understand the necessity of all those truths which we do
know. His claim is, rather, that a mind capable of grasping the world
as a whole, in all its interconnectedness, would be able to understand

every truth as a necessary truth.[19] In a complete understanding of the world, nothing would be unexplained, and there would be no element of contingency. This is the ideal towards which our knowledge aims, but which it never attains. Our knowledge is partial and incomplete, so that things which we take ourselves to know may have conditions which we do not know. This incompleteness of our knowledge is the explanation of the fact that most truths appear to us as contingent: '"physical necessity" is never absolute . . . since [a physical event] may depend on conditions which cannot be fully ascertained' (*Works*, iii. 88). Most truths as we know them lack necessity, because we are ignorant of the conditions upon which they depend. Where we can know all the conditions of a truth, as in the case of truths about our own intellectual constructions, then the necessity of the truth is evident to us:

Mathematical necessity is only more absolute [than physical necessity] because it makes hypothetical abstraction of certain conditions. . . . Of every new case with which the geometrician deals the conditions can be fully known, because constructed by himself. Once let a physical phenomenon be known with the same completeness, which in the nature of the case they cannot be by us, and it in like manner becomes necessary with the necessity of thought. (*Works*, ii. 88–9; cf. ii. 265)

This view of necessity is essentially connected with Green's holistic picture of the world. That picture is of the world as forming a system, each part of which is necessary to every other part, and can be fully understood only by reference to every other part. The world as a whole is necessary, and, in principle, intelligible to us because it is the expression of a mind analogous to ours. The necessity of a given fact derives from the role it plays in this systematic whole. If we do not appreciate the necessity of such a fact, this is simply because our knowledge is too limited to allow us to understand the way in which that fact determines and is determined by the whole of the rest of the world. It is only this incompleteness in our knowledge which prevents us from grasping the necessity of every truth. Fully adequate knowledge of the world would be knowledge of the world as a whole, and for such knowledge every truth is 'necessary with the necessity of thought'. Only God has such knowledge of the world, but this is the ideal which our knowledge presupposes and to which it aspires.

---

[19] Here there is a clear Spinozistic element in Green's thought, as in that of Hegel. By contrast with Spinoza, however, the Mind which constitutes the world is, for Green, distinct from it.

2

F. H. Bradley

F. H. Bradley was the most influential of the British Idealists. He was born in 1846, and in 1870 he was elected to a Fellowship at Merton College, Oxford. He retained this Fellowship, which did not require him to teach, until his death in 1924. His most ambitious book, *Appearance and Reality*, was published in 1893, and throughout the 1890s he was perhaps the most prominent philosopher in Britain. Certainly he was taken very seriously in the philosophical world inhabited by Russell and Moore in the early 1890s. Russell says of G. F. Stout, one of his teachers, that he 'thought very highly of Bradley; when *Appearance and Reality* was published, he said it had done as much as is humanly possible in ontology'.[1] Of himself, Russell says, 'I read Bradley at this time with avidity, and admired him more than any other recent philosopher'.[2] In an essay he wrote at this time, Russell called *Appearance and Reality* an 'epoch-making work'.[3] Moore makes an even more striking statement about Bradley. In the first version of his Research Fellowship Dissertation (written in 1896–7), he mentions Caird's *Critical Philosophy of Kant*, but says that he is prevented from sympathizing with certain features of this work 'by my far greater agreement with Mr. F. H. Bradley's general philosophical attitude. It is to Mr. Bradley that I chiefly owe my conception of the fundamental problems of Metaphysics.'[4] In view of this influence, it is important for our purposes to examine Bradley's philosophy.

[1] *The Philosophy of Bertrand Russell*, ed. P. A. Schilpp (Evanston, Ill.: The Library of Living Philosophers, Inc., 1946), p. 10; cf. *MPD*, p. 38.

[2] Schilpp, op. cit. n. 1 above, p. 10.

[3] 'The Free-Will Problem from an Idealist Standpoint', *The Collected Papers of Bertrand Russell*, i. ed. Kenneth Blackwell *et al.* (London: Allen & Unwin, 1983), p. 230. Dated, by Russell, 8 June 1895.

[4] Preface, p. 1. The manuscript of Moore's Research Fellowship Dissertation is owned by the University Library, Cambridge, and is currently on loan to Trinity College, Cambridge. I should like to thank the Librarian of Trinity College for making it available to me.

1. Experience, Relations, and Reality

We can perhaps best approach Bradley's philosophy by returning, in a more critical vein, to an aspect of Green's view which we have already touched on. We saw in the previous chapter that there are a number of questions which Green takes as more or less equivalent to one another: How is relatedness possible? How do diverse elements combine to form a fact? How is thought or judgement possible? How can unity be combined with diversity? The single question which Green takes as fundamental to all of these formulations is central to his philosophy.[5] Yet Green has, I shall argue, no answer to this question. In the end he has to accept unity-in-diversity as fundamental, given, and inexplicable. Although Green sometimes acknowledges this fact, he fails to reconcile it with other crucial aspects of his philosophy.

We saw in the last chapter that Green rejects Kant's dualism. Perhaps the most attractive feature of this dualism is that it holds out the promise of an explanation of relatedness, or of unity-in-diversity. Diverse elements are given to a single self-consciousness, which introduces unity among them—if in no other way, they are unified by the very fact of being given to a unified self-consciousness. In the idiom of relations, distinct objects are given to the mind which then creates relations among them by connecting or comparing them in thought.[6] To put it crudely, the dualist picture hopes to explain unity-in-diversity by attributing diversity to one side (the given) and unity to the other (the self to which it is given).[7] Green, as we saw in the last chapter, rejects this picture because (roughly) he finds the idea of a given which is prior to experience unintelligible. If human experience is, as Green takes it to be, a combination of unity with diversity, then diversity alone (and unity alone, or its source) is not a possible object of experience; speculation about there being such a thing is thus empty (see Chapter 1, above, pp. 33–4).

The rejection of dualism implies that neither the diversity of feelings nor the unity of thought can be considered as a separate and indepen-

---

[5] And not, of course, only to Green's philosophy. This issue, under one guise or another, has been traced back to Plato's *Philebus* and *Parmenides*; we shall find that it recurs at more than one point in Russell's work. See the present author's 'The Nature of the Proposition and the Revolt against Idealism', in Richard Rorty, J. B. Schneewind, and Quentin Skinner (eds.), *Philosophy in History* (Cambridge: CUP, 1984), pp. 375–97, where one aspect of the issue is examined.

[6] It is crucial to note that the concern here is with our knowledge or our experience of relations—relations as present to the mind. This is a crucial presupposition, both for Green and for Bradley; see Ch. 1, above, pp. 24–5.

[7] Crude as it is, there are passages of the *Critique of Pure Reason* which justify the attribution of this picture to Kant, e.g. A108.

dent entity, but that each must be considered as an aspect of, or abstraction from, human consciousness or experience as a whole. We cannot, therefore, explain human experience by saying that it results from a combination of thought and feeling, for these two elements in turn presuppose human experience, since they are not intelligible independently of it. This same line of thought leads naturally to the conclusion that any attempt to *explain* experience or consciousness will fail for the same reason: experience is that in terms of which everything is to be understood, so any purported explanation of experience is bound to be circular. This conclusion is one that Green explicitly accepts, at least at one moment: 'the consciousness itself . . . being that by means of which everything is accounted for, does not in turn admit of being accounted for' (*Prol. Eth.*, s. 50).

In spite of his rejection of dualism, and his acceptance of the further conclusion that consciousness must be taken as fundamental and inexplicable, however, Green talks in terms that are incompatible with these doctrines. He speaks, for example, of 'sensations which, as brought into relation by intelligence, become sensible objects or events' (*Prol. Eth.*, s. 29). This is simply the dualist picture over again: on the one hand the sensations, on the other hand the intelligence which relates them. Again, we examined the pressure which led Green to distinguish 'Thought' from 'mere thought' (see Chapter 1, above, pp. 37–9). Seen uncharitably, this distinction is a straightforward equivocation in which Green indulges in order to preserve the claim that thought is constitutive of experience. This claim seems to be refuted by the view, which Green accepts, that thought (in the ordinary sense) is intelligible only as an abstraction from experience; Green's response is that the Thought which constitutes experience is *not* thought in the ordinary sense ('Thought' appears rather to be consciousness or experience as a whole). Seen in this way, however, what Green has done is to preserve the formulation 'thought constitutes experience' by drastically changing its sense. On Green's view thought (in the only sense of the word that we really have) does *not* constitute experience. The equivocation between 'Thought' and 'mere thought' is simply an attempt to avoid this conclusion. It is perhaps not surprising that Green should, in these ways, fail fully to acknowledge the consequences of his rejection of dualism, for these consequences threaten to undermine his philosophy as a whole. If we can no longer speak of the need for 'combination' in the constitution of human experience, then we have no basis for the view that experience requires a combining agent or intelligence analogous to, but distinct from, the human. Green's argument for an eternal self-consciousness is thus cast in doubt.

The position in which we seem to be left, then, is that experience, and the unity-in-diversity which it manifests, must be taken as basic and inexplicable. This claim is, I think, a consequence of Green's rejection of dualism; as we have seen, however, it is a consequence that Green does not fully acknowledge. In Bradley's philosophy, by contrast, this same claim plays a fundamental role. Bradley speaks of the unity-in-diversity which is given as 'immediate experience' or 'feeling', and says: 'That on which my view rests is the immediate unity which comes in feeling' (*ETR*, pp. 230–1). Two points about immediate experience are crucial to Bradley's philosophy, and will be discussed at some length. The first is that the unity of immediate experience is non-relational. What is given is not made up of distinct objects with relations holding among them; it is, rather, a unified whole within which diverse aspects can be distinguished.[8] Secondly, immediate experience is not the only form of human consciousness. It is the foundation of all other forms, and is in some sense never absent; but not all human experience is of this kind ('immediate experience' might thus be contrasted with 'mediated experience').

The first point is based on the idea that to speak of two things as related to each other implies the distinctness of the things from one another, and of the relation from both of them. The things have, to a greater or lesser extent, a certain independence of the relational fact which is asserted; each of them, for example, will stand in other relations to other things. Analogously, the relation will be capable of relating other pairs of things, even if in fact it does not do so. To speak of a fact or situation as relational thus implies that it is made up of separate elements. On Bradley's view, however, what is merely felt does not consist of distinct elements with relations among them; it is a unified whole. We may distinguish elements within this whole, but to do so is to go beyond mere feeling: 'the unity of feeling contains no individual terms with relations between them, while without these [i.e. separate terms] no experience can be really relational' (*CE*, p. 642).

---

[8] Some idea of Bradley's influence on Russell can be gathered from this passage from one of the latter's undergraduate essays: 'If I lie in a field on a hot day with my eyes shut, and feel sleepily the heat of the sun, the buzz of the flies, the slight tickling of a few blades of grass, it is possible to get into a frame of mind which seems to belong to a much earlier stage of evolution; at such times there is only what Bradley calls "a vague mass of the felt"; I do not reflect on the outside causes of the various blurred and indistinct sensations, nor on the fact that I am feeling these sensations. Perhaps we may hope that there are also possible states of mind where we are above the distinction of subject and object, as in pure sensation we are below it; but to pursue such a possibility would be to plunge into mysticism' ('On the Distinction between the Psychological and Metaphysical Points of View', in op. cit. n. 3 above, p. 196. Dated by the editors as spring 1894.).

Relatedness implies some measure of independence, which does not exist at the level of immediate experience. Experience *comes* as a unified whole. Nothing in the feeling felt at a given moment, it would seem, could assure me that it is made up of elements which are capable of existing in other contexts, in other relations. I may analyse the feeling into such elements, but doing so seems to go beyond the feeling as merely felt.

The conclusion that immediate experience is non-relational in character can be better understood by drawing on an argument which Bradley presents in what appears to be a rather different context.[9] The argument occurs in Chapter III of *Appearance and Reality*. In a notorious passage, Bradley claims that relations involve a vicious regress: a relation can combine its terms only if it is *related* to each, but this requires two new relations, to each of which the same argument applies, so 'we are hurried off into the eddy of a hopeless process, since we are forced to go on finding new relations without end' (*A. & R.*, p. 28). This argument seems to leave Bradley open to the charge that he has failed to appreciate the difference between objects or things on the one hand, and relations on the other. Relations, it may be said, *relate*; we do not need to invoke other relations to explain how they combine their terms, for they would not be relations unless they had this combining power. This response, however, seems to miss the point of Bradley's argument. Relations do have the power to relate their terms, but the question is whether this power of combination is intelligible to us. Bradley's claim is that it can be made intelligible only if it is seen as dependent upon the non-relational unity with which we are acquainted in immediate experience. If we take the relational unity as independent and fundamental, as we do if we think of immediate experience as relational, then we find that we can make no sense of the power of relations to relate their terms. Thus one might put the point of the regress argument like this. If you think of relations as the fundamental source of unity and connectedness, then you cannot explain *how* relations relate (for what is fundamental cannot be explained). But then you cannot explain what is special about relations, or about the connection between a relation and its terms, so that *this* connection will seem to be on a par with any other, and thus to demand a further relation to effect it. Since this further relation is no more intelligible than the first, the regress is launched.

What Bradley's regress argument attempts to show, then, is that

---

[9] It has been claimed that Bradley in fact intended the argument to apply to immediate experience. See M. J. Cresswell, 'Reality as Experience in F. H. Bradley', *Australasian Journal of Philosophy* 55 (1977), 169–88.

relational unity is not fundamental. Relations and relational unity are intelligible only as abstractions from a more fundamental sort of unity. Support for this interpretation of Bradley's position comes from his unfinished article on relations,[10] where he says:

a relation in the strict sense is always an abstraction. The relation itself is not the entire fact of the relational situation, as actually experienced, but in every case omits and ignores more or less of what there is contained. (*CE*, p. 648)

We can understand relations and their relating power only by thinking of them as abstractions from an actual, given situation or fact. We cannot think of the given 'relational situation' as explicable in terms of relations, because relations must be explained in terms of the given situation.

Immediate experience must thus manifest a unity which is non-relational in character. A recognition of this feature of immediate experience makes plausible the second of the two facts that I mentioned, that immediate experience is not the only form of human experience. For whatever one may think about the status of relations, it is hard to deny that we *do* think relationally, or, as Bradley puts it, that we do have 'relational experience'. (As we shall see, Bradley, like Green, holds that all thought is relational, so that it is redundant to speak of 'relational thought'.) Relational experience, according to Bradley, develops out of immediate experience, and is only possible on the basis of immediate experience. Bradley says, for example, 'immediate experience, however much transcended, both remains and is active. It is not a stage which shows itself at the beginning and then disappears, but it remains at the bottom throughout as fundamental' (*ETR*, p. 161).[11] Now what is important here is not only the fact that there are forms of consciousness other than immediate experience, but also the suggestion that the development and existence of these forms can be explained by reference to immediate experience. The suggestion is that there are inadequacies or inconsistencies in feeling, and that thought, or relational experience, develops as a response to these inadequacies: 'feeling is compelled to pass off into the relational consciousness. It is the ground and foundation for further developments, but it is a foundation that bears them only by a ceaseless lapse from itself' (*A. & R.*,

---

[10] *CE*, pp. 630–76. In spite of its incompleteness, this article seems to me to be the best source for Bradley's views about relations.

[11] Bradley is willing to leave open the question whether there is in fact a stage of mental life which consists only of pure feeling, with no element of mediation. He seems to believe that there is such a stage, but the belief is not important for his wider views. See *ETR*, p. 174.

p. 407). In a more overtly Hegelian idiom: there are contradictions in immediate experience which lead to its transcendence.

One of Bradley's statements of the inadequacy of immediate experience runs as follows:

> Feeling has a content, and this content is not consistent within itself, and such a discrepancy tends to destroy and to break up the stage of feeling. The matter may be briefly put thus—the finite content is irreconcilable with the immediacy of its existence. For the finite content is necessarily determined from the outside: its external relations penetrate its existence, and so carry that beyond its own being.... This fleeting and untrue character is perpetually forced on our notice by the hard fact of change. (*A. & R.*, p. 497)

Several aspects of this seem to require comment. Implicit in it is the idea, to which I shall return, that what is 'determined from the outside' is therefore inadequate; that only the completely self-contained can be completely adequate (see pp. 52–4, below). More immediately puzzling, perhaps, is the idea that experience can be described as 'determined from the outside', or as not self-contained. This idea runs directly counter to the Humean dogma that a given experience is a discrete 'mental item', which has no intrinsic connection with anything else—all such connections being simply the result of our habitual association of one idea with another (see pp. 23–4, above). Bradley's rejection of this Humean, atomistic picture of experience is one of the fundamental points of his philosophy.[12] The last sentence of the passage quoted above gives us one way of understanding it. Bradley holds that the temporal, changing nature of our experience shows that this experience does not consist of discrete, self-contained mental items.

The given experience which, according to the Humean picture, is discrete and self-contained is, presumably, the experience of a single moment. One way in which to break the hold of that picture is to press the questions: What is a single moment? How long does such a moment last? If we take a period of arbitrary but short duration—a minute or two, Russell once suggested[13]—then we cannot avoid the continuity of one moment or specious present with the next. The temporal transition which takes place within our moment is one with transitions which lead beyond it to earlier and later moments. The second half of a given moment and the first half of the next presumably form a new moment, which is undeniably connected with each, and which forms a

---

[12] Again, we find this doctrine in an early essay of Russell's: 'Sense-particulars are not individuals: they are not completely differentiated from one another: in sensation there is nothing discrete, but one sensation merges into another'. ('Paper on Epistemology, I', in op. cit. n. 3 above, p. 122. Dated, by Russell, Nov. 1893.).

[13] See 'The Philosophy of Logical Atomism', in *Marsh*, p. 203.

natural transition between them. Thus thinking of moments in this way, as periods of short duration, seems incompatible with the idea that the experience of each moment is discrete and self-contained. Just as each moment (on this conception) is continuous with moments before and after it, so the experience of each moment will be continuous with the experience of moments before and after. Nor can we try to avoid this conclusion by finding genuine instants, moments with no duration. No experience could occur in a durationless moment, so the appeal to such moments will not help us to find a unit of experience which we can regard as self-contained (see *PL*, p. 52, for considerations akin to those advanced in this paragraph).

These considerations suggest that immediate experience does not come in discrete, self-contained units. What is experienced at any moment—however we conceive of moments—is continuous with what is not experienced at that moment. Nor can we appeal to the whole of immediate experience, for no such whole is given, at least in anything like ordinary experience—the experience of a moment is transitory and vanishing. It is precisely because of this sequential, successive character of experience that any given experience is not self-contained, but is connected with what it does not include, and is thus, by Bradley's lights, inadequate. This inadequacy can be seen as stemming from the limited, incomplete character of any given experience. But how are we to remedy this? Not by attempting to expand the given experience, say by opening our eyes wider—even if we could make immediate experience more inclusive, still something would be excluded, and the tactic of expanding the given would fail us at last. Bradley distinguishes the content of experience (*what* it is) from its existence (*that* it is). We cannot expand experience on the side of its existence beyond very narrow limits; but what we can do is to relate its content to the content of other experiences, past and future. Considered as existing, a past experience is gone—since it is past it no longer exists. But if we abstract the content of experience from its existence, the content of a past experience can be connected with a present experience. The expansion of experience which is a response to its incompleteness or relativity thus takes place on the side of its content, the 'what' of experience, not on the side of its existence. The expansion which is forced on us thus involves a separation, or abstraction, of the content of experience from its existence. For reasons that will concern us more later, this separation is identified with the beginnings of thought, or ideality:

the content of the given is for ever relative to something not given, and the nature of its 'what' is hence essentially to transcend its 'that'. This we may call the ideality of the given finite. It is not manufactured by thought, but thought itself is its development and product. The essential nature of the finite is that everywhere, as it presents itself, its character should slide beyond the limits of its existence. (*A. & R.*, p. 146)

The content of an experience, thought of as abstracted from the immediate existence of the experience, can be related to the contents of other experiences to form a more inclusive whole—no longer of experience but of thought or knowledge. (The fleeting character of each experience prevents this from being done until the content and the existence are separated.) While something is excluded from the system of our knowledge, that system will suffer from an inadequacy analogous to that of the content of a single experience. This inadequacy stems from incompleteness, and leads to a striving for a completeness in which it would be overcome. The ideal of thought, and the goal towards which it tends, is thus a holistic system of knowledge in which everything would be related to everything else, and nothing excluded (see *A. & R.*, pp. 315–16; cf. also Chapter 1, Section 3, above). This ideal is not one that Bradley believes we can in fact realize. More importantly, he holds that even if realized it would still not be wholly satisfactory because even a complete system of thought is still a system of *thought*, and thus confined to the content of experience, and unable to do justice to the immediacy of its existence. This is a matter that will occupy us at some length in the second section of this chapter.

In discussing the transcendence of immediate experience I appealed to the idea that only what is self-subsistent and not dependent upon anything else is fully adequate and truly real. This idea is one that Bradley relies upon more often than he explicitly states; it comes most clearly to the surface, perhaps, in this remark about the given: 'If the now in which the real appears is purely discrete, then we may say that, as characterised by exclusion the phenomenon, if apparent, is *not self-contained, and so not real*' (*PL*, p. 52; my emphasis). According to Bradley's conception of reality, to say that a thing is real implies that it is not dependent on anything else: it exists absolutely and unconditionally. Where something is conditioned by, or dependent upon, other things, true reality can be obtained only if we take the thing together with its conditions. Analogously, if a thing is real then the thought of that thing will be perfectly adequate and intelligible by itself. Thinking of it will not involve or imply other things: a real thing, on this view, is something we can comprehend in its own terms, without appeal to anything else.[14]

---

[14] This view has a long philosophical history, most obviously in Spinoza and in Hegel. Thus Spinoza defines substance as 'that which is in itself, and is conceived through itself; in other words, that of which a conception can be formed independently of any other conception' (*Ethics*, Pt. I, Definition III). Hegel explicitly endorses this attitude of Spinoza

One way to understand this doctrine is through the idea that our aim in metaphysics is absolute and unconditional truth (the 'study of first principles or ultimate truths' as Bradley puts it—*A. & R.*, p. 1). Now suppose we are considering something which is dependent upon another thing, or which is intelligible only in terms of something other than itself. To advance a proposition about such a thing as a metaphysical truth must always be incorrect. Since the thing itself, and our conception of it, is dependent upon other things, so also is the truth which we advance. It may, indeed, be true, but its truth is due to conditions which our statement leaves unexpressed. In one sense of the term, the truth is conditional. If metaphysics strives after truths which are, in this sense, absolutely unconditional, then that metaphysics will reject what is limited or dependent as unreal. To be a metaphysical truth, a statement about a limited thing would have to include statements about all the things on which it depends. In other words, to turn the limited thing into an object of metaphysical truth (and thus into something fully real) we have to take it together with all its condition (and their conditions . . .) and everything upon which it depends (and all the things upon which they depend . . .). Thus the objects which metaphysics counts as real, or as substances, will be sufficiently inclusive to contain all of their conditions, and to rely upon nothing else for their intelligibility. Such objects are thus self-contained or self-subsistent; the Reality we seek in metaphysics is a Reality which exists absolutely, and is not dependent upon anything else.

In Bradley, this way of conceiving Reality is manifested and illustrated in a passage in which he attacks those who accept what is limited, partial, or conditional as real. The basis of the attack is the idea that to accept a conditional way of thinking as real is to suppose it correct unconditionally. What may be valid within a particular sphere must nevertheless be called unreal, for otherwise we implicitly claim that it is valid outside its own sphere. It is only in this way that we can, so to speak, keep everything in its proper place:

Everywhere on behalf of the real Absolute I have been warning the reader against that false absolutism which in philosophy is to me another name for error. . . . It takes some distinction within the whole and asserts it as being real by itself and unconditionally; and then from this misconceived ground it goes on to deny or to belittle other complementary aspects of the same whole. But, as against such absolutism, the very soul of the Absolute which I defend is its

(see *Lectures on the History of Philosophy*, trans. E. S. Haldane and Frances H. Simon (London: Routledge & Kegan Paul, 1955; 1st edn. 1892), iii. 257); he also argues the same point in a different context (see *Science of Logic*, trans. A. V. Miller (London: Allen & Unwin, 1969), pp. 86, 130, 154–5).

insistence and emphasis on an all-pervading relativism. Everything is justified as being real in its own sphere and degree, but not so as to entitle it to invade other spheres . . . it is the Absolute alone that gives its due to every interest just because it refuses to everything more than its own due. (*ETR*, p. 470)

For Bradley, to call something 'real' is at once to assert its claim to be absolute and unconditional.

Two negative conclusions about what is (ultimately) real can be drawn from the parts of Bradley's philosophy which we have already examined. These are that neither immediate experience nor relations are real (from the unreality of relations, as we shall see, Bradley infers the unreality of all ordinary phenomena). In the case of immediate experience we have already reached this conclusion in a slightly different guise: the inadequacies of immediate experience which explain its transcendence (see p. 50, above) equally provide reasons why it cannot be real. To recapitulate briefly: what is given in immediate experience was found to be not self-contained, but limited by, and dependent upon, what is not given with it. From this, and from the conception of Reality sketched above, it at once follows that immediate experience is not real. The conclusion that relations are not real, or that Reality is not relational, also follows fairly straightforwardly from our previous discussions. Relations, we saw, are dependent upon the prior non-relational unity which is immediately given, and are comprehensible only as abstractions from some such unity. If this is correct, then that way of thinking about the world which sees it as made up of separate objects in various relations to one another cannot be the correct way of thinking to employ when our concern is with Reality. However useful this way of thinking may be—and Bradley does not deny its usefulness, and even its indispensability—it is not a way of thinking that can be adequate to Reality. Reality is not made up of separate objects with relations among them.

To this point I have discussed Bradley's view of relations without reference to the distinction between internal and external relations. It is in terms of this distinction that Bradley's view is usually explained and criticized; this emphasis, however, seems to me to be misplaced. Roughly, the distinction is that a relation is internal to an object if it is part of that object's nature or essence to be related in that way; if it is accidental or not a part of the object's inner nature to be so related then the relation is external. Until he comes to defend himself against criticism, however, Bradley makes no real use of this distinction. In his replies to criticism, he both rejects the ultimate validity of the distinction, and also denies that he accepts internal relations—on his view *all* relations are unreal (see *A. & R.*, p. 513, and *ETR*, pp. 239–40). Neither internal nor external relations are ultimately real on Bradley's view, because neither can succeed in attaining the non-relational unity which is fundamental. The difference between them is that in internal relations this defect is explicit. If *a* is internally related to *b*, then the relation to *b* is part of *a*'s internal nature. Since '*a*'s internal nature' is just what *a* essentially *is*, it follows that *a* is not independent, but is what it is only because of its relation to *b*. Internal relations are thus unstable: as relations they set up their objects as independent entities; as internal they make it clear that their objects are not independent, but can be considered only as part of a larger totality. Thus it is that 'internal relations ... point towards a higher consummation beyond themselves' (*ETR*, pp. 239–40). By their internality, internal relations make it manifest that they are destined to be transcended in a higher unity in which the separateness of the relata, and thus the relational nature of the whole, has disappeared. External relations, by contrast, are supposed to be relations in which the dependence of the relata is not acknowledged but is denied. Each object is taken to be what it is independently of the relation, and so external relations are not obviously unstable in the way that internal relations are. They thus 'cut us off in principle from any advance to a higher unity' (*ETR*, p. 240). Both internal relations and external relations are inadequate, but the internality of the former is an acknowledgement of this fact. Because external relations contain no such acknowledgement, they are less satisfactory than internal relations (*ETR*, p. 312). Internal relations, therefore, have a preferred status not because they are fully adequate but, on the contrary, because their inadequacy is the more obvious.

The unreality of relations is the basis of Bradley's other paradoxical conclusions. He condemns as unreal all of the fundamental features of what we take to be ordinary things—as well as things themselves. In Part I of *A. & R.*, Substantive and Adjective, Space and Time, Causality, Motion, Change, Activity, and the Self are all examined and found to be unreal. I shall not discuss the details of these arguments. Bradley employs various tactics, but his strategy is always the same: the phenomenon concerned is shown to be relational, or to depend upon relations, and thus to deserve the same fate as relations themselves. At the end of Chapter III of *A. & R.*, which deals with relations, Bradley puts the matter like this:

The reader who has followed and grasped the principle of this chapter, will have little need to spend his time upon those which succeed it. He will have seen that our experience, where relational is not true; and he will have condemned, almost without a hearing, the great mass of phenomena. (*A. & R.*, p. 29)

Another phenomenon which is relational, and thus unreal, is diversity or plurality. If there were a plurality of real objects, then they would have to be related, if only by the relation of difference (see *A. & R.*, p. 24); since the relation is not real, the plurality cannot be real either. I shall spell this out in a little more detail. All relatedness, we saw, is an abstraction from a non-relational unity. The supposition that there are two real things in some relation to one another leads at once to the idea of a non-relational unity from which the objects and the relation are abstractions. But as abstractions, neither the objects nor the relation are real; the non-relational unity alone is real. This argument can of course be applied to any supposition that there is more than one real thing. Bradley's monism follows from this: Reality is one.

Bradley's monism is to be understood in terms of the conception of Reality which I have already articulated. The real, on this conception, is that which is independent; since the order of explanation is assumed to follow the order of dependence, the real is that in terms of which everything is to be explained, whereas it is not to be explained in terms of anything external to it. One assumption embodied in Bradley's monism is thus that explanation is, so to speak, expansionist: the explanation of anything short of the world as a whole will involve other things; since these other things must be explained in turn, a *complete* explanation of anything, could we attain it, would involve the world as a whole. The world as a whole, by contrast, is self-explanatory in at least this sense: since there is nothing outside it in terms of which it could be explained, any explanation that it may have must be in its own terms. A second assumption of Bradley's monism is that everything *has* an explanation—i.e. some sort of Principle of Sufficient Reason is presupposed. This assumption can equally be seen as underlying Bradley's view of relations. This view presupposes that it cannot be an ultimate and inexplicable fact that two things are related; the fact must be explicable, and the explanation, at least in the first instance, is to be found in a more inclusive whole. Only in terms of some such whole can the supposed relational fact be made intelligible. These sorts of ideas surface in a strikingly rationalistic passage:

In mechanical explanation generally the connexion of the elements with the laws remains unknown and external.... But any such irrationality and externality cannot be the last truth about things. Somewhere there must be a reason why this and that appear together. And this reason and reality must reside in the whole from which terms and relations are abstractions, a whole in which their internal connexion must lie. (*A. & R.*, p. 517)

Bradley rejects 'the great mass of phenomena' because they are relational. He rejects relations because they are intelligible only as abstractions from a non-relational unity, because they are one-sided, partial, or incomplete. These reasons for rejecting relations, and the phenomena which depend upon relations, ought to connect with the sense that we can legitimately give to 'rejection' here, and thus also with the positive nature of Reality. In particular, it follows from the reasons which we have for rejecting relations that we cannot simply say that they do not exist at all. What is incomplete requires completion; what is partial or one-sided must be complemented; what is abstract requires to be restored to context. These processes will transform our objects, but they will not completely abolish them; a relation does not exist as such in the non-relational unity from which it is abstracted, but it must exist there in some guise and in some sense or it could not be abstracted from the non-relational unity. Reality must in some sense contain all of the phenomena, but in Reality each phenomenon is transformed, so as to be unified with all the others in a single whole. It is important to stress this point. Bradley speaks of phenomena as 'contradictory', and one natural conclusion to draw from this is that we should seek Reality in a realm completely divorced from the phenomenal. But such is not Bradley's view.[15] For him, Reality or the Absolute is not beyond all phenomena or totally distinct from them. On the contrary, all phenomena find their place within the Absolute, but are there so changed as to form a unified whole in which all things are harmoniously combined: 'Reality . . . is not the sum of things. It is the unity in which all things, coming together, are transmuted, in which they are changed all alike, though not changed equally (*A. & R.*, p. 432). We have already seen one reason why Bradley holds that Reality is not wholly distinct from phenomena, but made up from them in some sense: the basis on which he argues that phenomena are unreal would not justify the claim that they are completely separate from Reality. There is also a second reason for this view. If Reality and the phenomena formed two disjoint realms then there would, presumably, have to be some relation between them—if only the relation of difference. Given Bradley's views about relations, this would be absurd. If there were anything at all which were not included in Reality, then Reality would have to be related to that thing. Since this is impossible, Reality must include everything that exists in any sense at all. Things may be transformed in the Absolute, but they cannot be excluded from it: Reality is all-embracing.

Bradley's Absolute, as we have seen over the last couple of para-

---

[15] The view which is here contrasted with Bradley's is, in outline, Kant's. For Kant, the truly real, the world as it is in itself, is distinct from the phenomenal world, not implicit within it. See Ch. 1, above, pp. 32–3.

graphs, is a single, unified, all-embracing whole. But it is not an all-embracing whole in the way in which a fully comprehensive system of knowledge might be. Bradley's ideal, unlike Green's, is in no sense intellectual or made up of thought. This is because thought, as we shall see in more detail later (Section 2, below), is relational, and as relational it is not fundamental but depends upon a prior non-relational unity. Since Reality is dependent upon nothing else, it must possess a non-relational unity analogous to that of immediate experience. (If Reality were relational, it would depend upon a non-relational unity which it did not include.) This, indeed, is one of the roles that immediate experience plays in Bradley's thought. Immediate experience is, as we have seen, not itself Reality; but it supplies us with 'a low and imperfect example of an immediate whole' which is crucial if the idea of an immediate and non-relational unity is to make sense to us. We can see the Absolute as combining features of both immediate experience and thought. On the one hand, the Absolute must have the completeness which is potentially a property of a system of thought (a complete system of thought or knowledge, while perhaps unrealizable, is surely a coherent ideal); on the other hand the Absolute must be a non-relational unity and have the immediacy or givenness of immediate experience.

Emphasizing the immediacy or givenness of the Absolute helps to render comprehensible one of Bradley's more puzzling doctrines: that the Absolute is 'a single and all-inclusive experience' (*A. & R.*, p. 129). Bradley offers detailed arguments for this view which are not, however, very convincing.[16] One commentator has suggested that the view must be simply a 'basic assumption' of Bradley's view for which no argument can be given, that it functions as 'the foundation and presupposition of his whole metaphysics'.[17] It seems to me, on the contrary, that the view can be seen as stemming from the internal logic of Bradley's thought. Given the immediacy of the Absolute, for which I have already argued, it is natural to think of it as experience. One might, indeed, take immediacy or givenness as the defining characteristic of experience. Such an experience, however, is not to be equated with ordinary experience, such as we might have in sense-perception. The Absolute must be a single atemporal experience, in which everything is somehow given at once. Bradley never attempts to describe such an experience and it is, I think, part of his view that any descrip-

---

[16] *A. & R.*, pp. 126–9; for a thorough, but not very sympathetic, examination of these arguments, see R. Wollheim, *F. H. Bradley* (Harmondsworth: Penguin Books, 1969), pp. 197–200.

[17] Cresswell, op. cit. n. 9 above, pp. 169, 170.

tion of it is impossible. The experience which is the Absolute is accessible to thought and description only in its broadest outlines; ultimately it is ineffable in character. It is thus arguable that Bradley's philosophy should be thought of as a form of mysticism.[18] These ideas may seem to contradict the rationalistic elements which we have seen in his thought. The Principle of Sufficient Reason, the demand that the world must be intelligible, goes oddly with the idea of ultimate reality as a kind of *experience*, for experience cannot, presumably, be thought of as *intelligible*. But the paradox is not, I think, damning. Reality, for Bradley, is not ultimately accessible to thought, but in so far as it is accessible to thought it must be thoroughly intelligible. Indeed one might say that it is just because Bradley, like others in the idealist tradition, takes 'accessible to thought' in such a strong sense that he ultimately draws back and insists that Reality is not so accessible. The paradox here is that of the great rationalist, the indefatigable arguer, who finds that reason and argument are ultimately inadequate. But it is only ultimately that they fail. Bradley rejects rationalism in the end, but only because he takes it utterly seriously at every point along the way. The failure of rationalism in Bradley's hands is an internal failure, a failure of reason to live up to what Bradley at least construes as reason's own demands.

2. Ideas, Judgement, and Truth

Bradley's views about judgement, and related issues, may be best approached through his criticism of the Empiricists. Both Locke and Hume claim that a judgement or belief is an idea, or group of ideas (Locke, *Essay*, III. iv. 5; Hume, *Treatise*, I. iii); indeed, given the empiricist view of the mind, its contents, and its functions, it is hard to see what alternative would be open to them. Bradley attacks this view on two fronts. The first is the empiricist account of the idea in judgement. Ideas, both in Locke's account and in Hume's, are mental phenomena, particular mental objects or events which exist or occur in the mind of a given person at a particular time. But Bradley insists that an idea, in the sense in which ideas are even prima-facie candidates for being the constituents of judgement, cannot be identified with particular mental items:

In England at all events we have lived too long in the psychological attitude. We have taken it for granted and as a matter of course that, like sensations

---

[18] This is a claim to which we shall return at the end of this chapter.

and emotions, ideas are phenomena. And, considering these phenomena as psychical facts, we have tried (with what success I will not ask) to distinguish between ideas and sensations. But, intent on this, we have as good as forgotten the way in which logic uses ideas. (*PL*, p. 2)

The essential point here, for our purposes, is that we cannot identify logical ideas, ideas used in judgement, with psychological ideas or mental states. (Hereafter I use 'idea' always in the former sense, in which an idea is at least a prima facie candidate for a constituent of judgement.) In the sense in which mental states seem to be undeniable and unproblematic, a mental state is a particular, datable object or event, a unique mental phenomenon. Taken in this strict sense, a mental state is always the mental state of a given person at a given time, and we cannot speak of 'the same mental state' occurring in some other person or at some other time. An idea, by contrast, is general or universal. There could be no judgement at all if it made no sense to speak of two people as having the same idea, or one person having a given idea on two occasions. A non-repeatable item could not have the symbolic function of ideas. An idea is thus something repeatable, so that when a mental phenomenon is used as an idea it is at most the *content* of the phenomenon which is relevant, not its existence. (For Bradley's distinction between content and existence, see pp. 51–2, above.) Thus Bradley says: 'Meaning consists of a part of the content (original or acquired), cut off, fixed by the mind, and considered apart from the existence of the sign' (*PL*, p. 4). How much of the content of a mental phenomenon is relevant to its role as a logical idea may vary. The details of Bradley's theory here are not to the present point;[19] what is central is that all symbolism—and thus all thought or judgement— requires the separation of content from existence (see pp. 51–2, above). If we take the content with its existence we have a particular mental phenomenon, which cannot be an idea. Only when we abstract the content of the phenomenon from its existence is an idea formed. This abstraction is thus necessary to any thought or judgement.

An idea, as ideas are used in judgement, is thus an abstraction from particular mental phenomena. It does not, therefore, exist as such. There simply is no particular thing which *is* the idea:

[19] I have suppressed a good deal of complexity at this point. Bradley says that in any symbol we can distinguish three 'sides' or aspects: its existence, its content, and its signification; see *PL*, p. 3. Exactly what connection he sees between its content and its signification is hard to ascertain; see Wollheim, op. cit. n. 16 above, pp. 27–31. A version of Bradley's doctrine of the three aspects of an idea occurs in Russell's 'On the Distinction between the Psychological and Metaphysical Points of View': 'besides their existence and their nature, our ideas have what we may call meaning' (op. cit. n. 8 above, p. 196; cf. also p. 197).

an idea, if we use idea of meaning . . . can not as such exist. It can not ever be an event, with a place in the series of time and space. It can be a fact no more inside our heads than it can outside of them. And, if you take this mere idea by itself, it is an adjective divorced, a parasite cut loose, a spirit without a body seeking rest in another, an abstraction from the concrete, a mere possibility which by itself *is* nothing. (*PL*, pp. 7–8)

Unlike Locke's abstract ideas or Hume's substitutes for them, Bradley's ideas are not identified with any kind of mental particular. They are genuinely universal, and as such must be abstractions from the mental phenomena.

This, then, is the first part of Bradley's attack on the empiricist theory of judgement: the ideas used in judgement are not mental particulars. The second part of his attack is that a judgement cannot be a synthesis of ideas of any sort. In particular, Bradley argues against (what he takes to be) the traditional subject-predicate view of judgement. He speaks, for instance, of the 'superstition of subject, predicate and copula' (*PL*, pp. 13–14). The fact that Bradley represents himself as rejecting the subject-predicate view of judgement is striking, not least because Russell tends to blame the errors of his opponents—including Bradley—on the fact that they accept the subject-predicate view (see e.g. *Leibniz*, p. 12; *Principles*, 51; we shall return to this point in Chapter 4, below, pp. 136–46). It is, therefore, worth considering in what sense Bradley's view is, and in what sense it is not, a subject-predicate view.

The sense in which Bradley's *is* a subject-predicate view of judgement is relatively clear-cut. Judgement, on his view, consists of a predicate, or 'ideal content', ascribed to a subject (see e.g. *PL*, p. 10). To this point, however, two crucial qualifications must be made. The first is that Bradley does not suppose that accepting only judgements of the subject-predicate form enables him to dispense with relations. On the contrary, his view is that all judgement is relational; the subject of the judgement is related to the predicate (see *A. & R.*, Chapter II; also pp. 68–9, below). Russell later argues against the subject-predicate view by insisting on just this point: 'that judgments of subject and predicate are themselves relational'—but this is not something that Bradley denied.[20] The second qualification that must be entered is less straightforward. In the traditional theory, as Bradley sees it, the subject of the judgement is one of the constituents of the judgement and, if

---

[20] *Leibniz*, p. 15. Green too would not have denied this; indeed it is, as we saw, central to his attack on Empiricism (see pp. 26–31, above). Russell makes the point as if it contradicted Leibniz, Kant, and the post-Kantian Idealists; but in fact it is only Leibniz who straightforwardly disagrees with Russell here.

judgement is a synthesis of ideas, must therefore be an idea. In Bradley's theory, by contrast, the subject of the judgement is reality, which is not an idea and cannot be a constituent of the judgement: 'the ultimate subject is never an idea.... The subject, in the end, is always reality, which is qualified by adjectives of ideal content' (*PL*, p. 81). The first step in the argument is straightforward. A judgement is always about something which is not itself included in the judgement:

A judgment says something about some fact or reality.... We not only say something, but it must also be about something actual that we say it. For consider: a judgment is true or false, and its truth or falsehood can not lie in itself. They involve a reference to something beyond. (*PL*, p. 41)

The reality beyond the judgement, which the judgement is about and which determines its truth or falsehood, is what Bradley takes as the subject of the judgement: 'The actual judgment asserts that S-P [*sic*] is forced on our minds by a reality *x*. And this reality, whatever it may be, is the subject of the judgment' (*PL*, p. 41). In this sense every judgement must have a subject, for a judgement is not merely one or more ideas (an ideal content) but is the assertion that the idea holds of reality. It is on this basis that Bradley argues that the subject-predicate theory, or any other theory which makes judgement out to be a synthesis of ideas, must be incorrect. Judgement cannot be merely a synthesis of ideas, for judgement must also have a subject that is not an idea.

The argument above is only the first step towards the conclusion that judgement is not a synthesis of ideas. For as it stands the argument presupposes that a synthesis of ideas cannot, as such, be about reality. As against this, it is perhaps natural to suppose that our ideas designate (parts of) reality, and thus succeed in being about it. Bradley's claim that a synthesis of ideas cannot be a judgement is thus based upon an argument that ideas cannot designate reality, that the gap between ideas and reality cannot be bridged.

The argument against the possibility of designation is complex, but the basic thought on which it rests is simple. An idea is universal, in the sense that it may apply to many cases (even if in fact it should only apply to one); and this is an essential feature of ideas (cf. the discussion of the distinction between ideas and mental phenomena above, pp. 59–61). Reality, by contrast, is quite particular and unique. Bradley's claim is that ideas, just because they are universal and general, cannot succeed in designating particular and specific facts:

Ideas are universal, and, no matter what it is that we try to say and dimly mean, what we really succeed in asserting is nothing individual.... The fact given us is singular, it is quite unique; but our terms are all general and state a truth which may apply as well to many other cases ... the judgment will be true of any case of a certain sort; but it cannot be true of the reality; for that is a fact and not a sort. (*PL*, pp. 49–50)

Let us see how Bradley articulates this point in the case of three sorts of expressions which one might think of as designating in an unproblematic way: proper names, spatio-temporal locations, and indexical expressions.

The idea that a proper name is a guarantee of unique reference is one which Bradley treats with scorn. In opposition to Mill, he insists that if such a name is to play any role in judgement, it must do so by conveying an idea; but if it conveys an idea, then it is at once universal, and so might apply to objects other than the intended one. A name cannot simply and immediately fasten on to an object; it must be associated with some properties of the object. But then the name could apply equally to another object, if there were another object which had the relevant properties:

Now a sign can not possibly be destitute of meaning. Originally imposed as an arbitrary mark, that very process which makes it a sign and associates it firmly with the thing it signifies, must associate with it also some qualities and characters of that which it stands for. If it did not to some extent *mean* the thing, it could never get to *stand* for it at all. (*PL*, p. 60)

The more promising idea of assuring uniqueness of designation by specifying spatial and temporal location also gets short shrift from Bradley. The objection here is that if we have no guarantee of the uniqueness of our spatial or temporal series itself, then locating an object within this series will not necessarily locate it uniquely; there might be another spatio-temporal series just like our own. Bradley insists that our ideas alone can give us no guarantee of the uniqueness of our spatio-temporal series:

There is nothing whatever in the idea of a series to hint that there may not be any number of series, internally all indistinguishable from the first. How can you, so long as you are not willing to transcend ideas, determine or in any way characterize your series, so as to get its difference from every possible series within your description? (*PL*, p. 64)

Thus we cannot ensure that a synthesis of ideas has determinate content by building in a spatio-temporal reference, for there might be other spatio-temporal series, and no idea can ensure that our reference is to just *this* spatio-temporal series.[21]

This way of putting the matter suggests another way in which we

---

[21] The idea of alternative spatio-temporal series may seem implausible. Bradley's claim, however, is only that our ideas alone are insufficient to determine that their reference is to this spatio-temporal series; so the sense in which he has to hold alternative series possible is a very abstract one. It is perhaps worth adding that the idea of

might try to ensure that our ideas can uniquely designate, namely by
the use of indexical expressions—'this', 'now', 'here', 'I', and the like.
Thus our example would become: 'I have toothache now'. But again,
Bradley denies that we can achieve uniqueness of designation in this
manner. Like Green (see Chapter 1, pp. 30–1, above), Bradley insists
upon the universality of *all* language, including indexicals:[22]

> In 'I have a toothache' both the I and the toothache are mere generalities. The
> *actual* toothache is not any other toothache, and the *actual* I is myself as having
> this very toothache. But the truth I assert has been and will be true of all other
> toothaches as of my own.... It is in vain that we add to the original assertion
> 'this', 'here', and 'now', for they are all universals. They are symbols whose
> meaning extends to and covers innumerable instances. (*PL*, p. 49)

Indeed, Bradley claims that 'this', so far from being a uniquely designating expression, is the most universal term of all: anything whatsoever can be 'this', so the idea does not single out one thing rather
than any other (*PL*, p. 60).

At this point one may feel that the trouble arises because Bradley
attempts to divorce language from the fact that it is spoken by particular human beings in particular circumstances. He seems to demand
that a synthesis of ideas should, by itself and without regard for its
context, be capable of representing a particular fact; perhaps this demand is based upon too abstract a view of language and of judgement.
The abstract view of language, however, is not so much Bradley's
presupposition as his target. Accepting a less abstract view of language
involves accepting that a synthesis of ideas (or a sequence of words)
considered as such, i.e. as abstracted from its context, will fail to have a
determinate content. A synthesis of ideas, on this view, has the content that it has only in virtue of facts which it does not include. But this
is Bradley's point. His argument is in service of the conclusion that no
synthesis of ideas, by itself, could have a determinate content—so that
if a judgement is to have a determinate content it cannot simply be a
synthesis of ideas, but must depend upon some other fact.

We have now seen enough of Bradley's view of judgement to be able
to discuss the two ways in which he holds that judgement is inadequate. The first may be thought of as the *incompleteness* of judgement.
Here the difference between Bradley's view and Green's is largely a
matter of emphasis, for the fundamental point in each case is the

---

spatio-temporal series distinct from, but qualitatively like, ours is one that must be taken
seriously by those who advocate a realistic attitude towards 'possible worlds' other than
the actual world.

[22] Cf. also Hegel's 'Sinnliche Gewißheit', cited in Ch. 1 n. 7 above.

holism which we have seen to be central to both philosophies. One way of explaining the matter is this. In a judgement of the usual sort—that Socrates is wise, for example—we seem to single out a piece of reality (Socrates) and ascribe some predicate to him. But Socrates, since he is only a *part* of reality, is not self-subsistent. He is what he is only in virtue of his place in the whole of reality; and our judgement, if true, is still true only in virtue of the whole of reality. This means that the judgement depends upon conditions which it does not include. The judgement is thus at best conditionally true:

Judgments are conditional in this sense, that what they affirm is incomplete. It cannot be attributed to Reality, as such, and before its necessary complement is added. And, in addition, this complement in the end remains unknown. But while it remains unknown, we obviously cannot tell how, if present, it would act upon and alter our predicate.... The content in fact might be so altered, be so redistributed, and blended, as utterly to be transformed. And, in brief, the predicate may, taken as such, be more or less completely untrue. Thus we really have asserted subject to and at the mercy of, the unknown. And hence our judgment, always but to a varying extent, must in the end be called conditional. (*A. & R.*, p. 320)

Two ideas are combined here. The first, which we have already touched on, is simply that any object which we single out from the whole of reality, or any predicate (ideal content) which we ascribe to reality, is bound to be partial, and dependent upon other aspects of reality. But now what is dependent on something else does not, by Bradley's lights, exist as such. The things which it depends upon and to which it is related make a difference to it. This gives rise to the second, rather more obscure, idea, that the Absolute does not contain the limited things which we know in the form in which we know them. These things are 'combined and blended' to form the harmonious whole which is the Absolute, and in this process they will be altered, perhaps beyond all recognition. Thus all our judgements, except the truths of metaphysics, are inadequate because they represent as self-subsistent what is in fact dependent. This is an error both on its own account and because the dependence of a thing transforms it so that the thing as it really is (as it exists in the Absolute) is not the thing that we took ourselves to know. (This last statement is paradoxical, because the point is that the thing, as such and as a thing, does *not* exist in the Absolute. No non-paradoxical statement is possible here; by Bradley's lights, however, this is not an objection to his view, for he does not suppose that our statements can do justice to Reality. On the contrary, he argues that they cannot. The importance of this point will become apparent when we discuss Moore's arguments against Idealism; see Chapter 4, pp. 122–3, below.)

An important consequence follows from this first way in which judgement is inadequate: that truth and falsehood are not absolute properties, which a judgement either has or lacks, but are matters of degree, which a judgement has to a greater or lesser extent:

There will be no truth which is entirely true, just as there will be no error which is totally false. With all alike, if taken strictly, it will be a question of amount, and will be a matter of more or less. (*A. & R.*, pp. 320–1)

No judgement is absolutely true, since all will be to some extent modified in the Absolute. Neither Socrates, nor wisdom, nor anything else of the ordinary sort is contained in the Absolute without being transformed from the objects that we know. The more a judgement has to be transformed before it can be included in the Absolute the less true it is; but none will be wholly true just as it is (the truths of metaphysics, as we shall see, constitute an exception to this). The closer the ideal content that we predicate in a judgement comes to being a self-subsistent, i.e. all-inclusive, and harmonious, whole, the more nearly true it is, for it will require less transformation before it can be taken up into the Absolute:

to be more or less true, and to be more or less real, is to be separated by an interval, smaller or greater, from all-inclusiveness and self-consistency. Of two given appearances the one more wide, or more harmonious, is more real.... The truth and the fact, which, to be converted in to the Absolute, would require less rearrangement and addition is more real and truer. And this is what we mean by degrees of reality and truth. (*A. & R.*, pp. 322–3)

Falsehood too is not absolute. Judgement is the ascription of an ideal content to reality. We could not ascribe the ideal content to reality unless we possessed it and we could not possess it if we had not received it from reality. So reality must in some sense contain the ideal content, although not in the form which it has in the judgement. All our ideas, we might put it, have their ultimate source in reality. So, again, the only question is how different the ideal content is in the Absolute from the way in which it appears in the judgement:

Error *is* truth, it is partial truth, that is false only because partial and left incomplete. The Absolute *has* without subtraction all those qualities, and it has every arrangement which we seem to confer on it by our mere mistake. The mistake lies in our failure to give it also the complement. (*A. & R.*, pp. 169–70)

The difference between true judgements and false ones has to do with how much the content is transformed in the Absolute, and is thus a matter of degree.

The doctrine of degrees of truth enables Bradley to claim that his metaphysics is compatible with common sense. He even claims that it is the only way in which we can do philosophical justice to the various claims of common sense, without letting any one of them override the claims of the others (see pp. 53–4, above, and *ETR*, pp. 470–2). All our judgements in matters of common sense and ordinary science are merely relatively true, true under certain conditions or certain assumptions; but still these judgements are accommodated, and only their claim to absolute truth is denied:

In the realm of the special science and of practical life ... we are compelled to take partial truths as being utterly true. We cannot do this consistently, but we are forced to do this, and our action within limits is justified. And thus on the relative view [of truth] there is after all no collision with what may be called Common Sense. (*ETR*, p. 258)

The difficulty with this, as Wollheim points out,[23] is that Bradley gives us no idea of how we are to apply the notion of degrees of truth to our actual judgements, how we are to tell whether one judgement is in fact more true than another. The criterion of greater completeness or internal harmony is not one whose application is obvious, and Bradley does not help us here. His work is not dialectical in the Hegelian sense, for it makes no attempt to arrange ideas or concepts in order, according as they more or less nearly approach truth.[24]

While our ordinary judgements are only partially true, the truths of metaphysics are wholly true. The degree of truth of any judgement is a matter of the transformation which the content of that judgement must undergo before it can be accommodated within the Absolute. The more incomplete the subject of the judgement, the greater the transformation which is necessary. When the subject of our judgement is reality as a whole, then, no transformation at all will be necessary. Truths of this sort are not incomplete, so they are as true as any judgement can be:

anything is absolute when all its nature is conditioned within itself. It is unconditional when every condition of its being falls inside it. It is free from chance of error when any opposite is quite inconceivable. Such characters belong to the statement that Reality is experience and is one. For these truths are not subordinate, but are general truths about reality as a whole. They do not exhaust it, but in outline they give its essence. The Real, in other words, is more than they, but always more of the same. There is nothing which in idea you can add to it that fails, when understood, to fall under these general truths. (*A. & R.*, p. 475)

---

[23] Wollheim, op. cit. n. 16 above, p. 178.
[24] McTaggart criticizes *A. & R.* precisely because it does not adopt the dialectical method. See his review of it, *Revue de métaphysique et de morale* (1894), 98–112.

Only the most general truths of metaphysics are wholly complete, and therefore as true as any truth can be; other subjects can attain only to partial truth, but partial truth is also partial error (*A. & R.*, p. 169). Thus metaphysics is indeed the Queen of the Sciences: only her truths are as true as truths can be.

This first way in which Bradley finds (ordinary) judgement to be inadequate—by being incomplete—is not the most novel aspect of his philosophy. That our ordinary ways of thinking about the world are unable to do it justice, that it can only be adequately conceived of by means of certain philosophical concepts which enable us to represent it as a unified whole—these are perhaps familiar idealist thoughts. The second way in which Bradley finds judgement inadequate, however, is less familiar, although it perhaps has analogues in certain expressions of mysticism. All judgement, according to Bradley (and here there are no exceptions), is the ascription of ideal content to reality; the judgement, if true, is true in virtue of the reality. Thus the judgement is true in virtue of something which it does not contain, and so, by Bradley's lights, it is only conditionally true:

all our judgments, to be true, must become conditional. The predicate, that is, does not hold unless by the help of something else. And this 'something else' cannot be stated. (*A. & R.*, pp. 319–20)

What is to be emphasized is that the incompleteness of judgement which is at issue here is not an incompleteness which can be remedied by the addition to the judgement of any more *ideas* (contrast the incompleteness discussed above, pp. 64–7). What the judgement fails to include is not any idea but *reality* itself.

Even the most complete and perfect judgement—as complete and perfect as any *judgement* can be—still uses ideas. And ideas result from the separation of content from immediate existence, of the 'what' from the 'that', the severing of the immediate union of feeling. But reality, for Bradley, has the character of *immediacy*—that is, in reality, existence and content are not severed but are united. Hence judgement can never recapture or do full justice to that immediacy, that given non-relational unity, of which we have a presentiment in feeling and which is found in the Absolute. Ideas, judgement, thought, truth—these notions all hang together, and all fail to represent the immediate and non-relational unity which is essential to the Absolute. Thus Bradley says, 'in the end, no possible truth is quite true. It is a partial and inadequate translation of that which it professes to give bodily' (*A. & R.*, pp. 482–3).

Another way of putting this is to say that in judgement the subject is always different from the predicate (*A. &. R.*, p. 482). The use that

Idealists have made of this fact has been taken to show that they simply could not tell the difference between the 'is' of predication and the 'is' of identity.[25] A more sympathetic critic has seen Bradley as arguing that there is in fact no difference between identity and predication.[26] But the real basis of Bradley's complaint is deeper. If the predicate, the ideal content, is different from the subject, reality, then it must be *related* to reality. All relations are based upon a non-relational whole, but just because a judgement must be an ideal content which is separated from the whole and merely related to it, judgement cannot adequately represent the non-relational whole on which it is based. All judgement is relational, because in judgement we use an ideal content which has to be split off from reality before it can be used to make the judgement. There is thus a lack of fit between judgement and reality: no judgement can represent the non-relational nature of reality. The aim towards which thought and judgement tend, that which alone would satisfy them, is itself beyond thought or judgement. Bradley replies thus to what is perhaps the obvious objection to this:

We may be told that the End, because it is that which thought aims at, is therefore itself (mere) thought. This assumes that thought cannot desire a consummation in which it is lost. But does not the river run into the sea, and the self lose itself in love? (*A. & R.*, p. 153)

These images suggest the mystical strain in Bradley's thought. Intellectual activity, of which philosophy is the highest form, points the way towards the Absolute; but the Absolute is not to be understood by the intellect, although its general outlines are given by the most general statements of metaphysics. Thought is mediate and relational; the Absolute is immediate and non-relational. If the Absolute is to be known in other than broadest outline, then the source of this knowledge must be some kind of immediate experience or intuition (see pp. 58–9, above).

It may give us further insight into this view to compare it with that of Green. Let us begin by considering the concrete universal. We can conceive of this in two ways. Starting with the 'abstract universal', we can make it particular and concrete by relating it to other things and making distinctions within it; starting with the 'bare particular' of sense, we make it universal by relating it to others. Both processes end with the concrete universal, and because both end at the same point the dualism of thought and sense, or thought and reality, is ultimately overcome. The concrete universal is at once the culmination of thought

---

[25] e.g. Russell's *OKEW*, pp. 48–9.   [26] Wollheim, op. cit. n. 16 above, p. 74.

and the essential reality; the two coincide. In Bradley's work, especially after *Ethical Studies*, we hear very little about the concrete universal. There is good reason for this. The universal that we use in thought, according to Bradley, is irremediably abstract, since it involves the separation of content from existence (see pp. 59–61, above). When Bradley does refer to the concrete universal (e.g. *PL*, p. 188) he seems to mean by it simply reality as a whole.[27] But for Bradley this lacks one of the essential features of universals, namely that of accessibility to the intellect. The universals that we use in thought are, for Bradley, not concrete, not only because they fall short of the whole (as Wollheim suggests) but also because their abstractness cannot be overcome. The theory of the concrete universal was essentially a theory of the overcoming of the duality between thought and reality. The reasons that the concrete universal plays so little role in Bradley's thought is simply that he does not accept that this duality can be overcome.

Both Green and Bradley insist that thought is universal and relational in character; but the conclusions that they draw from this are quite different. Green's conclusion is that reality must therefore equally be universal and relational in character. Bradley, by contrast, holds that relational and universal thought itself indicates that there is something beyond it which is not universal or relational; and that thought is inadequate because it is unable to represent the immediate and non-relational character of this reality. This is the difference in the two views which I have already touched on in discussing Bradley's arguments to the effect that there is an element in experience which is prior to any relations, and which cannot be represented relationally. For the inadequacy of thought is precisely its inability to represent this element of immediacy, the fact that experience has not only a certain character but also a particular existence as immediately given; this immediacy is not a matter of its character or content, and so it is not something that can be represented in thought. One might put Bradley's point by saying that for him 'existence' is not a predicate. This is misleading because for Bradley all thought and all language (including the word 'exists') is ideal, universal, and predicative in character. But just for this reason our words do not succeed in conveying *existence* in its immediacy and particularity. (This cannot be stated without paradox because our words are unable to state what it is that they cannot state. As we have seen in another instance, however, Bradley would not count this paradox as an argument against his view.)

The difference which I am emphasizing between Bradley's philosophy and Green's, then, lies in Bradley's insistence that reality is

----

[27] Wollheim, op. cit. n. 16 above, p. 38.

immediate, is the harmonious union of content with existence which always escapes thought. So the ultimate satisfaction of the intellect which Bradley seeks is to be found not in thought, but beyond what is purely intellectual, in an experience which remains essentially ineffable. If this is mysticism, then the result of Bradley's philosophy (thought certainly not its *method*) is mystical. The belief that reality ultimately escapes the power of thought is expressed in a passage as deeply felt as anything in Bradley's work:

I must venture to doubt whether ... truth, if that stands for the work of the intellect, is ever precisely identical with fact. ... Such an idea may be senseless, such a thought may contradict itself, but it serves to give voice to an obstinate instinct. ... It may come from a failure in my metaphysics, or from a weakness of the flesh which continues to bind me, but the notion that existence could be the same as understanding strikes me as cold and ghost-like as the dreariest materialism. That the glory of this world in the end is appearance leaves the world more glorious, if we feel it is a show of some fuller splendour; but the sensuous curtain is a deception and a cheat, if it hides some colourless movement of atoms, some spectral woof of impalpable abstractions, or some unearthly ballet of bloodless categories. Though dragged to such conclusions we cannot embrace them. Our principles may be true, but they are not reality. They no more *make* that Whole which commands our devotion, than some shredded dissection of human tatters *is* that warm and breathing beauty of flesh which our hearts found delightful. (*PL*, pp. 590–1)

3

Russell's Idealist Period

Russell adopted idealist views under the influence of his teachers at Cambridge—James Ward, G. F. Stout, and, especially, McTaggart. He held views of this sort from early in 1894 until late in 1898. He later gave the following summary of his position towards the end of this period:

I was at this time a full-fledged Hegelian, and I aimed at constructing a complete dialectic of the sciences.... I accepted the Hegelian view that none of the sciences is quite true, since all depend upon some abstraction, and every abstraction leads, sooner or later, to contradiction. Wherever Kant and Hegel were in conflict, I sided with Hegel. (*MPD*, p. 42)

The purpose of this chapter is to give a general account of Russell's Idealism, and of the influence upon him of Kant, of Hegel, and of Bradley. It is important for our purposes to see how Russell interpreted these philosophers. My discussion will deal chiefly with issues which arise in Russell's *Foundations of Geometry*.[1] This book has two main philosophical conclusions, to which the two sections of this chapter will roughly correspond. The first has to do with the *status* of geometry: that certain features of space, and therefore certain geometrical axioms,[2] are known a priori, whereas others can only be known by experience. Here it is the influence of Kant on Russell that is most apparent, if only because Kant's idealist successors were not in general concerned with geometry (as Russell himself remarks: *FG*, p. 62). The second main philosophical conclusion of *FG* is that there are irremediable contradictions in the notion of space, and thus in any geometry.

---

[1] *An Essay on the Foundations of Geometry.*

[2] Notice that I here equate truths about space with truths of geometry, as Russell does in *FG*; we shall see him adopt a different attitude in *The Principles of Mathematics*. This equation of course implies that there is only one true geometry—the body of truths about space. But Russell also acknowledges that, in a rather different sense, alternative (i.e. non-Euclidean) geometries are possible. He calls non-Euclidean geometry 'Metageometry' because, I suspect, he thinks that *as* geometry, i.e. as putative truth about space, it is false; but that it is correct if taken as a theory *about* (Euclidean) geometry. Thus Metageometry shows, e.g., that the axiom of parallels could be replaced, and new theories developed on this basis.

This claim relies upon the Hegelian conception of the dialectic; *FG*, indeed, is explicitly presented as an exploration of one stage in the dialectic. I shall discuss this point at some length, for the dialectic is an important idealist notion which we have not yet touched on.

1. Geometry and the A Priori

The first main philosophical conclusion of *FG* is that it is true a priori that space is of constant curvature.[3] Space need not be Euclidean (of zero curvature), as Kant had thought; it could be Riemannian (of positive curvature) or Lobaschevskian (of negative curvature). Which of these characteristics space actually has is, Russell claims, an empirical matter; but, a priori, it must have one of them. By calling this a priori Russell says that he means that it is *'logically* presupposed in experience' (*FG*, p. 2; emphasis in the original), or that it is 'required to make knowledge possible at all' (*FG*, p. 3). This conception of the a priori, and its ramifications, will occupy us for much of this section.

Russell's conception of the a priori is Kantian. The conception makes essential use of the idea of the *presuppositions* of experience. Implicit in this idea is the view that there is an underlying structure to experience. Experience is made possible by certain very general truths, which are, in some sense, truths about the world, i.e. (as Russell puts it) truths with an empirical subject-matter. From the mere fact that there is experience, therefore, certain things follow. Not all truths about the world are answerable to experience—the presuppositions of experience cannot themselves be known by experience (compare Green's view, Chapter 1, above, pp. 24–6). A second point helps to make this first one more intelligible. This is that Russell seems to hold that experience is always judgemental in character. The two definitions of the a priori quoted in the previous paragraph seem to equate knowledge with experience (see also *FG*, p. 90). This must, I think, be seen as an implicit reliance upon the Kantian conception of experience as judgemental, so that the presuppositions of judgement are also the presuppositions of any experience whatsoever (again, see Chapter 1, pp. 24–6).

The first definition of the a priori which I quoted from *FG* was that something is a priori if it is *'logically* presupposed in experience'. The

---

[3] For a non-technical explanation of this and other geometrical notions, see e.g. L. Sklar, *Space, Time and Spacetime* (Berkeley, Calif.: University of California Press, 1976), Ch. II.

use of the word 'logically' is something that I shall dwell upon, because of the very sharp contrast between the way in which the Idealists used the word 'logic' (exemplified by this use of Russell's) and the way in which it has come to be used (exemplified by Russell's uses after 1900). The idealist use of the word 'logic' must be traced back to Kant. Kant distinguishes General Logic from Transcendental Logic. Central to the former is an account of patterns of inference which are valid for *any* subject-matter, and whose validity is not empirical. Logic in this sense, Kant says 'deals with nothing but the mere form of thought' (*Critique of Pure Reason*, A54=B78); I shall, therefore, call it Formal Logic. Formal Logic, for Kant, is analytic, and therefore, he claims (following Leibniz) it follows from the principle of contradiction alone (*Critique of Pure Reason*, A150–1=B189–91). Transcendental Logic, by contrast, was the name that Kant gave to the study of the a priori conditions of the possibility of any knowledge or judgement (see *Critique of Pure Reason*, A56=B80–1).[4]

For Kant, therefore, Formal Logic and Transcendental Logic were distinct subjects. Transcendental Logic was, among other things, an enquiry into the conditions of synthesis, and thus into the presuppositions of any synthetic judgement. Since Kant thought of Formal Logic as made up of analytic judgements, i.e. judgements not produced by synthesis and so not subject to these presuppositions, the truths of Formal Logic thus seemed to be wholly independent of Transcendental Logic. This independence, however, proved tenuous. Even the most Kantian of Kant's successors came to find it implausible that there could be any judgements at all which did not require synthesis, and thus that there could be any judgements at all which are not subject to Transcendental Logic. Formal Logic thus seemed to presuppose Trans-

---

[4] Kant's choice of the word 'Logic' to describe this enterprise is to be understood in terms of two kinds of reasons, of which the first is easier to sympathize with than the second. The first is that if Logic is about reasoning, and reasoning is about relations among judgements, then an examination of the nature and possibility of judgement may seem to be a natural subject to include under the heading of 'logic' (cf. e.g. Pt. I of A. Arnauld, *La Logique: ou L'Art de penser*, 1662; trans. J. Dickoff and P. James (Indianapolis: Bobbs-Merrill, 1964), under the title *The Art of Thinking*, but more commonly known as *The Port Royal Logic*, which deals with the notion of judgement). The second kind of reason has to do with one of the less plausible features of Kant's architectonic. Transcendental Logic is meant to bear a special relation to Formal Logic; very roughly, the principles of Transcendental Logic are meant to result from the principles of Formal Logic when these latter are restricted so that they deal not with the forms of thought in general but with the forms of thought about possible objects (see A55–6=B79–80). Because Kant holds that the principles of Transcendental Logic can be located in this way (though not thereby proved to be, indeed, the principles of Transcendental Logic—i.e. to be necessary for the possibility of experience), most commentators have found his account of the origin of these principles unsatisfactory. See pp. 91–2, below.

cendental Logic: before we can consider the formal, logical, relations among judgements, we must first discover the necessary conditions of all judgement, for these conditions must be obeyed throughout. Given the poverty of the Formal Logic of the period, its dependence upon Transcendental Logic seemed to leave it in danger of merging into the latter entirely—if you understand the necessary conditions of judgement, then the logical relations among judgements follow more or less automatically. Thus Kemp Smith, in a critical discussion of Kant, says:

Synthetic, relational factors are present in *all* knowledge, even in knowledge that may seem, on superficial study, to be purely analytic....

This is the reason why, in modern logic . . . the theory of judgment receives so much more attention than the theory of reasoning. For once the above view of judgment has been established, all the main points in the doctrine of reasoning follow of themselves as so many corollaries.[5]

and again:

Modern Logic, as developed by Lotze, Sigwart, Bradley and Bosanquet, is, in large part, the recasting of general logic in terms of the results reached by Kant's transcendental enquiry.[6]

'Logic', as the Idealists understood it, was in large measure the heir of Kant's Transcendental Logic, though usually with some discussion of the valid patterns of reasoning appended.[7]

When Russell speaks of his criterion of apriority as 'purely logical', it is this sense of 'logic' that he is relying upon. In the Preface to *FG* he says: 'In Logic I have learnt most from Mr. Bradley, and next to him, from Sigwart and Bosanquet'. In the main body of the text he proves himself to have been an apt pupil; he rejects the distinction between analytic and synthetic judgements, and argues that every judgement is both analytic and synthetic (see *FG*, pp. 57–8, 115).[8] Kant, like Leibniz,

---

[5] N. Kemp Smith, *A Commentary to Kant's 'Critique of Pure Reason'* (London: Macmillan, 1918; 2nd edn. London, 1923), p. xxxviii.

[6] Kemp Smith, op. cit. n. 5 above, p. 181.

[7] In this discussion I take no account of the Hegelian dialectical logic (see section 2, below) which threatens not merely the independence but also the very existence of Formal Logic. The claim of dialectical logic, very roughly, is that the concepts which we use in ordinary judgement are not fixed and stable, but contain contradictions which impel us to go from one concept to another. But if our concepts do not stay stable in use, then the patterns of reasoning which Formal Logic picks out will not be valid.

[8] It is obvious from this that Russell does not interpret 'analytic' and 'synthetic' as contradictories, and so that he does not take an analytic judgement to be one for which synthesis is not required. He thinks, rather, of analysis and synthesis as two separate processes, and claims that every judgement involves both: 'Every judgement—so modern logic contends—is both synthetic and analytic; it combines parts into a whole, and analyses a whole into parts' (*FG*, p. 58).

held that analytic judgements follow from the principle of contradiction (see *Critique of Pure Reason*, A151=B190–1). Russell insists that no judgement has this status: 'the principle of contradiction can only give fruitful results on the assumption that experience in general, or, in a particular science, some special branch of experience, is to be formally possible' (*FG*, p. 57; cf. p. 59).

Russell's insistence that by 'a priori' he means '*logically* presupposed in experience' thus records his adherence to a modified form of Kantianism. The stress on the word 'logically', however, does more than this. Russell is also rejecting what he sees as Kant's subjective or psychological view of the a priori: 'logically' contrasts with 'psychologically'. Thus he says, 'To Kant . . . *a priori* and *subjective* were almost interchangable terms'. He goes on to make it clear that he takes 'subjective' to be a term of empirical psychology, and that this is his reason for rejecting the Kantian understanding of the a priori:

To decree that the a priori shall always be subjective, seems dangerous, when we reflect that such a view places our results, as to the a priori, at the mercy of empirical psychology. How serious this danger is, the controversy as to Kant's pure intuition sufficiently shows.

I shall, therefore, throughout the present Essay, use the word a priori without any psychological implication. My test of apriority will be purely logical. (*FG*, p. 3)

Russell thus charges Kant with psychologism—with making philosophy dependent upon empirical psychology.[9] The basis of this charge is not obvious, especially in view of the fact that Kant himself attacked the Empiricists for their psychologism. In a famous passage he argued that a Lockean account of the origin of our concepts could not be a justification of the use of those concepts (A84–7=B116–19). The situation is further complicated by the fact that synthetic a priori judgements are, on Kant's account, of two different sorts: those due to the forms of our intuition—space and time—and those due to the pure concepts of the understanding, or categories (the categories may be thought of as the conditions under which synthesis can occur).

In the case of the forms of intuition, we can easily see why Russell interpreted Kant's a priori as psychologistic. The intuition of space, Kant says, 'must be a priori, that is, it must be found in us prior to the perception of any object' (*Critique of Pure Reason*, B41). How, Kant asks,

---

[9] A significant fact, which I do not discuss, is the development of psychology as an autonomous discipline, making explicit use of experimental techniques. This development took place almost entirely in the 19th century, i.e. between the period when Kant was writing and the time of *FG*. See, in particular, E. G. Boring, *A History of Experimental Psychology* (New York: Appleton-Century-Crofts, 1950).

'can there exist *in the mind* an outer intuition which precedes the objects themselves' (loc. cit.; my emphasis)? His answer is that this is possible only because 'the intuition has its seat in the subject only' (loc. cit.). Kant repeatedly speaks of space as 'subjective' (*subjektive*) (e.g. *Critique of Pure Reason*, A26–8=B42–4). Kant's claim, moreover, is only that space and time are forms of our (i.e. human) intuition. He explicitly allows that other creatures might have different forms of intuition (see especially *Critique of Pure Reason*, A27=B43). Equally, we can see why Russell should have rejected this psychologism about the a priori character of the form of spatial intuition. Kant, as Russell sees it, had appealed to the subjectivity of space to explain the a priori status of Euclidean geometry; but Russell claims that the subjectivity of space would in fact have a very different consequence:

the subjectivity of space ... so far from establishing the universal validity of Euclid, establishes this validity only after an empirical investigation of the nature of space as intuited by Tom, Dick or Harry. (FG, p. 93)

This consequence would have been as unwelcome to Kant as it was to Russell. A crucial part of the reason that Russell saw it as following from the subjectivity of space, while Kant did not, has to do with the development of non-Euclidean geometry. While Kant envisaged the possibility of beings with forms of intuition other than the spatial and temporal he did not, I think, envisage the possibility of forms of intuition which were *spatial* but not Euclidean.[10] If this is correct, then Kant held that all beings with a spatial form of intuition would have a Euclidean form of intuition—and thus that they would all have the same form of spatial intuition. Given the obviousness of the fact that human beings perceive things spatially, this Kantian assumption implies that all human beings have Euclidean space as a form of their intuition; the idea of examining different people to see what their form of spatial intuition is actually like does not arise. But the serious development of non-Euclidean gemoetry rules out the Kantian assumption. It becomes clear that it is possible for space to be non-Euclidean, and even to be very slightly non-Euclidean (so that very refined tests would be needed to discover that it is not, in fact, Euclidean). From the obvious fact that we all perceive things spatially, one can no longer infer that we all perceive things in Euclidean fashion, or even that we all perceive things in the same fashion. It is then hard to resist the idea that if geometry is concerned with the form of our spatial intuition, it must be an empirical science, based on an investigation into the spatial perceptions of a large number of individuals. It is

[10] See Kemp Smith, op. cit. n. 5 above, p. 117.

easy to understand why Russell might have taken this result as a *reductio ad absurdum* of Kant's view of space.[11]

Russell's view of Kant as unduly psychologistic does not, however, apply only to the latter's view of space. Russell seems to interpret Kant's views in general as psychologistic. He says, for example, that Kant holds 'the view that all certain knowledge is self-knowledge' (*FG*, p. 55). This tendentious interpretation of Kant is the same as that which Russell holds after he rejects Idealism;[12] it is worth noting that the interpretation is not a product of Russell's opposition to Idealism. In giving this sort of psychologistic reading to Kant, Russell is in fact following the former's idealist critics. Thus Hegel, for example, says, 'Kant remained restricted and confined by his psychological point of view and his empirical methods.'[13] Kant's description of intuitions, and concepts, and how they combine to form experience, lends itself to this interpretation. More important from our point of view, however, is the fact that it is unclear how we could know what Kant claims to know—that there are intuitions and concepts which combine to form experience—unless this knowledge is psychological in character. The moral to draw from this is that being non-psychologistic is not the straightforward matter that it might seem. Kant rejected the psychologism of Locke, but this is not enough to ensure that his own views are not, or will not be understood as being, psychologistic in turn. Kant did not intend his claims to be answerable to the findings of empirical psychology, but it remains open whether there is any other way of understanding them. Whether we can talk about the combination of intuitions and concepts in a non-psychological way depends upon the sort of metaphysical commitments we are willing to make. Whether a given view is to be interpreted as psychologistic depends, more generally, upon the implicit or explicit metaphysics of the interpreter (I return to this issue in the Introduction to Part II, pp. 106–7, below).

This complexity in the notion of psychologism is no less applicable to Russell's views in *FG* than it is to Kant's. Russell avoids what he sees as the Kantian commitment to the subjectivity of space. He emphasizes

---

[11] It is worth emphasizing that the kinds of difficulties for Kant's view of space which I have discussed in this paragraph do not arise from the mere fact that the denial of Euclidean geometry is not contradictory. This fact was known to Kant (it is clear, for example, in the work of Lambert, with whom Kant corresponded) and is allowed for in his system by the synthetic character of our knowledge of geometry. It is not equivalent to the claim that there are non-Euclidean theories which are nevertheless theories *about* space.

[12] An almost identical phrase occurs in his *Leibniz* (p. 74). See Ch. 4, below.

[13] *Lectures on the History of Philosophy*, trans. E. S. Haldane and Frances H. Simon (London: Routledge & Kegan Paul, 1955, 1st edn. 1892), iii. 431; cf. pp. 432–3.

that his concern is only with the necessity of space for the possibility of experience, not with the nature or origin of space:

the question of the subjective or objective nature of space may be left wholly out of account during the course of this discussion [of the status of geometry], which will gain by dealing exclusively with logical, as opposed to psychological, points of view. (*FG*, p. 57)

Russell's claim is that certain requirements as to the existence and nature of a form of externality must be met if experience is to be possible; but he is agnostic as to *how* these requirements are met:

How we are to account for the fortunate realization of these requirements— whether by a pre-established harmony, by Darwinian adaption to our environment, or by the subjectivity of the necessary element in sense-perception, or by a fundamental identity between ourselves and the rest of reality—is a further question, belonging rather to metaphysics than to our present line of argument. The a priori ... is that which is necessary for the possibility of experience, and in this we have a purely logical criterion. (*FG*, p. 187)

Russell thus wishes to be free to proceed with one subject (logic, in his sense) without making any commitments in another and more dubious subject (metaphysics). But in fact the two subjects are not separable in this way. The status, indeed the very existence, of Logic (in the sense that Russell uses here) turns on the metaphysics that he wishes to avoid. Russell's agnosticism allows the possibility of a world which is independent of our knowledge of it, and which thus obeys the conditions of knowability more or less by accident. Worse still, it may not in fact obey them at all. If it is admitted even as a possibility that the form of externality may be subjective, i.e. just a product of our psychological constitution, and not true of the world, then it must be granted that what is a priori in Russell's sense may not in fact be true of the world. (It may be said that this sort of speculation about the possibility that the world does not in fact obey the conditions of our knowledge is senseless because unverifiable. But this line of thought, if followed out, would, I think, lead to the metaphysics that Russell wishes to avoid. His agnosticism about metaphysics allows sense to the unverifiable speculation.)

The whole enquiry is thus in danger of taking on just that psychological cast which Russell so insistently tried to avoid. If it is possible that the world does not in fact conform to the conditions of our knowledge, or conforms to them only fortuitously, then an enquiry into these conditions may seem to be an enquiry into *us* and the nature of our minds. Passing remarks of Russell's actually encourage this view of his work—suggesting, perhaps, that his intuitions were realist before his doctrines were. Thus he says: 'necessity for experience can only arise from the nature of the mind that experiences' (*FG*, p. 179). And again, even more clearly: 'in any world, *knowable to beings with our laws of thought*, some such form [of externality], as we have now seen, must be given in sense-perception (*FG*, p. 186; my emphasis). But if there could be beings with other laws of thought and thus, presumably, other conditions of possible experience, then the conditions of *our* experience become just a psychological fact about us. Since the conditions of our experience might have been different (we might have been those other beings), what these conditions are becomes an empirical, psychological issue.[14]

Although Russell criticizes Kant, his conception of the a priori is, as we have seen, very Kantian in broad outline. In particular, Russell seems to take it for granted that there can be a priori truths whose subject-matter is empirical—i.e. which are truths about the spatio-temporal world. The truths of geometry are an example of this. (This is the view that Kant had advanced by insisting on the possibility of *synthetic* a priori truths. Russell did not use this expression because, as we have seen, he rejected the Kantian distinction between the analytic and the synthetic.) He criticized Erdmann and Helmholtz for the opposite view, characteristic of empiricism, that truths with an empirical subject-matter must themselves be empirical, i.e. answerable to experience and thus not a priori. Speaking of their work he says:

it seems to me completely to ignore the work of the Critical Philosophy. For if there is one thing which, one might have hoped, had been made sufficiently clear by Kant's Critique, it is this, that knowledge which is a priori applies ... to empirical matter. (*FG*, p. 71)

What is striking about this statement is its tone of impatience. This tone indicates that the point at issue is one which Russell takes to have been settled, for once and for all, by Kant. Russell is prepared to criticize Kant from an idealist standpoint, but certain Kantian doctrines, especially Kantian criticisms of Empiricism, seem to him beyond dispute. The remark, although casual, indicates very clearly that Russell is willing to take certain things absolutely for granted, and to assume the same attitude in his audience. Something similar can be said about another remark of Russell's, which also shows his assumption that no serious philosopher could be an Empiricist. Discussing the views of Benno Erdmann, Russell says:

[14] The potential weakness of *FG* which I have discussed in this paragraph was ruthlessly exploited by Moore in his review of the book, in *Mind* (1899), 397–405. See Introduction to Pt. II, pp. 108–9, below.
    A deep issue rises to the surface at this point: to what extent does a truly fundamental psychological question deserve the name 'philosophy' or 'epistemology'? Can we think of philosophy as a wholly non-psychological, wholly abstract, subject?

Indeed his logic seems—though I say this with hesitation—to be incompatible with any system but that of Mill: there is apparently no distinction, to him, between the general and the universal, and consequently no concept not embodied in a series of instances. Such a theory of logic, to my mind, vitiates most of his work. (*FG*, pp. 81–2)

I turn now from this examination of Russell's conception of the a priori to the discussion of his claim that certain aspects of space, and thus certain truths of geometry, are known a priori in this sense. In one way, as we have seen, Russell's claim here is stronger than Kant's claims about geometry; Russell hopes to show, as Kant did not, that certain geometrical truths are necessary for the possibility of experience. In another way, however, Russell's claim is weaker than Kant's. Kant had claimed that Euclidean geometry was a priori. Russell, writing after the development of non-Euclidean geometry (which he calls 'Metageometry'), does not claim so much. Russell does not in fact doubt the truth of Euclidean geometry (cf. e.g. *FG*, p. 98), but he accepts that it is an empirical issue, and that observation and experiment cannot rule out the possibility of space having a very small positive or negative curvature (cf. *FG*, p. 97; also pp. 175–6). But while Euclidean geometry is empirical, some facts about space are a priori: 'the axioms common to Euclid and Metageometry will be a priori, while those peculiar to Euclid will be empirical' (*FG*, p. 53). In particular, Russell thinks that he can show that some 'form of externality' is necessary for the possibility of experience; that this form of externality must have at least two dimensions if it is to make experience possible;[15] and that any form of externality must be 'relative', i.e. homogeneous or of constant curvature (Russell's use of the word 'relative' here is not self-explanatory, and will be discussed; it should be distinguished from Einstein's use of the same word).

I shall trace out in some detail the argument by which Russell hopes to show that a form of externality is necessary for the possibility of experience. This argument shows very clearly the ways in which Russell accepts and relies upon the work of Bradley; it also shows the kinds of considerations which he is willing to count as 'purely logical'. Russell's language, at this point, is reminiscent of Bradley's *PL*:

My contention is . . . that since all knowledge is necessarily derived by an extension of the *This* of sense-perception, and since such extension is only possible if the *This* has that fragmentary yet complex character conferred by a

---

[15] The *certainty* of the statement that space is three-dimensional, Russell says, 'is almost as great as that of the a priori' (*FG*, p. 163). Although the statement is empirical, small errors are impossible because we know that the number of dimensions must be an integer.

form of externality, therefore some form of externality, given with the *This*, is essential to all knowledge, and is thus logically a priori. (*FG*, p. 183)

The point here is that what is given must be complex, in the sense that parts can be distinguished within it. These parts must be mutually external: hence the need for a form of externality.[16] In arguing for this claim Russell explicitly draws on idealist logic; and here it is clear that 'logic' is taken primarily as an analysis of knowledge or judgement and their presuppositions:

my premiss, in this argument, is that all knowledge involves a recognition of diversity in relation, or, if we prefer, of identity in difference. This premiss I accept from Logic, as resulting from the analysis of judgment and inference. To prove such a premiss, would require a treatise on Logic; I must refer the reader, therefore, to the works of Bradley and Bosanquet on the subject. (*FG*, p. 184)

The object of knowledge (which Russell here takes as a 'mental object'—loc. cit.) must thus be complex. Russell then claims that 'knowledge must start from perception' (loc. cit.), and goes on to argue that the 'object of immediate perception' must also be complex. An important consideration here is that two things must be complex if we are to be able to contrast and compare them—they must be alike in some respects and unlike in other respects, so each must have more than one 'respect'. Russell thus takes himself to have shown the need for complexity in the object of immediate perception, and thus also for some kind of form of externality.[17] He goes on to claim that time alone cannot play this role. His arguments for this claim are obscure. They rely upon two things: first, the need for an explanation of the changes in one's perceptions (a form of the Law of Sufficient Reason), and second, the fact that we are conscious of ourselves as having experience. (These things are thus, presumably, to be accounted as part of logic.)

Russell thus takes himself to have shown that the possibility of experience requires a form of externality other than that of time. Earlier in the book he had already claimed that any form of externality must fulfil certain conditions; in particular, that any such form must be homogeneous or (equivalently, as Russell takes it) 'relative'. This claim, and the arguments that Russell offers for it, are worth discussing at

---

[16] In discussing Bradley we examined his view that the given must be a non-relational whole, related to what is beyond it (and thus not self-subsistent), and admitting of distinctions within it. There it was the first two aspects of the given which were stressed; here the last is the most important.

[17] For a recent discussion which is in some ways analogous to this claim of Russell's, see P. F. Strawson, *Individuals* (London: Methuen, 1959).

some length, in part because of the role that the relativity of space will play in the next section.

I shall begin by quoting a passage which will give a clearer idea of just what Russell means by a 'form of externality':

> In any world in which perception presents us with various things ... there must be, in perception, at least one 'principle of differentiation', an element, that is, by which the things presented are distinguished as various. This element, taken in isolation, and abstracted from the content which it differenti- ates, we may call a form of externality.... [W]hat we wish to study here ... is the bare possibility of such diversity [i.e. diversity 'of material content'], which forms the residuum ... when we abstract from any sense-perception all that is distinctive of its particular matter. This possibility, then, this principle of bare diversity, is our form of externality. (*FG*, p. 136)

Space is a form of externality in this sense because one way in which different things may differ is precisely by occupying different parts of space.

The next stage is an argument for the relativity of any form of externality; and here we begin to see what Russell means by 'relativity':

> externality is an essentially relative conception—nothing can be external to itself. To be external to something is to be another with some relation to that thing. Hence, when we abstract a form of externality from all material content, and study it in isolation, position will appear, of necessity, as purely relative— a position can have no intrinsic quality.... Thus we obtain our fundamental postulate, the relativity of position. (*FG*, pp. 136–7)

The relativity of space, or of position, as Russell understands it, is the view that any position (or other part of space) is distinguished from any other position *only* by the fact that the two positions have different relations to yet other positions.[18] Intrinsically, abstracted both from the content that fills it and from its relations to other positions, one posi- tion is just like another; more accurately, perhaps, the attempt to consider a position intrinsically in this way is doomed to fail, because a position simply has no intrinsic properties that can be considered. A form of externality was the *possibility* of diversity of content, abstracted from the actual diverse content. But when this abstraction is made, we are left with nothing but the mutual externality of different positions.

---

[18] On the face of it, at least, the relativity of space in this sense is not the same as what are currently called relational or (by Sklar) relationist views of space and time. These latter views claim that: 'properly understood, all spatial and temporal assertions should be seen not as attributing features to space or time or spacetime, but rather as attributing some spatial, temporal, or spatio-temporal relations to material objects' (Sklar, op. cit. n. 3 above, p. 167). The relations that Russell stresses hold among positions, parts of space, not among material objects.

A position is nothing but its distinctness from, and relatedness to, other positions. The homogeneity of space follows directly from its relativity:[19] if positions have no intrinsic qualities, two positions cannot differ except in their relations to other positions; there can be no intrinsic difference between them (*FG*, p. 137). In spite of this direct equivalence, Russell phrases his argument for homogeneity rather differently from the argument for relativity, and the alternative formulation brings out a different aspect of the point at issue:

The diversity of content, which was possible only within the form of externality, has been abstracted from, leaving nothing but the bare possibility of diversity, the bare principle of differentiation, itself uniform and undifferentiated. For if diversity presupposes such a form [i.e. of externality], the form cannot, unless it be contained in a fresh form, be itself diverse or differentiated. (*FG*, p. 137)

In dealing with the form of externality we are dealing with that which makes diversity possible. This 'bare possibility of diversity' cannot itself manifest diversity, because we have abstracted from anything that might constitute diversity within this possibility. Russell thus claims that it is true a priori that the form of externality is homogeneous, and thus that space, which is our form of externality, must be of constant curvature.

2. Geometry and the Hegelian Dialectic

The second main philosophical conclusion of *FG* is, as I have said, that there are contradictions in geometry. Russell's claim is not merely that this or that formulation of geometry is contradictory, or even that all formulations so far devised are contradictory; his claim is that the subject itself is inherently, and irremediably, contradictory. To say that any theory of space, i.e. any geometry, is contradictory is to say that contradictory things are true of space. But surely this is enough to show that there is no such thing as space; and if there is no such thing as space then there cannot, presumably, be any acceptable theory of space. Russell's attitude, I think, would be that the first part of this charge is correct, but that it amounts to an endorsement of his view and not a criticism of it; and that the second part of the charge does not follow from the first and is not correct. Russell, that is to say, takes something like the following view of the matter. He accepts that there

---

[19] The homogeneity of space in turn implies that space is of constant curvature. If space were of variable curvature, the variations would make one position intrinsically different from another.

is no such thing as space—if by this one means that space is not fully real. Space is an abstraction from a more inclusive and less abstract whole. Because it is an abstraction it is not consistent and intelligible as it stands, for it must ultimately be understood as an aspect of this more inclusive whole; this for Russell, is precisely what is shown by the contradictions. That space is an abstraction which is not fully intelligible on its own terms may imply that any theory of space will be open to some objection on this score, but it does not at once imply that no theory of space is possible, or that no distinction of truth from falsehood is possible within such a theory. We may be able to take the theory on its own terms and work within it. Difficulties or incoherencies ('contradictions' in some sense of the term) will arise at certain points, precisely because those terms are not fully intelligible as they stand, but this does not threaten our ability to develop the theory up to those points. The truths of the theory will be *relative* truths, i.e. truths which are true only given (or relative to) the abstraction which is implicit in the terms of the theory. The contradictions of the theory indicate that this abstraction is not ultimately acceptable; relative truths are not absolute truths. But this is compatible with there being a distinction between the relative truths of the theory and its relative falsehoods. Geometry as a whole may fall short of absolute truth, but we can still distinguish the truths of geometry from the falsehoods of geometry. All of this represents, I think, Russell's attitude towards geometry in *FG*.

In the first part of this section I shall discuss the contradictions which Russell claims to find in geometry. By doing so I hope to render his attitude towards the subject more intelligible than the description of the previous paragraph may have made it appear. Central to this task is an understanding of the idea that space is an *abstraction*; and of the claim that this fact gives rise to contradictions, in some sense of that term. The second, and longer, part of the section will be a discussion, at a much higher level of generality, of the Hegelian dialectic to which Russell at this time professed adherence, and which he takes to be exemplified by the case of geometry.

I begin, then, with the contradictions that Russell claims to find in space. It is perhaps important that, in finding these contradictions, Russell can see himself as continuing a long philosophical tradition. The idea of such contradictions, he says, is 'an ancient theme—as ancient, in fact, as Zeno's refutation of motion' (*FG*, p. 188). Among philosophers who had a more direct influence on Russell, both Kant and Bradley had explicitly argued that there are irremediable contradictions in space. The details of Russell's argument may be novel, but the claim itself was far from heterodox.

We saw in the last section that Russell argues for what he calls the *relativity* of space: that spatial positions have no intrinsic properties, so that one position differs from another only because the two positions have different relations to yet other positions (pp. 83–4, above). It is the relativity of space which Russell sees as the source of the contradictions in space: 'the relativity of space ... renders impossible the expression of ... [any principle] of pure Geometry, in a manner which shall be free from contradictions' (*FG*, p. 128).[20] Why should the relativity of space give rise to contradictions? According to that doctrine, a spatial position has no intrinsic qualities. Such a position is given solely by its spatial relations to other positions; and these other positions, in turn, equally lack intrinsic qualities. In default of any intrinsic qualities, it may seem that each position simply consists of the spatial relations that define it—for there seems to be nothing else of which it could consist. Now geometry, the study of space, considers space as an independent entity. Of what is this entity composed? The positions with which geometry deals seem, as we have just seen, to consist of nothing but spatial relations. Among what elements do these relations hold? The usual geometrical answer is that the elements of spatial relations are *points*.[21] But Russell insists that the notion of a point is contradictory. On the one hand a point must be without extension, for whatever has extension can be divided into parts which themselves have spatial relations to one another and to other points, so that extended points cannot be the elements that we seek. Yet on the other hand, how can space be composed simply of points which are not themselves spatial? This is what Russell calls 'the antinomy of the point':

After hypostatizing space, as Geometry is compelled to do, the mind imperatively demands elements.... But what sort of elements do we thus obtain? Analysis, being unable to find any earlier halting place, finds its elements in points, that is, in zero quanta of space. Such a conception is a palpable contradiction.... A point must be spatial, otherwise it would not fulfill the function of a spatial element; but again it must contain no space, for any finite

---

[20] Elsewhere (p. 188) Russell says that there are *two* kinds of contradiction in space—those due to the relativity of space and those due to the continuum. He does, however, add that the two kinds may not really be distinct, because any continuum 'in which the elements are not data' will exhibit relativity. In the contradictions that Russell discusses, the problems of the continuum do not play any role which is separate from that of relativity, though this may simply be a matter of Russell's method of expressing the contradictions.

[21] It is, as Russell remarks, possible to take *lines* as undefined rather than points; and to consider a point as the relation between two lines (their point of intersection, as we would say informally) rather than considering a line as the relation between two points. But this makes no difference to the basic argument.

extension is capable of further analysis. Points can never be given in intuition, which has no concern with the infinitesimal: they are a purely conceptual construction, arising out of the need of terms between which spatial relations can hold. If space be more than relativity, spatial relations must involve spatial relata; but no relata appear, until we have analyzed our spatial data down to nothing. (*FG*, pp. 189–90)

This argument closely resembles one of Bradley's arguments for the contradictoriness of space (*A. & R.*, pp. 31–2). It also has connections with Zeno's argument against the possibility of motion and, more distantly, with Kant's Second Antinomy. Russell discusses other contradictions in space, but they all, on his account, have the same origin. On the one hand, space consists merely of spatial relations. On the other hand, no aggregate consisting merely of relations can amount to an independent object. Yet in thinking of geometry as a subject which can be pursued without reference to others, we implicitly take space as just such an independent, self-subsistent object. Space, considered abstractly, is mere relations; but if considering it abstractly is to be justified, it cannot be mere relations: and this is the source of the contradictions that Russell discusses.

At this point we can introduce an idea which, in slightly different guise, plays a crucial role in the Hegelian dialectic. This is the idea that the contradictions which figure in the dialectic can be removed or overcome by introducing new elements into the theory which gave rise to the contradictions. A theory which contains a contradiction, according to this view, requires supplementation;[22] the new theory will then not be vulnerable to the contradiction (though it may be vulnerable to others). There is a difference between supplementing a theory and simply discarding it in favour of another. The new theory has a different subject-matter from the old: it is more inclusive. Moreover, the contradictions of the dialectic themselves indicate the way in which the contradictory theory is to be supplemented. One theory is vulnerable to contradictions, and the attempt to overcome these contradictions forces us to a specific new theory: one theory 'gives rise' to another, or there is a 'dialectical transition' from the one theory to the other,

---

[22] The Hegelian position does not require that all contradictions should be removable in this way. It is perfectly consistent with this position to admit that there may be contradictions which simply arise from mistakes in formulating a theory; and the correct response to these would be to reformulate the theory. What is essential to the version of Hegelianism that I am articulating here is that in any ordinary subject there should be *some* contradictions which are not due to any errors but are unavoidable and intrinsic to the subject; and that *these* contradictions can be overcome by extending the scope of the theory. See *FG*, p. 128; see also 'On the Idea of a Dialectic of the Sciences' (written 1 Jan. 1898, but published in *MPD*, pp. 48–53), pp. 44, 53.

because there is only one theory that can remove the contradictions of the original theory. From the point of view of the new theory, we can say that the old theory was an abstraction (from the new, supplemented, theory), and that its abstractness was what gave rise to the contradictions. Overcoming the contradiction means removing abstraction, i.e. going from the original theory to the new theory. In a certain sense the new theory thus follows from the old; given that we begin by accepting the old theory, we must replace it by the new theory if we are to avoid contradiction.

Let us see how the idea that contradictions can be overcome works in the case of the contradictions that Russell found in geometry. First we have to understand the sense in which space can be thought of as an abstraction. The argument for the apriority of some form of externality proceeded from the claim that experience is possible only if the given exhibits diversity, to the conclusion that there must be a form of externality if this diversity is to be possible (pp. 81–2, above). Space is thus abstracted from the existence of different and interrelated things. It is the form of externality which makes this 'diversity in relation' (*FG*, p. 184) possible for us. So space is neither a relation nor a thing, but is rather 'the bare possibility of relations between diverse things' (*FG*, p. 190); but 'a bare possibility cannot exist' (loc. cit.). Geometry is the attempt to study empty space, i.e. space in abstraction from any objects in space, or the *possibility* of diversity in abstraction from the things which are diverse. Now it is this abstractness, according to Russell, which is the source of the contradictions:

it is empty space ... which gives rise to the antinomy in question; for empty space is a bare possibility of relations, undifferentiated and homogeneous, and thus wholly destitute of parts or thinghood. (*FG*, p. 191)

Given that the contradictions arise from the attempt to study space in abstraction from spatial objects, the solution to the contradictions is 'to give every geometrical proposition a certain reference to matter in general' (*FG*, p. 190). This matter, according to Russell, cannot be the matter with which physics deals, since physics, on his view, is in turn dependent upon geometry (*FG*, p. 78). So we abstract from those properties of matter with which physics deals, and consider only 'a peculiar and abstract kind of matter, which is not regarded as possessing any causal qualities, as exerting or subject to the action of forces' (*FG*, p. 191). To free space from its contradictions, we suppose it full of simple, unextended atoms of this peculiar kind of abstract matter. These atoms at once provide us with relata for spatial relations, since unlike points the atoms are differentiated from one another by more than their relations. Now that we have non-geometrical relata for spatial relations, we replace the study of empty space with the study of spatial order, and this resolves all the contradictions which Russell found in space: 'the mathematical antinomies . . . arise only in connection with empty space, not with spatial order as an aggregate' (*FG*, p. 196). It is spatial order, according to Russell, that is actually given. Geometry, and its contradictions, arise because we are led, by 'an unavoidable psychological illusion' (*FG*, p. 196), to treat the given spatial relations as if they were independent of their relata and formed a subject which could be carried on without reference to any other (see *FG*, pp. 194, 196). The contradictions in geometry show the error of this view.

Before leaving Russell's views on geometry it is worth reiterating three points. First, geometry is *inevitably* contradictory. When the contradictions are removed by introducing the notion of matter, it is then no longer geometry which we are studying. Geometry is the study of space (not of matter in space—however abstract the matter); and this subject is contradictory. Secondly, geometry, although contradictory, is neither impossible nor useless. I have already emphasized that geometry will yield relative truth (p. 85, above). For certain purposes this relative truth may be exactly what we want, and the limitations to which it is subject may be unimportant. This second point is reinforced by the third, which is that this kind of inconsistency is not peculiar to geometry; other subjects too will be contradictory, and the attempt to eliminate the contradictions will lead us from one subject to the next. This position is not argued for in *FG*, but it is clearly a part of the view expressed in that book. Russell ends the book like this:

Finally, we discussed the contradictions arising out of the relativity and continuity of space, and endeavoured to overcome them by a reference to matter. . . . To deal with new contradictions, involved in such a notion of matter, would demand a fresh treatise, leading us through Kinematics, into the domains of Dynamics and Physics. But to discuss the special difficulties of space is all that is possible in an essay on the Foundations of Geometry. (*FG*, p. 201)

I turn now to a more general discussion of the Hegelian dialectic, of which Russell was at this time a proponent. My interest in the dialectic is largely an interest in the way in which Russell understood it. With this aim in mind, I shall rely upon McTaggart's interpretation of Hegel. It was under McTaggart's influence that Russell first became a Hegelian,[23] and *FG* is dedicated to McTaggart. McTaggart's *Studies*

---

[23] *MPD*, p. 38, B. Russell, *Autobiography* (London: Allen & Unwin, 1971; 1st edn. 1967), i. 63.

in the Hegelian Dialectic was published in 1896, and Russell read it the same year.[24] McTaggart's interpretation of Hegel is in certain respects eccentric, but I shall ignore this fact as irrelevant to our concerns. When I speak of Hegel, I should therefore be understood as speaking of Hegel-as-interpreted-by-McTaggart.

The Hegelian dialectic is a criticism of the categories by means of which we ordinarily understand the world.[25] In particular, the criticism is that these categories are contradictory. In the simplest case, the application of a category to the world involves or implies the applicability of a second category to the world, where the two categories in some way conflict or contradict each other. These contradictions force on us a progression of categories. In the simplest case, again, there will be a third category in which the two contradictory categories are reconciled, and what is correct about each is preserved. Then this third category is in turn shown to be contradictory, and so on. In other cases, only two categories are involved, and the advance is direct; the use of the first category by itself gives rise to contradictions which can be removed or overcome only by replacing it by the second category. As before, the category thus attained is then the start of a new stage in the dialectic. McTaggart speaks of a 'logical connection between the various categories which are involved in the constitution of experience' and goes on to say:

this connection is of such a kind that any category, if scrutinized with sufficient care and attention, is found to lead on to another, and to involve it, in such a manner that an attempt to use the first of any subject while we refuse to use the second of the same subject results in a contradiction. The category thus reached leads on to a third, and the process continues until we at last reach the goal of the dialectic in a category which betrays no instability. (*Studies*, p. 1)

[24] Evidence that Russell read the book in 1896 is in his notebook, 'What Shall I Read?'
[25] 'Categories' here is McTaggart's word; Hegel does not use 'Kategorien' in this context ('Kategorien' is the Kantian term that is almost invariably translated as 'categories'). Hegel's usual word for the stages of the dialectic (short of the final stage) is 'Denkbestimmung' (literally: 'thought-determination'). The choice of this word reflects the idea that the dialectic begins with the emptiest, most abstract way of thinking about things, and that each stage of the dialectic is less abstract and more determinate (*bestimmt*) than the preceding stage (I owe this insight to Dan Brudney). The use of the word 'category' in this context is, however, by no means unusual among English-speaking commentators. See e.g. Stace, *The Philosophy of Hegel* (London: Macmillan, 1924), e.g. p. 82; J. B. Baillie, *The Origin and Significance of Hegel's Logic* (London: Macmillan, 1901), e.g. p. vii; E. Caird, *Hegel* (Edinburgh and London: W. Blackwood & Sons, 1891), e.g. p. 157; and, more recently, Taylor, *Hegel* (Cambridge: CUP, 1975), e.g. p. 225.
   In speaking of 'the categories by means of which we understand the world' I do not mean to imply that our relation to the world is merely one of understanding it, rather than constituting it in some sense. This is an issue about which McTaggart says very little.

This brief sketch requires elaboration. I begin with the issue of the starting-point of the dialectic, and here a comparison with Kant may be illuminating. A Hegelian category, like a Kantian category, is in some sense involved in or presupposed by all judgement or thought. Not every concept is a category, but our employing the categories is a condition of our being able to employ any concept whatsoever. Those features of the world in virtue of which the employment of the categories is valid will thus have a kind of necessity: a world without such features cannot be coherently thought of or described. Kant claimed that there were exactly twelve categories, and that the list of categories could be more or less straightforwardly obtained from the list of forms of judgement drawn up by the formal logicians. In the Transcendental Deduction he offered an extremely involved argument for the necessity of these categories for the possibility of experience. Kant's method of drawing up the list of categories, and his method of justifying them, both received severe criticism in the immediate post-Kantian period. Kant purported to criticize, and find the presuppositions of, all knowledge. How could one be justified, in an enterprise of this absolutely fundamental character, in taking for granted the procedures of the formal logicians? Equally, what knowledge could one appeal to in order to argue for the necessity of the categories? If the knowledge to which one appeals itself presupposes the categories, then the argument appears circular: one must presuppose the validity of the categories in order to know that which one uses to argue for their validity. Yet if there is knowledge that does not presuppose the categories then the categories cannot be the presupposition of all knowledge; and then the fundamental question seems to be the status and presuppositions of this prior knowledge. To what, then, can we appeal when we claim to know that which is said to be the presupposition of all knowledge? Where can philosophy begin? Some features of the Hegelian dialectic are to be understood against the background of these sorts of criticisms of Kant.[26] The starting-point of the dialectic is the category of Being, the necessity of which is held to be peculiarly self-evident and undeniable:

All that is required is the assertion that there is such a thing as reality—that something is. Now the very denial of this involves the reality of the denial, and so contradicts itself and affirms our postulate. And the denial also implies the reality of the person who makes the denial. The same dilemma meets us if we try to take refuge from dogmatic assertion in mere doubt. If we really doubt,

---

[26] For an examination of early criticisms of *The Critique of Pure Reason*, see Frederick C. Beiser, *The Fate of Reason* (Cambridge, Mass.: Harvard University Press, 1987).

then the doubt is real, and there is something of whose reality we do not doubt. (*Studies*, pp. 20–1)

The necessity of the category of Being is put forward as the sole assumption of the dialectic. Reflection on what is involved in the employment of this category leads us on to other categories. At any given point in the dialectic we argue for the necessity of a given category using only the results established by the dialectic up to that point. The dialectic is thus a progression of categories, in which the necessity of the first is held to be self-evident, and the necessity of each subsequent category to follow from the necessity of the previous ones.

It is important to emphasize that, in the progression of categories which constitutes the dialectic, it is not merely the *validity* but also the *necessity* of a given category which follows from the necessity of the previous categories. If I have followed the dialectical progression of categories to a given point, then not only *may* I validly proceed to the next point—I am also forced to do so. This is unlike ordinary logical inference. If I know that Socrates is a person, and that all people are mortal, then I *may* validly infer that Socrates is mortal, but I am not logically forced to do so. There is nothing logically contradictory about my knowing both of the premises of a syllogism but never putting them together to draw the conclusion (it is of course contradictory for me to hold the negation of the conclusion; but that is quite a different matter). In this respect the dialectical advance from one category to the next is unlike the syllogistic advance from premises to conclusion. I might of course fail in fact to carry out the dialectical advance, but if I do so contradictions result. If I employ a given category, then not merely may I validly employ the next category in the progression; I am also forced to employ it, on pain of contradiction.

This makes it clear that the notion of a contradiction is central to the dialectic. It also suggests that the notion in this context is a problematic one—most obviously because the employment of any category (short of the final one) appears to be both necessary and contradictory. Before considering these issues directly, however, I shall return to a rather different aspect of the comparison between Kant and Hegel. Kant distinguishes the noumenal world, which is the world as it is in itself, from the phenomenal world, which is the world as it appears to us. Every item of (actual or possible) empirical knowledge is part of the world as it appears to us, no matter how remote or hard to discover—electrons as well as trees, as yet unobserved galaxies as well as mountains. The noumenal world, by contrast, is beyond the bounds of our knowledge; we know that it exists, but can know nothing else about it. Kant's Transcendental Deduction attempts to show only that his categories are necessary for possible experience, and thus that they are necessarily applicable to the phenomenal world, but not that they are applicable to the noumenal world. Kant further argues that certain of the categories would give rise to contradictions (Antinomies) if they were employed unconditionally or unrestrictedly. If the category of cause, for example, could be validly applied without restriction, then we should be forced to admit that the world as a whole (the entire causal series) either has a cause or lacks a cause. Each alternative conflicts with the universal validity of the category of causality. If the world as a whole has no cause then the applicability of causality has a limit; but if causality has unrestricted validity then the causal series cannot be caused by an event outside the series, for there is no such event (if the category of causality is unrestricted, then the causal series is all-embracing). Kant avoids the threat of contradiction by his insistence that the categories are valid only of a world which is not independent of us, and which does not, therefore, form a whole existing in itself. The existence of the Antinomies, Kant says,

affords indirect proof of the transcendental ideality of appearance.... This proof would consist in the following dilemma. If the world is a whole existing in itself, it is either finite or infinite. But both alternatives are false.... It is therefore also false that the world (the sum of all appearances) is a whole existing in itself. From this it follows that appearances are nothing outside our representations—which is just what is meant by their transcendental ideality. (*Critique of Pure Reason*, A506–7=B534–5)

Kant thus claims that (some of) the categories would give rise to contradictions if they were admitted as unrestrictedly valid; and he concludes from this that their validity must be restricted. Since the Transcendental Deduction had argued that the categories must apply to all possible experience, it follows that there must be a realm beyond all possible experience—and this is the Kantian noumenon or thing-in-itself. Now, as we have already seen, the rejection of the Kantian thing-in-itself, or any *jenseits* to which our thought cannot attain, was a theme common to post-Kantian Idealists (see Chapter 1, pp. 32–4, above). The idea of categories which are presupposed by all judgement allows us to put this criticism of Kant in a sharper form. If the categories are presupposed by *all* judgement, then they must apply to anything about which we can make a judgement. But to say that the thing-in-itself exists is to make a judgement about it. Thus McTaggart says:

The thing-in-itself as conceived by Kant, behind and apart from the phenomena which alone enter into experience, is a contradiction. We cannot, we are told, know what it is, but only that it is. But this is itself an important piece of knowledge relating to the thing. It involves a judgment, and a judgment involves the categories, and we are thus forced to surrender the idea that we can be aware of the existence of anything which is not subject to the laws governing experience. (*Studies*, p. 27)

The implication of this is that the idea of something to which the categories do not apply is unthinkable—literally so, since all thought involves the employment of the categories.[27] In McTaggart's interpretation of Hegel, this point is crucial, for the ontological validity of the dialectic rests entirely upon it:

as Hegel's theory, if valid at all, covers the whole sphere of actual and possible knowledge, any speculations on the nature of reality outside its sphere are meaningless, and the results of the dialectic may be predicated of all reality. (*Studies*, p. 109)

The results of the logic, McTaggart therefore claims, hold of reality as a whole. A Hegelian category which was itself satisfactory (i.e. not contradictory) would therefore provide insight into, and a satisfactory way of understanding, reality as a whole.

The Hegelian rejection of the thing-in-itself, and consequent insistence that the validity of the categories must be unrestricted, rules out the Kantian resolution of the contradictions. The contradictions in the Hegelian categories must be resolved in some other way; and this affects the way in which we are to understand the notion of contradiction which is involved in the dialectic. The contradictions which Kant discusses in the Antinomies (*Critique of Pure Reason*, A404–567=B432–595) arise, he claims, from employing the categories beyond their proper sphere (which is possible experience); but this casts no doubt upon the validity of the categories within that sphere. The contradictions in the Hegelian dialectic, by contrast, are taken to show that the categories which give rise to them are inherently faulty and must be rejected, at least when ultimate truth is our aim. But a category cannot be straightforwardly rejected in the way in which one might reject the concept *round square*, or the concept *phlogiston*, for the categories are said to be involved in all possible judgement. When a category gives rise to a contradiction, we cannot merely reject that category; rather we reject it in favour of a specific other category which preserves what was correct in the first but is not contradictory in the same way (unless it is the final category of the dialectic it will be contradictory in some other way). This is how the dialectical advance from category to category

---

[27] As we have already seen, this sort of criticism of Kant overlooks, or denies, a subtlety in Kant's view; see p. 33, and Ch. 1. n. 13, above.

takes place. One category, when employed unrestrictedly, gives rise to contradictions which are overcome or resolved only in some other category. This second category gives rise to further contradictions, which lead us to a third category, and so on until we reach the end point of the dialectic. This end point is the Absolute Idea, which is fully adequate to express reality as a whole, and which can thus be employed unrestrictedly without giving rise to contradictions.

This dialectical process is intelligible only in the light of two ideas. The first is that, at each stage, the lower category is an abstraction from the higher. McTaggart expresses this by saying that the higher category is in each case logically prior to the lower category (*Studies*, p. 94). Logical priority, as McTaggart uses the term here, has to do with the order of intelligibility: the lower category can only be fully understood if seen as an abstraction from the higher category; so an understanding of the lower category has an understanding of the higher category as a pre-condition. The second idea required to make the dialectic intelligible is that it is the abstractness of each category (short of the last) that gives rise to the contradictions in that category. The Absolute Idea alone is fully adequate to express the nature of reality. Any other category is merely an aspect of, or abstraction from, this ultimate category. But then if we take any lower category and attempt to employ it unconditionally and without restriction, the attempt will fail.[28] A lower category may be useful within a limited sphere and subject to certain conditions, but if we attribute unrestricted validity to it contradictions will arise. These two ideas together make it comprehensible that a dialectical contradiction in a lower category can be overcome by the transition from that category to a higher category. This is possible precisely because the contradictions arise from the abstractness of the lower category, and the higher category is that from which the lower category is an abstraction. If we think of the various categories as independent, then it will seem incomprehensible that the contradictions to which one category gives rise can be 'overcome' in another; or that two conflicting categories can be 'reconciled' in a third. But these things become intelligible (at least abstractly) when we recognize that the lower categories are simply abstractions from the richer and more complex higher categories. It is, therefore, not surprising that McTaggart should stress just this point:

the essence of the whole dialectic lies in the assertion that the various pairs of contrary categories are only produced by abstraction from the fuller category in

---

[28] Compare the way in which, according to Kant, the category of causality breaks down if accorded unrestricted validity. Kant's conclusion from this, however, is not Hegel's.

which they are synthesized. We have not, therefore, to find some idea which shall be capable of reconciling two ideas which originally had no relation to it. We are merely restoring the unity from which those ideas originally came. It is not, as we might be tempted to think, the reconciliation of the contradiction which is an artificial expedient of our minds in dealing with reality. It is rather the creation of the contradiction which was artificial and subjective. (*Studies*, pp. 93–4)

The two ideas which I have just emphasized are well illustrated by the contradictions which Russell claimed to find in the concept of space (pp. 86–9, above). Russell's claim was that these contradictions are due to the abstraction of space, as the mere possibility of diversity, from the actuality of diverse things in space. If this claim is correct, if there are contradictions in the concept of empty space which are due to its abstractness, then it is clear enough that the contradictions are to be overcome by undoing the abstraction. Hence Russell urges the need for a transition from the theory of empty space (geometry) to a theory of space with some material content. The feature of this example which gives it its clarity, however, also gives it a sort of triviality. In arguing for the necessity of some form of externality, Russell explicitly introduces space (our form of externality) as an abstraction from diverse things in space. When contradictions are found in the concept of empty space, this shows that the process of abstraction by which we arrived at that concept must be reversed. We undo the abstraction and thus end up back where we started.[29] Thus in the case of this particular dialectical transition we have, independently of the transition itself, some knowledge of the higher stage in the dialectic and of the way in which the lower stage is an abstraction from it. When the abstractness of the lower stage is found to lead to a contradiction, it is therefore perfectly comprehensible that this contradiction is to be overcome by a transition to the higher stage. All of this, which is true of the example in *FG*, cannot be thought to hold generally of the contradictions of the dialectic. In particular, it cannot be held that we have, independently of the dialectic, an explicit knowledge of the Absolute Idea (the highest stage of the dialectic) and of the way in which all the lower categories are abstractions from it. If we did have this explicit knowledge then the dialectic would be superfluous, for we should already understand the essential thing that it has to teach us. McTaggart does claim that we have an implicit knowledge of the Absolute Idea—he speaks of it as 'latent in the nature of all experience, and of the mind itself' (*Studies*, p.

---

[29] This is not strictly correct because, as we saw, the 'matter' which Russell adds to empty space to undo the abstraction is not matter in the ordinary sense. But this does little to save the example from triviality.

47).[30] But the only argument that there can be for this is the dialectic itself, the process of making the Absolute Idea explicit.

The two ideas upon which the intelligibility of a dialectical transition depends can only be appreciated from the point of view of the higher stage which we reach as a result of the transition. Only from that point of view can we see that the lower stage is an abstraction from the higher; and only when we see the lower stage as an abstraction from the higher can we recognize that the contradictions in that stage are due to its abstractness. In the case of the example from *FG* we were in possession of an understanding of the higher stage from the outset; this was what gave the example both its clarity and its triviality. But in general this will not be so. In general, therefore, the transitions of the dialectic must be carried out before we are in a position to understand them fully. If we are to avoid blatant circularity there must, therefore, be a distinction between the order of intelligibility and the order of knowledge or justification (see *Studies*, pp. 14–15). The dialectic can only be fully understood if we begin with its conclusion, the Absolute Idea, and see each lower category as an aspect of, or abstraction from, this ultimate category. But the justification of the dialectic must be justification to the ordinary, non-philosophical mind, which does not yet have (explicit) knowledge of the Absolute Idea. This ordinary consciousness, for which the Hegelian term is 'the Understanding', accepts the categories as fixed and stable. It works with them but does not concern itself with their interrelations, with the way in which one category passes over into another in the dialectic (this is the province of what Hegel calls 'Reason').[31] The dialectic, in these terms, must be justified to the Understanding. If this realm were satisfactory by its own standards, then the claim that there is some other standpoint from which it is unsatisfactory would not affect it; one could simply dismiss that other standpoint. But this is not the case. On the contrary; the categories of the Understanding are contradictory even by the standards of the Understanding.

---

[30] Cf. Hegel's remark: 'Common fancy puts the Absolute far away in a world beyond. The Absolute is rather directly before us, so present that so long as we think we must, though without express consciousness of it, always carry it with us and always use it.' *Hegel's Logic, Being Part One of the Encyclopedia of the Philosophical Sciences (1830)*, trans. William Wallace (Oxford: Clarendon Press, 1975; 1st edn. 1873), p. 40.

[31] The Hegelian contrast between Reason (*Vernunft*) and the Understanding (*Verstand*) is thus importantly different from (though connected with) the contrast that Kant marks in the same words. Reason and the Understanding, on the Hegelian understanding of the terms, are not ultimately separate. Reason is, rather, implicit in the Understanding. The contradictions indicate this, and Reason, when made explicit (in the dialectic), provides an explanation both of the contradictions and of the Understanding itself. See *Studies*, pp. 88–9.

The contradictions arise when the categories are applied generally, in the search for a complete explanation of the world. It is this demand for completeness which shows up the inadequacies of every category short of the Absolute Idea; and the demand for completeness must therefore be a demand of the Understanding itself, or of the ordinary non-philosophical consciousness. And McTaggart claims exactly this:

The Understanding, in its attempts to solve particular problems, demands a complete explanation of the universe, and the attainment of the ideal of knowledge.... For although we start with particular problems, the answer to each of these will raise fresh questions, which must be solved before the original difficulty can be held to be really answered, and this process goes on indefinitely, till we find that the whole universe is involved in a complete answer to even the slightest question.... For if a thing is part of a whole it must stand in some relation to the other parts. The other parts must therefore have some influence on it, and part of the explanation of its nature must lie in these other parts. From the mere fact that they are parts of the same universe, they must all be connected, directly or indirectly. (*Studies*, p. 82)

A holistic view of the world is thus implicit in the dialectic, as in the other idealist philosophies that I have discussed: since any one thing depends upon everything else in the universe, a *complete* explanation of any one thing would be a complete explanation of the universe as a whole, and short of this completeness the goal of knowledge is not yet reached. The Understanding, our ordinary ways of thinking about the world, thus more or less explicitly demands a complete explanation of the universe. But the Understanding cannot meet this demand, as the contradictions in the categories of the Understanding show. Reason can meet the demand, and is thus justified: 'the Reason is the only method of solving the problems which are raised by the Understanding, and therefore can justify its existence on the principles which the Understanding recognizes' (*Studies*, p. 88).

One consequence of the dialectic is worth emphasizing further: the relativity of the notions of truth and falsehood. McTaggart says:

in the sphere of our ordinary finite thought, in which we use the imperfect categories as stable and permanent, the dialectic gives us objective information as to the *relative amounts of truth and error* which may be expected from the use of various categories, and as to the comparative reality and significance of different ways of regarding the universe. (*Studies*, p. 100; my emphasis)

The rationale for this is much the same as the rationale behind Bradley's claim that judgements can be more or less true. All categories except the Absolute Idea are abstract, and in so far as they are abstract they are erroneous. But abstraction is something that comes in degrees. Judgements made using less abstract ideas are capable of a higher degree of truth than are judgements made using more abstract ideas. The dialectic gives us a clear method of application of the idea of the relative truth of a judgement.[32] The dialectic is a progression in which categories occur in a quite definite order, beginning with Being and ending with the Absolute Idea. The position of a category within this progression tells us how abstract it is, and thus how much truth we may hope for in judgements involving it. Only when our judgements concern the universe as a whole, and use the Absolute Idea, do they escape incompleteness, abstraction, and partial falsehood: 'The one category by which experience can be judged with complete correctness is the Absolute Idea' (*Studies*, p. 25). So the ordinary judgements of science or of common sense are at best partially true, while meta-physical judgements may attain complete truth.

This discussion of the dialectic will, I hope, be enough to give some idea of what is involved in Russell's claim to be an Hegelian, and in his belief in the dialectical method. In particular, we can now appreciate the way in which Russell thought of *FG*. His general philosophical project at this period can be gathered from the title of the notes written in January 1898: 'On the Idea of a Dialectic of the Sciences' (these notes are printed in *MPD*). The dialectic of the sciences was to be a dialectic, in the Hegelian sense, in which each stage was made up of the ideas of some science. These ideas would be examined philosophically and found to be involved in inescapable contradictions; the contradictions of any given stage would be removed by employing ideas from another science, which would in turn be examined and found wanting. In the notes to which I have referred, Russell gave the following overall statement of the project:

we have ... first to arrange the postulates of the science so as to leave the minimum of contradictions; then to supply, to these postulates or ideas, such supplement as will abolish the special contradictions of the science in question, and thus pass outside to a new science, which may then be similarly treated.

Thus, e.g., number, the fundamental notion of arithmetic, involves some-thing numerable. Hence geometry, since space is the only directly measurable element in sensation. Geometry, again, involves something which can be located and something which cannot move. Hence matter and physics. (*MPD*, p. 53)

As in the view of McTaggart, each stage of the dialectic purports to give a complete explanation of the universe: 'every science may be regarded as an attempt to construct a universe out of none but its own ideas' (*MPD*, pp. 52–3; cf. the discussion in Chapter 2 of Bradley's

---

[32] As we have seen, no analogue of this holds for Bradley's conception of relative truth and falsehood; see Ch. 2, pp. 66–7, above.

view that to allow that something is real is to exclude the reality of other things—pp. 53–4, above). But these attempts are bound to fail, since no science is in the requisite way complete and independent. Each is, rather, incomplete and at best partially true: 'from the stand-point of a general theory of knowledge, the whole science [i.e. the whole of any science], if taken as metaphysic, i.e., as independent and self-subsistent, is condemnable' (*MPD*, p. 53).

What has been described is a philosophical programme, and Russell's only attempt to carry it out is *FG*. But the same ideas can also be seen in an arithmetical context in two pieces which Russell published in *Mind* in 1897.[33] As we should expect, arithmetical concepts are found to be contradictory. In particular, the infinite, long held by philosophers to be a source of antinomies, is held to be contradictory. Couturat's book is criticized on the grounds that:

the possibility of contradiction in results to which the understanding appears forced, though peculiarly evident in the case of mathematical infinity, is stre-nuously denied throughout the work.[34]

Again, Russell pays considerable attention to the interrelations of the various categories which he discusses. Following Hegel, he speaks of extensive quantity passing over into intensive quantity, and quantity in general becoming measure (see Section 2 of Book I of Hegel's *Science of Logic*), while the relation of number to quantity is twice said to be the 'most fundamental' problem of mathematical philosophy.[35] Finally, the moral which Russell draws from the contradictions is that philosophi-cal truth is altogether of a higher order than the truth of the special sciences. Mathematical truth is, by philosophical standards, relative truth only:

That infinity follows necessarily from certain premisses—e.g., the reality of space and time as something more than relations—must be admitted; that infinity is useful and unobjectionable in mathematics is by this time almost self-evident; but that mathematical infinity is philosophically valid might, I think, be met by two converging lines of argument. The first and more usual argument would urge the contradictions of infinity, which M. Couturat, I think, has not succeeded in disproving; the second might urge that, in all cases where infinity is unavoidable, there has been some undue hypostasising of

[33] Review of L. Couturat, *De l'infini mathématique*, *Mind* (1897), 112–19; and 'On the Relation of Number and Quantity', *Mind* (1897), 326–41.

[34] Review, op. cit. n. 33 above, pp. 114–15.

[35] Review, op. cit. n. 33 above, p. 112; 'On the Relation of Number and Quantity', op. cit. n. 33 above, p. 326.

relations, which makes the attainment of a completed substantive whole impossible.[36]

This view of the contradictoriness of infinity, and of the status of mathematics, is, as we shall see in Chapter 5, in stark contrast to the view that Russell held a few years later.

[36] Review, op. cit. n. 33 above, p. 119.

PART II
Platonic Atomism

Introduction

My primary aim in Part I of this book was to make intelligible the sort of idealist doctrines that were familiar to, and in some measure accepted by, Russell and Moore before 1898. As a part of this aim I tried to make those doctrines sufficiently attractive and plausible to make it credible to us that Moore and (especially) Russell could have adhered to them, not as a brief aberration but genuinely and profoundly. In doing this, however, I hope also to have done something to contribute to a second aim, which I now bring to the fore. This is the aim of indicating some of the weaknesses in Idealism, and thus of suggesting ways in which it might come to seem vulnerable, or even incredible, as it did to both Russell and Moore. My claim here is not that either of them had a conclusive argument against Idealism; one of the things that I wish to convey, indeed, is that issues at the most fundamental level of philosophy are not decided by conclusive argument. For every argument that Moore or Russell could mount against Idealism, there is an idealist reply which points out a distinction that is being neglected, or one that is drawn erroneously; an assumption smuggled in, or the sense of a term distorted. It is not because of any one argument that Moore and Russell rejected Idealism—though once they had done so they certainly employed arguments, which they held to be conclusive, against it. What I wish to do here, then, is not to supply a refutation of Idealism but to give a sense of its potential weaknesses, of the way in which it can seem to be in danger of collapsing under its own weight. I shall go on from this to discuss, at a general level, some of the ways in which the views of Moore and Russell after 1898 were shaped by their rejection of Idealism. This general discussion will guide us in the more detailed material of the next two chapters.

In my discussion of idealist views I have already drawn attention to several points which, looked at uncharitably, will appear as points of weakness. To accept Green's philosophy one has to accept the existence of an eternal self-consciousness, in which all human minds 'partake'—where the sense of this last word remains, in the end, obscure. Again, we saw that Green can naturally be interpreted as equivocating on the term 'thought'; I argued that Bradley could be seen as responding to exactly the problem which this equivocation attempts to mask. In the case of Bradley's own views, the conclusion, that all thought, all judgement, is in the end inadequate to reality, may come to seem like a *reductio ad absurdum*. With no way of distinguishing the more nearly adequate judgements from the less nearly adequate, or the more nearly true from the less nearly true, this conclusion seems to leave us with no theoretical way of making the simplest, yet most vital, distinction among judgements. The danger is that from the lofty point of view which Bradley adopts all judgements will have the same status—the idea that some are correct and others incorrect is one that does not seem to receive its true weight. Again, the idea that all judgements are inadequate to reality may seem empty, a mere expression of scepticism and defeatism, unless contrasted with some view as to what might be adequate to reality. And at this point Bradley's conception of reality as a single, all-embracing experience revealed to us, perhaps, in transcendent and ineffable moments—all of this may seem incredible, and a more fit subject for scepticism than the ordinary judgements which Bradley attacks.

More generally, we may distinguish two pervasive features of Idealism which might seem, again to the uncharitable reader, to correspond to fatal weaknesses. The first is that Idealism is always in danger of seeming psychologistic. It is not that the Idealists mean to be making claims that are answerable to experimental psychology (their work is not psychologistic in the straightforward way in which, say, J. S. Mill's *Logic* is). On the contrary, as I emphasized in Chapter 3 (above, Section 1, pp. 76–9), many Idealists explicitly disavowed any appeal to empirical psychology in philosophy, and criticized Kant for failing (as they saw it) to exclude psychological considerations from his epistemology. But anti-psychologistic intentions are not enough to guarantee freedom from psychologism. Crucial to all the forms of Idealism which we discussed is a reliance, at some stage, upon claims about the nature of experience, the nature of the mind or of thought, the presuppositions of experience or of knowledge. Now it is clear enough, as I indicated in my more detailed discussions, that what the Idealists mean to be talking about is in no case something that might be the subject-matter of empirical psychology. It is not this or that particular person's experience or mind which is being discussed, but Experience as such, Thought as such, Mind as such. When the Idealists talk about the conditions of knowledge, their attitude is not that we have a fact on the one hand and a sentient being on the other hand and wish to know what must be true of this being if it is to know or to make judgements about that fact. Their interest is, rather, at the totally general level where it is at least possible to claim that the presuppositions of judgement and knowledge are equally presuppositions of fact. Their interest, we might say, is in the presuppositions of Judgement as such, Knowledge as such. This way of talking about the concerns of the Idealists is very crude, but it brings out the idea that I wish to emphasize: that Idealism avoids psychologism only at the price of certain metaphysical commitments—to there being, for example, such things as the nature of Thought as such, or Judgement as such, which are not part of the subject-matter of empirical psychology. (I invoked this idea when I claimed, in Chapter 3, that Russell's refusal to make such metaphysical commitments in *FG* left him peculiarly open to the charge of psychologism; see p. 79, above.) The other side of this idea is that if one does not accept at the outset that it is possible to talk about (say) Thought as such, then the Idealists may appear as psychologistic in spite of their protestations. Something like this, I think, lies behind the claims of Moore and of Russell that Idealism is psychologistic.

The second pervasive feature of Idealism that I wish to discuss has several closely interwoven strands. One is that our ordinary ways of thinking about the world are contradictory, or inadequate, or not fully intelligible—or in any case unsatisfactory in some profound sense. More or less explicit in this is some ideal of consistency, or perfect intelligibility, to which, it is held, the world must in fact conform, even though it may not appear to. Only the world as a whole can meet this standard of consistency and intelligibility; any part, taken by itself, is bound to be inadequate, and thus not fully real. Only metaphysics can give us an understanding of the world as it must be, of the world as it really is; any other subject is bound to be more or less inadequate. This doctrine is naturally, perhaps inevitably, accompanied by the view that truth and reality can be matters of degree, of more and less. The judgements of ordinary life, of (say) science or history or mathematics, are at best true only for certain purposes, under certain restrictions, subject to certain conditions; but they must surely be distinguished from out and out falsehoods. These ordinary judgements are thus held to be (at best) partly true, true to some degree. Similarly, the things which our ordinary ways of thinking take as real—the chairs we sit in, the food we eat, the books we read—can hardly be dismissed as wholly unreal, as if they were no better than illusions. They must be allowed to be real in some degree, even though they fall short of complete and ultimate reality.[1] It is a part of this view that nothing is ever, ultimate-

---

[1] This doctrine of the relativity of truth and reality can be seen as playing the same role for Bradley and Hegel as the distinction between the empirical and the transcendent does for Kant. There is a clear opposition between the doctrines, but from the distant perspective of Platonic Atomism the similarity stands out. Both allow you to speak of different points of view such that something may be true from one point of view but not from another. In particular, both allow you to say that ordinary empirical subjects are

ly, quite what it seems to be to the ordinary, unphilosophical mind; and that what something really is depends on how the question is interpreted, on how ultimate a notion of reality is in play. A situation that is correctly described in one way at a certain stage, for certain purposes, may demand a quite different description from another stage, with different purposes. And neither description will be acceptable in metaphysics, where the demand is for full, ultimate and complete Truth.

This view of Idealism is unsympathetic and extremely general. It excludes the subtlety which, from within Idealism, might seem to be crucial. Yet this crude view of Idealism is useful in the initial attempt to understand the philosophy which Moore and Russell developed after their rejection of Idealism. I give the name 'Platonic Atomism' to this philosophy. In the remainder of this Introduction I shall sketch some very general characteristics of Platonic Atomism, and indicate how these characteristics can be seen as rejections of—or responses to—those features of Idealism which I discussed above.

The anti-psychologism of Platonic Atomism, to begin with, is complete and thoroughgoing. Platonic Atomism does, as I shall point out, imply or suggest a picture of the mind and its capacities, but this picture is very much a by-product of the view. There is no overt concern at all with the nature of thought or the mind, or of experience, in any sense. It is not that Moore and Russell are concerned to advance a view of these notions which is different from that of the Idealists, it is rather that these notions almost cease to be the subject of explicit philosophical concern. This seems to be because the notions are looked on as psychological, and for this reason of no interest to philosophy. Thus Moore, in his review of *FG*,[2] makes the following comment about Russell's claim that some form of externality is necessary for the possi-

---

true in their way, but that their truth is somehow confined or limited or non-absolute. The sharpest point of contrast between the two doctrines is that for Kant all our knowledge (though not all our rational belief) is in this way non-absolute, whereas Hegel takes non-absolute knowledge as the route to the absolute. While there are, in a sense, two standpoints, or two points of view, for Kant, one of them cannot be attained by finite beings, and seems only to play the role of showing the other standpoint to be limited. For Kant, then, the only notion of truth which makes sense to us is that in which truth is not absolute or unconditioned. Hegel's rejection of the transcendent, of anything essentially beyond human knowledge, opens the way for his insistence that the notion of absolute and unconditioned truth does make sense, and that absolute knowledge must be available to us. In spite of these differences, we can say that for both Kant and Hegel there is a clear sense in which ordinary knowledge is *not* absolute. For a piece of ordinary knowledge to be as true as ordinary knowledge can be is still for it to be relative truth, truth only from a limited point of view. Moore's and Russell's opposition to this view is, as we shall see, fundamental.

[2] *Mind* (1899), 397–405.

bility of experience: 'To put the matter shortly, to show that a "form of externality" is necessary for the possibility of experience, can only mean to show that it is presupposed in our actual experience' (p. 399). What this suggests is that, however much Russell (in *FG*) may mean to be talking about the fundamental nature of Experience as such, he in fact only succeeds in telling us about our actual experience; and that what he says therefore carries no philosophical weight. A similar attitude towards knowledge and its presuppositions emerges slightly later in the same review. Moore cites a passage in which Russell assumes that one thing is presupposed by another if the falsehood of the first would leave the second 'inaccessible to our methods of cognition' (*FG*, p. 60). Moore comments as follows:

Now that which is 'inaccessible to our methods of cognition' would seem to mean only that which we cannot know: it cannot imply that the judgments in question cannot be true. But apart from a proof that they cannot be true (in which case of course they cannot be *known* in the sense in which knowledge is distinguished from belief), it would seem that the only possible way of showing that they cannot be known must be simply a psychological inquiry into the conditions that are necessary for the production of actual beliefs. (p. 400)

Moore refers to the assumption of Russell's that he is attacking as a 'Kantian fallacy'. The question of the limits and presuppositions of knowledge is for Moore, as it was for the Empiricists, a psychological one (see Chapter 1, pp. 22–4, above). The crucial difference is that Moore, writing after the Kantian and post-Kantian attacks on psychologism, takes this as reason enough to hold that such questions are philosophically irrelevant. Moore's attitude seems to be that in philosophy our concern is simply with what is true about a given subject-matter; whether it can be known or not is a separate question, relevant to psychology rather than to philosophy. (An Idealist might say that Moore writes as if *he* were not subject to the conditions of knowledge, as if he had a position from which he could talk about what is true without regard even for the psychological possibility of his knowing such things. But in fact, as I shall explain, there is a view of knowledge implicit in Platonic Atomism according to which there simply are no significant presuppositions or limits to knowledge.)

A crucial assumption is implicit in the remark of Moore's which I have just been discussing. This is that judgements, or propositions, as Russell later called them, are independent of our acts of judging, or acts of synthesis—or acts of any kind. Propositions, in short, are conceived of as objective and independent entities. If there are conditions or presuppositions of our acts of judgement, these are not in any sense conditions or presuppositions of the proposition or of the object of judgement, for that is independent of us. The significance of this distinction is clear if we recall the central role played, in the work of Kant and his idealist successors, by the issue of the possibility and presuppositions of knowledge or judgement. The separation of the object of judgement from the act of judgement makes it clear that these presuppositions, if such there be, are merely conditions of our being able to perform a certain kind of act; they are not conditions on what propositions there can be, and therefore they cannot be conditions on what truths there are. The investigation of such presuppositions plays no role in Platonic Atomism, presumably because such an investigation would have the status of psychology, rather than metaphysics.

In discussing the works of Green and Bradley I argued that the issue of the status and reality of relations is, in those works, inseparable from the issue of the status of the proposition. Given that propositions, within Platonic Atomism, are objective and independent of us, it is thus no surprise that relations have the same status. This doctrine about relations contrasts most obviously with Bradley's denial of the reality of relations; but the contrast with Green's position, though less striking, is equally important. Green admitted the reality of relations— indeed he insisted on it. But he also argued that relations are not independent of our minds, or of the eternal Mind of which ours partake. These claims gave him a basis on which to argue that reality is in some sense Mental or Spiritual. What is important to Platonic Atomism, therefore, is not merely the insistence upon the reality of relations but also the insistence upon their objectivity and their complete independence of the mind which knows them or fails to know them—in any sense of 'mind' at all.

One of the ways in which I phrased the Platonic Atomism doctrine of the independence of propositions was as an insistence upon the distinction between the *act* of judgement and the *object* of judgement. This can be seen as a special case (and the most important case) of the distinction between (mental) acts and their (objective, non-mental) objects. Moore and Russell seem to insist upon this distinction quite generally—in knowledge, belief, thought, perception, and even imagination. In the case of each of these mental acts or states, their view is that we are in contact with an object which is *not* mental.[3] And the object with which we are in contact is, in all such cases, unaffected by the fact that we are in contact with it. If we can say that Idealism is a

---

[3] This is not strictly correct in all cases. If I think of your mental state, or of a mental state of my own, then the object of my thought is of course mental. But it is distinct from my act of thought, and not affected by it; and this is the crucial point. In the future I shall sometimes leave this qualification unstated.

view according to which the mind (in some sense of 'mind') is *active*, and plays a role in the constitution of reality, then we can equally say that Platonic Atomism is a view according to which the mind is completely passive, and in no way creative. Even the processes of thought or imagination, which we might naturally think of as creative, are represented as processes in which the mind is in contact first with one object and then with another. We can, no doubt, direct our attention from one object to another, but the objects are there independently of us.

Although the explicit doctrines of Platonic Atomism say little or nothing about the nature of our knowledge, a view of knowledge is none the less implicit in those doctrines. According to this view, we have a direct relation to various objects; we are, as it were, in direct contact with them. Russell sometimes speaks of this sort of knowledge as *acquaintance*.[4] There is little more to be said about acquaintance than that it is an immediate relation between a mind and an object. Indeed one might say that the point of the notion is precisely that there is very little to be said about it: the point is that knowledge is both presuppositionless and unproblematic. Nothing needs to be said, or can be said, about *how* we know, we just do know; hence my stress on the relation being 'direct' and 'immediate'. (The contrast with the idealist view of knowledge is, I hope, clear. Consider, for example, the role played, in Russell's argument (in *FG*) for the need for a 'principle of differentiation', by the view that knowledge is always complex, and so demands a complexity in its object—Chapter 3, pp. 81–2, above.) The Preface to Russell's *Principles of Mathematics* shows a striking instance of the use of this notion of knowledge. The discussion of the indefinables of logic, Russell says, 'is the endeavour to see clearly, and to make others see clearly, the entities concerned, in order that the mind may have that kind of acquaintance with them which it has with redness or the taste of a pineapple' (*Principles*, p. xv).[5] The Idealists, as we saw especially in the case of Green, held that even the simplest kind of sensory knowledge—the kind to which Russell is appealing here—is implicitly judgemental in character, and that it therefore presupposes a complex structure from which philosophers can learn much about the character of the (knowable) world. Russell appeals to sensory knowledge,

---

[4] The use of this term in Russell's work after 1905 is well known; see e.g. 'On Denoting', or *The Problems of Philosophy*. In his earlier works the term appears less often because Russell has less concern with knowledge. The use of the term is, however, very much the same in the earlier and in the later works.

[5] In a somewhat similar vein, Moore compares *good* with *yellow*, as an idea which cannot be conveyed by any definition, but which we must know directly if we are to know it at all; see *PE*, p. 10.

however, because it is the most plausible case of knowledge which lacks such presuppositions; and Russell's claim is that all knowledge is of this sort.[6] It is not only simple sensory states with which we can have direct acquaintance, but entities of all kinds, including those that we should call abstract.[7] In particular, we have this kind of knowledge of propositions and of relations. A view of knowledge according to which it is a direct and immediate relation between a mind which is passively receptive and an object which is unaffected by being known—such a view is in some ways reminiscent of Empiricism (see Chapter 1, pp. 22–4, above). We saw that Green argued against Empiricism on the grounds that our ability to form judgements would not be accounted for by the view that our mind is passively receptive of the sensory given; and that since all knowledge is judgemental in character, Empiricism could therefore not account for knowledge at all. Such a line of thought could not, however, be advanced against Platonic Atomism, for on that view propositions are among the things with which we have immediate acquaintance.

Over the last few pages I have sketched some central ideas of Platonic Atomism in such a way as to emphasize their connection with opposition to psychologism—the first of the two pervasive themes of Idealism which I distinguished at the beginning of this Introduction. The second such feature of Idealism also provides us with a way of thinking about some elements of Platonic Atomism. By contrast with the idealist talk of degrees of truth or reality, Platonic Atomism adopts a straightforward and absolute attitude towards these notions: either a proposition is true or it is false. The idea that it might have some intermediate status, that it might be true for certain purposes but not for others, that it might be true from one point of view or stage of thought but false from others—these are ideas with which Moore and Russell have, after their rejection of Idealism, no sympathy whatsoever. Their view is similar in the case of reality. There are no degrees of

[6] Cf. his statement in *Principles*: 'the mind, in fact is as purely receptive in inference as common sense supposes it to be in perception of sensible objects' (s. 37).

[7] I put it in this way because the distinction between abstract objects and non-abstract objects in Platonic Atomism is one that cannot be taken for granted. I shall discuss this in detail later, but it is worth pointing out that Moore and Russell seem to see no more difficulty in accepting abstract objects than they do in accepting non-abstract objects. It is, of course, because of this untroubled acceptance of abstract objects that I refer to the view as '*Platonic* Atomism'. This is not to say that the view in fact has very much in common with Plato's. In particular, Plato's abstract objects are quite different in kind from non-abstract objects, whereas in Platonic Atomism non-abstract objects are, so to speak, just special cases of objects in general (the rest of which are abstract). The term 'platonism' has, however, been adopted as a label for any view that freely accepts abstract objects (especially in the philosophy of mathematics), and I concur in this usage.

reality. A thing is what it is, and it is not what it is not; it cannot be one thing from one point of view and something else from another, or one thing to the ordinary mind and something else to the more discerning eye of the metaphysician.[8] We may be wrong about what something is, but if we are wrong we are just wrong, not right from some other point of view. These ideas most obviously contrast with the Hegelian dialectic, which I discussed above (Chapter 3, Section 2). But there is also a clear contrast with the kind of holism that is characteristic of all the idealist views which I have discussed. According to that holism, the true nature of any thing, or the full significance of any judgement, depends upon the place that that thing (or judgement) occupies in the unified structure that is reality as a whole (or complete knowledge of reality). In so far as we are still in the process of discovering reality, in all its complexity and interrelatedness, we are also in the process of articulating the true nature of each thing. It is only from the point of view of reality as a whole that we can appreciate the ultimate truth about anything at all. The view of Moore and Russell is in direct opposition to this holism. According to them, knowledge and understanding come piecemeal. It would be possible to know a single proposition, or to understand the nature of a single thing, and to be otherwise completely ignorant; one's ignorance would in no way impugn the knowledge or the understanding that one had. The world can be known by separate and distinct acts of knowledge because it is made up of separate, distinct objects.[9] The nature of any one such object is independent of anything else. There are relations among these objects, but these relations do not affect the objects. An object which is related to another would be exactly the same if it were not so related; and this is usually phrased as the insistence on the *externality* of relations. These relations themselves are conceived of as object-like, as distinct entities which could, again, be known in isolation from everything else.

The doctrines of Platonic Atomism forbid any inference from the nature of our knowledge to the nature of reality. It is, nevertheless, natural that the ontological picture which I sketched in the last paragraph should fit with the view of knowledge which I considered in the paragraph before that. Just as each object is what it is, without regard

---

[8] It is in this context that we can understand why Moore took, as the motto to *PE*, Bishop Butler's dictum: 'Everything is what it is and not another thing'.

[9] Hence the name 'Platonic *Atomism*'. I use the word 'object' here, and below, broadly, to include e.g. relations and propositions. This usage is, as we shall see, a natural one within Platonic Atomism, for according to that philosophy the distinctions among various kinds of entities are not fundamental.

to anything else, so the relation of direct acquaintance is one that holds between a mind and an object, equally without regard to anything else. The independence and self-subsistence of objects corresponds to the fact that our knowledge of a given object is independent of everything except the mind which knows and the object which is known; the atomistic ontology corresponds to the atomistic view of knowledge. To put the matter negatively, the Platonic Atomism view of knowledge seems to leave no room for knowledge of a *structure* or a *system*, made up of parts but comprehensible only as a whole. On that view of knowledge we can know *a* and know *b* and know the relation between them, but each of these bits of knowledge is separate. There is no room for a knowledge of *a* which partly consists of knowing its relation to *b*, or a knowledge of *b* which partly consists of knowing its relation to *a*, or a knowledge of their relation which partly consists in knowing that it relates *a* to *b*. There is no room for the idea of knowledge of a whole, of a system, of what the Idealists called an Organic Unity, which amounts to more than the conjunction of the knowledge of one part with the knowledge of another part, and so on for each part.[10] The fit between the ontology and the epistemology emerges from the fact that just as the view of knowledge leaves no room for knowledge of a system (in the sense indicated above), so the ontological vision seems to leave no room for the existence of such a thing. There are objects, and relations among them, but each of these (the relations as well as the objects) is independent of the others. There is, therefore, no room for the idea of a whole which is more than the sum of each of its parts taken in isolation. The idea of such a system, a whole which is more than the sum of its parts because its parts make a difference to one another, is a commonplace of Idealism. The Idealists, indeed, conceive of the world as such a whole; but the doctrines of Platonic Atomism rule out the possibility of such a whole.

An important feature of Platonic Atomism can be understood in terms of its opposition to the idealist view that all our ordinary (i.e. non-metaphysical) ways of thinking about the world are contradictory or incoherent. This opposition needs to be stated with some care. It is

---

[10] The advocate of Platonic Atomism can say that such a whole is *one* thing, not many, and that it must therefore be known as a single thing, so that its unity is, after all, appreciated. But this kind of knowledge leaves no room for an account of the complexity of the whole, for the fact that it consists of parts and that we can have partial knowledge of the individual parts. One might say that Platonic Atomism cannot account for knowledge of unity-in-diversity, or of the one-in-the-many, which the Idealists had so stressed. Not surprisingly, this leaves Moore and Russell unable to give a satisfactory account of the unity of the proposition (see Ch. 5, pp. 175–9, below; also the author's 'The Nature of the Proposition and the Revolt against Idealism', in Richard Rorty, J. B. Schneewind, and Quentin Skinner (eds.), *Philosophy in History* (Cambridge: CUP, 1984), pp. 375–97).

not that Russell or (at this stage of his life) Moore held that our ordinary ways of thinking are invariably correct, or that the deliverances of common sense enjoy any special status. They did perhaps hold that the things of common sense should be taken as real in the absence of evidence to the contrary, but this is not an important aspect of their opposition to the idealist view. The crucial point is, rather, the idea that we can find (non-metaphysical) ways of thinking which are wholly correct and satisfactory, and not vulnerable to any philosophical criticism. We may or may not already be in possession of such ways of thinking, but they must be available. This doctrine is very closely associated with the rejection of the idea of degrees of truth. If one holds that a statement is always either absolutely true or absolutely false, then there must be absolute truths about any subject that is not to be wholly repudiated.[11] We may not yet know such truths, but they are what we aim at. I emphasize this point because it came to play a crucial role in Platonic Atomism. In *FG*, as we saw, Russell had argued for the contradictoriness of geometry, if taken as an independent branch of knowledge. By 1900 he had come to the opposite conclusion. He argued that all of the incoherences which had been found in geometry could be shown to be caused by mistakes, and were not inherent in the nature of the subject. He held that the logic which he derived in part from Peano was capable of showing the whole of mathematics, including geometry, to be perfectly coherent and consistent. The method by which this was to be achieved was the reduction of mathematics to logic—i.e., the demonstration that mathematical concepts can be understood as built up from the basic concepts of logic, and that mathematical truths can all be proved from the basic truths of logic. This demonstration was outlined and discussed, but not fully carried out, in *Principles*. The philosophy of mathematics was, for Russell, a sort of crucial experiment—a testing ground on which the relative merits of Idealism and Platonic Atomism could be definitively judged. The Idealists had claimed that any non-metaphysical knowledge must be subject to incoherence and contradiction, if taken absolutely and without limitation; Russell thought he had a clear and decisive refutation of this claim in the case of mathematics.[12] In this case at least, he held, it could be shown that the idealist position rested

---

[11] Moore and Russell thus hold that the notion of absolute or unconditioned truth makes sense. In this they agree with the Idealists and disagree with Kant (see n. 1, above). Where they disagree with the Idealists is in holding, at least after 1900, that this is the only notion of truth—that 'relative truths' are tantamount to falsehoods.

[12] The Idealists did not, of course, see the matter this way. McTaggart explicitly replies to Russell in s. 48 of *A Commentary on Hegel's Logic* (Cambridge: CUP, 1910). It is also worth noting that Russell himself, in his idealist phase, had been far more concerned with the status of geometry than were other post-Kantian Idealists.

simply on ignorance—both of mathematics itself and of the new logic which turned out to be continuous with it.

Platonic Atomism is thus, from 1900 on, interwoven with this new logic.[13] On the one hand, Russell holds that the new logic shows that mathematics, and geometry in particular, is not inconsistent. He takes this to undermine Idealism; it refutes a crucial claim of the Idealists and also removes a powerful argument for Idealism, an argument which could appeal even to those not predisposed in favour of Idealism. By undermining Idealism, the new logic indirectly strengthens the claims of Platonic Atomism. On the other hand, the new logic itself seems to make certain metaphysical demands. If we are to take that logic as ultimate truth, then we seem to have to accept the absoluteness of truth and falsehood, the reality of abstract objects, and at least a certain degree of atomism. The new logic, in short, seems to be incompatible with Idealism (and also with Empiricism) but perfectly compatible with Platonic Atomism. Because of the complexity of the relationship between the new philosophy and the new logic, Russell's appeal to logic and mathematics against Idealism is circular. Unless one already accepts Platonic Atomism—or at least rejects Idealism—the new logic will not appear to have the status which it must have if it is really to show that mathematics is fully coherent and consistent. But to call this appeal circular is by no means to say that it is without force. On the contrary, it is to suggest that if one item is accepted then everything else within the circle will fall into place, and in turn provide reasons for the initial acceptance. Russell's circle, moreover, has a number of points at which one might plausibly enter. The new view allows mathematics to be perfectly true, not subservient to some greater but vaguer truth. The reduction of mathematics to logic gives undeniable technical insight into the nature of mathematics, and clarifies concepts which had puzzled mathematicians themselves. The power of the new logic, and the apparent success of the reduction of mathematics to logic, makes it natural to think that technical work can have immediate metaphysical results—or that the division between the technical and the metaphysical is misconceived. It is this intimate link with the new logic that is, I think, most responsible for the appeal of Platonic Atomism and for its influence on later analytic philosophy.

[13] In *Principles* Russell combines the metaphysics of Platonic Atomism with the new logic, as we shall see in Ch. 5. The connection of these things, however, is not inevitable. Both Moore and Russell advocated the metaphysics, at first, independent of the logic; and Platonic Atomism is not the inevitable philosophical consequence of modern logic.

4

The Underlying Metaphysics

The concern of this chapter is the philosophy which Moore and Russell first developed in the course of their rejection of Idealism. In this development it was Moore who took the lead. In the Preface to *The Principles of Mathematics*, Russell says: 'on the fundamental questions of philosophy, my position, in all its chief features, is derived from Mr. G. E. Moore'. The greater part of this chapter is, therefore, devoted to an examination of the work of Moore from the period 1898–1903, especially the earlier part of this period. As in the rest of the book, I have confined my discussion to metaphysics, and excluded other issues except in so far as they are directly relevant to it. In the case of Moore this exclusion is important, for it means that I largely ignore his views on Ethics, which was perhaps his chief concern during this period. Moore's metaphysical views between 1898 and 1903 have a considerable degree of unity and inner coherence. Some changes occur, but I shall not emphasize these, for my aim is to convey the basic structure of Moore's metaphysics and its relation to Idealism. This discussion of Moore occupies Section 1 of this chapter; in the second, much briefer, section, I discuss Russell's *Philosophy of Leibniz* (1900).

1. Moore

G. E. Moore went up to Trinity College, Cambridge, in 1892, two years after Russell. He spent four years as an undergraduate, two working for the Classics Tripos (1892–4), and two working on Philosophy (1894–6). Early in 1894 he became a member of the society known as the Apostles (or simply as 'The Society'). The discussions of this society may have played as important a role in Moore's philosophical development as did his formal course of instruction.[1] Like Russell,

---

[1] McTaggart and Russell were among the more active members of the Apostles at this period, and the discussions of the society seem to have been largely philosophical. See P. Levy, *Moore: G. E. Moore and the Cambridge Apostles* (London: Weidenfeld & Nicholson, 1979), esp. Chs. 5 and 6.

Moore knew McTaggart, who was at once a fellow-member of the Apostles, a friend, and a teacher. Not surprisingly, Moore said that he was more influenced by McTaggart than by any of his other teachers at Cambridge.[2] After graduating in 1896, Moore began work on a dissertation to submit for a Prize Fellowship at Trinity. His first attempt, in 1897, was unsuccessful, so he submitted a second version, which was successful, in 1898.[3] Some pages are missing from the manuscript of the 1898 dissertation, and internal evidence strongly suggests that these pages were sent to the printer as part of the article 'The Nature of Judgment'.[4] Both versions of the dissertation are called 'The Metaphysical Basis of Ethics', and are far more concerned with metaphysics than with ethics. Both of them discuss Kant, especially the *Critique of Pure Reason* and the *Critique of Practical Reason*. The second incorporates almost all the material of the first, but adds to it considerably. This new material is of striking interest. Although it still contains many idealist doctrines, it takes what I shall argue is the crucial step in the rejection of Idealism. I turn to this step immediately.

In the context of discussing the meaning of 'Reason' in Kant's work, Moore considers what he takes to be Kant's argument for the necessary applicability of the Kantian categories. As we shall see later, Moore does not deny that some, at least, of the categories are 'involved in every judgment'—specifically he mentions the categories of substance and attribute, and of cause and effect, as being so involved (p. 38).[5] What he does deny is that Kant shows that the necessary applicability of the categories is due to their being in some way subjective, the imposition of the mind. Moore claims, indeed, that Kant does not even attempt to show this, but rather assumes the subjectivity of the categories from the start, and argues that their objective necessity can be explained in terms of their subjective origins. Moore concludes that Kant has not proved his claim. But Moore's case, so far, is not a strong one. He has not shown that the Kantian claim cannot be proved, nor has he produced an explanation of the necessary applicability of the

[2] *The Philosophy of G. E. Moore*, ed. P. Schilpp (Evanston and Chicago: Northwestern University, 1942), p. 18.

[3] Both versions of the dissertation are part of the Moore Archives in Cambridge University Library, but are on loan to Trinity College, Cambridge. I should like to thank the Librarian at Trinity for allowing me access to them.

[4] *Mind* (1898), 176–93.

[5] The pagination of the 1898 dissertation is problematic. Some pages have several numbers crossed out. Some groups of pages which are clearly consecutive, without gaps or omissions, are not numbered sequentially. Several different numbering systems seem to have been used, and no one of them uniformly imposed. I have, therefore, numbered the surviving pages in strict order, ignoring places where pages seem to be missing. It is by these numbers, and by chapters, that I shall refer to passages.

categories which does not rely upon the idea that they are subjective. To strengthen his case, and to discover how far Kant's conclusions rest upon the assumption of the subjectivity of the categories, Moore turns to a more general consideration of the role of subjectivity in Kant's argument. A crucial Kantian premiss, Moore claims, is that 'the unity of apperception is involved in any judgment whatsoever' (i.e., very roughly, that every judgement presupposes the unity of the mind which judges) (p. 38). Moore accepts that knowledge implies consciousness and therefore, presumably, the unity of consciousness. He then raises a crucial question:

Are we here concerned at all with knowledge? Will it not be sufficient for our purpose, if we can find out what is true? . . . If truth is something independent of knowledge and therefore of consciousness, no theory that tries to explain the validity of necessary propositions by showing them to be involved in knowledge or consciousness can possibly attain its purpose. It may be a true theory, but it cannot explain that which it professes to explain. (p. 39)

If propositions are what they are independent of our minds and our acts of judgement, and if their truth and falsity is equally independent, then a Kantian argument based upon the conditions of the unity of consciousness cannot succeed. The most that such an argument could show would be that there are conditions under which we have access to propositions. But if the propositions and their truth are independent of us, these conditions are only psychological facts about us, and not constraints on what the world must be like. Nothing more than this can follow from such a Kantian argument—*if* propositions are completely independent of us. Moore refers us to Chapter II of the dissertation for an articulation and defence of the view that propositions are in this way independent (this material occurs in *NJ* and I discuss it below, pp. 132–9), but it is already clear that he is willing to assert the strongest possible form of this position. He says, for example: 'to say that philosophical propositions are true logically implies nothing whatsoever with regard to consciousness, not even that they can be known' (p. 40).

We can best appreciate the importance of this idea by seeing how Moore used it to attack the crucial Kantian notion of the necessary conditions or presuppositions of knowledge. If our knowledge is wholly independent of what is known, then the two sorts of things have different sorts of presuppositions, or have presuppositions in different senses of the word, one logical and the other psychological or (more generally) causal. Thus Moore finds both 'knowledge' and 'condition' to be ambiguous:

By 'knowledge' what is meant? If 'truth', then it is difficult to see that there can be any other condition for a true proposition than some other true proposition. If empirical cognition, then does not empirical psychology investigate the conditions for the possibility of this? A similar ambiguity is involved in the word 'condition'. In what sense a 'condition'? If an existent be meant, upon which the existence of something else depends, then condition is equivalent to 'cause', and both reason and knowledge must be conceived under the category of substance, as in empirical psychology. But if a logical condition be meant, then it must be some true proposition, from the truth of which the truth of another can be inferred. If any third kind of condition can be pointed out, then, no doubt, the whole of this criticism must fall to the ground. (p. 53)

Moore thus insists that the Kantian notion of a condition or presupposition of knowledge is ambiguous. On the one hand, there are the empirical, causal conditions of our processes of cognition, to be investigated by empirical psychology; on the other hand, there are the logical conditions of the truth of a given proposition. Kant's notion of Reason, or the transcendental mind, Moore claims, is the product of the same ambiguity, for Kant 'regards it partly as something which can act and be acted upon, partly as a logical presupposition of true propositions' (p. 54).

Idealism in all its forms depends, as we have seen, upon a transition, at some stage, from the necessary structure of thought, or the necessary conditions of knowledge, to necessary features of reality. This transition may, perhaps, be eased by taking 'thought' or 'knowledge' in non-psychological senses, but it cannot be avoided completely. By making the objects of knowledge completely independent of us, our thought, and our knowledge, Moore is denying this fundamental presupposition of any sort of Idealism. This explains the vehemence with which Bosanquet, perhaps the most distinguished follower of Bradley, reacted to Moore's dissertation. The passage is worth quoting at some length:

In sum, the intellectual motive of the Dissertation, as I read it, is to dissociate Truth from the nature of Knowledge, and Good from the nature of the Will, so as to free Metaphysics from all risk of confusion with Psychology. The theory of the proposition and the concept which harmonises with the dissociation of Truth from the nature of Knowledge is set out in ch. 2. I confess that I feel a difficulty in regarding it as serious. It is necessary no doubt to distinguish, in the process and products of cognition, between their nature as knowledge and their psychological genesis. But the theory here propounded seems to reduce the world of truth to an immutable framework of hypostatised 'propositions' or 'Concepts' in relations, which are indeed possible objects of thought, but are entities not dependent upon thought, nor partaking of any character which distinctively belongs to thought.... Here it seems to me clear that 'the child has been thrown away in emptying the bath.' To get rid of mere psychology, the essential idea of consciousness and cognition as an endeavour towards unity has been abandoned.[6]

We have now seen Moore make two closely connected claims: first, that propositions are objective entities, wholly independent of any mind; second, that any notion of condition must be either causal or logical, i.e. that no other sense is available. These two claims are directly connected with his views as to the nature and status of relations. First, relations are objective and mind-independent. That propositions are relational, and that propositions must therefore have the same status as relations, was clearly recognized by Moore's idealist adversaries (but see Section 2, pp. 154–5, below, for more discussion of this). Green held judgement and relations both to be mental, but to exist in the world-constituting Universal Mind, and thus to be none the less objective; Bradley held both to be ultimately unreal. Moore follows the Idealists in giving relations and propositions the same status. He thus holds relations to be, like propositions, both real and non-mental. Second, all relations are external (I shall mention an exception to this later). Moore's dichotomy between the logical and the causal is directly connected with his opposition to internal relations. If all relations are either logical or causal, and neither logical nor causal relations are internal, then of course all relations are external. Let us begin discussion of this with the claim that logical relations are not internal. An internal relation is one that is in some way essential to, or constitutive of, the identity of the objects related, so that without the relation neither would be that object which it is. A logical relation, on Moore's view, is not internal in this sense. Propositions are prior to, and independent of, the nexus of logical relations in which they figure. To deny this we should have to see propositions as partly constituted by their places in that nexus. To see logical relations as internal we should, therefore, have to deny a fundamental feature of Moore's view of propositions.[7]

The claim that causal relations are not internal is more complex, for here the discussion is always likely to alternate between this claim and the claim embodied in the fundamental dichotomy between the logical and the causal. An insistence upon the purely external nature of the causal relation invites the reply: if *that's* what you mean by causality, it

---

[6] This is from a report which Trinity College asked Bosaonquet to write on Moore's 1898 dissertation; the report is with the dissertation in Trinity College Library (see n. 3, above).

[7] This argument hardly succeeds in meeting the Idealists on neutral ground, for the Idealists are unlikely to accept the independence of propositions, one from another.

may be external, but many relations which we might say are causal are not causal in that sense. An insistence that such relations *are* causal in form invites the reply that causality is then not a purely external relation. The claim that causal relations are external must thus be defended at the same time as the exhaustive nature of the dichotomy between the logical and the causal. Moore does this in a powerful passage from *Principia Ethica*[8] in which he tackles head-on an example which is paradigmatic of the notion of an organic unity, and thus of internal relations. The example is that of the relation of one part of the living body to the body as a whole. Moore thus confronts his opponents on their strongest ground. Where they had seen internal relations and an organic unity, he sees similarity ('partial identity') and a purely external sort of causal dependence:

if an arm be cut off from the human body, we still call it an arm. Yet an arm, when it is a part of the body, undoubtedly differs from a dead arm: and hence we may easily be led to say 'The arm which is a part of the body would not be what it is, if it were not such a part'.... But, in fact, the dead arm never was a part of the body; it is only *partially* identical with the living arm. Those parts [i.e., properties] of it which are identical with parts of the living arm are exactly the same, whether they belong to the body or not.... On the other hand, those properties which *are* possessed by the living, and *not* by the dead, arm, do not exist in a changed form in the latter: they simply do not exist there *at all*. By a causal necessity their existence depends on their having that relation to the other parts of the body which we express by saying that they form part of it. Yet, most certainly, *if* they ever did not form part of the body, they *would* be exactly what they are when they do. (*PE*, pp. 34–5)

The implication of the last sentence is that if, in violation of causal necessity, a living arm could survive in isolation from the body, i.e. all its properties could continue to exist (not a metaphor for Moore), then it would be, in isolation from the body, exactly what it is when attached to the body. Causal dependence, Moore is saying, is not the sort of constitutive relation which the Idealists had sought; yet causal dependence is all that we need in order to give an account of what the Idealists would have called an organic unity.

The analysis just quoted is, it seems to me, by far the strongest argument that Moore has against internal relations—it enables him to claim that they are simply unnecessary to account for the facts. He also offers various arguments for the claim that internal relations are absurd or self-contradictory. One of these arguments is worth examining in part for the sake of its presuppositions, which have to do with the

---

[8] *PE*, pp. 34–5. Moore's 1898 dissertation also implies a sceptical attitude, at the least, towards internal relations—as we shall see below, pp. 125–7.

nature of the truth. Moore claims that if a part were internally related to a whole, then we could never consistently say so. What we want to say is that *the part itself* is related to the whole; but if it were internally related to the whole then we could not consistently speak of the part in isolation at all—not even to say that it is related to the whole:

When we think of the part *itself*, we mean just *that which* we assert, in this case, to *have* the predicate that it is part of the whole; and the mere assertion that *it* is a part of the whole involves that it should itself be distinct from that which we assert of it. Otherwise we contradict outselves since we assert that, not *it*, but something else—namely it together with that which we assert of it—has the predicate which we assert of it. (*PE*, p. 33)

The conclusion of Moore's argument seems to be one that the Idealists might accept—their disagreement with Moore coming over the issue whether this conclusion constitutes a *reductio ad absurdum*. In the case of Bradley this is obvious: he is willing to say that all judgement is ultimately contradictory, including the judgement (on which this conclusion is based) that any given object is internally related to every other. Other Idealists too would, I think, agree with Moore's conclusion, even if they objected to his stark phrasing of it. As we saw in discussing T. H. Green's holism, he would find judgement about a limited part of the world (i.e. almost any judgement at all) to be, for that reason, inadequate. The crucial difference, in this respect, between Moore and the Idealists is that the latter held that judgements which were inadequate, or even contradictory, might none the less capture a part of the truth and be useful and admissible for certain purposes (including, as it turns out, almost all human purposes). Moore's attitude, by contrast, is that a judgement is either correct or incorrect, and if it is incorrect must simply be given up. Moore's argument thus presupposes one of the central doctrines of Platonic Atomism: that truth and falsehood are absolute, not matters of degree.[9]

The absoluteness of truth and falsehood does not follow inevitably from the dichotomy between the logical and the causal, or from the rejection of internal relations. In the 1898 dissertation, indeed, Moore grudgingly accepts that there are degrees of truth. The passage is worth examining with some care:

[9] It is important to note that this doctrine about truth and falsehood is closely connected with a less explicit view about the bearers of truth and falsehood, propositions. If each proposition is either absolutely true or absolutely false then each proposition must say something quite definite and explicit, something which quite clearly either is so or is not. For discussion related to this ideal of explicitness, see W. D. Hart, 'Clarity', in David Bell and Neil Cooper (eds.), *Meaning, Thought and Knowledge* (Oxford: Blackwell, forthcoming).

Can any meaning be given to ... comparative truth? It seems only possible to give it the meaning of consistency in falsehood; but that meaning is perhaps enough ... granted that all our propositions with regard to time and space are absolutely false, yet these may involve a greater or less number of false pre-suppositions, according as they are or are not logically consistent with one another in other details than their implication of the above-mentioned contra-diction. (Ch. II, pp. 66–7)

One striking feature of this is its statement that all propositions about space and time are absolutely false. At the time of the 1898 dissertation Moore follows Kant in holding that propositions about space and time cannot be absolutely and unconditionally true. Kant says that they are empirically true; later Idealists spoke of them as relatively true. Moore, who is more given to sharp edges and clear-cut dichotomies, says they are absolutely false. The second striking feature is that one is left with the impression that the most important thing about a comparative truth is that it is, in fact, false. Moore seems unable to avoid thinking of truth and falsehood as absolute, even in this passage, where he is ostensibly accepting the idea of degrees of truth. The implication of this is that by natural inclination Moore thinks of truth as absolute, and that the unconvincing air of the above passage is the result of this inclination being subordinated to a contrary philosophical theory. Why should anyone thus hold the doctrine of degrees of truth, even against his natural inclination? Drawing on what we have already seen, I think we can find two possible reasons. One is the idea that space and time are contradictory, so that propositions involving space and time, or spatio-temporal objects, cannot be absolutely true. This idea almost forces the doctrine that there are degrees of truth upon us. It is absurdly paradoxical to say that the proposition that the Thames flows through London is absolutely false, as false as its negation or as the claim that two and two is five. Even if the proposition cannot be absolutely true, because it involves spatio-temporal objects, yet it must be partially true, and more true than its negation. The second doctrine which might force one to hold that there are degrees of truth is the doctrine of the internality of relations. We said above that Moore's argument against internal relations (at *PE*, p. 33) is successful if we grant the absoluteness of truth; the corollary of this is that those who maintain the internality of relations must deny the absoluteness of truth. Thus in denying the internality of relations Moore has removed one of the two obstacles with might prevent him from acknowledging the absoluteness of truth. If this way of thinking about the matter is justified, one would expect to find that the removal of the other obstacle would be simultaneous, in Moore's thought, with his accept-ance of the absoluteness of truth. And this is indeed the case; both steps are taken in articles that Moore wrote for Baldwin's *Dictionary of Philosophy*,[10] very soon after the 1898 dissertation. (It is worth pointing out that Moore offers no argument against Kant's claim that space and time are contradictory; Russell, in *The Principles of Mathematics*, places great emphasis on the refutation of this Kantian claim—see Chapter 5, below.)

I turn now to Moore's view of knowledge. This issue is closely connected with that of the internality or externality of relations. If the relation between knowledge and its object is an internal one, then the object of knowledge is partially constituted by the knower and his consciousness; if the relation is external then the two are independent. I focus, to begin with, on a discussion of these issues in the 1898 dissertation.

Moore's discussion begins with a criticism of Kant that was, as he acknowledges, common in the work of Kant's idealist successors. In Kant's first *Critique* reason is both the criticizer and the criticized, and this, Moore complains, is circular (see Chapter 3, Section 2, pp. 91–2, above, for a discussion of the use of this criticism in the hands of the Idealists). If we are to criticize reason, he claims, we need to do so from a standpoint which is not itself subject to criticism of the same sort; but no such standpoint can be found (p. 40). Moore considers a response to this difficulty made by Edward Caird, in the Introduction to his *The Critical Philosophy of Immanuel Kant*.[11] Caird's reply to the argument is, very briefly, that reason is not to be criticized by a standard external to itself. The criterion by which reason is to be judged is an immanent or internal criterion; the idea of an external or transcendent standpoint is simply empty. By these means Caird shifts the ground of the discussion from the circularity of reason's criticism of itself to the claim that we do not, in knowledge, attempt to gain access to objects which are wholly independent of us. At one point, Caird phrases the claim like this: 'We can never know anything except as it is related to the conscious self within us; whatever we deal with, we are still dealing with our own consciousness of things' (p. 13). In characteristic fashion,[12] Moore seizes on this sentence. He accepts the first half but denies the second. He argues, indeed, that the first half contradicts the second:

[10] *Dictionary*. Moore's denial that space and time are contradictory is implicit at ii. 444; he explicitly denies the relativity of truth and falsehood at ii. 717.

[11] 2 vols. (Glasgow: James Macelhouse & Sons, 1889; 2nd edn. 1909). Moore refers, of course, to the 1st edn.; I have consulted the 2nd.

[12] Moore's later work is not, of course, my concern; but it seems to me that the cast of mind which he displays in this discussion is characteristic of that work as well as of the 1898 dissertation—completed when Moore was 25. See e.g. Moore's 'Proof of an External World', *Proceedings of the British Academy*, 25 (1939); repr. in G. E. Moore, *Philosophical Papers* (London: Allen & Unwin, 1959), for the extreme literalness of his late work.

that which is merely *related* to our self, or our consciousness, cannot *be* that consciousness. The relatedness which the first half of the sentence asserts implies the distinctness which the second half of the sentence denies. Moore imagines Caird's reply to be that consciousness is related to the objects of knowledge, but that we must not suppose this relation to be an external one. Moore finds this reply incomprehensible. Our knowledge of things, he insists, 'certainly does not seem to me to justify an implication that things are the same as our consciousness of things' (p. 41).

The movement of Moore's thought here is characteristic of his criticism of Kant in the 1898 dissertation. He begins with a criticism which was, and which he acknowledges to have been, part of the standard idealist response to Kant. In articulating this objection, however, he makes a realist claim that would be inimical to any sort of post-Kantian Idealism: that there is an absolute independence of the objects of knowledge from the knowing mind. It is, I think, clear from the context that Moore's claim is to be interpreted as strongly as this, for only then will it play the role that he attributes to it; but it is revealing that his phrasing is weaker than this. What he actually says is that there is no reason to think that 'things are the same as our consciousness of things'. It is precisely in the (supposed) middle ground between the strong claim and the weak claim that Idealism takes root. Absolute Idealists would admit—indeed, insist—that in some sense things are not the same as our consciousness of them—that there is an important distinction to be drawn here—but would go on to say that the distinction is not absolute, that it does not imply the complete independence of things from our minds. But Moore is implicitly denying the existence of this middle ground, insisting that the Idealist must be understood as simply identifying things with our consciousness of them. Moore moves, that is to say, from the weak claim that things are not simply the same as our consciousness of them to the strong claim that things are totally independent of us: he sees no gap between the two claims. Here we have a clear example of what one might call the absoluteness of Moore's thought. He seems to see only two possibilities: either things and our minds are simply the same, or else they are completely distinct and independent of one another. Idealism, as we have sufficiently seen, depends upon the subtlety—or the equivocation—which enables one to deny that these alternatives are exhaustive.

Moore insists, then, upon an absolute distinction between our knowledge, on the one hand, and the *object* of our knowledge, on the other. He takes the failure to make this distinction to be a pervasive philosophical error:

It is commonly supposed . . . to be obvious to direct inspection that what I know is always in my mind; whereas the only thing which is really thus obvious is that my consciousness of a thing is so. The history of philosophy exhibits a uniform inability to distinguish between that of which I am conscious and my consciousness of it.[13]

Moore's view here is a generalization of his insistence that propositions are distinct from our acts of judging (it might be more accurate to say that no generalization is involved, that we simply have the same position stated in two different ways; see p. 137, below). A part of this position is the fact that the cognitive relation is an external one. The objects of our knowledge—concepts and those complexes of concepts which are propositions—are not in any way altered or affected by the fact that they are known (see *NJ*, p. 179). One of Moore's reasons for holding this seems to have been that if the act of knowing changed the objects of our knowledge then they would not, in fact, be the objects of our knowledge at all. What we would know would be not the unchanged object (the object in itself, we might say) but rather the object as changed by its relation to the knower. In that case the actual object of our knowledge would be in part constituted by the act of knowing, and so would not be what we set out to know. That these considerations play a role in Moore's thought is apparent from a passage in which he is discussing the view that we know things by means of their effects on our minds:

inconsistencies follow from [the] fundamental false assumption that to be known is to produce an effect upon the mind, i.e., that the relation of knower to known is a causal relation; for it immediately follows from this that we never do know what we know, but always something else, which is to be regarded as the result of the interaction with our minds of the object we alter by knowing it. (*Dictionary*, ii. 451)

(This argument is closely analogous to the more general argument about internal relations, which we discussed above, pp. 122–3.)

The objects of knowledge are not known via their effects on our minds: knowledge is immediate. In knowledge we are, then, in direct contact with objects which are outside our minds and which are not affected by our minds. In view of this, it is unsurprising that Moore constantly uses perceptual (and especially visual) language, even in talking about our knowledge of very abstract matters. All knowledge, for him, ultimately has the characteristics of directness and immediacy which are, arguably, possessed by the perception of simple sensory

---

[13] 'Mr. McTaggart's *Studies in Hegelian Cosmology*', *Proceedings of the Aristotelian Society* (1901–2), 187.

qualities; as I have already pointed out, however, the Idealists specifically deny that any knowledge is of this kind (see Introduction to Part II). The pervasiveness of perceptual language in Moore's talk of abstract knowledge is striking, and the language seems quite literally meant. A complex concept may be known or understood (the difference seems hard to make out within Platonic Atomism) in virtue of knowledge or understanding of its components. A simple concept, however, must simply be perceived (either sensuously or non-sensuously); thus Moore says: 'What kind of relation makes a proposition true, what false, cannot be further defined, but must be immediately recognised' (*NJ*, p. 180). Again, Moore claims that the relation of logical priority 'needs . . . only to be seen in any instance, in order to be recognised',[14] and again, in discussing metaphysical ethics, he speaks of our perceiving that two questions are distinct, and says: 'In face of this direct perception that the two questions are distinct, no proof that they *must* be identical can have the slightest value' (*PE*, p. 126). It is a curious, but not vicious, example of circularity that the cognitive relation is itself, on Moore's account, a simple concept; it is, he says, an 'ultimate datum'. Like other simple concepts, it can only be known directly, by being perceived. The only way in which we can come to understand or know the cognitive relation is to stand in that very relation to it.

We have seen that Moore attacks the Kantian, and more generally idealist, notion of the presuppositions of knowledge (p. 120, above). The Moorean view of knowledge which I articulated in the previous paragraph complements this attack: it provides a picture of presuppositionless knowledge, an alternative to the Kantian view that Moore attacks. Although I shall have little to say about Moore's view of knowledge, its importance as part of his anti-idealism should not be underestimated. It is crucial, in this regard, that Moore includes propositions among the entities of which we can have immediate, direct, and presuppositionless knowledge. As we saw in discussing T. H. Green's version of Kantianism, one route to Idealism is via the claim that all genuine knowledge is judgemental or propositional in character; it can then be argued that, whatever may appear to be the case for simple sensory knowledge, judgement has a structure, a complexity, which imposes presuppositions on what can be judged. These presuppositions then appear as the presuppositions of all possible knowledge and so (given another leap) of knowable reality or (given the denial of the unknowable thing-in-itself) of Reality itself. Because Moore's view of knowledge applies to propositions, he can block this line of thought

----

[14] 'Necessity', *Mind* (1900), 301.

at its second step. He can agree that all knowledge is judgemental or propositional in character, but deny that this gives it any particular structure or presuppositions. Propositions are simply objective entities, independent of us; in judgement the mind stands in a simple and presuppositionless relation to one of these entities. Moore's view of knowledge has weight against the Idealists only because propositions (objects of thought) are on his account among the objects of knowledge. That this is so can be seen from the well-known article 'The Refutation of Idealism'.[15] The bulk of that article consists of an attack on Berkeley's doctrine that *esse* is *percipi* (to be is to be perceived) and, in particular, on the view that there is no distinction between a sensation and the object of the sensation. Given this description, it is clear why Moore should think that he has an argument against Berkeleian Idealism, but puzzling why he should think, as he clearly does, that the argument applies equally to Kantian and post-Kantian Idealism. The answer to the puzzle is that Moore holds that the objects of thought can be treated in exactly the same way as the objects of sensation, so that arguments which show the latter to be independent of our minds will show the former to be so too. I shall quote the relevant passage at some length:

I consider it to be the main service of the philosophic school, to which the modern Idealists belong, that they have insisted on distinguishing 'sensation' and 'thought' and on emphasising the importance of the latter. Against Sensationalism and Empiricism they have maintained the true view. But *the distinction between sensation and thought need not detain us here.* For, in whatever respects they may differ, they have at least this in common, that they are both forms of consciousness or . . . they are both ways of experiencing. Accordingly, whatever *esse* is *percipi* may mean, it does *at least* assert that whatever is, is *experienced*. And since what I wish to maintain is, that even this is untrue, the question whether it be experienced by way of sensation or thought or both is for my purpose quite irrelevant.[16]

Moore's view of knowledge, then, applies to the objects of thought just as much as to the objects of sensation; and this is essential if it is to have any force at all against post-Kantian Idealism. (If we include the constituents of propositions, as well as propositions themselves, among the objects of thought, then we may say that for Moore *all* objects are objects of thought. This indicates the sense in which for Moore, as for the Idealists (but not Bradley), the world is transparent to the intellect, see pp. 136–7, below.) The difficulties of this reified view of the objects of thought are not at all apparent in Moore's philosophy

---

[15] *Mind* (1903), 433–53; repr. in *Philosophical Studies* (London: 1922), pp. 1–30.

[16] Moore, op. cit. n. 15 above, p. 7; first emphasis mine.

of the period I am considering; they will emerge when we see the difficulty that Russell has in accounting for the nature of the proposition (see Chapter 5, pp. 175–9, below).

The passage quoted in the previous paragraph suggests that Moore agrees with the Idealists, and disagrees with the Empiricists, on some crucial issues. In particular he holds that Kant's claims about the presuppositions of knowledge are correct if interpreted as claims about the *logical* presuppositions of empirical fact; and that this constitutes a refutation of Empiricism. Moore holds these views throughout the period which is our concern. Perhaps their clearest expression is this passage from *NJ*:

> The Transcendental Deduction contains a perfectly valid answer to Hume's scepticism, and to Empiricism in general. Philosophers of this school generally tend to deny the validity of any propositions except those about existents. Kant may be said to have pointed out that in any of these propositions, which the Empiricists considered to be the ultimate, if not the only, data of knowledge, there was involved by the very same logic on which they relied to support their views, not only the uniform and necessary succession of time, and the geometrical properties of space, but also the principles of substance and causality. (p. 190)

Moore's rejection of Empiricism is unequivocal. What he means by Empiricism, however, and on what basis he rejects it, are less clear. I shall briefly return to these issues.

To this point we have seen that Moore holds a number of related anti-idealist positions: the objectivity and independence of propositions, the objectivity and externality of relations, the absoluteness of truth and falsehood, and the absolute distinctness of knowledge from what is known. What we have not yet seen is how these doctrines, and others, are combined into a metaphysical account of the world. It is to this that I now turn.

Moore's fundamental, and all-inclusive, ontological category is being. All things are, or have being. Some things, those which are temporal, also exist.[17] This is, as we shall see, not a fundamental distinction between different kinds of things; some of the things which

---

[17] One might suppose that existence, as distinct from being, was to be understood in terms of temporality. Moore gives no other way of understanding it, but he insists that they are distinct ideas even if they happen to coincide (1898 dissertation, Ch. II, pp. 69–70). This explains a curious passage in *PE* (pp. 110–12) where Moore criticizes the advocates of what he calls 'metaphysical ethics' (the Stoics, Spinoza, Leibniz, Kant, Hegel, Green, Bradley) for holding that some things exist without being temporal. Moore writes as if he were accusing his opponents of a factual error, but it seems as if they might reply that they use the word 'existence' where Moore uses the word 'being'. Perhaps Moore would have a response to this, but it is unclear what it would be.

do not exist are of the same kind as those things which do exist—indeed we might say that Moore recognizes no fundamental differences in kind among entities. (This position will be examined in detail below, pp. 138–9.) Moore's distinction between being and existence evolves out of the version of the Kantian distinction between noumena and phenomena which he advocates in the 1898 dissertation. I do not propose to discuss the steps by which this evolution took place,[18] but it is worth seeing that the fundamental move away from Kant in the 1898 dissertation implies that Moore's version of this distinction is bound to be quite unKantian in character. Crucial to Kant's distinction is the idea that the phenomenal is the world as it appears to us, while the noumenal is the world as it is in itself, and is necessarily inaccessible to our knowledge. This distinction relies upon the idea that knowledge has presuppositions which are partially constitutive of what is known. This idea makes the gap between phenomenal Appearance and unknowable noumenal Reality absolute and unbridgeable. The phenomenal, the knowable, is that which is subject to the presuppositions of knowledge, i.e. that which is partially constituted by the action of our minds. Noumenal Reality is that which is independent of the presuppositions of knowledge. As we have already seen, Moore rejects the Kantian view that knowledge has presuppositions which are constitutive of what is known (or, in fact, that it has presuppositions at all—p. 120, above). It is thus open to Moore to hold a view which for Kant would be absurd: that we do have knowledge of the noumenal, and that it can 'appear to us' in just the same sense as the phenomenal (see 1898 dissertation, pp. 68–9). Even in the 1898 dissertation, then, Moore's distinction has a very different character from Kant's, and after that time he dropped the Kantian terminology; the distinction became one between that which *is* and that which also exists. The claim that not everything which is exists is, as we shall see, crucial to Platonic Atomism.

We are now in a position to discuss Moore's anti-empiricism. Moore rejects the definition of Empiricism as a doctrine about the *origin* of our knowledge. Employing a distinction we have already examined, he finds this definition to be ambiguous as between the causal origin of our mental states, on the one hand, and the logical premises of the truths we know, on the other hand.[19] In neither case, he claims, do we obtain a definition which separates those philosophers who are usually

[18] The crucial step is Moore's rejection of the Kantian claim that space and time are contradictory. This allows for the possibility that there may be absolute truths about those things which exist in time, and this in turn alters the fundamental nature of the distinction.

[19] 'Nativism and Empiricism', one of Moore's contributions to the *Dictionary* and E. & E.

thought of as Empiricists from those who are not. Moore's understanding of Empiricism is, characteristically, not in terms of our knowledge and its origin, but rather in terms of the *objects* of our knowledge. He takes Empiricism to be the view 'that all known truths are truths about what exists at one or more moments of time' (*E. & E.*, p. 93; cf. *Dictionary*, ii. 130). As thus understood, Empiricism is directly contradicted by Moore's view that there are non-existent atemporal entities.

Among the atemporal non-existent entities which Moore explicitly recognizes are numbers, logical relations, and, paradigmatically, propositions. Propositions are a particularly important case, for their status as objective and non-mental entities depends on the idea that they do not exist in time. The view of propositions as objective and non-mental is, in turn, fundamental to Moore's rejection of Idealism, as I have already emphasized. One crux of Moore's early work is thus his argument, in *NJ*, that propositions and their constituents (which he calls 'concepts') cannot be explained in terms of anything that exists in time, but must be acknowledged as fundamental and irreducible. Moore's explicit target in this argument is Bradley's view of meaning, and of the 'logical idea' used in judgement; but he claims that Bradley's views here are very similar to Kant's, and clearly thinks that the argument applies to both. We saw that Bradley attacks the view which identifies logical ideas with mental states (Chapter 2, Section 2, above, pp. 59–61). Moore applauds this anti-psychologism, but complains that it does not go far enough. Although Bradley does not identify logical ideas with mental states he does, Moore claims, take them to be parts of, or abstractions from, such states. In support of this charge Moore quotes from *Principles of Logic*: 'A meaning consists of part of the content (original or acquired) cut off, fixed by the mind, and considered apart from the existence of the sign' (p. 4; cf. Chapter 2, Section 2, above, p. 60). It is against this element of abstractionism in Bradley's view that Moore argues, in two slightly different ways. First, Moore suggests that to 'cut off' a part of the content of a (psychological) idea we must first know what that content is. But this knowledge requires that we have already made a judgement about the content of our psychological idea or mental state. The formation of a constituent of judgement would thus require an actual prior judgement; but this prior judgement must contain constituents which would in turn require actual prior judgements for their formation, and so on. The theory, as Moore says, 'would therefore seem to demand the completion of an infinite number of psychological judgments before any judgment can be made at all' (*NJ*, p. 178). Moore's argument here presupposes that the abstraction by which a logical idea is formed is a conscious process, which takes place in accordance with a judgement. But there is no reason why a proponent of abstractionism should admit this point, as Bradley indeed pointed out in a letter to Moore.[20]

Moore's second argument begins by claiming that Bradley must allow it as possible that I should have two ideas which have part of their content in common. According to Bradley, Moore says, we have to understand this situation and the notion of 'having part of their content in common' by reference to a third idea—each of the two original ideas has part of their content in common with the third idea. (The third idea here is presumably the (psychological) idea from which the relevant logical idea was formed. To say that two ideas of mine have something in common because both are red, I must use the logical idea of redness, which was in turn formed from part of the content of the third idea.) Put like this, however, it is clear that nothing is gained by invoking a third idea, for the basic notion of two ideas having part of their content in common remains unexplained. We can, Moore says, hardly mean that one and the same existing psychological entity is part of two distinct psychological ideas. But if that is not what is meant, then the whole story is without explanatory force, and no account has yet been given of what it is for two ideas to have part of their content in common. In this second argument Moore seems to assume, in a rather plausible version, the essential point at stake between him and the Idealists—whether there are facts which are independent of the constitutive activity of the mind. What an explanation of the logical idea (or concept) has to explain in this case, Moore takes it, is what it is for two ideas to have part of their content in common, where this fact is objective and independent of our constitutive activity. Given this criterion, it is, as he says, useless to invoke a third idea. If we drop this Moorean criterion, however, the matter looks different. It is then open to us to claim that the fact that two ideas have part of their content in common is constituted by the fact that we *take* each to have a part of its content in common with a third idea— where we do not suppose that there is any fact of this latter issue which is independent of our taking it to be so. This move will be more plausible if we can claim that this constitutive activity of our minds (our 'taking it to be so') occurs on a transcendental rather than an empirical level—and here we are clearly back to the fundamental disagreement between Moore and the Idealists.[21]

---

[20] Bradley to Moore, 10 Oct. 1899, unpublished letter now in the Moore Archives in the University Library, Cambridge.

[21] A full treatment of this second Moorean argument would require more space than I have given it, especially in view of the fact that Moore's argument is very similar to that which Bradley uses against the Empiricists' account of abstractionism in *PL*, Pt. II, Ch. I. I shall make two brief comments on this. First, Bradley can (although many other

Moore compares his arguments with the 'third man' argument originally used against the Platonic Forms. He concludes from the arguments that the nature of concepts cannot be explained in other terms;
concepts must be accepted as basic. The difficulties which he found in
Bradley's view (and Kant's), he says, 'inevitably proceed from trying to
explain the concept in terms of some existent fact, whether mental or
of any other nature. All such explanations do in fact presuppose the
nature of the concept, as a *genus per se*, irreducible to anything else'
(*NJ*, pp. 178–9). We shall discuss Moore's views about concepts at
some length, but some preliminary points are worth making here.
Concepts, to begin with, may be simple or complex. A complex concept is made up of simple concepts, and is to be understood by
analysing it into its simple constituents. Simple concepts are not susceptible of analysis (see below, pp. 143–6, for some more discussion of
analysis as a philosophical method). Concepts stand in various relations to one another, and these relations are external (see pp. 121–3,
above). Both concepts themselves and the relations in which they
stand are, as Moore says quite explicitly, immutable (*NJ*, p. 180).
Propositions, finally, are 'complex concepts[s]' (loc. cit.); a proposition
'is constituted by any number of concepts, together with a specific
relation between them' (loc. cit.). I shall enlarge upon each of these
points below, but first I shall consider a doctrine which plays a fundamental role in Platonic Atomism and will be a crucial part of the
context of our later discussions.

The doctrine is that the constituents of propositions, 'concepts', as
Moore calls them in *NJ*, make up everything that is. 'The world', as
Moore puts it, is 'formed of concepts' (*NJ*, p. 182); in particular, 'All
that exists' is 'composed of concepts' (*NJ*, p. 181). At first sight, at
least, this is paradoxical: the constituents of propositions make up the
world; conversely, objects in the world are themselves among the
constituents of propositions (in particular, an object will be a constituent of those propositions which are about that object). Similarly, a
true proposition is itself a piece of reality; it does not correspond to a
fact, it *is* (the Moorean equivalent of) a fact. In Bradleyan terms, Moore
denies the distinction between the real and the ideal. We saw above
that Bradley argues against the possibility of designation (Chapter 2,
pp. 62–4, above). He argues, that is to say, that our logical ideas, the
constituents of our judgements, can never succeed in designating reality; this is one of the grounds on which he holds that all judgement is

Idealists cannot) accept the view that no ultimately coherent account of judgement is
possible. Indeed this is, as we have seen, central to his philosophy. Secondly, Idealists in
general can appeal to the fact that the processes which they describe occur on the
transcendental, or world-constituting, level, whereas the Empiricists took themselves to
be describing facts of empirical psychology.

unsatisfactory. Moore's response is *not* that designation is possible, that the gap between the real and the ideal can be bridged. It is, rather, that designation is unnecessary because there is no gap between the real and the ideal. Concepts, the analogue of Bradley's logical ideas, are the reality about which we judge. In judging we are in direct and unmediated contact with a proposition; the constituents of this proposition are the objects that our judgement is about. There are thus no intermediate entities—meanings, senses, or (logical) ideas—between our thought and its subject-matter.

This view, as Moore interprets it, has implications for the notion of truth; to bring these out I shall contrast it with a more familiar philosophical view, the correspondence theory of truth. Consider the (true) thought that my coffee-cup is red, and the (false) thought that my coffee-cup is green. According to the correspondence theory, the truth of the first thought consists in there being a corresponding fact, that my coffee-cup is red, while the falsity of the second thought consists in there being no such fact. If we wish to say, further, that the corresponding fact is the object of the first thought then we face the difficulty that the second thought appears to be left without an object; some further subtlety, at least, is called for. In any case, the notion of fact is here the crucial one. Contrast Moore's view. Here each thought has as its object a nexus of related concepts: the concept of my coffee-cup (taking this as simple), a colour-concept, the concept of existence, and the concepts of a number of moments of time. Here the concepts, remember, are not distinct from the things themselves: my coffee-cup is in a certain nexus with the colour green (etc.), just as it is in a certain nexus with the colour red (etc.). Each nexus (which is a proposition) is equally real. The distinction between them is simply that one is true and the other is false. Here there are no facts, independent of the propositions, to which we can appeal to explain the notions of truth and falsehood. The notion of a fact, if we continue to use it at all, is thus simply that of a true proposition. Hence the correspondence theory of truth is more or less obviously mistaken (*Dictionary*, ii. 717–18; Moore is able to be very cavalier at this point because the Idealists too rejected the correspondence theory). Truth is thus a simple concept, which 'cannot be further defined, but must be immediately recognised' (*NJ*, p. 180). This simple concept is, moreover, fundamental in Moore's ontology. The notion of reality, which one might expect to be ontologically basic, must itself be understood in terms of propositions and truth:

So far, indeed, from truth being defined by reference to reality, reality can only be defined by reference to truth: for truth denotes exactly that property of the complex formed by two entities and their relation, in virtue of which, if the entity predicated be existence, we call the complex real—the property, namely, expressed by saying that the relation in question does truly or really hold between the entities. (*Dictionary*, ii. 717)

Moore offers very little argument for the doctrine which I have articulated over the last two paragraphs. He seems to think, indeed, that the doctrine will be more or less obvious, once we have a correct understanding of the objectivity of the proposition. It is, he claims, only the identification of a proposition with a collection of words, or with a mental entity, that prevents us from recognizing the truth of his doctrine:

Once it is definitely recognised that the proposition is to denote not a belief or form of words but an *object* of belief, it seems plain that a truth differs in no respect from the reality to which it was supposed [by advocates of the correspondence theory of truth] merely to correspond: e.g., the truth that I exist differs in no respect from my existence. (*Dictionary*, ii. 717)

Because Moore offers so little argument for the doctrine, it is hard to see why he holds it. My discussion of this issue is, therefore, somewhat speculative. I begin with some remarks from *NJ*. However we may think of the 'matter' (i.e. content) of an idea, Moore says, 'its nature, if it is to enter into a true proposition, must . . . be the nature of a concept' (p. 181). Concepts, he says, 'are the only objects of knowledge. They cannot be regarded fundamentally as abstractions either from things or from ideas; since both alike can, if anything is to be true of them, be composed of nothing but concepts. A thing becomes intelligible first when it is analyzed into its constituent concepts' (p. 182). It is with propositions and their constituents that the mind is immediately and directly in contact; they are the primary objects of knowledge and of understanding. If we think of propositions and concepts as merely a medium, a means by which we come to have knowledge of facts and of objects distinct from them, then the relation of the propositions to the facts is problematic; Bradley, as we saw, thought the problem insoluble. On Moore's view there is no room for a problem here. The world is made up of concepts, with which the mind is in direct contact, and is thus transparent to the intellect.

We can put this in a different context by seeing how it is possible to understand Moore's doctrine as the result of combining certain idealist views with the claim that propositions are objective and non-mental. The attempt to do this is certainly encouraged by the fact that it is only this last issue which Moore seems to think he has to insist upon—as if his doctrine is obvious once this point is granted. The idealist views which I have in mind here are, first, that knowledge and experience are judgemental in character and, second, that the objects of our ordinary knowledge are in some sense immanent within our knowledge.[22] Given an idealist understanding of the notion of judgement these two views lead naturally to the result that our acts of judgement or synthesis are partially constitutive of the objects of our knowledge. Moore, by contrast, sees an act of judgement as an act in which the mind is in direct contact with an objective, non-mental entity—a proposition. Given the same two idealist views, this radically non-idealist conception of judgement leads to a quite different picture. Knowledge and experience must be thought of as being identical with, or at least very like, judgement—i.e. as being cases in which the mind is in direct contact with propositions or constituents of propositions. And the objects of our knowledge must be thought of as being, or being contained in, these entities with which we are in direct contact. Moore satisfies the first of these conditions because he thinks of perception as 'the cognition of an existential proposition' (*NJ*, p. 183) or, as he puts it later, that 'the kinds of objects which can properly be said to be experienced . . . must be true, and must be existential propositions' (*E. & E.*, p. 88). He satisfies the second of these conditions in virtue of his doctrine that everything is composed of concepts. It is worth emphasizing that, given Moore's denial of internal relations, and what I have called the 'absoluteness' of his mind, the only way that he could accept that 'the objects of ordinary knowledge are in some sense immanent within our knowledge' is by identifying propositions or their constituents outright with the reality which is their subject-matter.

For Moore, then, as for certain of the Idealists, the world is not alien to the mind but is, rather, transparent to the intellect. In the case of the Idealists this idea is based upon the claim that the world is constituted by our minds, or by a Mind of which ours is a part. In Moore's case the idea is based upon his doctrine that the world is made up of the objects of thought, with which the mind is in direct contact—propositions and their constituents. This is, I think, what Moore was expressing when he wrote (in a letter to Desmond MacCarthy, August 1898),[23] 'I am pleased to believe that this is the most Platonic system of modern times.' For both Moore and the Idealists, moreover, the same idea is expressed by the rejection of the correspondence theory of truth, i.e. of that theory according to which the truth of propositions depends upon something distinct from them and (usually) of a quite different sort.[24]

---

[22] It is worth emphasizing that Bradley rejects the first of these views, even at the price of the view that judgement is not an ultimately satisfactory means of knowledge. But both of these views are accepted by Kant, and by philosophers such as T. H. Green who read Kant through Hegelian eyes.

[23] This letter is now in the Moore Archives, in Cambridge University Library.

[24] For the Idealists' rejection of the correspondence theory, see e.g. Ch. I of H. H. Joachim's *The Nature of Truth* (Oxford: OUP, 1906); and Bk. II, Ch. IX of Bernard Bosanquet's *Logic* (Oxford: OUP, 1888; 2nd edn. Oxford: 1911). Bosanquet says: 'I cannot

Moore's metaphysics has a number of consequences which may, at first sight, strike the reader as counter-intuitive. Perhaps the most extreme of these is his claim that ordinary things, which exist in space and time, are to be identified with propositions (*NJ*, p. 183). Let us see how this claim follows from the metaphysics. Take, again, the example of my red coffee-cup. This object, on Moore's account, consists of a nexus of concepts: coffee-cup, red, existence, certain moments of time, and perhaps others. Now not just any relations among these concepts will have the result that they constitute an existing thing, for any group of concepts are related in some fashion. The relations which unite these concepts into an existing thing also unite them into a true pro-position.[25] Thus Moore, like the correspondence theorist, achieves the result that the proposition that my coffee-cup is red is true just in case my coffee-cup is indeed red. But Moore's route to this result is quite different from that of the correspondence theorist: for Moore the truth of the proposition constitutes the existence of the coffee-cup. All of these points are illustrated in a passage in which Moore discusses existential propositions, i.e. propositions which include the concept *existence*:

A proposition is constituted by any number of concepts together with a specific relation between them . . . . And this description will also apply to those cases where there appears to be a reference to existence. Existence is itself a concept; it is something which we mean; and the great body of propositions, in which existence is joined to other concepts or syntheses of concepts, are simply true or false according to the relation in which it stands to them. . . . But if [the proposition that this paper is white] is true, it means only that the concepts,

for my own part conceive how the doctrine of Correspondence can be adopted as a serious theory' (p. 263); and, again, 'Immanence is the absolute condition of a theory of truth. It is this that makes the fundamental contrast between the coherence and the correspondence theory' (p. 266). Kant's explicit statements about truth are all statements of the correspondence theory, but since he holds that the objects of our knowledge are immanent within the conditions of our judgement, it was natural for later Idealists to reinterpret him as really holding a coherence theory of truth. Kemp Smith, for example, says, 'Kant is the real founder of the *Coherence* theory of truth. He never himself employs the term Coherence, and he constantly adopts positions which are more in harmony with a *Correspondence* view of the nature and conditions of knowledge. But all that is most vital in his teaching, and has proved really fruitful in its after-history, would seem to be in line with the positions which have since been more explicitly developed by such writers as Lotze, Sigwart, Green, Bradley, Bosanquet, Jones and Dewey, and which in their tenets all derive from Hegel's re-statement of Kant's logical doctrines' (*A Commentary to Kant's 'Critique of Pure Reason'* (London: Macmillan, 1918; 2nd edn. London: 1923), p. 36).

[25] In *NJ* Moore seems to put forward two views of truth: first, that it is a matter of the way in which concepts are related, as if two (or more) concepts could be related either in 'the true way' or in 'the false way'; second that it is a property which is possessed (or not) by the whole formed by a group of concepts and their relations (*NJ*, pp. 180, 181, respectively). After *NJ* it is this second view that Moore consistently holds.

which are combined in specific relations in the concept of this paper, are also combined in a specific manner with the concept of existence. That specific manner is something immediately known, like red. (*NJ*, pp. 180–1)

Moore's understanding of existence, as just one more concept to which concepts may be related, suggests responses to two further objections to his doctrine. First the doctrine may appear to neglect the distinction between abstract objects and concrete objects—for it identifies physical objects, which exist in space and time, with propositions, which are surely abstract. Here the response is that Moore's doctrine does distinguish the concrete from the abstract. Everything is a concept, and everything has being; some concepts also exist, i.e. are related to the concept *existence* and to one or more moments of time, in the manner characteristic of *true* propositions; of these objects which exist at some moments of time, some are in space, i.e. are so related to points of space. The distinction between the abstract and the concrete is not neglected, but is differently understood: concrete objects become, as it were, special cases of abstract objects.

The second objection is that concepts are most naturally thought of as immutable, as Moore says they are (*NJ*, p. 180), whereas what exists may be begotten or created, and is notoriously prone to corruption and decay. So how, the objection goes, can concepts *be* existents, given that concepts are immutable, while existents change? The reply is that all concepts, including existents, are immutable; what we think of as change consists in the fact that complex concepts which include *existence* may be related (in the *true* manner) in a particular way to certain moments of time, and not so related to other moments of time. Thus when we say that a thing is different at one time from what it is at some later time, the situation could be more accurately described by saying that the complex concept of that thing together with *existence* has a particular relation[26] to the first moment of time, which it lacks to the second; and that another complex concept, at least slightly different from the first, together with *existence* has that same relation to the second moment of time but not to the first. Thus Moore describes change of this kind as 'the transition ... from the existence of something in time to the existence of something else in time, different from the first in some other respect than mere position in time' (*Dictionary*, i. 172). The same point is made, perhaps even more clearly, by Moore's understanding of motion:

[26] This relation is, as we have seen, that which holds among the constituents of a proposition when that proposition is true, for the true proposition *is* the reality with which we are concerned, in this case the existence of the given thing at the given moment of time.

if contiguous positions in space be occupied at immediately successive moments by things which differ in no distinguishable respect except their position both in time and space, these things are also said to be one thing, and that thing is said to have changed its position in space. This change constitutes motion. (loc. cit.)

The picture which Moore conveys, then, is of a static atemporal universe, made up of concepts atemporally related to one another in various ways. This is, of course, only possible because the moments of time, and *existence*, are concepts which have no special metaphysical status—though we are, no doubt, especially interested in them (see *NJ*, p. 180). Metaphysically, the primary notions are those of a concept, of a proposition, and of truth and falsity. For this reason, Moore's doctrine that existents are composed of concepts does not contradict his argument to the effect that we cannot 'explain the concept in terms of some existent fact, whether mental or of any other nature' (*NJ*, p. 178; see pp. 132–4, above for a discussion of this argument). What that argument purported to show was not so much the non-identity of concepts and existents but rather the irreducibility of concepts to existents. Moore's crucial claim was that concepts (and thus also propositions and their truth-values) cannot be explained away in terms of mental states (or anything else), but must be assumed outright 'as a *genus per se*, irreducible to anything else' (*NJ*, pp. 178–9). Moore's identification of existents with concepts takes concepts, propositions, and truth as basic, and explains everything, including existents, in terms of them.

One aspect of the doctrine that concepts make up the world is complicated by Moore's change of mind over the issue of a distinction between universals and particulars. In *NJ* there is no such distinction. Concepts include some things that fall on one side of this distinction— e.g. moments of time—and other things that fall on the other side— e.g. red. Where two ordinary physical things have (for example) the same colour, one and the same concept occurs in both. They are two, and not one, because the concept occurs in different relations in each. A physical thing is a nexus of relations among concepts (including, since the thing is physical, the concept *existence*, one or more moments of time, and one or more points of space). Two different physical things are, accordingly, two different such nexuses:

The material diversity of things, which is generally taken as a starting point, is only derived; and the identity of the concept, in several different things, which appears on that assumption as the problem of philosophy, will now, if it instead be taken as the starting point, render the derivation easy. Two things are then seen to be differentiated by the different relations in which their common concepts stand to other concepts. (*NJ*, p. 182)

This group of views changes after *NJ* because Moore distinguishes universals from particulars, which are instances of universals (see *Dictionary*, ii. 406–7, and 'Identity'[27]). At the same time he gives up the word 'concept', using instead the words 'predicate', 'property', 'quality', or even 'object of thought'. Why Moore changes his mind in this way is obscure, and I shall not discuss it further. The striking thing, from our point of view, is how much of Moore's *NJ* view survives this change of mind. In particular the distinction between universals and their instances does not coincide with that between the abstract and the concrete: particulars, even if they are of a sort which could exist, may be without existing.[28] (This will become evident shortly, when I discuss false propositions with non-existent subjects.) Nor does the universal–particular distinction coincide with a distinction between those things which can and those things which cannot be constituents of propositions. In the new theory, as in *NJ*, anything whatever can enter into a proposition, and if it could not nothing would be true of it. In spite of the use of the words 'predicate' and 'property', Moore also continues to hold that there is no entity which *has* these properties. Things, including existing things, are made up of their predicates or properties; there is nothing to a thing except its properties, no substratum or substance. In *NJ* Moore had put the point this way: 'in the end, the concept turns out to be the only substantive or subject' (pp. 192–3). This doctrine survives. Thus in *PE*, speaking of natural properties (i.e. those which can exist in time, unlike *good*), Moore says:

They are, in fact, rather parts of which the object is made up than mere predicates which attach to it. If they were all taken away, no object would be left, not even a bare substance: for they are in themselves substantial and give to the object all the substance that it has. (p. 41)

Finally, the static and atemporal quality of Moore's universe, which I discussed in connection with *NJ*, is unaltered by the introduction of the universal–particular distinction. Particulars, instances of universals, are no more subject to change than were the concepts of *NJ*; indeed, some of the passages which I quoted in my earlier discussion (from *Dictionary*, i. 172) postdate Moore's introduction of this distinction.

There is one final issue that I shall discuss in order to indicate the nature of Moore's distinction between being and existence; this issue may also correspond to one of Moore's motives for introducing the distinction, though this is not explicit. The issue is that of propositions

---

[27] 'Identity', *Proceedings of the Aristotelian Society* (1901–2), 103–27.
[28] Universals, however, do *not* exist—Moore is somewhat hesitant in asserting this (*Id.*, p. 115), but nothing in this theory demands that they should exist, and it is hard to see how an existing universal would differ from an instance.

with non-existent subjects—in particular, subjects which, as we would think of it, are the sorts of things which might exist, but which in fact do not. Moore treats propositions of this sort in just the same way as he treats other propositions:

When . . . I say 'This rose is red', I am not attributing part of the content of my idea to the rose, nor yet attributing parts of my ideas of rose and red together to some third subject. What I am asserting is a specific connexion of certain concepts forming the total concept 'rose' with the concepts 'this' and 'now' and 'red'. . . . Similarly when I say 'The chimera has three heads', the chimera is not an idea in my mind, nor any part of such an idea. What I mean to assert is nothing about my mental states, but a specific connexion of concepts. (*NJ*, p. 179)

We have already seen that Moore says everything must be a concept if anything is to be true of it (cf. *NJ*, p.182, quoted above, p. 136). What the passage just quoted suggests is that he also holds that everything must be a concept if anything is to be false of it: the chimera must be a concept because we can say, albeit falsely, that the chimera has three heads.[29] Although the chimera does not exist, there must, therefore, be an entity in the realm of being which *is* the chimera, prevented from existing (so to speak) only by the fact that it has the wrong relation to the concept *existence*. Moore's answer to the ancient puzzle, how can we form judgements (or appear to) about what is not, is that we cannot; everything about which we (appear to) form judgements in fact *is*—it has being, even if it does not exist. Thus '[being] is an absolutely universal term . . . propositions, whether true or false, and any terms that can be used in a proposition, have being or are entities' (*Dictionary*, ii. 421). Moore's ontology of being is clearly an extravagant one. Just how extravagant it is impossible to tell, for Moore does not discuss what is, from this point of view, the crucial issue: the nature of complexity. We can say that the golden mountain does not exist. Must we, therefore, say that the realm of being contains a golden mountain? Or can we, rather, say that our original proposition contains only the concepts golden and mountain, and does not commit us to accepting that there is a (non-existent) golden mountain? Or should we, again, say that once we admit that there are the concepts golden and mountain it is not a further step to say that there is a golden mountain—i.e.

---

[29] One might argue that the chimera must be a concept because some things are *true* of it: given Moore's understanding of existence, it is straightforwardly true of the chimera that it does not exist. Appealing to the principle that things must be concepts (and thus *be*) if anything is to be true *or false* of them, however, suggests that Moore's motivation may have to do not merely with the question how there can be true propositions about things, but rather with the question how there can be propositions at all (true or false) about things.

that the appearance of ontological extravagance which this last admission has is in fact illusory? Which of these is correct, or whether other possibilities are open to us, is primarily a matter of how we understand the ways in which complex concepts are formed from their simple constituents, of what account we can give of the sort of complexity involved here. Moore, as I have said, has nothing to say about this issue during the period which is my concern. The tone of his work sometimes suggests that he should be understood in the most ontologically extravagant way: but there is no sign that he considered the implications of this extravagance with any care. (The sorts of issues of complexity which I have mentioned in passing here will recur in Chapter 6, below, in connection with Russell's 'On Denoting'.)

I turn now to Moore's views on the related issues of analysis, definition, and philosophical method. In this context I shall also mention the one relation which Moore, at this period, holds to be internal: the relation of a complex whole to the parts of which it is composed.[30] The discussion of analysis will make it clear why Moore can accept the internality of this relation without it damaging his general philosophical position.

The question of the legitimacy of analysis as a philosophical method is directly connected with the issue of internal relations. The method of analysis is an attempt to understand a complex whole by seeing what parts compose it, and by gaining knowledge of each of those parts by considering it in isolation, abstracted from the whole. If the parts are internally related to the whole, each partially constituted by its position within the whole, then the abstraction of each part from the whole will not leave it unchanged. The parts, each of which we consider in isolation, will not suffice to reconstitute the whole that we wish to understand. For the Idealists, therefore, analysis would not have been acceptable as a method in philosophy. They could admit the legitimacy of analysis in areas of human knowledge which are, and must be, content with partial truth—the whole of science, for example. But in metaphysics, where our aim is complete and ultimate truth, they would reject analysis. Metaphysical insight, on this view, cannot be attained piecemeal, by first understanding one entity or one proposition, and then adding to this the understanding of a second entity or proposition. Such insight is, rather, a matter of an increasingly clear and articulated grasp of a complex whole. Now given the connection between analysis and internal relations, it is of no surprise to find that

---

[30] This relation must also, I think, be seen as an exception for Moore's claim that all relations are either logical or causal.

Moore advocates and uses analysis as a primary philosophical method. To see just how pervasive this is in his work, we shall first have to see the role played in that work by the notions of meaning and definition, and then to see how Moore understands these notions.

Moore's emphasis on meaning and definition and analysis, in his early work, is striking. He seems to hold that clarity about meaning would, by itself, suffice to settle many philosophical arguments. The Preface to *PE* opens with what is perhaps the boldest statement of this view.

It appears to me that in Ethics, as in all other philosophical studies, the difficulties and disagreements, of which its history is full, are mainly due to a very simple cause: namely to the attempt to answer questions, without first discovering precisely *what* question it is which you desire to answer.... The work of analysis and distinction is often very difficult.... But I am inclined to think that in many cases a resolute attempt would be sufficient to ensure success; so that, if only this attempt were made, many of the most glaring difficulties and disagreements in philosophy would disappear.

In the main body of the book, he says, in a similar vein, that '[the] question, how "good" is to be defined, is the most fundamental question in all Ethics' (p. 5). Nor is the emphasis on meaning, and the high estimate of what we can expect from it, merely a matter of abstract methodology. Time and again in *PE* he insists, with astonishing confidence, 'once the meaning of the question is clearly understood, the answer to it... appears to be so obvious, that it runs the risk of seeming to be a platitude' (p. 188); or 'It would hardly have been possible that such a gross difference of opinion should exist... if the meaning of the question had been clearly apprehended' (p. 173; cf. also pp. 134, 120–1, 99, and others). Although perhaps most evident there, this emphasis is by no means limited to *PE*. In the paper on necessity, for example, Moore says that his 'primary object... is to determine the *meaning* of necessity' (*Nec.*, p. 289; emphasis in the original).

Now it is important to emphasize that meaning and definition, as Moore understands these notions here, have nothing to do with language or with words. In the period which is our concern, Moore was not the ordinary language philosopher that he later became; he seems, rather, to have regarded questions having to do with words, with language, and with usage as trivial and of no philosophical interest: 'verbal questions are properly left to the writers of dictionaries, and other persons interested in literature; philosophy, as we shall see, has no concern with them' (*PE*, p. 2). Both in *PE* and in *Nec.* Moore is at some pains to distinguish the sense of definition which is his concern—'definitions which describe the real nature of the object or notion denoted by the word' (*PE*, p. 7)—from the merely verbal definitions which are of concern to the writer of dictionaries. After discussing two kinds of verbal definition, using the definition of 'horse' as an example, and saying of each that it is *not* what he means,[31] Moore says:

> But (3) we may, when we define horse, mean something much more important. We may mean that a certain object, which all of us know, is composed in a certain manner: that it has four legs, a head, a heart, a liver, etc., etc., all of them arranged in definite relations to one another. It is in this sense that I deny good to be definable. I say that it is not composed of any parts, which we can substitute for it in our minds when we are thinking of it. *We might think just as clearly and correctly about a horse, if we thought of all its parts and their arrangement instead of thinking the the whole* ... but there is nothing whatsoever which we could so substitute for good; and that is what I mean, when I say that good is indefinable. (*PE*, p. 8; my emphasis)

This is the philosophically important sense of 'definition'; and definitions, in this sense, 'are only possible when the object or notion is something complex' (*PE*, p. 7). Although definition or analysis is applicable to all complex entities, whether or not they happen to exist, Moore seems to think of the process as a direct mental analogue of the literal physical process of taking a thing to pieces, breaking it down into its constituent parts.

Against the background of this conception of analysis, we can understand why Moore's admission of the relation of whole to part as an internal relation is no concession to Idealism. First, this admission does nothing at all to cast doubt on the validity of the process of analysis, as Moore conceives it. This process requires that the simple parts, into which we analyse complex entities, be independent of everything else; no such requirement is imposed upon the complex wholes with which we begin. Second, and more profoundly, the validity of analysis makes it clear that we never in fact have to deal with complex wholes at all. Everything that we wish to say could be said just as well by talking about their simple parts and the external relation among them. As Moore puts it: 'We might think just as clearly and correctly about a horse, if we thought of all its parts and their arrangements instead of thinking of the whole' (*PE*, p. 8). Once the process of analysis has been carried out, complex wholes will be of no concern to us. Indeed, we might say—though perhaps Moore would not—that complex wholes are not ultimately real in Moore's view, and that their unreality con-

---

[31] It may be said that, whatever his official doctrine, Moore is forced to rely upon our use of words as his data in arriving at his definitions. This is no doubt correct; indeed, Moore comes close to acknowledging the point in *Nec.* (pp. 290–1). For him, however, the usage of words is only a guide to a subject-matter which is independent of it, and which is our real concern. It is this official doctrine, and the connected view of analysis, which is relevant to my interests here.

sists in the very fact that they are dependent upon other entities. These other entities, simple concepts and their relations, are real precisely because they are not dependent upon anything else. The criterion of reality here is precisely that which we saw in play in Bradley's thought; like Bradley's Absolute, or Spinoza's substance, Moorean simples are real because they are independent and self-sufficient (see Chapter 2, above, pp. 52–4). The crucial difference between Moore on the one hand, and Spinoza and the Idealists on the other, is that for the latter the search for reality leads to larger and larger units, until in the end only the world as a whole can be real; because Moore sees the only internal relation as that of whole to part, the search for reality leads to smaller and smaller units, and terminates with simple concepts. In Moore's view these are—almost literally—the building blocks from which everything else is composed. The method of composition here is a peculiarly simple one: it is conceived on the model of the relation of physical objects to its parts. It is just this relation which, in analysis, we mentally undo, decomposing the whole into its parts. Hence the status of complex wholes is not problematic for Moore. He can accept the truism that wholes are dependent upon their parts without accepting any of the claims which the Idealists had wanted to make by insisting upon the internality of relations.

The final issue that I shall discuss in this section is Moore's thought about the interconnected questions of the nature of necessity, the nature of logic, and, more generally, the existence of an a priori or necessary structure to the world. My claim will be that it is, within the metaphysics of Platonic Atomism, very hard to make sense of the idea of there being such a structure. The discussion will be complex, partly because Moore's view of necessity changes within the period which is our concern. In *NJ* Moore claims that all propositions are necessary (p. 189). (By saying that all propositions are necessary Moore means, of course, that true propositions are necessarily true and that false propositions are necessarily false.) One of the reasons that Moore offers for this view seems to presuppose that any proposition which implies a necessary proposition is itself necessary. This is a most implausible doctrine, which we are given no reason to accept (see *NJ*, p. 185). A second reason which Moore advances for the view that all propositions are necessary rests upon his claim that to be necessary is to have an unchanging truth-value: 'The test of [a proposition's] necessity lies merely in the fact that it must be either true or untrue, and cannot be true now and untrue the next moment' (p. 188). Given Moore's general views about change, it follows at once that propositions cannot change their truth-values, and thus that all propositions are necessary. A related consideration is that Moore may think of the truth-value of a proposition as in some sense a part of it, and thus as essential to it (as we have seen, Moore accepts that it is essential to a complex whole that it has the parts that it does have). Given these sorts of reasons for the view, Moore's claim that all propositions are necessary seems to be tantamount to the trivialization of the notion of necessity.[32] From our point of view it is of course significant that he has no non-trivial use for the notion.

The view of necessity which Moore advances in the article of that name is quite different from that discussed in the previous paragraph. According to the later view, necessity or a priority (they are identified: *Nec.*, p. 300) is to be analysed in terms of logical priority, i.e. implication. Necessity is thus a matter of degree: the larger the number of (true) propositions a given proposition is logically prior to, the more necessary it is.[33] Moore states the view thus:

any truth which is logically prior to some other true proposition is so far necessary . . . as you get more and more true propositions to which a given truth is logically prior, so you approach that region within which the given truth will be said to be absolutely necessary or *a priori*. There will, then, be only a difference of degree between the necessary truths and many others. . . . If there be any truths which have this logical relation [logical priority] to all other propositions, then, indeed, the application of these would be not merely wide but absolutely universal; such, it would seem, is the Law of Contradiction and, perhaps, some others. (p. 300)

This analysis of necessity in terms of logical priority, or implication, clearly pushes the important question back: what account can Moore

---

[32] I do not wish to be understood as maintaining that the claim that all propositions are necessary *ipso facto* involves the rejection or trivialization of the notion of necessity. It need not be so if one considers that property or group of properties (if such there be) which is usually thought to pick out just some among propositions as necessarily true, and then argues that, appearances to the contrary, *all* propositions have that property or group of properties. But this is not what Moore does. In the first place, it seems very dubious whether the notion of necessity can reasonably be thought to consist in having an unchanging truth-value. Secondly Moore does not *argue* that all propositions are timelessly true; it follows at once from his notion of a proposition. Someone holding this view can hardly claim in good faith that this feature is the basis on which necessary propositions are usually distinguished from others.

[33] This general strategy of thinking of the necessary propositions as those which are prior to, or presupposed by, many others, is directly analogous to the views of Kant, and some post-Kantian Idealists, on the same subject. Moore refers favourably to Kant in this context: 'what Kant showed is that there are a number of propositions logically prior to almost every true "empirical" judgment that we make' (*Nec.*, p. 301). See also Russell's view of the a priori in *FG* (Ch. 3, s. 1, above). The crucial difference is, as we have seen, that Moore's notion of logical priority—the analogue of the Idealists' notion of presupposition—contains no reference to the structure or presuppositions of our knowledge or of our capacity to judge, but only to the logical relations of the propositions themselves. See pp. 119–20, above.

give of the notion of logical implication? Here he has nothing to say of a theoretical nature. He confidently claims that the relation of logical priority 'needs, I think, only to be seen in any instance, in order to be recognised' (p. 301). He gives a number of examples, and then says: 'These then are cases of logical priority, and we can determine whether other supposed cases are also of this nature, by considering whether they are like or unlike these' (loc. cit.). This appeal to our ability to recognize cases which are like those given as examples may enable us to distinguish those pairs of propositions where one is logically prior to the other from those pairs which are not so related. But what Moore says does not amount to a theoretical account of logical implication or, therefore, of necessity. Being able to recognize logical implication when we see it is not the same as understanding what it is and how it is possible; nor does Moore's confident reliance upon our recognitional capacity leave him with any recourse against those who say that they simply lack any such capacity, or those who say that they have such a capacity but who hold views different from Moore's about some putative cases of logical implication. The sort of theoretical account of logical implication which Moore does not give is, I wish to claim, in principle unattainable, given the basic metaphysics of Platonic Atomism.[34] This claim will occupy us over the next two paragraphs.

The first point to make, in order to see why no theoretical account of logic or of necessity is available within Platonic Atomism, is that any such account would have to be entirely free of epistemic considerations. The rejection of such considerations, as being merely psychological, runs throughout Moore's discussions of necessity. We may, for convenience, think of the point under two headings. First, Moore rejects the attempt to understand necessity in terms of the way in which we come to know a proposition, how certain we are of it, and whether its opposite is conceivable. All of these notions are, for Moore, psychological, whereas the necessity of the proposition is independent of psychology:

It is perhaps inconceivable to us now that two and two should not make four; but, when numbers were first discovered, it may well have been thought that two and two make three or five. Experience, no doubt, must have been the means of producing the conviction that this was not so, that two and two made

---

[34] This claim needs to be qualified. It would, I think, be consistent with the metaphysics of Platonic Atomism to try to give an account of logical implication which relied upon the fact that one concept can be part of another, more complex, concept. Logical truths would, on such an account, be analytic. See below, pp. 150–2, for more discussion of this strategy, and of Moore's attitude towards analytic truths. Again, 'necessarily true' might be taken as fundamental and undefined, as 'true' is; but clearly this would not be an explanation of necessity.

four. The necessity of a proposition, therefore, is not called in question by the fact that experience may lead you to think it true or untrue. (*NJ*, pp. 187–8)

Second, Moore rejects the idea that necessity could be based upon the necessary structure of knowledge or of thought. This is an aspect of his view which we have already sufficiently examined (see pp. 111 and 119 above). It is perhaps worth adding that, just as Moore rejected the idea of basing necessity upon the structure of thought, so also would he have rejected necessity based upon the necessary structure of language. Language, after all, is *our* language, just as thought is *our* thought; Moore's concern is with how things really are, independent of us and our thought or language.

Logical or necessary connections must therefore, on Moore's view, be located in things themselves, wholly independent of our thought or knowledge. But now consider what, in very general terms, the world is like in Moore's metaphysics. It is composed of discrete and independent entities, with external relations among them.[35] Any pair of these entities will have some relation holding between them; but every such entity is what it is independent of all its relations. In particular, this will be true when the entities concerned are propositions. Now, given this vision of the world, what could be the force of the claim that some propositions are necessary and others contingent, some relations among propositions logical and others not? Suppose that a certain relation holds between one pair of objects (propositions), and also between a second pair. What could be meant by saying that in the first case it holds necessarily (logically) and in the second case not? It cannot, of course, be meant that it is a part of the nature of the entities making up the first pair that they stand in the given relation, for this would make the relation in question an internal one. Yet short of this there seems to be no way of making sense of the idea of necessity in the nature of things, or of two propositions being *logically* related. Moore's extreme atomism simply leaves no room for an account of these matters. This is not, of course, to say that it is inconsistent for Moore to insist that some pairs of propositions are logically related; it is only to say that he cannot explain what this means or how it is possible. He can give us no idea of how the relation of logical priority imposes a necessary structure upon propositions. The metaphysics of Platonic Atomism rules out any explanatory account of the notion of necessary structure.

I now take up the issues, which I postponed earlier, of analytic truth

---

[35] Here I ignore the internal relation of whole to part; the possibility of a notion of necessity based upon that relation will be under discussion when I talk, in the next two paragraphs, about Moore's attitude towards analytic truths.

and the internality of the relation of whole to part. These issues are directly connected. Since it is essential to a whole that it have just those parts which it has, a statement which says of a whole that it has a part which it has possesses an intelligible sort of necessity. Given Moore's view of complex concepts as having simple concepts for their parts, there will be many statements which we can interpret in this way, as saying of some whole that it has a part which it does, in fact, have. To use an example of Moore's, the proposition 'Horses have hearts' will, presumably, be analytic, for the concept *heart* is one of the constituents of the concept *horse* (see *PE*, p. 8 quoted above, pp. 144–5). This example seems to suggest that Moore's view should lead to the conclusion that *all* propositions containing complex concepts are analytic; Moore does not discuss this point, but, as we shall see, the conclusion might well be acceptable to him. In any case, it is clear that Moore does not think that analytic propositions are of any philosophical significance. Two kinds of propositions are worth distinguishing. First, there are—or so we might think—cases in which the subject of the proposition is simply the same as the predicate, or in which a thing is said to be identical to itself. The characteristic feature of these propositions is that they contain only a single entity (as well as a relation), which occurs twice over. In *Nec.* Moore simply denies that we do, in fact, have a proposition in such a case (p. 245). He offers no reason for the assumption that a proposition must contain two distinct terms; it is worth noting that it is an assumption that he shares with his idealist opponents.[36] Even apart from this view, it is clear that propositions of this first kind are likely to be simply too trivial to be of any philosophical interest.

Propositions of the second kind are far more promising as candidates for philosophically significant analytic propositions. Propositions of this kind are, paradigmatically, those in which the subject is a complex concept and the predicate is one of its component concepts, so that the subject contains the predicate (this was of course Kant's definition of an analytic proposition in the first *Critique*; Moore's view of the relation

---

[36] Thus Hegel says of the Law of Identity, A=A: 'The propositional form itself contradicts it: for a proposition always promises a distinction between subject and predicate: while the present one [i.e. the law of identity] does not fulfill what its form requires' (*Hegel's Logic, Being Part One of the Encyclopedia of the Philosophical Sciences (1830)*, trans.' William Wallace (Oxford; Clarendon Press, 1975; 1st edn. 1873), s. 115). In *Id.*, Moore attacks what Hegel says in this section—*not* on the grounds that there can be propositions which merely relate an object to itself, but rather on the grounds that to say of something that it is identical with itself is to say that it is a subject, i.e. can stand in the subject place in a subject-predicate proposition (*Id.*, pp. 120–1). This, of course, is something which is universally true, according to Moore. It is in this sense that Moore takes a version of the law of Identity as the motto to *PE*.

of a complex concept to its parts gives an almost literal sense to the notion of containment used here). Moore's attitude towards propositions of this sort is of considerable interest. He does not deny that they are propositions, but he claims that they are, or that they rest upon, synthetic claims:

take the definition that [the analytic proposition] is a proposition of which the predicate is contained in the subject ... [if this means] that the predicate is united in some way with the other predicates which along with it define the subject ... [then] the analytic proposition is as synthetic as you please. (*Nec.*, p. 295)

Moore's clearest discussion of the reasons for this view occurs in 'The Refutation of Idealism'. He is discussing the claim 'what is meant by *esse*, though not absolutely identical with what is meant by *percipi*, yet includes that latter as a *part* of its meaning'.[37] Now, since we can mean what we choose by our words, it is open to us to use *esse*, or 'reality', with a meaning that includes the meaning of *percipi*; Moore says that he does not think that the word 'reality' is commonly used in this way, but that he 'do[es] not wish to argue about the meaning of words' (loc. cit.). The important question is not about what we mean by our words but rather (though Moore does not put it exactly like this) about the reason or justification that we have for using words with a given meaning. In particular, Moore holds that the important question is whether the other parts of the meaning of 'reality' (other than *percipi*, that is) together imply *percipi*:

if the assertion that *percipi* forms part of the whole meant by reality is to have any importance, it must mean ... that the other constituent or constituents of it *cannot* occur without *percipi*.... Let us call these other constituents *x*. The proposition that *esse* includes *percipi*, and that therefore from *esse percipi* can be inferred, can only be important if it is meant to assert that *percipi* can be inferred from *x*. (Ibid. p. 10)

The only alternative to interpreting '*Esse* is *percipi*' in this way is to take it as having to do only with words and their actual use; Moore clearly regards these issues as of no philosophical interest. Correctly understood, then, '*Esse* is *percipi*' must be thought of as 'a *necessary synthetic* proposition' (ibid. p. 11). The point of this, I think, is as follows. If the concept *heart*, say, is in fact combined with other simple concepts in the complex concept that is a horse, then it is analytic that horses have hearts. But the proposition that they are so combined cannot itself be analytic.

---

[37] op. cit. n. 15 above, p. 9.

It is, I think, correct to see in this argument of Moore's the lingering influence of the idealist doctrine that there are no purely analytic judgements, because all judgement presupposes synthesis (see Chapter 3, Section 1, pp. 74–6). In this context, also, we can see that if Moore does hold that all propositions containing complex concepts are analytic (p. 150, above), he might still find the notion of analyticity insignificant. Here again there is precedent in the works of the Idealists. Russell in *FG*, for example, holds that all judgements are both analytic and synthetic (Chapter 3, n. 8). In any case, the important point, for present purposes, is that Moore gives no philosophical weight to the notion of analyticity.

2. Russell

In this section we shall discuss Russell's *Leibniz*,[38] which was published in 1900, and is based on lectures which Russell gave at Cambridge in 1899. One purpose of this discussion is to establish the influence of Moore on Russell in this period. I have said that it was Moore who took the lead in the rejection of Idealism, but I have not yet shown that Russell followed; the idea of a single rejection of Idealism by both Moore and Russell has not yet been justified. A more general purpose of the discussion is to see what Russell's philosophical views were in the brief period between his rejection of Idealism and his assimilation of the work of Peano. This latter event can be precisely dated: it took place at and immediately after the International Congress of Philosophy in Paris, in late July and early August 1900.[39] From that time onward, Russell took mathematical logic to be of the first philosophical importance, a source of solutions to philosophical problems and of refutations or confirmations of philosophical claims. To understand the difference that this made to Russell's philosophy, we need to examine his views before, as well as after, his attendance at the Paris Congress. Thus it would be easy to suppose, for example, that Russell's concern with the nature of the proposition has its source in a desire to give philosophical foundations to mathematical logic; but, as we shall soon see, the concern in fact predates Russell's philosophical interest in mathematical logic. This pattern, moreover, holds for many of Russell's concerns and claims immediately after 1900: the fundamental doctrines

[38] This book was based on a course of lectures that Russell gave in Cambridge in the spring of 1899.

[39] See *MPD*, pp. 65–6, and 'My Mental Development' in *The Philosophy of Bertrand Russell*, ed. P. Schilpp (Evanston, Ill.: The Library of Living Philosophers, Inc., 1946), p. 12.

were ones that he held before he was influenced by mathematical logic, and the chief effects of that influence were to enable (or force) him to articulate those doctrines further, to show him that they could play a role in the solution of problems which had previously seemed insoluble, and, especially, to enable him to defend those doctrines.

Russell's views in *Leibniz* include many points of striking superficial agreement with the views of Moore which we examined in Section 1. Russell insists that we must distinguish our mental states from their non-mental objects, and, in particular, that we must distinguish states of knowledge or belief from the propositions which are the objects of such states (e.g. see *Leibniz*, p. 178). He attacks Kant for failing to make this distinction, i.e. for holding 'that propositions may acquire truth by being believed' (p. 14). In accordance with the distinction, Russell divides the study of knowledge into a logical part, dealing with the nature of propositions and of truth, and a psychological part, dealing with our acquisition of knowledge (pp. 160–1). Although Russell does not yet articulate a distinction between Being and Existence, he does attack the idea that the constituents of propositions must exist (he refers to this idea as 'the existential theory of judgment'). He also attacks the view that there are analytic propositions of any significance at all (pp. 16–24); and he denies that the distinction of necessary propositions from contingent propositions has any force, holding, indeed, that all propositions are necessary (p. 24). He claims that all judgements, including subject-predicate judgements, are relational in character. Finally, Russell advances a view of analysis as a philosophical method which is very close to Moore's (pp. 170–1).

This bare list of doctrines suggests the extent of Moore's influence on Russell, but it does not convey the philosophy which underlies *Leibniz*. To do this, I shall set those doctrines, and others, in the context of the book as a whole, i.e. in the context of Russell's interpretation and critical discussion of Leibniz. The chief interpretative thesis of *Leibniz* is that 'Leibniz's philosophy follows almost entirely from a small number of premisses' (p. 3). A part of this thesis is that certain Leibnizian doctrines which are inconsistent with those premisses were held by Leibniz only 'through fear of admitting consequences shocking to the prevailing opinions' (p. 3), and should not be counted as a part of philosophy. The care and thoroughness with which Leibniz articulated his philosophy enables us, Russell claims, to draw a conclusion which is independent of that philosophy. This philosophical moral is that Leibniz's fundamental premisses are inconsistent, so that at least one of them must be false. Both the interpretative thesis and the philosophical moral are claims about Leibniz's premisses taken together

(Russell distinguishes five such premisses). But in both cases Russell singles out one premiss: that every proposition has a subject and a predicate. It is this Leibnizian premiss ('the subject-predicate theory', as I shall sometimes call it) which Russell chiefly relies upon in explaining Leibniz's philosophy; indeed, he explains two of the other premisses at least partly in terms of this one.[40] It is this premiss, too, which Russell holds is clearly shown by Leibniz's philosophy to be false.

The falsity of the subject-predicate theory of propositions is, in Russell's estimation, a result of the highest philosophical importance. He seems to have held that the theory was practically universal among philosophers:

In the belief that propositions must, in the last analysis, have a subject and a predicate, Leibniz does not differ either from his predecessors or from his successors. Any philosophy which uses either substance or the Absolute will be found, on inspection, to depend upon this belief.... Philosophers have differed, not so much in respect of belief in [the theory's] truth, as in respect of their consistency in carrying it out. (p. 15)

To these sweeping statements, Russell makes no exceptions. Besides Descartes, Spinoza, and Leibniz himself, Russell explicitly mentions Kant and Bradley as having held the subject-predicate theory; his tone is consistently that of one who holds himself to have uncovered a hitherto universal philosophical error. In the case of Bradley, there is some point to this charge. Bradley does hold that every judgement is to be thought of as ascribing a predicate to Reality. But it is by no means obvious that this view of Bradley's stems from the subject-predicate theory, rather than from metaphysical doctrines which are independent of it; the fact that Bradley holds that all propositions, including subject-predicate propositions, are relational in character militates against Russell's reading (see Chapter 2, Section 2, especially pp. 61–2 for discussion of Bradley's view of judgement, and of the extent to which it should be thought of as a subject-predicate view). In the case of Kant, and of post-Kantian Idealists other than Bradley, it is harder to make any defence of Russell's charge. In our discussion of Green, for example, we saw that the claim that all propositions are

---

[40] The five premisses which Russell distinguishes are: 'I. Every proposition has a subject and a predicate. II. A subject may have predicates which are qualities existing at various times. (Such a subject is called a *substance*.) III. True propositions not asserting existence at particular times are necessary and analytic, but such as assert existence at particular times are contingent and synthetic. The latter depend upon final causes. IV. The Ego is a substance. V. Perception yields knowledge of an external world, i.e., of existents other than myself and my states' (*Leibniz*, p. 4). Russell explains II and III in terms of I; he asserts that I is by itself inconsistent with both IV and V.

relational in character was a crucial part of his argument against Ideal-ism, and this is surely tantamount to a rejection of any form of the subject-predicate theory.

Why, then, did Russell take the subject-predicate view to be a nearly universal philosophical error? The most plausible answer, I think, is that he equated this issue with the issue of the reality and objectivity of relations. A proponent of the subject-predicate theory will, of course, deny that there are objective relations, either by claiming that ap-parently relational propositions are not genuinely relational, or by making relations into merely mental phenomena (Leibniz, according to Russell, uses both of these tactics). Russell seems to assume that the converse is also true, i.e. that one who denies that relations are (by Russell's standards) real and objective must do so because of the influence of the subject-predicate theory. This opinion of Russell's is in turn, perhaps, to be explained by his apparent attitude towards the idea that propositions might be in some sense mental entities. Late in the book Russell argues against this idea, but often he assumes its falsehood. If propositions are objective, non-mental, entities, then the question of the reality of relations can, presumably, be settled by seeing whether propositions contain relations. It is for this reason that Russell takes the nature of the proposition to be the crucial philo-sophical issue: 'That all sound philosophy should begin with an analy-sis of propositions is a truth too evident, perhaps to demand a proof' (p. 8); and again, a little more explicitly: 'The question whether all propositions are reducible to the subject-predicate form is one of fun-damental importance to all philosophy' (p. 12). Russell's emphasis on this point constitutes a clear difference between him and Moore. Moore's usual attitude is that it is uncontroversial that propositions contain relations, and the controversial point is whether propositions, and therefore also the relations that they contain, are objective, non-mental entities.[41]

Russell, then, takes the subject-predicate view of propositions to be philosophically crucial because he identifies this view with the doctrine that relations are not real, objective, non-mental entities. With this fact in mind, we can understand in more detail the relation between the two aspects of Russell's *Leibniz*, as an interpretation of Leibniz, on the

---

[41] But contrast the following passage from Baldwin's *Dictionary*, ii. 408: 'From Hegel proceeds a modern tendency to hold that the categories of quality, quantity, and relation are all self-contradictory . . . but at the same time, consciously or unconsciously, a pre-eminence is assigned to quality, since some philosophers avow the view that relations are to be interpreted as qualities of the things related, and most imply that the ultimate form in which all views can be expressed is as predicates of several subjects, or, by preference, of one'. This is, however, an atypical passage in Moore's writings—I know of no other in which the same view is expressed.

one hand, and as an independent philosophical argument, on the other hand. As an interpretation of Leibniz, the book argues, as I have already said, that most of Leibniz's doctrines follow from a small number of premisses of which, according to Russell, the subject-predicate theory is the most salient and the most controversial. From this argument two philosophical consequences flow. First, a number of Leibnizian doctrines are seen to be completely without foundation if the subject-predicate theory is rejected. Russell unhesitatingly extends this consequence from Leibniz's own doctrines to the less specific philosophical doctrines of which Leibniz's are, Russell thinks, particular versions. Given this extension, Russell's claim is that a number of philosophical doctrines, held in common by all of the major philosophers, have no support other than the subject-predicate theory, and collapse if we reject that theory (i.e., by Russell's lights, if we accept the reality of relations). Second, the inconsistency of Leibniz's view shows that the subject-predicate theory must indeed be rejected.

The first Leibnizian (and traditional) conception which Russell claims is derived from the subject-predicate theory is the notion of substance. Descartes and Spinoza had, Russell says, thought of substance as that whose existence is not dependent upon the existence of anything else (or sometimes, in Descartes, as that whose existence is not dependent upon the existence of anything else except God). Leibniz rejected this understanding of the notion (quite correctly, Russell implies), in favour of an understanding of it which is quite explicitly dependent upon the subject-predicate theory:

Leibniz perceived, however, that the relation to subject and predicate was more fundamental than the doubtful inference to independent existence .... He, therefore, definitely brought his notion of substance into dependence upon this logical relation. He urges against Locke that there is good reason to assume substance, since we conceive several predicates in one and the same subject. (p. 42)

The Leibnizian understanding of the notion of substance is thus as that which can be the subject of a subject-predicate proposition, but cannot be the predicate of such a proposition. This view of substance, Russell claims, gives rise to an important element in the ordinary view of substance, as that which persists through change:

Change implies some thing which changes; it implies, that is, a subject which has preserved its identity while altering its qualities. This notion of a subject of change is, therefore, not independent of subject and predicate, but subsequent to it: it is the notion of subject and predicate applied to what is in time. (p. 42)

Even the Cartesian and Spinozistic conception of substance, as that whose existence is independent, Russell implies, must itself be understood in terms of the logical distinction of subject from predicate: 'The attributes of a substance are the predicates of a subject; and it is supposed that predicates cannot exist without their subject, though the subject can exist without them. Hence the subject becomes that whose existence does not depend upon any other existent' (p. 41). Both the Leibnizian and the Cartesian conceptions of substance thus depend, directly or indirectly, upon logical doctrines about subject and predicate. In particular, it is only these logical doctrines which prevent us from identifying substances with the sum of their predicates, thereby eliminating the notion entirely:

The ground for assuming substances—and this is a very important point—is purely and solely logical. What Science deals with are *states* of substances, and it is assumed to be states of *substances*, because they are held to be of the logical nature of predicates, and thus to demand subjects of which they may be predicated. The whole doctrine depends, throughout, upon this purely logical tenet. (p. 49)

Since Russell rejects the logical tenet, he also rejects the notion of substance.

A second doctrine which Russell claims is a consequence of the subject-predicate theory is monism. In the context of a book on Leibniz the claim is a paradoxical one, for Leibniz was not a monist; Russell's claims is that Leibniz's pluralism is in fact inconsistent with his subject-predicate theory. The claim comes in the course of a discussion of Leibniz's argument for the identity of indiscernibles. Leibniz, according to Russell, infers the identity of indiscernibles from the subject-predicate theory. According to that theory, 'All that can be said about a substance consists in assigning its predicates. Every extrinsic denomination—i.e. every relation—has an intrinsic foundation, i.e. a corresponding predicate' (*Leibniz*, p. 58). But then it is absurd to suppose that there could be two distinct substances, A and B, which have exactly the same predicates. For A's being distinct from B is a relation which must be grounded in some predicate of A. Since B is not distinct from B, it lacks this predicate:

A differs from B, in the sense that they are different substances; but to be thus different is to have a relation to B. This relation must have a corresponding predicate of A. But since B does not differ from itself, B cannot have the same predicate. Hence A and B will differ as to predicates. . . . Indeed, if we admit that nothing can be said about a substance except to assign its predicates, it seems evident that to be a different substance is to have different predicates. (p. 58)

According to Russell, however, this argument threatens to prove too much—not only that there cannot be two indiscernible substances, but that there cannot be two substances at all. Given the subject-predicate logic, the argument goes, a difference between two substances must be a difference in their predicates. But, Russell objects, a difference in the predicates of two substances presupposes that they are different, that they are indeed two and not one—'the numerical diversity of substances is logically prior to their diversity as to predicates: there can be no question of their differing as to predicates, unless they first differ numerically' (pp. 58–9). The point here is that predication alone cannot ground diversity; but, according to the previous argument, the subject-predicate theory has the consequence that nothing other than predication can ground diversity. Russell draws the conclusion that Leibniz's pluralism is inconsistent with his subject-predicate logic; had Leibniz been consistent he would, like Spinoza, have held that there is only one substance. If we reject the subject-predicate theory, however, then the way is open for a consistent pluralism.

A third unpalatable conclusion which, Russell thinks, has been correctly drawn from the subject-predicate logic is that relations are purely mental entities, so that the truth of relational statements is dependent upon the mind. Relations, according to the subject-predicate logic, are not real; yet it is hard to deny that there are relational statements. Russell holds that this dilemma leads Leibniz to make truth dependent upon the mind: relations are unreal, but can have a mental reality in the mind of the percipient who perceives two or more objects at once. Thus an apparently relational truth becomes a subject-predicate truth, where the subject is the mind of a perceiver: 'Leibniz is forced, in order to maintain the subject-predicate doctrine, to the Kantian theory that relations, though veritable, are the work of the mind' (p. 14). This view comes to the fore particularly in considering attributions of number. What unites a collection of objects is that a certain relation holds among them; but since relations are unreal, or have only a mental reality, it follows that aggregates or collections likewise have, at best, a mental reality. As Russell puts it: '*One* is the only number that is applicable to what is real' (p. 115). This view, according to Russell, follows from the subject-predicate theory:

this position is a legitimate deduction from the theory that all propositions are to be reduced to the subject-predicate form. The assertion of a plurality of substances is not of this form—it does not assign predicates to a substance. Accordingly, as in other instances of a similar kind, Leibniz takes refuge, like many later philosophers, in the mind—one might almost say, in the synthetic unity of apperception. The mind, and the mind only, synthesizes the diversity of monads; each separate monad is real apart from the perception of it, but a collection, as such, acquires only a precarious and derived reality from simultaneous perception. Thus the truth in the judgment of plurality is reduced to a judgment as to that state of every monad which perceives the plurality. (p. 116)

As before, Russell draws the conclusion that, according to this view, the truth of many apparently non-mental propositions will consist in facts about the mind, or, as he puts it, 'that propositions derive their truth from being believed' (loc. cit.).

Apart from this argument, which depends upon the unreality of relations, Russell finds another source in Leibniz for this idea that 'propositions derive their truth from being believed'. This is the view that eternal (or, as we might put it, necessary) truths exist in the mind of God[42]—as if it were only thus that such truths could be explained:

It is a view commonly held that, as Leibniz puts it, the eternal truths would not subsist if there were no understanding, not even God's.... This view has been encouraged by Kant's notion that a priori truths are in some way the work of the mind, and has been exalted by Hegelianism into a first principle. Since it is self-contradictory to deny all knowledge and since, on this view, nothing can be true without being known, it has become necessary to postulate either a personal God, or a kind of pantheistic universal Mind. (p. 181)

Russell's response to the view that truth may depend upon the mind is to follow Moore in insisting upon a very sharp distinction between knowledge, which is a mental state, and what is known, which is a proposition, and which is wholly independent of all mental states. Like Moore, Russell argues that this distinction is necessary if we are to explain how two people can know the same thing:

if a truth be something existing in some mind, then that mind and another which knows the truth cannot be aware of the *same* truth. If we once admit that there is one and only one Law of Contradiction, which is the same whoever knows it, then the law itself is distinct from all knowledge, and cannot logically depend upon God's mind. *Unless truth be different from God's knowledge, there is nothing for God to know.* (p. 181, my emphasis)

Russell responds in similar fashion to Leibniz's view that relations exist in God's mind: by insisting that either a relational proposition *is* a proposition, in which case it needs no help from God, or else it is not, in which case Leibniz means to assert the absurdity that 'God ... believes in the truth of what is meaningless' (p. 15).

Russell sees the view that the eternal truths exist in God's mind as depending upon what he calls 'the existential theory of judgment', i.e. the theory that constituents of propositions must *exist*. 'The dependence of truth upon knowledge', he says, 'is really a particular case of the existential theory of propositions, and like that theory, involves the gross assumption that what does not exist is nothing, or even

---

[42] This view should be distinguished from the Cartesian view that the eternal truths are created by God's will. Leibniz consistently rejects this latter view, as Russell acknowledges (see *Leibniz*, p. 179).

meaningless' (p. 182). It is this assumption that misleads us into looking for *existing* entities which have truth as their property, and the only
such entities that we find are mental. To avoid this conclusion we have
to acknowledge that there *are* entities which do not *exist*—especially
propositions and their constituents. Russell puts forward an argument,
very closely resembling Moore's argument in *NJ*, for the claim that
ideas (the constituents of propositions) do not exist:

the only reason Leibniz had for saying ideas exist in the mind is that they
evidently do not exist outside it. He seems never to have asked himself why
they should be supposed to exist at all, nor to have considered the difficulty in
making them merely mental existents. Consider, for example, the idea of 2.
This is not, Leibniz confesses, my thought of 2, but something which my
thought is about. But this something exists in my mind, and is therefore not
the same as the 2 which someone else thinks of. Hence we cannot say that
there is one definite number 2, which different people think of; there are as
many numbers 2 as there are minds. These, it will be said, all have something
in common. But this something in common can be nothing but another idea
which will, therefore, in turn consist of as many different ideas as there are
minds. Thus we are led to an endless regress. Not only can no two people
think of the *same* idea, but they cannot even think of ideas which have
anything in common, unless these are ideas which are not essentially constituents of any mind. (pp. 165–6)

For Russell, as for Moore, it is a philosophically crucial step to acknowledge that entities may be real although they do not exist, and that
propositions and their constituents have this status.

   Besides the existential theory of judgement, Russell also considers
and rejects another view having to do with judgement, that there can
be purely analytic judgements. He associates this view directly with
the subject-predicate theory: 'An analytic judgment is one in which the
predicate is contained in the subject' (p. 17). Russell sees this view,
then, not as following from the subject-predicate theory, but as presupposing it. His argument against the view, however, is on different
grounds, and is, again, strikingly like Moore's argument for the same
conclusion (see Section 1, pp. 150–52). Except for pure tautologies of the
form 'A is A'—which, Russell says, are 'not properly propositions at
all' (p. 17)—the subject of an analytic proposition must be complex:
'The subject is a collection of attributes, and the predicate is a part of
this collection' (p. 18). But this fact shows that the supposedly analytic
proposition implicitly asserts, or at least presupposes, a synthetic
claim:

The collection, however,—and this is the weak point of the doctrine of analytic
judgments—must not be any haphazard collection, but a collection of compati-

ble or jointly predicable predicates.... Now this compatibility, since it is presupposed by the analytic judgment, cannot itself be analytic. (p. 18)

Along with the distinction between the analytic and the synthetic, Russell also rejects that between the necessary and the contingent. More fully, he claims that all propositions are necessary, but that this trivializes the notion of necessity:

Leibniz and Kant both held that there is a fundamental distinction between propositions that are necessary and those that are contingent.... It may be questioned whether, in fact, there is any sense in saying, of a true proposition, that it might have been false. As long as the distinction of analytic and synthetic propositions subsisted, there was some plausibility in maintaining a corresponding distinction in respect of necessity. But Kant, by pointing out that mathematical judgments are both necessary and synthetic, prepared the way for the view that this is true of *all* judgments. This distinction of the empirical and the a priori seems to depend upon confounding sources of knowledge with grounds of truth. There is no doubt a great difference between *knowledge* gained by perception and *knowledge* gained by reasoning; but that does not show a corresponding difference as to what is known ... it must be confessed that, if *all* propositions are necessary, the notion of necessity is shorn of most of its importance. (pp. 23–4)

Most of the salient points here are familiar from my discussions of Moore's views of necessity, and of the difficulty of giving any sense to this notion within the framework of Platonic Atomism. Besides rejecting analyticity, Russell also insists upon a very sharp distinction between knowledge and the proposition which is known, thereby rejecting any epistemic basis for the distinction between the necessary and the contingent. With these two supports for the distinction rejected, he simply sees no basis for it. When Moore, in *NJ*, discussed and rejected Kant's distinction of propositions into the a priori and the a posteriori, he went on to suggest that there was a genuine and important distinction upon which the misguided Kantian distinction is based. This genuine distinction, Moore says, is 'between concepts which can exist in parts of time and concepts which seem to be cut off from existence altogether' (*NJ*, p. 188). This distinction between kinds of concepts gives rise to a distinction between those propositions which contain one or more concepts of the first kind ('empirical concepts', Moore calls them) and those propositions all of whose constituents are of the second kind. Russell follows Moore:

We have now seen that Leibniz's division of propositions into two classes (necessary and contingent), in the form in which he gave it, is untenable.... Nevertheless, there is a most important principle by which propositions may be divided into two classes. This principle leads to the same division of propositions as that to which Leibniz was led . . . His division does, therefore, correspond to what is perhaps the most important classification of which propositions are capable. (p. 25)

Russell's distinction, like Moore's, is between those propositions which 'involve a reference to parts of time' (p. 25) and those which have no such reference (p. 26).

Thus far we have seen how Russell held the subject-predicate theory to be connected with various philosophical doctrines which, for independent reasons, he wished to oppose. What I have not yet done is to discuss those considerations which Russell held to be decisive against the subject-predicate theory; it is to this that I now turn. The first point to make about these considerations is that they are drawn from problems having to do with the nature of space, and of spatial extension and continuity. Russell sees these problems as having had a major influence on Leibniz's philosophy as a whole. Thus he says: 'Leibniz's theory of space is more or less involved in everything that can be said about his philosophy' (p. 112). And again:

We now reach the central point of Leibniz's philosophy, the doctrine of extension and continuity. The most distinctive feature of Leibniz's thought is its preoccupation with the 'labyrinth of the continuum.' To find a thread through this labyrinth was one main purpose of the doctrine of monads . . . And the problem of continuity might very well be taken . . . as the starting point for an exposition of Leibniz. (p. 100)

Both in Russell's interpretation of Leibniz, then, and in his argument that Leibniz's premisses are inconsistent, problems connected with the nature of space are crucial. This fact is significant, for it shows a continuity of concern on Russell's part, from the *Foundations of Geometry* to the discussions of continuity, of geometry, and of mathematical dynamics which occupy Parts V, VI, and VII of the *Principles of Mathematics*. As far as the details of Russell's views on these topics is concerned, however, his discussions in *Leibniz* are disappointing. What he does *not* say here is, as we shall see, quite as significant as what he says. First, however, I shall briefly discuss Russell's exposition of Leibniz's views on space, and of the objection which he holds to be decisive against those views.

   Like other aspects of Leibniz's philosophy, according to Russell, his theory of space must be understood against the background of his assumption of the subject-predicate theory ('the traditional logic', as Russell also calls it). This theory is inconsistent with the idea that space exists absolutely, independent of entities which occupy space. If space did exist in this fashion, then there would be irreducible truths of the form: such-and-such an object currently occupies such-and-such a spatial position. In a statement of this sort, the object and the position are taken to be independent of one another, so that we cannot understand one as the predicate of the other. So a statement of this sort cannot be accommodated by the subject-predicate theory: 'The relation, then, between a place and the substance occupying it, is one for which the traditional logic had no room' (pp. 118–19).[43] Leibniz's theory thus takes space to be an abstraction from objects:

there is no absolute position, but only mutual relations of things, from which position is abstracted. Space is an order according to which situations are disposed, and abstract space is that order of situations, when they are conceived as being possible. (p. 120)

The notion of a situation or place employed here is given content in terms of relations between objects:

When the relations of situation of a body A to other bodies C, D, E, etc. changes, while the mutual relations of situation of C, D, E, etc. do not change, we infer that the *cause* of change is in A, not in C, D, E, etc. If now another body B has to C, D, E, etc., a precisely similar relation of situation to that which A formerly had, we say that B is in the *same place* as A was . . . the identity implied in speaking of the *same place* is an illusion; there are only precisely similar relations of situation.[44] (pp. 120–1)

This eliminates relations among positions, and between positions and their occupants, in favour of relations among things. These latter relations must now be shown to be in fact attributes of the related terms. It is partly to this end, Russell claims, that Leibniz introduces monads and their perceptions (see p. 122). Properly understood, spatial relations do not hold between objects but are a function of the various perceptions which occur within each monad. Thus for Leibniz, Russell says, 'space is properly subjective' (p. 122). Objective space is to be understood in these terms: different monads have different perceptions, so a monad can be treated as a point from which the objective spatial world is viewed; these points of view correspond to different positions, so that 'the assemblage of possible points of view is the assemblage of possible positions' (p. 122). We thus obtain what Russell calls an 'objective counterpart' to subjective space. It is here that Russell objects:

The difficulty is, that the objective counterpart cannot consist *merely* in the difference of points of view, unless the subjective space is *purely* subjective; but it if *be* purely subjective, the ground for different points of view has dis-

---

[43] The above argument is, as Russell acknowledges, not explicitly given by Leibniz, who argues rather from the identity of indiscernibles and the Law of Sufficient Reason.
[44] Compare the notion of a 'logical construction' as it appears in Russell's own work after 1913.

appeared, since there is no reason to believe that phenomena are *bene fundata*. (p. 122)

Russell takes this argument as conclusive, and as showing that the subject-predicate theory is incompatible with objective space, which is in turn necessary if the idea that there is more than one substance is to be intelligible. Large conclusions thus follow:

The confusions into which Leibniz falls are the penalty for taking extension as prior to space, and they reveal a fundamental objection to all monadisms. For these, since they work with substance (and thus the subject-predicate theory), must deny the reality of space; but to obtain a plurality of coexistent substances, they must surreptitiously assume that reality. Spinoza, we may say, had shown that the actual world could not be explained by means of one substance; Leibniz showed that it could not be explained by means of many substances. It became necessary, therefore, to base metaphysics on some notion other than that of substance—a task not yet accomplished. (p. 126)

In one respect this passage is very curious. In an earlier chapter of the book Russell argued, as we have seen, that monadism collapses into monism. The conclusion of this passage then follows, without any need to discuss Leibniz's view of space. Why, then, does Russell not draw the conclusion at the earlier point? My speculation is that Russell held this argument to be crucial because of the central place that questions about the nature of space occupied in his own thought, quite independently of his reading of Leibniz. This centrality, I suggest, made him assume that an argument which involved Leibniz's view of space would get at what is essential in Leibniz—that an inconsistency at this point in his philosophy would be conclusive.

Although Russell emphasizes the nature of space in his interpretation and criticism of Leibniz, the book contains very little independent discussion of this issue. Two points, however, emerge clearly enough. The first is that Russell holds space to be absolute (as Newton thought), not relational (as Leibniz thought). His arguments on this score are not very revealing of his general view, and I shall pass over them. The second point is that Russell holds that there are unsolved difficulties and contradictions in all theories about space. This is worth dwelling on, for here there are clear contrasts with both his earlier work (*FG*) and his later work (*Principles*).

'There are', Russell says, 'two great types of spatial theory, the one represented by Newton, the other by Leibniz.' In spite of his adherence to a theory of the former type, Russell goes on to say that neither type of theory is satisfactory:

The objection to Newton's theory is, that it is self-contradictory; the objection to Leibniz's, that it is plainly inconsistent with the facts, and, in the end, just as self-contradictory as Newton's. A theory free from both these defects is much to be desired, as it will be something which philosophy has not hitherto known. (*Leibniz*, pp. 112–13)

The contradictions in the two types of theory are based on what Russell, apparently speaking in his own voice, calls 'the antinomy of infinite number' (p. 117 n.; p. 115) and 'the difficulties of the continuum' (p. 109). Russell's acceptance of these contradictions is in clear contrast to his attitude towards them a year or two later. *Leibniz* contains no indication that progress has been made in the treatment of these problems since Newton and Leibniz discussed them. Nor is there any sign of the idea that the philosophical difficulties raised by space, time, and motion might lend themselves to mathematical solution; in particular, Russell does not mention Weierstrass, Dedekind, or Cantor, although he was acquainted with the work of at least the last two (*MPD*, p. 35). The full force of the contrast between this and Russell's later work will emerge in the next chapter, but some idea of it can be gathered from 'Mathematics and the Metaphysician'.[45] The problems raised by space, time, and motion, Russell says there, are versions of the more abstract problems of the infinitesemal, the infinite, and continuity. Of these three problems Russell says: 'In our time, however, three men—Weierstrass, Dedekind and Cantor—have not merely advanced the three problems but have completely solved them'. This clarity and confidence is wholly absent from *Leibniz*. On the other hand, there is also a sharp contrast here between Russell's view in *Leibniz* and his view in *FG*. This difference does not concern the existence of contradictions and unsolved difficulties, for that is accepted in both books. The contrast is, rather, in Russell's attitude towards the contradictions. In *FG*, they were presented as contradictions in the nature of space, and as showing the need for a dialectical transition from our consideration of space in isolation to a more inclusive subject which would not be vulnerable to the same contradictions (see Section 2 of Chapter 3, above). In *Leibniz* the contradictions are presented as contradictions in every current *theory* of the nature of space. Presented in this way, the contradictions show only that no satisfactory theory has yet been found, that more work is needed. The difference between this attitude and that of *FG* shows the sharpness of the break in Russell's overall philosophy.

In drawing the first of the two contrasts of the previous paragraph— that between *Leibniz* and Russell's work of a year or two later—I said that the former work contained no sign of the idea that mathematics

[45] First published in 1901, in the *International Monthly*, under the title 'Recent Work in the Philosophy of Mathematics'; repr. under its present title in *Mysticism and Logic* (New York: Longmans, Green & Co., 1918), pp. 74–96.

might be a method of solving philosophical problems. This fact emerges in a passage worth quoting at some length, for it is in dramatic contrast with the later view. Russell is discussing Leibniz's project for constructing a *Characteristica Universalis*, which was to provide a method of solving philosophical problems:

What [Leibniz] desired was evidently akin to the modern science of Symbolic Logic, which is definitely a branch of Mathematics, and was developed by Boole under the impression that he was dealing with the 'Laws of Thought.' As a mathematical idea . . . Leibniz's conception has shown itself in the highest degree useful. But as a method of pursuing philosophy, it had the formalist defect which results from a belief in analytic propositions . . . For the business of philosophy is just the discovery of those simple notions and those primitive axioms, upon which any calculus or science must be based. The belief that the primitive axioms are identical leads to an emphasis on *results*, rather than premisses, which is radically opposed to the true philosophic method. There can be neither difficulty nor interest in the premisses, if these are of such a kind as 'A is A' or 'AB is not not-A'. And thus Leibniz supposed that the great requisite was a convenient method of deduction. Whereas, in fact, the problems of philosophy should be anterior to deduction. An idea which can be defined, or a proposition which can be proved, is only of subordinate philosophical interest. The emphasis should be laid on the indefinable and indemonstrable, and here no method is available save intuition. The Universal Characteristic, therefore, though in Mathematics it was an idea of the highest importance, showed, in philosophy, a radical misconception. (pp. 170–1)

Russell's positive views on philosophical method are, as this passage suggests, very close to Moore's. Complex ideas are composed of simple ideas, and can be analysed into those simple ideas (see e.g. p. 18). Simple ideas, however, are not analysable; such ideas must simply be 'perceived' or known by 'intuition'. Analysis locates the simple, indefinable ideas; intuition gives us knowledge of them. These two points of method are to be found equally in *The Principles of Mathematics*; but there they coexist with the view that mathematics (and logic) provides an essential philosophical method.

5

Russell's *Principles of Mathematics*

In the work of Russell from September 1900 on, the metaphysics of
Platonic Atomism became interwoven with mathematics and mathematical logic. This interweaving is one of the points of origin of a conception of philosophy which was to have a decisive influence on
the development of analytic philosophy, a conception according to
which the technical is not separable from the philosophical, and mathematical logic provides the crucial method of philosophy. Russell had a
long-standing interest in the philosophy of mathematics, especially of
geometry, but it was not until after he attended the Congress of
Philosophy in Paris, in July 1900, that he began to take a serious
interest in mathematical logic. He later described his attendance at this
Conference as 'the most important event' in 'the most important year'
in his intellectual life.[1] By his own account, Russell was so impressed
with Peano's performance at the Congress that he began to study his
work. Within a month he had mastered the logic of Peano and his
school, and had begun to extend the technique to new areas—most
notably to the logic of relations.[2] This phase of Russell's work includes
his discovery of the class paradox which bears his name, in June 1901,
and culminates in *The Principles of Mathematics*,[3] which was completed
in the summer of 1902.

Principles has, as Russell says in its Preface, two main objects. The
first is to present and discuss the basic concepts and principles of logic,
including the theory of classes. The second is to argue for logicism, i.e.
the claim that mathematics is logic. (More fully: that all concepts of
mathematics can be defined in terms of the basic concepts of logic, and

---

[1] *The Philosophy of Bertrand Russell*, ed. P. A. Schilpp (Evanston, Ill.: The Library of
Living Philosophers, 1946), p. 12.
[2] In 1901 Russell published 'Sur la logique des relations' in *Revue de mathématiques*,
7 (Turin), 12–43: this journal was dominated by the work of Peano and his school. A
translation of Russell's article appears in Marsh, pp. 3–38, under the title 'The Logic of
Relations'.
[3] Cambridge: Cambridge University Press, 1903; 2nd edn. London: Allen & Unwin,
1937. Except for the addition of an Introduction, and the consequent repagination of the
Preface, the 2nd edn. is unchanged from the 1st. Except for the Preface, my citations will
be by section number, *not* by page number.

that all truths of mathematics can be proved from the basic principles of logic.) The argument for logicism is not carried out rigorously; apart from other considerations, Russell does not present a definite solution to the class paradox. The informal exposition of the argument, however, is quite detailed. Cardinal numbers are defined as classes of similar classes, where similarity is understood in terms of the existence of a one–one correlation, finite cardinals are picked out from cardinals as a whole, rational numbers defined in terms of them, and real numbers are introduced as certain kinds of classes of rationals; the notions of continuity and limit are defined, and it is shown that these notions suffice for the calculus; transfinite cardinals are discussed, as are transfinite ordinals; complex numbers are introduced; and the use of this mathematical apparatus in geometry and dynamics is considered at some length. All of these matters are now more or less familiar, but much of it was new to Russell. Even where he drew on the logic of Peano or the mathematical work of Dedekind, Cantor, and Weierstrass, he modified and unified their techniques; the fundamental idea of showing mathematics to be reducible to logic was his own.[4] The book has an air of excitement and novelty to it. It shows an impatience with ideas—whether mathematical or philosophical—which are discredited by the new results, and an impatience also with the difficulties which seem to threaten those results—even where, as in the case of the class paradox, the difficulty is fundamental.

From our point of view the significance of *Principles* does not lie simply in the technical achievement which it embodies. Most of this work is well known, and is available in more accessible forms.[5] The salient characteristic of *Principles* is, rather, the way in which the technical work is integrated into metaphysical argument. On the one hand, Russell uses logicism as the basis of a complex argument against Idealism. The immediate target of this argument is Kant's theory of mathematics, but Russell takes it to be a refutation of Kant's philosophy in general and of any form of Idealism (see pp. 174–82, below). On the other hand, Russell takes his logicism to presuppose much of the metaphysics of Platonic Atomism. He claims, indeed, that this constitutes a reason to accept that metaphysics: that if we do accept it, we are then able to give a satisfactory account of the truth of mathematics. This claim is made in an important passage in the Preface, in which Russell acknowledges his debt, on metaphysical questions, to Moore:

[4] Here I assume that Russell arrived at his logicism independently of Frege. See p. xviii of the Preface to *Principles*.

[5] e.g. Russell's own *Introduction to Mathematical Philosophy* contains a clearer account of the basis of the reduction of mathematics to logic.

On fundamental questions of philosophy, my position, in all its chief features, is derived from Mr G. E. Moore. I have accepted from him the non-existential nature of propositions (except such as happen to assert existence) and their independence of any knowing mind; also the pluralism which regards the world, both that of existents and that of entities, as composed of an infinite number of mutually independent entities, with relations which are ultimate, and not reducible to adjectives of their terms or of the whole which these compose. Before learning these views from him, I found myself unable to construct any philosophy of arithmetic, whereas their acceptance brought about an immediate liberation from a large number of difficulties which I believe to be otherwise insuperable. The doctrines just mentioned are, in my opinion, quite indispensable to any even tolerably satisfactory philosophy of mathe-matics.... Formally my premises are simply assumed; but the fact that they allow mathematics to be true, which most current philosophies do not, is surely a powerful argument in their favour. (p. xviii)

This argument is unlikely to appeal to Idealists. When Russell says that his premises 'allow mathematics to be true' he is taking for granted one of the crucial points at issue between Idealism and Plato-nic Atomism: that truth is absolute, objective, and unconditioned. Russell recognizes no other sense of truth, and demands that we show mathematics to be true in this sense. But Kant, for example, could not be expected to agree that he had failed to provide even a 'tolerably satisfactory philosophy of mathematics' because he has failed to meet this Russellian standard. We might describe Russell's argument here as a circular one. If we accept the premises of Platonic Atomism then we can, given the success of the logicism of *Principles*, show that mathema-tics is true (always, now, in Russell's sense of 'true', except as indi-cated). If, on the other hand, we accept the truth of mathematics, then this, as Russell claims in the passage above, gives us a strong reason to prefer Platonic Atomism to any sort of Idealism. But why should we accept this circular argument as having *any* force against Idealism? There are, I think, two parts in the answer to this question. The first relies upon the idea that Russell's logicism gives us technical, mathe-matical, insight into the nature of mathematics which is not otherwise available, and, in particular, upon the claim that it shows Kant's theory simply to have been based on technical ignorance. The crucial idea here, which I shall explore at some length, is that advances in logic and in mathematics itself make Kant's reliance upon intuition unnecessary. The second part of the answer has to do with the idealist claim that their philosophy is implicit in our ordinary thoughts, and that contra-dictions in that ordinary thought make this fact manifest (see e.g. Chapter 3, Section 2, pp. 97–8, above). If the circle of Platonic Atom-ism, logicism, and mathematics is a consistent one then this idealist claim is undermined. The fact that our entry into the circle may be arbitrary seems less important, from this point of view, than the fact that if the circle is consistent then once in it we have no reason to leave it.

To conclude the introduction to this chapter, I shall emphasize two points which are implicit in the preceding discussion. The first is that Russell does not take the logic that he advocates as merely a technical apparatus, susceptible of philosophical discussion but in itself philosophically neutral. On the contrary: Russell accepts that the logic he expounds and uses has immediate philosophical implications, including (as we shall see) such apparently remote matters as the denial of the subject-predicate theory of judgement and his theory of denoting. As suggested by the previous paragraph, this is a point that cuts both ways. On the one hand it means that his logic, and his logicism, requires more philosophical defence than one might otherwise suppose; the distinction between philosophy and logic cannot, indeed, be a fundamental one for Russell. On the other hand it means that if we have reason to accept Russell's logicism then we are, on his account, committed to much of the apparatus of Platonic Atomism as Russell develops it in *Principles*. The second point is that a crucial role is played, in the argument against Idealism, by mathematical results. The fundamental claim of logicism is itself a mathematical claim. Once Russell's logic, whatever its philosophical presuppositions, is in place, the claim that this logic contains sufficient resources to define certain notions, and to prove certain theorems, is most plausibly thought of as being a mathematical claim. Again, it is a mathematical claim that we can now give clear and consistent definitions of certain notions, most obviously infinity and continuity, which were once thought to give rise to contradictions. Interwoven with the philosophical discussions of *Principles* we thus have certain technical results, established in the nineteenth century or claimed by Russell. As before, the very idea of the technical, as distinct from the metaphysical, is undermined by Russell's view that logic itself has metaphysical presuppositions. It may thus be misleading to speak as if we had, in the technical and the metaphysical, two separate elements whose connections could then be described (the problem, and the paradox, here are familiar from our discussion of internal relations). The interplay between the two elements—however exactly one should describe it—is what makes *Principles* both intellectually powerful and historically important.

Before discussing Russell's logicism and its implications, I shall consider a number of philosophical points which are more or less independent of logicism. These points will be to a large extent familiar from the previous chapter, but they also show the doctrines of Platonic Atomism being thought through with more care. Fundamental problems thus begin to emerge.

Russell, like Moore, takes propositions to be objective, non-linguistic, and non-mental entities. It is propositions, and their constituents, which are his concern, not sentences or words:

Words all have meaning, in the simple sense that they are symbols which stand for something other than themselves. But a proposition, unless it happens to be linguistic, does not itself contain words: it contains the entities indicated by words. Thus meaning in the sense in which words have meaning is irrelevant to logic. (*Principles*, 51)

Thus it is propositions, not sentences, which are true or false, and logic consists of propositions of a certain sort, not of sentences. Russell takes it that there is an approximate symmetry between sentences and their constituents, on the one hand, and propositions and their constituents, on the other (see *Principles*, 46). From Russell's perspective, this assumption means that words may be of some interest: while they are not what we want to talk about, they may be taken as a guide to it (loc. cit.). From our perspective, however, Russell's assumption makes it all the easier for him to ignore the linguistic. Language becomes, as it were, a transparent medium through which propositions may be perceived. The transparency of the medium makes it possible to ignore it. Russell sometimes appears to be talking about language, or moving back and forth between the linguistic and the non-linguistic. This is not, however, because he is at all unclear or ambivalent about what his real subject-matter is. It is, rather, because the assumed symmetry between the linguistic and the non-linguistic means that it is not important to keep the distinction clear in practice.

Russell refers to the constituents of propositions as 'terms'; terms, in *Principles*, are thus closely analogous to concepts, in *NJ* (we shall see one difference shortly). For Russell, as for Moore, constituents of propositions are not in general different in kind from ordinary things that we talk about (as one might say that Fregean senses are different). The things which the proposition is about are, in the ordinary case, among the constituents of that proposition (see Chapter 4, pp. 134–6). Perhaps the clearest statement of this view by Russell occurs in a letter to Frege written on 12 December 1904,[6] where Russell uses an example which Frege had introduced in an earlier letter:

[6] G. Frege, *Nachgelassene Schriften and wissenschaftliche Briefwechsel*, ii (Hamburg: Felix Meiner Verlag, 1976), pp. 250–1. I have followed the translation of Hans Kaal in *Philosophical and Mathematical Correspondence* (Oxford: Blackwell, 1980), p. 169, except for leaving 'Satz' untranslated. In its first occurrence one might substitute 'sentence' or 'statement'. In its second occurrence, Russell uses 'objektiver Satz' as German for (Russellian) 'proposition'. His claim is that the object of thought is objective, neither psychological nor made up of words, and can have things as concrete as mountains among its constituents.

Concerning *Sinn* and *Bedeutung*, I see nothing but difficulties which I cannot overcome. I explained the reasons why I cannot accept your view as a whole in the appendix to my book [*Principles*], and I still agree with what I there wrote. I believe that in spite of all its snowfields Mont Blanc itself is a component part of what is actually asserted in the *Satz* 'Mont Blanc is more than 4,000 metres high'. We do not assert the thought, for this is a private psychological matter: we assert the object of the thought, and this is, to my mind, a certain complex (an *objectiver Satz*, one might say) in which Mont Blanc is itself a component part. If we do not admit this, then we get the conclusion that we know nothing at all about Mont Blanc.

Propositions and terms are thus notions with immediate ontological significance. One point which is connected with this, and to which we shall return, is that *everything* is a term, for everything is a constituent of propositions. Given the ontological primacy of propositions and truth, this follows at once.

Russell, like Moore, takes for granted an extreme and naïve realism:

all knowledge must be recognition, on pain of being mere delusion; Arithmetic must be discovered in just the same sense in which Columbus discovered the West Indies, and we no more create the numbers than he created the Indians. The number two is not purely mental, but is an entity which may be thought *of*. Whatever can be thought of has being, and its being is a pre-condition, not a result, of its being thought. (*Principles*, 427)

Russell's naïve realism is connected with his view that not everything which *is*, *exists*. The distinction between being and existence is required to guarantee the objectivity of what does not exist in time—and thus, in particular, of the entities of mathematics. Only by making this distinction, Russell claims, can we avoid psychologism:

Misled by neglect of being, people have supposed that what does not exist is nothing. Seeing that number, relations, and many other objects do not exist outside the mind, they have supposed that the thoughts in which we think of these entities actually create their own objects. Everyone except a philosopher can see the difference between a post and my idea of a post, but few can see the difference between the number 2 and my idea of the number 2. Yet the distinction is as necessary in one case as it is in the other. (*Principles*, 427)

Lying behind these expressions of realism is the assumption, which we have already seen in Moore, that objectivity requires *objects*;[7] if these

---

[7] This is one quite general issue at stake between Moore and Russell, on the one hand, and Kant on the other. Is the notion of an object to be taken for granted, as with Moore and Russell, and objectivity explained in terms of it? Or is the notion of an object itself to be explained in terms of objectivity, of which some other account is given? This issue has most often surfaced, in subsequent philosophy, in the context of philosophy of mathematics, for many philosophers have found it harder to take for granted the concept

objects are to do what Russell requires of them, they must not be mental. Since they are certainly not physical either, they do not *exist* at all, and so must have some other status—being. Every term, every possible object of thought, has being: 'Numbers, the Homeric gods, relations, chimeras, and four-dimensional spaces all have being, for if they were not entities of a kind, we could make no propositions about them' (*Principles*, 427; I shall return to the argument which is implicit in this sentence, p. 212, below). Existence, by contrast, belongs only to some of the entities which are.

In one respect the metaphysics of *Principles* is like Moore's metaphysics in *NJ*, and unlike that of *Id*. Among terms, the fundamental entities of Russell's ontology, there is no distinction between universal and particular. Thus a single term may exist in many different places and times: a red coffee-cup and a red book each, at a given moment, represents a number of points of space at which the one term *red* exists (see *Principles*, 440). This view is combined with the Moorean doctrine that what we might think of as the predicates of a thing in fact constitute it. There is no entity *in which* colour exists; its existence is as independent as anything else. There is no substance in which attributes inhere (see, again, *Principles*, 440). It may seem paradoxical to say that a term, such as red, can both be an independent entity and exist in more than one place at a given time. The air of paradox is dispelled by the fact that Russell's ontology is an abstract one. The existence of an entity in space and time consists merely in a certain relation holding among that entity, *existence*, a moment or moments in time, and a point or points of space. Similarly, there is nothing absurd in supposing that a thing may exist and then simply cease to exist, or, reversing the process, simply come into existence. Given Russell's understanding of change, indeed, this does happen. What is normally called change is, as we shall see, understood as one thing ceasing to exist and a different, but perhaps very similar, thing beginning to exist (see pp. 194–95, below). To cease to exist is, in turn, given an atemporal reading: it

of an abstract object than that of a physical one. The issue can, however, be made into a quite general one—as in the work of Michael Dummett, who has extended his critical reflections on (what he calls) realism from the philosophy of mathematics to philosophy in general (many of the essays in *Truth and Other Enigmas* (Cambridge, Mass.: Harvard University Press, 1978) are relevant to this point, as are the unpublished William James Lectures given at Harvard in the spring of 1976).

This issue, of the primacy of the concept of an object, is connected with the issue of the unity of judgement (see below, pp. 174–7). Only those who take objects (in the most general sense) as fundamental are faced with the problem of saying how they combine to form propositions or judgements. This cannot be a question for those who, with Kant and Frege, take the concept of an object to be derivative upon the fundamental notion of a complete proposition or judgement (Fregean *Gedanke*).

is simply to be (timelessly) related to one stretch of time and not so related to subsequent stretches. All of this serves to emphasize that Russell's ontology is an atemporal ontology of Being, in which space, time, and existence have no distinguished ontological status: 'though a term may cease to exist, it cannot cease to be; it is still an entity, which can be counted as *one*, and concerning which some propositions are true and other false' (*Principles*, 443).

Russell's ontology, as we have just seen, has no ultimate distinction between substances and attributes. It does, however, have a distinction which is in some ways analogous to this distinction; and this is a point of contrast between Russell's views and the Moorean view which we examined in the previous chapter.[8] In Moore's theory of judgement, it seems that a proposition may consist of any two or more terms, in any order; no distinctions are made among terms on the basis of the roles they can play in propositions. Russell, however, does have such a distinction:

Among terms it is possible to distinguish two kinds, which I shall call respectively *things* and *concepts*. The former are the terms indicated by proper names, the latter those indicated by all other words. Here proper names are to be understood in a somewhat wider sense than usual. (*Principles*, 48)

The distinction is that things cannot play the predicate role in propositions, but can occur only as subject; concepts, by contrast, can play either role:

Socrates is a thing, because Socrates can never occur otherwise than as a term [i.e. subject] in a proposition: Socrates is not capable of that curious twofold use which is involved in *human* and *humanity*. (*Principles*, 48)

(Note that there is no use-mention confusion here: Socrates, the man himself, occurs in propositions about Socrates; see p. 171–2, above).

The most important thing about this Russellian distinction, from our point of view, is what it is *not*: it is not a distinction between things which can play the role of subject in a proposition and things which cannot play that role. It is Russell's view that *everything* can be a logical subject. This view lies behind Russell's use of the word 'term'. This word, says Russell, 'is the widest word in the philosophical vocabulary.... A man, a moment, a number, a class, a relation, a chimera, or anything else that can be mentioned, is sure to be a term; and to deny that such and such a thing is a term must always be false'[9] (*Prin-*

---

[8] It may be because of this difference that Russell speaks of his notion of a term as 'a modification' of Moore's notion of a concept in *NJ* (*Principles*, 47 n.; cf. also 426 n.).

[9] We shall see an exception to this below, p. 212.

ciples, 47). Russell then raises the question of the utility of a word so general, and answers the question like this:

A term is, in fact, possessed of all the properties commonly assigned to substances or substantives. Every term, to begin with, is a logical subject: it is, for example, the subject of the proposition that itself is one. Again, every term is immutable.... *Term* is, therefore, a useful word, since it marks dissent from various philosophies. (*Principles*, 47)

Everything, then, is capable of being a logical subject in Russell's metaphysics. He explicitly considers an alternative to this view, the idea that:

a distinction ought to be made between a concept as such and a concept used as a term [i.e. as a subject], between e.g., such pairs as *is* and *being*, *human* and *humanity*, one in such a proposition as 'this is one' and 1 in '1 is a number.' (*Principles*, 49)

Russell rejects this alternative to his view. He argues that if anything is to be true or false of concepts as such then they must be capable of being logical subjects:

suppose that one as an adjective differed from 1 as a term. In this statement, one as an adjective has been made into a term; hence either it has become 1, in which case the supposition is self-contradictory; or there is some other difference between one and 1 in addition to the fact that the first denotes a concept not a term while the second denotes a concept which is a term. But in this latter hypothesis, there must be propositions concerning one as a term, and we shall have to maintain propositions concerning one as adjective as opposed to one as term; yet all such propositions must be false, since a proposition about one as adjective makes one the subject, and is therefore really about one as term.... But this state of things is self-contradictory. (*Principles*, 49)

The view which Russell is here arguing against may be compared with the Fregean distinction between concepts (*Begriffe*) and objects (*Gegenstände*). This comparison is, indeed, one that Russell himself makes in his discussion of Frege in Appendix A of *Principles* (see especially sections 481, 483). In this Fregean context we might explain Russell's argument by saying that Russell takes very seriously what Frege dismisses as 'an awkwardness of language',[10] namely that the concept horse (to use Frege's own example) is not a concept. Since a Fregean concept can never occupy the subject position in a proposition, the phrase 'the concept horse', which does occupy the subject-place in

---

[10] From 'Über Begriff und Gegenstand', translated as 'On Concept and Object' in *Translation from the Philosophical Writings of Gottlob Frege*, ed. P. Geach and M. Black (Oxford: Basil Blackwell, 1952), pp. 42–55.

sentences, cannot refer to a concept, as the phrase '. . . is a horse' does. Thus, for Frege the two phrases 'the concept horse' and '. . . is a horse' do not refer to the same thing: as one might put it, the concept taken as predicate is for Frege different from the concept taken as subject. (This way of putting it would of course be unacceptable to Frege; but it is parallel to Russell's mode of expression.) How, then, can Frege say, as he does, that 'The concept . . . is predicative', or that 'A concept is the reference of a predicate'?[11] The word 'concept' in these sentences, since it occupies subject position, refers to an object (as Frege would say), or indicates a concept taken as subject, not as predicate (as Russell would put it). But then each of the sentences is false. Frege's response is to speak of an awkwardness of language, but if this implies that there is here some coherent thought which for some trivial reason cannot be put into words, then it is quite unjustified. Frege says that he is 'relying on a reader who would be ready to meet me halfway— who does not begrudge me a pinch of salt'.[12] But for Russell, no quantity of salt can make a false proposition true; and the fact that a theory contains propositions which according to that very theory cannot be true means, quite simply, that the theory cannot be true and must be rejected.

Frege's insistence that a concept cannot be the subject of a subject-predicate sentence arises from his claim that concepts are incomplete, unsaturated (*ungesättigt*), or essentially predicative in nature, whereas the subject of a sentence must be something that is in this sense complete, is not predicative in nature. One reason why Frege makes this claim has to do with what Russell calls 'the unity of the pro-position'—how terms combine to form propositions. A list of terms, say Socrates, mortality, does not form a proposition; nor does it appear to help to say that the proposition is the terms with some relation, say predication, between them—for it needs to be explained why this does not just give us the longer list: Socrates, mortality, predication, which is no more a proposition than is the previous list. Russell spends considerable space worrying about this problem (see *Principles*, 38, 52, 82, 136, *et al.*); although it may seem to be trivial, it in fact cuts deep, for any relation which could do what is needed here would share with Frege's concepts the property that it could not be the subject of a sentence; yet we have seen Russell argue that nothing could have this property, for having a property is after all having something be *true* of the thing in question; but anything which had the property could, for Russell, have nothing be true of it. Russell's position on these issues

---

[11] op. cit. n. 10 above, pp. 43, 48.
[12] op. cit. n. 10 above, p. 54.

remains confessedly unsatisfactory. He does invoke and use the notion of an *assertion*, which is:

everything that remains of the proposition when the subject is omitted: the verb remains an asserted verb . . . [and] retains that curious indefinable relation to the other terms of the proposition which distinguishes a relating relation from the same relation abstractly considered. (*Principles*, 81)

But such a relation, and the notion of an assertion given in terms of it, is contradictory, given Russell's metaphysics. When he first introduces the notion of an assertion (in this sense) he is quite explicit about this fact:

There appears to be an ultimate notion of assertion, given by the verb, which is lost as soon as we substitute a verbal noun. . . . Thus the contradiction which was to have been avoided, of an entity which cannot be made into a logical subject, appears to have here become inevitable. This difficulty . . . is one with which I do not know how to deal satisfactorily. (*Principles*, 52)

It is worth pointing out, further, that the Russellian notion of a propositional function has no role to play in this context. The point can be seen most clearly in section 482 of *Principles*, where Russell compares his own theory of propositional functions with Frege's theory of functions (Fregean concepts are special cases of Fregean functions; they share the essential feature of unsaturatedness). From this discussion it is clear that the closest analogue of the Fregean concept in Russell's thought is not that of a propositional function but that of an assertion. This notion is, as we have just seen, contradictory. Russell, moreover, does not hold that every proposition can be analysed into assertion and argument, so that no general solution to the problem of the unity of the proposition could be gained from the notion of an assertion (we shall return to the issue of assertions and propositional functions; see pp. 215–21, below).

I have discussed the issue of the unity of the proposition at such length not primarily for the sake of the role that it plays in *Principles* but for the sake of its connection with both earlier and later developments. A consistent theme, and motivation, of Idealism is the need to account for unity—in particular the unity exemplified in a proposition or judgement. This is implicit in the Kantian view of the categories as derived from 'the functions of unity in judgment' (*Critique of Pure Reason*, A69=B93–4), and in Kant's statement that 'The same function which gives unity to the various representations *in a judgment* also gives unity to the mere synthesis of various representations *in an intuition*' (*Critique of Pure Reason*, A79=B104–5). We have seen the point made explicit in Green's attack on Empiricism, which revolves around the nature of the proposition and its unity (Chapter 1, Section 1, above). The fact that Russell has no consistent view of these matters therefore undermines much of the force of his opposition to Idealism.[13]

Connected with the issue of the unity of the proposition is a further problem, also implicit in the fundamental metaphysics of Platonic Atomism, which comes to the surface in a very confusing section of *Principles*.[14] The problem concerns the notion of truth; it is important to bear in mind that in Platonic Atomism this is an ontological notion as well as a semantic or linguistic one. One way in which the problem arises is as follows.[15] An object's having a property, according to Platonic Atomism, consists in a proposition's being true. Thus the term, *my coffee-cup*, is related to the term *red* to form one nexus (i.e. proposition), and related to the term *green* to form a second nexus. The fact that my coffee-cup has the property red, and lacks the property green, is the fact that the first nexus of terms is true, and the second is false. Hence the ontological significance of truth. The problem arises when this account is applied to truth as a property of propositions.[16] For a given proposition, call it *a*, to have the property truth is for another proposition, that *a* is true, to have the property truth; for this to be so, the proposition that the proposition that *a* is true is true must in turn have the property truth, and so on. The ontological primacy of propositions and of truth arises from the fact that for an object to have a property (or for two objects to be related by a given relation) is taken to consist in the truth of the corresponding proposition. But if truth is itself taken as a property of propositions (or as a relation among their constituents), the view is clearly useless. The only escape from this difficulty would be to deny that truth is a property of propositions. Russell experiments with the view that propositions cannot be made into logical subjects to which truth or falsehood can be ascribed. This view, however, conflicts with his own argument that anything can be a logical subject:

Thus the contradiction . . . of an entity which cannot be made a logical subject, appears to have here become inevitable. This difficulty, which seems to be inherent in the very nature of truth and falsehood, is one with which I do not know how to deal satisfactorily. . . . The nature of truth, however, belongs no

---

[13] On these issues, see also the author's 'The Nature of the Proposition and the Revolt against Idealism', in Richard Rorty, J. B. Schneewind, and Quentin Skinner (eds.), *Philosophy in History* (Cambridge: CUP, 1984), pp. 375–97.

[14] S. 52. My remarks by no means amount to a full interpretation of this section.

[15] In the following I am particularly indebted to Thomas G. Ricketts.

[16] The difficulty cannot, however, be avoided by taking truth as a relation among the constituents of a proposition.

more to the principles of mathematics than to the principles of everything else. I therefore leave this question to the logicians. (*Principles*, 52)

In fact the problem here seems quite inescapable, given the metaphysics of Platonic Atomism; elsewhere, as we have seen, Russell suggests that his logicism is inseparable from that metaphysics.

I turn now to the central theme of this chapter: Russell's logicism, and his use of logicism as an argument against Idealism. The argument is directed, in the first instance, at Kant's theory of mathematics. Russell, as we shall see, does not deny Kant's claim that mathematics is synthetic. He does, however, deny that mathematics is based on the forms of our intuition, forms which impose spatiality and temporality upon the objects we intuit. From Russell's perspective, to say that a proposition of mathematics is true in virtue of the form of our intuition—or any other fact about our minds—is a confusion. Since the proposition is not about our minds, its truth cannot be explained by facts about our minds. All that could be explained in this way is our *belief* in the proposition. If Kant's explanation of our belief were correct, moreover, the proposition would not be true, but would be false. Writing about the example of supposedly a priori propositions about space, Russell says:

the Kantian theory seems to lead to the curious result that whatever we cannot help believing must be false. What we cannot help believing, in this case, is something as to the nature of space, not as to the nature of our minds. The explanation offered is, that there is no space outside our minds; whence it is to be inferred that our unavoidable beliefs about space are all mistaken. Moreover we only push one stage farther back the region of 'mere fact', for the constitution of our minds remains still a mere fact. (*Principles*, 430)

Russell's objection to Kant, then, is that his theory does not allow mathematics to be (absolutely and unconditionally) true, because it claims that mathematics is dependent upon space and time, and thus on the forms of intuition. Russell's argument against Kant's theory consists in the demonstration that mathematics is *not* dependent upon space and time. Given that logic is itself independent of space and time (a point to which I shall return), the demonstration that mathematics is reducible to logic shows that mathematics too is independent of space and time. Logicism is thus to constitute a definitive refutation of Kant's view of mathematics.

An important point here is that Russell takes logicism, and thus the refutation of Kant, to have the certainty of mathematics rather than the doubtfulness of philosophy. In other contexts, as we have seen, Russell emphasizes the philosophical presuppositions of logic; here this point is not stressed. Thus Russell says of Kant's view of mathematics: 'Thanks to the progress of Symbolic Logic, especially as treated by Professor Peano, this part of the Kantian philosophy is now capable of a final and irrevocable refutation' (*Principles*, 4). I shall return to the technical aspects of Russell's logicism; for the present my concern is with the use of logicism as part of an argument against Idealism.

Russell's argument against Kant's theory of mathematics may seem to be a relatively narrow point. It is not clear on the face of it why this argument should carry any weight against Kant's philosophy as a whole, or against Kant's idealist successors. But in Russell's hands the argument against Kant's view of mathematics serves as the basis for a general attack on Kantianism and on post-Kantian Idealism. According to Kant's philosophy in general, we can have no knowledge of the world as it is in itself, independently of us; all our knowledge is confined to the world as it appears to, and is partially constituted by, our minds (see Chapter 1, above). A direct consequence of this claim is that our knowledge is confined to what can be given in intuition, i.e. to actual or possible objects of sensible experience (see e.g. the preface to the second edition of the *Critique of Pure Reason*). Russell takes logicism to show that this Kantian claim is false: because it shows mathematics to be independent of intuition, it shows that we do have knowledge which is, in Kant's terms, unconditioned, not confined to the world as it appears to us. This argument presupposes two points. First, mathematics, and so also, given logicism, logic, must be genuine knowledge. This presupposition is met by Russell's view that logic is synthetic (*Principles*, 434; see pp. 196–7, below). Second, logic must be unconditioned. This presupposition is met by Russell's view of logic as unrestrictedly general (see pp. 198–205, below). This argument against Kant has force also against post-Kantian Idealism. Here the relevant claim is that all of our *ordinary* knowledge, i.e. all of our knowledge except for that special kind of knowledge of the world as a whole which metaphysics affords us, is inadequate and at best partially true. Ordinary sorts of knowledge, if thought through with rigour, are held to lead to contradictions. The most obvious articulation of this claim is the Hegelian dialectic, which we briefly examined in Section 2 of Chapter 3 (above); a similar claim is, however, implicit in the philosophies of Green and Bradley, which are not explicitly dialectical (in Bradley's philosophy, indeed, we find the stronger claim that anything which could, strictly speaking, be called *knowledge* will be inadequate). As against this general idealist claim as to the inadequacy of our ordinary (non-metaphysical) thought, *Principles* set out to show that mathematics is true—not true as one stage in the dialectic, or more or less true, but absolutely true; not true if put in a wider context, or seen as part of a larger whole, but true just as it stands; not—to revert to the Kantian idiom—true only from the empirical standpoint and not from the transcendental standpoint, but flat-out true, with no distinctions of standpoints accepted. Mathematics thus functions as a counter-example to a claim which is a necessary part of any form of Idealism.

If mathematics is absolutely true, and is independent of space and time, then a further, and more general, point can be made. In Kant, and in many of his idealist successors, claims about the inconsistency of space and time play the crucial role of showing that the ordinary spatio-temporal world is not fully real (or is, in Kantian terms, empirically real but transcendentally ideal); and that apparent truths about the world are only relative truths. This conclusion is of the utmost generality, and immediately establishes the sort of contrast between appearance and reality that is characteristic of Idealism. In particular, it establishes that the spatio-temporal world falls on the side of appearance. To overthrow this very general conclusion, Russell claims in *Principles* that space and time are consistent, and that modern (i.e. nineteenth-century) mathematics demonstrates this beyond doubt. To be more precise: Russell's claim is that modern mathematics makes available consistent theories which may represent the truth about space and time; whether they in fact do so is a matter on which he is willing to remain agnostic. The crucial point is that mathematics makes consistent theories of space and time available. The importance of this point to Russell can be gathered from the fact that space, which is hardly an obvious subject for a book on the foundation of mathematics, is the subject of Part VI of *The Principles of Mathematics*, and occupies nearly a hundred pages of that book. This part of the book concludes with a discussion of Kant's antinomies, and claims that they are 'disproved by the modern realization of Leibniz's universal characteristic' (section 436). Russell's claim that there are consistent mathematical theories of space and time draws, as one would expect, upon the treatment of real numbers and of continuity made available by Cantor, Dedekind, and (especially) Weierstrass. It is important, however, to see that it also depends upon the central claim of Russell's logicism, that mathematics is wholly independent of the Kantian forms of intuition. It is only if mathematics is in this way independent of space and time that it can be used, in non-circular fashion, as an argument for the consistency of the latter notions. Russell thus takes the central claim of logicism, and the claim of the consistency of space and time, as crucial to his opposition to Kant:

The questions of chief importance to us, as regards to Kantian theory, are two, namely, (1) are the reasonings in mathematics in any way different from those of Formal Logic? (2) are there any contradictions in the notions of space and time? If these two pillars of the Kantian edifice can be pulled down, we shall have successfully played the part of Samson towards his disciples. (*Principles*, 434)

I turn now to some of the technical aspects of Russell's reduction of mathematics to logic. The aim here is not to give an exposition of the reduction but simply to illustrate some of its philosophically significant features. It is important, to begin with, to see why Russell puts so much weight on advances in logic.[17] The logic available to Kant was syllogistic logic, which can handle only (part of) monadic quantification theory, i.e. quantification theory which deals with one-place predicates, not with two or more place predicates (relations). Russell's logic, by contrast, contains a general treatment of polyadic quantification theory.[18] The difference between monadic and polyadic quantification is crucial: monadic quantification theory is inadequate for mathematical reasoning. The difference is clearest if we consider reasoning about the infinite. Even elementary branches of mathematics—natural number theory or Euclidean geometry—require an infinite number of objects (natural numbers, points). But using monadic quantification theory we cannot infer the existence of an infinite number of objects from any axioms which do not already contain the notion of the infinite; so our reasonings will shed no light on this notion. The case of polyadic quantification theory is quite different. We can, to take a simple example, lay down two axioms ensuring that a certain relation, R, is transitive and asymmetrical.

$$(x)(y)(z)(xRy.yRz \supset xRz) \tag{1}$$
$$(x)(y)(xRy \supset -yRx) \tag{2}$$

A third axiom then ensures that there are infinitely many objects:

$$(x)(\exists y)\, xRy \tag{3}$$

To see why there must be infinitely many objects if (1)–(3) are all true, reason as follows: we begin with the supposition that there is one object, a. Since (3) is universal, we know $(\exists y)aRy$, i.e. a has R to something. Call that thing b. By the asymmetry of R((2)), a and b are

---

[17] Here and in what follows I am indebted to Michael Friedman, 'Kant's Theory of Geometry', *Philosophical Review*, 94 (1985), 455–506; also, less directly, to papers by Charles Parsons ('Infinity and Kant's Conception of the "Possibility of Experience"' and 'Kant's Philosophy of Arithmetic', both repr. in *Mathematics in Philosophy* (Ithaca, NY: Cornell University Press, 1983)) and Jaakko Hintikka (especially 'On Kant's Notion of Intuition (*Anschauung*)' in T. Penelhum and J. MacIntosh (eds.), *The First Critique* (Belmont, Calif.: Wadsworth, 1969); and 'Kant Vindicated', in *Logic, Language-Games and Information* (Oxford: OUP, 1973), pp. 174–98). These papers raise issues beyond the scope of this book.

[18] This is clearer in 'Sur la logique des relations', cited n. 2 above, than it is in *Principles*.

distinct. Repeating this reasoning, *b* has R to *c* and is distinct from it; since *a* R *b* and *b* R *c*, *a* R *c* (by (1)), so *c* is also distinct from *a*. Similarly there must be a *d* to which *c* has R which is distinct from *a*, *b*, and *c*; and *e* to which *d* has R. . . . Thus, for example, the fact that there are infinitely many natural numbers follows at once from the assertions that the relation 'greater than' is transitive and asymmetrical, that there is at least one number, and that for every number there is a greater one. Crucial to this sort of reasoning, and to the question of the infinity of any series, is the fact of quantifier dependence: in (3), the existential quantifier is within the scope of the universal quantifier. Every formula equivalent to (3) also manifests this quantifier dependence, but in monadic logic every formula is equivalent to some formula in which no quantifier is within the scope of another (e.g. $(\exists x)(y)(Fx.Gy)$ is equivalent to $(\exists x)Fx.(y)Gy$).

The facts which I have emphasized in the previous paragraph do not, of course, imply that arithmetic and geometry could not exist in the absence of a formulation of polyadic quantification theory. People were capable of carrying out the sort of reasoning embodied in this part of logic before the logic was formulated. We might, however, expect to find that the theoretical accounts of this reasoning would look, in retrospect, unnatural—if only because such reasoning would not be counted as part of logic. This is what Russell claims about Kant's use of intuition in mathematics, that it was necessary because the logic available to Kant was inadequate:[19]

There was, until very lately, a special difficulty in the principles of mathematics. . . . Not only the Aristotelian syllogistic theory, but also the modern doctrines of Symbolic logic, were either theoretically inadequate to mathematical reasoning, or at any rate required such artificial forms of statement that they could not be practically applied. *In this fact lay the strength of the Kantian view*, which asserted that Mathematical reasoning is not strictly formal, but always uses intuition, i.e., the a priori knowledge of space and time. Thanks to the progress of Symbolic Logic . . . this part of the Kantian philosophy is capable of a final and irrevocable refutation. (*Principles*, 4, my emphasis)

In discussing the difference between monadic and polyadic quantification theory I said that a transitive asymmetrical relation could be used to generate an infinite series. One way to express this is to say that such relations impose an *order* on the objects among which they hold (as the relation 'taller than' imposes an order on people; a different relation, such as 'heavier than', may impose a different order on the same objects). We can then say that the set of objects is infinite by

---

[19] This interpretation of Kant's view of geometry has been convincingly argued for by Friedman, op. cit. n. 17 above. Friedman is, however, far more sympathetic to Kant than is Russell.

saying that for every object there is one that has the ordering relation
to it (thus we could say, falsely, that for every person there is a taller
one; if this were true it would follow that there are infinitely many
people). For these reasons, the notion of order receives much emphasis
in *Principles*. Part IV of the book is devoted to this notion, and Russell
says, for example, 'the whole philosophy of space and time depends
upon the view we take of order' (187), and again, 'the solution of the
most ancient and respectable contradictions in the notion of infinity
depends mainly upon a correct philosophy of order' (224). It is of great
importance to Russell that the notion of order requires transitive asymmetrical relations. Relations of this kind in particular, Russell argues,
cannot be reduced to predicates. Previous philosophers, he claims,
could not give a coherent account of mathematics because they did not
accept relations of this irreducible sort:

> asymmetrical relations are unintelligible on both the usual theories of relation.
> Hence, since such relations are involved in Number, Quantity, Order, Space,
> Time, and Motion, we can scarcely hope for a satisfactory philosophy of
> Mathematics so long as we adhere to the view that no relation can be 'purely
> external'. As soon, however, as we adopt a different theory, the logical puz-
> zles, which have hitherto obstructed philosophers, are seen to be artificial.
> (*Principles*, 216)

For Russell this is a paradigm case of the interrelation of the philosophical and the technical. A coherent account of mathematics requires
the notion of order, which in turn requires irreducible relations; hence
we have a reason to adopt a philosophy which accepts such relations.
(See, however, the discussion of Russell on the subject-predicate
theory for some doubts as to whether the philosophical lines are quite
as clear as Russell takes them to be; Chapter 4, pp. 154–5, above).

I turn now to a different technical development, that which began to
put the calculus on a rigorous basis. Here again we can see the force in
Russell's claim that Kant's philosophy is based on mathematical ignorance, and is refuted by mathematical advances; here again, also, we
see the significance of polyadic quantification theory. Kant follows one
line of thought in Newton's work, and puts forward an understanding
of the calculus in dynamical terms. The key notion here is that of the
continuous motion of a point in space. If we think of a curve as generated in this way, we can give sense to the idea of the derivative of
a curve ('fluxion' is Newton's word) in terms of the idea of the velocity
of the point at a given instant.[20] Given this understanding, the calculus

---

[20] See Friedman, op. cit. n. 17 above, s. III. H. J. M. Bos has no hesitation in
attributing a dynamical understanding of the calculus to Newton: 'The terms "fluents"
and "fluxions" indicate Newton's conception of variable quantities in analytical geometry: he saw these as "flowing quantities", that is, *quantities that change with respect to time*'

is dependent upon the notions of space, time, and motion, for these notions are presupposed in the explanation of the fundamental notions of the calculus. In Kantian terms, the calculus presupposes the a priori intuitions of space and time.

The dynamical or kinematic approach to the calculus has the advantage of avoiding the Leibnizian appeal to infinitesimals.[21] The kinematic approach has serious mathematical drawbacks, however. An obvious example is that it leads naturally to the conclusion that a continuous curve is everywhere differentiable (except at, at most, a finite number of points).[22] This conclusion, however, is false. During the nineteenth century a number of mathematicians produced counter-examples to it, i.e. curves which are continuous but fail to be differentiable at an infinite number of points.[23] This sort of difficulty led to a movement to put the calculus on a more rigorous basis, which would be independent both of the infinitesimal and of dynamical notions. Bolzano, Cauchy, and Weierstrass, in particular, produced definitions of the fundamental notions of the calculus which satisfied these two criteria. Thus it is that Russell can claim that 'modern mathematics' shows that Kant is simply mistaken in thinking that the calculus presupposes space and time:

It was formerly supposed—and herein lay the real strength of Kant's mathematical philosophy—that continuity had an essential reference to space and time, and that the Calculus (as the word *fluxion* suggests) in some way presupposed motion or at least change. In this view, the philosophy of space and time was prior to that of continuity, the Transcendental Aesthetic preceded the Transcendental Dialectic, and the antinomies (at least the mathematical ones) were essentially spatio-temporal. All this has been changed by modern mathematics. (*Principles*, 249)

The developments which Russell emphasizes here again show the significance of polyadic quantification theory for mathematics. Although the crucial definitions precede the development of modern

('Newton, Leibniz and the Leibnizian Tradition', in I. Grattan-Guinness (ed.), *From the Calculus to Set-Theory, 1630–1910* (London: Duckworth, 1980), p. 58, emphasis in the original). For some qualifications to this view, see Morris Kline, *Mathematical Thought from Ancient to Modern Times* (Oxford: OUP, 1972), Ch. 17, s. 2.

[21] The use of infinitesimals was widely attacked by philosophers and mathematicians. Hegel, for example, found the notion of an infinitesimal to be contradictory (see S. II, Ch. 2, s. C of *Hegel's Science of Logic*). It has been argued that the work of Abraham Robinson on non-standard analysis has provided a coherent understanding of this notion. See *Non-Standard Analysis* (Amsterdam: North-Holland, 1966).

[22] As Friedman puts it: 'A curve generated by continuous motion (drawn by the continuous motion of a pencil, as it were) automatically has a tangent or direction of motion at each point. So the class of continuous curves is assimilated to the class of what we now call *smooth* (differentiable) curves' (op. cit. n. 17 above, p. 30).

[23] See Kline, op. cit. n. 20 above, Ch. 40; the point is emphasized by Russell in *Principles*, 305.

logic, they make essential use of the sort of quantifier dependence which was logically intractable without that logic. Thus we can define the concept of *continuity* by saying that a function, f(x), is continuous at a point, x_0, if and only if the absolute value, $|f(x) - f(x)_0|$ (i.e. the difference between f(x) and $f(x_0)$) can be made as small as you like by considering only those values of x which are sufficiently close to x_0. This is more perspicuous if put in quantifier notation:

$$(\varepsilon)(\exists\delta)(x)[|x - x_0| < \delta \supset |f(x) - f(x_0)| < \varepsilon]$$

This represents a great advance over definitions of the eighteenth and early nineteenth centuries. Here there is no use of infinitesimals. Nor is there talk of variables getting closer and closer to a certain value (such talk suggests that variables are numbers whose magnitude changes over time; this is confusing about variables, and also suggests that continuity is an essentially temporal notion). The definition assumes only the real numbers, the simplest statements about them, and logical operations on such statements. Our focus is on the last of these points, and in particular on the crucial role of quantifier dependence. The definition works only because the universal quantifier '(ε)' precedes the existential quantifier '$(\exists\delta)$'. (Note that if we reverse the order of quantifiers we obtain a criterion which no function satisfies. The only way to avoid this consequence is to say that the quantifier '$(\exists\delta)$' ranges over numbers which are smaller than any real number—i.e. over infinitesimals.) A second example is that of the *limit* of an infinite series, which emerged as a fundamental concept of calculus (as Russell emphasizes: *Principles*, 262). Suppose we have a function whose value for each natural number, n, is a non-negative real number, a_n. For each natural number, n, let S_n be $a_1 + a_2 + \ldots + a_n$. Then we give a definition of the claim that the infinite series, $a_1 + a_2 + \ldots$ converges to a limit by using what is now known as the Cauchy convergence criterion: a series 'converges to a limit if and only if $S_{n+r} - S_n$ can be made less in absolute value then any assignable quantity for all r and sufficiently large n'.[24] Again, the point can be put more perspicuously in quantifier notation. The series converges if and only if for every real number, k, there is a natural number, n, such that for every natural number, r, $|S_{n+r} - S_n| < k$, i.e.

$$(k)(\exists n)(r)(|S_{n+r} - S_n| < k)$$

(Here I have assumed that k ranges over real numbers, while n and r range over natural numbers; clearly these assumptions can be made explicit, by taking them as antecedents in a conditional.) Here again, polyadic quantification theory is required, for quantifier dependence is

---

[24] Kline, op. cit. n. 20 above, p. 963.

crucial: if we invert the order of the first two quantifiers we obtain a criterion which will not in general be satisfied by convergent infinite series.

The discussion of the last few pages indicates why Russell puts so much emphasis on logic, and on the rigorization of the calculus in the nineteenth century. These developments suggest, at least, that some of Kant's reasons for thinking that mathematics depends on the intuition of space and time are incorrect. To show this, however, is not yet to show that mathematics is independent of space and time; to make out this latter point Russell argues that mathematics is wholly reducible to logic. In this argument Russell is again indebted to the work of earlier mathematicians. Cauchy, Dedekind, and Cantor showed that the real numbers could be understood in terms of the rational numbers, and that the rationals could in turn be understood in terms of the integers. In each case, set-theoretic ideas were presupposed; Cantor had articulated these ideas explicitly, laying the basis for modern set-theory.[25] Russell was, as we shall see, critical of some details of this work, but he accepted it in a modified form. The two obvious tasks necessary to turn this work into a reduction of (large portions of) mathematics to logic are thus, first, the reduction of the integers themselves to logic and something analogous to set-theory; second, the argument that the analogue of set-theory either is part of logic or can be reduced to logic. Russell acknowledges that the second of these tasks is not satisfactorily carried out in *Principles*. Russell did not, when he published the book, have what he took to be a satisfactory solution to the paradox which he had discovered in May 1901. We shall discuss Russell's notion of a class, and some of the difficulties attending it, later; for the moment I put these issues on one side. *Principles* does, however, indicate how the first of the two tasks can be carried out, i.e. how the theory of integers can be reduced to logic (understood as including the theory of classes). A brief discussion of this reduction will give us at least the flavour of Russell's technical work.

Russell begins the reduction of the theory of finite integers by reflecting philosophically upon the nature of such a reduction. He distinguishes the mathematical from the philosophical sense of definition. The latter is 'the analysis of an idea into its constituents' (*Principles*, 108), but for the former we need only give necessary and sufficient conditions for an entity to fall under the concept with which we are

[25] There is, of course, a complex history here which I am passing over; see Kline, op. cit. n. 20 above, Ch. 41. I speak of *understanding* one kind of number in terms of another because it is not clear that all—or any—of the authors that I have mentioned thought of themselves as giving a *reduction* of (say) the real numbers, as opposed to a justification for introducing them.

concerned. It is, Russell insists, only the mathematical sense of definition which will be relevant in what follows. (The contrast between the two senses of definition raises issues to which we shall return; see pp. 233–6, below.) Russell next claims that numbers are 'applicable essentially to classes' (*Principles*, 109). He then shows that we can define the idea of two classes having the same number (or being *similar*) using only concepts of logic. In particular, we use the logic of relations, which Russell had developed. Two classes are similar just in case one is the domain, and the other the converse domain, of a one–one relation. A relation, R, is one–one if it fulfils these conditions: for every x there is a y such that xRy, and if xRy and zRy then x and z are identical; if xRy and xRw then y and w are identical. Thus we can define 'A has the same number of members as B' without the use of specifically arithmetical notions (and, as Russell points out somewhat contemptuously, without appeal to the idea that we can count the members of a class). A crucial point, whose significance will emerge when we come to discuss the consistency of the infinite, is that this definition holds equally for finite and for infinite classes.

Having defined the notion of similarity, Russell takes a step which is explicitly critical of Peano. The relation of similarity is what is now called an equivalence relation: because it is reflexive, symmetrical, and transitive it divides classes into groups in which a member of any group is similar to all other members of that group and is not similar to any class which is not a member of that group. These properties of a relation, Russell says, 'are held by Peano and common sense to indicate that when the relation holds between two terms, these two terms have a certain common property, and vice versa. This common property we call their number. This is the definition of number by abstraction' (*Principles*, 109). Russell, however, objects to this procedure of definition by abstraction. The crucial point is that the procedure assures neither the existence nor the uniqueness of what it is supposed to define. The classes similar to a given class may have many things in common, and definition by abstraction fails to single out one of them as *the* number of the given class: 'every class will have many numbers, and the definition wholly fails to define *the* number of a class' (*Principles*, 110). Russell's solution is simple: he identifies the number of a given class with the class of all classes similar to it. (Like Russell's objection to definition by abstraction, this technique is perfectly general.) Although he has some doubts about its philosophical correctness, Russell claims that this definition is perfectly adequate for all mathematical purposes: 'Mathematically, a number is nothing but a class of similar classes: this definition allows the deduction of all the usual properties of numbers, whether finite or infinite' (*Principles*, 111). This latter statement, that all of the usual properties of numbers can be deduced from this definition, is one that Russell begins to justify in the following chapter (XII), where he defines addition, multiplication, and exponentiation for numbers as defined in the previous chapter. I shall not expound these definitions.

Everything that Russell has said, to this point, about cardinal numbers applies equally to finite and to infinite numbers. He therefore proceeds to show how the two can be distinguished, offering two definitions which he claims are equivalent.[26] The first is that if a class is infinite, then it is similar to a class containing all but one of the members of the original class (and nothing which was not a member of the original class). In other words, taking away one member of an infinite class leaves you with a class which is similar to the one you started with. This is not true of finite classes. The other definition is based on the fact that the finite integers are the ones which can be obtained from zero by successive applications of the 'add one' operation—this operation having been defined in logical terms (using this definition of finite integers, it follows immediately that mathematical induction holds of them).

All of this puts Russell in a position to define the fundamental concepts of arithmetic. The definition of 'finite integer' is that indicated in the previous three paragraphs:[27] '0' is defined as the class containing only the null class: 'successor of' is defined as follows: if n is the number of a class a, and b is an object which is not a member of a, then the successor of n is the number which is the number of the class which contains all the members of a and also contains b, and contains nothing else. These three concepts, finite integer, zero, and successor, are the ones that Peano had taken as indefinable in laying down axioms for arithmetic (these axioms are still known as 'Peano's Postulates', but were first formulated by Dedekind). Russell concludes his discussion by showing that his definitions enable one to prove Peano's axioms; this proves the adequacy of the definitions.[28]

The discussion of the last few pages, though simplified, gives us an indication of how Russell is able to reduce the theory of finite integers to logic. In carrying out the reduction of other branches of mathematics

---

[26] In fact the two definitions can only be proved to be equivalent if one assumes the axiom of choice—as Russell himself points out in the Introduction to the 2nd edn. of *Principles* (pp. viii–ix).

[27] The exposition is importantly simplified at this point. In particular, to define the finite integers as zero and the objects which can be attained from zero by successive applications of the successor function requires a definition of the ancestral of the successor relation.

[28] Assuming, of course, the adequacy of Peano's Postulates.

to logic, he relies upon the reducibility of arithmetic and upon earlier mathematical work. Rational numbers are defined as ratios of finite integers, i.e. particular one–one relations between finite integers (*Principles*, 144–5). Russell then defines real numbers as certain sorts of classes of rationals. The hard work is then to show that real numbers, as thus defined, will indeed play the roles that are required of them, especially in the calculus. I have said that in defining the real numbers Russell both draws on and criticizes the work of his predecessors, especially Weierstrass, Cantor, and Dedekind. I shall not discuss the details of his criticisms of their views, and his consequent modifications. One recurrent criticism, however, is significant from our point of view. In the case of all three, Russell argues that they put forward definitions of the real numbers but do not prove that these definitions apply to anything. The requisite existence proofs are lacking, and Russell insists that they are necessary (*Principles*, 267–9).[29] (Note that 'existence' here cannot be existence in the sense of our earlier discussion, in which it was distinguished from being, p. 172, above. See pp. 211–12, below, for Russell's account of the sense of existence which *is* relevant here.)

Russell's emphasis on existence proofs is noteworthy in part because it might seem to be in conflict with one of his general claims about the nature of mathematics. Chapter I of *Principles* begins with the following claim:

Pure Mathematics is the class of all propositions of the form 'p implies q', where p and q are propositions containing one or more variables, the same in the two propositions, and neither p nor q contains any constants except logical constants.

This claim suggests a view of mathematics according to which it would be unnecessary for the mathematician to prove, for example, that there are real numbers. The supposition that there are such numbers would, according to this view, be the antecedent of the conditional, and the theorem about the real numbers would be the consequent. Definitions of the real numbers, on this view, would still be needed (for the implication is to contain only logical constants), but existence proofs would not be. We thus have at least a prima-facie conflict between Russell's general claim about mathematics and his actual practice. The resolution of this conflict, I think, is that Russell's general claim misrepresents his own considered view; the mistake is caused by the fact that when he makes the claim he is thinking about geometry and

---

[29] Cantor, unlike Dedekind and Weierstrass, does put forward an existence proof; but Russell claims that it is fallacious.

taking it as a model for mathematics as a whole. (This is exactly what Russell himself says about the matter in the Introduction to the second edition of *Principles*, written in 1937. See p. vii.) Russell's view that geometry is to be thought of as made up of hypothetical statements is in opposition to the idea that the subject tells us something about the nature of actual existing space. Thus a paradigm geometrical statement would be *not* 'The angles of triangle add up to 180°' but rather 'If space is Euclidean, then the angles of a triangle add up to 180°'. What is explicitly hypothesized (and therefore need not be proved or assumed) is existence in the temporal or spatio-temporal sense, not existence in the mathematical sense. The statements of geometry, if presented categorically, may look like statements about actual existing space; presenting them hypothetically makes it clear that they are not. Statements of other branches of mathematics are not likely to present this misleading appearance, and so do not need to be hypothetical.

The considerations of the previous paragraph indicate an important point. The independence of mathematics from space, time, and motion makes possible a quite general distinction, which requires particular emphasis in the case of geometry: the distinction of pure mathematics from applied mathematics. As long as geometry, or the calculus, was held to be dependent upon our knowledge of space or of motion it could not be presented as a wholly abstract subject, without reference to the spatio-temporal.[30] Given Russell's claim of the independence of mathematics from intuition, however, the way is open to make the distinction. In the case of geometry, in particular, this distinction is of great historical importance.[31] Geometry comes to be considered in two separate ways, as a branch of mathematics or as an empirical science. As a branch of mathematics geometry has nothing to do with the space of the actual world; it is the study of abstract structures of a certain kind. As an empirical science, geometry investigates the properties of the space of the actual world. In particular, it is concerned to discover which of the various kinds of abstract mathematical structures is that of actual space. Thus in one sense geometry is a priori, and in another it is a source of knowledge about the space of the actual world; in no

[30] Friedman (op. cit. n. 17 above) points out that Kant had *a* distinction between pure and applied geometry, but not our distinction. For Kant, pure geometry is concerned with (actual) space, applied geometry with the behaviour of objects in space (see *Critique of Pure Reason*, B155 n.).

[31] Einstein, speaking of this view of geometry, says, 'without it I should have been unable to formulate the theory of relativity' ('Geometrie und Erfahrung', 1919, translated as 'Geometry and Experience' in *Ideas and Opinions* (London: Souvenir Press, 1973), pp. 232–45). It is not surprising, in view of Einstein's prestige and the importance of relativity theory, that the distinction came to be widely accepted—almost taken for granted—by philosophers of science.

sense is it both.[32] It is of course geometry as a branch of mathematics that is Russell's concern in *Principles*. It is worth pointing out that in making this distinction Russell sides against Kant, and with the Empiricists, on one crucial issue: whether it is possible to have a priori knowledge of the actual (spatio-temporal) world. This fact is important to the understanding of the relationship between *Principles* and twentieth-century versions of Empiricism; it is, however, perfectly consistent with the fact that Russell, in *Principles*, is as strongly opposed to Empiricism as he is to Kantianism.

I began my discussion of Russell's logicism in *Principles* by emphasizing that Russell deployed logicism as an argument against Idealism. Let us now return to this issue, and consider some aspects of Russell's direct responses to idealist charges of the inconsistency of mathematics, and of space and time. I shall discuss three points. First, Russell's discussion of the infinite, in opposition to the idealist claim that this notion is irremediably contradictory. Second, his comments upon, and the philosophical conclusions he draws from, a purported argument of Zeno's—the sort of argument that the Idealists had appealed to in their attempts to show the notions of space, time, and motion to be inconsistent. Third, Russell's response to some arguments of Lotze's against the coherence of the notion of a geometrical point. Lotze's arguments are sufficiently close to those which Russell himself had put forward in *The Foundations of Geometry* to give us a sense of Russell arguing with his earlier self.

I begin, then, with the notion of the infinite. Russell's concern, here, is to show that the notion is consistent, and so mathematics is not vitiated by the use that it makes of it. The idea that mathematics is so vitiated, and is therefore not ultimately true, can be seen quite clearly in Russell's own notes, written in January 1898 under the title 'On the Idea of a Dialectic of the Sciences' (see Chapter 3, Section 2, pp. 99–101, above). It is with the fervour of a recent convert, then, that Russell rejects what he clearly thinks is the orthodox philosophical view:

Almost all mathematical ideas present one great difficulty: the difficulty of infinity. This is usually regarded by philosophers as an antinomy, and as showing that the propositions of mathematics are not metaphysically true. From this received opinion I am compelled to dissent. Although all apparent difficulties ... are ... reducible to the one difficulty of infinite number, yet this difficulty itself appears to be soluble by a correct philosophy of *any*, and to

---

[32] Contrast Russell's position in *The Foundations of Geometry*. There he had called geometry 'an impregnable fortress of the idealists' (p. 1) because it was, as he then thought, both a priori and a source of information about the world.

have been generated very largely by confusions due to the ambiguity in the meaning of the finite integers. (*Principles*, 79)

We shall see what Russell means by 'a correct philosophy of *any*' and why he thinks it is important to our understanding of the infinite. More to the present point is 'the ambiguity in the meaning of the finite integers', to which Russell in fact attributes the view that there are contradictions in the infinite; at this point we see the significance of the fact that Russell's definitions of cardinal number, addition, and multiplication apply equally to finite and infinite numbers, this distinction being subsequent (see pp. 188–9, above). The problem, as Russell sees it, is that previous philosophers who discussed the infinite lacked the mathematical knowledge necessary to know what they were talking about:

Of all philosophers who have inveighed against the infinite, I doubt whether there is one who has known the difference between finite and infinite numbers. The difference is simply this. Finite numbers obey the law of mathematical induction; infinite numbers do not. (*Principles*, 183)

In their ignorance, philosophers have relied upon a principle which Russell calls the 'axiom of finitude'. Though usually employed in some other form, such as the principle that 'every well-defined series of terms must have a last term', this is in fact equivalent to the simple assertion that all numbers are finite. Russell undertakes what he calls 'the analysis' of this principle both to show that it is nothing more than a flat denial of the possibility of infinite numbers, and to show that there is no reason to hold it: the philosopher 'will have to admit that the more precisely his principle is stated, the less obvious it becomes' (*Principles*, 183). An important point of method is that the 'analysis' which is to show this is a process at once philosophical and mathematical; the substantial point is that there is no reason to maintain the axiom of finitude.

One striking feature is Russell's tone throughout these discussions. He writes with a sense of liberation, of exhilaration—now, at last, we are free of our bondage to false ideas. The things responsible for the liberation are always said to be either his own philosophical innovations (the acknowledgement of relations, the theory of denoting) or recent mathematical work. In the case of the infinite, it is Cantor who is singled out:

The mathematical theory of the infinite may almost be said to begin with Cantor. . . . Cantor has established a new branch of Mathematics, in which, by mere correctness of deduction, it is shown that the supposed contradictions of infinity all depend upon extending, to the infinite, results which, while they can be proved concerning finite numbers, are in no sense necessarily true of *all* numbers. (*Principles*, 283)

The second issue I shall consider in this part of the chapter is Russell's discussion of an argument of Zeno's, and the philosophical conclusion that he draws from this discussion. The context is the claim that the understanding of the calculus made available by nineteenth-century mathematics, and Russell's own demonstration that all of this mathematics can be reduced to logic, enables us to give consistent theories of space, time, and motion. (In spite of the class paradox, Russell assumes that reduction to logic ensures truth.) This claim is perfectly general, but Russell specifically considers the mathematical forms of Zeno's paradoxes (in Chapters XLII and XLIII) and of the first and second of Kant's Antinomies (in Chapter LII; the first and fourth Antinomies rely upon causality, and so do not have purely mathematical forms). It is Russell's attitude towards Zeno that I wish to call attention to:

In this capricious world, nothing is more capricious than posthumous fame. One of the most notable victims of posterity's lack of judgment is the Eleatic Zeno. Having invented four arguments, all immeasurably subtle and profound, the grossness of subsequent philosophers pronounced him to be a mere ingenious juggler, and his arguments one and all sophisms. After two thousand years of continual refutation, these sophisms were reinstated, and made the foundation of a mathematical renaissance, by a German professor.... Weierstrass, by strictly banishing all infinitesimals, has at last shown that we live in an unchanging world, and that the arrow, at every moment of its flight is truly at rest. The only point where Zeno probably erred was in inferring ... that, because there is no change, therefore the world must be in the same state at one time as at another. This consequence by no means follows. (*Principles*, 327)

What is striking here is Russell's immediate leap from Weierstrass's mathematics to the metaphysics of change. We have already seen, in our discussion of Moore, that Platonic Atomism implies an atemporal, and therefore static, way of thinking of the world. Russell, however, claims that this way of thinking is forced on us by modern mathematics, at least if we wish to employ this subject to give us a consistent theory of motion.

Because Russell does not, of course, think that the world is in the same state at all times, he puts forward what he calls 'a theory of change which may be called *static*' (*Principles*, 332; Russell refers us to Part VII of the book for this theory). His statements of this theory are so vivid and striking that I shall simply quote two passages without comment:

Change is the difference, in respect of truth or falsehood, between a proposition concerning an entity and a time T and a proposition concerning the same entity and another time T', provided that the two propositions differ only the by the fact that T occurs in the one where T' occurs in the other. (*Principles*, 443)

It has been supposed that a thing could, in some way, be different and yet the same: that though predicates define a thing, yet it may have different predicates at different times. Hence the distinction of the essential from the accidental, and a number of other useless distinctions.... Change, in this metaphysical sense, I do not at all admit. The so-called predicates of a thing are mostly derived from relations to other terms; change is due, ultimately, to the fact that many terms have relations to some parts of time which they do not have to others. But every term is eternal, timeless and immutable; the relations it may have to parts of time are equally immutable. (*Principles*, 443)

The third and final issue of this part of the chapter is one which is interesting because of its relation to Russell's earlier, idealist, work. According to Russell's *Foundations of Geometry*, the concept of space is contradictory, because of what he there calls the 'relativity' of space (see Chapter 3, Section 1, p. 83, above). Russell in *Principles* does not explicitly consider his earlier views, but he does discuss a closely related position. He considers various arguments advanced by Lotze against the possibility of a space composed of points, and two of these arguments are sufficiently like Russell's own earlier views to make them of considerable interest to us. These arguments, the third and fourth on Russell's list, are:

(3) All points are exactly alike, yet every pair have a relation peculiar to themselves; but being exactly like every other pair, the relation should be the same for all pairs....
(4) The being of every point must consist in the fact that it distinguishes itself from every other, and takes up an invariable position relatively to every other. Hence the being of space consists in an active mutual conditioning of its various points, which is really an interaction. (*Principles*, 424)

Both of these arguments turn on the claim, emphasized in *The Foundations of Geometry*, that one point is intrinsically just like any other—or at least that some account must be given of their distinctness. Russell in *Principles* denies this claim, supporting his denial with fundamental tenets of Platonic Atomism:

This argument [i.e. Lotze's third] will be found to depend again upon the subject-predicate logic.... To be exactly alike can only mean—as in Leibniz's Identity of Indiscernibles—not to have different predicates. But when once it is recognized that there is no essential difference between subjects and predicates, it is seen that any two simple terms simply differ immediately—they are two, and this is the sum-total of their differences. (*Principles*, 428)

Russell argues, further, that even if there were an 'ultimate distinction' between subject and predicate, still difference as to predicates could not be the ground of the distinction of two subjects, for 'before two subjects can differ as to predicates, they must already be two' (*Principles*, 428; we have seen Russell make this same point in a different context; see Chapter 4, Section 2, pp. 157–8). Two points of space, for Russell, differ simply because they differ; like any two items, each is what it is and is distinct from the other. This fact cannot be, and does not need to be, grounded in any other. The opposite view, he holds, is 'a psychological illusion'. We cannot distinguish one spatial point from another, but this is simply a fact about us, and shows nothing about the nature of space:

though we are perpetually moving, and thus being brought among new points, we are quite unable to detect this fact by our senses, and we recognize places only by the objects that they contain. But this seems to be a mere blindness on our part. (*Principles*, 428)

Lotze's fourth argument is disposed of in much the same way. It contains, Russell says, 'what may be called the ratiocinator's fallacy, which consists in supposing that everything has to be explained by showing that it is something else'. In opposition to this Russell claims: 'So far from being explained by something else, the being of a point is presupposed in all other propositions about it, as e.g., in the proposition that the point differs from other points' (*Principles*, 429). In arguing against Lotze—and, implicitly, against the author of *The Foundations of Geometry*—Russell thus relies upon the fundamental metaphysics of Platonic Atomism. What is most interesting from our point of view is that both this metaphysics and the technical results of logicism and of the arithmetization of the calculus are invoked in Russell's argument that there is a consistent mathematical theory of space, time, and motion. The two sorts of consideration, in his view, are complementary, and both are required for the result.

So far I have discussed Russell's logicism, but have not explicitly raised the issue of his conception of logic. This is an important issue. Russell's conception of logic is very different from the model-theoretic conception, which is central to the modern view of the subject. Much that he says can be understood only in the light of these differences. His conception of logic is also, as we shall see in some detail, closely connected with the anti-idealist significance which he attributed to logicism.

I begin with some largely negative points concerning the status of logic. Russell takes logic to be synthetic a priori, and (it seems) to be necessary, but neither of these notions is, in his hands, of any real philosophical significance. Let us take first the claim that logic is synthetic a priori. Russell does not discuss the distinction between the analytic and the synthetic in *Principles*; he refers the reader to section 11 of *Leibniz*, which we considered above (Chapter 4, pp. 160–1; cf. also Chapter 4, pp. 150–2 for Moore's views on the same topic). As we saw there, Russell holds that no truths, except possibly those of the form 'A is A', are analytic. Logic is thus not analytic, so it must be synthetic.[33] The notion of the a priori also seems to have a negative and non-explanatory function for Russell: it is simply the denial of the relevance of ordinary sense-perception. Calling logic synthetic a priori thus has, and is intended to have, no explanatory force for Russell. He offers no discussion at all of what synthetic a priori knowledge is, and how it is possible. Logic is synthetic because everything is, and it is a priori because its truths are perceived with the eye of the mind rather than with the eyes of the body—this is all, from a Russellian standpoint, that can be said about the matter. The idea that the truths of logic are necessary is also one which, in *Principles*, carries little significance and no explanatory power. As in *Leibniz* (see Chapter 4, pp. 161–2, above), Russell says that every true proposition is necessary, and that the notion of necessity is more or less trivial:

Everything is in a sense a mere fact. A proposition is said to be proved when it is deduced from premisses; but the premisses, ultimately, and the rules of inference, have to be simply assumed. Thus any ultimate premiss is, in a certain sense, a mere fact. On the other hand, there seems to be no true proposition of which it makes sense to say that it might have been false. One might as well say that redness might have been a taste and not a colour. What

---

[33] This makes it clear that the motivation of Russell's logicism is very different from that of the Logical Positivists—although both Russell and the Positivists draw an anti-Kantian moral from logicism. The latter sought to defend Empiricism by showing that mathematics, which is not easily accounted for along empiricist lines, is analytic and therefore (by their lights) empty of content and therefore not a genuine branch of knowledge which needs to be accounted for. Russell's use of logicism against Kant and the Idealists, by contrast, presupposes that mathematics *is* a genuine branch of knowledge. Only thus can mathematics be a counter-example to Kantian claims about the necessary limits of human knowledge (see pp. 179–80, above).

  At the deepest level, it might be said, the Logical Positivists and Kant have more in common with each other than either does with Russell. In particular, they share an interest in knowledge, and a conception of what it is to account for it, which is not to be found in Russell's work of the period discussed in this chapter. This is why Russell can accept that some truths are synthetic a priori without feeling any need to go on and discuss the possibility of truths with this status. For some further discussion of this issue, see the present author's 'Logic in Russell's Logicism', in David Bell and Neil Cooper (eds.), *Meaning, Thought and Knowledge* (Oxford: Blackwell, forthcoming).

is true is true; what is false is false; and concerning fundamentals, there is nothing more to be said. (*Principles*, 430)

Immediately after this passage Russell suggests a more useful meaning for the word 'necessary', derived from Moore's article of 1900 (discussed in Chapter 4, pp. 147–8, above). This is that 'A proposition is more or less necessary according as the class of propositions for which it is a premiss is greater or smaller'. As I said about the corresponding view of Moore's, however, this theory depends upon a prior understanding of what it is for one proposition to be a premiss for another, i.e. for the second to follow from the first; it depends, therefore, on a prior understanding of the nature of logic, and certainly can play no role in an explanation of logic—and Russell does not attempt to use it in this way.

Russell takes the logical truths to be those truths which contain only variables and logical constants (see *Principles*, 12).[34] We can therefore raise the question of the status of logic as a question about the logical constants. What is it that characterizes the logical constants, and makes them different from any entities which are not logical constants? Clearly Russell thinks that the propositions of logic have a special status not enjoyed by, say, propositions about colours. The two sorts of propositions differ in that the former contain colours (colour-constants, so to speak) while the latter contain only logical constants. What is the difference between colour-constants and logical constants, such that propositions containing only the latter have a special status, while propositions which also contain the former do not have that status? What is special about logical constants? This is a question which Russell would have to answer in order to give an account of logic.[35] Here again, however, what Russell says is largely negative in character. He has no answer to the question; indeed, he suggests an argument for the claim that no answer is possible. What he says is this:

---

[34] It is important to note that Russell does not think of variables as linguistic. A failure to appreciate this point is, I think, responsible for the common view that Russell is often unclear as to whether he means to be talking about linguistic or non-linguistic items. Thus Russell commonly speaks of variables as occurring in propositional functions. If one assumes variables to be linguistic, it is reasonable to infer that propositional functions are also linguistic; in other contexts, however, they appear as non-linguistic. Hence the idea that Russell is confused or ambiguous about the status of propositional functions. (See especially Quine's introduction to Russell's 'Mathematical Logic as Based on the Theory of Types', in van Heijenoort, pp. 150–2.) We shall return to these issues, both later in this chapter and in Ch. 7.

[35] Wittgenstein avoids, rather than answers, this question in his account of logic in the *Tractatus* by denying that logical constants (in the linguistic sense) refer to anything (i.e. denying that there are logical constants in Russell's non-linguistic sense). For Wittgenstein there is no special kind of objects, the logical constants. He calls this denial his 'fundamental thought'—*Tractatus*, 4.0312.

The logical constants themselves are to be defined only by enumeration, for they are so fundamental that all the properties by which the class of them might be defined presuppose some term of the class. But practically, the method of discovering the logical constants is the analysis of symbolic logic. (*Principles*, 10)

Now one might think that this argument could be used to give a sort of quasi-definition of the logical constants, that we could pick them out precisely by this feature, that they are 'so fundamental that all the properties by which . . .' and so on. But this will not do. For one thing, a simple term such as *yellow* is, on Russell's account, indefinable, so that it could presumably be said of this term too that the properties by which the (one-member) class containing it might be defined presupposes the member of that class. To say that something is definable only in terms of itself, after all, is just a long way of saying that it is indefinable. A second problem is that what Russell says applies to the *class* of logical constants: that any definition of the class presupposes some member of it. But how is this class to be picked out? The question demands an answer, for it will presumably be true that if we add some arbitrary object, say *a*, to the class of logical constants, still the properties by which the resultant class might be defined will presuppose some member of that class (even if it is never *a* which is presupposed). Thus what Russell says will not play the role of a (quasi) definition of logical constant; it applies to things other than logical constants, and it requires that we already have a way of picking out the logical constants. His statement must therefore be taken simply as the claim that the notion of logical constant cannot be defined, and that therefore no account of the nature of logic is possible. This position is one that Russell holds consistently in *Principles*—he does not attempt such an account (nor does he argue against the possibility of an account except in the sentence I have quoted). Given the central role of logicism in *Principles* this fact may seem surprising. It is important to note, however, that Russell's use of logicism in the argument against Idealism does not require that he have any account of how the logical constants differ from other entities. For this purpose all that is necessary is that the logical constants be independent of spatio-temporal notions; Russell, I think, takes this fact to be evident.[36]

The question of the special character of the logical constants (now in the linguistic sense) became a focal point of the debate between Carnap and Quine over the status of logical truth; Quine challenged Carnap to produce a general, i.e. language-independent, definition of 'logical constant'. See esp. Quine's 'Carnap and Logical Truth', in *The Philosophy of Rudolf Carnap*, ed. P. A. Schilpp (LaSalle, Ill.: Open Court, 1963).

[36] It is, after all, not only propositions about the spatio-temporal which stand in logical relations to one another. This feature is, rather, wholly independent of the subject-matter of the propositions: hence the generality of logic.

The philosophical use that Russell makes of logicism is a guide to the way in which he thought of logic. To play the philosophical role that Russell uses it for, logic must above all be *true*. Its truth must be absolute, unconditioned, and unrestricted (in particular, it must be independent of space and time). These features may appear to be uncontroversial, but in fact they mark a crucial difference between Russell's conception of logic and the model-theoretic conception, which is an element, at least, in any modern view of the subject. Logic, for Russell, was a universal language, a *Lingua characteristica*, not a mere calculus which can be thought of as set up within a more inclusive language.[37] He thus conceives of logic as universal and all-inclusive. I shall explain both this conception of logic and its connection with Russell's use of logicism against the Idealists.

The idea of logic as made up of truths already marks a difference between Russell's conception and the modern one. The modern logician sees logic as made up of a formal system which contains schemata which are subject to interpretations, where each schema has a truth-value in each interpretation. The crucial notion is thus *truth in all interpretations* or validity. For Russell, by contrast, the crucial notion is simply truth. Logic on his conception does not consist of schemata whose truth-values wait upon the specification of an interpretation; it consists of propositions which have a content and a truth-value on their own account.[38] In particular, logic consists of those true propositions which contain only logical constants and variables; the variables, as we shall see, must be unrestricted, i.e. range over everything.[39]

Note too that Kant also thought of logic as not confined to the spatio-temporal. As Charles Parsons points out, the applicability of logic to things-in-themselves is implicit in Kant's view that we can *think* of things-in-themselves (see 'Kant's Philosophy of Arithmetic', repr. in *Mathematics in Philosophy*, op. cit. n. 17 above, pp. 115–19). For Kant, however, logic is analytic, so not genuine knowledge, so not a counter-example to the view (discussed above, pp. 179–81) that all knowledge is confined to possible objects of intuition.

[37] For discussions of this conception of logic, see J. van Heijenoort, 'Logic as Language and Logic as Calculus', *Synthese*, 17 (1967), 324–30; and W. D. Goldfarb, 'Logic in the Twenties: The Nature of the Quantifier', *Journal of Symbolic Logic*, 44: 3 (Sept. 1979), 351–68.

[38] A similar view is advanced by Frege, when he insists that his logic *expresses a content*. See esp. 'On the Aim of the "Conceptual Notation"' (trans. in T. W. Bynum (ed.), *Conceptual Notation and Related Articles* (Oxford: OUP, 1972)): 'my aim was different from Boole's. I did not wish to present an abstract logic in formulas, but to express a content through written symbols'. To say that a statement of logic expresses a content is presumably also to say that it is true or false on its own account, without the need for an interpretation.

[39] A consequence of this is that if, for some number n, there are exactly n entities, then it is a truth *of logic* that there are exactly n entities. (We can say that there are exactly n entities using only variables and logical constants, provided that identity either is a logical constant or can be expressed somehow. Where n is not finite, 'logic' must be

The notion of an interpretation, and the correlative idea of an un-interpreted formalism, are wholly alien to Russell's thought at this period. He simply never mentions such ideas; the conception of logic as universal is not something that Russell articulates and defends, but something that he seems to take entirely for granted. He does, how-ever, defend one feature of his conception. On Russell's conception of logic, as I have already said, there is no question of our specifying what the variables are to range over; they range over everything. It is thus a part of his conception that there is no room for the specification of a universe of discourse. (We might say that the only universe of discourse, on Russell's conception of logic, is *the* universe, the actual universe, comprising everything that there is. To say this, however, is to reject the notion of a universe of discourse within which the range of the variables is confined.) Thus the propositions of logic are wholly general: they contain variables, and the variables range over every-thing. Russell's argument against the idea of (restricted) universes of discourse is revealing, and I shall examine it at some length.

The basic argument is one that Russell makes not only in *Principles* but also in a number of other works in the period leading up to *Principia Mathematica*.[40] In *Principles* he puts it like this:

It is customary in mathematics to regard our variables as restricted to certain classes: in Arithmetic, for instance, they are supposed to stand for numbers. But this only means that *if* they stand for numbers they satisfy some formula, i.e., the hypothesis that they stand for numbers implies the formula. This, then, is what is really essential, and in this proposition it is no longer necessary that our variables should be numbers: the implication holds equally when they are not so.... Thus in every proposition of pure mathematics, when fully stated, the variables have an absolutely unrestricted field. (*Principles*, 7)

The point of this argument is that if we are to have a restricted uni-verse of discourse (i.e. something other than simply *the* universe) then we must establish this universe of discourse by means of a statement which says what the variable is to range over. But in *that* statement there is no reason to suppose that we are using a restricted universe of discourse. Nor, indeed, can we be doing so unless there is yet another

higher-order, but, as we shall see, Russell presupposes this.) In *Principles* Russell seems to accept this consequence; he offers a 'formal proof' that there are infinite classes (s. 339; see also s. 474). In his later work, however, the theory of types blocks this result; see Ch. 7, below, pp. 318–19.

[40] See e.g. 'Mathematical Logic as Based on the Theory of Types', repr. in Marsh, p. 71; 'On "Insolubilia" and their Solution by Symbolic Logic', repr. in Lackey, p. 206, and *Principles*, s. 7.

It is arguable that Russell's theory of denoting in *Principles* (see pp. 206–12, below) renders the argument less cogent in the context of *Principles* than it is in the context of his later (post-1905) views. I shall not discuss this point here, however.

statement in which the restrictions on the first statement are made explicit; and then, of course, exactly the same point will apply to the second statement. Thus it is, on this view, possible to use restricted variables, but the use of such variables presupposes the use of unrestricted variables, which simply range over everything that there is. Thus we can conclude that it is the unrestricted variable which is fundamental. We can also conclude that only propositions using such variables should be thought of as propositions of logic, at least by Russell's standards of what is to count as logic. A proposition which uses a restricted variable is made within the context of some other statement which establishes the universe of discourse. Its meaning, and its truth if it is true, are thus conditional upon that other statement. To say this, however, is to say that it is not unconditionally true. By Russell's standards it thus has no right to be thought of as a proposition of logic; such propositions must be unconditionally true, and this in turn requires that they contain all their conditions within themselves.

This argument of Russell's takes it for granted that the statement which establishes the universe of discourse is on the same level as the assertion which is made once the universe of discourse is established. Thus the former can be taken as antecedent and the latter as consequent in a single conditional statement. Russell, that is, assumes that all statements are on the same level; this contrasts with the view of the modern logician that we must distinguish some as object language statements and some as meta-language statements. Intrinsic to Russell's conception of the universality of logic is the denial of the meta-linguistic perspective which is essential to the modern conception of logic. This makes a crucial difference to the way in which one thinks of logic. Consider, for example, the question of the completeness of a system of logic, which is so natural for us. This question relies upon the idea that we have, independently of the logical system, a criterion of what the system ought to be able to do, so it relies upon the essentially meta-theoretic notion of an interpretation, and of truth in all interpretations. These meta-theoretic ideas, however, are foreign to Russell's conception of logic; the question of the completeness of a system simply could not arise for him. Logic for him was not a system, or a formalism, which might or might not capture what we take to be the logically valid body of schemata; logic for him was, rather, the body of wholly general truths. Another illustration of Russell's conception of logic is to be found in his discussion of the independence of the truth-functional axioms. He denies that we prove the independence of one of these axioms by finding an interpretation for the negation of the given axiom together with the other axioms. The point is that if we deny such an axiom, reasoning itself becomes impossible:

it should be observed that the method of supposing an axiom false, and deducing the consequences of this assumption, which has been found admirable in such cases as the axiom of parallels, is here not universally available. For all our axioms are principles of deduction; and if they are true, the consequences which appear to follow from the employment of an opposite principle will not really follow, so that arguments from the supposition of the falsity of an axiom are here subject to special fallacies. (*Principles*, 17)

The fact that Russell does not see logic as something on which one can take a meta-theoretical perspective thus constitutes a crucial difference between his conception of logic and the model-theoretic conception. Logic, for Russell, is a systematization of reasoning in general, of reasoning as such. If we have a correct systematization, it will comprehend all correct principles of reasoning. Given such a conception of logic there can be no external perspective. *Any* reasoning will, simply in virtue of being reasoning, fall within logic; any proposition that we might wish to advance is subject to the rules of logic. This is perhaps a natural, if naïve, way of thinking about logic. In Russell's case, however, we can say more than this to explain why he should have held such a conception. Given the philosophical use that Russell wishes to make of logicism, no other conception is available to him. If logic is to be unconditionally and unrestrictedly true, in the sense that Russell must require it to be, then it must be universally applicable. This in turn implies that statements about logic must themselves fall within the scope of logic, so the notion of a meta-theoretical perspective falls away. If this were not so, if logic were thought of as set up within a more inclusive meta-language, then by the standards which Russell and the Idealists share, it would appear that logic is not absolutely and unconditionally true. Logic, on this modern picture, is not unrestricted, for it is set up in a more inclusive language which must fall outside its scope. Nor can the truth of logic, thought of in this way, be thought of as absolute and unconditioned, for it is dependent upon the meta-language within which it is set up. There is no reason to believe that Russell ever considered anything like the modern conception of logic—at least as a conception of *Logic*—but if he had done so, the use he wishes to make of logicism would have given him reason to reject it in favour of the conception of logic as universal. The universality of logic is a consequence of the idea that logic is, by Russell's standards, absolutely true.

The conception of logic as universal can, I think, be usefully compared with certain idealist lines of thought. We saw above that McTaggart argues against the Kantian distinction of noumena from phenomena in the following way: to say that there is something—the noumenal—to which our categories of thought do not apply is presumably to make a judgement in which our categories of thought *are* applied to the noumenal (see pp. 93–4, above). A judgement of this sort is thus self-defeating: if it were true it could not be made; the fact that it is made shows that it cannot be true.[41] Put like this, McTaggart's argument bears a striking resemblance to the argument which we saw Russell use against the idea that some things cannot be logical subjects of propositions (see pp. 174–7, above). One can also put the point like this: if what the philosopher says about knowledge or judgement is to be of real philosophical interest then it must apply to all knowledge, or all judgement—including the knowledge which the philosopher claims to have, or the judgements he makes. The generality of the subject gives it a certain reflexive character; we cannot philosophize as if we occupied a position to which what we say does not apply. The relevance of this to Russell's conception of logic is that one could equally argue that if logic is to be of philosophical significance it too must have this reflexive character, and so must apply to what we should call its meta-theory. Russell seems to take for granted this conception of logic; his familiarity with idealist arguments against Kant may explain why he does so.

Earlier in the discussion of the universality of logic I emphasized the idea that the variables of logic are unrestricted.[42] We can now see how seriously Russell takes this idea. Unrestricted variables, for Russell, range over absolutely all entities—tables, numbers, spatial points, propositions, classes, propositional functions, and so on. Any restriction on the variable would have to be stated, but then the truth of the statement using the restricted variable is not absolute, but is dependent on the statement restricting the variable. The absolute truth of logic and mathematics thus demands absolutely unrestricted variables. The passage from section 7 of *Principles* quoted a few pages back continues like this:

in every proposition of pure mathematics, when fully stated, the variables have an unrestricted range: any conceivable entity may be substituted for any one of our variables without impairing the truth of the proposition. (*Principles*, 7)

'Any conceivable entity' here is to be taken in the strongest possible sense. It is for this reason that Russell states his axioms for truth-

---

[41] We saw above that it is by no means clear that Kant is vulnerable to this argument. The argument would also have little force against a philosopher such as Bradley, for whom our knowledge of ultimate reality is not obtained by thought or judgement.

[42] Logic is not unique in this respect; by making any desired restrictions explicit in an antecedent, with the original statement as consequent, it seems that any statement at all could be put in a form where its variables are unrestricted. It is, however, the absolute truth of logic (and mathematics) which Russell is chiefly concerned with, and so it is only in the context of logic that he makes this point.

functional logic in the way that he does, for example: '(5) If p implies p and q implies q, then pq implies p' (*Principles*, 18). The antecedent here is required by the fact that the letters 'p' and 'q' are taken as unrestricted variables, ranging not only over propositions but over everything. For values other than propositions, the antecedent will invariably be false (this is assured by Russell's axiom (2): 'Whatever implies anything is a proposition') and hence the axiom as a whole will be true for those values.

The idea that there is only one sort of variable in logic, and that it is absolutely unrestricted, is reminiscent of the idea that there is only one fundamental ontological category, and that it includes everything (pp. 173–8, above). From our present vantage-point, indeed, we can see that these ideas are not really distinct. The variables of logic range over everything that there is; logic, as Russell conceives it, is not separate from ontology.

The emphasis, in the preceding discussion, on generality brings to the fore a problem which is inherent in the Platonic Atomism account of propositions. I emphasized that propositions, according to that account, contain the things they are about: the proposition that Socrates is wise contains Socrates. The problem is that this account is not directly applicable to general propositions, such as the proposition that all philosophers are wise. One response would be to say that this latter proposition contains Socrates and Thales and Plato and Aristotle . . . This response treats general propositions more or less as if they were singular propositions (or conjunctions or disjunctions of them). The response is perhaps implausible in any case,[43] but Russell's emphasis on logic and mathematics makes it quite unacceptable to him. The propositions of logic and mathematics all contain unrestricted variables—Russell speaks of the variable as '*the* characteristic notion of Mathematics' (*Principles*, 87). If construed in the fashion suggested, each such proposition would thus contain every entity. One objection to this is that a consequence of this construal is that our minds must be able to grasp the infinitely complex. Russell, as we shall see, denies that this is so (*Principles*, 72, quoted pp. 206–7, below). A second objection to the suggested response is that the distinguishing feature of logic (and thus of mathematics too) is lost. What is distinctive about a

---

[43] To say that something holds of a, b, c . . . z is not obviously the same as saying that it holds of everything, even if a, b, c . . . z are all the things which there are. For one thing, the first statement does not *say* that a, b, c . . . z are all the things that there are, and to say this demands just the sort of generality which the first statement avoids, generality which goes beyond a list, even an exhaustive list (Russell himself later put forward a very similar argument for the unavoidability of generality; see 'Lectures on Logical Atomism', Lecture V, p. 236 of Marsh).

proposition of logic, for Russell, is that it contains only logical constants and (unrestricted) variables. On the suggested construal, however, such a proposition contains every entity. This will also be true of
any other proposition which contains an (unrestricted) variable; the
demarcation of logic from what is not logic would no longer work.

Given Russell's purposes, then, it is crucial that he find a genuine
account of generality—i.e. an account which does not simply treat
general propositions as if they were singular propositions. This account
is the theory of denoting. Before discussing this theory it is worth
emphasizing that the issues here are crucial for Russell because they
are directly connected with the central project of reducing mathematics
to logic and, even more generally, of achieving a consistent understanding of the infinite. In the Preface to *Principles* he gives this description of the origin of the book, beginning with his work in the
philosophy of Dynamics: 'I was led', he says, 'to a re-examination of
the principles of Geometry, thence to the philosophy of continuity and
infinity, and thence, with a view to discovering the meaning of the
word *any*, to Symbolic Logic' (p. xvii). And again, he says:

With regard to infinite classes, say the class of numbers, it is to be observed
that the concept *all numbers*, though not itself infinitely complex, yet denotes
an infinitely complex object. This is the inmost secret of our power to deal with
infinity. An infinitely complex concept, though there may be such, certainly
cannot be manipulated by the human intelligence; but infinite collections,
owing to the notion of denoting, can be manipulated without introducing any
concepts of infinite complexity.[44] (*Principles*, 72)

The notion of generality makes it clear that one principle tenet of
Platonic Atomism does not in fact hold without exception. The tenet in
question is that the things which a proposition is *about* are among its
constituents. Denoting is Russell's explanation for—or at least his
name for—the cases in which it does not hold. Let us see how the
explanation works in the case of a proposition expressed using the
phrase 'every term'. Such a proposition does not, for the reasons given
above, contain every term. On Russell's view, what corresponds, in
the proposition, to the phrase 'every term' is a single entity (a denoting
concept, which we may call *'every term'*).[45] But then we must say

---

[44] Note that Russell is certain that we do not grasp infinite concepts or propositions,
yet agnostic as to whether there are such things. This shows his realism very clearly:
what propositions there are is nothing to do with us and what we understand.

[45] It has been argued that *Principles* contains several versions of the theory of denoting, of which this is only one; see Paulo Dau, 'Russell's First Theory of Denoting and
Quantification', *Notre Dame Journal of Formal Logic*, 27 (1986), 133–66. The account that I
have given, however, seems to fit most of what Russell says, and to be more cogent than
the alternatives.

something about the connection of this single entity to the totality of terms. It is, after all, the totality that we wish to talk about. As Russell puts it: 'the proposition "any finite number is odd or even" is plainly true; yet the concept "any finite number" is neither odd nor even' (*Principles*, 56). Russell expresses this sort of relation between the single concept and the totality by saying that the former *denotes* the latter.

Denoting is thus—to speak more generally—Russell's way of acknowledging that there must be exceptions to the rule that the things which a proposition is about are among its constituents. If a term (always a concept) denotes a given entity (or collection of entities) then, when the denoting term occurs in a proposition, the subject-matter of the proposition will be not the denoting term but rather the denoted entity—even though it does not occur in the proposition. As Russell puts it: 'A concept denotes when, if it occurs in a proposition, the proposition is not *about* the concept, but about a term connected in a certain peculiar way with the concept' (*Principles*, 56). This 'peculiar way' in which the concept is connected with the term is that it denotes it. It is worth stressing that the relation of denoting, which one entity may have to another, is not due to us or to our use of words, but is intrinsic to the entities concerned. Here, as throughout *Principles*, psychological considerations of all sorts are ruled out:

The notion of denoting, like most of the notions of logic, has been obscured hitherto by an undue admixture of psychology. There is a sense in which *we* denote, when we point to or describe, or employ words as symbols for concepts; this, however, is not the sense that I wish to discuss. But the fact that description is possible—that we are able, by the employment of concepts to designate a thing which is not a concept—is due to a logical relation between some concepts and some terms, in virtue of which such concepts inherently and logically *denote* such terms. It is this sense of denoting which is here in question. (*Principles*, 56)

Thus the proposition corresponding to the sentence 'The first President of the USA is wise' contains a denoting concept, *The First President of the USA*, which denotes George Washington (strictly speaking, the denoting concept should be specified by reference to a particular moment of time). In virtue of this fact the proposition is *about* Washington, who is not a constituent of the proposition; it is *not* about the denoting concept which it contains (the proposition corresponding to the sentence 'George Washington is wise', by contrast, both contains and is about George Washington; no denoting concept occurs in this proposition). Phrases formed with a predicate and one of the six words 'any', 'a', 'some', 'all', 'every', and 'the' are denoting phrases, i.e. the presence of such a phrase in a sentence indicates that the corresponding proposition contains a denoting concept (see *Principles*, 57 and 58).

I spoke above of a denoting concept denoting 'a given entity (or collection of entities)'; the parenthesis here conceals difficulties which I shall now briefly indicate. The mechanism of denoting may seem unproblematic if we consider a phrase such as 'The first President of the USA'. One term—a denoting concept—denotes another—a human being. But the cases of phrases using 'all', 'any', 'every', and so on are more problematic. In each case it is, roughly speaking, the totality of terms (if it is 'all terms' etc. which we are dealing with) which is relevant. But the phrases function differently in some contexts, so that it cannot be the same thing which is denoted in each case. For any given predicate, each of the five denoting concepts (excluding that indicated by 'the') denotes a different combination of the entities possessing that predicate. The effort to define and distinguish these various combinations, and to work out the consequences for sentences which combine two denoting phrases, leads to some of the most tortuous discussion of the book (see sections 61, 62).[46] As Russell himself puts it, at the end of this discussion:

There is, then, a definite something, different in each of the five cases, which must, in a sense, be an object, but is characterized as a set of terms combined in a certain way, which something is denoted by *all men, every man, any man, a man*, or *some man*; and it is with this very paradoxical object that propositions are concerned in which the corresponding concept is used as denoting. (*Principles*, 62)

What makes these objects 'very paradoxical' is not simply their peculiarity. These objects are essentially plural; each one is not a term but a combination of terms. It is this fact, that these objects are not terms, that causes the paradox: 'I shall use the word *object* in a wider sense than *term*, to cover both singular and plural. . . . The fact that a word can be framed with a wider meaning than *term* raises grave logical problems' (*Principles*, 58 n.).

Even apart from any difficulty in understanding the nature of the denoted objects, the introduction of denoting constitutes a major alteration in the earlier metaphysics of Platonic Atomism. The significance of the change is not remarked in *Principles*, and Russell may not have been aware of it at that time; it is, however, important for our understanding of his later work (see Chapter 6, below). We can approach the issue by noting that the theory of denoting places heavy demands on the notion of *about*: a term is a denoting concept just in case the presence of that term in a proposition results in the proposi-

---

[46] Again see Dau, op. cit. n. 45 above, for an account of some of the complexities which I am ignoring at this point.

tion not being about the term, but rather about some other term (or combination of terms). This notion of aboutness may appear familiar to us, but within the context of earlier Platonic Atomism it is quite novel.

What is it for a proposition to be *about* a given term (or combination of terms)? Two very similar lines of reply suggest themselves. One is that for a proposition to be about (say) Socrates is for the truth of the proposition to depend upon whether Socrates has a certain property, or stands in a certain relation to such-and-such another object. According to the fundamental doctrines of Platonic Atomism, however, Socrates' having a given property simply is a certain proposition's being true. For paradigmatic propositions, those which contain the entities which they are about, speaking of truth dependence is thus quite vacuous: the truth of such a proposition depends solely upon itself. For a proposition containing a denoting concept, however, the point is far from vacuous. A proposition containing, say, the denoting concept *the teacher of Plato* is about Socrates because the truth of the original proposition depends upon the truth of a different proposition, namely one which contains Socrates where the original proposition contains the denoting concept. A more complex version of this idea is needed to handle cases where the denoting concept corresponds to an indefinite, rather than a definite, description. The truth of, say, the proposition expressed by 'All people are mortal', would presumably depend upon the truth of many propositions, or of a combination of propositions, e.g. the conjunction of 'Socrates is mortal' and 'Xantippe is mortal' and 'Plato is mortal', and so on. The upshot of this line of thought is thus that the truth or falsehood of a proposition containing a denoting concept depends upon the truth or falsehood of another proposition (or combination of propositions) which does not contain a denoting concept. (Note that if the truth or falsehood of the first proposition depended upon a proposition which *did* contain a denoting concept, then this proposition would depend for its truth or falsehood upon a third, and so on until at last we found a proposition which conforms to the Platonic Atomism paradigm, and does not contain a denoting concept. Since the 'depends on' relation is presumably transitive, the result follows.) The idea of the truth or falsehood of one proposition depending upon that of another is clearly quite alien to Platonic Atomism. It amounts, indeed, to the introduction of something like the correspondence theory of truth for the special case of those propositions which contain denoting concepts: whether such a proposition is true depends upon whether there is a corresponding fact, where a fact is a true proposition which does not contain a denoting concept, or a combination of such propositions. The propositions (putative facts) which are the corresponding ones are presumably those which are obtained from the original by replacing the denoting concept by the denoted object(s). (Thus the proposition expressed by 'The teacher of Plato is wise' corresponds to that expressed by 'Socrates is wise'. The latter has its truth-value directly, the former has its truth-value by virtue of its correspondence with the latter.)

A second way of making sense of the idea of aboutness may seem, at first sight, to be a less drastic modification of Platonic Atomism. According to this second line of thought, we have to distinguish what a proposition *is*—a certain combination of terms—from what it *says*, or its content. A proposition which contains a denoting concept, *the teacher of Plato*, say, *says* something about Socrates. What the content of a given proposition (i.e. a given combination of terms) is will depend upon facts external to the proposition—facts about what denotes what. The distinction between a proposition and its content is, however, no less alien to Platonic Atomism than is the correspondence theory of truth. It also seems that this second line of thought may in fact imply the first. Given the constraints of Platonic Atomism it seems natural, if not inevitable, to identify the content of a proposition with a proposition. In particular, it seems natural to identify the content of a proposition which contains a denoting concept with the proposition which is obtained when the denoting concept is replaced by the denoted object. But then it follows that the truth-value of the first proposition depends upon that of the second, and so we are back with the consequences of the first line of thought.

I should stress that the sort of considerations advanced in the three previous paragraphs do not occur explicitly in *Principles*. Perhaps the closest that Russell comes to them is in a passage in which he speaks of 'what is asserted' by a proposition, a notion surely very close to that of the content of a proposition. The passage is as follows:

Consider again the proposition 'I met a man.' It is quite certain, and is implied by this proposition, that what I met was an unambiguous perfectly definite man.... But the actual man whom I met forms no part of the proposition in question.... Thus the concrete event which happened is not asserted in the proposition. What is asserted is merely that some one of a class of concrete events took place. The whole human race is involved in my assertion: if any man who ever existed or will exist had not existed or been going to exist, the purport of my proposition would have been different. (*Principles*, 62)

For the most part, however, Russell in *Principles* rests content with the notion of aboutness, without considering the implications of this notion. But, as I have tried to bring out, it seems that any way of thinking about the notion must lead to conclusions which are quite inimical to Platonic Atomism. This fact, if fact it be, will play no further role in our discussion of *Principles*, but we will return to it in Chapter 6.

Russell, as I have indicated, introduces denoting to account for generality and the variable. I shall return to this point, but first it is worth noting that he also exploits it for two purposes which are at least not obviously connected with generality. The first has to do with identity. He explains how it can be worth while to assert identity by saying that the typical proposition asserting identity contains either a denoting concept formed with *the* and an object, or else two such denoting concepts. What is asserted, of course, is that the object contained in the proposition is identical to the one denoted by the denoting concept; or, in the other case, that the two denoting concepts denote the same object (see *Principles*, 64). Closely connected with this theory of identity is the discussion of denoting concepts formed with *the*. Russell declares this notion to be essential to an understanding of mathematical definition, for we define something by saying that it is *the* entity or *the* class satisfying certain conditions (see *Principles*, 63; for a discussion of the difference between mathematical and philosophical definition, pp. 232–3, below).

Another way in which Russell uses the notion of denoting has to do with existence-proofs in mathematics. Russell lays great stress on the necessity for such proofs, constantly criticizing earlier mathematicians for failing to provide them (as we have seen, he criticizes the treatment of irrational numbers offered by Dedekind and Weierstrass because they assume, but do not prove, that converging series of rationals must have limits; see *Principles*, 267–8). It may seem, however, as if Russell's metaphysics makes the demand for such proofs unintelligible. Consider the sense of existence at stake in the existence-proofs of mathematics. Existence in this mathematical sense must be distinguished from the sort of existence which is contrasted with being. Apart from other considerations, existence of the latter sort is temporal, whereas the entities of mathematics are atemporal. Russell, following Peano,[47] defines the notion of existence which is relevant to mathematics as follows:

Another very important notion is called the *existence* of a class—a word which must not be supposed to mean what existence means in philosophy. A class is said to exist when it has at least one term. (*Principles*, 25)

It may, however, seem as if Russell's metaphysics makes it trivially true that every class has a member and, indeed, infinitely many members. According to some of his explicit statements, it could never be true to say that there is no such thing as the member of the class K, for

[47] See 'Studies in Mathematical Logic' in *Selected Works*, ed. and tr. H. C. Kennedy (Toronto: University of Toronto Press, 1973), pp. 190–205. Peano uses '∃a' to mean 'the class a is non-empty'.

the very use of the phrase 'the member of the class K' would imply
that there is such a thing; similarly, presumably, the phrase 'the two
members of class K' and so on. One such statement is this:

Being is that which belongs to every conceivable term, to every possible object
of thought—in short to everything that can possibly occur in any proposition,
true or false. . . . 'A is not' must always be either false or meaningless. For if A
were nothing, it could not be said not to be; 'A is not' implies that there is a
term A whose being is denied, and hence that A is. Thus, unless 'A is not' be
an empty sound, it must be false. (*Principles*, 427)

In spite of the implication of the latter half of this statement, however,
Russell can, consistently with his fundamental tenets, deny that there
is (say) such a thing as the member of the class K. Whatever can occur
in a proposition must, indeed, be. But if one makes an assertion using
the words 'the member of K' then the corresponding proposition contains not the member of K but rather the denoting concept, *the member
of K*. And it is perfectly possible for there to be a denoting concept
which denotes nothing. Significantly, the only acknowledgement, in
Principles, of this latter fact occurs in a chapter on classes (Chapter VI),
and in a section discussing the null class in particular (73). It is thus the
notion of denoting which enables Russell to make sense, within the
metaphysics of Platonic Atomism, of the fact that mathematics may
require existence-proofs.

At the beginning of the discussion of denoting I emphasized that this
notion was introduced by Russell primarily to explain (or at least allow
for) the possibility of generality. It turns out, however, as Russell
reluctantly acknowledges, that the notion is not adequate to this task.
The issue here is not whether denoting can really *explain* anything at
all. Even granting this, the idea of denoting does not suffice for an
explanation of generality; in particular, it is inadequate to explain the
crucial fact of multiple generality. A number of points are important
here. We need to understand why Russell is often tempted by the idea
that denoting can explain generality; why this explanation, as Russell
sees, will not work; and, finally, how he does seek to explain generality, at those times when he realizes that it cannot be explained by
denoting. These points will require extended discussion.

In the logic which is described—though not explicitly formulated—in
Principles, it is what Russell calls 'formal implication' that carries the
burden of generality. Formal implication is a notion that Russell took
over from Peano. It amounts to the introduction of quantification in
one limited context, that typified by '$(x)(Fx \supset Gx)$'.[48] At the cost of a

---

[48] In Peano, and in Russell's 'The Logic of Relations', this notion is symbolized by
using the variable or variables concerned as subscripts to the '$\supset$'. This notation survives
in *PM* where it is, however, introduced explicitly as an abbreviation; see *10.02.

little artifice, formal implication can be made to serve all the purposes of quantification. The details here are complex and need not concern us; the crucial point is that Russell introduces (the analogue of) quantification under the guise of formal implication. He recognizes quite explicitly that for mathematical purposes this notion gives us all that we need by way of generality—we do not require denoting in addition to formal implication (see sections 87, 89). Non-mathematical propositions are of less concern to Russell, but here too his position is interesting. He suggests rather casually that a proposition containing a denoting concept involving *all* or *any* or *every* is equivalent to, though not identical with, one involving formal implication. Certainly in logic and mathematics, which are at the centre of Russell's concern, it is formal implication which, in the first instance, conveys generality. (It is perhaps for this reason that Russell's discussion of 'every', 'any', etc. seems poorly worked out; in the end the differences between these notions play no role in his logic, or in his account of mathematics. It is for this reason, also, that I have not thought it worth while to attempt to follow out his discussion of these matters in detail.) Russell is, however, not content to take formal implication as an indefinable notion. He seeks, rather, to analyse it. It is here that Russell attempts to explain generality (the fact that it is only generalized conditionals that are explicitly at issue is not, however, significant for our purposes).

Russell's discussion of generality takes place, of course, within the context of his general view of propositions. Among other things, this implies that the sort of explanation wanted is not a linguistic explanation of sentences which express generality; he seeks, rather, an explanation which functions on the non-linguistic level. What are the constituents of a general proposition? Socrates and wisdom are the constituents of the proposition expressed by 'Socrates is wise'; what are the constituents of the proposition expressed by 'All philosophers are wise'? As we have already seen, Russell rejects the idea that such a proposition simply contains all philosophers (see pp. 205–6, above). Rather it must be the case that some constituent or element of the proposition is not an entity of the ordinary sort, such as Socrates, but is itself in some way variable or ambiguous, so that containing such an element makes the proposition general. Now Russell is quite clear about the fact that this role cannot be played by a variable entity. He is in no doubt about the absurdity of such entities:

Originally, no doubt, the variable was conceived dynamically, as something which changed with the lapse of time, or, as is said, as something which successively assumed all values of a certain class. This view cannot be too soon dismissed. If a theorem is proved concerning n, it must not be supposed that n is a kind of arithmetical Proteus, which is 1 on Sundays and 2 on Mondays, and so on. Nor must it be supposed that *n* simultaneously assumes all its values. (*Principles*, 87)

If there are no variable entities then, again, how are we to account for general propositions? An answer which Russell constantly suggests is that we can do so in terms of the sort of denoting concepts that we have examined. The issue is confused by the fact that, although Russell sees that this answer will not in fact work, he constantly reverts to it. His remarks on this subject have influenced the interpretation of his work, adding confusion to matters which in any case would not be straightforward. I shall endeavour to explain the issues.

The answer which tempts Russell is that we can explain generality as it were head-on, by means of the variable; this latter notion in turn is to be explained as a denoting concept. Thus the proposition expressed by 'All philosophers are wise' contains wisdom and the denoting concept *all philosophers*. In this spirit, the passage quoted in the last but one paragraph continues as follows:

If *n* stands for any integer, we cannot say that *n* is 1, nor yet that it is 2, nor yet that it is any other particular number. In fact *n* just denotes *any* number, and this is something quite distinct from, each and all of the numbers.... The variable, in short, requires the indefinable notion of *any* which was explained in Chapter V [titled 'Denoting']. (*Principles*, 87)

In logic and mathematics the generality will, Russell claims, always be unrestricted. The relevant denoting concept will thus always be *any term* or (more or less equivalently) *every term*. These notions Russell identifies with the variable as it is used in mathematics: '*Any term* is a concept denoting the true [i.e. unrestricted] variable' (*Principles*, 88; cf. 86, and also 44).

According to this (misleading) picture, then, the variable as it is used in logic is a quite definite (non-linguistic) entity, namely a certain denoting concept. This entity is fundamental in the proposed explanation of generality; the theory of denoting is thus, as Russell constantly implies, crucial to his enterprise because it provides an account of generality. The proposed account, however, will not work, as Russell himself argues in two rather different contexts. The first context is one in which Russell is considering whether the notion of a propositional function is definable. An important role is played by the notion of an *assertion*. As Russell uses the word, an assertion is, roughly, what is left of a proposition when the subject is removed:[49]

---

[49] One issue that this raises is that of the unity of the proposition. I have already argued that Russell can give no consistent account of this. I do not discuss the issue

every proposition may be divided, some in only one way, some in several ways, into a term (the subject) and something said about the subject, which something I call the *assertion*. Thus 'Socrates is a man' may be divided into *Socrates* and *is a man*. (*Principles*, 43)

In some cases, Russell claims, the analysis of a proposition into subject and assertion is certainly correct, but will it work for all propositions? Russell takes as an example the proposition expressed by 'Socrates is a man implies that Socrates is mortal'. In the case of a proposition of this sort, he asks, can the analysis be carried out? He argues, at some length, that it cannot:

An assertion was to be obtained from a proposition by simply omitting one of the terms occurring in the proposition. But when we omit Socrates, we obtain '. . . is a man implies . . . is mortal'. In this formula it is essential that, in re-storing the proposition, the *same* term should be substituted in the two places where the dots indicate the necessity of a term. It does not matter what term we choose, but it must be identical in both places. Of this requisite, however, no trace whatever appears in the would-be assertion, and no trace can appear, since all mention of the term to be inserted is necessarily omitted. (*Principles*, 82)

The relevance of this to the definability of propositional functions is as follows: *if* the analysis into subject and assertion were one that worked for all propositions, then we could presumably explain a propositional function by saying that it is what results from a proposition when an entity in it is replaced by a variable. Similarly, of course, we could explain general propositions by means of denoting and the notion of an assertion. (The difference between propositional functions and general propositions is not clear on this view; perhaps they involve different denoting concepts.) But in fact, as Russell's own argument shows, the proposed analysis does not work.

The second context in which the same point emerges is Russell's discussion of the notion of the variable. Here it becomes clear that the problem with the idea of explaining generality in terms of denoting

---

further in this context because it seems to play no role in his thinking about the notions of an assertion and a propositional function; it plays no role here, I suspect, because Russell recognized that no alteration in his views about the latter pair of notions can make any difference to the underlying problem. He does raise the issue in contrasting assertions and propositional functions, but he raises it only to drop it. The passage reads as follows: 'We say . . . that when a proposition is completely analyzed into its simple constituents, these constituents taken together do not reconstitute it. A less complete analysis of propositions into subject and assertion has also been considered; and this analysis does much less to destroy the proposition. A subject and assertion, if simply juxtaposed, do not, it is true, constitute a proposition; but as soon as the assertion is actually asserted of the subject, the proposition reappears' (*Principles*, 81).

arises from complex propositions and propositional functions. In particular, Russell's earlier suggestions that we can identify the variable with the denoting concept *any term* proves to be inadequate to account for complex propositions. Consider, for example, the distinction between saying that every object stands in some given relation to itself, and saying that every object stands in that relation to every object. Thinking in terms of the variable, as explained by the denoting concept *any term*, cannot capture this essential distinction. Russell puts the point like this:

Thus *x* is, in some sense, the object denoted by *any term*; yet this can hardly be strictly maintained, for different variables may occur in a proposition, yet the object denoted by *any term* is, one would suppose, unique. . . . Thus variables have a kind of individuality. This arises . . . from propositional functions. When a propositional function has two variables, it must be regarded as obtained by successive steps. If the propositional function $\phi(x,y)$ is to be asserted for all values of *x* and *y*, we must consider the assertion, for all values of *y*, of the propositional function $\phi(a,y)$, where *a* is constant. This does not involve *y*, and may be written $\psi(a)$. We then vary *a*, and assert $\psi(x)$ for all values of x. . . . The individuality of variables is thus explained. A variable is not *any term* simply, but any term as entering into a propositional function. (*Principles*, 93)

The 'individuality' of variables cannot be explained simply by means of denoting concepts; the moral, again, is that the notion of a propositional function must be taken as the fundamental one.[50]

In spite of the arguments which we have examined in the last two paragraphs, however, Russell continues to believe, or to talk as if he believes, that there are variables, or the variable, in more than a linguistic sense.[51] This habit continues, as we shall see, even as late as *Principia Mathematica*. It adds unnecessary confusion to Russell's view, and has, I think, influenced the way in which his work has been interpreted. I shall enlarge on both of these points.

Russell's constant reversion to the view that there are variables

[50] Russell's thought here is perhaps surprisingly close to Frege's. Frege rejects the idea that we can explain the nature of functions in terms of variables, and says: 'If the letters "*x*" and "*y*" designated different variables, we should be able to say how they are distinguished; but this no one can do. . . . Hence it is impossible to explain what a function is by referring to what is called a variable. *It is rather the case that when we seek to make clear to ourselves what a variable is, we come back again and again to what we have called a function*' (*Posthumous Writings* (Oxford: Blackwell, 1979), p. 238; *Nachgelassene Schriften und wissenschaftliche Briefwechsel*, i (Hamburg: Felix Meiner Verlag, 1969), p. 256; emphasis in the original).

[51] Here there is a contrast between Russell and Frege, for the latter always insisted that a variable is only a letter, and cannot coherently be thought of as standing for anything. Besides the material around the previous citation, see section II of *Begriffsschrift*, and the revealing discussion around p. 181 of Gottlob Frege, *Philosophical and Mathematical Correspondence*, op. cit. n. 6 above. At this last reference, as at some other later writings, Frege urges that we avoid the word 'variable' altogether.

which are non-linguistic entities is the source of considerable confusion in his thought. A brief discussion will indicate why this should be. Distinctions which are quite clear on the symbolic level become intractable if we take them to be no more than indications of distinctions which must be understood on the non-linguistic level. The point emerges, again, from a consideration of complex propositional functions. Take as an example the distinction between '$\phi x, x$' and '$\phi x, y$'. On the level of symbolism the distinction is clear: there is no difficulty in saying that there is a distinction between the letter 'x' and the letter 'y'. But suppose we say that there is a corresponding, and more fundamental, difference on the non-linguistic level, between what 'x' stands for and what 'y' stands for. Then we seem forced to say that there is a corresponding difference between what '$\phi x, x$' stands for and what '$\phi x, y$' stands for, but, unless we are presupposing some wider context, there clearly is no such difference. Taken out of context, 'x' and 'y' do not stand for different things; if this makes the problem of distinguishing between what '$\phi x, x$' stands for and what '$\phi x, y$' stands for intractable then the proper moral to draw is that the whole idea that we can talk of 'x' and 'y' standing for things is misguided from the outset. Russell's insistence on the ultimate and indefinable nature of the propositional function is, I take it, a way of acknowledging this fact; in particular, it is a way of acknowledging that the distinction between the propositional functions $\phi x, x$ and $\phi x, y$ must be taken as inexplicable. Yet in spite of this acknowledgement, and in spite of the arguments that we have seen, Russell continues to talk of (non-linguistic) variables, and of variables occurring in propositional functions. So the confusion remains, at least on the surface of his work.

I emphasize Russell's frequent assumption that variables are non-linguistic entities partly because it is, I suspect, largely responsible for one of the most influential interpretations of Russell—an interpretation that I hold to be misleading. According to this interpretation, Russell's logic, not only in *Principles* but in the entire period up to and including *PM*, is mired in use/mention confusions; his use of the key terms 'variable', 'propositional function', and even 'proposition' is irremediably confused as between the linguistic and the non-linguistic, as if he were simply unable to distinguish them. Thus Quine, for example, speaking of Russell's use of 'propositional function' deplores Russell's '[f]ailure to distinguish thus between open sentences on the one hand and attributes or relations on the other'.[52] Now an important motive

---

[52] Introduction to Russell's 'Mathematical Logic as Based on the Theory of Types', in van Heijenoort, p. 151. See also Quine's 'Russell's Ontological Development' in R. Schoenman (ed.), *Bertrand Russell; Philosopher of the Century* (London: Allen & Unwin, 1967), pp. 304–14.

behind this interpretation, I suspect, is that clear-minded logicians such as Quine take for granted that talk of variables is talk of letters—linguistic objects. They then construe Russell's statements that propositional functions contain variables as implying that propositional functions too must be linguistic. Thus Quine, again, speaking of Russell's type theory in 'Mathematical Logic as Based on the Theory of Types', says, 'Variables, in the easiest sense, are letters; and what contain them are notational expressions. Is Russell then assigning types to his objects or to his notations? The confusion persists as he proceeds to define nth-order propositions' (loc. cit.). What this view of Russell's work overlooks is that Russell often writes as if he possessed an understanding of variables as non-linguistic objects. It is, I think, this idea that he relies on when he speaks of propositional functions as containing variables. I have argued above that Russell's own arguments show that there is no coherent idea, of the sort that he seems to rely on, of variables as non-linguistic objects. Nevertheless, the idea is one that constantly tempts him, and constantly recurs in his work (see the discussion of *Principia Mathematica* in Chapter 7, below, especially pp. 191–2).

According to the view that I have put forward above, Russell's talk of variables as non-linguistic objects represents merely a blind alley. In spite of Russell's temptations, he does at least on occasion clearly perceive that this idea leads only to confusion. We shall thus do well to ask how we can understand his thought without representing it as relying on this idea. What, then, is Russell's account of generality? What is the element in a general proposition that is somehow general or variable in nature? The answer is that it is a propositional function; and, as we have indicated, this notion must be taken as indefinable, not as explicable in terms of propositions and variables. The crucial fact about a propositional function is that it stands in some kind of special relation to a number of propositions—those which are its instances or values.[53] By means of this 'special relation', we can use a proposition containing a propositional function to assert all or some of the values of that function. Russell's account of quantification is thus best thought of as representing a quantified proposition as one in which a property is ascribed to a propositional function. Such a property achieves its effect

[53] It is not only propositions but also propositional functions that must be seen as values of propositional functions. A propositional function with more than one place, such as that represented by 'x loves y', does not merely have as values a class of propositions. It also has as values two distinct sets of propositional functions: those of the form 'x loves Socrates', 'x loves Plato', etc. and those of the form 'Socrates loves y', 'Plato loves y', etc. The ability to make the distinction between these two classes is vital to any account of multiple generality.

in virtue of a 'special relation', not further explicable, between a propositional function and its instances. As we shall see, this special relation is in some ways analogous to the relation of denoting, since it
enables a proposition containing one object (a propositional function)
to be about a multiplicity of others. This relation, however, is not
salient in Russell's account, and he does not use the word 'denoting' in
this context. The entities which he does speak of as denoting, however, play no role in his account as I have reconstructed it.

Russell often reverts to the picture of there being an entity, the
variable, which is crucial to generality, thereby implicitly contradicting
the account that I have attributed to him. What I attribute to him can,
however, be extracted from his discussion of propositional functions.
The most extended discussion is in Appendix A, where he compares
his propositional functions with Frege's concepts. The most directly
relevant passage is phrased in terms of what Russell calls 'unities'; for
our purposes we can think of all unities as propositions,[54] though
Russell wants to leave open the possibility of there being non-
propositional unities (see *Principles*, 136). He then goes on to distinguish six putative entities which may derived from a unity (a
proposition); the first four will be relevant to our discussion:

(1) What remains of the said unity when one of its terms is simply removed . . . This is what Frege calls a function.

(2) The class of unities differing from the said unity, if at all, only by the fact
that one of its terms has been replaced, in one or more of the places where it
occurs, by some other terms, or by the fact that two or more of its terms have
been thus replaced . . .

(3) Any member of the class (2)

(4) The assertion that every member of the class (2) is true. (*Principles*, 482)

Russell identifies (1), Frege's function (of which a Fregean concept is a
special case), with his own notion of an assertion.[55] He refers back to
his argument that the analysis into argument and assertion can only
be carried out in special cases, where the proposition with which we
begin is a simple one. On this basis, he dismisses Frege's notion: 'what
Frege calls a function, if our conclusion was sound, is in general a
non-entity' (loc. cit.). Here we could say that Russell simply misunder-
stands, or entirely misses, Frege's notion of unsaturatedness. This is,
however, no simple misreading on Russell's part, but a sign of a fun-

---

[54] Russell speaks here of 'propositional concepts'; the death of Caesar is the propositional concept corresponding to the proposition that Caesar dies. I shall ignore this
complication.

[55] One should perhaps think of the identification as being with the *Sinn* of a function-
expression, rather than with its *Bedeutung*. Russell's rejection of the notion would apply
to either case.

damental difference between him and Frege. The idea of an entity, or a quasi-entity, which is not self-subsistent but is incomplete, is so alien to Russell's metaphysics at this time that he does not seem able to understand it, even as the idea of another. Here, if anywhere, we reach bedrock. Having dismissed the first of the four notions distinguished above, Russell goes on to make it clear that it is the other three which figure in his theory of propositional functions: 'Instead of the rump of a proposition considered in (1), I substitute (2) or (3) or (4) according to circumstances' (loc. cit.).

Now one can hardly suppose that Russell here is simply identifying a propositional function with a class of propositions, or with an arbitrary member of that class, or an assertion of every member of the class—still less with all three at once. Apart from other objections to this idea, it is clear that the class of propositions involved will invariably be infinite; we should also have to accept that any proposition containing a propositional function (e.g. a quantified statement) is of infinite complexity. The best way to interpret what Russell says is, as already suggested, in terms of a relation which is analogous to denoting. A propositional function is related to the given class of propositions in very much the same way as the denoting concept *any term* is related to the class of terms. The denoting concept can be used to make statements about the class, or at least about all its members, or to make statements about an arbitrary member of the class: which entity is concerned in a given case is simply a matter of the context in which the denoting concept occurs. Similarly, I suggest, if we think of a propositional function as denoting any member of a certain class the apparent ambiguity in Russell's statement ceases to be mysterious (the idea that we can use a propositional function to make an assertion will have to be introduced *ad hoc*; but the present line of thought at least leaves room for it). The view that propositional functions are to be understood through the notion of denoting is reinforced by the consideration that it is denoting, in Russell's thought, that allows propositions to be about things which they do not contain. For it seems plausible to suppose that a proposition containing a propositional function is not typically *about* that propositional function, but is rather about a class of propositions (and thus indirectly about what those propositions are about). This point may be illustrated by Russell's discussion of formal implication. He argues that 'x is a man implies x is mortal' must be construed as a single propositional function, not as a relation of two. He goes on to say:

Thus our formal implication asserts a class of implications, not a single implication at all. We do not, in a word, have one implication containing a variable, but rather a variable implication. We have a class of implications, no one of which contains a variable, and we assert that every member of this class is true. (*Principles*, 42)

The formal implication contains a propositional function but is, in virtue of this fact, about (or an assertion of) every member of an infinite class of propositions. We should therefore think of the propositional function as standing in a relation at least formally analogous to that of denoting, to the infinite class.

I conclude this discussion of propositional functions with two related points. The first is that for Russell the notion of a propositional function is not a special case of a more general notion of a function. Clearly one might take for granted the general notion of a function, and then explain propositional functions as those functions all of whose values were propositions.[56] This, however, is not Russell's procedure. On the contrary: he defines ordinary functions, and the general notion of a function, in terms of propositional functions; the latter notion is taken as undefinable. (If xRy is a two-place propositional function which for each value of x becomes a true proposition for one and only one value of y, then we can define $f(x)$ as the value of y such that xRy is true. Clearly this procedure can be generalized: any $n+1$-place propositional function with the relevant uniqueness property will give rise to an n-place function in the ordinary sense.) This view of the priority of propositional functions is one that Russell maintains not only in *Principles* (see e.g. section 80) but throughout the period which is our concern in this book; in the next chapter I shall suggest a possible rationale for it. The second of the two present points is that a propositional function, as Russell understands it, has a definite internal structure. Like a proposition, it contains certain entities combined in certain ways. A propositional function shares this structure with the propositions which are its values or instances; one might almost say that a propositional function *is* a certain structure, and that its instances are precisely those propositions which have this structure. This is clearly indicated by a passage from the section in which Russell introduces the idea of a propositional function:

In any proposition . . . we may imagine one of the terms, not a verb or an adjective, to be replaced by other terms: instead of 'Socrates is a man' we may put 'Plato is a man', 'the number 2 is a man' and so on. Thus we get successive propositions all agreeing except as to the one variable term. Putting x for the variable term, 'x is a man' expresses the type of all such propositions. A propositional function in general will be true for some values of the variable and false for others. (*Principles*, 22)

---

[56] Frege's procedure, in explaining concepts in terms of functions, is analogous to this. For Frege, concepts are functions all of whose values are truth-values.

I turn now to the issues connected with classes and the class paradox. An important preliminary point is that there are two separable problems here. First, the notion of a class would have been problematic for Russell even if he had not discovered the contradiction. The very idea of a class seems to be in conflict with the fundamental metaphysics of Platonic Atomism. Second, it is a mistake to think of the contradiction as being, from Russell's point of view, a special problem about classes. The contradiction, or close analogues, arise from, again, the fundamental metaphysics of Platonic Atomism. Although these two problems are thus separable, they are not, of course, unrelated. Each exacerbates the other; in particular, Russell thinks that the existence of the class contradiction makes it clear that the nature of classes is a mystery. Thus he says in the Preface that the discussion of indefinables in general is 'the endeavour to see clearly, and to make others see clearly, the entities concerned, in order that the mind may have that kind of acquaintance with them which it has with redness or the taste of a pineapple'. He goes on to say:

In the case of classes, I must confess, I have failed to perceive any concept fulfilling the conditions requisite for the notion of *class*. And the contradiction . . . proves that something is amiss, but what this is I have hitherto failed to discover. (pp. xv–xvi)

Russell introduces classes via 'the notion of *such that*' (*Principles*, 20), which he takes as one of the indefinables of logic. The crucial point is this:

The values of x which render a propositional function ϕx true are like the roots of an equation . . . and we may consider all the values of x which are *such that* ϕx is true. In general, these values form a *class*, and in fact a class may be defined as all the terms satisfying some propositional function. (*Principles*, 23)

In Chapter VI, however, he introduces what may appear to be a different approach, in which 'a class is a numerical conjunction of terms' (*Principles*, 67). Russell himself distinguishes the two approaches, using the terminology 'intensional' and 'extensional'. It is important to note that he does *not* mean by these words what a modern author would mean; he is quite clear from the start that the identity criterion from classes is (what we would call) extensional (see *Principles*, 24). What is at stake is, rather, how we should understand the notion of a class. Russell puts the point like this:

Class may be defined either extensionally or intensionally. That is to say, we may define the kind of object which is a class, or the kind of concept which denotes a class: this is the precise meaning of the opposition of extension and intension in this connection. (*Principles*, 71)

It may seem as if Russell is here considering two quite distinct ways of understanding the notion of a class. This appearance, however, seems to me to be mistaken.[57] The considerations which unify the two approaches are, first, that numerical conjunctions in general must be defined by being denoted, for only finite classes can be defined by enumeration (see section 66). Second, the denoting concepts which the intensional approach takes as central must, at least in some cases, denote something. What each such denoting concept denotes is a numerical conjunction. Russell insists, moreover, that it makes no difference to a numerical conjunction that we regard it as denoted by a class concept:

It is evident that a numerical conjunction considered as denoted is either the same entity as when not so considered, or else is a complex of denoting together with the object denoted; and the object denoted is plainly what we mean by a class. (*Principles*, 72)

Russell's final position thus seems to be that a class is a numerical conjunction, but that except for finite classes we must think of classes as denoted by class concepts.

This discussion of classes illustrates what I have called Russell's object-based metaphysics. For Russell, it is not enough that we have an understanding of when a denoting concept denotes a class, and when two denoting concepts denote the same class. What we require is an independent understanding of the notion of a class. The most obvious contrast here is with Frege. Frege's metaphysics, we may say, is judgement-based: the notion of a judgement is taken as basic, and the notions of object and concept understood essentially in terms of the analysis of judgement.[58] One consequence of this is what is often called the context principle: only in the context of a judgement [*Satz*] does a word have meaning; closely related to this is Frege's injunction: never to ask for the meaning of a word in isolation.[59] Frege thus introduces his analogue of classes (*Wertverläufe*, which Russell trans-

---

[57] For another view, see Linsky, 'Russell's "No-Classes" Theory of Classes', in J. J. Thomson (ed.), *On Being and Saying* (Cambridge, Mass.: MIT Press, 1987), pp. 21–39, especially ss. I and II. In spite of my disagreement, I am indebted to Linsky's discussion.

[58] See Michael Dummett's 'Nominalism', repr. in *Truth and Other Enigmas* (Cambridge, Mass.: Harvard University Press, 1978), pp. 38–49; for a detailed examination of the idea of Frege's metaphysics as judgement-based, see T. G. Ricketts, 'Objectivity and Objecthood: Frege's Metaphysics of Judgment', in L. Haaparanta and J. Hintikka (eds.), *Frege Synthesized* (Dordrecht: D. Reidel, 1986), pp. 65–96.

[59] Frege, *Die Grundlagen der Arithmetik* (Breslau: Verlag von Wilhelm Koebner, 1884), trans. by J. L. Austin as *The Foundations of Arithmetic* (Oxford: Blackwell, 1953; 1st edn. 1950), ss. 60, 62; also p. x of the Introduction.

lates as 'ranges') into his logic by means of Axiom V of the *Grundgesetze*:

$$(\hat{x}(Fx) \equiv \hat{x}(Gx)) \equiv (x)\ (Fx = Gx)$$

This axiom (which I have written in non-Fregean notation) states that the class of Fs is identical with the class of Gs just in case F is true of all and only those things of which G is true. For Frege this axiom is sufficient to introduce *Wertverläufe* (though not, of course, sufficient to guarantee that the resulting theory is consistent). It fixes the meaning of identity statements involving *Wertverläufe*,[60] and this tells us everything that we need to know in order to theorize about them: no further questions about their nature are appropriate. Russell, by contrast, cannot accept that Frege's Axiom V suffices to introduce *Wertverläufe*:

What Frege understands by a range [i.e. *Wertverlauf*]...he endeavors to explain in his *Grundgesetze der Arithmetik*. He begins by deciding that two propositional functions are to have the same range when they have the same value for every value of x ... *But this only determines the equality of ranges, not what they are in themselves.* (*Principles*, 484; my emphasis)

And again:

The chief difficulty which arises in the above [i.e. Frege's] theory of classes is as to the kind of entity that a range is to be.... It would certainly be a very great simplification to admit, as Frege does, a range which is something other than the whole composed of the terms satisfying the propositional function in question: but for my part, inspection reveals to me no such entity. (*Principles*, 486)

For Russell, then, a satisfactory explanation of classes is required to tell us what a class is in itself.

A class, for Russell, must thus be a definite entity; he explains it as a numerical conjunction or collection of terms. The expression 'numerical conjunction' is one that Russell introduced earlier, in his discussion of denoting. A numerical conjunction, according to that discussion (*Principles*, 59), is what is denoted by A and B, where we mean to assert something of A and B collectively, not individually (e.g. the sense of 'John and Mary are friends' in which it cannot be equated with 'John is a friend and Mary is a friend'). A collection, similarly, Russell takes to mean 'what is conveyed by "A and B" or "A and B and C", or any other enumeration of definite terms' (*Principles*, 71). (The meaning of 'and' causes Russell considerable worry, chiefly because he thinks of it

---

[60] One might object that the axiom does not fix the meaning of a sentence which has a *Wertverlauf* expression on one side of the identity sign and an expression of a different form on the other, as for example '$\hat{x}(Fx) = a$'. I shall not, however, press this point here.

as one more entity, which seems to have the undesirable result that 'A and B' names a collection of three terms, not two. In the end he accepts the notion of *and* as *sui generis*—'a definite unique kind of combination, not a relation, and not combining A and B into a whole which would be one' *Principles*, 71.) These discussions, however, do not explain what a class is. All they tell us is how a class is denoted; by Russell's standards they are thus inadequate. A sign of this inadequacy is that Russell is left unclear as to whether a class is one term or many. (In the ensuing discussion I assume that we are considering only classes containing more than one term. The null class and unit classes pose special problems for Russell, as we shall see.) Russell puts the question as follows:

Taking the class as equivalent simply to the numerical conjunction 'A and B and C and etc.,' it seems to be plain that it is many; yet it is quite necessary that we should be able to count classes as one each, and we do habitually speak of *a* class. Thus classes would seem to be one in one sense and many in another. (*Principles*, 74)

In the main body of *Principles* Russell argues that there is 'an ultimate distinction between a class as many and a class as one' (loc. cit.), and goes on to suggest that we may be able to use this distinction to avoid the class paradox. The idea here is that some classes as many have no corresponding classes as one which could be logical subjects (see *Principles*, 104). A more general issue lies behind the question whether classes are one or many. We may think of this issue as that of the unity of a class: what makes it possible to think of *many* terms as forming a collection which is *one* term? This question is unavoidable, even in the case of the class as many. Such a class must surely have some degree of unity. Russell accepts this point, but it is apparent that he has nothing informative to say here:

In a class as many, the component terms, though they have some kind of unity, have less than is required for a whole. They have in fact, just so much unity as is required to make them many, and not enough to prevent them from remaining many. (*Principles*, 70)

The difficulties which Russell faces over the unity of a class are by no means adventitious. The issue of unity, or of the one and the many, is one of the major themes of the rejection of Idealism by Moore and Russell. In opposition to the idealist insistence on internal relations and organic wholes, Moore and Russell adopted an extreme atomism. But this doctrine makes the question of the unity of a class an intractable one for Russell. No account he can give will both give him the classes he needs for logicism and be compatible with his general metaphysics.

It is not surprising, therefore, that Bradley should have seized on the problem of the unity of a class in criticism of Russell:

the inconsistency of such an idea as 'class'. . . . It is still the old problem of the universal, of the one and the many . . .

The class is many. It *is* its members. There is no entity external to and other than its members. The class is a collection.

The class is One, but the One is not something outside the members. The members even seem to be members because of what each is internally. And this apparent quality in each cannot be a relation to something outside the class. . . . On the other hand, a quality merely internal to each member seems to leave the class without any unity at all. The unity, therefore, not being external, must be taken as itself a member of the class. And since this seems once more to be senseless, the class appears to be dissolved. (*ETR*, pp. 283–4)

I said above that unit classes and the null class pose difficulties for Russell's view. He takes classes to be numerical conjunctions, but a conjunction requires more than one object. Thus he says that if one makes a sharp distinction between classes and class concepts, two consequences follow:

The first consequence is, that there is no such thing as the null-class, though there are null class-concepts. The second is, that a class having only one term is to be identified . . . with that one term. (*Principles*, 69)

Both of these consequences, but especially the second, seem to present considerable difficulty for the theory of classes. At one point Russell responds to them by saying that 'Symbolic Logic ought to concern itself, as far as notation goes, with class-concepts rather than with classes' (loc. cit.). He also suggests, however, that the role of the null class can be played by 'the class of all null class-concepts or of all null propositional functions' (*Principles*, 73). These ideas could be explored further; their chief interest from our point of view, however, is that they indicate how puzzling the crucial notion of a class was for Russell.

Our discussion of classes in *Principles* has, so far, made no mention of the contradiction which Russell discovered in June 1901; it is to this contradiction, and its analogues, that I now turn. The class contradiction, now known as Russell's paradox, can be briefly stated as follows. Most classes one thinks of are clearly not members of themselves: the class of books is not a book, and so is not a member of the class of books. But some classes do seem to be members of themselves: since there are, presumably, infinitely many classes with an infinite number of members, the class containing all classes which have infinitely many members must, it seems, contain itself; since the class of all classes is itself a class, it presumably belongs to itself; and so on. Now consider the class which contains all normal classes, i.e. all those classes which do *not* belong to themselves. Call this class *W*. Is *W* a member of *W* or not? From either answer we can infer the opposite one: no consistent answer is available. This paradox, as I have stated it, makes essential use of the notion of a class. For Russell, however, analogues of the paradox arise which are independent of that notion. Russell states the paradox for predicates, for example, as follows:[61]

If *x* be a predicate, *x* may or may not be predicable of itself. Let us assume that 'not predicable of oneself' is a predicate. Then to suppose either that this predicate is, or that it is not, predicable of itself, is self-contradictory. (*Principles*, 101)

A predicate, here, is not a linguistic entity,[62] but a constituent of a proposition.

It is important to see that this paradox arises not from special assumptions about predicates but from fundamental features of Russell's metaphysics. In particular, we can distinguish two principles which between them make the paradox almost inescapable. First: everything is a term, i.e. is the subject of propositions. We have already seen Russell's argument for this principle. It is, he claims, self-contradictory to say of anything that it cannot be the subject of a proposition, for to say this is to express a (false) proposition of which the given thing is the subject. Second: all terms have the same ontological status, in the precise sense that if any term which is the subject of a proposition is replaced by any other term then what we obtain is still a proposition. As Russell puts it: 'It is characteristic of the terms of a proposition that any one of them may be replaced by any other entity without our ceasing to have a proposition' (*Principles*, 48). The argument for the first principle also goes a long way towards demonstrating this second principle. If everything is a term, then in the proposition that Socrates is a term, any entity may be substituted for Socrates to yield a new proposition. Thus the notion of a term, one of the central concepts of Platonic Atomism, runs counter to the view that entities divide into types such that we only obtain a proposition if we replace an entity in a proposition by another of the same type. Note also that if

---

[61] In his first letter to Frege, informing him of the paradox, Russell states the paradox first for predicates and then for classes. See Russell's letter to Frege of 16 June 1902, trans. in *The Philosophical and Mathematical Correspondence* of Frege, op. cit. n. 6 above, pp. 130–1.

[62] Even if it were, paradox might result: compare Quine on the contradictory nature of '"does not produce a true statement when appended to its own quotation" produces a true statement when appended to its own quotation'; *From a Logical Point of View* (Cambridge, Mass.: Harvard University Press, 1961; 1st edn. 1953), pp. 133–4. Predicates in the linguistic sense are not, however, Russell's concern.

we introduce the relation *is of the same type as* then we have a relation
which must make sense whether it is true or false, i.e. which itself
threatens to violate type distinctions (we shall return to this point; see
Chapter 7, below, pp. 314–18).

We can see these Russellian principles as arising from the rejection of
any idea of degrees of reality: they give a precise sense to the otherwise
vague idea that all entities are on the same level, all real in exactly the
same sense. More specifically, however, I think the principles arise
from the rejection of the idealist view that certain things cannot be
said, or cannot be said with full and literal accuracy. Platonic Atomism
enshrines an ideal of clarity and explicitness which is in direct opposition to this idealist view. This idea is expressed, for example, in the
view that a fact is simply a true proposition: the idea of a fact which
cannot be fully stated becomes absurd. Similarly, within Platonic
Atomism it is natural to argue that if there were anything which could
not be a subject of propositions then there would be a proposition
which stated this; and in that proposition, of course, the alleged entity
would be the subject.

Given the two principles, the paradox of predicates which are not
predicable of themselves follows almost immediately, without the use
of any obviously dubious assumptions. Since the predicate *mortal*, say,
is a term, and since terms are intersubstitutable, we can substitute this
predicate for Socrates in the proposition that Socrates is mortal. We
thereby obtain a proposition in which the predicate is ascribed to itself.
This proposition is false: the predicate *mortal* is not predicable of itself.
Since we can say this, there must be such a predicate as *not predicable
of itself*. So the paradox seems irresistible, given the two very general
principles of Russell's philosophy. We may, again, helpfully contrast
Russell with Frege on this point. Frege did not hold (the analogue
of) the first of the two Russellian principles which I distinguished: he
did not hold that the objective correlates of (linguistic) predicates—
Begriffe—are capable of being logical subjects (see 'Concept and Object';
also *Principles*, 483, where Russell considers and explicitly rejects this
view of Frege's). Thus in Frege's philosophy (the analogue of) the class
paradox does not arise without special assumptions. Only when Frege
embarks upon (the analogue of) the theory of classes does paradox
arise, for then he makes the assumption embodied in the notorious
Axiom V of *Grundgesetze*, which, as we have seen, states that the
Wertverläufe (value-ranges) of two concepts are equal just in case the
concepts are co-extensive. Given Frege's assumption that there is a
Wertverlauf associated with every concept, this leads directly to Russell's paradox. For Russell, however, the paradox arises without the
use of any special assumption or axiom; what corresponds to the

words (say) '. . . is a horse' (or '. . . is a non-self-member') is already an object, not merely something with which an object is associated, for on Russell's view whatever can occupy the predicate position in a proposition can also occupy the subject-position, and so must be recognized as an object.

The paradoxes to which Russell's view is vulnerable can be avoided if there are distinctions in ontological type among the various entities concerned (classes, propositional functions, predicates, and, as we shall see, propositions). Russell sees this fact quite clearly in *Principles*, but is nevertheless reluctant to admit all the type restrictions which would be necessary to avoid contradiction. Although the book contains various suggestions for avoiding contradiction, it thus ends without claiming success in this enterprise. Let us look at these matters in slightly more detail.

The main body of *Principles* contains an inchoate theory of types based on the distinction between the class as many and the class as one (see sections 103–4; and pp. 224–5, above). Appendix B contains a more articulated theory, which applies to propositional functions as well as to classes. The fundamental claim of Appendix B is that '[e]very propositional function $\phi(x)$ . . . has, in addition to its range of truth, a range of significance, i.e. a range within which x must lie if $\phi(x)$ is to be a proposition at all' (*Principles*, 497). A type is then defined as the class of objects which belong to the range of significance of a given propositional function. The first type consists of terms or individuals, i.e. any objects which are not ranges or classes. For individuals the principle of universal substitutivity *salva significatione* holds: 'If such an object—say a certain point in space—occurs in a proposition, any other individual may *always* be substituted without loss of significance' (loc. cit.; emphasis in the original). The next type is that of 'ranges or classes of individuals' (loc. cit.); the next after that is classes of classes of individuals; and so on. For classes, the doctrine is thus very like that of simple type theory, where the types are not cumulative. An important difference from simple type theory, however, is that the hierarchy of individuals, classes of individuals, classes of classes of individuals, etc., does not include all the types. A second hierarchy begins with ordered pairs of individuals. Numbers form a problematic type not included in either of the hierarchies. A number is, on Russell's account, a class of similar (or equinumerous) classes: the number seven is the class of all seven-membered classes. But there are seven-membered classes at every type (or almost every type) in the class hierarchy. Since all classes or ranges can be numbered, Russell also assumes that some propositional functions have all ranges (i.e. roughly, all classes) within their range of significance:

Since all ranges have numbers, ranges are a range; consequently $x \varepsilon x$ is sometimes significant, and in these cases its denial is also significant. Consequently there is a range w of ranges of which $x \varepsilon x$ is false: thus the contradiction proves that this range w does not belong to the significance of $x \varepsilon x$. (*Principles*, 498)

The importance of this doctrine of types, from our point of view, does not lie in its details, which are, in any case, rather sketchily indicated. What it shows is, rather, that Russell is willing at least to consider a view according to which entities are not all of the same type. *Principles*, however, contains no articulation of this view, much less a defence of it. Russell's commitment to type-theory is, in any case, as I have indicated, half-hearted. At two points, in particular, he seems to find it incredible. The first concerns the general notion of object, and is clearest in Russell's discussion of Cantor's proof that there is no greatest cardinal number.[63] The crux of Cantor's argument is that a class always has more sub-classes (i.e. classes all of whose members are also members of the given class) than it has members. Applied to the class of all terms, this argument shows that there are more classes than terms. Russell finds this to be, at least prima facie, paradoxical: 'If we assume, as was done in s. 47, that every constituent of every proposition is a term, then classes will be only some among terms' (*Principles*, 348). He suggests that distinctions of type (which I shall discuss shortly) may remove this seeming paradox; yet the paradox immediately recurs when he invokes a more general notion of object which would, presumably, not be subject to type distinctions. It is almost as if Russell cannot believe that objects in the most fundamental sense are subject to type distinctions:

But if we admit the notion of all objects of every kind, it becomes evident that classes of objects are only some among objects, while yet Cantor's argument would show that there are more of them than there are objects. (loc. cit.)

The notion of 'all objects of every kind' is one which it is hard for Russell to exclude: we seem to need this notion even to say that objects are *not* all of the same type.

The second point at which Russell finds distinctions of type to be clearly unacceptable concerns propositions. Russell claims in Appendix B that propositions form a single type, i.e. that there are no type distinctions among them. The basis for this claim is, at least in part,

---

[63] In 'Mathematics and the Metaphysician', written in the first half of 1901, Russell says that Cantor 'has been guilty of a very subtle fallacy, which I hope to explain in some future work' (*Mysticism and Logic* (New York: Longmans, Green & Co., 1918), p. 69). In *Principles*, however, Russell accepts at least one version of Cantor's proof (see ss. 344–9).

that 'propositions can significantly be said to be true or false' (498; cf. 349 where a similar point is made in a similar context). Russell also insists that we can form classes or ranges of propositions 'for we often wish to assert the logical product of such ranges' (500). Given these two claims, the way is open for a paradox which is closely analogous to the class paradox. With any class of propositions, m, we can correlate the proposition m^*, which says that every member of m is true. In some cases m^* will itself be a member of m, in other cases not. Consider the class of propositions of the form m^* (i.e. which say of some class that all its members are true) which are *not* members of the corresponding class m. Call this class w. Then there is a proposition w^* which says that every member of w is true. Then w^* is a member of w just in case w^* is *not* a member of w, i.e. contradiction results. I shall not here discuss the question whether this paradox can be thought of as 'semantic' rather than 'logical', and thus dismissed (see Chapter 7, below, for some discussion of related issues). The important point, for the moment, is that Russell remained dissatisfied with his doctrine of types. He contemplates the idea of escaping the paradox by thinking of propositions as stratified into types, but finds it incredible:

It is possible, of course, to hold that propositions themselves are of various types, and that logical products must have propositions of only one type as factors. But this suggestion seems harsh and highly artificial.

[the class paradox] is solved by the doctrine of types, but . . . there is at least one closely analogous contradiction which is probably not soluble by this doctrine. The totality of all logical objects, or of all propositions, involves, it would seem, a fundamental logical difficulty. What the complete solution of the difficulty may be, I have not yet succeeded in discovering. (*Principles*, 500)

Russell thus pays a high price for his failure to embrace type distinctions in a thoroughgoing fashion. This failure must, I think, be seen not as adventitious but as the result of a metaphysics which appears, at least, to leave no room for distinctions of type. Without type distinctions, however, the metaphysics generates contradictions. What the various contradictions cast in doubt, from Russell's point of view, is not simply the theory of classes; it is the fundamental metaphysics of Platonic Atomism.

I shall conclude this chapter with a brief discussion of an issue to which I have already alluded: the conception of philosophy embodied in *Principles*. Of particular interest here is a certain tension in Russell's thought, arising from his philosophical use of technical arguments. This tension enables us, in retrospect, to see *Principles* as foreshadowing a conception of philosophy which is quite different from that which it officially advances.

In the previous chapter I sketched a view of the nature of philosophy held by both Russell and Moore: there are simple terms and complex terms which are composed of simple ones. Philosophy consists of two activities: first, analysis of complex terms into their simple constituents, and secondly, non-sensuous perception of simple terms (see Chapter 4, pp. 144–6, above). This same conception of philosophy persists in *Principles*, but is there combined with views as to the philosophical importance of mathematics—views which were to be immensely influential in later analytical philosophy.

One of the tasks of philosophy, according to the view mentioned above, is to discover the indefinable entities and the indemonstrable propositions of any given subject; and the method by which this is performed is analysis:

The definition [of mathematics] professes to be, not an arbitrary decision to use a common word in an uncommon signification, but rather a precise analysis of the ideas which ... are implied in the ordinary use of the term. Our method will therefore be one of analysis, and our problem may be called philosophical—in the sense, that is to say, that we seek to pass from the complex to the simple, from the demonstrable to its indemonstrable premisses. (*Principles*, 2)

Russell does not identify the analysis of a notion with a set of necessary and sufficient conditions: on the contrary, he contrasts philosophical definition, which gives 'an actual analysis' of a notion, with mathematical definition, which gives 'merely a set of conditions insuring its presence' (*Principles*, 196): 'definition in mathematics does not mean, as in philosophy, an analysis of the idea to be defined into constituent ideas' (*Principles*, 31). Thus philosophical definition, genuine analysis, is possible only when our terms are complex; with simple terms, the philosopher can only endeavour to perceive them, and to get others to do so too:

The discussion of indefinables—which forms the chief part of philosophical logic—is the endeavor to see clearly, and to make others see clearly, the entities concerned, in order that the mind may have that kind of acquaintance with them which it has with redness or the taste of a pineapple. (*Principles*, p. xv)

The perceptual metaphor is one which Russell takes very seriously—as indeed he is bound to do, for he has nothing else to say about how we can know entities which do not exist:

entities which are not regarded as existing in space and time ... if we are to know anything about them, must be ... in some sense perceived, and must be distinguished one from another; their relations also must be in part immediately perceived.... [In philosophy] all depends, in the end, upon immediate perception; and philosophical argument, strictly speaking, consists mainly of an endeavor to cause the reader to perceive what has been perceived by the author. The argument, in short, is not of the nature of proof, but of exhortation. (*Principles*, 124)

Again, Russell attributes the class contradiction to the fact that 'I have failed to perceive any concept fulfilling the conditions requisite for the notion of a *class*' (*Principles*, pp. xv–xvi).

Besides this conception of philosophy, as being concerned with analysis of complex terms and perception of simple terms, Russell in *Principles* also holds that mathematics is itself a method in philosophy:

in one respect not a few of our discussions will differ from those that are usually called philosophical. We shall be able, thanks to the labors of the mathematicians themselves, to arrive at certainty in regard to most of the questions with which we shall be concerned, and among those capable of an exact solution we shall find many of the problems which, in the past, have been involved in all the traditional uncertainty of philosophical strife. The nature of number, of infinity, of space, time and motion, and of mathematical inference itself, are all questions to which in the present work, an answer professing itself demonstrable with mathematical certainty will be given. (*Principles*, 2)

This is characteristic of one powerful line of thought in later analytic philosophy: that central philosophical problems, such as the nature of mathematics, the reality of space and time, and the contradictions in the infinite, can be *solved* by pure mathematics and logic (which are, of course, not separable for Russell). At least at this time it was the nature of mathematics itself which Russell took as the most important of these problems, and which became the paradigm case of the solution of a philosophical problem by mathematical means; and this paradigm dominated the thought of Russell, and of later philosophers influenced by him, when he, and they, attempted to solve other philosophical problems.

It is, however, not entirely clear what the relationship is between, on the one hand, the philosophical use which Russell makes of mathematics and, on the other hand, the conception of philosophy as consisting of analysis to locate the indefinables and non-sensuous perception of these indefinables. If we wish to reconcile them, we might say that there is *pure* philosophy, which consists in the attempt to perceive the indefinables, and there is analysis, which is a process in which philosophy makes essential use of mathematics and mathematical logic (see above). The crucial fact is that philosophy for Russell now becomes a thoroughly technical subject, one in which the methods and results of mathematics may be relevant at any point, except when we are merely trying to perceive an indefinable—and even here, a mathematical result may show or suggest that we are trying to perceive the wrong thing, and so redirect our attention. Not only is mathematics and mathematical logic relevant to philosophy, but its relevance cannot be circumscribed in advance—any philosophical question may turn out to have an answer that draws upon mathematics and logic. Two points in particular illustrate this. The first is the use of formal methods to solve not only major philosophical problems but also small-scale issues. Russell is faced with a problem over the existence of the null class, because he wants to treat classes extensionally, and believes that doing so rules out the existence of the null class (although there are of course null class-concepts, i.e. concepts under which nothing falls). The solution he offers is to take as a surrogate for the null class the class of all null class-concepts, which can then play the same role in the symbolism as the null class would have played if there had been such a thing. Once technical tricks of this sort are recognized as legitimate means of solving philosophical problems, philosophy has become inextricably mixed with mathematics and logic.

The second point can be seen as a generalization of the first, and is connected with the whole question of what goes on when one tries to reduce mathematics to logic; presumably the aim is to find among the classes a domain of classes which will play the role of (say) the real numbers. But what if one does find such a domain? On Russell's view of mathematics and its relation to philosophy, it ought to remain open to some philosopher to say that while there are classes which are isomorphic to the reals, these classes are certainly not the real numbers themselves, for he can see these quite distinctly in, as it were, another place in the realm of being. In the face of the mathematical fact of the isomorphism, however, this appeal to bare perception seems to carry no weight. The claim that there is another class of objects, the reals themselves, as well as the isomorphic class of classes which has been defined, looks like an unnecessary hypothesis, which should be rejected as a pointless complication. But on Russell's official theory, the rival view is a genuinely different one, which might be true even though more complicated. Russell in fact considers a case of just the kind that I have been discussing:

there is no logical ground for distinguishing segments of rationals from real numbers. If they are to be distinguished, it must be in virtue of some immediate intuition, or of some wholly new axiom.... The above theory, on the contrary, requires no new axiom, for if there are rationals, there must be segments of rationals; and it removes what seems, mathematically, a wholly unnecessary complication, since, if segments will do all that is required of irrationals, it seems superfluous to introduce a new parallel series with precisely the same mathematical properties. I conclude, then, that an irrational actually *is* a segment of rationals. (*Principles*, 270)

Arguments of this form are very hard to resist; yet once one is willing to accept such arguments on what is, officially, a philosophical question, Russell's distinction between a philosophical definition, which gives 'an actual analysis' of a notion, and a mathematical definition, which gives 'merely a set of conditions insuring its presence' (*Principles*, 196, see pp. 187–8, above) becomes very hard to maintain.

To put the point more generally, we might say that in *Principles* Russell invokes facts of acquaintance, but does not take them seriously. By facts of acquaintance here I mean facts of the form: so-and-so is acquainted with such-and-such (or, as in the above example, so-and-so is *not* acquainted with such-and-such). Clearly Russell's view has implications of this form—psychological implications, one might say, since facts of acquaintance are psychological facts. Yet Russell does not take facts of this form seriously enough to allow that they might impose constraints on philosophical theory: he almost invariably assumes that such facts simply are as his theory demands, so that they play no independent role.

Russell's attitude makes two developments natural. One, which does not explicitly occur in the period discussed in this book, is towards the view that facts of acquaintance have no role at all to play, even in principle. This development is perhaps most appealing in the case of acquaintance with abstract objects; its naturalness makes it possible to see in *Principles* the embryonic form of a quite different conception of philosophy. If we have found a model for sentences about (say) the real numbers, a domain of objects in which those sentences have an interpretation which preserves truth and deducibility relations (and makes sense of the application of such sentences), then even on the view of *Principles* it is hard to take seriously the idea that there is a philosophical question about the real numbers which has not been answered. Yet if no such question arises we are left with a view according to which the question, what are the numbers *really*? does not arise. In short, *Principles* can be seen as preparing the way for an anti-metaphysical view which is quite alien to Russell's explicit thought during the period discussed in this book. A second development is to begin to take facts of acquaintance seriously, and to accept them as imposing constraints on philosophical theory. As we shall see in Chapter 6, and especially Chapter 8, Russell's attitude undergoes just such a change. Rather than simply assuming that the facts of acquaintance are what the philosophical theory suggests, Russell comes to be more sceptical about such facts, especially in cases where it is claimed that we are acquainted via sense-perception with existent (concrete) objects. Thus he comes to think that philosophical theory must be shaped around such (alleged) facts; this shift in attitude was to have the greatest importance for his philosophical views in general. Each of these two developments—towards an anti-metaphysical view, and towards a view which treats the (psychological) facts of acquaintance as an important source of data—is, as I have said, a natural development from the view of *Principles*. But note that neither is present to any significant extent in that book: there the facts of acquaintance are, in principle, required for the philosophical theory, but are, in practice, ignored as a source of data, or of constraints on theory.

6

'On Denoting'

In the previous chapter we briefly examined the notion of denoting as it appears in *The Principles of Mathematics*. The point of that notion, as we saw, is to allow a proposition to be *about* an object which it does not *contain*. The theory is that there are certain entities, called 'denoting concepts', which have the following property: if a proposition contains a denoting concept then it is not about that concept but is rather about an object to which the concept stands in a special relation, called 'denoting'. In such a case the object which the proposition is about, 'the denotation' or 'the denoted object', as we might call it, may be either a single term (as is that denoted by the denoting concept *The First President of the USA*) or a complicated sort of collection of terms (as is that denoted by *Any Republican*); there may even be denoting concepts which do not in fact denote anything. Our understanding of the issues surrounding the theory of denoting concepts, as I shall call it, is impeded by a complexity which we have already discussed. Russell often seems to assume that this theory suffices to explain generality—in particular, that we can understand unrestricted variables by means of the denoting concept *any term*, and that this is all that is needed. At other moments, however, Russell explicitly—and convincingly—argues that the theory of denoting concepts will *not* explain multiple generality. At such moments it appears that the crucial step in the explanation of generality is the postulation of propositional functions as indefinable entities standing in a particular relation to the propositions which are their values. The theory of denoting concepts is more or less irrelevant to this explanation. We shall return to this complexity. For the moment the relevant point is that Russell rejects the theory of denoting concepts in 'On Denoting'.[1] The aim of this chapter is to examine the nature of this change in Russell's views, and other changes which took place around the same time. Our discussion will draw on as yet unpublished manuscripts written by Russell between 1903 and 1905.[2]

---

[1] *Mind* (1905). Reprinted in both Marsh and Lackey.
[2] 'On Meaning and Denotation', 'Points About Denoting', both written in 1904 or early 1905; 'On Fundamentals', dated June 1905.

As a preliminary step, let us make some terminological remarks in the hope of avoiding unnecessary confusion. As we have seen, Russell introduces the word 'denoting' as a relation between a non-linguistic entity, a denoting concept, and the object which it denotes (the latter will in most cases also be non-linguistic, but not in all—e.g. *the first word of 'On Denoting'* denotes the word 'By'). As a natural extension of this he speaks of 'denoting phrases', which are phrases whose presence in a sentence indicates the presence of a denoting concept in the proposition expressed by the sentence. As an extension of *this* he sometimes speaks of the phrase itself as denoting, so that denoting appears as a relation between a linguistic item and the object which is denoted (in the original sense) by the denoting concept corresponding to that linguistic item. After the rejection of the theory of denoting concepts Russell has, at least according to his explicit doctrine, no use for the word 'denoting' in its original sense, but he continues to use it as the name of a relation between phrases and things. I shall use the word exclusively in its original sense, as the name of a relation between denoting concepts and the objects they denote, except in the self-explanatory phrase 'denoting phrase'. I shall also call the theory which Russell develops in *OD* to take the place of the theory of denoting concepts 'the *OD* theory'. I begin my discussion with a brief statement of that theory.

The *OD* theory is a theory of denoting phrases, or descriptions, as Russell calls them, both indefinite descriptions (such as 'everything', 'any person', 'some black dog', 'every fast car', etc.) and definite descriptions (such as 'the book you are reading', 'the man who broke the bank at Monte Carlo', 'the greatest number', etc.). The difference between these two is, of course, that the latter purport to pick out a single object whereas the former do not. Both in *OD* itself, and in most discussions of it, definite descriptions receive much more attention than do indefinite descriptions; I shall briefly discuss the reasons for this later. A salient feature of the theory is that it makes no overt use of the notion of denoting, or of a denoting concept. The fundamental and indefinable notions are, rather, said to be that of the (unrestricted) variable and that of a propositional function's being always true, or true of every object (see Marsh, p. 42; Lackey, pp. 104–5).[3] Russell also assumes the notion of falsehood, and thus derives the notions of a

---

[3] Russell often speaks of the *OD* theory as taking the variable as fundamental. It is more accurate to say that the theory takes as fundamental the notions of a propositional function, and of a propositional function's being *always true*, or true of every object; the connection is that Russell thinks of a propositional function as obtained from a proposition by replacing one or more constituents with variables. See *OD*; Marsh, p. 42; Lackey, p. 104. As in *Principles* Russell is always inclined to adopt the view that generality requires only 'the variable'; but he sees that he cannot in fact hold this view.

propositional function's being true of no objects, and of a propositional function's being true of some (one or more) objects. Given this apparatus, the explanation of sentences containing indefinite descriptions proceeds straightforwardly, along lines which are now familiar from elementary quantification theory. Thus the sentence 'Every person is mortal' is to be understood as expressing a proposition whose form is more accurately mirrored by the sentence 'The propositional function "If x is a person then x is mortal" is always true', and so on. The analysis of definite descriptions is more complicated, but almost equally familiar. A sentence ascribing a certain property to a definitely described object is understood as asserting that the predicate from which the definite description was formed is uniquely satisfied, and that whatever object satisfies it has the property in question. Thus, to use Russell's own example, the sentence 'The father of Charles II was executed' expresses a proposition whose form is more accurately mirrored by the sentence 'It is not always false of x that x begat Charles II and that x was executed and that "if y begat Charles II, y is identical with x" is always true of y' (Marsh, p. 44; Lackey, p. 106). This latter sentence is more perspicuous if expressed in quantifier notation:

$(\exists x)[x$ begat Charles II .x was executed. $(y)(y$ begat Charles II $\supset y=x)]$.

The *OD* theory explains descriptions by explaining the form of the propositions expressed by sentences in which such descriptions occur. The explanation does not give us an entity in the proposition which corresponds to the description. According to the theory of denoting concepts, the denoting concept *every person*, say, was such an entity; according to the *OD* theory, however, there is no such entity. Russell emphasizes this point, and expresses it by saying that descriptions 'are not assumed to have any meaning in isolation', and that they 'never have any meaning in themselves, but that every proposition in whose verbal expression they occur has a meaning' (Marsh, pp. 42–3; Lackey, p. 105).[4]

---

[4] It is, however, consistent with Russell's theory to construe a denoting phrase as 'having a meaning in isolation' (i.e., roughly, as indicating the presence of an entity in a proposition) if we take that entity to be a propositional function. Thus the phrase 'every person' can be taken to correspond to a (second-level) propositional function which is true of a (first-level) propositional function just in case the latter is true of every person, the phrase 'the man who broke the bank at Monte Carlo' to a propositional function true of a propositional function just in case the latter is uniquely true of the man who broke the bank at Monte Carlo. This possibility does not, as I shall argue, undermine the point that Russell is trying to make by means of the expression 'have no meaning in isolation'; see n. 17 below.

The importance of allowing for this possibility has been urged on me by my colleague Nathan Salmon.

Before discussing the details of the *OD* theory I shall take up two issues which are, I shall argue, independent of that theory. Between *Principles* and *OD* Russell's views on ontology and epistemology underwent significant changes. These changes are often thought to depend upon the change that occurred when he adopted the *OD* theory, but this idea seems to me mistaken in both cases. Arguing this point in each case will enable us to see how Russell's views were evolving between *Principles* and *OD*; it will thus put us in a position to evaluate the significance of *OD*.

I begin with an ontological issue: how are we to account for sentences containing definite descriptions (or names) which do not in fact uniquely describe (or name) anything? Must we suppose that there is a present King of France (say) in order to give a plausible account of sentences containing the expression 'the present King of France'? This issue has been thought, by some commentators,[5] to be the crucial feature of *OD*, and to provide the motive for the change which that article represents in Russell's thought. Some encouragement for this view can be found in Russell's own later statements of the significance of *OD*:

Meinong... pointed out that one can make statements in which the logical subject is 'the golden mountain' although no golden mountain exists. He argued, if you say that the golden mountain does not exist, it is obvious that there is something that you are saying does not exist—namely the golden mountain; therefore the golden mountain must subsist in some shadowy Platonic world of being, for otherwise your statement that the golden mountain does not exist would have no meaning. I confess that, until I hit upon the theory of descriptions, this argument seemed to me convincing. (*MPD*, p. 84)

This is misleading, because the theory of denoting concepts also has the consequence that definite or indefinite descriptions do not function in the same way as names, i.e. the presence of a description in a sentence does *not* show that the sentence expresses a proposition which contains the object described. For this reason it is also clear that according to the theory of denoting concepts a definite description may have a role in significant sentences even though it does not in fact pick out a unique object. According to that theory a definite description, 'the present King of France', say, functions by indicating a denoting concept, *the present King of France*. If the phrase occurs in a sentence, the denoting concept will occur in the proposition expressed by the

---

[5] e.g. W. V. O. Quine, 'Russell's Ontological Development', in R. Schoenman (ed.), *Bertrand Russell: Philosopher of the Century*, (London: Allen & unwin, 1967), p. 305; A. J. Ayer, *Russell* (London: Fontana 1972), pp. 53–5.

sentence (at least in the usual sort of case). This is enough to give the phrase a meaning, both in the sense of showing what non-linguistic entity it corresponds to and in the sense of explaining how it can have a role in significant sentences. Nothing in the theory of denoting concepts demands that the denoting concept *the present King of France* must actually denote something in order to occur in propositions. Thus the theory of denoting concepts explains how we can meaningfully say 'The present King of France is bald', and can truly say 'there is no present King of France', without presupposing that there is a present King of France subsisting (even if not existing) in the realm of being.

This issue is confused because Russell's ontological views undergo an important change between *Principles* and *OD*, but the change is in fact independent of, and slightly earlier than, the change from the theory of denoting concepts to the *OD* theory. Russell's account of mathematics demands that the notion of denoting must, from the outset, allow for the possibility of denoting concepts which do not denote anything. We must be able to say that there are no members of a given class, that there is no greatest number, and so on. Since the sort of putative entities that these statements deny are not spatio-temporal, this is not simply a denial of existence as distinguished from being. In terms of that distinction, it is a denial of being, and Russell uses the possibility of denotationless denoting concepts to make sense of this (see *Principles*, 73, and Chapter 5, pp. 211–12, above). Russell seems, however, to lose sight of this possibility in those portions of *Principles* where more general metaphysical questions are under discussion. Even though the theory of denoting concepts would enable Russell, in *Principles*, to deny that the present King of France has being, there is no sign that he realizes this fact. More important, perhaps, there is no sign there that he sees any reason to deny being to the present King of France. In that book he is, notoriously, willing to attribute being to any putative object we can name. In section 427 he argues quite generally that: ' "*A* is not" must always be either false or meaningless' (see Chapter 5, above, pp. 172–3, where this argument is discussed). This section is far from a grudging admission of the being of every putative entity. On the contrary: outside the context of mathematics, Russell willingly asserts that every expression which seems to refer to something does in fact refer to a real entity, which has being even if it does not exist in space and time. (This attitude is no doubt to be explained, at least in part, by the fact that Russell is reacting against idealist claims that such-and-such is not real, or not fully real.)

Russell's attitude towards this issue changes between *Principles* and *OD*. We saw in Chapter 5 that the theory of denoting concepts can be used to deny that certain names and definite descriptions succeed in naming or describing anything. The present point is that Russell came to recognize this fact and take advantage of it outside the context of mathematics. This is quite clear in an article published in *Mind* for July 1905, 'The Existential Import of Propositions':[6]

[nectar and ambrosia] are substances having such and such properties which, as a matter of fact, no substances do have. We have thus merely a defining concept for each, without any entity to which the concept applies. In this case, the concept is an entity, but it does not denote anything . . . 'The present King of England' is a complex concept denoting an individual; 'The present King of France' is a similar concept denoting nothing. The phrase intends to point out an individual, but fails to do so: it does not point out an unreal individual, but no individual at all. The same explanation applies to mythical personages, Apollo, Priam, etc. These words have a *meaning*, which can be found by looking them up in a classical dictionary; but they have not a *denotation*: there is no entity, real or imaginary, which they point out. (*EIP*, p. 100)

This view is in direct conflict with that of *Principles*. The difference, however, does not depend upon the *OD* theory, which Russell clearly did not hold when he wrote the article. It is a change of attitude which is independent of the later technical change.[7]

Russell's ontological views thus undergo a major shift. He now implicitly accepts that some objects are, so to speak, intrinsically spatio-temporal: if they have any kind of ontological status at all then they exist in space and time. Not all objects are intrinsically spatio-temporal, of course, for Russell continues to accept that there are propositions and propositional functions, for example, which are fully real but are not spatio-temporal. What he no longer accepts, however, is that there are objects, such as the King of France, which might exist but which in fact do not. This shift of doctrine is usually associated with the change of theory that took place when Russell rejected the theory of denoting concepts in favour of the *OD* theory; I have argued, however, that the doctrinal shift is independent of the change in theory.

We can see something of the significance of this change of doctrine by seeing how it alters the distinction between being and existence. Russell continues to use these words to mark a distinction (see e.g. *Problems of Philosophy*, Chapter IX), but the nature of the distinction changes. It becomes a distinction between the ontological status which

---

[6] *Mind* (1905), 398–401; repr. in Lackey, pp. 98–102.

[7] My view is thus just the opposite of Quine, who says: 'The reform [from a Meinongian position] is no simple change of heart; it hinged on his discovery of a means of dispensing with the unwelcome objects [i.e. on the *OD* theory]', op. cit. n. 5 above, p. 305.

one kind of object has, and that which another kind of object has. One kind of object is intrinsically non-spatio-temporal; if an object of this sort has any kind of reality it has *being*. Another sort of object is intrinsically spatio-temporal; if an object of this sort has any kind of reality it *exists*. Russell no longer accepts that there are objects such as the putative present King of France, which are just like existent objects except that they happen not to exist. Because there are no such objects, we no longer have to think of being and existence as two different ontological statuses which a given object may have. We can instead think of a single notion of existence which applies unequivocally to objects of two different sorts. In the idea that objects are of these two different sorts we can see what came to be called the distinction between abstract objects and concrete objects.

To this point I have said nothing about the reasons for Russell's change of doctrine. If in early 1905 Russell used the theory of denoting concepts to eliminate the need to suppose that there is a present King of France, why did he not do so in 1902, when he wrote *Principles*? Part of the answer to this question is that after writing *Principles* Russell became aware of certain problems which arise from the assumption that every apparent referring expression does indeed refer. The reason that Russell became aware of these problems at this stage is, I suspect, that he read Meinong's ontological works.[8] Meinong shared the ontological generosity of *Principles*, but had thought it through more rigorously, and was more aware of its potential problems. It is plausible to suppose, therefore, that reading and reflecting upon the ontological work of Meinong (and, later, his followers) made Russell realize the difficulties of his own ontological attitude, and led him to give it up. This change did not, however, occur immediately. In the long article which Russell published on Meinong in April, July, and October of 1904,[9] he endorses the ontological attitude of *Principles* (and also of Meinong). In particular, he argues that any proposition which attributes being to some putative entity must be true. If such a proposition is false, he says, 'it affirms the being of what, *ex hypothesi*, does not have being, and therefore there is nothing of which it affirms the being, and therefore it affirms nothing and is meaningless' (*MTCA*, pp. 48–9; cf. pp. 72–3). Russell now sees difficulties in this view,

---

[8] In the main body of *Principles* Russell refers to Meinong a number of times, but not to the ontological doctrines for which he is now known. *Über Annahmen*, perhaps the chief source for those doctrines, was not published until 1902; Russell mentions it in a footnote in Appendix A (476) but does not discuss it.

[9] 'Meinong's Theory of Complexes and Assumptions', *Mind* (1904), 204–19; repr. in Lackey, 21–76.

however, which he does not seem to have been aware of when he wrote *Principles*. Thus he says:

> when we consider such complexes as 'the difference between *a* and *b*' which must be admitted by some door, it seems plain that, when *a* and *b* are identical, there is no difference between *a* and *b*, which seems equivalent to saying 'the difference between *a* and *b* does not have being'. (*MTCA*, p. 62)

In this article the problem is left as unsolved; Russell is, however, beginning to be aware that there are problems caused by the attitude of *Principles*.

To this point I have argued that Russell's change of mind about whether there is (in any sense) a King of France is independent of the change from the theory of denoting concepts to the *OD* theory. Because Russell published almost nothing manifesting the new onto-logical attitude until he published *OD*, however, it has often been assumed that the ontological attitude and the technical change are directly connected. This is the assumption that I have argued against. Very similar remarks can be made about another Russellian change of attitude that took place around the same time. This concerns questions of epistemology and psychology, in broad senses of those words. It concerns, that is to say, not how things are in the world which is independent of us, but how we come into contact with those things, how they affect our minds. In the period after *Principles* we see the beginning of a quite general shift in attitude and interest which was to be of increasing importance over the following decade or more.

Russell by no means abandons his anti-psychologism after *Principles*, but he does begin to take some interest in questions which he might there have dismissed as merely psychological. In arguing against Meinong's view that false propositions are not objective entities, for example, Russell analyses the notion of awareness with a view to discovering what the objects of awareness must be like (*MTCA*, pp. 65–7). This sort of argument embodies the idea that the objects of a psychical state, though they may be entirely independent of that state, must be capable of being its objects. This idea is quite trivial once stated, and certainly Russell would never have *denied* it. But neither would the Russell of *Principles* have relied upon it; in that book he eschewed all concern with the psychological, in any sense, almost as if psychologism might be contagious. There are other signs in *MTCA* of a new-found interest in 'psychological' questions. The notion of percep-tion is analysed at some length (pp. 30–7), and Russell considers such questions as: can complexes be perceived? (pp. 24, 29–30); are internal perceptions more certain than external perceptions? (p. 33); is material-ism 'derived from perception of what belongs to psychology' (p. 33)?

Again, the discussion of denial and affirmation manifests a more psychological bent than that in *Principles*. In the earlier work Russell insists that he is not interested in the psychological sense of assertion, but only in a curious and totally non-psychological sense of the notion (a sense of assertion which implies, among other things, that an asserted proposition is true; see *Principles*, 38, 478). In the later work, by contrast, the notion of assertion is clearly understood psychological-ly: 'the state of mind in which we reject a proposition is not the same as that in which we accept its negation' (p. 41). In this turn towards the psychological Russell is, I suspect, influenced not only by Meinong but also by Moore.[10]

Russell's concern with the psychological, in the period after *Prin-ciples*, must not be exaggerated. He is as far as ever from seeing the objects that make up the world as in any sense constituted by the action of the mind. His new concern represents the beginning of a shift not so much in doctrine as in interest. It also, however, introduces a new kind of constraint in his philosophical theorizing, that of psycho-logical plausibility. This is clearest, and most significant, in the case of the crucial notion of acquaintance. This notion is, as we saw, presup-posed throughout *Principles*. In that work, however, it does not play a substantive role, because it carries with it no constraints. Russell there seems to assume that every term (in his sense) is a possible object of acquaintance; the notion thus functions simply as a way of avoiding any discussion of epistemological or 'psychological' questions. After *Principles* Russell's attitude shifts. Questions of psychological or episte-mological plausibility intrude, and lead to the conclusion that not every object that we seem to be able to talk about is a possible object of acquaintance. This in turn leads to various attempts to show how we can (at least apparently) talk about things which are not possible objects of acquaintance. (These issues have their greatest effect on Russell's work in the period after *Principia*; see Chapter 8, below, especially Section 2.)

In *OD* and after Russell puts forward what I shall call 'the principle of acquaintance'; in connection with this he introduces a distinction between knowledge by acquaintance and knowledge by description. The principle of acquaintance states that I must be acquainted with every constituent of any proposition which I understand. The distinc-tion between knowledge by acquaintance and knowledge by descrip-

---

[10] See in particular the two articles 'The Refutation of Idealism' and 'Experience and Empiricism'. Moore's concern in both is not with the timeless world of propositions and concepts but with the relation of that world to human beings, and in particular with the notion of sense-perception.

tion is introduced to allow for the possibility of my having knowledge about an object with which I am not acquainted. Thus I may know that the man who broke the bank at Monte Carlo is bald, even though I am not acquainted with him. According to the *OD* theory, this is possible because the proposition that I know does not contain the man who is its subject-matter. It contains, rather, the propositional functions $\hat{x}$ *is a man*, $\hat{x}$ *broke*, $\hat{x}$ *is a bank*, $\hat{x}$ *is at Monte Carlo* (as well as the propositional function $\hat{x}$ *is bald*, and logical entities). This technique came to be crucial to Russell's theory of knowledge, as we shall see; in *OD* he appears to claim that the principle of acquaintance is a result of this technique and of the *OD* theory which makes it possible. The penultimate paragraph of *OD* begins as follows:

One interesting result of the above theory of denoting [i.e. of the *OD* theory] is this: when there is anything with which we do not have immediate acquaintance, but only definition by denoting phrases, then the propositions in which this thing is introduced by means of a denoting phrase do not really contain this thing as a constituent, but contain instead the constituents expressed by the several words of the denoting phrase. Thus in every proposition that we can apprehend (i.e. not only those whose truth or falsehood we can judge of, but in all that we can think about), all the constituents are really entities with which we have immediate acquaintance. (Lackey, pp. 118–19; Marsh, pp. 55–6)

In spite of this statement, I do not think that either the principle of acquaintance or the distinction between knowledge by acquaintance and knowledge by description is intrinsically connected with the *OD* theory. Russell does not state the principle of acquaintance in *Principles*, but it is, I think, implicit in that work. It receives no formulation because Russell simply has no interest in issues of this sort. Nor is there any reason for him to formulate it, since at this stage in his work it imposes no constraints and is thus quite trivial. The one exception to this is the case of propositions about the infinite, for Russell denies that we are acquainted with any such propositions. How, then, can we understand and know propositions about the infinite? Russell's answer is that what we understand in each such case is a finitely complex proposition, one of whose constituents *denotes* infinitely many terms (see *Principles*, 141). Implicit in this answer is an analogue of the distinction between knowledge by acquaintance and knowledge by description.[11] The theory of denoting concepts allows for such a dis-

[11] This distinction is also implicit in Russell's use of the theory of denoting concepts to explain how there can be informative (true) statements of identity: the propositions expressed by such statements do not simply contain the same object twice, but contain at least one denoting concept which denotes the object. See *Principles*, 64, and Chapter 5, above, p. 211.

tinction just as does the *OD* theory. According to the theory of denoting concepts, the proposition that the man who broke the bank at
Monte Carlo is bald does not have among its constituents the man
whom it is about. It has, rather, the denoting concept *the man who broke*
the bank at Monte Carlo. Clearly this kind of case, where what is known
is a proposition containing a denoting concept which denotes an object, can be distinguished from the kind of case in which what is
known is a proposition containing the object itself. This distinction is
directly analogous to that which Russell later called the distinction
between knowledge by acquaintance and knowledge by description.
Russell does not articulate any such distinction in *Principles*, because he
has no interest in knowledge and because his assumptions about acquaintance mean that he would in any case have very little use for the
distinction.

Given what has been said so far, one might expect that when Russell
begins to accept implicit constraints on the notion of acquaintance he
would also become self-conscious about both the principle of acquaintance and (the analogue of) the distinction between knowledge by
acquaintance and knowledge by description. And this, indeed, is exactly what we do find, in unpublished material written between *Principles*
and *OD*, most explicitly in 'Points About Denoting' (written late in
1904 or early in 1905, but in any case clearly before Russell invented the
OD theory). The first of these 'Points' is 'That sometimes we know that
something is denoted, without knowing what'; under this rubric Russell argues 'that to be known by description is not the same as to be
known by acquaintance' (fo. 2). A little later he writes as follows:

It is necessary, for the understanding of a prop[osition] to have *acquaintance*
with the *meaning* of every constituent of the meaning [i.e. the denoting con-
cept]; it is not necessary to have acquaintance with such constituents of the
denotation which are not constituents of the meaning.... In the proposition
'there is one and only one instance of *u*', the said instance is not a constituent
of the meaning, hence the proposition may be known without our being
acquainted with the instance. Thence we can define the instance as 'the *u*', and
make props about it, while yet remaining unacquainted with it. (fo. 6)

(See also 'On Fundamentals', fo. 17, where Russell uses the expression
'denotative knowledge' for knowledge which comes via denoting concepts.) In this material, written before *OD*, we see Russell beginning to
use the principle of acquaintance in argument. Rather than merely
responding to philosophical claims held for other reasons, the notion
of acquaintance becomes itself a source of philosophical claims. Consider, for example, the following passage from 'On Meaning and Denotation':

If we say, for instance, 'Arthur Balfour advocates retaliation', that expresses a thought which has for its object a complex containing as a constituent the man himself; no one who does not know what is the designation of the name 'Arthur Balfour' can understand what we *mean*: the object of our thought cannot, by our statement, be communicated to him. But when we say 'the present Prime Minister of England believes in retaliation', it is possible for a person to understand this completely without knowing that Mr. Arthur Balfour is Prime Minister, and indeed without his even having heard of Mr. Arthur Balfour. On the other hand, if he does not know what England is, or what we mean by *present*, or what it is to be Prime Minister, he cannot understand what we mean. This shows that Mr. Arthur Balfour does not form part of our meaning, but that England and the present and being Prime Minister do form part of it. Thus the *meaning* of the two propositions is different: a man may know either without knowing or even understanding the other. (fo. 3)

This style of argument is familiar in the post-*OD* works of Russell, but not the pre-*OD* works. As this quotation suggests, however, the emergence of this sort of argument is the result of a shift in attitude which is not intrinsically connected with *OD*.

Epistemologically there is thus no evident difference between the *OD* theory and the theory of denoting concepts. Just as the former enables one to distinguish knowledge by acquaintance from knowledge by description, so the latter enables one to distinguish knowledge by acquaintance from knowledge by denoting, or 'denotative knowledge'. The difference is in the sorts of entities with which one has to be acquainted: propositional functions in the one case, denoting concepts in the other. When Russell turns his attention to the issue of our knowledge, and especially of our knowledge of the spatio-temporal world, the distinction between direct knowledge (acquaintance) and indirect knowledge becomes crucial to his thought. Because he holds the *OD* theory at that time, and not the theory of denoting concepts, indirect knowledge is called 'knowledge by description' and understood in accordance with the *OD* theory. It is thus easy to have the impression that it is only in terms of the *OD* theory that we can understand the notion of indirect knowledge. This impression is incorrect. The initial phase of Russell's thought about our knowledge of the physical world (1909–13, say) could have been carried out equally well if *OD* had never been written and Russell had continued to hold the theory of denoting concepts. This is not so clearly true of his treatment of knowledge after 1913, as we shall see (Chapter 8, Section 2, below).

In *OD* Russell gives up one theory, which I have called the theory of denoting concepts, and adopts another, which I have called the *OD* theory. I turn now to the question, why he makes this change. What we have said so far rules out one answer to this question: clearly

Russell does not, as has sometimes been supposed, adopt the *OD* theory in order to avoid having to assume the being of entities such as the King of France. We have shown that the theory of denoting concepts equally enables one to avoid this consequence, and that Russell fully appreciated this fact. This point is, from the perspective of the present question, purely negative. Why, then, does Russell reject the theory of denoting concepts? The most important consideration, I think, is one having to do with the relation of a denoting concept, or 'meaning', as Russell calls it, to the object which it denotes. Russell says exactly this at the start of a famous passage of 'On Denoting':

The relation of the meaning to the denotation involves certain rather curious difficulties, which seem in themselves sufficient to prove that the theory which leads to such difficulties must be wrong. (Lackey, p. 111; Marsh, p. 48)

What is the relation of the meaning to the denotation, which leads to such difficulties? It is, of course, that the meaning *denotes* the denotation. To take an example: *the teacher of Plato* denotes Socrates. Facts of this sort are of course crucial for the theory of denoting concepts. Given the metaphysics of Platonic Atomism, the fact that *the teacher of Plato* denotes Socrates simply *is* the (true) proposition that *the teacher of Plato* denotes Socrates. But now consider this proposition. What are its constituents? We might suppose that its constituents would be: the denoting concept *the teacher of Plato*, the relation of denoting, and the man Socrates. But this cannot be correct, for the presence in a proposition of a denoting concept indicates that the proposition is not about that denoting concept but is about the denoted object (if any). So we cannot have a proposition which is about a denoting concept in virtue of containing that denoting concept. If we put a denoting concept into a proposition then the proposition is about the denoted object, not about the denoting concept. As Russell says: 'The difficulty in speaking of the meaning of a denoting complex may be stated thus: The moment we put the complex in a proposition, the proposition is about the denotation'. (*OD*: Lackey, p. 112; Marsh, p. 49).[12]

The obvious response to this argument is to say that the proposition which expresses the fact that *the teacher of Plato* denotes Socrates does not contain the denoting concept *the teacher of Plato*, but is *about* that denoting concept in virtue of *containing* some other entity.[13] This other

---

[12] Russell is also at some pains to establish this point in the unpublished work from the period immediately before *OD*. See *OMD*, fos. 16–18, and *OF*, fos. 2, 7, 35–6.

[13] Here again, these are ideas which are explored in the unpublished work. Thus in *OF* Russell says: 'To speak of C [some arbitrary denoting complex] itself requires either a concept which denotes C, or else some further kind of occurrence.... And a concept which denotes C must not contain C as entity (as is the case, e.g., with "the meaning of

entity must of course also be a denoting concept, but one whose denotation is itself a denoting concept—the one that our proposition is to be about. Russell considers just this idea, taking the third letter of the roman alphabet, upper case, as indicating an arbitrary denoting concept:

to speak of C itself, i.e. to make a proposition about the meaning [the denoting concept], our subject [i.e. the constituent of the proposition in subject-position] must not be C, but something which denotes C. (Lackey, p. 112; Marsh, p. 50)

Russell uses single quotation marks around the third letter of the roman alphabet, upper case, to indicate when he is speaking of this something which denotes C:

Thus 'C', which is what we use when we want to speak of the meaning [i.e. of the original denoting concept, C], must not be the meaning, but something which denotes the meaning. (loc. cit.)

But now we are faced with the problem of the relation of 'C' to C, which is no more tractable than was our original problem, that of the relation of *the teacher of Plato* to Socrates:

Thus it would seem that 'C' and C are different entities, such that 'C' denotes C; but this cannot be an explanation, because the relation of 'C' to C remains wholly mysterious. (Lackey, p. 113; Marsh, p. 50)

Let us put these issues in terms of our example. We began with the idea that *the teacher of Plato* denotes Socrates. A proposition which states this, we saw, cannot itself contain the denoting concept which it is about. If there is to be such a proposition, it must contain a further denoting concept, a second-level denoting concept, we might say, which denotes the denoting concept *the teacher of Plato*. But now it is clear that we are faced with an infinite hierarchy of denoting concepts. There must be a proposition which states that the second-level denoting concept denotes the first-level denoting concept, and in order to be *about* the second-level denoting concept, this proposition must presumably *contain* a third-level denoting concept. Since the third-level denoting concept must denote the second-level denoting concept, there must be a proposition which expresses this; in order to be *about* the third-level denoting concept, that proposition must presumably *contain* a fourth-level denoting concept—and so the hierarchy is launched.

C''), for then we get the denotation of C occurring where we meant to have the meaning.' The reference to different kinds of 'occurrences' here is to the idea that a denoting complex may 'occur' in a proposition either 'as entity' or 'as meaning'; see pp. 253–4, below.

It is not hard to see why Russell might have found these consequences of the theory of denoting concepts implausible. To begin with, the infinite hierarchy of denoting concepts is completely *ad hoc*: apart from the exigencies of the theory of denoting concepts, there is no reason at all to accept it. The existence of such an infinite hierarchy may seem, at the least, implausible ('where', asks Russell, 'are we to find the denoting complex 'C' which is to denote C'). Worse, the infinite regress which generates the hierarchy appears to be vicious. For there to be any cases of denoting, there must be facts of the form: *the teacher of Plato* denotes Socrates. But a fact here is just a true proposition, and for there to be such a proposition there must be a second-level case of denoting. But for this to be possible there must be a fact that the second-level denoting concept denotes the first-level denoting concept. But again, a fact is just a true proposition, and for there to be such a proposition there must be a third-level case of denoting, and so on. For denotation to occur at any level, it must occur at a higher level. Russell himself, in *Principles*, distinguishes regresses of implication, which he takes to be benign, from 'regresses of analysis', which are vicious (*Principles*, 55). A regress of the latter sort is one which 'arises in the analysis of the actual meaning of a proposition'. The regress that we have been discussing is surely of the latter, vicious, sort. The very possibility of one case of denoting requires another, and so on without end. At no stage do we have any reason to believe that denoting is indeed possible; the attempt to resolve our doubts in any one case only leads us to another case of the same sort, for which the same doubts arise.

We can make what is at bottom, I think, the same point in a somewhat different way. The crucial idea for understanding denoting is that a proposition may be *about* an object which it does not contain. It is by no means obvious how to make sense of this idea within the context of Platonic Atomism. We saw in Chapter 5 that a natural way to do so is to say that for a proposition containing a denoting concept to be about some other entity is for the truth-value of that proposition to be dependent upon the truth-value of the proposition obtained from it by replacing the denoting concept by the denoted entity (see pp. 208–10, above). Let us call this the principle of truth-value dependence. Given this principle, there cannot be a proposition which says that *the teacher of Plato* denotes Socrates. We have already seen that such a proposition cannot itself contain the denoting concept *the teacher of Plato*, but would rather have to contain a second-level denoting concept denoting it. But now the effect of the principle of truth-value dependence is to say that the proposition containing the second-level denoting concept depends for its truth-value upon the proposition containing the denoted object.

In this case, the denoted object is the first-level denoting concept, so we get back to a proposition containing the first-level denoting concept, *the teacher of Plato*. Applying the principle once more shows that this proposition (containing the first-level denoting concept) depends for its truth-value upon the corresponding proposition containing the denoted object, i.e. upon the absurdity that Socrates denotes Socrates.[14] Clearly the same argument works if we consider a proposition containing a third-level (or higher-level) denoting concept: according to the principle, that proposition is dependent for its truth-value upon the corresponding proposition at the previous level, and so on down until we reach a proposition without any denoting concepts. The principle of truth-value dependence thus has the consequence that there are no true propositions which say that one entity denotes another; but clearly there must be such propositions if the theory of denoting concepts is correct.

The argument above shows that if denoting is to be understood in accord with the principle of truth-value dependence, there can be no true propositions of the form *a* denotes *b*. One might respond to this by saying that the theory of denoting concepts is in some way unstatable. The metaphysics of Platonic Atomism, however, equates facts with true propositions, so the idea of an unstatable fact need not even be considered. Given that metaphysics, there can be no facts of the form *a* denotes *b*. The attempt to introduce the notion of denoting into Platonic Atomism thus results in an incoherence; *OD*, on this way of looking at the matter, is Russell's removal of the incoherence (though it might be questioned, as we shall see, whether the new doctrine in fact succeeds in removing the incoherence). Now the incoherence only arises in the straightforward fashion that we discussed in the last paragraph if denoting is indeed to be understood in accord with the principle of truth-value dependence. We saw in Chapter 5 that it is hard to find any other way to understand the idea. Furthermore *OD* contains a second argument against the theory of denoting concepts, which also suggests that Russell held the principle of truth-value dependence.

The second kind of argument that *OD* contains against the theory of denoting concepts goes like this:

---

[14] One might be tempted at this stage to suggest modifying the theory of denoting concepts so that every object other than a denoting concept denotes itself, i.e. every object becomes a denoting concept of one kind or the other. The drawback to this idea is that it is characteristic of a denoting concept that its presence in a proposition refers us to some other proposition, that on which the truth-value of the first proposition depends. But this requires that some propositions are simply true or false in their own right, and this requires that some propositions do not contain denoting concepts of any kind.

The proposition 'Scott was the author of *Waverley*' has a property not possessed by 'Scott was Scott', namely that George IV wished to know whether it was true. Thus the two are not identical propositions; hence the meaning of 'the author of *Waverley*' must be relevant as well as the denotation, if we stick to the point of view to which this distinction belongs. Yet . . . so long as we adhere to this point of view, we are compelled to hold that only the denotation can be relevant. (Lackey, p. 113; Marsh, pp. 50–1)

At first sight this is puzzling. Platonic Atomism has no trouble in distinguishing the proposition that Scott is Scott from the proposition that Scott is the author of *Waverley*. The two propositions have different constituents; one contains a denoting concept and the other does not. If we have two distinct propositions, why should they not have different properties? This puzzle is removed if we suppose that Russell is taking for granted something like the principle of truth-value dependence: that the truth-value of a proposition containing a denoting concept depends upon the truth-value of the corresponding proposition with the denoted object replacing the denoting concept. While the principle holds for the proposition that Scott was the author of *Waverley*, it clearly fails when this proposition is embedded in the more complex proposition that George IV wanted to know whether Scott was the author of *Waverley*.

The principle of truth-value dependence fails, as the above example shows, for idioms of propositional attitude (John thinks that . . . , Mary wonders whether . . . , etc.). This sort of failure, however, is not an isolated phenomenon in Russell's philosophy. The notion of a proposition is, as we have seen, fundamental to Russell's thought, and this notion immediately gives rise to many contexts for which the principle of truth-value dependence fails, e.g. that such-and-such a proposition contains Socrates, or contains a given propositional function, etc. On the other hand, the failure of truth-value dependence is not, as Russell rather suggests in *OD*, a knock-down argument against the theory of denoting concepts.

The unpublished manuscript 'On Fundamentals' shows Russell attempting to accommodate the failure of the principle of truth-value dependence. He distinguishes different ways in which a denoting concept may occur within another complex: as being or as meaning, depending on the nature of the complex, and position within the complex, in which the denoting concept occurs. Russell puts the distinction like this, using the word 'complex' where we have been using 'denoting concept':

When a complex occurs as being, any other complex having the same denotation, or the denotation itself, may be substituted without altering the truth or non-truth of the complex within which the said complex occurs. (*OF*, fo. 18)

A denoting concept occurs *as meaning* in a complex, presumably, if this is not so.

Russell also has, however, another criterion to distinguish the two kinds of occurrence: when a denoting concept occurs as being (i.e. where we have what he calls an 'entity-occurrence'), it must be possible to replace it with any other entity without loss of significance; not so when it occurs as meaning. The two criteria, however, do not precisely coincide; as Russell says: 'there would seem to be a third mode of occurrence of a complex, in which the occurrence is an entity-occurrence as regards significance, and a meaning occurrence as regards truth' (*OF*, fo. 19).

There is also another source of complication in Russell's theory. The distinction between 'occurring as meaning' and 'occurring as being' is one that he makes for denoting concepts, not for all entities. In particular, no such distinction applies to propositions (we shall briefly return to this point; see pp. 263–4, below). For this reason, it makes a crucial difference whether the complex in which the denoting concept occurs (as being or as meaning) is a denoting complex or a propositional complex. As soon as Russell begins to take this issue into account, the resultant theory becomes very complicated. He draws six interrelated distinctions to keep track of the various ways in which denoting concepts can occur within more complex entities (see *OF*, fos. 23–7). Even so, it appears that the theory needs to be yet more elaborate if it is to do what is required of it. Thus there is, as I have said, no knock-down argument here. There is, however, a discussion which is so complex, and so lacking in explanatory power, that one gets the sense of a theory about to collapse under its own weight. The arguments that Russell takes as decisive against the theory of denoting concepts appear to be those involving the relation of meaning to denotation. Reading the relevant pages of *OF*, however, makes it easy to understand why Russell should have welcomed the possibility of replacing that theory by the far simpler *OD* theory.

Russell's arguments against the theory of denoting concepts leave him in a peculiar and complex situation. Let us recall three facts, each of which puts *OD* in a somewhat different light. First, according to most of his explicit statements in *Principles*, Russell introduced the theory of denoting concepts primarily in order to 'explain the variable', where he assumes that such an explanation will account for quantification theory. In the light of this fact it is striking that one thing which the *OD* theory does not offer is an alternative explanation of the variable; on the contrary, it takes that notion for granted. Thus we might say that Russell eliminates denoting only by assuming the crucial case of it—i.e. that he does not eliminate denoting but simply reduces it to the one case of the variable. Second, at least at some moments Russell recognizes that the theory of denoting concepts will not account for quantification theory, and that the indefinable notion of a propositional function is required. Focusing on this fact might lead us to say that in *OD* Russell accepts that the sort of account that he had hoped, in *Principles*, to give of quantification theory is simply not obtainable, and that he realizes that if we once accept quantification theory we do not also need to postulate denoting—that the idea is simply otiose. Third, propositional functions are related to other entities—their values—by a relation which is analogous to denoting. The analogy here seems close enough to ensure that the problems of the relation of meaning and denotation will arise here, for a propositional function, like a denoting concept, has the crucial property that a proposition which contains it is not thereby about it, but is rather about other entities. This fact, like the first, suggests that Russell has not so much eliminated denoting as reduced it to a special case—but now to the special case of the propositional function and its values, rather than that of the variable.

Russell's own attitude towards the achievement of *OD* in relation to generality is primarily the first of those indicated above. This does not emerge from *OD* itself, but is clear in various unpublished works. I spoke above of Russell as reducing denoting to the single case of the variable. He himself puts the matter exactly this way in a passage from 'On Fundamentals' which immediately follows the first formulation of the new theory. I shall quote this passage at some length:

It seems imperative to find some meaning for x and $\phi'x$ ... which shall not involve us in the difficulties of denoting. The interesting and curious point is that, by driving *denoting* back and back as we have been doing, we get it all reduced to the one notion of *any*, from which I started at first. This one notion seems to be presupposed always, and to involve in itself all the difficulties on account of which I rejected other denoting concepts. Thus we are left with the task of concocting *de novo* a tenable theory of *any*, in which denoting is not used. The interesting point which we have elicited above is that *any* is genuinely more fundamental than other denoting concepts; they can be explained by it, but not it by them. And *any* itself is not fundamental in general, but only in the shape of *anything*.

Anything seems to be exactly the same as *the variable*. When we say 'f'anything', we say just the same as when we say 'f'x'. We should, of course, simply say that 'anything' is a primitive idea, if it were not for the fact that we cannot get clear as to the relation of its meaning to its denotation. (*OF*, fo. 44)

A very similar point is made in an exchange of letters between Moore and Russell, after Moore had read *OD*. Moore comments on *OD* as follows:

What I should chiefly like explained is this. You say '*all* the constituents of propositions we apprehend are entities with which we have immediate acquaintance.' Have we, then, immediate acquaintance with the variable? And what sort of an entity is it? (Moore to Russell, 23 October 1905)

Russell responds to the comment, in a letter dated two days later.

I am glad that you agreed to my main contentions in the article on Denoting. I admit that the question you raise about the variable is puzzling, as are all questions about it. The view I usually incline to is that we have immediate acquaintance with the variable, but it is not an entity. Then at other times I think it is an entity, but an indeterminate one. In the former view there is still a problem of meaning and denotation as regards the variable itself. I only profess to reduce the problem of denoting to the problem of the variable. This latter is horribly difficult, and there seem equally strong objections to all the views I have been able to think of.

'On Fundamentals' contains lengthy discussions of the nature of the variable, but Russell finds no view that he regards as satisfactory. From this point on he simply says that the variable is to be taken as fundamental and unexplained. Given that it is in fact the propositional function which is used in the account of generality, both before and after *OD*, it may seem as if there is little change here. Still, Russell's new rhetoric about treating the variable as fundamental is a considerable shift from the emphasis, in *Principles*, on finding 'a correct philosophy of *any*'.

Our discussion to this point makes it hard to see what real change in Russell's views is effected by *OD*. The need to account for generality appeared in *Principles* to be the crucial reason for introducing denoting, but on this issue there is no new theory (instead there is either the assertion that the variable is fundamental, or there is the same theory of propositional functions as was given at some points in *Principles*). And given that both the variable (on Russell's usual account) and propositional functions (in his more careful discussions) involve something like denoting, it is not clear that his new view avoids the difficulties of the relation of meaning to denotation. Nevertheless *OD* does change Russell's view in a significant way. To understand the nature of this change we have to consider what I shall call the phenomenon of (non-propositional) complexity. What I mean by this is the fact that there are complex ways of talking about objects, where the complexity of the way of talking may not reflect a corresponding complexity in the objects themselves. Thus 'the (positive) square root of nine' contains 'nine', but three does not contain nine; 'the teacher of Plato' contains 'Plato', but Socrates does not contain his pupil. Now facts of this sort, as well as the need to handle the notion of generality, might be thought to be enough to force a modification of the naïve view of Platonic Atomism in the direction of something like a distinction between meaning and denotation. Clearly we need to be able to explain the fact that (say) 'The teacher of Plato is wise' follows from 'All teachers are wise', and this we cannot do if we construe the former sentence as expressing a proposition which simply contains Socrates as its subject. On the other hand, however, since 'The teacher of Plato is identical with Socrates' is true, it seems impossible, according to naïve Platonic Atomism, to construe 'the teacher of Plato' as indicating a constituent of the proposition other than Socrates.[15] The theory of denoting concepts removes this apparent difficulty: 'the teacher of Plato' indicates the presence in a proposition of a denoting concept which denotes Socrates; since propositions which contain denoting concepts are about the denotation rather than the denoting concept, the identity statement is literally true. But now if the theory of denoting concepts is also to explain why 'The teacher of Plato is wise' follows from 'All teachers are wise', then we must assume that some denoting concepts have a kind of structure, that they can be complex in the sense of containing various objects and even other denoting concepts. This sort of complexity must hold not only for definite descriptions but also for indefinite descriptions, e.g. the denoting concept expressed by 'every student who ever admired the teacher of Plato' is one which we shall be forced to recognize as having a definite structure.

The phenomenon of complexity thus provides a reason for the theory of denoting concepts which is to some extent separable from the problem of explaining generality and the variable. In *Principles* there is no sign at all that Russell was influenced by these sorts of considerations. In the period immediately after that book, however, he clearly was:

It is to be observed that, in such a phrase as 'the present Prime Minister of England', the various words employed merely designate their objects, and do not, taken singly, express anything other than what they designate. The fact from which our whole discussion [of meaning and denotation] starts is embodied in this, that the whole phrase designates something of which the designations of the parts are not parts. There is *some* object involved, of which England etc. are parts; but this object is not the designation of the phrase, since England is not part of Mr. Balfour. Thus we were led to assume an object, called the *meaning* of the phrase, of which England, etc., were parts. (*OMD*, fo. 13)

---

[15] Notice that nothing in this argument turns on whether an identity statement is informative; the point has nothing to do with information content or other cognitive matters. The issues here are ontological, not epistemological; this is not to deny, of course, that the change I am discussing has epistemological implications.

Russell seems here to suggest that what I am calling the phenomenon of complexity is the primary or fundamental basis for the introduction of meanings which denote entities other than themselves. This attitude is perhaps even more clearly manifested in a brief passage from the end of the same manuscript: '"The father of Socrates" contains Socrates, but his father did not. This is the ultimate ground for distinguishing meaning and denotation; and this ground seems irrefutable' (*OMD*, fo. 96).

The phenomenon of complexity, as we have discussed it, requires us to recognize that constituents may combine into a unity in a way which is distinct from their combination into a proposition. The nature of this unity is as problematic for Platonic Atomism as is the unity of a proposition. The unity of a proposition is not dispensable, but it turns out that non-propositional unity is. This is a clear achievement of the *OD* theory: it completely eliminates the need for non-propositional complexity.[16] This is perhaps most straightforward in the case of indefinite descriptions. Take the sentence 'Every student who admires Socrates is wise'. According to the theory of denoting concepts, this sentence expresses a proposition which contains the complex denoting concept *every student who admires Socrates*. According to the *OD* theory it contains the variable and the propositional functions $\hat{x}$ *is a student* and $\hat{x}$ *admires Socrates* (as well as $\hat{x}$ *is wise* and logical entities). The whole combines into a unity, but it is a propositional unity. There is no complex referring expression, which would require explanation in terms of a non-propositional kind of unity, for there is no complex referring expression at all. Similarly in the case of a definite description. According to the theory of denoting concepts, 'The man who broke the bank at Monte Carlo is bald' expresses a proposition which contains a complex denoting concept corresponding to the words 'the man who broke the bank at Monte Carlo', and this denoting concept has a unity which is non-propositional in character. According to the *OD* theory, however, the proposition contains only the variable, various logical entities, and the relevant (non-complex) propositional functions; the only kind of complexity is propositional. It is for this reason, I think, that Russell so insists on the idea that (what appear to be) complex referring expressions 'have no meaning in isolation'. If 'the man who broke the bank at Monte Carlo' had meaning in isolation, i.e. when not part of a sentence expressing a proposition, it

---

[16] It is presumably for this reason that Russell speaks throughout *OD* of 'denoting *complexes*'. Because of the doubt about whether the variable (or propositional function) is not itself a denoting concept, Russell might well be reluctant to say that *OD* eliminates all denoting concepts; but clearly it does eliminate complex denoting concepts.

would also have unity in isolation, and this unity would be of a non-propositional sort.[17] The insistence that such phrases have no meaning in isolation is the insistence that there is no non-propositional unity which needs to be explained.

The elimination of non-propositional complexity is not simply a matter of avoiding something which cannot be explained. Propositional complexity is, as we emphasized in Chapter 4, no more metaphysically explicable. But Russell's logic gives him a method of handling and exploiting propositional complexity, whereas he has no such method of handling non-propositional complexity. According to the theory of denoting concepts, the inferences from 'Rover is a black dog' to 'Rover is a dog' and from 'Rover is the best dog' to 'Rover is a dog' depend upon the structure of denoting concepts. But this kind of structure is not one into which we have any insight, except that it must give certain results. In particular, the theory of denoting concepts gives us no reason to count the above inferences, and others like them, as logical in character. The elimination of non-propositional complexity in favour of propositional complexity completely changes this situation. Russell's logic exploits the structure that we have been calling propositional complexity. Both of the inferences above, which are obscure if we accept the theory of denoting concepts, are transparent if we accept the *OD* theory. It becomes transparent also that the inferences are logical in character. The *OD* theory thus meshes with Russell's logic in a way that the theory of denoting concepts had not done. The effect of the introduction of the new theory is to give a new account of the propositions expressed by sentences containing definite and indefinite descriptions; the new account makes it clear that such sentences have a structure which Russell's logic can exploit.

The considerations of the previous paragraph might make it appear as if Russellian logic could not be applied at all by one who consistently held the theory of denoting concepts—as if only the *OD* theory made the development of that logic possible. What this idea overlooks, however, is the fact that according to *Principles* the variables of logic and mathematics are universal. This means that a sentence which says that all prime numbers are so-and-so is understood as expressing a proposition which contains the unrestricted variable and says of any term that if it is a number and if it is prime then it is so-and-so. Here there is no problem in applying logic; we obtain in effect the same

[17] It is for this reason, also, that the possibility mentioned in n. 4 above seems to me to be, from a Russellian point of view, an unimportant one. Since the 'meaning in isolation' suggested there is itself a propositional function, it does not threaten to introduce a non-propositional kind of complexity.

analysis that we obtain according to the *OD* theory. (If we analysed the sentence as containing the denoting concept *all prime numbers* then Russell's logic would not be applicable to it; but so analysed the sentence contains a restricted variable.) In virtue of his view that logic and mathematics use unrestricted variables, then, Russell is able to exploit the insights of logic even before the development of the *OD* theory. (Although there is no direct textual evidence, it is tempting to suppose that this is another reason for his insistence that logic and mathematics must use unrestricted variables.) Even before *OD* he is, moreover, clearly aware that the same treatment can be given to indefinite descriptions quite generally, i.e. not only to those in logic and mathematics (see 'On Meaning and Denotation', fo. 33). The technique which enables definite descriptions to be treated the same way, however, is one that Russell seems to work out in the course of thinking about the relation of meaning to denotation (see *OF*, fo. 38). As soon as he does so he gives up the theory of denoting concepts, and on the next page draws the conclusion:

The above theory leads to the result that *all* denoting functions are meaningless in themselves, and are only significant when they occur as constituents of propositions. Hence all complexes become undenoting: they will be such as propositions, propositional functions, modes of combination, etc. (fo. 39)

This is one reason why *OD* so emphasizes *definite* descriptions. The elimination of indefinite descriptions, in favour of the variable and propositional functions, is a possibility of which Russell had long been aware. The possibility of eliminating definite descriptions, by contrast, was the result of a technical insight which was quite new to Russell as he worked out the *OD* theory. (We shall shortly see a second reason why Russell so emphasizes definite descriptions.)

I said above that the *OD* theory eliminates complex referring expressions; expressions which are complex are not construed as referring. There is one kind of apparent complex referring expression which is of particular importance to mathematics, namely functional expressions. How is Russell able to construe an expression such as '5 + 7', or '3^2', without accepting them as complex referring expressions? A philosopher who takes the notion of a function in the ordinary sense to be fundamental, as Frege does, is bound to acknowledge phrases of this sort as complex referring expressions. For a philosopher who holds this view it is, therefore, very natural, if not inevitable, to make a distinction analogous to Russell's distinction between meaning and denotation. Russell, however, does not take the ordinary notion of a function as fundamental. He uses the notion of a definite description to define functions in terms of propositional functions. This is a second reason for the importance that Russell attributes to definite descriptions: both in *Principles* and in *PM* they are used to define ordinary mathematical functions in terms of propositional functions.[18] Suppose that a given relation, or two-place propositional function, $\hat{x}R\hat{y}$ satisfies this condition: for each entity y, there is only one entity x that makes the proposition $\hat{x}R\hat{y}$ true. Then we can derive a function from the relation as follows: for any y, the value of the derived function is to be the entity x which makes the relation true for the given value of y. (If $\hat{x}R\hat{y}$ does not satisfy the condition I laid down, we can still carry out the definition; but what we get will not be a function in the usual sense.) Similarly, if $f(x)$ is the function derived from $\hat{x}R\hat{y}$, '$y = f(x)$' is to mean 'y = the z such that zRx'. Before *OD*, Russell therefore calls non-propositional functions 'denoting functions', because they involve the denoting phrase 'the entity which makes the relation true...' (see *OMD*, fos. 34–40); after *OD* he calls them, for analogous reasons, 'descriptive functions':

the ordinary functions of mathematics... are not propositional. Functions of this kind always mean 'the term having such and such a relation to y.' For this reason they may be called *descriptive* functions, because they *describe* a certain term by means of its relation to their argument....

The general definition of a descriptive function is:

*30.01 $R'y = (\imath x)\,(xRy)$ Df

(*PM*, *30)

The symbol '$\imath$' in the above is of course Russell's definite description operator. In *PM* it is given a contextual definition (in *14) along the lines laid down in *OD*, but the use of the notion to obtain ordinary functions from propositional functions is the same before *OD* as after.

The previous paragraph makes clear a point that has been implicit throughout our discussion of the phenomenon of complexity. For Russell, a propositional function is not a special case of a more general notion of function, which is antecedently understood. Again there is a clear contrast here between Russell and Frege. For Frege the notion of a function, in something like the ordinary mathematical sense, is the fundamental one, and concepts are understood as special cases of functions.[19] For Frege a sentence has the same kind of unity as a

---

[18] Some of the intervening manuscripts show Russell considering taking the notion of an ordinary (non-propositional) function as fundamental, but this ceases to be an option for him after *OD*, because it is plausible for Russell only in the light of a distinction between meaning and denotation.

[19] Fregean concepts (*Begriffe*)—the Fregean analogues of propositional functions—are those functions whose values are always truth-values. Frege's treatment of logic, and his analysis of language, are thus more mathematical than Russell's; in order to reduce mathematics to logic Frege first mathematizes logic. This difference between Fregean functions and Russellian propositional functions has important consequences for Russell's theory of types; see below, Chapter 7, pp. 279–80.

complex referring expression; hence it is entirely natural for Frege to say that sentences *are* complex referring expressions. Russell denies each of these Fregean doctrines (see the correspondence between Frege and Russell, from October 1902 to December 1904; these letters are of considerable interest, but they do not show a meeting of minds on these issues). What gives substance to Russell's views here is that propositional functions, as he conceives of them, are not like other functions. The general notion of a function is such that, for a given argument, a function may yield a value of which the argument is in no sense a constituent, and which stands in no very particular relation to the function itself. Thus, as already remarked, three is the positive square root of nine, but three does not *contain* nine; Socrates is the teacher of Plato but does not contain him. The crucial idea here is that a function takes an argument and yields a (possibly quite distinct) value. This crucial idea, however, does not apply to propositional functions. For a given entity as argument, a propositional function yields as value a proposition which contains that entity (according to Russell's usual account, indeed, the proposition differs from the propositional function only in that it contains the given entity in place of the variable). The sense in which a propositional function takes an argument and yields a value is thus more perspicuous than is the sense of this idea for functions in general.

The fact that the notion of a propositional function is in this way more perspicuous than that of a function in general is, I think, one reason why Russell takes the former notion as fundamental and the latter as derived. There is also a somewhat different consideration, which is more explicit in Russell's discussion. By Russell's lights, the proposition that Socrates is wise is a different proposition from the proposition that the teacher of Plato is wise, even though Socrates *is* the teacher of Plato.[20] A function in the usual sense does not share this feature of the propositional function $\hat{x}$ *is wise*. It follows from '$3^2 = 9$' that '$(3^2)+1 = (9)+1$', and so on for functions other than the successor function. We may express this by saying that, for ordinary (non-propositional) functions, the substitution of co-referential expressions within a functional expression does not change the reference of the expression as a whole (the language here is not Russell's, but nothing is said that could not be said in Russellian terminology). If we interpret linguistic predicates as expressing functions (as Frege does), this principle implies e.g. that '$3^2 > 5$' refers to the same thing as '$9 > 5$', or

---

[20] Note that the theory of denoting concepts, understood in terms of the principle of truth-value dependence, threatens to blur this distinction. The *OD* theory, by contrast, makes the difference clear-cut.

'the number of the planets > 5', and so on. By repeating this sort of procedure, we can show that we are forced to treat as co-referential sentences which seem, at first sight, to have nothing in common except their truth-value.[21] Just as Frege held that concepts are functions, so also he held the reference of a sentence is its truth-value. It was on this basis, indeed, that Frege distinguished concepts from other functions: a concept is a function whose values are truth-values. Russell finds the idea that sentences refer to truth-values simply incredible. In a letter to Frege he says, for example, 'For me there is nothing identical about two propositions that are both true or both false' (24 May 1903). In *OMD* Russell considers the view, which is more or less equivalent to Frege's, that a proposition is a meaning which has a distinct denotation—at least if it is true. He considers this view because he is attracted by the idea that true propositions denote facts. He decides against the view because he sees that propositions which do not in any intuitive sense express the same fact will nevertheless have to be counted as denoting the same thing. The considerations here are roughly those which lead, on the Fregean view, to the conclusion that all true sentences refer to the same thing. Russell objects to the view he is considering as follows:

the fact does not remain the same when a different description is substituted. It is difficult to think that 'Felton killed Buckingham' denotes the same fact as is denoted by 'Charles I's Lord High Admiral was assassinated at Southampton when he was about to embark on an expedition for the relief of the Huguenots'. (*OMD*, fo. 28)

Over the last few pages I have been discussing the phenomenon of non-propositional complexity, and I have argued that one clear change which *OD* makes in Russell's thought is that it eliminates the need for such complexity. The arguments against the theory of denoting concepts, and thus for the *OD* theory, which I discussed above (pp. 249–53), however, have nothing to do with this issue. Those arguments apply equally to simple (non-complex) denoting concepts, such as the variable (this fact explains the worries which we saw Russell express at *OF*, fo. 44). Hence the question arises: does the phenomenon of complexity have anything at all to do with Russell's rejection of the theory of denoting concepts in favour of the *OD* theory? The answer to this question is not straightforward. Russell does not take the issues arising from the phenomenon of complexity as the source of (what he takes to be) a conclusive argument against the

---

[21] See e.g. Ch. I of A. Church, *Introduction to Mathematical Logic* (Princeton: Princeton University Press, 1944) for a more detailed discussion.

theory of denoting concepts. In particular, little role seems to be played by the idea that non-propositional complexity is inexplicable, given the metaphysics of Platonic Atomism.[22] The sorts of issues that I have been discussing do, however, seem to play some role in Russell's dissatisfaction with the theory of denoting concepts. The crucial point here is one already discussed, namely that Russell is not willing to accept any analogue of the distinction between meaning and denotation for sentences, i.e. that the notion of a proposition remains fundamental to his thought. As we have already indicated, this fact ensures that Russell's theory of meaning and denotation must, at best, be extremely complex; this complexity may have played a role in his willingness to abandon the theory (see pp. 253–4, above).

I turn now to the question of the significance of *OD* for Russell's philosophy, and I begin with the issue of its *ontological* significance. We have seen that the ontological progress of *OD*, as compared with the theory of denoting concepts, is not that it enables one to account for sentences using the words 'the King of France' without supposing that there is a King of France. This task can equally be performed by the theory of denoting concepts. The real ontological importance of *OD* cannot be understood if we concentrate on its analysis of definite (or indefinite) descriptions. Let us look again at the consequences of that analysis. According to the *OD* theory, neither the Queen of England nor the denoting concept *the Queen of England* occurs in propositions expressed by sentences using the expression 'the Queen of England'. Nevertheless, it is a consequence of the *OD* theory—and of the theory of denoting concepts—that there must *be* a Queen of England if there are to be interesting[23] *true* sentences which contain that expression. The two theories differ over what there must be in the proposition but not, one might say, over what there must be in the world, to account

---

[22] Russell makes something like this point in considering the view that sentences have both meaning and denotation, and that the denotation of a true sentence is the fact that makes it true. He says that if we hold this view then 'we must suppose that [the constituents of the proposition] are combined in one way by the denotation, and in another way by the meaning. But inspection reveals, to me at least, no such twofold combination' (*OMD*, fo. 12). Here, however, the difficulties raised by the issue of complexity are applied only to the case of sentences; Russell does not seem to realize that difficulties as to the nature of the complexity involved exist also for the case of referring expressions.

[23] I say '*interesting* true sentences' to exclude such cases as 'The present King of France does not exist', 'It is not the case that: the King of France is bald', 'Either the King of France is bald or grass is green', etc. All of these are true, according to the theory of descriptions, but they are not to the present point. Note that all of them except the first are truth-functionally complex, and that in these cases the non-complex sentence containing 'the King of France' is false.

for the possibility of interesting truths expressed using the words 'the Queen of England'. The notion of an incomplete symbol, which Russell formulated to account for definite and indefinite descriptions, lends itself to a more profound ontological use which has just that feature which its use in the case of definite descriptions lacks. It allows us, that is, to account for the possibility of interesting truths which are expressed using an (apparent) referring expression, without supposing that this expression in fact refers to anything. The crucial example here is Russell's attitude towards classes in his mature type theory, developed from 1906 onwards. Russell's claim here is that there are no classes: phrases which appear to refer to classes are to be explained without supposing that there are classes; yet what he wishes to explain about such phrases is not merely how they can occur in *significant* sentences but rather how they can occur in sentences which are (putatively) true. This is clearly a rather different use of the notion of an incomplete symbol from that which is involved in the analysis of definite descriptions. The definition which introduces symbols which appear to refer to classes is this:

$$f\{\hat{z}(\psi z)\} = \text{df } (\exists\phi)[(x)(\phi!x \equiv \psi x) \ \& \ f(\phi!\hat{z})]$$

(The symbol '!' here indicates that $\phi!x$ is a *predicative* function, i.e., roughly, that it is of the next order above that of its highest-order argument. What this means, and why it matters, will be discussed in Chapter 7, below, pp. 308–10.) In virtue of this definition, the truth-value of '$f\{\hat{z}(\psi z)\}$' depends only upon the extension of the propositional function $\psi\hat{z}$. The symbol '$\hat{z}(\psi z)$' thus operates (in the context '$f\{\hat{z}(\psi z)\}$') as if it stood for an extensional entity—the class of objects of which the propositional function $\psi\hat{z}$ is true. But in fact the symbol '$\hat{z}(\psi z)$' does not stand for any kind of entity: it is an incomplete symbol. The definition gives a sense to expressions of the form '$f\{\hat{z}(\psi z)\}$', and shows that some such expressions can be true, without implying that there is an entity for which '$\hat{z}(\psi z)$' stands. Sentences which appear to be about classes are shown to be in fact about propositional functions; the quantifier on the right-hand side ranges over propositional functions, not over classes. The truth of these sentences is thus shown not to imply the existence of classes. Analysing sentences (which appear to be) about classes shows that they do not in fact imply the existence of classes. In such a case, analysis is elimination.

The general ontological significance of *OD* thus comes from the notion of an incomplete symbol, which leads quite naturally to the idea of analysis as elimination. This technique can be used to claim that a given body of theory, which one wishes to hold as true, does not in fact have the ontological implications which it appears to have. It is partly for this reason that Russell speaks of the *OD* theory as crucial to the theory of types, a connection which is otherwise quite obscure.

> When the *Principles of Mathematics* was finished, I settled down to a resolute attempt to find a solution to the paradoxes . . . Throughout 1903 and 1904, my work was almost wholly devoted to this matter, but without a vestige of success. My first success was the theory of descriptions . . . This was, apparently, not connected with the contradictions, but in time an unsuspected connection emerged. (*MPD*, p. 79)

Strictly speaking, the connection here is not directly with the theory of descriptions but rather with the notion of an incomplete symbol. But Russell introduced the notion of an incomplete symbol in the context of the descriptions, and once introduced the notion rather obviously lends itself to the sort of ontological use that makes the elimination of classes possible. As we shall see in Chapter 8, the conception of analysis as elimination also comes to play a central role in other aspects of Russell's philosophy (most obviously in his epistemology, from 1913 or 1914 onwards).

There is, I think, no doubt that *OD*, and the notion of an incomplete symbol developed there, played a crucial role in enabling Russell to achieve everything that he wished to achieve by a theory of classes without assuming that there are classes. Without disputing this claim, however, it is perhaps worth pointing out that the same effect could in fact have been achieved by the theory of denoting concepts—though it is perhaps only with hindsight that this could be understood. Suppose we say that '$\hat{z}(\psi z)$' indicates a denoting concept which denotes a predicative propositional function, $\phi!\hat{x}$, which is co-extensive with $\psi\hat{x}$. *Which* such predicative propositional function (assuming there to be more than one) is denoted by our denoting concept is left open, just as the *Principles* theory left it open which person is denoted by the denoting concept *some person*. Then '$f\{\hat{z}(\psi z)\}$' will be true just in case '$f(\phi!\hat{x})$' is true for some predicative function, $\phi!\hat{x}$, which is co-extensive with $\psi\hat{x}$, just as it is according to *20.01 of *PM*. One might think that the falsity conditions of the two interpretations would not coincide in this way, because of the existence of propositional functions which are not co-extensive with any predicative propositional function. If there were such cases they could perhaps be handled by a suitable choice of a default denotation, but in fact this is unnecessary. The axiom of reducibility asserts that every propositional function is co-extensive with a predicative propositional function, so a denotation would be assured for every denoting concept of the sort under discussion. The difference between using the theory of denoting concepts to eliminate classes, in this way, and using Russell's technique, can best be thought of as follows. According to Russell's method, a sentence which appears to ascribe a predicate to a class is replaced by the assertion that there is a propositional function which has the property indicated by the predicate and also satisfies certain conditions (it is predicative, it is co-extensive with the original sentence). According to the theory of denoting concepts method, these conditions are not explicitly asserted but are built into the denoting concept, making it complex. It is precisely this sort of non-propositional complexity which, as I have said before, the *OD* theory eliminates.

The fact that the theory of denoting concepts could have been used to eliminate classes in favour of propositional functions is of no direct relevance to understanding the development of Russell's thought, for it is a possibility of which he does not seem to have been aware. I mention the point partly for any intrinsic interest which it may have, but partly also because it can be used to illustrate something which is important for the understanding of Russell's thought. The *OD* theory is directly connected with a shift in Russell's conception of philosophical analysis. Let us again consider sentences of the form '$f(\hat{z}(\psi z))$', i.e. sentences which appear to ascribe a certain predicate to a class, and contrast the two methods of showing that we can accept such sentences without assuming the existence of classes. The crucial point of contrast is that according to the method suggested by the theory of denoting concepts the analysis does not change the superficial logical form of the sentences which are to be analysed. The proposition expressed by such a sentence has the subject-predicate form of the original sentence. All the work of analysis goes into understanding the subject. The expression '$\hat{z}(\psi z)$' is understood not as indicating that the proposition contains a certain class, but as indicating that it contains a denoting concept which denotes a propositional function (or a combination of such) which satisfies certain conditions. Analysis, on this conception, goes referring expression by referring expression, and predicate by predicate. According to the conception introduced by *OD*, however, analysis must be thought of as going sentence by sentence. Russell's post-*OD* way of understanding a sentence of the form '$f(\hat{z}(\psi z))$' is as expressing a proposition the form of which is most accurately reflected by the sentence '$(\exists \phi)((x)(\phi!x \equiv \psi x) \mathbin{\&} f(\phi!\hat{z}))$'. Analysis thus leads us from a sentence of subject-predicate form to one of quite different logical form.

The point illustrated in the previous paragraph is quite general, and marks a second aspect of the significance of *OD* for Russell's philosophy. With that article he begins to develop a conception of analysis according to which the logical form of the sentences involved is crucial. Analysis, on this conception, will typically lead to a sentence of a quite different logical form from that with which we began, and the chief task of analysis is that of finding the underlying logical form of the proposition, a logical form which may be masked by the sentence expressing the proposition. This is in contrast to Russell's earlier conception of analysis, where the logical form of the sentence, or the way in which it divides up into units, is usually accepted as being the logical form of the underlying proposition. On this earlier conception, the work of analysis goes into giving an account of these units, not into questioning the division. Thus we saw that in analysing '$f(\hat{z}(\psi z))$' according to the theory of denoting concepts we assumed that '$\hat{z}(\psi z)$' corresponded to an entity in the subject place of a subject-predicate proposition, and all the work was in saying exactly what this entity might be. Russell's emphasis, in *OD* and after, on the notion of an incomplete symbol is, I think, to be understood as a way of insisting upon the new conception of analysis.[24] He calls an expression an incomplete symbol as a way of emphasizing the fact that where such a symbol occurs in a sentence, say as the subject of a subject-predicate sentence, we may have to understand that sentence as expressing a proposition of quite different logical form, one which may not have a subject, or whose subject does not correspond to the given symbol. The crucial idea here is that analysis may lead us to a proposition with a quite different logical form from that of the sentence with which we started. Over the decade or so after *OD*, this view of analysis, and its associated notion of logical form, came to dominate Russell's view of philosophy as a whole. Thus he came to speak of philosophy as consisting largely, at least, of discovering, investigating, and cataloguing logical forms. The study of logical forms is, Russell claims, a part of logic; and it is this part of logic that he has in mind when he speaks of logic as the essence of philosophy,[25] or when he says that 'Philosophy . . . becomes indistinguishable from logic'.[26] Contrasting Philosophy with the synthetic method of the special sciences, Russell says:

in philosophy we follow the inverse direction: from the complex and relatively concrete we proceed towards the simple and abstract by means of analysis, seeking in the process, to eliminate the particularity of the original subject-matter, and to confine our attention entirely to the logical *form* of the facts concerned.[27]

[24] Here again it is, I hope, clear that the suggestion of n. 4 above does not undermine what is important in Russell's position.
[25] See e.g. *Our Knowledge of the External World* (London: Allen & Unwin 1914; 2nd edn. (1926), Ch. II, esp. p. 67.
[26] 'Scientific Method in Philosophy', in *Mysticism and Logic* (New York: Longmans, Green & Co., 1918), p. 84.
[27] op. cit. n. 25 above, pp. 189–90; emphasis in the original.

Thus far I have discussed two aspects of the general significance of *OD* for Russell's subsequent philosophy: the use of the techniques suggested by *OD* to eliminate certain ontological assumptions, and the shift in the conception of analysis. Both of these contribute to a third aspect, which is that Russell begins to pay explicit attention to words and sentences: language becomes a subject of philosophical interest. In my discussions of the last two chapters I emphasized that both Moore and Russell, in the period under discussion, paid little overt attention to language. Propositions were not thought of as constructs, or as entities which were to be inferred from our use of language. They were held, rather, to be directly and immediately accessible to the mind. Propositions, on this view, were themselves the data for philosophy. Both Russell and Moore simply assumed this view, and did not even articulate it. From the outside, however, one can see that it depends on the further assumption that there is a congruence between sentences and the propositions that they express, so that language is a transparent medium through which propositions can be perceived. It is the very transparency of the medium, as they assume, which enables Russell and Moore to ignore it. The effect of the *OD* theory is to undermine these assumptions. A symptom of this is that 'incomplete symbol' becomes an important technical term in Russell's philosophy— the first such term that is explicitly linguistic in its reference. In my discussions of the two earlier aspects of the significance of *OD* I constantly talked about language, about expressions and symbols. There is simply no other way to present those matters. To describe the ontological use of the theory one must say that *sentences* which appear to be about classes can be held true without assuming that there are classes; or that *expressions* which appear to refer to classes can be explained, in context, within the same constraints. The case of the new conception of analysis is perhaps even clearer, though more complicated. One way in which this conception of analysis forces attention to words is through the contrast that it brings between the logical form of the sentence which is to be analysed (superficial logical form, or grammatical form) and the logical form of the underlying proposition (logical form *simpliciter*). If grammatical form can no longer be assumed to coincide, more or less, with real logical form then we must attend to grammatical form, if only to avoid being misled by it. Russell's early view of propositions as data, and language as a transparent medium, is in sharp contrast with his later emphasis on the dangers of being misled by grammar. His later attitude is that the grammatical form of the sentence will usually be quite different from the logical form of the proposition; and that many philosophical mistakes arise precisely from the neglect of this distinction. Thus in Lecture One of 'The Philosophy of Logical Atomism' he says: 'Some of the notions that have been thought absolutely fundamental in philosophy have arisen, I think, entirely through mistakes as to symbolism' (in Marsh, pp. 185–6). Because Russell comes to believe that symbols are fundamentally misleading, he also comes to think that symbolism is of great philosophical importance—not because it is really the thing we mean to talk about in philosophy but because it will mislead us if we do not pay attention to it. This is quite explicit in a well-known passage, also from Lecture One of 'The Philosophy of Logical Atomism':

There is a good deal of importance to philosophy in the theory of symbolism, a good deal more than at one time I thought. I think the importance is almost entirely negative, i.e. the importance lies in the fact that unless you are fairly self-conscious about symbols, unless you are fairly aware of the relation of the symbol to what it symbolizes, you will find yourself attributing to the thing properties which only belong to the symbol. That, of course, is especially likely in very abstract subjects such as philosophical logic, because the subject-matter that you are supposed to be thinking about is so exceedingly difficult and elusive that . . . you do not think about it except perhaps once in six months for half a minute. (Marsh, p. 185)

Perhaps more important than this somewhat grudging overt admission of the importance of language is the pressure which Russell is under, contrary to his explicit doctrines, to take language as the real subject with which he is dealing. To understand this, let us put matters in the wider context of the general issue of the analysis of language. Platonic Atomism may be seen as based on the paradigm of a simple two-stage analysis of language: on the one hand the words making up the sentence, on the other hand the proposition which they express, which is identical with the reality which the sentence is about; in the case of expressions other than sentences the same two-stage analysis holds: on the one hand the word, on the other hand the reality. In neither case is there a third entity, intermediate between the words and the reality they are about. There is thus a clear contrast between Platonic Atomism and a Fregean view, according to which there are senses intermediate between the words and the reality. A Fregean view puts forward a three-stage analysis, whereas Platonic Atomism puts forward a two-stage analysis, at least for the paradigm cases. A crucial fact confronting the advocate of Platonic Atomism, however, is that the paradigm cases are not the only kind. Other kinds of cases do not seem to permit the simple two-stage analysis.

One kind of case in which the two-stage analysis seems at least too simple is that of sentences involving generality. This reason for abandoning the two-stage analysis is quite clear to Russell in *Principles*, and leads to the theory of denoting concepts. Other reasons, which begin to be significant in the period after *Principles*, are ontological and epistemological. The ontological reason against the two-stage analysis is based on the fact that this analysis has the consequence that a word which fails to correspond to anything—e.g. a name which names nothing—has no role in language, but is merely an empty noise. The epistemological reason is based on the fact that the two-stage analysis suggests that in order to understand an expression I must know the corresponding reality—in Russell's view, must be acquainted with it. These facts are ones which Russell would accept in *Principles* as well as in the period after that book. The difference is that in the later period, as we have already seen, Russell begins to take a narrower view both of what things there are and of what things we can suppose ourselves to be acquainted with. (If one accepts, as Russell comes to, that we cannot suppose ourselves to be acquainted with anything whose existence we can doubt, then it is clear that the ontological assumptions play no separate role; it will suffice to talk about the epistemological assumptions; see Chapter 8, below, especially Section 2.) On these new assumptions the two facts greatly restrict the sentences to which the simple two-stage analysis is applicable. It is no longer explicit generality alone which gives rise to exceptions to the paradigm; on the contrary, cases conforming to the paradigm come to seem exceedingly rare.[28]

In the earlier part of this chapter, I argued that the theory of denoting concepts can in fact handle the problems which Russell's new epistemological assumptions pose for the two-stage analysis of language. It is important to see, however, that the theory of denoting concepts involves a departure from the paradigm. In particular, it involves a denial of the crucial identification of the proposition expressed by a sentence and the reality which the sentence is about. Almost every sentence will express a proposition which contains a denoting concept; the sentence is not, however, about the denoting concept but about what it denotes. Thus the theory of denoting concepts seems to lead us to a three-stage analysis of most, though not all, sentences of a language: for most sentences we have, as well as the sentence itself, the proposition which it expresses and, distinct from this, the reality which the sentence is about (this reality should perhaps be thought

---

[28] The idea that *some* cases, at least, conform to the paradigm persists in Russell's philosophy. This is the significance of what Russell later speaks of as names 'in the strict logical sense of the word' ('Philosophy of Logical Atomism', in Marsh, p. 201). A sentence consisting of a name in this sense and a (logically) simple predicate would be one for which a two-stage analysis is appropriate. From this point of view we can say that in *Principles* Russell held almost every grammatical name to be a logical name. His changing ontological and epistemological assumptions undermined this view, and as time went by his increasingly stringent epistemological views had the consequence that almost nothing could count as a name in the logical sense.

of as another proposition, or collection of propositions, distinct from
the one expressed by the sentence). Similarly for most, though not all,
names: we have the name itself, the denoting concept corresponding to
it, and the object (if any) which the denoting concept denotes.

In *OD* Russell ostensibly rejects the three-stage analysis of language
which was being increasingly forced upon him. I say 'ostensibly' here
because it is arguable that the use of propositional functions to explain
generality involves a kind of three-stage analysis. A sentence expressing generality corresponds to a proposition containing a propositional
function; but this proposition must in turn stand in some special
relation to a number of other propositions (in the simplest case, the
proposition containing the propositional function asserts the truth of
all, or some, or none, of the propositions which are the values of the
propositional function). In spite of this qualification, Russell usually
writes as if he has given up the attempt to explain generality, and is
thus free to adopt a two-stage analysis of language; I shall explain how
things look from this perspective. There are still epistemological
reasons for being dubious of the two-stage analysis of language, but
Russell now attempts to show that those reasons can in fact be
accommodated within the two-stage analysis. The crucial point here is
the idea that if we are dealing with the right sentences then the
two-stage analysis (modified by taking generality as unproblematic)
will apply. The sentences to which the analysis seems not to apply are
to be transformed into sentences to which the analysis does apply.[29]
Sentences of the former kind are one and all equivalent to sentences of
the latter kind in the strictest possible sense: they express the same
proposition. More than this, sentences of the latter kind express the
proposition in a less misleading fashion: their structure corresponds to
the structure of the proposition; the very fact that the analysis seems
not to apply to other sentences shows that they express the proposition
in a misleading way.

These points make it clear why Russell after *OD* increasingly insists,
as we have seen, on the misleadingness of language. In the case of
almost every sentence, considerable work is needed to get it into a
non-misleading form, i.e. into the form of a sentence to which the
two-stage analysis can be directly applied. Our discussion also shows
that the new conception of analysis is one in which language is crucial-

---

[29] Notice that to try to do this directly for sentences expressing generality would
require that we transform such a sentence into an infinite conjunction or disjunction, or
possibly into a sentence with an infinitely complex subject (assuming that the generality
is expressed over an infinite domain). This would have been reason enough for Russell
to reject this idea.

ly involved. On the new conception, analysis is a process of trans-forming one sentence into another. A single proposition, after all, is expressed equally by the unanalysed sentence and by the fully an-alysed sentence and by all the sentences which constitute the various stages of analysis between the two. So philosophical progress may consist in the transition from one sentence to another. Russell may say that this is progress only because the second sentence more nearly reflects the form of the proposition, but nothing in the process of analysis itself gives these words any force. Once the relation between sentences and the propositions that they express becomes problematic, the idea that one sentence can 'reflect' the form of a proposition more accurately than another has to carry more weight than it can bear. As Russell becomes more conscious of symbols—of words and sentences —it becomes clear that analysis essentially concerns sentences; the references to propositions become *pro forma*.

Finally, in this chapter, I shall discuss *OD* in the light of what I have called Russell's 'object-based metaphysics' (see Chapter 5, above, pp. 172–8). We have seen that the shift in Russell's philosophy from the theory of denoting concepts to the *OD* theory brings with it a change in focus. For certain purposes, at least, it is complete sentences, rather than sub-sentential expressions, which come to occupy the centre of attention. This fact may make it plausible that the *OD* theory marks at least a partial retreat from an object-based metaphysics. Some such view is perhaps suggested by Quine's statement that, with *OD*, Russell joins Frege in recognizing that it is the complete sentence which is 'the primary vehicle of meaning'.[30] At least on one interpretation, this idea is, I think, incorrect. Russell does not retreat from his earlier object-based metaphysics. The principle of acquaintance is, as I have re-marked, not new with *OD*. From around the time of *OD* it does, however, come to occupy a more prominent place in Russell's thought; this prominence is a sign that Russell's basic metaphysics is, if any-thing, held even more strongly. One can, after all, hardly demand that we be acquainted with all the constituents of the propositions that we understand unless one supposes that a proposition really has consti-tuents, and that they are genuine entities which are independent of the proposition. The primary relation between the mind and everything else continues to be not one of judgement but one of acquaintance, and acquaintance is paradigmatically a relation between a mind and an object. (To the extent that Russell holds that we are acquainted with

[30] Quine, op. cit. n. 5 above, pp. 53–4.

propositions, he treats propositions as themselves object-like.[31] This, as we have already seen, is why he is unable to account for the difference between propositions and other entities.) At the same time, however, the application of the *OD* theory undoubtedly has some of the consequences of a judgement-based metaphysics such as Frege's. One obvious example concerns the issues which I raised in the last chapter about the nature of classes, and the unity of a class. Given Russell's contextual definition of (symbols for) classes, these questions simply do not arise. To that extent, Russell's definition functions like Frege's Axiom V. Both allow us to use symbols for classes (or *Wertverläufe*) without raising questions about the nature of the entities which correspond to these symbols; both achieve this by specifying the meaning of (at least some of the) sentences which contain those symbols. Why, then, is Russell's underlying metaphysics still very different from Frege's? A superficial answer is that classes, for Russell, are not real, whereas for Frege *Wertverläufe* are as real as anything else (I speak here, of course, of Frege's attitude before he recognized the inconsistency introduced by Axiom V). The deeper answer, which lies behind this, is that symbols for classes, in Russell's philosophy, are introduced by explicit definition; and that this means that they are eliminable in favour of symbols which Russell recognized as having a different status. Russell's definition, unlike Frege's Axiom V, enables us to eliminate class symbols from all contexts in which they can legitimately occur (this is, indeed, the criterion for the legitimacy of the occurrence of such a symbol in a given context). It is this fact, rather than some general adoption of a judgement-based metaphysics, that would justify Russell in saying of class symbols that we must not ask for their meaning in isolation (or, as he does say, that they *have* no meaning in isolation). But when all eliminable symbols have been eliminated we are left with symbols for which Russell, unlike Frege, clearly thinks these questions are legitimate, and must have an answer.

---

[31] As we shall see in Ch. 8, s. 1, below, Russell gives up the idea that we are acquainted with propositions; he adopts what he calls the 'multiple relation' theory of judgement. This theory, as we shall see, introduces judgement or understanding as a relation distinct from acquaintance. It does not, however, mark a retreat from the primacy of acquaintance, for it is part of the new view that we must be acquainted with every object which is a constituent of a proposition that we understand. Propositions are no longer objects of acquaintance because they are no longer objects at all—expressions which appear to express propositions are analysed to show that they are incomplete expressions which have meaning in context, but do not indicate genuine objects. The multiple relation theory of judgement, then, does not indicate a retreat from the idea that the primary relation between the mind and objects is that of acquaintance; if anything, it reinforces this idea.

Thus the problem of the nature of a propositional function, for example, is not one that Russell thinks he can avoid.

Russell's metaphysics is no less realistic, and object-based, after *OD* than before. He continues to hold that whatever entities there actually are in a proposition are genuine and independent entities, whose being is in no way dependent upon their being constituents of propositions: each is what it is. A sign of this is his continued, and more emphatic, insistence that we must be acquainted with such entities if we understand the proposition. The shift is, rather, in what entities he now holds are really in the proposition expressed by a given sentence. Thus sentences containing class symbols are no longer held to express propositions containing classes. Russell's use of the techniques of *OD* thus enables him to simulate a judgement-based metaphysics for the particularly troublesome case of classes,[32] and, as we shall see, for other troublesome (apparent) entities. This is only possible in certain cases, however: classes can be eliminated, but propositional functions must be accepted as genuine entities.

---

[32] As I have already suggested, it seems that this *could* have been done even with the theory of denoting concepts. See pp. 266–7, above.

PART III
Logic, Fact, and Knowledge

Introduction

The metaphysical vision behind Platonic Atomism is a simple one. The world is made up of objects: *object* is a fundamental metaphysical category, into which everything falls. Objects are not intrinsically spatio-temporal but just atemporally *are*. Each object is quite distinct from and independent of every other; objects are related, but not intrinsically. They combine to form objects of a special kind, propositions, which are either true or false. The truth or falsity of a proposition is not a matter of its corresponding, or failing to correspond, to anything else, for the combination of objects *is* the proposition and there is nothing beyond it to which it may or may not correspond. Objects, including both true and false propositions, are real and objective. The truth and falsity of propositions is equally a real and objective matter. All of this is nothing to do with us or our minds, or with anything in any sense analogous to the mental. Our relation to the objects that make up the world, including propositions, is simply that of passively perceiving them, in some sense of perceive which is not intrinsically tied to any sense organ; we are acquainted with them.

We have already discussed one crucial point at which this simple vision is clouded. The idea that a proposition is simply a combination of objects is threatened by the existence of general (quantified) sentences: such sentences surely express propositions, but not ones that fit easily into the Platonic Atomist picture. We shall return to this issue. Other difficulties are also apparent, even from our simple and uncritical statement of the view. Most obvious is a problem which Russell himself explicitly recognized: how do objects combine to form propositions? What room does this atomistic metaphysics have for a kind of object which is a combination of objects? A second problem, less straightforward, concerns truth. This notion bears the whole weight of the metaphysics of Platonic Atomism. Existence, or being, according to that metaphysics, is to be understood in terms of certain propositions being true. Ontological questions, we may say, simply turn out to be questions about the truth and falsity of propositions, and cannot be understood independently of these. Hence truth cannot be understood simply in terms of there being, or not being, a fact or entity of some kind, for the being of anything is understood in terms of truth. The notions of truth, and of a proposition, are *ontologically* fundamental; the notion of being is derivative. Truth, the notion which bears all this ontological weight, is itself understood simply as a simple and indefinable property, which some propositions have and others lack. No further explanation is possible. Now this is in itself implausible rather than being, as the first problem is, a straightforward conflict of two crucial tenets of the metaphysics.[1] But this second problem is connected with the first in a way which aggravates the implausibility. The first problem concerns the notion of a proposition, and the second problem concerns the notion of truth; the two are connected because propositions are the bearers of truth. No account of propositions can be satisfactory which does not explain why it is propositions, and not other objects, which are true or false; and the account of truth and falsity is similarly constrained. Neither problem can be satisfactorily resolved without resolving the other at the same time. A third problem implicit in the simple statement of the metaphysics of Platonic Atomism concerns the implausibility of the idea of non-senuous 'perception' of any object whatsoever. In its general form this might not appear to be a problem to an adherent of Platonic Atomism; certainly it generates no threat of internal inconsistency in the metaphysics. It does, however, have a multitude of problematic special cases. The metaphysics appears to require us to perceive or be acquainted with many objects; in each particular case we can ask how plausible it is that we are in fact acquainted with that object. This multitude of individual questions may not undermine the general idea of acquaintance, but it is likely to force us to find a method of showing that the metaphysics does not in fact require us to be acquainted with as many kinds of objects as may at first appear.

Further difficulties, moreover, become apparent when Platonic Atomism is combined with modern logic to form a single view. One issue here has been mentioned: that of generality. A second issue is the paradox which bears Russell's name. In each case it is, I think, a mistake to suppose that we have simply a problem of the new logic which is not intrinsic to Russell's metaphysics. If we think of the metaphysics as independent of logic, then we have in each case a problem in the metaphysics which becomes more obvious, and more pressing, when the metaphysics is combined with the logic; the distinc-

---

[1] As we have seen, however, there is a problem with the notion of truth which threatens real incoherence, not mere lack of explanatory power; see Ch. 5, above, pp. 178–9. I do not discuss this further because there is no evidence that it plays a role in Russell's own thought.

tion between logic and metaphysics, however, is artificial in the context of Russell's thought. Let us consider the issue of generality. In spite of his frequent discussions of 'the variable', Russell's response to this issue in fact relies upon the idea of a propositional function. This idea is obscure. The obscurity is, moreover, not incidental, but is connected with fundamental features of Platonic Atomism. The characteristic feature of a propositional function—practically, its only feature—is that it stands in a peculiar relation to certain propositions (its values), so that a proposition containing a propositional function can somehow assert all of those propositions (the values of the propositional function) at once, or deny them all at once, and so on. Yet the metaphysics demands that each object be what it is independent of all others, so that all relations are external. The tension implicit here is brought out when we consider the issue of the paradox, which is connected with that of generality. Taken as a paradox about classes, Russell's paradox can be considered as arising from the assumption of the existence of classes, where this assumption need not be thought of as intrinsic to Platonic Atomism. But when propositional functions are postulated, in order to allow for generality, the paradox arises without any assumption of the existence of classes. Russell's response, as we shall see in detail, is to accept that there are ontological differences between objects and propositional functions (and, indeed, among propositional functions). But then it is arguable, as we shall see, that these differences cannot be accommodated within the object-based metaphysics characteristic of Platonic Atomism.

It is in Russell's responses to the various difficulties confronting Platonic Atomism that many of the familiar features of later analytic philosophy emerge: the theory of types; the theory of descriptions; the more general exploitation of the idea of an incomplete symbol to facilitate eliminative definition of ontologically or epistemologically awkward entities; an increasing concern with, and sophistication about, language, in the sense of symbols; a concomitant insistence on the distinction between superficial or grammatical structure and deep structure or logical form; an increasing concern with the objects of knowledge, and the means by which we can know what we appear to know; the self-conscious application of the constructional method to philosophy in general; and a concern with such issues as the status of logic and the nature of truth and the nature of judgement which is recognizably continuous with subsequent discussions of the same issues. All of these doctrines and themes are to be seen in Russell's work in the decade after *Principles*. It might be said, indeed, that it is in Russell's responses to the problems posed by Platonic Atomism that the characteristic methods, questions, and doctrines of later analytic philosophy emerge. We have already seen the emergence of some of these themes in Chapter 6, where we indicated something of their significance for Russell's later work. (Chapter 6 might thus be thought of as a transitional chapter—as perhaps 'On Denoting' can be thought of as a transitional work.) Let us now survey some of the main developments discussed there and in the final two chapters of this book.

To begin with, as already indicated, Russell abandons the idea that all entities are objects with the same ontological status. The theory of types is developed in 'Mathematical Logic as Based on the Theory of Types', and culminates in *Principia Mathematica*. In these works Russell puts forwards categorial distinctions between propositional functions and individuals, and among various propositional functions. He also exploits the idea of contextual definition which first emerges in 'On Denoting' to argue that the assumption of the existence of classes is unnecessary: symbols which appear to indicate classes can be taken as incomplete symbols, and explained, in context, in terms of propositional functions. As we saw in Chapter 6, this step places heavier weight on the idea of an incomplete symbol than 'On Denoting' does, and Russell becomes correspondingly more self-conscious about the role of symbolism in general. This is not exactly a change in doctrine, but rather something forced on Russell, especially by his response to the paradox: here we see one of the roots of the attention to symbolism which is sometimes taken as characteristic of twentieth-century analytic philosophy.

A further fundamental shift in Russell's metaphysical view is that the concepts of proposition and truth lose their fundamental metaphysical status. The new view, which evolves from 1906 on, is connected with what Russell calls the multiple relation theory of judgement. More than judgement, however, is at stake in the change which occurs in Russell's metaphysics. The concept of a fact now becomes fundamental. Truth is defined in terms of the correspondence of belief or sentence with a fact. The new view threatens to undermine what we have called Russell's object-based metaphysics, for it appears that facts cannot be understood as a species of object. Here, in embryo, we see the line of thought that was to issue in Russell's 'Lectures on Logical Atomism' and in Wittgenstein's *Tractatus Logico-Philosophicus*. Russell does not seem to realize that the new view requires fundamental changes in the metaphysics of Platonic Atomism. Nor, as we shall see, does he ever arrive at a version of the multiple relation theory which satisfies him. Both in this case and in the case of the theory of types, Russell continues to presuppose his old object-based metaphysics, even while he is putting forward theories which are arguably inconsistent with it.

A further line of development can be seen as a working out of the principle of acquaintance. This principle itself is not new; we have seen that it is explicit in 'On Denoting' and, at least arguably, implicit earlier. In our discussion in Chapter 6 we saw that Russell begins to accept that this principle imposes significant constraints on philosophical theorizing. This idea emerges more strongly in Russell's work after *PM*. The psychological facts of acquaintance are no longer treated as mere appendages, to be assumed as needed. Instead Russell comes to think that we have independent access to these facts, presumably by some sort of 'introspection', and that philosophical theory must conform to these facts. While Russell continues to think that the subject-matter of philosophy is wholly independent of psychology, psychological facts come to be a crucial kind of data for philosophy. The clearest example here is Russell's work on knowledge. As he becomes interested in the way in which we can know the physical world, he becomes convinced that we cannot simply suppose ourselves to be acquainted with the ordinary things that we (seem to) know about. The constraints that Russell imposes on acquaintance are, indeed, sufficient to make it clear that whatever I am acquainted with when I know that my coffee-cup is on my desk must be an object, or a multiplicity of objects, of a quite extraordinary kind. It thus becomes a problem to show how our acquaintance with objects of the extraordinary kind issues in our (real or apparent) knowledge of objects of the ordinary kind. Russell attempts to solve this problem by means of the idea of contextual definition, and of other constructional techniques used in the reduction of mathematics to logic; these techniques thus become central to Russell's philosophy in general, not merely to his philosophy of mathematics. This idea of the constructional method in philosophy, based on the techniques of mathematical logic, is perhaps the deepest of Russell's legacies to subsequent analytic philosophy. This sort of method, I suspect, is one of the bases for the idea of analytic philosophy as a distinctive tradition within philosophy.

The nature and tone of our discussion in Part III are rather different from those of the earlier portions of the book, both because of the subject-matter of this Part and because it is the last part of the book. In discussing British Idealism I was not concerned to point out the weaknesses of that view; in so far as they are relevant to our purpose they were given due weight in Part II. Similarly, the weaknesses of Platonic Atomism are as much the subject of Part III as they were of Part II, for our concern in the next two chapters is with the views that evolved by way of response to these weaknesses. There is, however, no Part IV in which we can see how Russell and other philosophers responded to the views discussed in Part III.[2] Our discussion is therefore to some extent more critical, and more forward-looking, in order to convey some sense of the sort of response that these views evoked. Also relevant is the fact that the issues discussed here, and the implicit standards and methods that Russell relies on and employs, are closer to those of contemporary analytic philosophy. As before, however, my concern is not primarily to engage in debate about this or that view of Russell's which is of current interest. My concern is, rather, with understanding of Russell's views, and with the way in which the history of analytic philosophy has unfolded.

---

[2] The most relevant works here would include Russell's 'The Philosophy of Logical Atomism', to which I refer at a number of points; Wittgenstein's *Tractatus*; Carnap's *The Logical Structure of the World*; Ramsey's 'The Foundations of Mathematics'; and Russell's Introduction and Appendices to the 2nd ed. of *Principia Mathematica*.

7

The Logic of *Principia Mathematica*

The Principles of Mathematics, as we saw in Chapter 5, contains many admittedly unsolved problems. By far the most serious of these arise from Russell's paradox. We can think of the paradox as posing two distinguishable problems for Russell. One is logical or mathematical: the paradox casts doubt on the coherence of the very notion of a class, yet this notion seems inescapable. Classes were, obviously, central to Russell's logicism. Worse, the notion of a class, or something like it, is presupposed in much nineteenth-century work which had appeared as purely mathematical, and so as free from philosophical doubts. As a result of the rigorization of analysis, reasoning that appealed to arbitrary classes of real numbers was seen as fundamental to mathematics. Russell's paradox threatened the notion of an arbitrary class. This aspect of the problem arises quite independently of Russell's philosophical views. The second aspect of the problem is logical or metaphysical.[1] In the view of *Principles* there are no ultimate distinctions of ontological category among entities; all are conceived of as object-like. Once the notion of a propositional function is introduced to allow for generality, and to explain the validity of certain patterns of inference, a paradox follows immediately, unless special restrictions are laid down. One has only to see that certain propositional functions cannot be truly applied to themselves and note that since we can say this, there is presumably a propositional function expressed by the words '...is a propositional function which can (not) be truly applied to itself' (see pp. 227–9, above, and pp. 298–9, below). For Russell this problem would, in principle, have remained even if he had given up logicism and abandoned all interest in the philosophical status of mathematics. The contrast between Russell and Frege, which we have already noted,

---

[1] It is, of course, no accident that it is natural, in explaining these views of Russell's, to speak both of 'logical or mathematical' and 'logical or metaphysical'. For Russell there were no clear distinctions between these subjects: logic was at once composed of ontological or metaphysical truths and able to encompass mathematics. This is one way of thinking of the presuppositions of Russell's use of logicism against the Idealists. If Russell had been completely successful, the distinction drawn above between mathematics and metaphysics would have only heuristic value.

is helpful at this point. For Frege, the distinction between concept and object ensures that no analogue of Russell's paradox threatens his philosophical view, in so far as this is independent of mathematics. The threat of paradox arises, for his view, only when he adds the notorious Axiom V of *Grundgesetze*, which asserts the existence of an object (*Wertverlauf*) corresponding to every concept. For Russell, by contrast, the object-based metaphysics gives the effect of Frege's Axiom V without the use of any special assumption: a propositional function, in *Principles*, is already in the relevant sense an object.

The two kinds of problem arising from Russell's paradox are dealt with, in *Principia Mathematica*,[2] in two connected steps. First, Russell acknowledges the inevitable consequence of the paradox: he abandons the claim that there are no ultimate ontological distinctions among entities. He sets up a distinction of ontological category, or *type*,[3] between propositional functions and individuals (simple entities, neither propositions nor propositional functions). There is also an extremely complex array of distinctions among propositional functions. The exact nature of these distinctions of category, and their justification, will occupy much of this chapter. Second, *PM* eliminates classes: it exploits the ideas of *OD* and treats symbols which appear to refer to classes as incomplete symbols. Such symbols, as we saw in the last chapter, are given contextual definitions; statements ostensibly about classes are transformed into statements about propositional functions.[4] Thus the

---

[2] A. N. Whitehead and B. Russell, *Principia Mathematica*, i (Cambridge: CUP, 1910; 2nd edn. 1927). Except as specified, all of my references are to material printed in the 1st edn. and reprinted 'unchanged except as regards misprints and minor errors' (Introduction to the Second Edition, p. xiii). I make the simplifying assumption that it is Russell, rather than Whitehead, who is responsible for the parts of *PM* which are my chief concern. One piece of evidence for this is Russell's own statement (*MPD*, p. 74). A second piece of evidence is that many of the basic ideas of *PM* are to be found in Russell's 'Mathematical Logic as Based on the Theory of Types', first published in the *American Journal of Mathematics*, 30 (1908), 222–62; repr. in Marsh, pp. 59–102. See also A. N. Whitehead, *Process and Reality* (London: Macmillan, 1929), p. 10, and n. 6, below.

[3] I use the word 'type' quite generally, to speak of any distinction of ontological category. Russell's use is similar, but a different use has since become common; see the discussion of Copi's interpretation of *PM*, pp. 310–12, below.

[4] *PM* thus embodies what Russell sometimes calls the 'no-class' theory. It is important, however, to distinguish the theory of *PM* from another, somewhat earlier view of Russell's, which he also calls the 'no-class' view. The earlier theory presupposes the existence neither of classes *nor* of propositional functions; besides propositions and individuals, the key notion is that of substituting an individual for another individual in a proposition to attain a second proposition. See 'On Some Difficulties in the Theory of Transfinite Number and Order Types', *Proceedings of the London Mathematical Society*, ser. 2: 4 (7 Mar. 1906), 29–53, 'On the Substitutional Theory of Classes and Relations', read before the London Mathematical Society on 10 May 1906 (scheduled for publication by that Society but withdrawn by Russell in Oct. 1906), 'On "Insolubilia" and their Solution by Symbolic Logic', published in French under the title 'Les Paradoxes de la logique',

distinctions of category among propositional functions automatically transfer to (symbols which appear to refer to) classes, and these distinctions, as we shall see, suffice to block Russell's paradox and its analogues. At bottom, then, *PM* is a theory not of classes but of propositional functions; the definition of class symbols, however, enables the theory to simulate the theory of classes.

On the apparently unpromising basis of the theory of propositional functions, Whitehead and Russell erected a unified and detailed treatment of considerable portions of mathematics. They produced the first (consistent) detailed reduction of the essential concepts of arithmetic, finite and infinite, cardinal and ordinal, and of real analysis, to the concepts of (the analogue of) set theory. They also showed that the reduction translates the truths of these branches of mathematics into truths of (the analogue of) set theory.[5] Whatever one may think of the underlying philosophy, and in spite of its technical flaws, *Principia Mathematica* is an extraordinary achievement. Its influence, not surprisingly, has been great. Philosophically, it played a crucial role in forming the views of Wittgenstein and of the Vienna Circle, and so directly or indirectly influenced much subsequent work in analytic philosophy. More narrowly, its technical influence is unparalleled: it founded a subject. This foundational role is not without its price. *PM* has been extensively criticized by those who have wished to appropri-

---

Revue de métaphysique et de morale, 14 (Sept. 1906), 627–50. All three articles are reprinted in Lackey, pp. 135–64, 165–89, 190–214, the third in Russell's original English version. I have discussed this earlier view in some detail elsewhere, and shall not repeat this discussion here; see 'Russell's Substitutional Theory', *Synthese*, 45 (1980), 1–31. Russell had abandoned the substitutional theory by late 1906 or early 1907. 'Mathematical Logic as Based on the Theory of Types' was published in May 1908; in a letter to Philip Jourdain, Russell complains that the *American Journal of Mathematics* 'kept the manuscript a year before printing it'. See I. Grattan-Guinness, *Dear Russell–Dear Jourdain* (London: Duckworth, 1977) p. 111.

[5] A more precise picture will emerge, but some qualifications should be noted immediately. First, the reduction is to the *analogue* of set theory because *PM* is, as we have seen, a theory of propositional functions, not of sets or classes; the theory of classes is reduced to the theory of propositional functions, and from that point on the reduction proceeds as if classes had been assumed outright. Second, in the case of many mathematical truths, what is shown, strictly, is that one can infer from the theory of propositional functions a conditional in which the mathematical truth is consequent and the antecedent is the statement that there are infinitely many individuals (see pp. 318–20, below).

A full assessment of the achievement of *PM* would also have to consider Gödel's incompleteness theorem, proved in 1930, which shows that no formal theory can prove every arithmetical truth. I shall not discuss this in any detail, but will make a few comments here. If logic is taken to be a formalism then Gödel's theorem shows at once that mathematics is not identical with logic, i.e. that logicism is false. From a Russellian point of view, however, there is no reason to identify logic with a formalism. Rather Gödel's theorem seems, from this point of view, to show that the theory of propositional functions—logic itself—cannot be completely formalized. This situation may be peculiar, but there is no evident reason why it should be fatal to the project of *PM*.

ate it for their own ends, most notably Ramsey, Gödel, and Quine.[6] These critics sought to reinterpret *PM* so as to obtain a clearer and simpler system which would accomplish roughly what *PM* accomplished. My aims are quite different. I wish to show how Russell attempts to maintain the logicist thesis, in spite of the difficulties posed by the paradox; and how this attempt both draws upon the metaphysics we have examined and reshapes that metaphysics. This discussion will provide a perspective from which we can consider the internal coherence of Russell's project.

PM is a theory of propositional functions, not of classes. One reason for this is that Russell holds that the ontological distinctions which must hold among entities can be understood and justified if the entities concerned are individuals and propositional functions; whereas if classes were assumed outright no such distinctions could be justified. A second reason is that Russell holds that the theory of propositional functions is logic, whereas the theory of classes (assumed as independent entities) is not. A third reason is that dispensing with the assumption that classes exist allows Russell to avoid questions about the nature of classes—questions which he had found unanswerable in *Principles*. Let us postpone consideration of the first of these reasons, for it will require considerable background discussion. The second and third, by contrast, are familiar, and may be considered briefly.

Logic, on Russell's account, is the study of absolutely general truths and of universally correct patterns of inference. For Russell this directly implies that logic must assume the existence of, and include truths about, propositional functions. Propositional functions are, on Russell's view, required for an account of complex quantification, and of inference involving such quantification (see Chapter 5, above, pp. 212–19). On this view, to make sense of the inference from 'Brutus killed Brutus' to '$(\exists x)$ (x killed x)' (and to see why the latter does *not* follow from 'Brutus killed Caesar'), we must accept that there is a propositional function $\hat{x}$ *killed* $\hat{x}$. For Russell, the inference from 'Brutus killed Caesar' to '$(\exists R)$ (Brutus R Caesar)' is as immediate as that from

---

[6] To this list of critics one other notable name might be added: that of Russell himself. The 34-page 'Introduction to the Second Edition', and the three appendices to vol. i, suggest fundamental changes to the 1st edn. of *PM*. In making these changes Russell was greatly influenced by Ramsey. Although I shall sometimes note points where relevant, I shall not discuss Russell's changes in any systematic fashion. (My assumption that they are Russell's changes, rather than Whitehead and Russell's, is borne out by Whitehead's repudiation of the new Introduction in a letter to the editor of *Mind*, published in that journal for 1926, p. 130. Besides saying that he had no involvement in the production of the 2nd edn., Whitehead also says that Russell was solely responsible for the corresponding, i.e. the fundamental, parts of the 1st edn., except for *10.)

the former sentence to '($\exists x$) (x killed Caesar)'.[7] Thus, rather than stating comprehension axioms guaranteeing the existence of propositional functions, Russell implicitly adopts inference rules that license the inference from '*Fa*' to '($\exists \phi$) ϕa'.[8] Thus, also, quantification over propositional functions is introduced without fanfare, not as a new subject but as an extension of an old one. From a consideration of first-order propositional functions (all of whose arguments are individuals), Russell introduces the idea of an arbitrary function of this sort and thus of a matrix (quantifier-free propositional function) one of whose arguments must be such a function. He then casually remarks: 'From these matrices, by applying generalisation to their arguments, whether to such as are functions or to such (if any) as are individuals, we obtain new functions and propositions' (*PM*, i. 163). Russell can afford to be casual here, for from his point of view no new principle is involved.

There are thus reasons, from a Russellian point of view, to think that the theory of propositional functions is logic. Russell in *Principles*, however, also held that the theory of classes is logic, and Frege held the closely analogous position that the theory of *Wertverläufe* is logic. The latter wrote: 'we can transform the generality of an identity into an identity of *Wertverläufe*, and vice versa. This possibility must be regarded as a law of logic[9]'. Frege, however, wrote this before Russell's discovery of the class paradox. The discovery of the paradox, and of its

---

[7] It is tempting to reinforce this argument by the claim that propositional functions are *constituents* of the propositions that are their values. Thus $\hat{x}$ *is wise* would be seen as a constituent of the proposition that Socrates is wise; then it could be persuasively argued that the propositional function in a proposition should be accessible to generalization in just the same way that the object in a proposition is. But in fact Russell denies that propositional functions are constituents of propositions (*PM*, i. 54–5) and there are good reasons for him to do so. First the rationale he gives for the hierarchy of types would be destroyed by this view; see n. 23, below. Second, the view seems to require an account of the variable as an entity which may replace Socrates in the latter's occurrence in the proposition that Socrates is wise. As we saw in Ch. 5, Russell in fact has no such account of the variable, although he often writes as if he did. Third, while the suggestion under consideration may seem to lead to a relatively straightforward account of the structure of propositions, this semblance is in fact deceptive. If a proposition contains those propositional functions of which it is a value, then the proposition that Brutus killed Brutus, for example, will contain the propositional functions $\hat{x}$ *killed Brutus*, *Brutus killed* $\hat{x}$, $\hat{x}$ *killed* $\hat{x}$, $\hat{x}$ *killed* $\hat{y}$, *Brutus* $\hat{R}$ *Brutus*, and so on. There is no straightforward picture to be had of a proposition as a complex in which all these entities are in some fairly literal sense constituents.

[8] This point is made by W. D. Goldfarb, 'Russell's Reasons for Ramification', in *Rereading Russell: Essays in Bertrand Russell's Metaphysics and Epistemology* (vol. 12 of Minnesota Studies in the Philosophy of Science) (Minneapolis: Minnesota University Press, 1989), p. 32.

[9] G. Frege, *Grundgesetze der Arithmetik, begriffsschriftlich abgeleitet*, 2 vols (Jena: Verlag Hermann Pohle, 1893–1903), vol. i, s. 9. I follow the translation of Montgomery Furth, published under the title *The Basic Laws of Arithmetic* (Berkeley and Los Angeles: Univer-

intractability, made a crucial difference to the plausibility of his claim. Axiom V cannot be true as it stands; it must be subject to some restrictions. Restrictions of Axiom V which will have the desired results, however, lack the complete generality which, for Frege and Russell, is characteristic of logic.[10] The fact that the method of forming classes is restricted makes it hard to think of the theory of classes as logic; as restricted, the method does not seem to represent perfectly general facts, but rather facts which hold only when our subject-matter is classes.

The strategy of defining symbols for classes in terms of propositional functions also enables Russell to avoid the questions about the nature of classes which he had failed to answer in *Principles*. There were, in particular, two such questions: to what extent should a class be thought of as intensional and to what extent as extensional? And: how can *one* class contain *many* objects? (For these questions, see Chapter 5, above, pp. 222–6.) Russell comments on both of these issues in *PM*. On the first:

It is an old dispute whether formal logic should concern itself mainly with intensions or with extensions.... The facts seem to be that, while mathematical logic requires extensions, philosophical logic refuses to supply anything except intensions. Our theory of classes reconciles these two apparently opposite facts, by showing that an extension...is an incomplete symbol, whose use always requires its meaning through a reference to intension. (i. 72)

On the second problem Russell says that though we cannot dogmatically assert that there are no classes, 'arguments of more or less cogency can be elicited from the ancient problem of the One and the Many' (loc. cit.). A footnote summarizes the arguments:

---

sity of California Press, 1967), p. 44. The law is Frege's infamous Axiom V, which in Russellian notation states:

$$\hat{x}\{F(x)\} = \hat{x}\{G(x)\} \: . \: \equiv \: . \: (x)(Fx \equiv Gx)$$

Although not explicitly cast as a definition, this axiom introduces the notion of a *Wertverlauf* (roughly equivalent to a class in Russell's terminology). This makes it clear that the axiom implies that for every open sentence there is a class of objects satisfying it; the axiom thus plays the same role in Frege's system that the comprehension axiom plays in set theory.

[10] Frege's own restriction may seem to escape this structure. The version he offers in Appendix II to vol. ii reads, in Russellian notation, as follows:

$$\hat{x}\{F(x)\} = \hat{x}\{G(x)\} \: . \: \equiv \: .(y)([y \neq \hat{x}\{F(x)\} \: . \: y \neq \hat{x}\{G(x)\}] \supset [Fy \equiv Gy])$$

The generality of this is perhaps arguable, but it is in any case moot. Frege's proposed modification will not allow the crucial proof of the infinity of the series of natural numbers; furthermore it yields a contradiction if we assume that there are at least two objects. See W. V. O. Quine, 'On Frege's Way Out', Ch. xii of *Selected Logic papers* (New York: Random House, 1966).

If there is such an object as a class, it must be in some sense *one* object. Yet it is only of classes that *many* can be predicated. Hence, if we admit classes as objects, we must suppose that the same object can be both one and many, which seems impossible. (i. 72 n)

The issue here is how one class can contain many objects; equivalently, it is the problem of the unity of a class—what unites the many objects into a single class.[11]

The strategy of giving contextual definitions of class symbols means that problems over the nature of classes do not arise: since we do not assume that there are any classes, we do not need to account for the nature of classes. On the other hand, the strategy makes it all the clearer that the notion of a propositional function is crucial for Russell's work. It is to propositional functions that we now turn.

Russell's discussion of propositional functions is greatly complicated by the fact that in *PM* propositional functions play a role which had little prominence in *Principles*. For reasons which we shall examine in detail later, it is important to Russell to be able to make sense of the idea of asserting an arbitrary proposition of a given form. He speaks of 'asserting a propositional function', meaning thereby that one of the values of the propositional function is asserted, but that it remains indeterminate which one. Such an 'indeterminate assertion' can of course only be true if each value of the propositional function is true; but Russell distinguishes this sort of assertion of *any* value from the universally quantified assertion of *all* values. In *PM* the idea of 'asserting a propositional function' is interwoven with Russell's explanation of propositional functions from the outset. Chapter I of the Introduction to *PM* contains a brief discussion of propositional functions, but the detailed account is in Chapter II. It begins like this:

By a 'propositional function' we mean something which contains a variable x, and expresses a proposition as soon as a value is assigned to x. That is to say, it differs from a proposition solely by the fact that it is ambiguous: it contains a variable of which the value is unassigned....

The question as to the nature of a [propositional] function is by no means an easy one. It would seem, however, that the essential characteristic of a function is *ambiguity*.... When we speak of 'ϕx', where x is not specified, we mean one value of the function, but not a definite one. We may express this by saying that 'ϕx' *ambiguously denotes* ϕa, ϕb, ϕc. (i. 38–9)

---

[11] Note that this problem is much more pressing after *OD*, when Russell comes to hold that all complexity is propositional in character. We might say, indeed, that just as *OD* eliminated the problem of the complexity of denoting concepts by reducing it to propositional complexity, so the no-class theory eliminates the problem of the unity of a class by reducing it to the unity of a proposition.

As in *Principles*, Russell suggests here that the notion of a propositional function can be explained in terms of propositions and the variable; as in *Principles*, however, this idea is misleading. Russell has no account of the variable (as a non-linguistic object) which would allow it to play this sort of explanatory role.[12] This passage is significant, however, as suggesting that a propositional function should be thought of as having the same sort of complexity as a proposition; this point is important, and we shall return to it. As in *Principles*, again, it is clear that the crucial aspect of a propositional function is the fact that it stands in a special relation—of an undefined kind—to certain propositions, namely its values. Less familiar is the emphasis on the propositional function as picking out one of its values 'but not a definite one'; and, relatedly, on the idea of a propositional function as therefore being an ambiguous entity. This last idea is crucial to Russell's view of the justification of his distinctions of ontological category, as we shall see.

One of Russell's requirements in *PM* is to allow for the possibility of asserting, or saying something about, an arbitrary one of the values of a propositional function. This idea is pressed into service to explain a difficulty that the theory of types creates for our ability to state logic (see pp. 315–16, below). The origin of the idea in Russell's thought, however, is independent of this later use of it.[13] Russell is greatly influenced by the mathematical practice of reasoning about 'any triangle' or 'any number'. He assimilates this to the use of free ('real') variables, which he holds to be essential to deductions of logic. Thus he writes, in *ML*, as follows:

deduction can only be effected with *real* variables, not with apparent variables. In the case of Euclid's proofs, this is evident: we need (say) some one triangle *ABC* to reason about, though it does not matter what triangle it is. . . . If we adhere to the apparent variable, we cannot perform any deductions, and this is why in all proofs, real variables have to be used. Suppose, to take the simplest case, that we know 'ϕx is always true', i.e. '$(x).\phi x$', and we know 'ϕx always implies ψx', i.e. $(x).\{\phi x$ implies $\psi x\}$'. How shall we infer 'ψx is always true', i.e. '$(x).\psi x$'? . . . In order to make our inference, we must go from 'ϕx is always true' to ϕx, and from 'ϕx always implies ψx' to 'ϕx implies ψx', where the *x*, while remaining any possible argument, is to be the same in both. Then from 'ϕx' and 'ϕx implies ψx', we infer 'ψx'; thus ψx is true for any possible argument, and therefore is always true. . . . This process is required in all mathematical

---

[12] It is, I suspect, because he has no explanation of the variable as a non-linguistic entity that Russell is careless in his discussions of it, sometimes implying that variables are linguistic entities (e.g. *PM*, i. 4.).

[13] Thus the idea of *any*, as distinct from *all*, is already to be found in 'On Fundamentals', written in June 1905; see especially fos. 51–4. The role of the idea there is much the same as the role attributed to it in the passage from *ML* quoted below.

reasoning which proceeds from the assertion of all values of one or more propositional functions to the assertion of all values of some other propositional function.... In a word, *all deduction operates with real variables* (or with constants). (van Heijenoort, pp. 157–8; Marsh, pp. 66–7; emphasis in the original)

The point here is not, of course, only a technical one about deductions. If a deduction includes a sentence containing a free variable (to use the modern idiom), that sentence must, for Russell, express a proposition just as it stands. (In particular, the ability of the sentence to express a proposition is not dependent on an interpretation, or an assignment of values to variables.) On the other hand, this proposition cannot be straightforwardly identified with a statement about a particular definite object; nor is Russell willing to identify it with the corresponding universal quantification. Russell therefore feels the need to make sense of the use of free variables; the distinction between *any* and *all* is his attempt to do so.

In *PM*, the distinction between *any* and *all* also looms large, but here there is little emphasis on its role in explaining the use of free variables. This is, I think, a change of emphasis rather than of doctrine. Certainly Russell gives the same account of free (or real) variables, in terms of *any* or of ambiguous assertion. And the role of this notion in deduction, although not stressed, continues unchanged. Thus a crucial primitive proposition in the introduction of quantification theory is *9.13, which states: 'In any assertion containing a real variable, this real variable may be turned into an apparent variable of which all possible values are asserted to satisfy the function in question.'[14] In the second

---

[14] Strictly speaking, the expression 'the introduction of quantification theory' is a misnomer, for Russell offers two separate ways of introducing quantification theory, one in *9 and one in *10. The proposition quoted in the text above is also numbered *10.11, and is a primitive proposition of both methods.

*9 and *10 are different ways of dealing with one difficulty which arises from the fact that not all propositions are of the same type. According to the most stringent version of the type distinctions, which Russell seems to presuppose in these sections, elementary or quantifier-free propositions differ in type from those containing quantifiers. Hence the truth-functions and truth-functional axioms introduced in *1 for elementary propositions cannot be transferred directly to quantification theory. (It is worth noting, however, that Russell seems to see no difficulty in applying the theory of truth-functions to elementary propositional functions.) The difference between *9 and *10 is, roughly, as follows. According to the view of *9 there are no propositions in which truth-functions hold among propositions containing quantifiers. Sentences which appear to express propositions of the non-existent kind are defined as in fact expressing propositions in which the quantifiers all have greater scope than any truth-functions; the latter hold among elementary propositional functions. (In effect every statement of logic is identified with its prenex equivalent, i.e. with an equivalent statement in which all quantifiers have greater scope than any truth-functional connective; but the identification is by definition, rather than by proof of equivalence.) In *10, by contrast, disjunction and negation are

edition of *PM* Russell rejects the idea of 'assertion of a propositional function' (see *PM*, i. xiii). It is noteworthy, however, that he does not argue that the use of free variables is independent of any such idea. Instead he introduces quantification theory by a new method, given in a new section, *8, which wholly avoids the use of free variables in deduction. (The crucial step, in this regard, is the introduction of a new axiom which permits by fiat what the passage quoted above argued was possible only by means of real variables. The axiom *8.12 states: 'From "$(x).\phi x$" and "$(x).(\phi x \supset \psi x)$" we can infer "$(x).\psi x$", even when ϕ and ψ are not elementary'.) In the first edition of *PM*, however, deductions do require free variables; even though the point is not emphasized there, it seems clear that Russell requires the notion of ambiguous assertion to make sense of the use of free variables in deduction.

The most obvious difficulty with this explanation of the use of free variables is in the idea that we can assert a proposition without there being a particular definite proposition that is asserted. We cannot explain this idea in the way that Quine and others have attempted to explain the situation that obtains if, for example, I want a cat without having my heart set on any particular cat.[15] That kind of explanation presupposes that we can, in ordinary cases, generalize unproblematically over the entities concerned. In Russell's use of the idea of ambiguous assertion, however, there are no unproblematic cases. As we shall see, he uses the idea in an attempt to evade the fact that we cannot generalize over propositions (unless they are all of the same order); thus it will not help to explain ambiguous assertion in terms that presuppose such generalization.

Ambiguous assertion must thus be accepted as rock bottom, with no explanation possible; it is, as Russell says, 'a primitive idea' (*PM*, i. 17). The most helpful comparison is with one aspect of the theory of denoting concepts, as this occurs in *Principles*. Denoting concepts corresponding to expressions formed with 'any' seem to have just the feature of ambiguous assertion that is most puzzling: that some entity can be picked out without any particular entity being picked out. Thus Russell says: '*Any a* denotes only one *a*, but it is wholly irrelevant which it denotes, and what is said will be equally true whichever one it may be. Moreover, *any a* denotes a variable *a*, that is, whatever particu-

---

permitted to hold among quantified propositions. Strictly these are not the same disjunction and negation as those introduced in *1 but 'new primitive ideas' (*PM*, p. 138); Russell assumes, however, that the truth-functional laws of *1 apply equally to the new versions of disjunction and negation.

[15] See W. V. O. Quine, 'Quantifiers and Propositional Attitudes', in *Ways of Paradox* (New York: Random House, 1966), pp. 183–94.

lar *a* we may fasten upon, it is certain that *any a* does not denote that one; and yet of that one any proposition is true which is true of any *a′* (*Principles*, 60). What is striking here is that the most problematic and puzzling aspect of the theory of denoting concepts reappears, in more or less the old form, in *PM* and this in spite of 'On Denoting', where the theory of denoting concepts was apparently rejected.

Let us now return, from this discussion of ambiguous assertion, to a more general consideration of the notion of a propositional function. There is, to begin with, a distinction between using a propositional function to assert or say something about an arbitrary one of its values, and saying something about the propositional function itself. This is the basis of a crucial feature of *PM*, which Russell himself sometimes neglects, namely the distinction between 'ϕx' and '$\phi \hat{x}$'. The distinction is introduced in the following passage:

It is necessary practically to distinguish the function itself from an undetermined value of the function. We may regard the function itself as that which ambiguously denotes, while an undetermined value of the function is that which is ambiguously denoted. If the undetermined value is written 'ϕx', we will write the function itself '$\phi \hat{x}$'. . . . Thus we should say 'ϕx is a proposition', but '$\phi \hat{x}$ is a propositional function'. . . . The function itself, $\phi \hat{x}$, is the single thing which ambiguously denotes its many values; while ϕx, where x is not specified, is one of the denoted objects. (i. 40)

If we understand the relation between a propositional function and its values by analogy with that of denoting, we can express Russell's view as follows: a propositional function denotes an arbitrary one of those propositions ϕa, ϕb, ϕc, etc., which are the values of the propositional function. When the propositional function is asserted, or is the subject of a proposition, the assertion is the assertion of such an arbitrary proposition or the proposition is about such an arbitrary proposition. Like a denoting concept, the role of a propositional function is to enable the proposition which contains it to be about something other than itself—an arbitrary proposition of the given form. Thus the sentence 'If x is human, x is mortal' is not an assertion *about* a propositional function; it is the assertion of an arbitrary one of the propositions expressed by 'If Socrates is human, Socrates is mortal', 'If the moon is human, the moon is mortal', etc. The presence of a propositional function in a proposition thus indicates that the proposition is about an arbitrary instance of the function (just as the presence of a denoting concept in a proposition indicates that the proposition is about the denoted object). But then if we are to talk *about* the propositional function itself we must, presumably, use a proposition containing another entity, one which stands in the analogue of the denoting relation to the propositional function (just as to talk about a denoting concept we must use another entity, a further denoting concept which denotes it; see Chapter 6 above, pp. 249–50). Russell introduces the circumflex as standard notation which indicates that a proposition does not contain but is *about* the propositional function. (Although Russell is sometimes quite precise about the distinction between 'ϕx' and '$\phi \hat{x}$', as in the passages quoted above, he treats it very casually at other times, e.g. p. 40 n.)

A crucial characteristic of propositional functions, on Russell's account, is that they are intrinsically ambiguous entities. As he says: 'the essential characteristic of a propositional function is ambiguity' (*PM*, i. 39), and again: 'A [propositional] function, in fact, is not a definite entity . . . it is a mere ambiguity awaiting determination' (p. 48). The rationale for this idea is set out in a passage which we have already quoted in part:

When we speak of 'ϕx', where x is not specified, we mean one value of the function, but not a definite one. We may express this by saying that 'ϕx' *ambiguously denotes* ϕa, ϕb, ϕc, etc., where ϕa, ϕb, ϕc, etc. are the various values of 'ϕx'.

When we say that 'ϕx' ambiguously denotes ϕa, ϕb, ϕc, etc., we mean that 'ϕx' means one of the objects ϕa, ϕb, ϕc, etc., but an undetermined one. It follows that 'ϕx' only has a well-defined meaning (well-defined, that is to say, except in so far as it is of its essence to be ambiguous) if the objects ϕa, ϕb, ϕc, etc. are well-defined. That is to say, a function is not well-defined unless all of its values are already well-defined. (*PM*, i. 39)

This idea is, as we shall see, crucial for understanding the ontological distinctions set forth in *PM*. Its relation to Russell's general metaphysical view is, however, quite problematic (we shall return to this last issue at the end of this chapter).

Propositional functions are used in *PM* to account for generality. More clearly than in *Principles*, it emerges that a quantified or general proposition is one which makes a statement *about* a propositional function: that all or some or none of its values are true. Russell introduces the quantifiers like this:

corresponding to any propositional function $\phi \hat{x}$, there is a range, or collection, of values, consisting of all the propositions, true or false, which can be obtained by giving every possible determination to x in ϕx. . . . Now in respect of the truth or falsehood of propositions of this range three important cases must be noted and symbolised. These cases are given by three propositions of which at least one must be true. Either (1) all propositions of the range are true, or (2) some propositions of the range are true, or (3) no proposition of the range is true. The statement (1) is symbolised by '$(x).\phi x$', and (2) is symbolised by '$(\exists x).\phi x$'. (*PM*, i. 15)

Later Russell makes explicit the distinction between asserting a propositional function (i.e. asserting an arbitrary value) and asserting the universal quantification. The latter is an assertion *about* the propositional function, and so is introduced using '$\phi\hat{x}$':

We will denote by the symbol '$(x).\phi x$' the proposition 'ϕx always', i.e. the proposition which asserts *all* the values for $\phi\hat{x}$. This proposition involves the function $\phi\hat{x}$, not merely an ambiguous value of the function. The assertion of ϕx, where x is unspecified, is a different assertion from the one which asserts all values for $\phi\hat{x}$, for the former is an ambiguous assertion, whereas the latter is in no sense ambiguous. (i. 41)

It is worth noting that Russell's account of quantification as an assertion about a propositional function is very similar to the Fregean account of it as an assertion about a concept. What complicates Russell's account is his idea that it must be possible to make sense of asserting an arbitrary value of a propositional function (as already indicated, this is an idea to which we shall return; see pp. 315–16, below).[16]

In introducing Russell's notion of a propositional function we saw that he thinks of such entities as having the same sort of complexity as propositions.[17] One consequence of this is that co-extensive propositional functions are not identical. Distinctions among propositional functions are as fine-grained as those among propositions. If Fa is a distinct proposition from Ga, then $F\hat{x}$ and $G\hat{x}$ are distinct propositional functions, even if they should happen to be co-extensive. The fact that co-extensionality is not the identity criterion for propositional functions is not an arbitrary or an isolated fact within the context of Russell's philosophy. On the contrary: it stems from one of the most fundamental elements of his thought, the notion of a proposition. A proposition is a complex entity, which is either true or false. Its identity-criteria are given not by its truth-value but by its constituents and their ar-

---

[16] The idea of asserting an arbitrary value of a propositional function relies, as we have seen, upon something like the *Principles* theory of denoting concepts. It is arguable that it is only this use of the propositional functions that relies upon denoting in this way, i.e. that Russell's use of propositional functions to account for generality does not make the same presupposition. This is a subtle point, however, and there is no indication that Russell makes the distinctions that it would require.

[17] As was also implied above, however, this view is one that may be hard to maintain, given the fact that Russell has no account of the variable. This latter fact is one that Russell does not seem fully to absorb. At some points he holds views which may not be tenable without an account of the variable (as a non-linguistic object). This is one of those points; as we shall see, however, the idea of the complexity of a propositional function is essential to Russell's account of the distinctions of category among propositional functions.

rangement.[18] Thus 'Grass is green' expresses a different proposition from the proposition expressed by 'Snow is white'; the importance of the arrangement of the constituents is seen from the fact that 'Desdemona loves Cassio' expresses a different proposition from that expressed by 'Cassio loves Desdemona'. Just as we can talk of the constituents of a proposition, so we can talk of the constituents of a propositional function. Cassio is a constituent of the propositional function $\hat{x}$ *loves Cassio*, just as he is of the proposition that Desdemona loves Cassio. This is implicit in Russell's assertion that a propositional function 'differs from a proposition solely by the fact that it is ambiguous' (see p. 291, above). A special case of this which is of particular importance is the fact that a propositional function, like a proposition, may contain a quantifier; $(\exists y)\hat{x}$ *loves y* contains the existential quantifier in just the same sense as does the proposition that $(\exists y)$ Desdemona loves y. Thus we may say of a propositional function itself, and not merely of the phrase which expresses it, that it does or does not contain a given quantifier.[19] This is important because, as we shall see, Russell makes distinctions among propositional functions not only on the basis of the kinds of objects they take as argument but also on the basis of the kinds of object which the quantifier that they contain ranges over. The idea of such distinctions is intelligible only if we recognize the present point, that propositional functions may contain quantifiers.

I turn now to the large and complex issue of the distinctions of category which Russell establishes among propositional functions. The purpose of these distinctions is, of course, to prevent the theory of propositional functions from giving rise to contradictions. Russell gives a number of examples of the contradictions which he is concerned to block (*PM*, i. 60–5; cf. *ML*, pp. 59–63 of Marsh, pp. 153–5 of

---

[18] The Fregean idea that two sentences which have the same truth-value mean or refer to the same object is plausible only in the context of a distinction between meaning or reference, on the one hand, and sense or what is expressed, on the other hand. In *Principles*, as we saw, Russell holds such a distinction for some expressions, but not for sentences. Some of the unpublished manuscripts from 1904 and early 1905 show him considering the distinction for sentences, but he never adopts it in a settled fashion. The effect of 'On Denoting' is, as was emphasized in the last chapter, to reject such a distinction for any expressions (except perhaps propositional function expressions).

[19] In accordance with the previous account of generality, it would be more accurate to say: a propositional function may contain another propositional function, together with the assertion that all, or some, or none, of the values of that other propositional function are true. And of course the other propositional function may itself contain yet another propositional function, in the same way, and so on. While I shall continue, where convenient, to speak of a propositional function containing a quantifier, it is important to bear in mind that this conceals a more complex, and perhaps less paradoxical, idea.

van Heijenoort). It will be helpful to have two of these paradoxes before us. First and foremost there is the Russell paradox of the class of classes which are not members of themselves; this class, it seems, both is and is not a member of itself. Since this paradox is stated in terms of classes, it cannot arise in this form in a no-class theory. A directly analogous paradox arises for propositional functions, however. Let us say that a propositional function *holds of* an object if the value of that propositional function for that object is a true proposition. We achieve the direct analogue of the class paradox by considering the propositional function which holds of a propositional function if, and only if, it does not hold of itself. This propositional function, it seems, both does and does not hold of itself. A second paradox is that of the Liar. Russell takes the simplest form of this paradox to be that of 'the man who says "I am lying"; if he is lying, he is speaking the truth, and vice versa' (*PM*, i. 60).

Russell claims that a single error lies behind all of the paradoxes which he considers: 'they all result from a certain kind of vicious circle' (*PM*, i. 37). Russell states the error involved as follows:

Vicious circles arise from supposing that a collection of objects may contain members which can only be defined in terms of the collection as a whole.... More generally, given statements about any set of objects such that, if we suppose the set to have a total, it will have members which presuppose this total, then such a set cannot have a total. (*PM*, i. 37)

To avoid paradox we must, therefore, restrict our reasoning in such a way that we avoid vicious circles; the injunction to do so is called the vicious-circle principle. Now this principle has been the subject of much criticism by commentators on Russell, most notably Ramsey and Gödel.[20] This criticism is all, I think, based on the fact that Russell sometimes formulates the principle (as we have seen) using the word 'definability' and its cognates. Formulated in this way the principle might appear to apply only to entities that do not exist independently of our definitions or constructions of them. Both Ramsey and Gödel reject this view of mathematical entities, and it is for this reason that they reject the vicious-circle principle. Within the context of our earlier discussion of Russell's philosophy, however, it is most implausible that Russell is even considering a view of mathematical entities which

---

[20] See Ramsey, 'The Foundations of Mathematics', *Proceedings of the London Mathematical Society*, ser. 2, 25/5: 338–84; repr. as Ch. I of F. P. Ramsey, *The Foundations of Mathematics*, ed. R. B. Braithwaite (London: Routledge & Kegan Paul, 1931); the latter edn. is used here. See esp. p. 41; and Gödel, 'Russell's Mathematical Logic', *The Philosophy of Bertrand Russell*, ed. P. A. Schilpp (Evanston, Ill.: The Library of Living Philosophers, Inc., 1946), esp. pp. 133–8.

makes them dependent upon any human activity of definition or construction. And certainly *PM* contains no discussion of definition or construction which could play the sort of role which an alternative view would require. Within the context of *PM*, we should, therefore, treat the principle as a principle about presupposition, or the metaphysical dependence of one kind of entity upon another kind of entity.[21]

Understood as a principle about presupposition, the vicious-circle principle is, I think, quite uncontroversial. It is perhaps best thought of less as a substantive claim than as a partial explanation of the difficult idea of presupposition. (Russell's own discussion of the principle does not suggest that he thinks of it as controversial, for he does not argue for it. His emphasis on it seems to be due to his wish to find a single error at the root of the various paradoxes, and also to the polemic that he engaged in with Poincaré around 1905–8.[22]) The principle is, after all, conditional in this sense: it makes no claim about what presupposes what, but simply says what follows from such a claim. The claim about presupposition which is central to the theory of types is that which we have already seen in our discussion of propositional functions: that a propositional function presupposes its values. This gives rise to the crucial use of the vicious-circle principle:

a [propositional] function is not a well-defined function unless all its values are already well-defined. It follows from this that no function can have among its values anything which presupposes the function, for if it had, we could not regard the objects ambiguously denoted by the function as definite until the function was definite, while conversely, as we have just seen, the function cannot be definite until its values are definite. This is a particular case, but perhaps the most fundamental case, of the vicious-circle principle. A function is what ambiguously denotes some one of a certain totality, namely the values of the function; hence this totality cannot contain any members which involve the function, since, if it did, it would contain members involving the totality, which, by the vicious-circle principle, no totality can do. (*PM*, i. 39)

Our discussion to this point puts us in a position to understand the basic principles of the type theory set out in *PM*. The idea that a propositional function presupposes its values gives rise to distinctions of category which, following Russell, I shall call distinctions of order. The basic principles are two. First, a propositional function is of higher

---

[21] For a more extended discussion to the same effect, see Goldfarb, op. cit. n. 8 above, pp. 32–3.

[22] See W. D. Goldfarb, 'Poincaré against the Logicists', in W. Aspray and P. Kitcher (eds.), *Essays in the History and Philosophy of Mathematics* (Minneapolis: University of Minnesota Press, 1987), s. II.

order than any object which it can take as argument; second, a propositional function is of higher order than any object within the range of a quantifier contained in that propositional function. The first follows almost immediately from the idea that a propositional function presupposes its values. Since each value includes the relevant argument (*Fa* includes *a*, etc.), a propositional function also presupposes the objects which it can take as arguments (since presupposition is presumably a transitive relation). Hence, by the vicious-circle principle, a propositional function and its arguments do not 'have a total', i.e. a propositional function belongs to an ontological category distinct from that of its arguments. The argument for the second basic principle is slightly more complex; Russell's understanding of generality is relevant, as well as the fundamental idea that a propositional function presupposes its values. According to this understanding, a propositional function which expresses generality (*x̂ has all the properties of a great general* is Russell's example) contains another propositional function (*φ is a property of a great general*). So the first propositional function presupposes the second, which (by the first principle) presupposes the entities which are its arguments. Hence the original propositional function must be of an ontological category distinct from that of those entities (hence *x̂ has all the properties of a great general* is of a different category from *x̂ is brave*, *x̂ is resourceful*, and other propositional functions which fall within the range of the quantifier 'all the properties . . .'). So a propositional function is of higher order than any object within the range of a quantifier contained in that propositional function.[23]

It is worth emphasizing that the two basic principles which we have discussed are both based on the idea that a propositional function presupposes its values, and hence its arguments. This fact makes it non-arbitrary to suppose, as Russell does, that it is the same classification of propositional functions—by order—that is at stake in each principle (i.e. these two principles, taken by themselves, yield a clas-

---

[23] We appeal, in the reasoning of this paragraph, to the principle that a proposition presupposes the entities which it contains. Now if an elementary proposition (e.g. that Socrates is wise) contained the propositional function of which it is a value (e.g. *x̂ is wise*), then such a proposition would presuppose all of the values of that propositional function—including itself. Since presupposition is an asymmetrical relation, this result would undermine the whole idea of presupposition. For Russell, however, a proposition does *not* contain the propositional function of which it is a value, as he says explicitly (*PM*, i. 54–5). This position is one which he must hold if the idea of presupposition is to play any role in grounding the type hierarchy. It seems, however, to leave him without a clear account of the structure and constituents of propositions. The proposition that Socrates is wise contains some constituent other than Socrates, but it is unclear what this is, and how it is related to the propositional function *x̂ is wise*.

sification along a single dimension). The first principle is based on the potential arguments of a propositional function. The second is based on the objects generalized over by a propositional function. One immediate consequence is that propositions, as well as propositional functions, will have an order, based on the ontological category of the objects which the proposition generalizes over.

Let us briefly see how these two principles block the two paradoxes that we mentioned above. Russell's paradox, stated for propositional functions, depends upon the possibility of a propositional function being its own argument (i.e. upon there being a proposition, true or false, in which a propositional function is its own argument). But, by the first principle, a propositional function presupposes its values; they must be determinate independent of it. So it immediately follows that a propositional function cannot have a value which contains that propositional function. So the putative proposition considered above is not possible. Now consider the Liar paradox. Russell interprets the liar's statement as meaning: 'There is a proposition which I am affirming and which is false.' It thus contains a quantifier ranging over propositions. Hence, by the second principle, it must itself express a proposition of higher order than any of those over which its quantified variable ranges. Thus for some n the liar expressed an $n+1$th order proposition which says that he is now affirming a false nth order proposition. This proposition is itself false, since he is not affirming any nth order proposition at all. The falsehood of the liar's assertion, however, is not paradoxical, since it is a falsehood of $n+1$st order and therefore does not supply an nth order falsehood which would verify the assertion.

The two principles which we have discussed establish the main outlines of a hierarchy of *orders* among propositions and propositional functions. Call a quantifier-free propositional function a *matrix*. Thus '$\hat{x}$ loves $\hat{y}$' expresses a matrix, but '$(\exists x)$ (x loves $\hat{y}$)' does not. Call the process of quantifying of a free variable *generalization*. Thus generalizing on a free variable will turn an n-place propositional function into an $(n-1)$-place propositional function, and will turn a 1-place propositional function into a proposition; propositions may thus be thought of as special cases of propositional functions, those with zero argument places. (In Russellian terms a matrix is a propositional function without apparent variables, and generalization turns a real variable into an apparent variable.) If we remove the quantifiers from any propositional function (or proposition) we obtain a matrix. The hierarchy of orders is governed by two ideas, first, that a matrix is one order higher than its highest-order argument; second, that the order of any propositional function (or proposition) is that of the matrix which would be obtained from it by removing all its quantifiers. These ideas are related to our fundamental principles in a relatively straightforward fashion. The first principle ensures that a matrix which has entities of order n as argument is itself of higher order than n. (There is an element of arbitrariness in inferring from this principle that if the highest-order argument of a matrix is n, then the order of the matrix is $n+1$; $n+2$ would clearly respect the principle equally well. One might say that we raise orders as little as possible, consistent with the fundamental principle.) The second principle ensures that generalizing on a matrix will yield a propositional function whose order is that of the matrix. (Again there is an element of arbitrariness. The second principle would be respected if we said that generalizing on one or more argument positions in a matrix yields a propositional function whose order is *higher* than that of the matrix itself. But again we can think of the hierarchy of orders as obtained if we raise orders as little as possible, while still respecting the fundamental principle.)

More than one hierarchy of orders is consistent with the ideas that we have examined. I shall explain one, which is slightly different from those that Russell puts forward in *PM* (see n. 26, below). Call a matrix *first-order* if all of its variables take individuals as values. Call a propositional function *first-order* if it could be derived from a first-order matrix by generalizing on zero or more of the variables in that matrix (the zero case is to allow that first-order matrices are themselves first-order propositional functions).[24] Call a proposition *first-order* if it could be derived from a first-order matrix by generalizing on *all* of the variables in that matrix.[25] Thus $\hat{x}$ *loves* $\hat{y}$ is a first-order matrix; $(\exists x)$ $(x$ *loves* $\hat{y})$ is a first-order propositional function; $(\exists x)$ $(\exists y)$ $(x$ *loves* $y)$ is a first-order proposition. Now we can define the second level of the hierarchy. Call a matrix *second-order* if it contains variables taking as values first-order propositional functions, but contains no variables which take values other than first-order propositional functions and individuals (thus a second-order matrix invariably contains one or more variables which take first-order propositional functions as values; it may or may not also contain variables taking individuals as values).[26] Second-order

---

[24] This explanation applies directly only to propositional functions and propositions which are in prenex form, i.e. which consist of a string of quantifiers followed by a matrix. Since every schema of quantification theory, open or closed, is equivalent to a prenex schema, this involves no loss of generality. Russell does not explicitly note this fact. As remarked above, however, his introduction of quantification theory in *9 has the consequence that there are only prenex propositions and propositional functions; apparent exceptions are abbreviations for symbols which directly express prenex propositions and propositional function. In *10 Russell has explicitly available the equivalences (not here definitions) which show that every proposition and propositional function has a prenex equivalent.

[25] Elementary, or quantifier-free, propositions may be thought of as zero-order.

[26] It is at this point that the version of the hierarchy of orders given here differs from Russell's, since our hierarchy allows second-order matrices (and hence propositional

propositional functions and propositions are those which could be derived from second-order matrices just as their first-order counterparts are those which could be derived from first-order matrices. Let '$\phi\hat{x}$', etc. represent variables ranging over first-order propositional functions (in practice we use 'ϕ', but the longer form is strictly correct; see *PM*, i. 165). Then $\hat{\phi}Socrates$ is a one-place second-order matrix: it becomes a proposition as soon as a first-order propositional function is specified as argument. Similarly, $\hat{\phi}\hat{x}$ is a two-place second-order matrix (one variable takes individuals as values, the other first-order propositional functions), $\hat{\phi}Socrates \supset \psi\hat{x}$ is a three-place second-order matrix, and so on. $(\exists\psi)$ $(\hat{\phi}Socrates \supset \psi\hat{x})$ is a second-order propositional function which is not a matrix, since it is derived from a second-order matrix $(\hat{\phi}Socrates \supset \psi\hat{x})$ by generalizing on one of its variables. Generalizing on all of the variables of a second-order matrix will of course yield a second-order proposition: since every second-order matrix contains at least one variable taking first-order propositional functions as values, every second-order proposition contains at least one apparent (i.e. quantified) variable which ranges over first-order propositional functions. Thus $(\exists\phi)$ (ψ) $(\phi\ Socrates \supset \psi Plato)$ is a second-order proposition. The third level of the hierarchy is generated from the second as the second was generated from the first. A third-order matrix will contain at least one variable taking second-order propositional functions as values; it may or may not contain variables taking first-order propositional functions as values, and may or may not contain variables taking individuals as values. Third-order propositional functions and propositions are those which could be derived from third-order matrices, by generalizing on zero or more, but not all, of the variables of the matrix in the case of propositional functions, by generalizing on all of the variables of the matrix in the case of propositions. We thus have a hierarchy of propositional functions, up to arbitrarily high order.[27]

functions in general) to contain variables ranging over first-order propositional functions without restriction. Russell's version restricts those variables to such as take first-order *predicative* propositional function as arguments. We shall briefly return to this issue after we have discussed the idea of predicativity; see n. 34, below.

[27] But not, it should be noted, of infinitely high order: 'Since the orders of [propositional] functions are only defined step by step, there can be no process of "proceeding to a limit", and [propositional] functions of an infinite order cannot occur' (*PM* i. 53). The reason for this limitation is, I suspect, that Russell thought that the operation of taking to a limit is a mathematical operation which must be shown to be available in logic. To presuppose a mathematical idea of this sort at the base of the logical system would undermine the idea of a reduction of mathematics to logic. (Poincaré used just this sort of argument against logicism, arguing especially that the logic which makes logicism possible has to presuppose mathematical induction. See Goldfarb, op. cit. n. 22 above, s. II.)

From the point of view of the subsequent history of logic, the limitation to finite types is of the first importance. For some indication of its significance, see n. 48a of

Distinctions of order are introduced to avoid vicious-circle fallacies, and thus to avoid paradox. It is therefore these distinctions that loom largest when Russell's attention is focused on propositions and propositional functions and the need to avoid paradoxes. Thus he says, for example: 'In practice we may without risk of reflexive fallacies treat first-order [propositional] functions as a type, since the only totality they involve is that of individuals' (p. 162). As this remark implies, however, the hierarchy of types—i.e. of ontological categories in general—is not simply identical with the hierarchy of orders that we have examined.

Besides distinctions of order, there seem to be at least two other determinants of type that Russell considers. One of these, however, is not generally reflected in his practice. Let us take this one first. Russell suggests that two propositions or propositional functions differ in type if they contain a different *number* of quantifiers, even if the entities in the range of the quantifiers, and the propositional functions themselves, are of the same order. Thus he says, for example: 'First-order propositions are not all of the same type, since ... two propositions which do not contain the same number of apparent variables cannot be of the same type' (*PM*, i. 162). This idea, if followed out, would give very fine-grained type distinctions. It seems, however, to play little role in Russell's thought, and I shall in general ignore it.[28] The second determinant of type, other than order, is more significant. It is based on the idea that the type of a propositional function is determined not only by its order but also by the number of argument places that it has. Thus a first-order propositional function of one argument will be of different type from a first-order propositional function of two arguments. This idea is not very clearly articulated by Russell in *PM*, but it is consistently exhibited in his practice; thus *21 reiterates for two-variable propositional functions what *20 does for one-variable propositional functions. Although the fundamental idea here is simple, the complexity that it introduces into the type hierarchy is considerable. Since type is not determined by order alone, the type of a propositional function will be determined not only by its order and the number of its argument places; it will also be determined by the *type* of its argument places. Thus a second-order one-place propositional function which takes as arguments first-order one-place propositional functions of

Gödel's paper 'Über formal unentscheidbare Sätze der *Principia Mathematica* und verwandter Systeme I' (first published in *Monatshefe für Mathematik und Physik*, 38 (1931); reprinted, with English trans., in Kurt Gödel, *Collected Works*, ed. Solomon Feferman *et al.* (Oxford: OUP, 1986)), pp. 144–94.

[28] For discussion of this idea, and of why it appears in *PM*, see Goldfarb, op. cit. n. 8 above, pp. 36–8.

individuals will differ in type from a second-order one-place propositional function which takes as arguments first-order two-place propositional functions of individuals. In general, then, the type of a
propositional function will be determined by its order and by the
number and type of its argument places.

It is important for our purposes to note that Russell's discussion of
types is inconclusive or incomplete: it is left undetermined whether
we should think of types as affected by the first of the ideas of the
previous paragraph. Where convenience calls for some assumption on
this score, however, I shall assume that this idea does not affect types
(while assuming that the second idea of that paragraph does). This
yields a theory of types that is broadly the same as that attributed
to Russell by Church in his rigorous discussion;[29] it is, however, significantly different from that attributed to Russell by some other commentators.[30]

Distinctions of order, and the distinctions of type which are based
upon them, are, as we have seen, foremost when Russell is considering propositional functions and paradoxes. These distinctions do not,
however, appear natural when the mathematical purposes of *PM* are
salient. For those purposes, Russell's interest in propositional functions
is that they enable him to simulate the theory of classes; it is in terms
of this theory that all the mathematical work is done. The theory of
classes that Russell wishes to simulate is, of course, a theory according
to which the identity of a class is determined by the entities which are
members of the class; and according to which two classes which have
members of the same ontological category are themselves of the same
ontological category.[31] For these purposes distinctions of order are too
fine-grained: two one-place propositional functions may be significantly (i.e. truly or falsely) applicable to the same objects, yet of different
type (because they contain different quantifiers, and are thus of different order). The issue here is not simply one of redundancy—of unnecessary distinctions. For the purposes of reducing mathematics to
logic, as we shall see, we need to be able to generalize over arbitrary
classes of which a given object can be said, with sense, to be a mem-

---

[29] 'Comparison of Russell's Resolution of the Semantical Antinomies with that of
Tarski', *Journal of Symbolic Logic*, 41(1976), 747–60.

[30] See particularly I. M. Copi, *The Theory of Logical Types* (London: Routledge & Kegan
Paul, 1971), Ch. 3; see below, pp. 310–12.

[31] Note that the second point here is not an inevitable consequence of the first. In the
2nd edn. of *PM* Russell treats co-extensive propositional functions as identical, so that he
ceases to distinguish between propositional functions and classes (see p. xxxix). Nevertheless, the theory presented there does not always allow generalization over the classes
of which a given object can be a member.

ber. But we cannot generalize over the propositional functions which can with sense (truly or falsely) be applied to a given object, for these propositional functions form an illegitimate totality: there are distinctions among them based on the range of quantifiers that each contains.

Let us consider the above issue with more care. According to Russell's theory of types, the propositional functions which can take a given object as argument are themselves of various orders, and hence of various types. We saw one example of this in the contrast between $\hat{x}$ *is brave* and $\hat{x}$ *has all the properties of a great general*. Both are one-place propositional functions applying (truly or falsely) to human beings, but they are themselves of different order, and hence of different type. We are therefore prevented from generalizing over all one-place propositional functions which take (say) human beings as arguments: we can generalize over all such first-order propositional functions, all such second-order propositional functions, and so on, but not over *all* of them (note that I am here generalizing in just the way that the theory of types prevents; this raises issues to which we shall return). But we need to be able to generalize over the propositional functions which take a given entity as argument. Most obviously, perhaps, the definition of *natural number* from zero and successor requires that we say that an object is a natural number if it has *every* property which zero has and which is possessed by the successor of every object which possesses it. Russell's type theory prevents the required generalization. Without further modification it does not allow us even to give a definition of natural number;[32] quite elementary parts of mathematics thus cannot be constructed.

Russell's response to these issues is to introduce the notion of predicativity; and to add the axiom of reducibility to the logical theory. On the account which I shall follow, a propositional function is predicative if it is of the lowest order compatible with its taking the arguments that it has (and is therefore also of the lowest type compatible with its taking those arguments). While we cannot generalize over all the propositional functions which are applicable to a given object (pair of objects, etc.), we clearly can generalize over all predicative propositional functions of this kind. The contextual definition of class symbols in terms of propositional functions, as we shall see, defines the class

---

[32] In Appendix B to the 2nd edn. of *PM*, Russell presents what he claims is such a definition. Gödel points out that Russell does not in fact establish the adequacy of the definition (see 'Russell's Mathematical Logic', op. cit. n. 20 above); John Myhill shows that no such definition can be carried out in *PM* without the axiom of reducibility (see 'The Undefinability of the Set of Natural Numbers in the Ramified *Principia*', in George Nakhnikian (ed.), *Bertrand Russell's Philosophy* (New York: Barnes & Noble, 1974), pp. 19–27).

corresponding to a given propositional function in terms of a co-extensive predicative propositional function. The role of the axiom of reducibility is to ensure that there are enough predicative propositional functions to allow the definition of class symbols to do what is required, and to ensure that generalizing over the predicative propositional functions applicable to a given object can for mathematical purposes play the role of generalizing over all such propositional functions. What is required, and what is asserted by the axiom of reducibility, is that for every propositional function there is a co-extensive predicative propositional function.[33]

A more detailed discussion of these issues is complicated by the fact that Russell gives two different ways of understanding the key idea of predicativity. In *12 he defines predicative propositional functions as quantifier-free functions, i.e. matrices (see pp. 164, 167). In the Introduction, by contrast, he says: 'We will define a function of one variable as *predicative* when it is of the next order above that of its arguments, i.e. of the lowest order compatible with its having that argument' (p. 53). This is clearly a weaker notion: all functions which are predicative in the *12 sense are also predicative in this sense, but not vice versa. In *12 Russell is presumably influenced by the idea that the type of a propositional function is affected by the number of quantifiers that it contains. This idea would provide a reason for working entirely with quantifier-free functions (see n. 35, below). Otherwise there seems to be no reason for the *12 version of predicativity. In what follows we shall use 'predicativity' in the weaker sense, that of the Introduction; this decision, however, is purely for the sake of convenience.[34]

---

[33] Russell states two separate axioms: *12.1 asserts reducibility for one-place propositional functions, *12.2 for two-place propositional functions. (This is one point at which it is clear in Russell's practice that he thinks of the number of argument places as influencing the type of a propositional function.) The axioms of reducibility for one- and two-place propositional functions allow you to infer a corresponding statement for n-place propositional functions; and using Norbert Wiener's later device of the ordered pair in fact would have allowed Russell to dispense with the axiom for two-place functions (see Wiener, 'A Simplification of the Logic of Relations,' *Proceedings of the London Mathematical Society*, 17: 387–90; repr. in van Heijenoort, pp. 224–7). Note that since reducibility must hold for propositional functions regardless of the type of their arguments, each of Russell's two axioms must be thought of as ambiguous as to type, and as thus making infinitely many assertions at once. See pp. 314–16, below, for some discussion of this issue.

[34] Now that we have discussed the idea of predicativity we can revert to the point made in n. 26: in his versions of the hierarchy of orders, in the Introduction and in *12, Russell requires that a matrix contain only variables ranging over individuals and *predicative* propositional functions. Our version of the hierarchy imposed no such restriction. In *12, Russell's restriction issues in the demand that variables range only over matrices, since predicative propositional functions are there identified with matrices. Russell appears to claim that no loss results from restricting variables to predicative propositional

Russell symbolizes predicative propositional functions by an ex-
clamation mark between the function sign and the variable sign, thus:
'φ!x'. Predicative propositional functions play a crucial role in the
contextual definition of class symbols. The definition, recall, is as
follows:

$$f\{\hat{z}(\psi\ z)\} = (\exists\phi)\ (x)\ (\phi!x \equiv \psi x.)\ f(\phi!\hat{z})$$

What plays the role of a statement ascribing a property to the class
corresponding to a propositional function, $\psi\hat{x}$, is the assertion that
there is a co-extensive predicative propositional function, $\phi!\hat{x}$, together
with a statement ascribing that same property to this propositional
function. Now this definition will not do what is required unless it
is true that for every one-place propositional function there *is* a co-
extensive predicative propositional function. If there were a propositional function not meeting this condition, all assertions about the class
corresponding to that propositional function would be false, according
to the definition of classes. The axiom of reducibility asserts that for
each propositional function there is indeed a co-extensive predicative
propositional function. Given this axiom, we can achieve the effect
of generalizing over all classes of which a given object is or is not a
member by generalizing over all one-place predicative propositional
functions which apply, truly or falsely, to that object. Such generaliza-

functions (see pp. 53, 165). This claim, however, is incorrect. Consider the following
argument:

    (x)(x is a successful general ⊃ x is brave)
    (x)(x is a successful general ⊃ x is decisive)
    Smith is brave.
    Jones is decisive.

From these premisses it follows that:

    (∃φ)([(x)(x is a successful general ⊃ φx). φ(Smith)]

and:

    (∃φ)([(x)(x is successful general ⊃ φx). φ(Jones)]

From these two sentences, in turn, it follows that

    (∃ψ)[ψ(Smith). ψ(Jones)]

The existential generalization of the last step requires that we be able to generalize over
all second-order propositional functions of a given type; the argument cannot be repro-
duced if we confine ourselves to generalizing over predicative propositional functions.
Our earlier discussion of the status of the theory of propositional functions indicates that
it is natural, from a Russellian perspective, to allow such existential generalization
without restriction; see pp. 288–9, above. (For this argument, and related discussion, I
am indebted to Thomas G. Ricketts.)

It is important to note that because *PM* contains the axiom of reducibility the above
restriction makes no difference to the reduction of mathematics to logic: all the work of
the reduction is done by the simulated theory of classes, and so in effect by predicative
propositional functions.

tion is possible within the constraints of type theory, for all such propositional functions will be of the same type.[35]

Predicative propositional functions, and the classes which are based on them, form a hierarchy which is simpler than the hierarchy which we discussed above. This simpler hierarchy uses a different notion of type, according to which the type of any propositional function is determined solely by the type and number of its arguments (so type, in this sense, is not affected by the quantified variables in propositional functions). For one-place propositional functions this yields the hierarchy: individuals, propositional functions which apply (truly or falsely) to individuals, propositional functions which apply (truly or falsely) to propositional functions which apply to individuals, and so on (i.e. a hierarchy where each level after the first consists of propositional functions which apply to entities at the previous level). This simpler hierarchy is, in effect, the hierarchy of classes in *PM*. According to the definition of classes, it is only the distinctions that obtain among predicative propositional functions that are inherited, so to speak, by classes. Notation for these distinctions among classes is given in *63, but the distinctions themselves are implicit from the definition of classes.

All of the mathematical work of *PM* is done in terms of the relatively simple hierarchy indicated above. This may in part explain the fact, noted above, that *PM* contains more than one version of the full hierarchy of propositional functions, and that within each there appear to be questions whose answers are vague. The issues left open are not ones that affect the hierarchy of classes, in terms of which the construction of mathematics is actually carried out. The full hierarchy is fundamental in that it holds among propositional functions in general, and (at least according to Russell) arises from the crucial characteristic of such functions. But the actual work of construction uses the simpler hierarchy of classes (or, equivalently, of predicative propositional functions).

The existence of a simple hierarchy of predicative propositional functions within the full hierarchy of types has affected the interpretation of *PM*. Ramsey argued that the full hierarchy is unnecessary (and, in fact, that the full hierarchy with the axiom of reducibility collapses into the simple hierarchy). Since Ramsey's work, commentators have contrasted the simple theory of types with the ramified theory of

---

[35] Note that this does not hold for a system in which type is affected by the number of quantifiers in a propositional function, *unless* we adopt the *12 understanding of predicativity. It is thus natural, as remarked, to think of that understanding of predicativity as motivated by the fine-grained version of type distinction.

types.[36] We cannot consider all of the issues of exegesis and interpretation which are relevant here, but a brief discussion of some points may help to explain the interpretation adopted above.

The full ('ramified') hierarchy is often explained as the result of imposing distinctions upon the simpler hierarchy.[37] This influential interpretation, which I shall call 'the Copi view', uses the word 'type' to speak of the distinctions imposed by the simple hierarchy; the word 'order' is used to refer to the (allegedly) additional distinctions imposed by the more complex hierarchy. According to this view, then, distinctions of type (in this sense) are fundamental. The ramified hierarchy is to be obtained by imposing distinctions of order *within* each type. From the perspective of our interpretation of *PM*, this alternative view is misleading in a number of respects. To begin with, it conceals the fact, emphasized above, that for Russell all of the distinctions of the full hierarchy have the same basis. All arise from the same fundamental idea of the ambiguity of a propositional function. More important, the Copi view will not yield the hierarchy which we have discussed. Let us for the moment speak the language of that interpretation, using 'type and 'order' in the senses indicated. Translating the full hierarchy we discussed into this language, it is clear that the type of a propositional function depends not only upon the type of its arguments but also upon their order. Thus, for example, there will be one type of one-place propositional function which takes as argument propositional functions of type 1 and order 1, another type which takes as argument propositional functions of type 1 and order 2, and so on. Within each of these types there will be different orders, and among the propositional functions to which these may be arguments there will be type distinctions corresponding to these distinctions of order, and so on. So distinctions of type (in the Copi sense) are not independent of distinctions of order (in the Copi sense). What this indicates is that the attempt of the Copi view to reconstruct the full Russellian hierarchy in terms of a fundamental stratification of type distinctions, with distinctions of order superimposed, will not work. If we are indeed to reconstruct the full hierarchy, we cannot conceive of orders as super-

---

[36] I have avoided the expression 'ramified type theory' because it seems to me tendentious. It strongly suggests that the theory is best understood as the result of imposing complications (or ramifications) upon a simpler underlying theory. Once this is accepted, it becomes natural to ask whether we cannot avoid the complications by using only the simpler theory.

[37] See esp. Copi, op. cit. n. 30 above, Ch. 3. Copi follows Ramsey in distinguishing the simpler from the more complex version of type distinctions; it is important to note, however, that Ramsey's aim was not so much to interpret *PM* as to modify it in the light of his own philosophical views.

imposed on more fundamental distinctions of type. In Russell's hierarchy of propositional functions, distinctions based on the number and type of argument places (distinctions of type, in the Copi sense) do not appear as independent of other distinctions.[38]

Ramsey's discussion of *PM* is, as we have noted, in service of an argument that we should adopt the simple theory of types rather than the full Russellian type hierarchy. This argument is based in part on Ramsey's philosophical views, and cannot be discussed here.[39] One issue, however, is worth exploring briefly for the light that it throws on Russell's views. This is the issue of the paradoxes. Simple type theory does not suffice to block the derivation of all of the paradoxes. Of the three that we discussed, the arguments for two, the Liar and the Berry paradoxes, are unaffected by the distinctions imposed by simple type theory (this is particularly obvious in the case of the Liar: simple type theory, since it stratifies propositional functions on the basis of their argument places, imposes no distinctions at all on propositions; yet it is these distinctions that are required to block the argument for the Liar). A crucial part of Ramsey's discussion is thus his claim that the paradoxes fall into two distinct groups, those (such as Russell's paradox) which are properly logical or mathematical, and those which 'are not purely logical, and cannot be stated in logical terms alone; for they all contain some reference to thought, language, or symbolism'.[40] These latter are what have come to be known as the semantic paradoxes.

Ramsey's claim that the paradoxes divide into two kinds, only one of which is the proper concern of logic, is widely accepted. We can gain a different perspective on Russell's philosophy by seeing why these ideas would not have been acceptable to him. One consideration is that it is by no means clear, from a Russellian point of view, that every paradox which is not solved by the simple theory of types can be held to be independent of logic, and attributed to concepts of 'thought, language, or symbolism'. An example here is the paradox which Russell discusses in section 500 of *Principles*. There are propositions which

---

[38] There is one passage, on pp. 48–9, where Russell seems to advance something like the Copi view. That view is, however, inconsistent with the more detailed explanation in the Introduction (pp. 50–4) and with that of *12. I think that Russell gives the earlier explanation only for heuristic purposes.

[39] Ramsey was greatly influenced by (his understanding of) the views of Wittgenstein's *Tractatus*. Thus, for example, he holds that all propositions are truth-functions of elementary propositions, and that expressing the same such truth-function is the criterion of propositional identity. This leads him naturally to a view that the criterion of propositional function identity is co-extensionality. Again, the above view leads him to hold that general propositions are infinitary truth-functions. Connected with this, he accepts the idea of an infinitary language, and this makes it possible for him to hold that propositional functions and propositions are linguistic entities.

[40] Ramsey, op. cit. n. 20 above, p. 20.

assert every member of some class of propositions; call these *class assertions*. Of class assertions some are members of the class all of whose members they assert (call these *self class-assertions*); others are not (*non-self class assertions*). Now consider the class w of non-self class assertions. Let p be the proposition which asserts every member of w. p is a class assertion, but is p a self class-assertion? It is a self class-assertion if it is a member of the relevant class; but this class is the class of *non*-self class assertions. So paradox results. This paradox cannot be blocked by simple type theory: blocking it requires that we stratify propositions, which simple type theory does not do. On the other hand, the paradox makes no very obvious use of concepts of 'thought, language, or symbolism'. From the Russellian point of view, indeed, it is clear that the concept of a proposition, and the assumptions about what propositions there are, which the paradox relies upon are intrinsic to logic.[41]

A second consideration is of a somewhat different kind. To say that the semantic paradoxes are not the concern of logic is presumably to say that they indicate the need for a reformulation of ideas outside logic—the ideas of semantics, most obviously. The reformulation most often suggested is that ideas such as truth, designation, and so on, should be stratified in some way, e.g. that strictly speaking the concept of truth in a given language L should be formulated only in some higher-level language.[42] But now consider these ideas from a Russellian perspective. The ideas connected with the universality of logic obviously give him reason to resist the view that there are different languages and no inclusive language of which each is simply a sublanguage. And if we accept that there is a single language, and various concepts of truth within it, then we can ask whether this stratification of the concept of truth is a *logical* matter or not. If it is, then we are back with something like the (full ramified) type hierarchy.[43] If, on the other hand, the stratification of the concepts of truth is said not to be a matter of logic, then we have a language with various notions of truth: $truth_1$, $truth_2$, $truth_3$ ... But now what is to prevent us from introducing into the language the single, unstratified, concept of truth, by saying that an entity is true if for some i it is $true_i$? The technique of summing up a number of predicates will be one that is generally available, and if it violates no logical restrictions it is unclear how its

[41] For discussion of this paradox, see L. Linsky, 'Terms and Propositions in Russell's *Principles of Mathematics*', *Journal of the History of Philosophy*, 26(1988), 621–42.
[42] The most obvious source of these ideas is Tarski's 'The Concept of Truth in Formalised Languages', in his *Logic, Semantics and Metamethematics* (Indianapolis, Ind.: Hackett, 1983; 1st edn, Oxford: 1956), pp. 152–278.
[43] Compare Church, op. cit. n. 29 above.

prohibition is to be justified.[44] A related point is that although *PM* does not itself contain any semantic or intensional concepts, it is intended as a framework within which such concepts might be used consistently. This might be surmised from what we have already said about Russell's conception of logic as universal (see Chapter 5, above, pp. 200–205). It is also stated quite explicitly. Russell introduces the idea of a truth-function, and then goes on to say:

Such functions are by no means the only common functions of propositions. For example, '*A* believes that *p*' is a function of *p* which will vary its truth-value for different arguments having the same truth-value.... Such functions are not excluded from our consideration, and are included in the scope of any general propositions we may make about functions. (*PM*, i. 8)

This passage, and the related considerations that we have discussed, indicate that Russell would reject the idea that the so-called semantic paradoxes need not be taken into account in constructing a system of logic.

Ramsey's rejection of Russellian type theory is motivated in part by his refusal to accept the axiom of reducibility.[45] From a Russellian perspective, too, the axiom is problematic. We argued above that Russell has reason to regard the existence of propositional functions as a matter of logic (see pp. 288–9). There seems, however, to be no comparable reason to accept the existence assumptions embodied in the axiom of reducibility. These assumptions are not required to explain the possibility of elementary logical relations among propositions. Whether the axiom of reducibility is compatible with Russell's conception of logic is a complicated question, because that conception seems, at times, to shift under pressure of the need to accommodate the axiom of reducibility. We shall discuss this issue later (pp. 320–5, below).

We have noted in passing that Russell's theory in fact requires infinitely many axioms of reducibility. We need to ensure that for every propositional function, *of whatever type*, there is a co-extensive predicative propositional function. To conform with the restrictions of type theory, it would thus appear that we need distinct axioms for propositional functions of distinct types. The problem that this poses is a special case of a more general problem of stating logic within the confines of type theory. This problem arises because of two features of Russell's logic. First, that logic imposes distinctions of type on the entity that it generalizes about. Second, Russell conceives of logic as universal, and thus as not merely a system which is set up within a

---

[44] Compare Goldfarb, op. cit. n. 8 above, pp. 28–9.
[45] See Ramsey, op. cit. n. 20 above, p. 29.

more inclusive meta-language. The first of these points has the immediate consequence that within *PM* we cannot straightforwardly generalize over all the entities that we need to generalize over in logic: we cannot, for example, make assertions about *all* propositions, for propositions are not all of the same type. The second point has the consequence that we cannot retreat to the meta-language in order to do there what cannot be done within *PM*, for there is no meta-language. Equivalently, we might say that the meta-language is subject to the same logic, including type distinctions, that *PM* itself is subject to. This way of making the point brings out the connection between the universality of logic and the idea of logic as representing the truth about the world: if there really are those distinctions of ontological category which *PM* establishes then obviously we cannot legitimately ignore them when it suits us. If, on the other hand, type distinctions are simply rules made up for the purposes of one symbolic system, then the claim of that system to be *Logic* in Russell's sense, i.e. to be a source of metaphysical truth about the world, is undone.

Russell is most explicitly aware of the problem of stating logic within type theory as it affects truth-functional logic. The full type hierarchy includes distinctions among propositions. How, then, can we assert the laws of truth-functional logic, e.g. that every proposition is either true or false? Russell attempts to answer this question by means of the idea of ambiguous assertion, which we have already examined. The hope here is that the fundamental characteristic of propositional functions, their ambiguity, can be invoked to explain how we can manage to make assertions about *all* propositions without vicious-circle fallacies. We assert the relevant propositional function: since this is not itself a proposition, it is not a generalization over a totality of which it is a member. It is for this reason that Russell states the laws of truth-functional logic not as universal quantifications, with the quantifiers ranging over propositions, but rather as the assertions of propositional functions (see especially *PM*, i. 129, for a statement of this rationale).

Russell attempts to use ambiguous assertion to allow for, or simulate, generalization over entities which according to type theory have no total. This use, however, faces considerable difficulties. All of the values of a single propositional function will be of the same type; therefore asserting an arbitrary value of a (single) propositional function is asserting an arbitrary one of a number of propositions which are all of the same type. But this clearly is not what is required. Our assertion must rather somehow be of many propositional functions at once. Russell implicitly accepts this point. In discussing the assertion of $p \lor - p$, he says: 'we may give to p a value of any order, and then give

to the negation and disjunction involved those meanings appropriate
to that order' (*PM*, i. 129). Here it is clearly not simply a case of
asserting a propositional function, for there is not a single propositional function of which an arbitrary instance is asserted. There are, rather,
many propositional functions involved (many meanings of negation
and disjunction). But this sort of ambiguity has nothing to do with
ambiguous assertion, or with the sense in which a propositional function is an essentially ambiguous entity. Here is one point at which we
can see why the next generation of philosophically minded logicians
took a more linguistic approach to the subject than Russell, for it is
hard to see how to make his point clearly without talking about the
assertion of all sentences having a certain form. If we do reinterpret
Russell in this way, however, there seems no longer to be a reason to
say that the sentence concerned must contain only *free* variables.

The conclusion of the previous paragraph is reinforced by recalling
that the axiom of reducibility itself contains quantifiers:

$$(\exists f)\ (x)\colon \phi x . \equiv . f!x$$

At some points in *PM* (though not in connection with the axiom of
reducibility) Russell invokes the idea of typical ambiguity: what is
asserted is supposed to be ambiguous as to type, and so to play the
role of infinitely many assertions (one at each type). But we are entitled
to ask what, exactly, is being said to be ambiguous. And again we can
see why it is hard to resist the idea that it is the expression, the
symbols, that are ambiguous in such a case.[46]

We have been discussing the issue of stating the axioms (and, indeed, the theorems) of *PM* within the constraints of type theory. There
is also a rather different issue which falls under the general heading of
the difficulty of stating logic. This issue concerns not the axioms and
theorems of logic, but rather the formulation of type theory itself. The
notion of predicativity, for example, is one that applies across types: if
the notion is to do any work at all, it must be truly applicable to some
propositional functions and falsely applicable to others (i.e. there must
be both predicative and non-predicative functions). But then a single
propositional function (ϕ *is predicative*) is applicable (truly or falsely) to

---

[46] It may appear that even if we reinterpret *PM* in this linguistic fashion, still the
axiom(s) of reducibility will pose difficulties. We may be able to pick out all the sentences
of the relevant form, but to say that all are *true* would require a univocal concept of truth.
Russell speaks of truth as being a typically ambiguous concept (*PM*, i. 41 ff.), but the
point of the linguistic move was to explain or to avoid appeal to typical ambiguity. Here,
perhaps, we see pressure to give up the idea of logic as universal, and to think rather in
terms of a system formulated with a meta-language; in the meta-language we can of
course talk freely about the truth of any sentence of the object-language.

entities of different type: this contravenes type restrictions. Another example concerns the notion of type itself. Proposition *9.131 is a definition of 'being the same type as'. The primitive proposition (axiom) *9.14 makes essential use of this notion, asserting, 'If "ϕx" is significant, and if a is of the same types as x, then "ϕa" is significant, and vice versa'. This proposition, and others which depend upon it, are essential for Russell's extension of logic from (what we should call) the truth-functional to the quantificational.[47] The relation 'is of the same type as' is one which itself violates type restrictions. The clause of *9.14 which states 'a is of the same type as x' must be true in some cases and false in others (if it were always true, which it is not, it could be simply omitted; if it were always false the whole axiom would be unnecessary). If we take some fixed entity a, we can truly assert that b, say, is of the same type as a; we can also falsely, but with sense, assert that an entity of another type, c, say, is of the same type as a. So both b and c can be arguments to the same propositional function (that expressed by 'is of the same type as a'). By the 'vice versa' clause of *9.14 itself, it ought to follow from this that b and c are themselves of the same type; but this is contrary to the initial assumption that b is of the same type as a while c is not. What this shows is that we cannot consistently treat 'is of the same type as', and other notions that Russell employs in setting up type theory, as being themselves subject to type theory. But Russell's conception of logic gives him no other way to treat them.

What Russell's position requires is that type theory should somehow go without saying. He acknowledges this, in a passage in which he argues that the fundamental notion of the variable is that of the unrestricted variable, ranging over everything. He qualifies the point as follows:

We shall find that the unrestricted variable is still subject to limitations imposed by the manner of its occurrence, i.e. things which can be said significantly concerning a proposition cannot be said concerning a class or relation, and so on. But *the limitations to which the unrestricted variable is subject do not need to be explicitly indicated, since they are the limits of significance of the statement in which the variable occurs, and are therefore intrinsically determined by this statement.* (*PM*, i. 4; my emphasis)

---

[47] This point is complicated, because this extension is done twice over, in two rather different ways, once in *9 and once in *10 (see n. 14 above). *10 does not contain a definition of 'is the same type as', but it appears to rely on the definition given in *9, for it does contain propositions which make explicit use of the notion (*10.121, which is identical with *9.14; *10.13). These propositions, and those which depend on them, play a crucial role in *10, so that the reliance on the notion 'is the same type as' is required by both methods.

Restrictions imposed by limits of significance, Russell is claiming, go without saying: they do not need to be stated (a similar point is made in *ML*; see van Heijenoort, pp. 160–1; Marsh, p. 71). This claim, however, cannot be sustained. In fact limits of significance do need to be explicitly stated; hence the need for a definition of 'is the same type as'.

There is a further difficulty which Russell faces, also as a result of the type distinctions of *PM*. The difficulty concerns the existence of infinitely many entities, which is essential for even quite elementary parts of mathematics. In *Principles* Russell had claimed that there is what he called a 'formal proof' that there is an infinite class.[48] Thus he offers the following proof that for any (finite) number n, n cannot be the number of the natural numbers:

> if n be any finite number, the number of numbers from 0 up and including n is $n+1$, whence it follows that n is not the number of numbers. (*Principles*, 339)

As it stands, this proof seems to assume that natural numbers exist as independent entities, whereas the doctrine of *Principles*, as we saw, is that such numbers are classes. In particular, natural numbers are classes of classes all of which have the same number of members, i.e. are *similar*, where the notion of similarity is defined in a way that does not presuppose the notion of number (see *Principles*, 109, 111). What Russell says, however, can be easily adapted to this doctrine, to give the following argument in terms of classes. Whether or not there are individuals, there is the null class, i.e. the class containing no objects. The class containing only the null class is the number 0 (only the null class is similar to the null class). Since there is the number 0, there is at least one one-membered class, that containing 0 and nothing else. The number 1 can then be defined as the class containing this paradigmatic one-membered class, and all classes similar to it, if any. In like fashion, the class containing only 0 and 1 functions as a paradigmatic two-membered class, enabling us to define the number 2, and so on.[49]

The above argument can easily be rephrased in terms appropriate to *PM*. (For the sake of convenience I shall continue to talk of classes,

---

[48] Note that from the present point of view the emphasis is not on questions of *class* existence. If at any type there are infinitely many entities, then the presuppositions and definitions of *PM* guarantee that at the appropriate higher type there will be an infinite class. This inference might be controversial in some systems, but is not so here; so our focus is on the infinitude of entities.

[49] This sort of argument, implicit in Russell's *Principles*, is explicit in Frege's *Die Grundlagen der Arithmetik* (Breslau: Verlag von Wilhelm Koebner, 1884), trans. as *The Foundations of Arithmetic* (Oxford: Blackwell, 1933, 1st edn. 1950); see s. 82.

rather than propositional functions, and shall accordingly for the moment use 'type' in the sense applicable to classes. Except for some additional complexity, nothing is altered if we talk rather in terms of propositional functions.) When so rephrased, however, it is clear that the argument involves an unlimited ascent of the type hierarchy. The null class is of type 1; the class which contains it alone—i.e. the number 0—is thus of type 2. The number 1 is a class which contains (possibly among other things) a class whose sole member is the number 0; the number 1 is thus a type 4 class. Similarly, the number 2 will be of type 6, and so on. Thus at any given (finite) type only a finite number of natural numbers can be proven to exist by anything like the *Principles* strategy. Only at transfinite type could we prove the existence of infinitely many entities. But Russell, as we have seen, rejects the notion of transfinite types (see n. 27, above). The consequence of this is that Russell, in *PM*, has no way of proving the existence of infinitely many entities. Thus the system cannot prove, for example, the existence of enough numbers to make number theory possible. At each type there will be a simple numerical inequality, e.g. $8 \neq 9$, which cannot be proved at that type. Even quite elementary parts of mathematics are impossible unless this difficulty can be circumvented in some way.

Russell's response is the so-called 'axiom of infinity'. It must be made clear at the outset that this is not in fact an axiom of *PM*. It is rather a statement, guaranteeing the existence of an infinite class, which is 'adduced as a hypothesis [i.e. taken as antecedent to a conditional] whenever it is relevant'; what *PM* thus enables us to prove, in many cases, is not a mathematical theorem itself but rather a conditional, of which the antecedent is the axiom of infinity and the consequent is the theorem in question (see *PM*, ii. 183).[50] Even if *PM* is accepted as completely successful on its own terms, and as constituting logic, it might thus be thought that it still does not amount to a demonstration of logicism. The need for the so-called 'axiom of infinity' does not affect the *analysis* of mathematics, including the infinite, in terms of logic. It does not, that is to say, affect the idea that we can translate the theorems of mathematics into the vocabulary of logic (understood as the theory of propositional functions). It does, how-

---

[50] In this respect the axiom of infinity has the same status in *PM* as does the axiom of choice, which Russell calls 'the multiplicative axiom'. In its attitude towards the axiom of choice, however, it could be argued that *PM* accurately reflects mathematics, as it was practised in the early 20th century. At that time the axiom of choice was not generally accepted among mathematicians, so its appearance as the antecedent of a conditional might seem to be appropriate. Clearly no analogous argument could be made about the axiom of infinity.

ever, constitute an acknowledgement that the theorems of mathematics cannot be proved from principles which are true by logic.[51] *PM*, the culmination of Russell's logicism, thus also marks his retreat from his earlier logicist claims.

In *Principles* we saw a fairly straightforward view of logic, of logicism, and of its philosophical significance. Logic consists of absolute truths of unrestricted generality; logicism shows that, contrary to appearances, mathematics also consists of such truths; and this result is the basis for an argument against Idealism. The only cloud in this clear blue sky was the paradox, which *Principles* essentially left unresolved. The need to resolve the paradox gave rise to the theory of types, and this in turn gave rise to the need for the axiom of reducibility to be accepted as part of logic, and for the use of the axiom of infinity as an hypothesis. These two features of *PM* threaten the apparently straightforward view of *Principles*, in two ways. The need for the axiom of reducibility casts Russell's conception of logic in doubt: on what view of logic is this axiom a truth of logic? Given this conception of logic, what is the more general philosophical significance of the reduction of mathematics to logic? The use of the axiom of infinity, on the other hand, seems to amount simply to abandonment of logicism in favour of the weaker position that mathematics is reducible to logic *if* we add a relatively weak existence hypothesis. What philosophical significance does this weaker position have?

These questions are, surprisingly, scarcely raised by Russell. His writings from the period during which he was writing *PM* (and indeed for some years after) contain almost no discussion of the nature of logic, or of the general significance of logicism. *Principles* contains a not very clearly articulated view of logic as consisting of the most general truths, i.e. truths which contain only variables and logical constants. This, however, does not seem to be Russell's view in the later period. According to the *Principles* criterion, the axiom of infinity is a truth of logic, if it is true at all. In *PM*, however, Russell takes that axiom as 'empirical', and as definitely not part of logic (nor, strictly, as an axiom; see above, pp. 318–19). Russell's change of mind stems from the

---

[51] Given the anti-idealist motives of the logicism of *Principles*, two points are worth noting here. First, the need for the axiom of infinity does not affect the earlier claims that idealist arguments against the infinite are mistaken; these claims require only the analysis of mathematics, and especially the infinite. Second, the need for the axiom of infinity arguably does affect the earlier claim that logic/mathematics is an independent subject with a content of its own. I do not investigate these issues in detail because there is no sign that the anti-idealist motives are important in *PM*; on the contrary, Russell seems to regard that battle as won.

introduction of the theory of types, and of the notion of an individual as an ontological category. (In *Principles*, as we saw, Russell claims that it is a logical truth that there are infinitely many entities.) In spite of this implicit rejection of the earlier view of logic, Russell does not offer a new view to replace it. He does, however, briefly discuss a related question: our knowledge of logic, or at least of the fundamental principles of mathematics. His interest in this may stem partly from the fact that he has nothing to say about the intrinsic nature of logic; it may also stem in part from a more general interest in epistemological (even, in a sense, psychological) questions (see Chapter 6, above, pp. 244–247, and Chapter 8, below, pp. 329–33). In any case, it is to Russell's discussion of these matters that I now turn.

Russell discusses our knowledge of the fundamental principles of mathematics in 'The Regressive Method of Discovering the Premises of Mathematics'.[52] According to this discussion, there is no difference in principle between our knowledge of mathematics and our knowledge of anything else. All knowledge, to begin with, has the same kind of basis. This basis is what Russell calls 'intrinsic obviousness'. Some facts we simply find obvious.[53] Russell calls these facts the 'empirical premises' of knowledge, but there is no implication that these facts are empirical rather than logical or mathematical; on the contrary, while he notes this distinction it seems to play no role at all. Thus he says:

The function of intrinsic obviousness in any body of knowledge demands some consideration. It is to be observed that it gives necessarily the basis of all other knowledge: our empirical premises must be obvious. In the natural sciences, the obviousness is that of the senses, while in pure mathematics it is an a priori obviousness, such as that of the law of contradiction. (Lackey, p. 279)

---

[52] Read before the Cambridge Mathematical Club, 9 Mar. 1907; repr. in Lackey. It may be significant that Russell never published this piece; on the other hand this may be more or less a matter of accident. The lack of extensive discussion of these issues elsewhere in his work around this time makes it hard to confirm or refute that the ideas advanced in this piece represent a settled view. As we shall see, however, some of the same ideas occur in *PM*, and also in *Problems*.

[53] It might seem natural to us to ask whether this is simply a psychological fact about us or whether it also confers some degree of probability or credibility upon the proposition that we find obvious, i.e. whether 'intrinsic obviousness' has merely descriptive force or also justificatory force. Since Russell has no account of the justificatory force of intrinsic obviousness, pressing this question may make it seem as if his is an account not of knowledge, but merely of how we come to take ourselves to know certain propositions. This matter is, however, not so clear-cut. One line of thought, somewhat developed in *Problems*, goes as follows: since Russell sees intrinsic obviousness as the source of *all* knowledge, he presumably sees us as faced with the alternatives of according justificatory force to this notion or else accepting a total scepticism. If an account of knowledge must include a decisive refutation of scepticism then, indeed, Russell has no account of knowledge; but by this standard, he would insist, no account is possible (see Chapter 8, pp. 381–2, below, for a slightly more detailed discussion).

Other beliefs, which are not obvious, are justified because they enable us to systematize our obvious knowledge. Thus the empirical premisses of knowledge, the obvious truths from which we in fact begin, are contrasted with the logical premisses, which are the logically simpler and more general truths which we believe because they imply the empirical premisses. Our justification for believing the logical premisses is thus inductive, not only when the premisses are those of the empirical sciences but also when they are those of mathematics:

in dealing with the principles of mathematics . . . we tend to believe the [logical] premisses because we can see that their consequences are true, instead of believing the consequences because we know the premisses to be true. But the inferring of premisses from consequences is the essence of induction; thus the method in investigating the principles of mathematics is really an inductive method, and is substantially the same as the method of discovering general laws in any other science. (Lackey, p. 274)

There thus emerges a picture of knowledge applicable to the mathematical and the non-mathematical alike. This picture is fallibilist, in the sense that there are no incorrigibly certain claims, and holist, in the sense that any one claim draws part of its support from its relations with others (see Lackey, p. 279).

The picture of knowledge which Russell sketches in 'The Regressive Method' is tailor-made for the axiom of reducibility. It is surely a description of something like the way in which Russell in fact came to formulate this axiom: not because it struck him as intrinsically obvious, but because he needed it in order to permit inferences to logical or mathematical claims which did strike him in this way. The effect of the discussion is to elevate this method not merely into a general method of discovery but also into a justification. In *PM* Russell mentions this method of justification in explicit connection with the axiom of reducibility. In a section of the Introduction entitled 'Reasons for Accepting the Axiom of Reducibility', he says:

That the axiom of reducibility is self-evident is a proposition which can hardly be maintained. But in fact self-evidence is never more than part of the reason for accepting an axiom, and is never indispensable. The reason for accepting an axiom, as for accepting any other proposition, is always largely inductive, namely that many propositions which are nearly indubitable can be deduced from it, and that no equally plausible way is known by which these propositions could be true if the axiom were false, and nothing which is probably false can be deduced from it. If the axiom is apparently self-evident, that only means, practically, that it is nearly indubitable; for things have been thought to be self-evident and have turned out false. (*PM*, i. 59)

In denying that apparent self-evidence is a guarantee of truth Russell explicitly refers to the paradoxes, which show that what seems self-evident may in fact conflict with so many other apparently self-evident truths that we conclude that it is false. While he is very confident of the truth of the axiom of reducibility, he allows the possibility that it might be 'found to be deducible from some other more fundamental and more evident axiom' (*PM*, i. 60). It is clear, however, that Russell does not see this position as differing in principle from that in which the not very evident axiom of reducibility is an axiom in its own right.

Logic has a complex role in the view of knowledge which we are discussing. To begin with, it is not entirely clear whether we should see that view as taking logic for granted. The reason for seeing it this way is that the justification of non-obvious propositions is that from them we can *deduce* obvious propositions. So it might seem as if the notion of deduction, and hence of logic, is presupposed, and is a constraint on knowledge. This cannot, however, be right. Russell intends to apply the view of justification to the axiom of reducibility, which he apparently counts as an axiom of logic; if the view of justification is to apply to knowledge of logic, it cannot require that logic be taken for granted. Remarks of Russell's also suggest that even elementary claims of logic are to be justified in the same way as everything else (see Lackey, pp. 278–9). The implication of this is that logic is not presupposed, and that 'intrinsic obviousness' is thus the only constraint on knowledge. To put it a different way: the goal, and the justification, of knowledge is to systematize the various propositions that we naturally believe, discarding some because they do not fit, adding others solely for the sake of a more coherent system. To take the view above seriously is to say that in this attempt, the standards of coherence of a system with which we try to accord are not given, but are as much in question as anything else. There is, however, no sign that Russell faced up to the full consequences of this view.[54]

The view of knowledge suggested in 'The Regressive Method', and echoed in one section of *PM*, seems to blur or even totally to efface the distinction between logic and other subjects. The view is based on the

---

[54] One such consequence is that the view may be vulnerable to arguments akin to those which Russell himself uses against the coherence theory of truth (see especially 'The Monistic Theory of Truth', originally published in *Proceedings of the Aristotelian Society* for 1906–7, where it constituted the first two sections of a piece called 'The Nature of Truth'; repr. in Russell's *Philosophical Essays* (London: Allen & Unwin, 1966; 1st edn. 1910)). The crux of these arguments is the idea that more than one system might be coherent, but only one can be correct. Two further points are worth noting. First, the view of Russell's discussed here is in some ways very like Quine's view, advanced in, for example, Ch. 1 of *Word and Object* (Cambridge, Mass.: MIT, 1960). Quine has a deep and subtle response to the idea that there might be more than one system of knowledge (or at least belief) which meets the relevant constraint. Second, in *Introduction to Mathematical Philosophy* (London: Allen & Unwin, 1919) Russell makes a distinction between the axioms essential

idea of intrinsic obviousness. At bottom this seems to be an unequivocal idea, applying equally to, say, the Law of Contradiction, to '2 + 2
= 4', and to my belief that the sun is now shining outside my study
window.[55] But if there is no fundamental distinction at the base of
the system then there will be no fundamental distinction at all; the
structure is the same for knowledge of all kinds. Now Russell does
suggest *a* distinction between kinds of obviousness. I do not think that
he intends this distinction to be fundamental (certainly he does not say
enough to justify the idea that it is), but it is in any case worth our
while to see why his distinction cannot help. In a passage we have
already quoted, Russell distinguishes 'the obviousness...of the
senses' from '*a priori* obviousness' (Lackey, p. 279). Now the problem
here is that '*a priori* obviousness' does not distinguish between the
obviousness of mathematics and the obviousness of logic; Russell's
own statement of the matter, indeed, makes it clear that he intends no
such distinction. Thus mathematics and logic will not appear as distinct
at any stage. Now if logicism is correct then mathematics and logic are
not in fact distinct; nevertheless, the conclusion that we have just
reached is disastrous for logicism. If there is to be any significance in
the reduction of mathematics to logic then we must have some conception of logic which frames the task of reduction; and that conception
must give logic a prima-facie distinctness from mathematics. To take an
obvious example: if logic is simply defined as the fundamental premisses and methods of reasoning of mathematics, then logicism is
clearly true, but equally clearly without significance. On such a view of
logicism, the definition of natural number in terms of classes (or pro-

for deduction and the axiom of reducibility. Using this distinction one could claim that
the former axioms are presupposed in knowledge, but that the axiom of reducibility, and
perhaps other logical axioms, can be justified along the lines indicated. This would mean
that the theory of deduction, at least, still acted as an external constraint upon knowledge, so the view would be far less radical. The distinction which Russell draws in
Introduction to Mathematical Philosophy, however, seems to result from a more sceptical
view of the axiom of reducibility in general; there seems to be no justification for reading
this view back into the earlier position.

[55] The issue of varieties of obviousness recurs in the debate between Carnap and
Quine over analyticity or truth in virtue of meaning. In his 'Carnap and Logical Truth'
Quine makes use of the notion of obviousness. In his reply, Carnap insists that obvious-
ness comes in two quite distinct varieties: he distinguishes 'the sense in which someone
might say "it is obvious that I have five fingers on my right hand"' from 'the sense in
which the word ["obvious"] is used in "it is obvious that, if there is no righteous man in
Sodom, then all men in Sodom are non-righteous"' (in Carnap's reply to Quine, *The
Philosophy of Rudolf Carnap*, ed. P. A. Schilpp (LaSalle, Ill.; Open Court, 1963), p. 916;
Quine's article, referred to above, is at pp. 385–406 of the same volume). Quine returns
to the theme in his *Philosophy of Logic* (Englewood Cliffs: Prentice-Hall Inc., 1970), where
he insists that he uses the word unambiguously 'in an ordinary behavioural sense' (p.

positional functions), or the definition of real number in terms of classes and natural numbers, would seem to be completely unnecessary to show the truth of logicism (such definitions might have significance from some other perspective, but this is not to the present point).

Russell's general discussions thus seem to show no concern with a distinction between logic, on the one hand, and other sorts of a priori knowledge, on the other hand. Although he does suggest that there is a distinction between a priori knowledge and non-a priori knowledge, this distinction seems to play little systematic role in his thought.

To this point I have been chiefly concerned, as Russell was, with the problem posed by the axiom of reducibility. It is, however, also worth considering the axiom of infinity in the context of the sort of justification that Russell suggests for the axiom of reducibility. Here the remarkable thing is that Russell does *not* attempt such a justification. One might have thought that just the same sorts of inductive reasons which Russell offers for the axiom of reducibility would hold equally for the axiom of infinity. The latter proposition is, after all, required by the axiomatization of mathematics; why does this not provide us with a justification, even a sufficient justification, of the proposition? The answer, I suspect, is that Russell is implicitly presupposing an understanding of the distinction between the a priori and the empirical which is distinct from (and, indeed, in conflict with) that suggested by 'The Regressive Method'. Given this other criterion, the axiom of infinity cannot be a priori—even if it is required for the systematization of the a priori subject of mathematics. (We shall return to this issue in Chapter 8, below, pp. 382–4.)

We have been discussing, implicitly and explicitly, Russell's conception of logic, in the light of the technical changes forced on him in *PM*. From our point of view, the most striking thing about this issue is how little Russell discusses it. *PM* attempts to integrate logic with metaphysics, to unify the technical and the philosophical. But the attempt does not seem to have been carried through, perhaps simply because the obstacles to it were too great. While Russell does, as we have seen, suggest a philosophical view which would accommodate the axiom of reducibility, he does not connect this view with others; he does not, for example, consider what the general significance of logicism might be on such a view. It is perhaps plausible to suppose that Russell became caught up in the technical aspects of the project of reducing mathematics to logic, and ceased to focus on questions of the conception of logic in play, or on the general significance of logicism. The technical endeavour of logicism, in short, seems to have taken on a life of its own. It is, in consequence, hard to attribute to Russell any one consistent view of the philosophical significance of *PM*.

Finally, in this chapter, we shall discuss an issue which is crucial to Russell's attempt to integrate logic and metaphysics. In discussing the basis of the type hierarchy, we saw that Russell explains the hierarchy in terms of the ambiguity of propositional functions. He takes this to be the fundamental characteristic of propositional functions, and to imply that a propositional function presupposes its values. This fact, in turn, gives rise to the hierarchy. Now our focus is on the fundamental idea of the ambiguity of a propositional function.

Let us look again at the crucial passage in which Russell asserts the ambiguity of a propositional function:

'ϕx' means one of the objects ϕa, ϕb, ϕc, etc., but an undetermined one. It follows that 'ϕx' only has a well-defined meaning (well-defined, that is to say, except in so far as it is of its essence to be ambiguous) if the objects ϕa, ϕb, ϕc, etc. are well-defined. That is to say, a function is not well-defined unless all its values are already well-defined. (*PM*, i. 39)

At first sight this passage seems to ignore the distinction which Russell himself draws between the use of 'ϕx' and the use '$\phi \hat{x}$': 'The function itself, $\phi \hat{x}$, is the single thing which ambiguously denotes its many values; while ϕx . . . is one of the denoted objects, with the ambiguity belonging to the manner of denoting' (*PM*, i. 40). Any expression which uses 'ϕx' is ambiguous, in a sense, for it allows us to assert (or say something about) one of a number of propositions without specifying which one we are asserting. But this does not imply that the propositional function itself, which we talk about by means of the symbol '$\phi \hat{x}$' is in any sense an 'ambiguous entity'.

Russell, indeed, makes exactly this contrast:

When we say 'ϕx is a proposition', we mean to state something which is true for every possible value of x, though we do not decide what value x is to have. We are making an ambiguous statement about any value of the function. But when we say '$\phi \hat{x}$ is a function', we are not making an ambiguous statement. . . . The function itself, $\phi \hat{x}$, is the single thing which ambiguously denotes its many values; while ϕx is one of the denoted objects, with the ambiguity belonging to the manner of denoting. (*PM*, i. 40)

The apparent confusion here between ϕx and $\phi \hat{x}$ is not an accidental act of carelessness on Russell's part. It is, rather, the symptom of a deep tension in his thought. If we attempt to restate the idea while retaining the distinction between ϕx and $\phi \hat{x}$ we obtain the position that an entity of one kind, a propositional function, presupposes or is dependent upon entities of another kind, the values of the propositional function. This position is clearly in conflict with the object-based metaphysics that we have attributed to Russell. According to that metaphysics, each thing is what it is, independent of every other thing;

there is no room here for the idea of one entity being dependent upon another. Russell does not suggest, much less articulate, any alternative to his earlier metaphysics. The earlier position seems to remain, as an increasingly implicit assumption; and for Russell to shift his position on this point would be a drastic change indeed. The idea of one entity presupposing or being dependent upon others is precisely that for which the Idealists had used the phrase 'internal relation'. The arguments which Moore advanced, and Russell endorsed, against the intelligibility of internal relations apply equally here. For Russell to acknowledge the full implications of his use of the idea of presupposition would be for him to undo the most fundamental elements in the rejection of Idealism.

It is perhaps because Russell cannot incorporate the idea of presupposition consistently into his metaphysics that he discusses it in constructive or temporal language—saying, for example, that a function is not well defined unless all its values are *already* well defined. As I have remarked, this language should not be taken literally. Certainly Russell at this time would have denied any view even suggesting that propositional functions come into being as we define them. On the other hand, his use of misleading language here is not an accident. On the contrary: it takes place because this issue, of the relation between a propositional function and its values, is a point of tension in Russell's thought.

The relation between a propositional function and its values, as it occurs in *PM*, is analogous to the relation between denoting concept and denoted object(s) as it occurred in *Principles*. Both were intended primarily as a way of handling the issue of generality, or 'the nature of the variable'; both are subject to the same sorts of problems from a Russellian perspective. In each case we have an entity (a denoting concept, a propositional function) which is, on the one hand, to be understood simply as that which has a certain relation to other objects (the denoted objects, the values of the propositional function) but which must, on the other hand, be an independent and self-subsistent object, a subject of propositions in its own right. We saw that in Russell's attempt to deploy logicism against Idealism he placed great stress on 'a correct philosophy of *any*', or on the nature of the variable. Seen through idealist eyes, it is no surprise that the metaphysics underlying the attempt should falter at just this point. From that perspective the problem here is an instance of the more general problem of the One and the Many, which must inevitably defy an attempt to understand it in terms of self-subsistent objects and external relations.

8

Judgement, Belief, and Knowledge: The Emergence of a Method

This final chapter deals with two separate developments in Russell's thought in the period 1906–13. One concerns fundamental metaphysical issues. Here Russell's views undergo a definite change: the notion of truth, and of a proposition, are displaced from their central metaphysical role, which is increasingly occupied by the notion of a fact. For reasons which are not immediately obvious, but will emerge, Russell's adoption of what he calls 'the multiple relation theory of judgment' is intrinsic to this change. The second development is, I think, not a change of doctrine on Russell's part but rather a shift of interest. He comes to be increasingly concerned with the question of knowledge: how, and to what extent, we can know the things that we take ourselves to know. The emphasis here is not on our (putative) knowledge of logic and mathematics, but rather on our knowledge of the physical world—from humble statements about there being a table in front of me to the most esoteric assertions of physics. Both of these developments of Russell's thought give rise to much subsequent work. My purpose in this chapter is not to give a full account of his thought on these matters but to indicate the main lines of the developments that I have mentioned, and especially their relation to Russell's earlier work.

The two developments mentioned above are distinct and I shall discuss them separately. There are, however, two themes which connect them. The first is quite general, and of great significance from our point of view. It is in the two developments which are the subject of this chapter that one begins to see the emergence of what we might call 'constructionalism' as a general method in philosophy. The general idea of constructionalism is of course familiar from the project of reducing mathematics to logic (or constructing mathematics from logic). In the two developments discussed in this chapter, most obviously in the second, we see something new: constructionalism becomes a general philosophical method. This method came to be an important strand running through the tradition of analytic philosophy;

it is perhaps most evident in later works of Russell, and in works by such authors as Carnap and Goodman.[1] The emergence of constructionalism as a general philosophical method is a theme that we shall return to throughout the chapter, and especially at the end of Section 2.

The second theme connecting the two developments discussed in this chapter requires more detailed consideration at the outset. This theme is Russell's new-found concern with the psychological. In particular, he begins to subject the notion of acquaintance to increasing psychological constraints. It is important to understand what sort of change this involves. According to Russell's view in *Principles*, say, certain entities, such as the indefinable notions of logic, are possible objects of acquaintance, and some people (including of course Russell himself) are in fact acquainted with them. At this stage he takes any uncertainty about which are the indefinable notions of logic to be simply an uncertainty over the possibility of giving definitions of a given notion in terms of others that seem simpler. Once the theory of logic has definitely generated the indefinables, there is no left-over worry about whether anyone is, as a matter of psychological fact, acquainted with them. In *Principles* such a question scarcely arises. Russell's view at that time does, however, require that the psychological facts—e.g. that Russell is acquainted with the notion of truth—should line up in the right way. The reason that such facts are never called in question is not that the theory does not require them; it is, rather, that Russell takes it for granted that if we can find the theory of (say) logic which seems best by internal (i.e. non-psychological) criteria, then the psychological facts just will (must) turn out to be those that this theory requires.[2] This point is simply assumed, without investigation. Russell's early view thus relies on an unexamined notion

---

[1] Among Russell's works, most obviously, the book *Our Knowledge of the External World*; less obviously, perhaps, *Analysis of Matter* (London: Routledge, Kegan Paul, Trench, Trubner & Co., 1927). All of Carnap's work may be seen as falling within the constructionalist tradition, but see especially *Der logische Aufbau der Welt* (Berlin: Welt-kreis Verlag, 1928), English translation published under the title *The Logical Structure of the World* (Los Angeles: University of California Press, 1967). In the case of Goodman, the most obvious source, but again not the only one, is *The Structure of Appearance* (Cambridge, Mass.: Harvard University Press, 1951).

[2] There is an apparent exception to this claim. In the Preface to *Principles* Russell says that he has 'failed to perceive' one of the indefinables which his view of logic clearly does require, namely the concept *class* (pp. xv–xvi). The exception, however, is apparent only. Russell's reasons for saying that he fails to perceive the concept *class* have nothing to do with a supposed psychological fact about his own perception; he is, rather, basing his statement simply on the fact that he has not found a consistent and satisfactory theory of classes. He infers immediately from the theoretical difficulty to the psychological fact. This point thus illustrates, rather than contradicts, the idea that for Russell, at this time, claims about perception or acquaintance are simply adjuncts to a theory which is worked out independently.

of acquaintance, or immediate perception. It is not only the notion itself which is unexamined; so also are particular implicit claims about what we are in fact acquainted with. Such claims are taken for granted, as and when needed. It is this last element which begins to change after *Principles*. This is not a change in the structure of Russell's view. It is, rather, a change in the standards by which he assesses one kind of claim that his view was committed to right from the start. The use of the new standards leads him to reject some claims which he had formerly accepted, explicitly or implicitly; hence the need arises to change his view so that those claims are no longer required by the theory.

Russell's turn towards the psychological is thus, as I see it, not a change in doctrine of the ordinary sort. It is never directly expressed, much less argued for, in his writings. It is, moreover, a change which appears to happen gradually; its consequences, at all events, occur in his work not all at once but little by little. In Chapter 6 we saw something of the beginning of the shift in emphasis, and the change becomes more marked as time passes. The manuscript entitled *Theory of Knowledge*,[3] written in May and early June of 1913, provides a dramatic illustration of the extent of the shift. Even the titles of the chapters show a psychological concern that is in marked contrast with *Principles*. Chapter I, for example, is called 'Preliminary Description of Experience', Chapter III 'Analysis of Experience'. Again, in Chapter II of Part II, Russell places considerable emphasis on the question whether we can be acquainted with a complex without being acquainted with its constituents (see pp. 120ff.). Throughout the book, especially Part I, questions as to the nature and contents of experience are explicitly at issue. In Russell's earlier view, and his earlier practice, such issues received no attention at all.

Philosophical theories therefore appear to be answerable to the data of experience, to facts about what is or can be plausibly supposed to be present to our minds. This is clearly a considerable concession to psychologism, one that it would have been hard to imagine Russell granting when the battle with Idealism loomed large in his mind.[4] But the concession is limited. While his philosophical theories become

---

[3] This was a projected book, of which Russell completed the first two of three proposed parts. He abandoned it following criticisms by Wittgenstein, but published the first six chapters in the *Monist* for 1914 and 1915. The book has been reconstructed from the published articles and from manuscript and published as vol. vii of *Russell's Collected Papers*, ed. Elizabeth Ramsden Eames with Kenneth Blackwell (London: Allen & Unwin, 1984).

[4] It is, I think, plausible to speculate that the end of this battle, as Russell saw it, facilitated the shift in emphasis that we are discussing. Once he had ceased to worry about Idealism, and its claims about Experience or The Mind, he could face the psycholo-

answerable, in part, to psychological facts, their subject-matter remains non-psychological. It might be said that the concern of philosophy remains not the nature of human experience but rather the most fundamental features of the world; the difference is that the former is now investigated as a clue to the latter. In terms of acquaintance, the crucial point is that while it is a psychological fact that, say, Russell is acquainted with so-and-so, the objects of acquaintance themselves are not in general mental. On the contrary: the point of acquaintance is still, as it was in *Principles*, to be an unproblematic meeting ground between the mind and what is outside it (this point will be further discussed in Section 2 of this chapter, below). Russell's insistence on his notion of acquaintance is the insistence that the fundamental cognitive relation does not demand two homogeneous objects; just because one of the relata is mental, we may by no means infer that the other is mental.[5] Thus in an essay written in 1910 Russell says: 'In all cognitive acts, such as believing, doubting, disbelieving, apprehending, perceiving, imagining, *the mind has objects other than itself* to which it stands in some one of these various relations'.[6] A similar remark occurs in the first paragraph of *ThK*, where Russell says: 'It will be maintained that acquaintance is a dual relation between a subject and an object, which need not have any communality of nature. The subject is "mental", the object is not known to be mental except in introspection' (p. 5).

I turn now to the question whether Russell's new emphasis constitutes a move towards Empiricism. In one obvious sense it does not:

gical implications of his own view clearly. The shift seems to have been reinforced by Russell's reading of William James and other American philosophers whom he referred to as Neutral Monists. See e.g. Ch. II of *ThK*. The influence on Russell of Neutral Monism, and Pragmatism, is not an issue that I can discuss in this work.

[5] The Neutral Monists, on Russell's account, are led to their view by the idea that what the mind can be in immediate contact with must itself be homogeneous with the mind, and indeed a part of it. Where they differ from the Idealists (again according to Russell) is in not inferring from this that what is known must always be mental, but in allowing rather that the mind and what is known may both be 'neutral', i.e. neither intrinsically mental nor intrinsically non-mental. This conclusion is of course more congenial to Russell than is that of the Idealists, but he sees the two schools as sharing a single false premiss: 'it is just at this point that neutral monism finds itself in agreement with idealism in making an assumption which I believe to be wholly false. The assumption is that, *if anything is immediately present to me, that thing must be part of my mind*' (*ThK*, p. 22; emphasis in the original).

[6] 'On The Nature of Truth and Falsehood', written esp. for the vol. *Philosophical Essays* (London: Allen & Unwin, 1966; 1st edn. 1910), p. 150 (emphasis added). It is in this essay that Russell first advocates the multiple relation theory of judgement. He wrote it to take the place of the third section of an essay originally titled 'The Nature of Truth', the first two sections of which are reprinted in *Philosophical Essays* under the title 'The Monistic Theory of Truth'. The third section of the original essay is the first published work in which Russell mentions the multiple relation theory, but he does so in a tentative and agnostic spirit; hence the need to replace that section in 1910, when he is no longer in doubt about the truth of the new theory.

while current sensory perception provides perhaps the most obvious example of acquaintance, there is no implication that it is the only such example. This is, indeed, explicitly denied. Thus the passage quoted at the end of the last paragraph continues like this: 'The object [of acquaintance] may be in the present, in the past, or not in time at all; it may be a sensible particular, or a universal, or an abstract logical fact.' Russell's shift in emphasis thus does not lead him to the view that our only contact with the world is through the senses; at least according to one account of what is essential to Empiricism he is thus not an Empiricist.[7] It might be thought that the new emphasis on psychological plausibility would bias Russell's views towards Empiricism, since it is easier to attribute psychological reality to (supposed) acts of acquaintance with sensory objects than to acts of acquaintance with abstract objects or facts. In the period which is my concern in this book, however, Russell has no hesitation in speaking of acquaintance with the abstract (besides the passage quoted from *ThK*, see e.g. *Problems*, Chapter X). He later came to have doubts, but does not quickly find a way of avoiding the doctrine. In *Our Knowledge of the External World*, for example, Russell confines the word 'acquaintance' to our immediate knowledge of what is given in sense (see pp. 35, 151). Nevertheless, the doctrines of that book require that we have direct knowledge of objects which cannot be given in sense—of logical forms, for example (see e.g. p. 53); eschewing the word 'acquaintance' for knowledge of this sort indicates a certain unease about such knowledge, but does not avoid it. A further point is that any bias towards sensory knowledge and Empiricism is not a result of new doctrine, but of old doctrine being thought through with more care. In the Preface to *Principles* Russell said that the purpose of the discussion of the indefinables of logic was 'that the mind may have that kind of acquaintance with them which it has with redness or the taste of a pineapple' (p. xv). Right from the start, the notion of acquaintance was conceived of by analogy with (Russell's conception of) the simplest sort of sensory knowledge.[8] If there is a prejudice, or an awkwardness, about extending the model of simple sensory knowledge to cover the case of knowl-

---

[7] I do not claim that 'the view that our only contact with the world is through the senses' is an adequate account of Empiricism. But it is hard to think that there could be much point in calling someone an Empiricist who did not hold this view. (This does not imply that all who hold the view should be called Empiricists.) Thus Quine, for example, mentions two 'cardinal tenets of empiricism'; one of these, which 'remain[s] unassailable' is that 'whatever evidence there *is* for science is sensory evidence' (*Ontological Relativity and Other Essays* (New York: Columbia University Press, 1969), p. 75).

[8] I say '(Russell's conception of) the simplest sort of sensory knowledge' because others are available. In particular, as we saw, the Idealists would hold that even the simplest sensory knowledge has a complexity, or a structure, which Russellian acquaintance excludes. See especially the Introduction to Part II, pp. 111–12, above.

edge of the abstract, it is a prejudice, or an awkwardness, which is implicit in Russell's views from his rejection of Idealism on. What is new is that the system is further developed, and its implications unfolded.

There is perhaps something which might be thought of as a different kind of Empiricism which Russell's work seems to illustrate more clearly. This is an 'Empiricism' of philosophical method. This too is perhaps implicit in his earlier work, but he speaks now more explicitly of (philosophical) 'theories' accounting for certain 'data'. Thus his view of philosophy openly construes the subject on the model of (one idea of) a natural science: here the data, there the theory to account for them; here a datum which does not fit, there a modification to the original theory, or a new theory with a different basis, to take account of the datum. But, in spite of his claims, Russell's philosophy does not exactly fit this model. His account of what the data are, or at least of which data are salient, shifts; as we shall see in a few instances, the theory seems to affect the data at least as much as the data the theory. There is also a question, which Russell does not confront directly, as to the status of the enterprise. The data, presumably, are more or less ordinary facts, often psychological facts; the theory sought, however, is not to be a psychological theory, or anything like a science. Thus the idea arises that the familiar facts of our psychological life, say, require not only the sort of explanatory theory that a psychologist hopes to offer but also a quite different sort of 'account'—a peculiarly philosophical account. Implicit here is the question of what distinguishes a *philosophical* account of these matters from a psychological or scientific account; given Russell's approach this question seems to require an answer. It may seem that this requirement can be met by the idea that scientific and psychological theories are empirical, while philosophical theories are not. But the term 'empirical', and other terms in which it seems natural to answer our question, are themselves terms that get their force from some philosophical theory, and it is in fact unclear that any adequate theory is available. Certainly Russell in 1910 or 1912 does not articulate any such theory. I shall not discuss these issues further here, for they receive no overt attention in the works of Russell that are my concern. They are, however, latent both in Russell's methodological remarks (e.g. *ThK*, p. 5) and to some extent in his method.

1. The Multiple Relation Theory of Judgement

The so-called multiple relation theory of judgement, as I have already indicated, represents a fundamental shift in Russell's general metaphysical views. In the view that we examined in Part II, the basic metaphysical notions were those of truth and of the proposition. The introduction of the multiple relation theory changes this view drastically. Russell ceases to hold that there are propositions in the old sense; symbols which appear to represent or express propositions are said to be incomplete symbols, which make sense in context even though there are no propositions. Truth ceases to be an indefinable property of propositions and becomes a property of beliefs, definable in terms of correspondence with fact. If there were no minds there would, clearly, be no beliefs; in making truth and falsehood properties of belief, Russell is accepting that if there were no minds there would be no truth. All of this clearly represents a drastic shift away from the view of *Principles*, with its insistence on the objectivity of propositions and of truth. Let us, then, examine the change in a more systematic fashion, beginning with a brief discussion of judgement.

The notion of judgement plays no significant role in Platonic Atomism. The account of propositions has, as a by-product, a very simple account of judgement. Implicitly, to make a judgement, or understand a proposition, involves being acquainted with a proposition. Towards the propositions with which one is acquainted, and which one therefore understands, one may have any one of a number of relations: belief, doubt, disbelief, and so on. These points are left implicit, for what later came to be called the propositional attitudes were not important enough to Russell to give him a reason to state them. This is unsurprising, for there is no reason for the notion of judgement to be of any particular positive philosophical interest within Platonic Atomism (the notion is perhaps of some negative importance, since Platonic Atomism requires opposition to a Kantian or idealist view of judgement). Nor is the account controversial, given the Platonic Atomist notion of a proposition. This situation changes not because Russell comes to have a particular interest in propositions of the form '*A* believes that *p*' but rather because Russell comes to doubt that there are propositions in the Platonic Atomist sense. Propositions are thus no longer the bearers of truth and falsehood; this role is rather to be played by beliefs or judgements.[9] There is also the more general need to show that even though there are no propositions, we can form beliefs which are genuinely about the world. For both of these reasons, Russell needs an account of judgement or belief which does not assume that there are propositions. This account is the 'multiple relation theory of judgment'.

---

[9] In his later works Russell speaks of truth and falsehood as properties of sentences or statements. In the works which are my concern in this book it is usually beliefs which are the primary bearers of truth and falsehood.

To get a general idea of this theory, let us consider a simple judgement. Suppose I form the belief or judgement that John is taller than Mary. According to the Platonic Atomism picture, there is a single objective entity, the proposition that John is taller than Mary, and in judging I am related to it. Judgement is thus a two-place relation, holding between a person (or mind) on the one hand, and a proposition on the other. When Russell gives up the view that there are propositions, he has to find another account of judgement or understanding. (Now that these notions are the subject of explicit attention, the various propositional attitudes emerge as a group, united by the fact that the notion of understanding is fundamental to each of them; see *ThK*, p. 107. Although Russell continues to speak, as I sometimes shall, of judgement, it is clearly understanding that is at issue.) In the new account I am, paradigmatically, separately acquainted with John, and with Mary, and with the *taller than* relation; I bring these objects together to form the judgement.[10] Judging will always involve a mind bringing together at least two other objects (three in our example).[11] It is thus a relation that holds among a mind and at least two other objects—hence it is a *multiple* relation, not a binary relation.

One point of continuity between the old view and the new is that it is the objects themselves with which we are in contact when we judge—not ideas or concepts of the objects. (The continuity here is with the fact that according to the old view it was the objects themselves which were the constituents of propositions.) All of the objects of my judgements must be things with which I am acquainted. Most—perhaps almost all—of our judgements seem to falsify this claim, but this shows only that appearances are deceptive: we have not found the true form of a judgement until it conforms to the doctrine of acquaintance. Short of that point further analysis is required. This immediately shows that most of our judgements do not have the form which they appear to have—that quite drastic changes may be required to reveal their true form. (See Chapter 6, pp. 244–8, above, for related discussion; also pp. 363–9, below, for Russell's continued emphasis on the idea of the immediacy of our contact with objective things.)

---

[10] This paradigm applies directly only to singular judgements, i.e. those not involving generality (quantification). It is a consequence of Russell's views, as we shall see more clearly in Section 2, that most judgements are not of this kind. Nevertheless, the paradigm remains crucial.

[11] It is not simply a matter of stipulation that judging is the relation of the mind to more than one object. The salient characteristic of judgement, as distinct from, say, perception, is that judgements can be true or false. According to the new view, as we shall see, this fact about judgements is to be explained in a way which requires that judgement be a relation among a multiplicity of objects.

A point of difference between the old view and the new is that according to the latter, but not the former, there need be no objective combination formed of the objects John, Mary, *taller than* (there will be such a combination, a fact, if the judgement is true but not if it is false; in any case its existence is not essential for the judging to be possible). There may be nothing other than a subjective combination of these elements: in judging I unite them in thought. Now since it is the objects themselves that we are concerned with, this sort of unity must be different from the unity that the objects have in the fact, if the judgement is true. By uniting the objects in thought I do not create the fact; since the judgement and the fact have the same objects, it is the uniting which must be different (this notion of uniting in thought is, as we shall see, quite problematic for Russell; see below pp. 345–346). Rather than mind-independent propositions to which various people are related, we thus have acts of judgement or, more helpfully, facts of the form: *A* judges that *a* is *F*, or *A* judges that *a* has *R* to *b*, etc.[12]

Russell suggests at one stage that rather than say that there are no propositions, we can find entities which will play the role of, and may be identified with, propositions. The entity which he proposes is a fact: the fact that there is a mind and there is a judging relation (i.e. a relation presupposing understanding) such that the mind stands in that relation to the various entities (the constituents of the putative proposition). The 'chief merit' of this view, he says, is that 'it provides propositions, both true and false, as fast as we can think of them, and that it gives something in common between all mental events which seem to be concerned with the same proposition' (*ThK* p. 113; as we shall see, it is not clear that this view allows enough propositions for the requirements of logic; see pp. 355–6, below). This suggestion illustrates one of the themes of what I have called Russell's constructivism: it suggests that we can identify propositions with any entities which will play a certain role, i.e. will meet certain constraints. In this particular case, the construction has a striking consequence: it makes propositions into a special case of *facts*.[13] This neatly demonstrates the switch from the old view to the new: according to the old view the

[12] Note that these are themselves not facts of the same form (in the two examples given, one is a fact in which three objects are related, another a fact in which four objects are related). Thus belief will have various logical forms, depending on what is believed. Russell acknowledges this consequence in 'The Philosophy of Logical Atomism'; see Marsh, p. 226.

[13] Here there is clearly an anticipation of Wittgenstein's view of the *Tractatus*, that a proposition (*Satz*) is a fact (*Tatsache*). See *Tractatus*, 2.14, which states that a picture (*Bild*) is a fact; a thought, which is what is expressed by a proposition, is in turn a kind of picture, and thus also a fact.

notion of a proposition is fundamental, and facts are singled out as a special case of propositions (the true ones); according to the new view, the notion of a fact is the fundamental one, and propositions—or at least acts of judgement—are to be singled out as a special case of facts. The job of the multiple-relation theory is to do this singling out, i.e. to find the distinguishing characteristics of those facts which are (the making of) judgements.[14]

One issue which our sketch of the new theory raises is this: I emphasized earlier that Russell's and Moore's insistence on the objectivity of propositions was a central element in their rejection of Idealism. Yet now Russell asserts a view according to which there is no such thing as a proposition (as distinct from an act of judgement); how can he avoid idealist consequences? The answer is that, according to Platonic Atomism, propositions played the role of constituting reality: given that view, to admit the mind-dependence of propositions would have been to admit the mind-dependence of reality. Hence Russell had to insist on a sharp distinction between the subjective or mental act of judgement and the objective non-mental correlate of judgement. The multiple relation view of judgement is a concomitant of a new metaphysical view. According to this view it is not propositions which make up the world; it is rather *facts*. On the old view the notions of proposition and of truth are primary; a fact is simply a true proposition. On the new view, the notion of a fact becomes primary. This shift is no mere relabelling of propositions as facts. For one thing, as noted, propositions were the correlates of judgement: in judging, the mind was said to be immediately related to a proposition. Facts do not play this role. A second difference is related. Propositions come both true and false, according to the old view, and both species have equal status. For facts, by contrast, there is no duality of true and false: a fact is a fact. So when the notion of a fact replaces that of a proposition, truth no longer has a fundamental metaphysical role to play. Certain passages in Russell's early expositions of the multiple relation theory indicate the importance of the notion of a fact in guarding against Idealism. In 'On the Nature of Truth and Falsehood', for example, Russell writes as follows:

The first point upon which it is important to be clear is the relation of truth and falsehood to the mind. If we were right in saying that the things that are true

---

[14] This shift in emphasis from propositions to facts goes along with a shift from talk about the logical form of propositions to the logical form of facts; increasingly it is the latter which forms the focus of Russell's enquiries. In these terms the multiple relation theory may be seen as an attempt to discover the logical form of a particular kind of fact—namely the fact that a given judgement is made.

and false are always judgments, then it is plain that there can be no truth or falsehood unless there are minds to judge. Nevertheless it is plain, also, that the truth or falsehood of a given judgment depends in no way upon the person judging, but solely upon the facts about which he judges. If I judge that Charles I died in his bed, I judge falsely, not because of anything to do with me, but because in fact he did not die in his bed.[15]

(For a similar point, see *Problems*, pp. 129–30.) The care that Russell takes to explain the point is due to the fact that he has only recently abandoned a view according to which the mind-dependence of (the objects of) judgement would have involved the mind-dependence of reality. As he makes clear, however, this dependence does not hold if we take as fundamental the notion of a fact, in a sense in which facts are independent of the objects of judgement.

We can put some of the points of the previous paragraph in a broader context by talking very generally about the contrast between Idealism and Platonic Atomism. For the Idealists, as we saw, there is a sense in which judgement plays the role of constituting the world. The judging mind is thus world-creating; constraints or limits on judgement give rise to a priori truths about the world. The Platonic Atomism reaction is to make the mind purely passive in judgement by distinguishing the object of judgement, which is mind-independent, from the act of judging, which is a matter of passive apprehension. Although the idealist consequence is now removed, it remains true that (the objects of) judgements—now called propositions—constitute the world: this assumption is common to Idealism and Platonic Atomism. When Russell adopts the multiple relation theory of judgement, he gives up this assumption. Facts come to assume the central metaphysical role. Judgement can now be thought of as a psychological act without objective correlates, for this no longer threatens us with Idealism. (The avoidance of Idealism requires that uniting objects in thought be distinct from uniting them in fact; we have already touched on this point, and shall return to it.)

To this point, I have emphasized the change in Russell's metaphysics which underlies his adoption of the multiple relation theory. I have not, however, said anything about his reasons for making this change: why does he give up the view of Platonic Atomism and adopt the new view? Russell offers two kinds of reason. One is what he calls the 'instinctive feeling' that there are no propositions, or at least no false ones (*ThK*, p. 109). The appeal to 'instinct', which is common throughout *ThK*, might seem unaccountable from a Russellian point of view:

---

[15] *Philosophical Essays*, op. cit. n. 6 above, p. 149.

what have the instincts of human beings to do with the objective truth about the world? We should perhaps see this sort of appeal as connected with the idea that all knowledge is based upon certain claims simply striking us as intrinsically obvious (see Chapter 7, above, pp. 321–5; and Section 2, below, pp. 382–4). The second reason that Russell offers for the new view is drawn from considerations having to do with truth. The two reasons, as we shall see, are not wholly separate.

In 'On the Nature of Truth and Falsehood' Russell expresses the first kind of reason like this:

it is difficult to believe that there are such objects as 'that Charles I died in his bed', or even 'that Charles I died on the scaffold'. It seems evident that the phrase 'that so and so' has no complete meaning by itself, which would enable it to denote a definite object as (e.g.) the word 'Socrates' does. We feel that the phrase 'that so and so' is essentially incomplete.... This argument is not decisive, but it must be allowed a certain weight.[16]

In *Theory of Knowledge* Russell similarly appeals to what he evidently takes to be shared intuitions: 'We might be induced to admit that *true* propositions are entities, but it is very difficult, except under the lash of a tyrannous theory, to admit that *false* propositions are entities' (p. 109).

At one stage Russell attempts to reinforce what he takes to be the instinctive belief that there are no propositions. The considerations that he advances apply directly only to false propositions. Their application to propositions as a whole depends upon an argument to the effect that belief must be the same sort of relation when the believed proposition is true as it is when it is false. It cannot be that true belief is a two-place relation, involving a mind and a proposition, while false belief is accounted for in some other way, e.g. by a multiple relation theory. If there were an intrinsic difference of this sort between true belief and false, Russell claims, the believer would be able to tell the difference. 'Unfortunately', as Russell says, we cannot do so (see *ThK*, p. 109). So if there are no false propositions, there are no propositions of any kind. Russell argues against there being false propositions as follows:

Let us take some very simple false proposition, say '*A* precedes *B*', when in fact *A* comes after *B*. It seems as though nothing were involved here beyond *A* and *B* and 'preceding' and the general form of a dual complex. But since *A* does not precede *B*, these objects are not put together in the way indicated by

---

[16] *Philosophical Essays*, op. cit. n. 6 above, p. 151.

the proposition. It seems, therefore, that nothing which actually is composed of these objects is the proposition; and it is not credible that anything further enters into the proposition. (*ThK*, p. 110)

This presents Russell's 'instinctive feeling' in what is perhaps its strongest form: if a belief about a certain combination of objects and relations (e.g. that *A* precedes *B*) is false, it is not because that combination of objects (*A* preceding *B*) has one property (falsehood) and lacks another (truth). It is, rather, simply because there is no such combination. Like some of Russell's other 'instinctive feelings' this is of course a flat denial of something which he had been willing to assert earlier. It presents the contrast between the two views, however, in a way which makes it easy to find the old view incredible. It also suggests that the 'feeling' that there are no propositions is not independent of the concepts of truth and falsehood. If it is peculiarly obvious that *false* judgements have no corresponding propositions, then there must be something about the difference of truth and falsehood that is relevant to the alleged intuition that there are no propositions. This brings us, therefore, to the issue of truth and falsehood, which is the second sort of reason that Russell offers against his old view of propositions.

    Truth and falsehood, according to Platonic Atomism, are ultimate and indefinable properties of propositions. Every proposition has one of these properties, and no proposition has both; these facts, however, cannot be explained. Equally inexplicable is the difference between truth and falsehood, and why these properties are of particular importance.[17] This inexplicability is not an adventitious fact within Platonic Atomism. According to that view, everything that might be used to explain the notion of truth—notions such as fact or existence or reality—is itself to be understood in terms of the truth of propositions. The notions of truth and falsehood thus represent rock bottom. Now these ideas about truth and falsehood may not be incoherent, but we can see how Russell came to find them implausible. Surely there should be something to be said about why belief aims at truth, or about the difference between truth and falsehood? And can we really take it as a matter of brute fact that every proposition is either true or false, as it would be a brute matter of fact that every rose is either red or white, if it were true at all? At one point, at least, these considerations seemed

---

[17] In this spirit Russell says: 'It may be said—and this is, I believe, the correct view—that there is no problem at all about truth and falsehood; that some propositions are true and some false, just as some roses are red and some white' (*MTCA*, p. 75; cf. also p. 77).

to Russell to be the most important ones leading to the abandonment of his earlier view of propositions. Speaking of that earlier view (he cites *MTCA*), he says:

it is very difficult to believe that there are objective falsehoods, which would subsist and form part of the universe even if there were no such thing as thought or mind. But the chief objection is that the difference between truth and falsehood, on the theory in question, has to be accepted as ultimate and inexplicable, whereas it seems obvious that the difference between truth and falsehood must be explicable by reference to *fact*, i.e. to what is actually in the universe whatever we may see fit to believe. (*ThK*, p. 153)

These considerations, of course, are ones that by no means seemed obvious to Russell in 1904. It is hard to know how to account for the difference. We have already noted that in giving up the Platonic Atomism view of propositions in favour of the multiple relation view Russell gives up an idealist doctrine about (the objects of) judgement playing a role in constituting the world; perhaps his giving up this doctrine is a delayed effect of the rejection of Idealism. Or perhaps it is simply that the notion of a fact, which is pivotal to the shift to the multiple relation theory, came to seem obvious and inevitable to Russell. This last idea is reinforced by the way in which Russell deploys the notion quite naturally, before he has publicly adopted the multiple relation theory. In criticism of the pragmatism of William James, for example, he claims that paradox 'is an inevitable result of the divorce which they [pragmatists] make between fact and *truth*'.[18] It may have been his reading of the pragmatists which made him see that to say what he wanted to say he had to take the notion of a fact as fundamental.

Whatever may be the reasons for Russell's change of mind about the fundamental metaphysical issue, a new understanding of judgement and of truth is required; this is the role of the multiple relation theory. When a judgement occurs the mind which judges is related to a number of objects; the judgement is a mental act which occurs when a mind is so related. According to the old view certain phrases had meaning in virtue of the fact that they expressed propositions. According to the new theory most such phrases (all those which must be accepted as meaningful) are incomplete symbols. Just as Russell sought to mimic the theory of classes without supposing that there are classes, by defining class symbols in those contexts where the theory requires them, so symbols which were formerly construed as expressing pro-

---

[18] 'James's Conception of Truth', *Philosophical Essays*, op cit. n. 6 above, p. 123. This essay was first published in the *Albany Review* for Jan. 1908.

positions are now understood in context. Most obviously, the multiple relation theory explains how a sentence has meaning when it is asserted (or denied, etc.). Here the context is supplied by the *act* of assertion, rather than by further words (see *PM*, i. 44). Ascriptions of judgements to others (e.g. *A* believes that *p*) are also expressions that the multiple relation theory enables us to understand without assuming that there are propositions; such phrases therefore also provide contexts of the right kind.

As in the case of classes, Russell sometimes employs a shorthand which may be misleading. He says that *propositions* are incomplete symbols—meaning that phrases which express propositions are incomplete symbols. Thus in a passage on p. 44 of *PM* he begins by stating quite carefully that 'the phrase which expresses a proposition is what we call an "incomplete symbol"'. Having said this, he concludes by saying that 'propositions are "incomplete symbols"'. In the context, however, it seems clear that there is here no confusion or uncertainty as to whether propositions are linguistic entities (symbols). Russell simply uses the second phrase as shorthand for the first and more cumbersome phrase (see *ThK*, p. 109, where Russell also introduces the misleading shorthand, but immediately explains it by an accurate statement). Russell has frequently been accused of superficial use/mention confusions. In this case, at least, these charges seem unfounded; there is looseness of expression, but no sign of confusion. When Russell, in the works that we are discussing, denies that there are propositions he is using the word in precisely the same sense as in his earlier works. What he is denying is that there are objective non-linguistic and non-mental entities which paradigmatically contain the things that they are about (this last point is clear from the passage from *ThK*, p. 110, quoted a few pages back; Russell says there that it is not credible that the proposition that *A* precedes *B* should contain anything other than *A*, *B*, and the *preceding* relation). Later the word 'proposition' shifts, and Russell comes to use it in a straightforwardly linguistic sense; but then, of course, he does not deny that there are propositions.[19]

The function of the multiple relation theory of judgement is to explain how, in the absence of propositions, judgement is possible. In the light of the last paragraph we can equally say that it is to explain how phrases which appear to express propositions can be meaningful,

---

[19] The use of the word 'proposition' in the linguistic sense is explicit, and consistent, in 'The Philosophy of Logical Atomism' (*Monist* (1918), 495–527; (1919), 32–63, 190–222, 345–80; repr. in Marsh, pp. 177–281).

at least in certain contexts, even though there are no propositions. How does the theory accomplish this task? Russell never found an answer to this question that satisfied him.[20] It is not my purpose here to give a full account of his various attempts and of the difficulties that they faced; a brief discussion of these issues will, however, be relevant.

Russell's statements of the multiple relation theory in *PM* and in 'On the Nature of Truth and Falsehood' suggest a simple picture. In judgement the judger is related to the various entities (including relations) which are mentioned in the expression of the judgement; i.e. to what on the earlier account would have been called the constituents of the judged proposition. Thus he says: 'When we judge that Charles I died on the scaffold, we have before us, not one object, but several objects, namely, Charles I and dying and the scaffold' (p. 153).[21] Similarly in *PM* Russell speaks of a judgement as 'a relation of four terms, namely *a* and *b* and *R* and the percipient [i.e. the one who judges]' (i. 43; a similar picture is presented in *Problems*; see Chapter XII, 'Truth and Falsehood'). In the later and more extended discussion of *ThK*, however, a more complicated picture emerges:

Let us take as an illustration some very simple proposition, say '*A* precedes *B*', where *A* and *B* are particulars. In order to understand this proposition it . . . is obviously necessary that we should know what is meant by the words which occur in it, that is to say, we must be acquainted with *A* and *B* and with the relation 'preceding'. It is also necessary to know how these three terms are meant to be combined; and this . . . requires acquaintance with the general form of a dual complex. (*ThK*, p. 111)

The difference between this statement of the matter and the earlier ones is of course that a new idea is now invoked: that of (logical) *form*. The fact which is an act of judgement relates a judger not merely to the constituents of the proposition (to speak loosely) but also to its form. Two questions thus arise: why does Russell now see this notion as necessary for an account of judgement? and what is logical form?

Let us begin with the first question, to which Russell offers what appear to be two connected answers (at one stage he suggests that they

---

[20] The unfinished *Theory of Knowledge* seems to have been abandoned because Wittgenstein's criticisms convinced Russell that the theory of judgement advanced in Part II of that work is untenable; see pp. 357–61, below. In 'The Philosophy of Logical Atomism' Russell's discussion is admittedly tentative and inconclusive; see Marsh, pp. 246–7.

[21] Note that this cannot really be an example of judgement, since Charles I is not an object of acquaintance. The same point perforce holds for all of Russell's examples. Given his view, indeed, there will be few judgements which can be made by more than one person.

are in fact the same; see *ThK*, p. 116).[22] The first is that to be able to make a judgement we need acquaintance not only with constituents of the proposition (to speak loosely again) but also with the way in which these constituents are to be united:

Let us suppose that we are acquainted with Socrates and with Plato and with the relation 'precedes', but not with the complex [i.e. the unanalysed fact] that Plato precedes Socrates. Suppose now that some one tells us that Socrates precedes Plato. How do we know what he means? It is plain that his statement does not give us *acquaintance* with the complex 'Socrates precedes Plato'. What we understand is that Socrates and Plato and 'precedes' are united in a complex of the form '*xRy*' where Socrates has the *x*-place and Plato the *y*-place. It is difficult to see how we could possibly understand how Socrates and Plato and 'precedes' are to be combined unless we had acquaintance with the form of the complex. (*ThK*, p. 99)

There is a complication here that must be disposed of before we can get to the point that concerns us. In spite of the suggestion of this passage, the form—the way the constituents are combined—is not what determines the order of constituents in a relational statement, i.e. what distinguishes judging, say, that Socrates precedes Plato from judging that Plato precedes Socrates. Russell discusses this issue separately. He argues that the correct understanding of the above proposition is complex; it asserts that there is a temporal sequence complex (i.e. a fact in which one object temporally precedes another) and that Socrates precedes in this complex, and Plato succeeds in this same complex. To the objection that each of these last two judgements is itself sensitive to the order of constituents, he replies that the object and the complex 'differ *logically*' (i.e., presumably, in ontological type), so that to attempt to reverse their order would result in nonsense (i.e. that the complex precedes in Socrates; this may be thought to violate type restrictions, and to be nonsense, whereas the same could not be claimed for the statement that Plato precedes Socrates; see *ThK*, pp. 111–12). I shall not go into this matter further.[23] The present point is that Russell treats the order of constituents as a separate problem, one that is not solved by the notion of form. He also makes it clear that form is required for

[22] Russell also offers a third reason. Typically (for *ThK*), he claims that it is simply obvious that form is required: 'It is obvious, in fact, that when *all* the constituents of a complex have been enumerated, there remains something which may be called the "form" of the complex, which is the way in which the constituents are combined' (*ThK*, p. 98).

[23] It is, however, worth noting the device that Russell employs to solve the difficulty of determining the order of constituents in a judgement. This sort of device is characteristic of what I have called the constructional method.

all judgements, including subject-predicate judgements and those involving symmetrical relations. The form is simply the manner in which the constituents are said to be united; strictly speaking this must not be taken to include their order in a relation. A form, understood in this way, is the form of the fact which corresponds to the judgement (i.e. the fact which is asserted by the judgement, or the fact which obtains if the judgement is true).[24] For the crucial point about a judgement and its 'corresponding' fact is that the judgement is to be true if (but only if) there is such a fact; and this requires that the judgement should not merely have the same objects as the fact, but should also represent them as combined in the way that they are combined in the fact (if there is one). So the logical form which figures in the judgement is the form of the corresponding fact.[25]

I turn now to Russell's second argument for the necessity of form. What he says is this:

> Suppose we wish to understand '*A* and *B* are similar'. It is essential that our thought should, as is said, 'unite' or 'synthesize' the two terms and the relation; but we cannot *actually* 'unite' them, since either *A* and *B* are similar, in which case they are already united, or they are dissimilar, in which case no amount of thinking can force them to become united. The process of 'uniting' which we *can* effect in thought is the process of bringing them into relation with the general form of dual complexes. (*ThK*, p. 116)

The issue here is what it can mean to say that in judgement the mind which judges unites the objects of the judgement in thought. It is, after all, the objects themselves that we are concerned with here: the judging mind has acquaintance with (what used to be called) the constituents of the proposition, so there are no intermediate entities which might be 'united in thought' without uniting the corresponding objects in reality. (This point is quite explicit in 'Knowledge by Acquaintance and Knowledge by Description'; see pp. 363–72, below, where the general significance of acquaintance as ensuring direct knowledge is discussed). Moreover, in accordance with the discussion of the previous paragraph, the judgement must represent the objects as combined in the same way that they are actually combined in the

---

[24] It might be thought that this opens up further problems in the case of false judgements. If a judgement is false, there is no fact corresponding to it; so where do we find the form that the judgement required? The answer, as will emerge more clearly, is that a false judgement will have the same form as many other judgements, at least one of which will be true.

[25] Note that if I make a judgement then it is a fact that, say, Hylton judges that the cat is on the mat. This fact has a logical form, which we might call the form *of* the judgement. That form, however, is not a constituent of that fact. The form which is a constituent of it is rather the form of the putative fact that the cat is on the mat.

corresponding fact (if there is one). If the judgement does this simply by bringing it about that the objects are so combined, then this no longer appears to be uniting them in thought only. So we seem to be in danger of losing the crucial distinction between uniting the objects in thought and uniting them in reality, so that to bring *A* and *B* and similarity into relation with one another would be to *make A* similar to *B*. But clearly this will not do. How can we give a meaning to 'unite in thought' which keeps this notion clearly distinct from uniting in reality? Russell's answer is that the judgement represents the constituents as combined in the right way not by so combining them but by including 'the way they are to be combined' as a further entity, the logical form, which the judging mind combines with the others. And the mode of combination of all of these entities (*including* the form) clearly need not be (and in fact cannot be) the same as that of the fact corresponding to the judgement, so we are in no danger of having to identify uniting in thought with bringing about the corresponding fact.

Russell's reasons for invoking the notion of form in his discussion of judgement lay down some constraints on what form can be. Form, to begin with, is the form of facts or complexes, and must be something that can be plausibly supposed to represent the way in which the objects which make up a fact are combined in that fact. Russell takes the notion of having the same form to be more tractable than the notion of form itself: 'two complexes have the same form if the one becomes the other when the constituents of the other are successively substituted for the constituents of the one' (*ThK*, p. 113).[26] The notion of form thus has to yield the answers suggested by this criterion. Since we are to be acquainted with forms, moreover, they must be actual entities (not merely *façons de parler*, as classes are). In response to these requirements Russell takes a strikingly imaginative step. He takes the form of an ordinary fact to be another fact, of a peculiarly abstract kind: namely the fact that there are facts of the given form. The general statement here sounds circular, but this difficulty is only apparent, as becomes clear when we consider a particular case. The form of the fact that Socrates precedes Plato, for example, is the abstract fact that something has some relation to something. More generally, a statement of the fact which is the form of a fact stated by a given sentence

---

[26] It might be thought that Russell is here illegitimately transferring to facts or complexes a notion of substitution that makes clear sense only when confined to the linguistic level. Whatever may be the merits of this view, talk of substitution in facts surely makes exactly as good sense as talk of substitution in propositions (as Russell earlier conceived of them). Russell had no qualms of speaking of obtaining one proposition from another by substitution, so his remarks here represent nothing new.

may be obtained by existentially generalizing on each name (of an object, a predicate, a relation, etc.) in the given sentence.[27]

Now the facts which are forms are quite unlike other facts. For one thing, they must be objects of acquaintance, a point which I shall discuss shortly. Also, they cannot themselves have forms, or contain constituents, or be analysable. Russell clearly recognizes these features:

the form of all dual complexes will be the fact 'something has some relation to something'. The logical nature of this fact is very peculiar . . . . [it] contains no constituent at all. . . . In a sense, it is simple, since it cannot be analysed. At first sight, it seems to have a structure, and therefore not to be simple; but it is more correct to say that it is a structure. Language is not well adapted to speaking of such objects. (*ThK*, p. 114)

Perhaps the most puzzling feature of the forms is that they are facts, and yet according to the theory must be simple. Surely a fact has some complexity? Russell recognizes the perplexity here, but has no way to resolve it; the question is raised only to be put aside (*ThK*, p. 130).

Forms are facts, and there are judgements which assert them (we have encountered examples above). These judgements, however, cannot be accounted for by the multiple relation theory of judgement: apart from anything else, they have no forms. In this case, as Russell acknowledges, understanding is a dual relation (*ThK*, p. 130); he identifies this relation with acquaintance. An abstract fact which is a form is thus also an object of acquaintance; in this one kind of case, we might say, Russell retains the Platonic Atomism picture of propositions, so that a (true) proposition is also a fact. Now in the general case Russell's objection to that picture of propositions hinged largely on the issue of truth and falsehood. Crucial to his view of our understanding of propositions without constituents (i.e. propositions suitable for expressing forms), therefore, is the claim that the duality of truth and falsehood does not apply to them; all such propositions are true.[28] Moreover it is only because they are true that we can understand them, for here understanding is a dual relation between a judger and a fact; if

---

[27] This assumes that the sentence expressing the original fact is not misleading—i.e. that it has a name for each constituent of the fact. What is needed here is thus a *fully analysed* sentence, i.e. one containing a name for every entity which must be an object of acquaintance for one who understands the sentence.

[28] There are issues lurking here which can be brought out by noting that constituent-less propositions can, presumably, be negated or combined with other propositions to form new propositions. If we negate a constituentless proposition then negation, presumably, is one constituent of the resulting proposition: what are its other constituents, if any? These issues are connected with the view of Wittgenstein in the *Tractatus*, that negation and the other so-called logical constants are not objects, i.e. not constituents of propositions at all.

there were no fact there would be no understanding, but since there is a fact the proposition is true.

We have seen that in Russell's view we can be acquainted with constituentless facts (i.e. forms). It is also possible for us to be acquainted with complexes. Thus in *PM* Russell says:

Some of the objects which occur in the universe are complex. When an object is complex, it consists of interrelated parts. Let us consider a complex object composed of two parts *a* and *b* standing to each other in the relation *R*. The complex object '*a*-in-the-relation-*R*-to-*b*' may be capable of being *perceived*; when perceived it is perceived as one object. Attention may show that it is complex; we then *judge* that *a* is in the relation *R* to *b*. Such a judgment, being derived from perception by mere attention, may be called a 'judgment of perception'. (i. 43)

Since a judgement of perception is (defined as being) based on the perception of a complex, it cannot be mistaken—though we may be mistaken as to whether a given judgement really is a judgement of perception:

The perception . . . is a relation of two terms, namely '*a*-in-the-relation-*R*-to-*b*', and the percipient. Since an object of perception cannot be nothing, we cannot perceive '*a*-in-the-relation-*R*-to-*b*' unless *a* is in the relation *R* to *b*. Hence a judgment of perception, according to the above definition, must be true. (loc. cit.)

It is thus Russell's view in general that facts may be perceived, and that the judgements corresponding to perceived facts must be true. In *ThK* the discussion of self-evidence is based on this idea (see Part II, Chapter VI, 'Self-Evidence'). Nevertheless, forms, and the constituentless judgements which express them, have special features. Judgements expressing other facts may be made under circumstances which guarantee their truth (when they result simply from attention paid to perception); but equally they may be, and usually are, made under other circumstances, which do not guarantee their truth. Constituentless judgements can only be made under circumstances which guarantee their truth. For this special case, judging always demands acquaintance with the fact that makes the judgement true, for only such acquaintance makes the judgement possible.

We have now examined enough of Russell's 1913 multiple relation theory, and the associated notion of logical form, to enable us to raise some further issues. In particular, we need to see how the new view accounts for truth and falsehood. This is crucial, for Russell's reasons for rejecting the old view had to do with its inability to explain these notions; the new theory must do better. The relation of understanding is now sharply distinguished from that of acquaintance. While complexes are in some instances objects of acquaintance, being acquainted with a complex is not the same as understanding the relevant proposition.[29] Russell deploys the difference between understanding and acquaintance to suggest that the fact that propositions, but not other entities, exhibit a duality of truth and falsehood is not accidental:

understanding and acquaintance... are very widely different in logical form....

The fundamental characteristic which distinguishes propositions (whatever they may be) from objects of acquaintance is their truth and falsehood. An object of acquaintance is not true or false, but is simply what it is: there is no dualism of true and false objects of acquaintance. And although there are entities with which we are not acquainted, yet it seems evident that nothing of the same logical nature as objects of acquaintance can possibly be true or false. (*ThK*, p. 108)

The suggestion made above depends, of course, upon our being able to give a definition of truth for judgements. This definition must exploit the structure of judgement, and in particular the fact that judging, unlike acquaintance, is a multiple relation. Russell attempts to give just such a definition. He sets out the fundamental idea like this:

It is obvious that the question whether a belief is true or false depends only upon its *objects*.... The belief is true when the objects are related as the belief asserts that they are. Thus the belief is *true* when there is a certain complex which must be a definable function of the belief, and which we shall call the *corresponding* complex or the *corresponding fact*. Our problem, therefore, is to define the correspondence. (*ThK*, p. 144)

This problem is one to which Russell offers a relatively simple solution for one class of judgements. This is the class of judgements for which the corresponding complexes are, as he says, 'completely determined by their constituents'. The point here is that in the case of some judgements, 'permutative', as Russell calls them, we can obtain a different judgement by rearranging the constituents: that Socrates precedes Plato is one judgement, that Plato precedes Socrates is another. In the case of other judgements, the non-permutative, no such rearrangement is possible. We have already seen that Russell's account of judgement is more complex in the case of permutative judgements; it might be said, in fact, that he reduces judgements of this form to a conjunction of non-permutative judgements. His account of truth for permutative judgements is correspondingly more complex than that for

---

[29] Constituentless judgements, corresponding to logical forms, are an exception to this, as we have seen. For constituentless judgements, however, there are not two possibilities, truth and falsehood; all are true.

non-permutative, and again the solution can be looked on as a reduction of the more complex case to the less complex (see *ThK*, pp. 145–7). Since the details are not our concern, I shall not consider the more complex case. For non-permutative judgements, then, Russell is able to give a rather simple definition of truth, as follows:

let our belief be

$$J(S, F, x_1, x_2, \ldots x_n)$$

where J is the relation 'belief' or 'judgement', S is the subject, F the form, and $x_1, x_2, \ldots x_n$ the objects of the belief; and suppose that F is a form such that there cannot be more than one complex having this form and composed of the given constituents. . . . [this is the assumption of non-permutativity] Then, if there is any complex whose constituents are $x_1, x_2, \ldots x_n$ there can only be one; this may therefore be defined as the *corresponding* complex. If there is such a complex the belief is true; if there is not, it is false. (*ThK*, p. 144)

The definability of truth is vital to Russell's new view. The simple definition above is not only limited to non-permutative judgements; it also has another limitation, which is less easy to overcome. The definition does not apply directly to judgements which are general, i.e. which are correctly expressed using quantified variables. This is a crucial limitation in any case, but especially for Russell. His doctrine that we must be acquainted with the objects of our judgements, together with the increasingly narrow view of what we are in fact acquainted with, leads to the view that many judgements which we express using names are more correctly expressed when those names are treated as Russell treats definite descriptions. But his analysis of definite descriptions replaces them, in context, by statements involving variables and quantifiers. So, for Russell, it is clear that almost none of our actual judgements are correctly expressed by quantifier-free sentences. So the problem of extending the definition of truth to apply to general judgements is crucial. Unfortunately, *ThK* contains no discussion of this issue; Russell abandoned the book before he reached that portion which was to have dealt with generality.[30] There is a brief discussion of this issue in *PM*, but nothing like a definition emerges. Russell says:

But take now such a proposition as 'all men are mortal'. Here the judgment does not correspond to *one* complex, but to many. . . . Our judgment that all

---

[30] For a table of contents of the unwritten portion of the book, as well as some discussion of the written portion, see Douglas Lackey, 'Russell's 1913 Map of the Mind', in Peter A. French *et al.*, *Midwest Studies in Philosophy*, vi: *The Foundations of Analytic Philosophy* (Minneapolis: University of Minnesota Press, 1981), pp. 125–42. For reasons given earlier in the paragraph, it seems to me an overstatement to say, as Lackey does, that Russell's manuscript contains 'a predecessor of the semantic theory of truth' (p. 141).

men are mortal collects together a number of elementary judgments. It is not, however, composed of these. (*PM*, i. 45)

There is no discussion of how a general judgement can 'collect together' elementary judgements, without being 'composed of' them (perhaps as a conjunction is composed of its conjuncts). More seriously, perhaps, there is no discussion of the mechanism of the collecting together: the truth of a general judgement may depend on the truth of various elementary judgements, but we need an account of how to go from the general judgement to the right elementary judgements.

The multiple relation theory of judgement is in one obvious way a denial of the fundamental Platonic Atomist notion of a proposition: according to the multiple relation theory there are no propositions. More subtly and indirectly, the new theory also threatens a vaguer and more general idea that stands behind Russellian propositions. This is the idea that the criteria which must be satisfied for two sentences to say the same thing are extremely stringent. This idea is manifest, before the introduction of the multiple relation theory, in the view that two sentences which are intuitively very alike in meaning may nonetheless express different propositions. Thus, to take an extreme example, it appears that a sentence expresses a different proposition from the double negation of that same sentence. A proposition is defined by its constituents (and their order), and on Russell's account the proposition expressed by a given sentence has different constituents from that expressed by the double negation of that sentence (the latter contains two more occurrences of negation than does the former). Although most naturally explained in terms of propositions, the same intuitive idea can also be explained in terms of the multiple relation theory. Thus it might be said that in understanding the unnegated sentence we are in contact with different entities from those that we are in contact with in understanding its double negation. Talk about constituents of propositions can in this way be translated directly into talk about the entities with which we are in contact when we understand, and the same distinctions made. The idea that what we express is susceptible of extremely fine-grained distinctions is thus formally compatible with the multiple relation theory. Nevertheless, the new theory threatens to undermine that idea. The subversive claim is that truth is definable in terms of the more fundamental idea of *fact*. This claim makes it natural to think that when two sentences are true (or false) in virtue of the same fact then they say exactly the same thing; it thus becomes hard to maintain that they express different propositions. The effects of this are not immediately apparent, because the identity-criteria for facts are by no means clear. Consider, again, the case of an arbitrary sentence (or belief) and the double negation of that sentence. In the new view we cannot maintain that the sentences differ in expressive power unless we can believe that the complex corresponding to the one (so that the sentence is true if there is such a complex, false if not) is different from the complex corresponding to the other. Once articulated, however, this position is quite implausible. The same complex whose existence makes true the belief that the cat is on the mat also makes true the belief that it is not the case that it is not the case that the cat is on the mat: it is the same objects in the world, and the same configuration of those objects, which is at stake in each case. It thus becomes natural to think that two sentences or beliefs which are made true (or false) by the same fact have the same expressive power; and to distinguish facts less finely than the old view distinguished propositions. This is a tendency which, as indicated, is hardly manifest in the works discussed in this book. It leads, however, to the view of Wittgenstein's *Tractatus*. This view deviates from that of Platonic Atomism in, for example, its treatment of the truths of logic; according to that view it is natural to say that all truths of logic say the same thing, namely nothing, and that logical constants are not constituents of propositions (objects of judgements), i.e. that there are no logical constants.[31]

Another issue worth discussing in connection with the new theory is that which we have called 'the unity of the proposition'; a discussion of this issue also illuminates the new theory from a slightly different angle. It might be thought that the old issue of the unity of the proposition is solved by the notion of logical form as 'the way the constituents of the judgment are combined'; or at least that logical form becomes the locus for this problem. These ideas are encouraged by the fact that Russell sometimes speaks of logical form in the sort of way that he used to speak of whatever it is that unifies a proposition, as something which must be part of any proposition but cannot be considered as a *part* in the same sense as anything else — for it is what unifies the parts. Thus he says:

[in the form of a subject-predicate fact] 'is' represents merely the way in which the constituents are put together. This cannot be a new constituent, for if it were, there would have to be a new way in which it and the two other constituents are put together, and if we take this way as again a constituent, we find ourselves embarked on an endless regress. (*ThK*, p. 98)

---

[31] An articulation of the view which Russell's work prefigures is also likely to have the consequence that two propositional functions which are true of the same objects cannot be distinguished. The type hierarchy of *PM* would have to be fundamentally reworked if it were to be made consistent with that doctrine. Ramsey's criticisms of *PM* may be thought of as presenting such a reworking.

While it may for these reasons be appropriate to think of part of the problem of the unity of a proposition as relocated in the notion of logical form, this point is relatively superficial. One consideration which points in this direction is the fact that all of the constituents of a judgement-fact (the objects, the form, and the judger) are related by the relation of judging (or understanding); it is this relation, not the logical form, that unites these various entities into a whole—into a fact. And this is the heart of the matter. Just as the notion of a fact takes over much of the metaphysical burden formerly borne by the notion of a proposition, so the issue of the unity of a proposition is replaced by that of the unity of a fact. Russell still needs to distinguish between relations considered abstractly, and relations considered as actually relating their relata: 'An entity which *can* occur in a complex as "precedes" occurs in "*A* precedes *B*" will be called a *relation*. When it does occur in this way in a given complex, it will be called a "relating relation" '(*ThK*, p. 80). The general issue here is that of the nature of a fact, or the unity of a fact: how are the various elements in a fact united? The occurrence of an act of judgement is a fact, and its unity is therefore a special case of the more general issue of the nature of a fact—not the general metaphysical problem that it was in Platonic Atomism.[32]

To this point we have discussed Russell's multiple relation theory quite independently of his logic. There are connections here, however, which we should at least indicate. One connection has to do with the idea of attributing a special status to logic and our knowledge of it, a status which would distinguish it from all other kinds of (actual or potential) knowledge. What I have been calling constituentless judgements have obvious affinities with what Russell, in *Principles*, thought of as the propositions of logic. In both, all the constituents, at least of the usual kind, have been made into variables and generalized. In each case, the truths are not about any object in particular but are of the most general possible kind. It is also true that our knowledge of constituentless judgements is quite unlike our knowledge of other sorts of judgement; in the case of the former, understanding is enough to guarantee knowledge (and thus truth). In view of these affinities, we

---

[32] This is not to deny that the unity of judgement might be a peculiarly intractable special case of the unity of a fact. If I believe that Socrates precedes Plato, then my act of belief creates a certain unity among me, Socrates, Plato, preceding, and the form of a two-place relational fact. What I believe, however, is that there is a certain unity created by the relation of preceding between Socrates and Plato. Thus it might seem as if a belief-fact (so to speak) has two sources of unity; and that this makes it quite unlike any other kind of fact. See Russell's later discussion in Lecture IV of 'Philosophy of Logical Atomism', titled 'Propositions and facts with more than one verb; Beliefs etc.', Marsh, pp. 216 ff.

might expect Russell to try to exploit the special status of constituent-less judgements to explain what he takes to be the special status of logic. And it is clear that he hoped to do exactly that:

The importance of the understanding of pure form lies in its relation to the self-evidence of logical truth. For since understanding is here a direct relation of the subject to a single object, the possibility of untruth does not arise, as it does when understanding is a multiple relation. (*ThK*, p. 132)

As well as some old points there is something new here. Russell speaks of logical forms as 'logical objects' (e.g. *ThK*, p. 99); he insists that 'acquaintance with logical form, whatever its ultimate analysis may be, is a primitive constituent of experience, and is presupposed, not only in explicit knowledge of logic, but in any understanding of a proposition '(loc. cit.). These ideas are like those of *Principles* in that the crucial notion continues to be direct knowledge of abstract logical objects; unlike the earlier view, however, his 1913 remarks clearly articulate the idea that knowledge of logic is somehow implicit in the understanding of any proposition. The new views are never explored in more detail; Russell postpones discussion to a later stage which was not reached before the book was abandoned. (The passage at p. 132 suggests that the topic will be considered in connection with self-evidence; but it does not arise in the chapter of that name.) Since Russell's new ideas about logic are left in this undeveloped state, it is hard to assess them.

Even though Russell does not develop the idea that logic might be seen as made up of constituentless judgements, we can see that this idea is in conflict with the picture of logic that emerged in the last chapter. According to that picture, logic does not seem to have a unique status; our knowledge of logic, as of any other subject, is taken as a result of the need to systematize the propositions that strike us as obvious. Such a view goes naturally with the idea that logic has a wide compass. Since little turns on the claim that a proposition is a proposition of logic, there seems to be no reason to withhold this title from, say, the axiom of reducibility, or even the axiom of infinity (see Chapter 7, above, pp. 322–5). The present inchoate idea stands in contrast to that view. If the propositions of logic are constituentless judgements then there is presumably a sharp line between the propositions of logic and all other propositions. There is here a tension, to which we shall return in Section 2, in Russell's view of logic. Given the significance of logic and logicism in his thought it is natural for him to be attracted to a view, such as the constituentless judgement view, which would give logic a unique and distinctive status (he finally adopts such a view, it might be said, when he accedes to Wittgenstein's characterization of logic in the *Tractatus*). On the other hand, however, what Russell requires of an account of logic is an account not merely of quantification theory but of logic in the sense required for logicism (the logic of *PM*). So an account of logic must include a justification of type theory. To achieve this result, Russell is also attracted to a broader and looser view of logic—even at the price of the unique philosophical status of that subject. These remarks raise a further issue to which I shall now turn: the relation between type theory and the multiple relation theory of judgement. The idea that propositions are not genuine entities seems to occur to Russell in the course of his attempts to solve the paradoxes. A 1906 manuscript entitled 'The Paradox of the Liar' contains a version of the multiple relation theory. Russell attempts to use that theory to dissolve the Liar, but decides that this attempt will not succeed.[33] The idea that there is a connection between the multiple relation theory of judgement and the solution to the paradoxes recurs, though in muted form, in *PM*. Russell introduces the theory there in the context of the fact that his type theory requires that propositions be of various types, and that the notions of truth and falsehood are correspondingly ambiguous. The multiple relation theory, as we have seen, had the implication that the account of truth given for quantifier-free propositions does not apply directly to propositions containing quantifiers. It can thus be used to explain one of the distinctions required by type theory (Russell does not, however, claim that it is the only possible such explanation, or that the multiple relation theory is required by type theory).

While the multiple relation theory may in one way reinforce type theory, it threatens more directly to subvert it. Russell's logic contains (what appear to be) generalizations about propositions.[34] The use that he makes of these generalizations requires that they be true not merely of all judgements that have been made, or even of all judgements that ever will be made, but of all judgements that *could* be made. This way of putting the point suggests that Russell might be able to avoid propositions by appeal to a notion of possibility; but it is clear that he is not willing to accept any such notion as fundamental.[35] So it seems that Russell's new theory does not allow him to give, by his own

---

[33] Russell Archives, McMaster University, Hamilton, Ontario, fos. 4–6.

[34] Compare Alonzo Church, 'Comparison of Russell's Resolution of the Semantical Antinomies with that of Tarski', *Journal of Symbolic Logic*, 41(1976), 747–60 n. 4. Note that the problem here is not one of generalizing over propositions of various ontological categories; the problem is rather that there are no propositions (even within a single category) over which to generalize.

[35] Thus: 'But the notion of what is "logically possible" is not an ultimate one, and must be reduced to what is *actual* before our analysis can be complete' (*ThK*, p. 111).

standards, a satisfactory account of generalizations about propositions. A second and somewhat more subtle point has to do with the propositional functions. In *PM*, as we have seen, Russell introduces propositional functions by such remarks as these: a propositional function containing the variable x 'becomes a proposition when x is given any fixed determined meaning '(i. 14); a propositional function 'differs from a proposition solely by the fact that it is ambiguous: it contains a variable of which the value is unassigned' (i. 38); 'a [propositional] function is not a well-defined function unless all its values are already well-defined' (i. 39). All of these ways of talking seem to require a realm of propositions—or of possible judgements—which is already complete; none of them will do what is wanted if only those judgements which have been (or will be) made have any kind of ontological status (note that, presumably, only finitely many judgements are actually made, while there must be indenumerably many propositional functions if *PM* is to do what is required of it). A closely connected point is that Russell's account of quantification seems to demand that every propositional function have 'a range, or collection, of values' (i. 15) which is fixed and complete from the outset. Universal quantification can then be understood as asserting that all propositions in the range of values of the given propositional function are true, and so on (see i. 15, 41). Here again the explanation simply will not work if we take seriously the idea that there are no propositions but only acts of judgement.

The considerations presented in the last paragraph certainly weighed with Russell, although he does not articulate them as I have done. In *ThK* he lists and responds to a number of objections to his new view. His response to the last is as follows:

The last of the above objections to our theory, namely that non-mental 'propositions' are, after all, indispensable, belongs to logic, not to theory of knowledge. It is, to my mind, much the most serious. . . . I do not profess to be able to answer all the arguments in favour of 'propositions' in this sense. I can only say that, to me personally, no such entities are visible. . . . Until, then, the arguments in favour of non-mental 'propositions' are presented in some more unanswerable form than any now known to me, I shall continue to reject them, and to believe that the apparent reasons in their favour are fallacious, even if I cannot always detect the fallacy. (*ThK*, p. 155)

This seems to show that Russell has no answer to the problem that (Russellian) logic requires propositions which are independent of our acts of judgement. Clearly, however, the attraction that the multiple relation theory has for Russell is by now so strong that he continues to believe it even though he cannot answer this objection. This situation is particularly odd in view of the fact, emphasized in Chapter 5, above, that in *Principles* the major argument offered in favour of Platonic Atomism, and the accompanying notion of a proposition, was that this philosophy is required for logic and for logicism. The rejection of propositions, even though they appear to be required for logic, suggests that Russell's philosophical views are less directly answerable to the needs of logic in 1913 than they were in 1902. One reason for this may be, paradoxically, that logic is now taken for granted; since it is not threatened, it does not have to be guarded diligently on all fronts. There is also, I suspect, another reason, which is connected with a point made at the start of this chapter. The constraints of psychological realism which Russell now attempts to impose on the notion of acquaintance may conflict with the (real or apparent) requirements of logic. Logic thus no longer serves as a royal road to the metaphysical truth about the world. Logic—or what we take to be our knowledge of logic—is rather one of a number of data which are the evidence for our metaphysical theory, and which that theory must account for if it is to be acceptable.[36] And clearly one may think or come to believe that logic is by no means the most important datum for metaphysics. According to one's point of view this may look like a step towards sanity, or a falling away from purity; in any case it is a considerable shift from Russell's views of a decade before.

The final issue that I shall discuss in this section is Russell's reasons for abandoning the version of the multiple relation theory set out in *ThK*.[37] Russell stopped work on the book early in June 1913. This fact is clear from letters that he wrote to Ottoline Morrell at the time.[38] These letters, and one written three years later,[39] make it clear that the proximate cause of the abandonment of the book was criticism by Wittgenstein, delivered late in May. A letter from Wittgenstein to Russell written in July 1913 at least strongly suggests that the criticism

---

[36] For talk of data and theories see e.g. the first lecture of 'The Philosophy of Logical Atomism' (Marsh, pp. 178–88). What there count as data are facts more obvious to commonsense, or less theoretical, than Russellian logic. Perhaps in these terms it is our ordinary practices of reasoning and (our knowledge of) mathematics which are data, and logic is an explanation—but one which in turn raises further questions, which may require metaphysical answers.

[37] The issues here are very complex, and I do not attempt more than a brief sketch. See David Pears's 'Wittgenstein's Picture Theory and Russell's *Theory of Knowledge*', *Third International Wittgenstein Symposium* (Vienna: Hölder-Pichler-Tempsky), and Stephen Somerville's 'Wittgenstein to Russell (July 1913)...', *Fourth International Wittgenstein Symposium* (Vienna: Hölder-Pichler-Tempsky).

[38] See in particular a letter postmarked 20 June 1913, quoted in Ronald W. Clark, *The Life of Bertrand Russell* (New York: Alfred A. Knopf, 1976), p. 205.

[39] See Russell, *Autobiography* (London: Allen & Unwin, 1968), ii. 57. In the letter printed there Russell described Wittgenstein's criticism dramatically: '[It was] an event of first-rate importance in my life.... I saw he was right, and I saw I could not hope ever again to do fundamental work in philosophy.'

had to do with the theory of judgement. Replying to a letter of Russell's which is lost, Wittgenstein says, 'I am very sorry to hear that my objection to your theory of judgement paralyses you.[40] What was this objection? The basis for an answer to this question is given in two letters from Wittgenstein, one in January and the other in June 1913. If these letters express a single objection, as they appear to, then it is plausible to think that this was the paralysing objection that Wittgenstein made to Russell in May of the same year. In January, Wittgenstein wrote as follows:

every theory of types must be rendered superfluous by a proper theory of symbolism: for instance if I analyse the proposition Socrates is mortal into Socrates, mortality and $(\exists x, y)\phi (x, y)$ I want a theory of types to tell me that 'mortality is Socrates' is nonsensical, because if I treat 'mortality' as a proper name (as I did) there is nothing to prevent me to make [*sic*] the substitution the wrong way round.

And in June:

I can now express my objection to your theory of judgment exactly: I believe it is is obvious that, from the proposition 'A judges that (say) a is in relation R to b', if correctly analysed, the proposition 'aRb, v . $-aRb'$ must follow directly *without the use of any other premiss*. This condition is not fulfilled by your theory. (emphasis in the original)

Various points suggest themselves on the basis of these passages. One is that Wittgenstein may at one time have held a view like the theory of judgement put forward in *ThK*. If so he had clearly abandoned it by January of 1913. More to the present point is the fact that both letters seem to suggest a single objection to that theory, which may be the objection that led Russell to abandon the theory, and the book, in June 1913.[41] Nothing in the theory of judgement makes it impossible to judge nonsense. Yet it is surely a legitimate requirement for such a theory that what can be judged must make sense. The problem here is that the theory describes the various objects of a judgement (e.g. Socrates, mortality, or a, b, and *similarity*) as on a level,

---

[40] The surviving correspondence between Wittgenstein and Russell is published in *Letters to Russell, Moore and Keynes* (Oxford: Blackwell, 1974). The parts of the correspondence that I shall cite are also published in Appendix III to Wittgenstein, *Notebooks 1914–16* (Oxford: Blackwell, 1961 and 1979). I shall cite the letters by date, rather than page of either source.

[41] I say that this *may* have been the crucial objection because this supposition seems to me dubitable: if Russell had this objection from Wittgenstein in writing in Jan. of 1913, why should it have seemed to him so devasting in May 1913? It is of course possible that Russell did not appreciate the point until Wittgenstein explained it to him in person, but it seems also possible that a somewhat different objection emerged in the course of the conversation.

as simply being entities with which we may be acquainted. Given this feature, there seems indeed to be nothing in the theory taken by itself that has the result that I can predicate mortality of Socrates, but cannot predicate Socrates of mortality. And this is fatal. Within Platonic Atomism it was possible to claim that the one sentence corresponded to a proposition, but that the other did not. Even if this could not be explained, still it could be reasonably maintained, and it has the desired result that the impossibility of judgement that mortality is Socrates is a logical or metaphysical matter. The new theory, however, threatens to turn the question into a psychological one. The new theory cannot distinguish the two sentences in the way that the old one did: neither corresponds to a proposition in the old way. The claim that now has to be made is that the one sentence does, and the other does not, correspond to a judgement that can in fact be made. But this looks like a psychological question, and nothing in the theory of judgement gives it any plausibility.

The obvious answer, of course, is to modify the theory so as to build in the necessary distinctions. But there are various objections to this strategy.[42] One objection, emphasized by Somerville (see n. 37, above) is that the suggested modification is tantamount to building the theory of types into the theory of judgement. Any hope that the theory of judgement might be able to support the theory of types is destroyed, for the theory of judgement clearly presupposes type distinctions. A second objection, emphasized by Pears (see n. 37, above) has to do with the nature of acquaintance. The various objects of a judgement (Socrates, mortality, etc.) are objects of acquaintance to the judger. Acquaintance is supposed to be direct and immediate knowledge *of* an object, which need carry with it no knowledge *about* the object (see *Problems*, p. 46). The idea of building type distinctions into the theory of judgement, however, seems to require that the judger have a good deal of knowledge about an object which can figure in his or her judgements. For the judger must, in knowing (being acquainted with) the object, also know what its type is, and this looks like a piece of quite complex knowledge about the object. Indeed it is a piece of knowledge that threatens the whole atomistic structure of Russell's philosophy, for if the type of an object is thought of as its possibilities of combination with other objects then it appears that we could not have the required sort of knowledge of a single object in isolation. What is required is the knowledge of a structure, and of the place within the structure of the given object. It even seems as if the object itself cannot be thought of as

---

[42] I do not say which of these objections would have most weighed with Russell. This is an extremely complex issue which need not concern us here.

independent of its place in the structure; we are in danger of saying that what is required is knowledge of an organic whole. These ideas not only run counter to Russell's earlier thought; they also contradict the view that the only fundamental epistemological relation is that of the direct contact between a person and an individual object which is outside that person's mind. The problem here is that because judgement is an act of the mind, it is not enough to say that objects *have* certain possibilities of combination and lack others; we must also show that these possibilities of combination are necessarily present, in some decisive way, in the act of judging. But there seems to be no way of doing this which is compatible with Russell's fundamental ideas.

Beyond these specific objections there is simply the difficulty of explaining how the various objects of a judgement differ from one another. Something of this difficulty can be seen from Russell's inconclusive discussion in 'The Philosophy of Logical Atomism'. In a passage explicitly critical of his earlier versions of the multiple relation view, Russell stresses the need for observing distinctions among the various objects of judgement, in particular between what he calls the 'verb' and the other objects ('verb' is, as he has already said, a word which he uses both in the linguistic and the non-linguistic senses; see Marsh, p. 217):

There are really two main things that one wants to notice in this matter that I am treating of just now. The *first* is the impossibility of treating the proposition believed as an independent entity . . . the *other* is the impossibility of putting the subordinate verb on a level with its terms as an object of belief. That is a point in which I think that the theory of judgment which I set forth once in print some years ago was a little unduly simple, because I did then treat the object verb as if one could put it as just on object like the terms, as if one could put 'loves' on a level with Desdemona and Cassio as a term for the relation 'believes' (Marsh, p. 226)

Russell's discussion on the previous page, however, makes it clear that while he recognizes the error of treating the 'verb' on a level with the other objects of judgement, he has no idea how to avoid this error. In Russell's mind, at least, the issue is not simply one of type distinctions. It is also an issue of the distinction between 'verbs', which combine or unify objects, and (other) objects which lack this capacity. Let me quote the relevant passage at some length:

Suppose I take . . . 'Othello believes that Desdemona loves Cassio.' There you have a false belief. You have this odd state of affairs that the verb 'loves' occurs in that proposition and seems to occur as relating Desdemona to Cassio whereas in fact it does not do so, but yet it does occur as a verb. I mean that when *A* believes that *B* loves *C*, you have to put a verb in the place where 'loves' occurs. You cannot put a substantive in its place. Therefore it is clear that the subordinate verb (i.e. the verb other than believing) is functioning as a verb, and seems to be relating two terms, but as a matter of fact does not when the judgement happens to be false. That is what constitutes the puzzle about the nature of belief. (Marsh, p. 225)

It is a puzzle which Russell never solved. Its chief significance for our purposes is as suggesting, at least, the sorts of reasons that he may have had in 1913 for abandoning the theory of judgement put forward in *ThK*.

2. Knowledge of the External World

After the completion of *PM* Russell became increasingly interested in philosophical issues having to do with knowledge, especially knowledge of the physical world.[43] This issue is a major theme of *The Problems of Philosophy*. It is also the subject of a number of substantial papers: 'On Matter', written in April and May 1912, heavily revised in October of that year; 'The Relation of Sense-Data to Physics', written in January 1914; 'On Scientific Method in Philosophy', given at Oxford in November 1914; and 'The Ultimate Constituents of Matter', given in Manchester in February 1915. Besides this, the subject was to have formed the second half (or possibly volume ii) of the uncompleted *Theory of Knowledge*. And it did form the main subject of the Lowell Lectures which Russell gave in Boston in March and April 1914, which were published as *Our Knowledge of the External World as a Field for Scientific Method in Philosophy*.[44] As this list suggests, Russell's work on this topic is a large and complicated subject; I shall, however, treat it relatively briefly. My aim is to show the sort of problems that knowledge of the physical world presented for Russell, the constraints within which he attempted to solve these problems, and, especially, the method which evolved in this process. I shall not discuss any of the details of his proposed solutions, though I shall mention some general points.

Russell's concern, from 1910 onwards, with the issue of knowledge, is new in his work. His earlier works show no sign at all of any such

---

[43] In the remainder of this chapter I shall often simply speak of Russell's concern with knowledge, taking it for granted that it is knowledge of the physical or external world which is in question.

[44] 'On Matter', unpublished, in the Russell Archives (dating due to Kenneth Blackwell, and based on Russell's correspondence with Ottoline Morrell); 'The Relation of Sense-Data to Physics', first published in *Scientia* of 1914 and repr. in *Mysticism and Logic* (New York: Longmans, Green & Co., 1918), pp. 145–79; 'On Scientific Method in Philosophy', first published by Clarendon Press, and repr. in *Mysticism and Logic*, pp. 97–124; and 'The Ultimate Constituents of Matter', first published in the *Monist* for 1915, and repr. in *Mysticism and Logic*, pp. 125–44; *Our Knowledge of the External World as a Field for Scientific Method in Philosophy* (London: Allen & Unwin, 1914; rev. ed. 1926).

interest. His concern with this question thus represents a shift not in doctrine but in interests; an issue which he had previously neglected came to seem important to him, and came for a time to be the major focus of his work. Why did this occur? The completion of *PM*, in the autumn of 1909, no doubt left Russell looking for a philosophical task of a somewhat different kind. In the autumn of 1910 Gilbert Murray invited him to write a book on philosophy for the Home University Library. This book—*The Problems of Philosophy*—was to be more or less a book for the general reader. Preparation for the task of writing it may have sent him back to authors and issues which he had not thought about seriously since the 1890s. A book of this sort could hardly be undertaken without discussing the issue of knowledge of the physical world. It may also be that his affair with Ottoline Morrell, and the desire to read philosophy with her, influenced him. She knew something of philosophy, but nothing of mathematics or (post-Fregean) logic; they could hardly discuss *PM*, but Plato and Descartes and Berkeley might be a different matter.[45] It also seems very likely that Russell was influenced by Moore, whose central concerns at this time definitely included problems of perception and of our knowledge of physical objects. This is clear from *Some Main Problems of Philosophy*,[46] which is the text of lectures that Moore gave at Morely College in London in the winter of 1910–11. In the Preface to *Problems* Russell says that he 'derived valuable assistance from unpublished writings of G. E. Moore'. According to Moore's Preface, those writings are the first ten of Moore's twenty lectures, which are largely concerned with issues having to do with perception and with knowledge of physical objects. There is of course a question here about the origin of Moore's interest in these issues. This interest dates back almost as far as Moore's initial rejection of Idealism.[47] Why this should be so, and why Moore's rejection of Idealism led in this direction at once and Russell's did not, are questions which we cannot investigate here.

Whatever may be Russell's reasons for becoming interested in issues of knowledge about the physical world, it is clear that his philosophical views in 1910 give him some reason to take these issues seriously. The notion of acquaintance seems to have been introduced more or less casually by Russell, as a way of avoiding problems about knowledge and understanding (of the abstract as well as of the concrete). There is,

---

[45] See Russell's letter to Ottoline Morrell, 9 June 1911; quoted in Clark, op. cit. n. 38 above, p. 149.

[46] *Some Main Problems of Philosophy* (London: Allen & Unwin, 1953).

[47] See e.g. 'The Refutation of Idealism', *Mind*, NS 12 (1903), 433–54; 'Kant's Idealism', *Proceedings of the Aristotelian Society*, NS 4 (1903–4), 127–40; 'The Nature and Reality of Objects of Perception', *Proceedings of the Aristotelian Society*, NS 6 (1905–6), 68–127.

nevertheless, a serious question whether this notion, and the view of knowledge and understanding that is implicit in it, are adequate. What it is for a view of knowledge to be adequate is of course not fixed in advance of an investigation; still there is a need for investigation if Russell is to be able to defend his presupposition that acquaintance is the only fundamental epistemological relation (we shall later discuss this presupposition explicitly). Acquaintance, as we have seen, came to play an increasingly explicit role in Russell's thought. It would thus be unsurprising if Russell came to think of knowledge of the external world as a field in which his view of knowledge could be fruitfully applied—and indeed as a field to which this view must be applicable if the view is ultimately defensible.

I have spoken above of Russell's view of knowledge and understanding, for both are implicit in his use of the notion of acquaintance. Understanding is the more fundamental, since a statement must be understood before it can be known (whereas most kinds of statements, at least, can be understood by those who do not know them). And it is not only our ability to know statements about the external world which is in question, but also our ability to understand such statements. As we shall see, the two go hand in hand in Russell's treatment—a fact of the greatest importance not only for understanding Russell but also for understanding his successors. Let us begin, however, with the question of understanding.

Understanding, for Russell, is constrained by a principle, which we called the principle of acquaintance: 'Every proposition which we can understand must be composed wholly of constituents with which we are acquainted' (see pp. 244–8, above; this version of the principle is from *Problems*, p. 58). This principle, is, as we saw, explicit in *OD* and at least arguably implicit throughout the earlier phase of Platonic Atomism. Although it is stated (above and elsewhere) in terms of propositions, it survives the change that occurs when Russell adopts the multiple relation view of judgement (the multiple relation view is asserted in *Problems*, where the above statement occurs). The change to the multiple relation view perhaps even strengthens the reasons for this principle, for according to the new view, a judgement clearly requires that the judger be epistemically related to each object of the judgement; given the role that acquaintance plays in Russell's thought, the epistemic relation here can only be that of acquaintance. (Given the Platonic Atomism view of propositions, one might try to argue that one could be acquainted with a proposition without being separately acquainted with each constituent; clearly no such argument is possible given the multiple relation view, for there are no propositions to be acquainted with.) A further point is that the first-person plural in which Russell states the principle of acquaintance is hardly appropriate. Clearly we are not all acquainted with the same entities; perhaps a more accurate, though less elegant, statement of the principle would be, 'Every proposition which a given person can understand must be composed wholly of constituents with which that person is acquainted'. Understanding, for Russell, is at bottom an individual and not a social phenomenon. The significance of this point will emerge later (see pp. 374–5, below).

Russell sees the principle of acquaintance as indubitable. He admits that there are objections to it, and responds:

it must be possible to meet these objections, for it is scarcely conceivable that we can make a judgment or entertain a supposition without knowing what it is that we are judging or supposing about. We must attach *some* meaning to the words we use, if we are to speak significantly and not utter mere noise; and the meaning we attach to our words must be something with which we are acquainted. (*Problems*, p. 58)

In 'Knowledge by Acquaintance and Knowledge by Description',[48] Russell says, 'the truth of this principle must be evident as soon as the principle is understood' (p.160). (These remarks may suggest that Russell takes the principle to be a priori. He does not say this, however, and we should perhaps not be quick to infer it. There is, as was suggested in the last chapter, even reason to doubt whether 'a priori' names any firm and stable category in his thought.)

Why does the principle of acquaintance seem so obvious to Russell? One crucial element in the answer is that for him acquaintance is the only fundamental epistemological relation. All knowledge, if it is to be worthy of the name, must be based upon direct and unmediated contact between the mind and the object which is known. In this unquestioned view of Russell's we can see two doctrines that we stressed throughout Part II of this work. The first is his insistence that knowledge requires direct contact between the mind and what it knows: if there were a medium between them then our knowledge would really be merely of the medium, and not of the object (see also the discussion of 'ideas', pp. 371–2, below). A second doctrine is what we have called Russell's object-based metaphysics. The word 'metaphysics' here is too narrow if taken as excluding epistemology, for the two subjects go hand in hand. In the present case the point is that

---

[48] This paper was given to the Cambridge Moral Sciences Club in the spring of 1910, and later to the Aristotelian Society; it was first published in the *Proceedings of the Aristotelian Society*, NS 11 (1910–11), and repr. in *Mysticism and Logic*, op. cit. n. 41 above, pp. 209–32. A part of it is included in *Problems*, where it forms the bulk of Ch. V; when quoting from this material I shall give references to both works.

knowledge is ultimately always knowledge of an object, rather than being propositional in character; our knowledge of propositions is to be explained in terms which presuppose knowledge of objects.[49]

The idea discussed above, that acquaintance is the only fundamental epistemological relation, makes it natural to reason as follows: since we must have some kind of knowledge of the objects of our judgement (if we are not to utter 'mere noise'), and since all knowledge is based upon acquaintance, therefore we must be acquainted with the objects of our judgements. Spelled out like this, however, it is apparent that the argument contains a lacuna. All knowledge may be *based* on acquaintance, but clearly not all knowledge *is* acquaintance. To make the same point in a slightly different way: while all knowledge may ultimately depend upon acquaintance, it seems clear from the outset that Russell will have to allow for non-ultimate knowledge. For it seems undeniable that we can know things about Julius Caesar, say, although no one now alive is acquainted with him.[50] So we can ask: if there is non-ultimate knowledge, i.e. knowledge which is not acquaintance, why can we not have this kind of knowledge of the objects of our judgements? Why does the knowledge that we have of the objects of our judgements (the constituents of the propositions that we can understand) have to be *acquaintance*, rather than the less direct knowledge that we have of Julius Caesar? Here an issue discussed in Chapter 6 is relevant, namely that according to Russell's post-1905 view all complexity is propositional complexity.[51] Once again, the point is epistemological as well as metaphysical. The knowledge that I have of Julius Caesar is to be analysed or explained by saying that what I know is in

[49] The contrast drawn here is blurred in Russell's earlier work by the view that propositions are themselves objects. In the context of that view, the problem of accounting for propositional knowledge takes the form of the problem of the kind of unity or complexity of a proposition. With the multiple relation theory, the contrast between objects and propositions emerges more clearly.

[50] Perhaps on the *Principles* view it would be possible now to have acquaintance with Julius Caesar, for although he does not exist now he still (timelessly) has being, and thus is presumably a potential object of acquaintance. The doctrine which makes this possible is, as we saw, dropped after 'On Denoting': Russell ceases to believe that entities capable of existing in space and time (concrete objects) may have being even though they do not exist; see pp. 241–3, above. Even in *Principles*, Russell consistently holds that our knowledge of concrete objects is always dependent on sense-experience; and this might suggest that he would resist the suggestion that we understand propositions about Julius Caesar in virtue of non-sensory acquaintance with the man himself.

[51] The same point is expressed in a slightly different way in the later 'Philosophy of Logical Atomism': 'The analysis of apparently complex *things* . . . can be reduced by various means to the analysis of facts which are apparently about those things' (Marsh, p. 192). The shift from talk of propositions to talk of facts is implicit in the shift to the multiple relation theory: it is now facts, not propositions, that have logical forms. The old way of talking, as we have seen, persists in Russell's texts.

fact a number of propositions *about* Julius Caesar. Now it is clear that none of these propositions can contain Julius Caesar, or else the explanation of my indirect knowledge of Julius Caesar will simply presuppose such knowledge.

A similar argument can be made against the supposition that any proposition that I understand contains any entity with which I am not acquainted. The knowledge of such an entity, while of course possible, consists in the knowledge of a number of propositions, which do not contain the entity in question. In judgement, the knowledge that we have of the objects of the judgement must be direct knowledge, for what appears to be indirect knowledge is to be explained by showing that the apparent judgement is not the actual judgement. (I shall allow myself to continue to talk of propositions, as Russell does, in contexts of this sort.) Hence if we have any kind of knowledge of the objects of our judgements, this knowledge is of the fundamental kind— acquaintance. For Russell, then, to admit that someone might fail to be acquainted with one of the objects of his or her judgement would be to say that that person had no epistemic relation at all to that object. But in that case, how could it be an object of that person's judgement? So we must be acquainted with the objects of our judgements, or, to speak loosely, with the constituents of the propositions that we understand. A terminological point is worth making here. In Russell's later usage, according to which propositions are linguistic entities (sentences), we should have to speak of being acquainted not with the constituents of a proposition but with the objects named by the words occurring in the proposition. Given this same usage we should also, more significantly, have to speak of *fully analysed* propositions, i.e. sentences ('propositions', in the linguistic sense) which truly represent the form of the corresponding fact. Only of fully analysed sentences can we say that each constituent is the name of an entity with which we are acquainted (this is, indeed, the decisive criterion which shows that it is a fully analysed sentence). When we speak of judgements, however, or of propositions in the non-linguistic sense (as Russell continues to do, as shorthand, for some years after he adopts the multiple-relation theory), no such qualification is necessary. There is such a thing as a less than fully analysed sentence, but in Russell's uses of 'judgment' there is no such thing as a less than fully analysed judgement (or, therefore, proposition in the non-linguistic sense).[52]

---

[52] A fully analysed sentence is one which accurately reflects the judgement which it expresses. Since the judgement is present to the mind of one who judges, it might be thought that the fully analysed version of any sentence one understands would be immediately accessible. Clearly this is not so on Russell's account; he does not discuss why it is not.

The principle of acquaintance has consequences for an account of our knowledge and understanding of statements about physical objects. Take some mundane statement that I (presumably) understand, and am at least capable of knowing: My coffee-cup is on my desk. What are the objects of the judgement corresponding to this statement? (In older parlance: what are the constituents of the proposition expressed by this statement?) Given the principle of acquaintance, we have a severe constraint on acceptable answers: any such objects must be ones with which I am acquainted.[53] The stringency of this constraint emerges when we see that for Russell it is clear that we are not acquainted with physical objects, such as my coffee-up and my desk. The reasons for this are based on the possibility of sensory illusion. Acquaintance gives complete and indubitable knowledge of its objects. Dubitable knowledge is therefore not knowledge by acquaintance. Yet clearly (notoriously, indeed) the knowledge that we have of physical objects is dubitable: we may be subject to delusions, or hallucinations, or mistaken in some more ordinary way. Russell does not articulate this argument as carefully as one might like, no doubt because the point quickly came to seem obvious to him. It seems to me not entirely straightforward. I shall explain the argument, and the complications that I see.

Acquaintance is a genuine relation: it cannot occur without the existence of both relata, i.e. both the mind and the thing to which it is related. I can, however, be in exactly that state that I am in when I perceive my coffee-cup without there being at that moment a coffee-cup that I perceive, for I may be subject to sensory delusions. Whatever the objects of acquaintance may be, they must be things about which it is, in a sense, impossible to be mistaken. The knowledge which acquaintance gives us, it gives us perfectly and indubitably. Thus Russell, discussing our knowledge of a colour with which we are acquainted:

The particular shade of colour that I am seeing [i.e., in the context, am acquainted with] may have many things said about it—I may say it is brown, that it is rather dark, and so on. But such statements, though they make me know truths *about* the colour, do not make me know the colour itself better than I did before: so far as concerns knowledge of the colour itself, as opposed to knowledge of truths about it, *I know the colour perfectly and completely when I*

---

[53] It follows from this that it is only objects of acquaintance whose existence is presupposed by the truth of what we say. This epistemological point might in turn suggest the metaphysical view that it is only objects of (actual or possible) acquaintance which exist. It could be said that Russell moves towards such a metaphysical view throughout the period discussed in this chapter, but that he does not unequivocally espouse the view.

see it, and no further knowledge of it itself is even theoretically possible. (*Problems*, p. 47; long emphasis added)

Some qualification is necessary here, however. While acquaintance must bring certain knowledge, it does not invariably bring with it knowledge of truths about the objects with which I am acquainted:

Knowledge of things, when it is of the kind we call knowledge by *acquaintance*, is essentially simpler than any knowledge of truths, and logically independent of knowledge of truths, though it would be rash to assume that human beings ever, in fact, have acquaintance with things without at the same time knowing some truth about them. (*Problems*, p. 46)

Now the complication that I see in understanding the application of the argument from illusion to the case of acquaintance is that the possibility of illusion—i.e. the dubitability of a given claim—is a matter of the possibility of being wrong, or making a mistake. But the only way that Russell has of understanding the idea of a mistake is that we make a judgement (believe a proposition) which is false. In other words, in the distinction between acquaintance with an object, on the one hand, and hopeful knowledge of putative truths, on the other hand, the notion of a mistake makes sense only about the latter category. It is only judgements or acts of belief—attempts at attaining truth—that can give rise to mistakes; an act of acquaintance cannot be right or wrong, mistaken or correct: it simply occurs or does not occur.

Let us be clear on the sort of difficulty that these points cause for the application of the argument from illusion. Suppose I judge that I am seeing a round tower when in fact I am looking at a square tower. This cannot be a case of acquaintance with a round tower, for acquaintance demands an object and there is (we are supposing) no round tower before me (and perhaps none in the universe). But why can the situation we are imagining not be a case of acquaintance with a square tower, together with the false judgement that it is round? Similarly for other cases of illusion. Seeing a straight stick in water could be counted as acquaintance with a straight stick, however bent the stick may look; the victim of a mirage could be said to be acquainted with sand and hot currents of rising air. In some cases, a similar tactic may lead us to say that some mistaken perceivers are acquainted with certain drugs in their blood stream, and so on. This last conclusion, in particular, may seem quite unintuitive, but then I am not advocating a notion of acquaintance which would license the various statements above. What I am doing is, rather, suggesting that the non-propositional character of acquaintance—its total separation from knowledge of truths—causes difficulty in what Russell represents as a quite straightforward line of thought. Some further principle or assumption is needed if we are to attain the conclusion that seems so obvious to Russell. Often in Russell's writings it seems that the further assumption is simply a flat denial of the non-propositional character of acquaintance: he often seems to assume that to be acquainted with an object in sense is to have the indubitable (propositional) knowledge that it has the obvious sensory qualities which it does have. So if one believes that a certain stick is bent, say, when it is not, then one is not acquainted with the stick itself; and even if one believes that the stick is straight, this is not indubitable knowledge, so the same conclusion follows.

Whatever exactly the principle involved, it is clear that Russell holds that the objects of (sensory) acquaintance are not physical objects but something more like the appearances of physical objects. Taking as an example the perception of a table, he says:

Although I believe that the table is 'really' of the same colour all over, the parts that reflect the light look much brighter than the other parts, and some parts look white because of reflected light. I know that, if I move, the parts that reflect the light will be different, so that the apparent distribution of colours on the table will change. It follows that if several people are looking at the table at the same moment, no two of them will see exactly the same distribution of colours, because no two see it from exactly the same point of view. (*Problems*, p. 8)

After making similar points about the shape of the table, and about the way it sounds when tapped, he concludes:

Thus it becomes evident that the real table, if there is one, is not the same as what we immediately experience by sight or touch or hearing. The real table, if there is one, is not *immediately* known to us at all, but must be an inference from what is immediately known. (*Problems*, p. 11)

Russell introduces the expression 'sense-data' for 'the things which are immediately known in sensation: such things as colours, sounds, smells, hardnesses, roughnesses, and so on (*Problems*, p. 12).

It is clear that which sense-data I am acquainted with at a given moment will depend not only on the external circumstances—the disposition of the objects around me—but also on the state of my sense-organs, and of my body more generally. To take an obvious example: if I shut my eyes my visual sense-data change drastically. More subtly, but no less clearly, an excess of certain drugs, or a deficiency of certain nutrients, will also lead to an alteration in my sense-data. As Russell says, sense-data thus do not 'exist independently of us' (*Problems*, pp. 12, 13). Again, he says:

Berkeley was right in treating the sense-data which constitute our perception of the tree as more or less subjective, in the sense that they depend upon us as much as upon the tree, and would not exist if the tree were not being perceived. (*Problems*, p. 41)

Now it would be easy to infer from this that Russellian sense-data are mental entities, akin to Berkeleian ideas. If this were correct it would be an utter repudiation of his earlier naïve realism. But it is not correct; and the notion of a sense-datum, although apparently anti-realistic, is in a curious way not a repudiation but an affirmation of naïve realism. I shall explain these points.

Acquaintance, for Russell, continues to play the role which it played from his first rejection of Idealism: it is the point of contact between the mind and what is outside the mind. Thus he says:

The faculty of being acquainted with things other than itself is the main characteristic of a mind. Acquaintance with objects essentially consists in a relation between the mind and something other than the mind; it is this that constitutes the mind's power of knowing things. (*Problems*, p. 42)

The first sentence here makes it clear that Russell continues to hold the anti-idealist view that in its essential characteristics the mind is passive rather than active (reasoning, synthesizing). He also continues to insist on the distinction between the mental act of acquaintance (sensation, in the case of sensory acquaintance) and the object of acquaintance, the sense-datum (see e.g. *Problems*, p. 41). The act is of course mental; but it does not follow that the object is mental. Indeed Russell seems to think that if we bear the distinction steadily in mind it will be evident that the object is not (in general) mental.

If the object of acquaintance is not mental, what of the arguments that the sense-datum depends upon the perceiver? Russell takes this argument to show only that a sense-datum depends upon the perceiver's *body* (sense-organs, etc.).[54] He insists that it does not follow from this that the sense-datum depends upon the perceiver's mind, or that it is mental:

Our previous arguments concerning the colour did not prove it to be mental; they only proved that its existence depends upon the relation of our sense organs to the physical object.... They did not prove that the colour is in the mind of the percipient. (*Problems*, p. 41)

---

[54] Note that both the issue and Russell's response to it are phrased in terms which presuppose such commonplace facts as that people are not disembodied minds, that bodily changes can affect perception, and so on. It is, I think, unclear at what stage such presuppositions are legitimate and at what stage they are not; certainly Russell does not confront this sort of question. The unclarity here has been exploited by Quine, who argues that our talk about knowledge must always presuppose the actual knowledge that we (take ourselves to) have. See especially Ch. 1 of *Word and Object* (Cambridge, Mass.: MIT, 1960).

The point is made more dramatically in a later discussion, with the aid of the idea of *sensibilia*, which are objects exactly like sense-data except that no one is in fact acquainted with them. (Later we shall briefly examine Russell's reasons for introducing entities of this sort.) Russell says:

> I regard sense-data as not mental... There are arguments... for their subjectivity, but these arguments seem to me only to prove *physiological* subjectivity, i.e. causal dependence on the sense-organs, nerves, and brain.... We have not the means of ascertaining how things appear from places not surrounded by brain and nerves and sense-organs; but continuity makes it not unreasonable to suppose that they present some appearance at such places. Any such appearance would be included among *sensibilia*. If—*per impossibile*—there were a complete human body with no mind inside it, all those sensibilia would exist, in relation to that body, which would be sense-data if there were a mind in the body. What the mind adds to *sensibilia* is *merely* awareness: everything else is physical or physiological. (*RSDP*, p. 111)

The most significant point here is in the last sentence: what the mind adds is simply awareness of an object which is independent of the mind.[55] This shows that Russell's notion of acquaintance in 1914 is in the crucial respect the same as his notion of acquaintance in 1903: in each case the notion encapsulates, and ensures, Russell's realism, for it is the point of direct epistemic contact between the mind and what is alien to it.

The best way to think of Russell's notion of a sense-datum is thus as the result of his extreme and naïve realism, subject now to certain epistemological constraints which played no role in the earlier work. When Russell turns his attention to physical objects he finds that we cannot suppose that we are in direct and immediate contact with the objects themselves. Given well-known facts about the fallibility of perception, this supposition, as we have seen, violates the epistemological constraints which he (now) takes to be built into the idea of direct and immediate contact. Russell's response is not to abandon the view that we are in direct and immediate contact with objects outside our minds, but to hold this notion fast and to look for objects which are

---

[55] There is an important assumption here: that while the state of one's body may affect one's perceptions (i.e. act as a medium through which one perceives), the state of one's mind does not. Once articulated this assumption appears dubitable: it might be argued that one's expectations and beliefs, for example, affect one's perception in the same sort of way as does the state of one's body. One line of response here is to deny that we have access to our unmediated perception, claiming rather that there is an unconscious inference from these perceptions to what we usually think of as perceptions. Thus the latter may be affected by the state of one's mind while the former are not. Carnap appeals to the idea of unconscious inference in *Der logische Aufbau der Welt*, and his reasons appear to be of the sort suggested.

suitable to play the role of relata to this relation. This is where the notion of a sense-datum comes from. Epistemological arguments show that the object which the mind confronts is not independent of the body of the perceiver. Indeed a natural way to understand Russell is perhaps as saying that the sense-datum is in the body of the percipient, more specifically in the central nervous system.[56] There must be no medium through which the object is apprehended. Any such medium would run counter to the idea of direct contact between mind and object. The medium is avoided by positing the sense-datum as an entity that exists, so to speak, on the same side of any putative medium as the perceiving mind; our acquaintance with it thus does not take place through any medium but is direct.

The rejection of any medium through which we are acquainted with the world is explicit in a passage in *KAKD* in which Russell discusses 'the view that judgements are composed of something called "ideas", and that it is the "idea" of Julius Caesar that is a constituent of my judgment' when I make a judgement about Julius Caesar. Russell rejects this view, and argues that it has the consequence that real knowledge is impossible, for we know only our ideas:

> The view seems to be that there is some mental existent which may be called the 'idea' of something outside the mind of the person who has the idea, and that, since judgment is a mental event, its constituents must be constituents of the mind of the person judging. But in this view ideas become a veil between us and outside things—we never really, in knowledge, attain to the things we are supposed to be knowing about, but only to the ideas of those things. The relation of mind, idea, and object, on this view, is utterly obscure, and, so far as I can see, nothing discoverable by inspection warrants the intrusion of the idea between the mind and the object. (*KAKD*, p. 160)

To ensure that our contact with objects is immediate, Russell adopts the general strategy of postulating such objects on the perceiving mind's side of any medium through which one might think perception would occur. This strategy is adopted even in the case when the 'medium' is the perceiver's own sense-organs and body. The result is the curious picture which we saw, of the mind existing inside the body and passively surveying the sense-data which the bodily organs and nervous system deliver to it. Only by driving the object of acquaintance inwards, in this way, can Russell maintain the idea that the contact between the mind and (at least some entities in) the world, where it

---

[56] Compare D. F. Pears, *Bertrand Russell and the British Tradition in Philosophy* (London: Fontana, 1967), p. 34.

occurs, is direct and unmediated. The curious nature of Russellian sense-data is thus required by the logic of Russell's conception of direct and immediate contact between the mind and the world. Given the relation of acquaintance, and well-known facts about perception, the objects of sensory acquaintance must have the features of Russellian sense-data. Sense-data are on the one hand independent of the mind, but are on the other hand right next to the mind, so to speak, so that no possibly distorting medium can interfere with the mind's knowledge of them. It is for this reason that Russell says that although in fact no two people can have the same sense-data, there is nothing in the nature of sense-data, or of acquaintance, that makes this idea incoherent. Given the way in which minds are dependent for their sensory perceptions on physical sense-organs, and on the location and condition of these sense-organs, it just happens that no two minds will ever be acquainted with the same (as distinct from very similar) sense-data.[57] Thus Russell can say, 'so far as can be discovered no sensible [sense-datum-like object] is ever a datum to two people at once' (*RSDP*, p. 117; emphasis added); the 'privacy' of sense-data must be a contingent privacy, for it must be compatible with sense-data being independent of the mind which is acquainted with them. In similar spirit, Russell says that there is nothing intrinsic or inevitable in the fact that it is not ordinary physical objects which are the objects of acquaintance.[58] There is nothing intrinsic to the relation of acquaintance that demands that the objects with which we are acquainted must be out of the ordinary, much less that they must be mental. Russell's insistence on our direct contact with those objects, together with facts about perception and the sense-organs, show that we are not in fact acquainted with ordinary objects. Russell's conception of sense-data is as objects which precisely do meet the constraints which ordinary objects cannot meet.

The central fact about Russell's view of knowledge of the physical world is that according to that view the objects of direct knowledge

---

[57] In these remarks I disagree with Sainsbury, who implies that Russellian sense-data are mind-dependent, and says, in particular, that 'Since sense-datum tokens are individuated, in part, by who experiences them, it is a necessary truth that no sense-datum token is experienced by two people' (*Russell* (London: Routledge & Kegan Paul, 1979), p. 40; cf. also p. 35). Sainsbury sees an ambiguity in Russell as between sense-datum types and tokens. Such an ambiguity is perhaps required if we are to reconcile the interpretation of sense-data as mind-dependent with Russell's clear statements to the contrary; in my view, however, it is Sainsbury's interpretation which is at fault, and Russell can be consistently read as talking of tokens, and as holding, as he says, that they are *not* mind-dependent.

[58] 'The Nature of Sense-Data—a Reply to Dr. Dawes Hicks', *Mind* (1913), p. 78.

are not ordinary physical objects but sense-data.[59] Accepting this fact
straightaway poses the questions: given that our *direct* knowledge is
of sense-data, do we have any knowledge at all of ordinary physical
objects? If so, how? Two points must be made immediately about these
questions. First, it is not only the extent and means of our knowledge
that are at issue. The very concept of a physical object, or of matter, as
Russell usually says, is one that now appears to be, at the least, in
need of philosophical discussion. The fact that we are not in direct
contact with ordinary physical objects indicates that it is in question
what meaning words which appear to refer to such objects have, and
how they come to have it. It is of no help here to say that physical
objects are in space, for the objective or physical space that they
occupy is no more an object of acquaintance than is the physical thing
said to be located in it. Each of us is perhaps acquainted with a visual
space and a tactile space, but objective space cannot be identified with
any person's 'private' space of sight or touch (see *Problems*, pp.
29–30).

A second point about the above questions is more complex. The
questions above are phrased in the first-person plural, as Russell
almost always phrases such questions, but, as in the case of the principle of acquaintance, this is not strictly correct. Each of us has direct
access only to his or her own sense-data. Knowledge of the minds of
others and, in particular, of the sense-data of others, comes only via
knowledge of their bodies, which must first be known in the way that
any physical objects are known:

What goes on in the minds of others is known to us through our perception of
their bodies, that is, through the sense-data in us which are associated with
their bodies. (*Problems*, p. 49)

[59] I contrast sense-data with *ordinary* physical objects in order not to rule out the
position that sense-data themselves should be thought of as physical objects of some
extraordinary kind. We saw one version of this position: the idea that sense-data can be
thought of as events in the human body. Later, as we shall see, Russell comes to hold a
more radical version of the thesis that sense-data are physical. He comes to hold, indeed,
that they are the only real physical objects; see *RSDP*, pp. 111 ff. The basis of this view is,
I think, as follows. Russell takes the notion of a physical object as one that has little
coherent pre-theoretical meaning: modern atomic physics, together with his own philosophy, shows that almost everything that we hold to be true of physical objects is not.
So the notion can mean little more than whatever is the ultimate subject-matter of
physics. And in 1914 Russell holds that sense-data are the ultimate subject-matter of
physics, a view that he did not hold when he wrote *Problems*. It is of course quite
compatible with this position to contrast sense-data with ordinary physical objects; in the
article mentioned above Russell makes the contrast by speaking of 'the "thing" of
commonsense or ... the "matter" of physics' (p. 113). I shall sometimes omit the word
'ordinary' where there appears to be no likelihood of confusion.

Even though Russell still speaks of *our* knowledge, the point here is an individualistic one: each of us knows of the existence of others, and of the minds of others, only indirectly, through first knowing his or her own sense-data. Even to put the point like this presupposes that we have already carried out the inference to the bodies, and thus to the minds, of others. The only way that we can avoid this presupposition, and thus the only way that we can pose the problem confronting us before the investigation begins, is by speaking in the first-person singular. The problem that confronts me is to give an account of my knowledge of the physical world, and of other people, beginning with the fact that I have direct sensory knowledge only of my own sense-data.[60] We thus arrive at the position later known as methodological solipsism. The existence of others, and my knowledge of their existence, is not denied; on the contrary, if the account of my knowledge is successful, one of the things which will be accounted for is the fact that I know of the existence of other people (and that I know that they know of my existence, and so on). But it is, in the first instance, *my* knowledge which is to be accounted for, on the basis of the sense-data with which *I* am acquainted. Russell does not stress this point; in *Problems*, at least, he invariably speaks of *our* knowledge. The point is, nevertheless, inescapable, given his position. We shall briefly return to these issues; meantime I shall as convenient adopt Russell's plural idiom.

In *Problems* Russell assumes that a satisfactory explanation of our (apparent) knowledge must show how we know that there are ordinary physical objects which exist quite independent of our sense-data. According to this view, ordinary physical objects are the causes of our sense-data. That sense-data have causes with the right sorts of properties (persistence through time, for example) is a hypothesis recommended on the grounds of simplicity; and also because it is an 'instinctive belief', and as such should be accepted unless we have an argument against it (see *Problems*, e.g. pp. 23–6; cf. also Chapter 7, above, pp. 321–3). Thus Russell speaks of 'our instinctive belief that there *are* objects *corresponding* to our sense-data'. He goes on to say:

Since this belief does not lead to any difficulties, but on the contrary tends to simplify and systematize our account of our experiences, there seems no good reason for rejecting it. We may therefore admit—though with a slight doubt derived from dreams—that the external world does really exist, and is not

---

[60] Here, as elsewhere, it is clear that the results of the epistemological enquiry are given in advance. The question is not so much *whether* we know what we take ourselves to know, but rather *how* we know these things. See n. 54, above, where a connected issue emerges.

wholly dependent for its existence upon our continuing to perceive it. (*Problems*, pp. 24–5)

It is a consequence of this view that physical objects, and physical space, are known only as what cause or, more generally, correspond to our sense-data. Russell takes it that physical entities have 'an intrinsic nature' (*Problems*, p. 34), but that this is something of which we can know nothing. Speaking of physical space, for example, he argues that this must have a certain correspondence with our various private spaces but that we can know nothing more about it than that it has the structural features required to ensure this correspondence: 'we can know nothing of what it is like in itself' (*Problems*, p. 31).[61]

It is now clear why Russell at this period puts so much emphasis on the idea of knowledge by description, and on the distinction between this kind of knowledge and knowledge by acquaintance. As we have seen we can have no knowledge by acquaintance of ordinary physical objects, so if any knowledge of them is to be possible there must be another way of knowing: knowledge by description. Suppose we know, in virtue of some general principle, that if sense-data of such-and-such a kind occur, then they are caused by a physical object. Then if sense-data of the appropriate kind do occur, we know that there is a physical object which causes them. And we may also know that the cause of such-and-such sense-data also has some other property, e.g. it is the cause of so-and-so other sense-data. In this case, according to Russell's analysis of definite descriptions, we know that there is exactly one object which is the cause of such-and-such sense-data, and that this same object is also the cause of so-and-so other sense-data. This sort of knowledge is extremely important. Although in one sense knowledge by acquaintance remains the paradigm of knowledge, almost all the knowledge which we actually express is clearly not of this kind, for we are acquainted with almost none of the entities that we (apparently) talk about. Thus most of our overtly expressed knowledge is some version of knowledge by description.

In *Problems*, and in that part of 'Knowledge by Acquaintance and Knowledge by Description' which overlaps it, Russell puts forward an

---

[61] The knowledge which we have of ordinary physical objects, according to this view of Russell's, is thus like the knowledge that we have of Kantian things-in-themselves according to one popular line of interpretation. Clearly Russell holds this sort of interpretation of Kant, for he makes the comparison himself (*Problems*, p. 86 n.). This point is, however, equally enlightening if put the other way round: philosophers directly or indirectly influenced by these views of Russell's, including of course Russell himself, have been inclined to interpret Kant as if Kantian things-in-themselves were like the physical objects of Russell's *Problems*.

odd twist on the basic idea of knowledge by description. According to these texts, what is described is not (directly) the object that we possess (putative) knowledge about, but rather the proposition that we should like to know—a proposition containing the given object. We cannot directly assert this proposition, for our lack of acquaintance with the object makes that proposition inaccessible to us; what we can do is to describe the proposition, and say that it is true (or that it is false, or dubious, etc.). Thus Russell says:

> It would seem that, when we make a statement about something only known by description, we often intend to make our statement, not in the form involving the description, but about the actual thing described. That is to say, when we say anything about Bismark, we should like, if we could, to make the judgement which Bismark alone can make, namely the one of which he himself is a constituent. In this object we are necessarily defeated, since the actual Bismark is unknown to us. But we know that there is an object B, called Bismark, and that B was an astute diplomatist. We can thus *describe* the proposition we should like to affirm, namely, 'B was an astute diplomatist', where B is the object which was Bismark.... What enables us to communicate in spite of the varying descriptions we employ is that we know there is a true proposition concerning the actual Bismark, and that however we may vary the description (so long as the description is correct) the proposition described is the same. This proposition, which is described and is known to be true, is what interests us; but we are not acquainted with the proposition itself, and do not know *it*, though we know it is true. (*Problems*, pp. 56–7; *KAKD*, p. 158)

Russell's reason for holding this idea is, I suspect, a wish to find a sense in which two people can know, or dispute, the same proposition. This is problematic because no two people will have the same sense-data; no judgement involving sense-data which one person makes can be made by another. Hence, perhaps, the idea that two people may at least be talking about a single proposition, so that their agreement or disagreement is at least over a single claim. Whatever may be the reasons for this view, it seems flatly inconsistent with the multiple relation theory of judgement, for it requires that there be propositions which may be described. Clearly there will not be enough actual judgements to play the role of these propositions. In Russell's example there may well be an actual judgement, for no doubt Bismark occasionally thought of himself as an astute diplomatist (though it is hard to think that whether he carried out such an act of judgement has anything to do with my ability to make such an assertion a hundred years later). In most cases, however, there will be no such judgement; if Russell is right, *no one* has ever been in a position to make a judgement in which an ordinary physical object was one of the objects of judgement. No one has ever been acquainted with such an object, so there is no judgement which has a physical thing among its objects. Perhaps because of its conflict with the multiple relation theory, the idea above is not encountered in any of Russell's later writings. It has the virtue, however, of making it clear that in *Problems* Russell attempts only, so to speak, an epistemological reduction of physical objects, not an ontological reduction. He is concerned to explain how we can know truths (apparently) about physical objects without being acquainted with such objects; he is not concerned to show how there can be such truths without there *being* physical objects. For Russell, at this stage, our apparent knowledge, if it is indeed to be knowledge, requires that there be physical objects, entities altogether independent of our sense-data. This aspect of Russell's view, as we shall see shortly, changes after 1912.

The general picture of knowledge suggested in *Problems* is interesting and influential. Knowledge, according to this view, has two sources. On the one hand there is experience, which gives us acquaintance with sense-data. On the other hand there is our knowledge of the general principles which allow us to infer beyond sense-data. This latter sort of knowledge is a priori, in the sense that it 'is *logically* independent of experience (in the sense that experience cannot prove it)' (*Problems*, p. 74).[62] On the basis of this distinction between two sources of knowledge, Russell adjudicates between the claims of the 'Empiricists' (taking Locke, Berkeley, and Hume as representative) and the 'Rationalists' (Descartes and Leibniz).[63] Each group erred by maintaining that only one of the two factors is involved in knowledge. The

---

[62] If we take this literally then it follows that all knowledge which cannot be known without the help of an a priori principle is itself a priori. Thus if there is an a priori principle that enables us to infer to the existence of physical objects, all our knowledge about physical objects would be a priori. This result would be as unacceptable to Russell as to us; I think we must read him as meaning that knowledge is a priori if it can be neither proved nor disproved by experience. He makes it clear that he takes this to be the status of the principle of induction; see *Problems*, p. 68.

[63] Russell also discusses Kant at some length in *Problems*. He expresses agreement with Kant on some points, but criticizes him, as before, for holding that a priori knowledge is subjective or 'contributed by us' (p. 87). It is worth noting the picture of the history of philosophy which Russell's remarks suggest: Descartes and Leibniz as Rationalists, Locke, Berkeley, and Hume as Empiricists, Kant as attempting to reconcile the claims of both parties. We need only add Spinoza as a somewhat marginal figure to obtain the canon of great modern philosophers that is still standard within the analytic tradition. See Bruce Kuklick, 'Seven Thinkers and how they Grew: Descartes, Leibniz, Spinoza; Locke, Berkeley, Hume; Kant', in Richard Rorty, J. B. Schneewind, and Quentin Skinner (eds.), *Philosophy in History*, (Cambridge: CUP, 1984), pp. 125–39. Except for some remarks about his much later *History of Western Philosophy* (New York: Simon and Schuster, 1945), Kuklick does not mention Russell. Given the importance of *Problems* in the pedagogy of philosophy (apart from its other influence), however, it is hard not to think that this book played a role in the formation of the canon that Kuklick describes.

Empiricists wrongly denied that there is knowledge which cannot be proved from experience. The Rationalists, who are rather less sympathetically treated, wrongly supposed that knowledge of what exists (i.e., presumably, is in space and time) was possible without experience. Russell's view is of course that general principles are necessary for any kind of knowledge that goes beyond bare acquaintance; and that experience is necessary for any knowledge of what exists:

All the knowledge that we can acquire *a priori* concerning existence seems to be hypothetical: it tells us that *if* one thing exists, another must exist.... All knowledge that something exists must in part be dependent on experience. (*Problems*, p. 75)

Russell's general view of knowledge, as outlined above, faces two evident difficulties. The first is one that plays no overt role in Russell's considerations, and I shall not discuss it in any detail. Since I am not acquainted with any ordinary physical object, any knowledge that I have of such an object is knowledge by description. Suppose I have knowledge of this sort of a certain physical object: I know that there is one and only one object which causes such-and-such sense-data, and that this object has some further property. Clearly having this knowledge requires that I make a general judgement about physical objects (i.e. a judgement most correctly expressed by a sentence containing a quantified variable which ranges over physical objects). But how is this possible? As remarked in Section 1 of this chapter, the incompleteness of *Theory of Knowledge* leaves us without a Russellian account of understanding which would apply to general judgements (i.e. those most perspicuously expressed by sentences using quantifiers). Remarks in *PM* suggest, however, that being about to make a judgement of that sort presupposes being able to make a judgement which is an instance of it. If anything of this sort is correct, then there is a grave problem here for Russell's view, for, again, presumably no one has ever made a judgement one of the objects of which is a physical object.[64] This point is, however, not one that I shall pursue.

The second evident difficulty with Russell's view in *Problems*, by contrast, is one that was of great concern to Russell himself, and will require more extended discussion. The difficulty concerns the nature of the general principles by which we can infer from sense-data to ordin-

---

[64] While this difficulty, as remarked, plays no overt role in Russell's thought, it is worth pointing out that he quickly gives up the view for which it is a difficulty. As we shall see, Russell shifts from the idea of inferring physical objects to the idea of constructing them. The new view does not require that we be able to quantify over ordinary physical objects; it thus avoids the difficulty mentioned above. This might suggest that some awareness of that difficulty plays an unacknowledged role in Russell's thought.

ary physical objects. This issue concerns not only our *knowledge* of physical objects but also our ability to form judgements about them, for such judgements require that we know that physical objects stand in certain relations to our sense-data. For example, a judgement purporting to ascribe a certain property to the physical object which causes such-and-such sense-data misses its mark altogether if in fact such-and-such sense-data are not caused by any one thing (in that case any such judgement will be false; but it will not in the ordinary sense even be a false claim *about* a physical object). It need not, of course, be causality, but if we are to be able to form judgements about physical objects there must be some relation which we know physical objects have to sense-data, so that we can pick out a physical object by describing it as the object which has that relation to such-and-such sense-data. In raising the question of general principles connecting physical objects to sense-data, then, we are raising not merely the question of our knowledge of ordinary physical objects, but also the question of our ability to form judgements, true or false, about such objects. Thus the question of knowledge is intertwined with the question of understanding, in a way that is characteristic of Russell's work of this period.[65]

It is clear, then, that if Russell's view is to succeed we must know general principles which connect sense-data with ordinary physical objects. Russell's discussion in *Problems*, however, contains little that is directly relevant. As I have indicated, he mentions in passing both the idea that physical objects are the causes of our sense-data, and the idea that they afford the simplest explanation of the occurrence of sense-data. Each of these ideas might be thought to correspond to a general principle of the required type. In neither case, however, does Russell formulate such a principle, much less discuss its justification. He does discuss the principle of induction, devoting a whole chapter to a formulation of the principle (Chapter VI). Although induction is not exactly a principle of the required sort, for taken by itself it does not connect sense-data with physical objects, it is likely to be one of a number of principles which taken together would form the required connections. Russell's discussion of the justification of the principle, however, is extremely cursory. As we have seen he asserts that the

---

[65] Russell's views might thus be said to have implicit verificationist consequences. These consequences are much less drastic than those drawn by later verificationists, partly because Russell assumes that we are acquainted with abstract objects of various sorts. This assumption is one which later philosophers found easy to question; hence there is a connection at this point between Russell and others whose views appear quite different.

principle is a priori. This characterization is purely negative: it says that the given principle cannot be proved (or disproved) by experience (see p. 378, above). Saying this does not provide a method of justification for general principles. In the chapter of *Problems* on the knowledge of general principles (Chapter VII), Russell mentions the principle of induction in passing, but then switches to the discussion of logical principles. Now it is unclear whether Russell thinks of this as a change of subject, for some of his remarks about logical principles would apply equally to the principle of induction. Thus he takes as examples three of the traditional laws of thought, the law of identity, the law of contradiction, and the law of the excluded middle, and says:

The name 'laws of thought' is . . . misleading, for what is important is not the fact that we think in accordance with these laws, but *the fact that things behave in accordance with them.* (*Problems*, p. 73; my emphasis)

He also explicitly asserts that logical deduction is the source of new knowledge (see *Problems*, p. 79). Russell's general view of knowledge clearly requires an account of our knowledge of general principles, not only those of logic but also such as a principle of induction or of causality. The remarks above suggest that Russell tends to assimilate principles of this latter sort to those of logic.

Russell thus sometimes suggests that a single pattern of justification can be used for various general principles, logical and non-logical alike. There is some indication of how this pattern of justification might run. He suggests at one stage that our various 'instinctive beliefs' can only be evaluated by judging their coherence with other beliefs of the same sort:

All knowledge . . . must be built up upon our instinctive beliefs, and if these are rejected nothing is left. . . .

Philosophy should show us the hierarchy of our instinctive beliefs, begin-ning with those we hold most strongly, and presenting each as much isolated and as free from irrelevant additions as possible. It should take care to show that, in the form in which they are finally set forth, our instinctive beliefs do not clash, but form a harmonious system. There can never be any reason for rejecting one instinctive belief except that it clashes with others; thus, if they are found to harmonize, the whole system becomes worthy of acceptance. (*Problems*, p. 25)

The idea suggested here is, I think, not that the general principles that we need for inferring physical objects from sense-data are themselves instinctive beliefs, but rather that their justification comes from the fact that they have a role in explaining how our instinctive beliefs in physical objects fit into a coherent system. Their justification is that they have a role in a system of knowledge which is, as a whole, consonant with our instinctive beliefs.[66]

Russell's view here is very like that suggested by 'The Regressive Method' (discussed in Chapter 7, pp. 321–3, above, in the context of Russell's view of the justification of logic, and particularly the axiom of reducibility). The discussion of this view in *Problems* (and in the completed portions of *ThK*) is too brief to advance our understanding of it in general. In one respect, however, the view is clarified: it becomes more evident that it is indeed a view of the *justification* of knowledge, rather than merely of the acquisition of belief. This point emerges in Russell's discussion of scepticism. He accepts that '[t]here is no logical impossibility in the supposition that the whole of life is a dream, in which we ourselves create all the objects that come before us' (*Problems*, p. 22). He clearly thinks, however, that whatever justification there *is* for our beliefs is of the sort indicated. He also claims that scepticism is 'a less simple hypothesis, viewed as a means of accounting for the facts of our own life' (loc. cit.); and this, he says, allows us to accept that there is an external world (see *Problems*, pp. 24–5, quoted above, p. 375). This is hardly convincing as a response to scepticism (since it relies on some principle that the simpler hypothesis is the more likely to be true; a principle which is itself in need of justification). It does, however, make it clear that it is indeed justification that is at issue here.

The coherentist view of justification which Russell suggests is thus nowhere presented in worked-out form. It is, nevertheless, clear that this view of the justification of a priori principles is in conflict with Russell's claims that the requisite general principles would be neither proved nor disproved by experience (*Problems*, p. 68), that they would be a priori (p. 74), and that 'All a priori knowledge deals exclusively with the relations of universals' (p. 103). Even more clearly, perhaps, there is a conflict between the view discussed in the last two paragraphs and the inchoate ideas we examined in the first section of this chapter, that our knowledge of logic is somehow based on our acquaintance with constituentless forms. If this latter is the source of our knowledge of logic, and if logic is the paradigm of a priori knowledge, then it is hard to see how we could have a priori knowledge of e.g. the principle of induction, for certainly this principle does not look like a constituentless form. For Russell, the question of our knowledge of general principles, and of the a priori, is, at the least, a point of

---

[66] This may be thought of as a coherentist theory of justification; but note that it is not, and is not accompanied by, a coherentist theory of truth.

unresolved tension. Two distinct views attract him.[67] On the one hand, he is clearly drawn (e.g. in passages from *ThK* discussed above, pp. 353–5) to a view whose consequences are like those of Wittgenstein's view in the *Tractatus*: that the only general principles we know are those of logic; and that these principles are quite unlike any others (so perhaps not genuine principles, or the targets of genuine knowledge, at all). This view, however, leaves vital parts of his logic unjustified (most obviously the axiom of reducibility, but also type theory more generally); it also does not supply any hope of justifying the general principles which are required by his view of knowledge as a whole. On the other hand, he is drawn towards the coherentist view we have just discussed, which is more akin to Quine's.[68] This view, however, gives no special status to logic, and so casts doubt on the significance of logicism. It also, as we shall see, threatens to be useless, since it seems likely that if one set of general principles can be justified because they permit the required inferences then so also can others; this would have the consequence that no one set of such principles is uniquely justified.

Although it takes us, strictly, beyond the scope of this book, it is worth pointing out that Russell became increasingly drawn towards the first of the two views above, no doubt partly under the influence of Wittgenstein. Take, as an example, the principle of induction. Any reconstruction of our knowledge of physics will presumably require some version of the principle of induction or of causality. Wittgenstein's view of logic as consisting of tautologies, in a precise sense, is clearly not applicable to the principle of induction. On such a view the principle cannot be justified in the same sort of way that logic is; to insist that it has its own a priori justification is obviously *ad hoc*. Hence in *OKEW* Russell's attitude towards induction is agnostic; he sees, as clearly as in *Problems*, that it cannot be justified by experience, but he does not know whether it is justified at all: 'I do not say that any such principle is known: I only say that it is required to justify the inferences from experience which empiricists allow, and that it cannot itself be justified empirically' (*OKEW*, p. 46; a later discussion is no less agnos-

---

[67] I do not, of course, mean to assert that these are the only two possible views. Indeed one might think that there was a natural compromise between them: take logic as quite different from everything else, but then be coherentist about everything else. Russell, however, shows no sign of having considered such a compromise, and we can see why it might not have appealed to him. First, it creates a split between what is logic and what is not which leaves the axiom of reducibility, and perhaps type theory as a whole, stranded on the wrong side. Second, given the role of logic as a paradigm, in Russell's mind, of knowledge and truth, the coherentist justification of other general principles would appear weak and *ad hoc* by contrast.

[68] See esp. Ch. 1 of *Word and Object*, op. cit. n. 54 above.

tic; see p. 225). Even Russell's agnosticism here may be more than is justified. Given the view of logic, and of a priori knowledge in general, which he is moving towards under Wittgenstein's influence, it is hard to see how he can avoid Wittgenstein's conclusion that belief in causality or induction is superstition.[69]

Russell returns to the general issue of our knowledge of the physical world in the important unpublished paper 'On Matter', written in April and May of 1912 and presented at University College, Cardiff, and extensively rewritten in the autumn of that year. In this paper we see Russell examining the *Problems* view of knowledge more critically, and working his way towards the understanding of the issues which is manifest in the papers and the book of 1914 and 1915. He begins with something very must like the *Problems* view:

All the knowledge we possess as to what exists rests upon two kinds of foundations: (1) immediate acquaintance, which assures us of the existence of our own thoughts and feelings and sense-data ... (2) general principles, according to which the existence of one thing can be inferred from that of another. (*OM*, fo. 2)

As before, the need for these two sources of knowledge is used to argue against both Empiricists and Rationalists (fos. 2–3). Russell then raises the question whether we can in fact know of the existence of anything other than the objects of acquaintance and, in particular, whether we can know of the existence of matter. This in turn leads to the question: what is matter? As before, it is of no immediate help to invoke the notion of space, for this raises the same issues: the space which matter occupies is not any experienced space (nor is it the mathematician's abstract space); it is, rather, 'that space, whatever it may be, which physical science assumes and uses' (fo. 7). This in turn suggests that the way to think of matter is as 'that which satisfies the hypotheses of physics' (fo. 8). He expands upon this idea in an important passage, which I shall quote at length:

Physics may be studied, to begin with, as a piece of pure mathematics; the space and matter concerned in this study are variables, concerning which certain hypotheses are made; that is to say, they are not definite given entities, but merely anything having certain properties. But if physics is to be *applied*, as for example in calculating the motions of the moon, it must be possible to derive, from the sense-data which we have when we see the moon, some object either inferred or constructed, which satisfies the hypotheses of abstract physics. Sense-data themselves do not satisfy these hypotheses; yet physics enables us to deal with sense-data ... Thus the matter which physics deals

---

[69] See *Tractatus*, 5.1361.

with, though not identical with sense-data, is connected with them and infer-rible from them. Matter, therefore, may be defined as that class of objects, if any, which are inferrible from sense-data and satisfy the hypotheses of phys-ics. The problem then arises whether there is any such class of objects, and, if so, what is their relation to sense-data ...

It is important to realize that, whenever mathematics is *applied* to the real world, there must, if the analysis is pushed far enough, be some substitution of actual particular sense-data for the variables of pure mathematics. (*OM*, fos. 8–9)

Here emerges the crucial idea that a central task of the theory of knowledge is to find an *interpretation* for the formulas of physics.[70] In this task we do not take the statements of physics (or any expressions which might be thought to refer to ordinary physical objects) at their face value, and try to decide whether they are true. Instead we take them as true, at least provisionally and approximately, and then try to find entities of which they are true. The crucial constraint, of course, is that those entities must be objects of acquaintance. The idea of reinter-preting the expressions of physics is the same as the idea that we are trying to give *logical constructions* of the entities of physics. There is a crucial analogy with logicism, which thus emerges as a paradigm of philosophical achievement, a model to follow not merely in logic and the philosophy of mathematics but quite generally. Thus the reduction of arithmetic to logic and the theory of classes can be phrased as the task of finding an interpretation of arithmetic mentioning only classes and the entities and operations of logic. (Equally, the point can be phrased in terms of logical construction: we logically construct arith-metical entities.) Similarly in dealing with our knowledge of the ex-ternal world, the task is one of reinterpreting the non-logical constants of physics in the realm of sense-data or objects which can be inferred from sense-data. Now in one way this attitude towards matter is simply an articulation of what is implicit in *Problems*; if matter is something whose intrinsic nature is unknowable, but about which we have certain structural or relational beliefs, then of course we are free to take as matter anything which satisfies the structural or relational statements that we believe. On the other hand, conceiving of the problem as one of reinterpretation, analogous to the problem of inter-

---

[70] There is an important qualification to be made here. Russell does not see these formulas as uninterpreted in the sense in which logicians today speak of uninterpreted formalisms; his view of logic, and thus of mathematics, does not at this stage shift in that direction. The point is rather that in a formulation of physics we can look on the non-logical (and thus also non-mathematical) constants as uninterpreted—as variables, as Russell says—and attempt to find an interpretation for them which makes the hypoth-eses true.

preting the theory of classes, say, changes Russell's understanding of the issues. In *Problems* it seems that the statements of physics are to be taken more or less at face value, as being about entities with which we are not acquainted; the question is then whether we can infer from sense-data to objects of which these statements are true. But now it is clear that the statements of physics need not be taken at face value, but may be drastically reinterpreted. Just as a simple statement of class theory, saying that a certain entity is a member of a certain class, was reinterpreted as a more complex statement about propositional functions, so statements apparently about physical objects may be reinterpreted. It thus becomes possible that a sufficiently drastic reinterpretation of the statements of physics will show that these statements are in fact true of sense-data themselves, so that no inference from sense-data to objects of a wholly different kind is required.

The possibility which opens up for Russell is thus that of showing that statements which are apparently about matter are in fact more complex statements about sense-data—that is, that matter is a logical construction from sense-data. This possibility gives him another way, besides inference, in which our apparent knowledge of matter can be explained on the basis of our knowledge of sense-data:

there are only two alternatives in regard to matter, if we are to have any reason to believe in matter. (1) It may happen that a piece of matter is a mere logical construction from certain sense-data, for example a combination of visual, tactile, and other sense-data associated together by some experienced relation. (2) It may happen that we know some a priori principle by which, from sense-data, we can infer the existence of entities of a sort with which we are not acquainted, but which we know to possess the kind of properties that physics assigns to matter.... At a later stage we must attempt to decide between these alternatives. (*OM*, fo. 12)

As the discussion continues, however, both of these alternatives seem problematic to Russell. The inductive argument in favour of matter now seems much less strong than it had previously seemed to him (fo. 15). In particular, he finds that principle of simplicity that he had casually relied upon in *Problems* quite fallacious: only if we knew that 'the universe had been created for the purpose of delighting mathematicians' would we have reason to suppose that 'of two hypotheses which both fit the data, the simpler is more likely to be true' (fo. 16). Not surprisingly, therefore, he turns to the idea of the logical construction of matter: 'Would it be possible, without assuming the existence of some non-sensible thing behind the sense-datum, to give to the symbols of dynamics a definition in terms of sense-data alone?' (fo. 18). It is clear that at least at one stage Russell takes himself to have grounds for a negative answer to this question: 'Matter as used in science can apparently not be defined in terms of sense-data alone' (fo. 19).[71] His reasons for this pessimistic view are not entirely clear. He does, however, argue that our sense-data do not determine the truths of physics. More than one hypothesis about the physical world is compatible with the sense-data that occur; so there must be something beyond the sense-data which can distinguish the true hypothesis from the false one:[72]

If, as we have contended, the relation of the world assumed by physics to our own sense-data is many–one, not one–one, then it must be impossible, however we may interpret our symbols, to preserve the truth of physics without assuming anything beyond sense-data. If, on the other hand, the relation had been one–one, it would have been possible to interpret our symbols in such a way that matter should be a purely logical function of sense-data. (*OM*, fo. 18d)[73]

Russell finds a possible way out of this impasse in the idea that 'qualities which are or resemble sense-data, or at least those of sight and touch, exist at times when they are not given in sense' (fo. 30). Thus:

matter will be composed of entities of the nature of sense-data, but not only of those which one observer perceives; it will consist of all the sense-data which all possible observers would perceive in perceiving the same thing. (*OM*, fos. 30–1)

This view, as Russell points out, still requires an a priori principle of inference, from sensed sense-data to unsensed sense-data-like entities. The required principle, he thinks, is 'less precarious' than those required to infer to matter wholly distinct from sense-data; it also has the advantage 'that it avoids an unknowable noumenon, since matter will

---

[71] The status of this remark is unclear. The whole of fo. 19 is scored through, suggesting that it was a page from the first draft which was discarded upon rewriting. The remark quoted, however, is an addition to the original version of fo. 19, where Russell is agnostic about the issue. The most reasonable conclusion is that he wrote fo. 19, in a spirit of agnosticism about the possibility of the logical construction of matter; that sometime before the major rewriting of (presumably) Oct. 1912 he came to think that the proposed logical construction was not possible; and that the whole page was discarded at the later rewriting.

[72] These ideas suggest the issue of the underdetermination of theory by evidence, an issue which has emerged most explicitly, perhaps, in the writings of Quine. (Very roughly the point is that there might be two competing theories of some subject each of which successfully accounted not merely for the evidence available at a given time but for all the evidence, available or not.) In this regard Quine cites Duhem (see e.g. 'Two Dogmas of Empiricism', in *From a Logical Point of View* (New York: Harper & Row, 1963; 1st edn. Cambridge, Mass.: 1953), p. 41; there is no evidence that Russell knew of the latter's work.

[73] This material appears to be from the final rewriting of this paper.

consist entirely of things of the kind with which we are acquainted' (fo. 32). Thus rather than having to infer vertically, from sense-data to entities wholly unlike them, we infer horizontally, from the sense-data that we actually have to other sense-data. The idea of matter as a logical construction from sense-data seemed to be ruled out by the paucity of our actual sense-data, which made them compatible with too many hypotheses about the physical world. The abundance of actual and possible sense-data together will, presumably, overcome this obstacle. The way is thus open for Russell to advance the view that matter is a logical construction not simply from actual sense-data but from these together with similar entities that are not sensed.[74]

The ideas adumbrated in 'On Matter' are more fully developed in Russell's writings of 1914; since these writings take us beyond the scope of this book, I shall simply sketch the salient points, drawing chiefly on 'The Relation of Sense-Data to Physics'. In that paper, Russell introduces the word 'sensibilia' to refer to 'those objects which have the same metaphysical and physical status as sense-data without necessarily being data to any mind' (p. 110). He argues that since 'the existence of a sense-datum is . . . not logically dependent upon that of the subject', there is no a priori reason why sense-data should not continue to exist when no longer perceived, or why sensibilia should not exist though never perceived (pp. 112–3). He insists, more clearly than before, on the virtues of the method of logical construction, rather than inference. In particular he introduces what he calls 'the supreme maxim in scientific philosophising': 'Wherever possible, logical constructions are to be substituted for inferred entities' (*RSDP*, p. 115). The example of the philosophy of mathematics serves as a demonstration of the power of the idea:

Some examples of the substitution of construction for inference in the realm of mathematical philosophy may serve to elucidate the uses of this maxim. Take first the case of irrationals. In old days, irrationals were inferred as the supposed limits of series of rationals which had no rational limit; but the objection to this procedure was that it left the existence of irrationals merely optative, and for this reason the strict standards of the present day no longer tolerate such definition. We now define an irrational as a certain class of ratios, thus constructing it logically by means of ratios, instead of arriving at it by a doubtful inference from them. Take next the case of cardinal number. (*RSDP*, p. 115)

---

[74] One is reminded here of Mill's view of objects as 'permanent possibilities of sensation'; Russell's sensibilia, however, seem quite clearly not to be mere possibilities but to be actual objects, on a par with any others. The notion of possibility is quite generally one with which Russell has little sympathy at this period. See n. 35. above.

Implementing the maxim is thus set out as a task for the scientifically minded philosopher, the task of actually coming up with the logical constructions which would 'exhibit matter wholly in terms of sense-data, and even, we may say, the sense-data of a single person, since the sense-data of others cannot be known without some element of inference'; the ideal is thus 'to establish physics upon a solipsistic basis' (*RSDP*, p. 116). It is clear, however, that Russell is sceptical whether this can be done, and certainly does not think that it can be carried out soon. For the present, at least, he is willing to accept an inferential element in his view of knowledge, but he insists that 'the inferred entities should . . . be similar to those whose existence is given, rather than, like the Kantian *Ding an sich*, something wholly remote from the data which nominally support the inference' (*RSDP*, p. 116). Thus in constructing the external world Russell admits inferences to 'the sense-data of other people' and to 'the "sensibilia" which would appear from places where there happen to be no minds' (*RSDP*, p. 116). It is on this basis that Russell sketches the constructivist programme in the remainder of *RSDP*.

I shall not discuss the details of Russell's sketch of the programme of logical construction of matter or of the physical world. There are more or less evident difficulties both about the appeal to unsensed sensibilia and about the justification of the general principles necessary to the programme.[75] From our point of view, however, the crucial issue is not any particular aspect of the programme of logical construction, but rather the impact that the existence of this programme had on Russell's conception of philosophy—and on the view of the subject by those who were influenced by him. The programme of logical construction of the external world is above all a programme, a task to be carried out. The constraints within which this task is framed—the points which I have been discussing throughout this section—are of course controversial. But even if we assume the correctness of these constraints, the task is not over, but is only beginning: there is work to do. The logical construction must actually be carried out. The work presents itself as a philosophical enterprise which has many of the more desirable aspects of a technical or scientific enterprise: its problems can be split up and tackled piecemeal, until definite and non-controversial results are

---

[75] On the first point, note that if it is natural to assume that there are appearances where there are no sentient beings to have them, it is so only because we presuppose that there are objects which would present various appearances from various points of view. This is a presupposition which is presumably not legitimate at the outset of the constructional enterprise. On the second point, note that however successful constructionalism might be, still the justification of physics—or even of commonsense—will require some general principle of induction or causality.

reached; it can thus be a co-operative endeavour in which one research-
er can build upon the work of another, rather than simply discarding
it and beginning anew; the enterprise is thus progressive and cumulative. Rather than rushing headlong at large problems and achieving
nothing of lasting worth, we now have a method, a technique, which
allows us to tackle them little by little:

Philosophy . . . has made the mistake of attacking the interesting problems at
once, instead of proceeding patiently and slowly, accumulating whatever solid
knowledge was obtainable, and trusting the great problems to the future. Men
of science are not ashamed of what is intrinsically trivial, if its consequences
are likely to be important; the *immediate* outcome of an experiment is hardly
ever interesting on its own account. So in philosophy, it is often desirable to
expend time and care on matters which, judged alone, might seem frivolous.
(*OKEW*, p. 244)

The method or technique which is to have these consequences is of
course logic. The new logic of Frege and, more particularly, of *PM*
established its worth in the reconstruction of mathematics and is now
to be applied to philosophical problems quite generally. Logic is the
method which will at last enable us to establish philosophy on a
scientific basis, just as Galileo used mathematics to effect a similar
revolution in physics:

the study of logic becomes the central study in philosophy: it gives the method
of research in philosophy, just as mathematics gives the method of research in
physics. And as physics . . . became a science through Galileo's fresh observation of facts and subsequent mathematical manipulation, so philosophy, in our
own day, is becoming scientific through the simultaneous acquisition of new
facts and logical methods. . . .
    [Galileo's] few facts sufficed to destroy the whole vast system of supposed
knowledge handed down from Aristotle . . . so in philosophy: though some
have believed one system, and others another, almost all have been of the
opinion that a good deal was known; but all this supposed knowledge in the
traditional systems must be swept away, and a new beginning must be made.
(*OKEW*, pp. 243–4)

Here Russell vividly expresses the idea that there is now a method
which will, at last, enable us to put philosophy on a scientific basis.
Philosophy is to become co-operative and cumulative, as the natural
sciences are; first, however, it must make a complete break with its
past.

The idea that philosophy can break decisively with its past, and make
a new beginning, is not original with Russell. The idea is a recurrent
hope, or temptation, within the subject. It is, however, characteristic of
such attempted revolutions that in trying to escape from the past they

paradoxically demonstrate its power. So it is in the case of Russell's ideal of scientific philosophy. That ideal does not emerge all at once, fully formed. On the contrary, as this book attempts to demonstrate, Russell's philosophy is in crucial ways shaped by earlier views. His relation to these earlier views, some of them his own, is not simple. On some points he takes over assumptions without question; on other points his need to avoid an earlier doctrine is so extreme that it leads him to an opposing dogmatism. In either case, if we are to understand his thought correctly we need to see it not as the product of a new beginning but rather as the outcome of a process of historical evolution. The need for such understanding is suggested by the fact, emphasized in the Introduction to this book, that philosophy does not *refute* previous philosophy in any way that commands general assent.

Russell's ideal of scientific philosophy, with logic as its method, has been immensely important to subsequent philosophy in the English-speaking world. The manner of its influence illustrates previous claims about the difference between philosophy and science. The programme of logical construction has not been influential in the way in which one might think of a research programme in natural science as being influential. It has not resulted in teams of workers setting out to fulfil small parts of the Russellian programme, accepting the task as Russell framed it and proceeding to do the work that would fill this frame; it has not given rise to the philosophical analogue of what Kuhn calls normal science.[76] On the contrary, the influence of the Russellian programme has been of a quite different, and less direct, kind. Some were inspired by it, and produced more or less different programmes, also in the name of scientific philosophy; others opposed it, and attempted to articulate reasons for thinking such a programme to be misguided from the outset. This sort of indirect influence is characteristic of even the most successful philosophy: where it presents itself as programmatic, the primary focus of subsequent attention is not on the task of implementing the programme but rather on the significance and coherence of the programme itself. In spite of the pleas of Russell and other programmatic philosophers, discussion rarely leaves the controversial programmatic level. Rather than accepting the terms of this debate and engaging in it, I have tried in this book to suggest that we can come to terms with the past in another way—not by attempting to refute earlier philosophy but by attempting to understand it and to become aware of its continuing influence on us.

---

[76] See T. S. Kuhn, *The Structure of Scientific Revolutions* (Chicago: Chicago University Press, 1970; 1st edn. 1962).

Bibliography

Arnauld, Antoine *The Art of Thinking*, trans. J. Dickoff and P. James (Indianapolis: Bobbs-Merrill, 1964).
Ayer, A. J. *Bertrand Russell* (London: Fontana, 1972).
—— *Russell and Moore: The Analytical Heritage* (Cambridge, Mass.: Harvard University Press, 1971).
Baillie, Sir James Black *The Origin and Significance of Hegel's Logic* (London: Macmillan, 1901).
Baldwin, James M. (ed.) *Dictionary of Philosophy and Psychology*, 3 vols. (New York: Macmillan, 1901–5).
Beiser, F. C. *The Fate of Reason* (Cambridge, Mass.: Harvard University Press, 1987).
Boring, E. G. *A History of Experimental Psychology*, 2nd edn. (New York: Appleton-Century-Crofts, 1950).
Bos, H. J. M. 'Newton, Leibniz and the Leibnizian Tradition', in *From the Calculus to Set Theory, 1630–1910*, I, ed. Grattan-Guinness (London: Duckworth, 1980), pp. 49–93.
Bosanquet, Bernard *Logic*, 2nd edn. (Oxford: Oxford University Press, 1911).
—— Untitled, unpublished report on G. E. Moore's 'The Metaphysical Basis of Ethics' (1898).
Bradley, F. H. *Appearance and Reality*, 2nd edn. (Oxford: Clarendon Press, 1968; 1st edn. 1893).
—— *Collected Essays* (Oxford: Clarendon Press, 1935).
—— *Essays on Truth and Reality* (Oxford: Clarendon Press, 1914).
—— *Principles of Logic*, 2nd edn. (London: Oxford University Press, 1922; 1st publ. London: Kegan Paul and Trench, 1883).
—— Letter to G. E. Moore, 10 October 1899, unpubl.
Caird, Edward *The Critical Philosophy of Immanuel Kant*, 2 vols., 2nd edn. (Glasgow: James MacLehose & Sons, 1909).
—— *Hegel* (Edinburgh and London: W. Blackwood & Sons, 1883).
—— *Philosophy of Kant* (Glasgow: James MacLehose, 1877).
Carnap Rudolf *The Logical Structure of the World* (Los Angeles: University of California Press, 1967).
Cavell, Stanley *Must We Mean What We Say?* (New York: Scribner, 1969).
Church, Alonzo 'Comparison of Russell's Resolution of the Semantical

Antinomies with that of Tarski', *Journal of Symbolic Logic*, vol. 41 (1976), pp. 747–60.

—— *Introduction to Mathematical Logic* (Princeton: Princeton University Press, 1956).

Clark, Ronald W. *The Life of Bertrand Russell* (New York: Alfred A. Knopf, 1976).

Copi, Irving M. *The Theory of Logical Types* (London: Routledge and Kegan Paul, 1972).

Cresswell, M. J. 'Reality as Experience in F. H. Bradley', *Australasian Journal of Philosophy*, vol. 55 (1977), pp. 169–88.

Dau, Paolo 'Russell's First Theory of Denoting and Quantification', *Notre Dame Journal of Formal Logic*, vol. 27 (1986), pp. 133–66.

Dummett, Michael *Truth and Other Enigmas* (Cambridge, Mass.: Harvard University Press, 1978).

Einstein, Albert *Ideas and Opinions* (London: Souvenir Press, 1973).

Frege, Gottlob *The Basic Laws of Arithmetic*, trans. Montgomery Furth (Berkeley and Los Angeles: University of California Press, 1967).

—— *Collected Papers on Mathematics, Logic, and Philosophy*, trans. Max Black, et al., ed. Brian McGuinness (Oxford: Basil Blackwell, 1984).

—— *The Foundations of Arithmetic*, 2nd edn., trans. J. L. Austin (Oxford: Basil Blackwell, 1953).

—— *Nachgelassene Schriften und Wissenschaftliche Briefwechsel*, vol. 2, eds. G. Gabriel, et. al.(Hamburg: Felix Meiner Verlag, 1976).

—— 'On the Aim of the "Conceptual Notation"', trans. T. W. Bynum, in *Conceptual Notation and Related Articles*, ed. T. W. Bynum (Oxford: Oxford University Press, 1972), pp. 90–100.

—— *Philosophical and Mathematical Correspondence*, trans. Hans Kaal, eds. Gottfried Gabriel, et al. (Oxford: Basil Blackwell, 1980).

—— *Posthumous Writings*, trans. Peter Long and Roger White (with the assistance of Raymond Hargreaves), eds. Hans Hermes, Friedrich Kambartel, and Friedrich Kaulbach (with the assistance of Gottfried Gabriel) (Oxford: Basil Blackwell, 1979).

—— *Translation from the Philosophical Writings of Gottlob Frege*, eds. Peter Geach and Max Black (Oxford: Basil Blackwell, 1952).

Friedman, Michael 'Kant's Theory of Geometry', *Philosophical Review*, vol. 94 (1985), pp. 455–506.

Gödel, Kurt *Collected Works*, *vol. I*, eds. Solomon Feferman, et al. (Oxford: Oxford University Press, 1986).

—— 'Russell's Mathematical Logic', in *The Philosophy of Bertrand Russell*, ed. P. A. Schilpp (Evanston, Ill.: The Library of the Living Philosophers, 1946), pp. 125–53.

Goldfarb, Warren 'Logic in the Twenties: The Nature of the Quantifier', *Journal of Symbolic Logic*, vol. 44, no. 3, pp. 351–68.

—— 'Poincaré Against the Logicists', in *Essays in the History and Philosophy of Mathematics*, eds. W. Aspray and P. Kitcher (Minneapolis: University of Minnesota Press, 1987), pp. 61–81.

—— 'Russell's Reasons for Ramification', in *Rereading Russell: Essays in Bertrand Russell's Metaphysics and Epistemology*, eds. C. Wade Savage and C. Anthony Anderson (Minneapolis: University of Minnesota Press, 1989), pp. 24–40.

Goodman, Nelson *The Structure of Appearance* (Cambridge, Mass.: Harvard University Press, 1951).

Grattan-Guinness, I. *Dear Russell, Dear Jourdain* (New York: Columbia University Press, 1977).

—— (ed.), *From the Calculus to Set Theory, 1630–1910* (London: Duckworth, 1977).

Green, Thomas Hill *Prolegomena to Ethics*, ed. A. C. Bradley (Oxford: Clarendon Press, 1883).

—— *The Works of Thomas Hill Green*, 3 vols., 3rd edn. (London: Longmans, Green & Co., 1894).

Hegel, G. W. F. *Hegel's Logic, Being Part One of the Encyclopedia of the Philosophical Sciences (1830)*, trans. William Wallace (Oxford: Clarendon Press, 1975).

——*Hegel's Phenomenology of Spirit*, trans. A. V. Miller (Oxford: Clarendon Press, 1977).

—— *Hegel's Science of Logic*, trans. A. V. Miller (London: George Allen and Unwin, 1969).

—— *Lectures on the History of Philosophy, vol. III*, trans. E. S. Haldane and Frances H. Simon (London: Routledge and Kegan Paul, 1955).

Hintikka, Jaakko 'On Kant's Notion of Intuition', in *The First Critique*, eds. Terence Penelhum and J. J. MacIntosh (Belmont, Calif.: Wadsworth Publishing Co., 1969), pp. 38–53.

—— *Logic, Language-Games, and Information* (Oxford: Oxford University Press, 1973).

Hume, David *A Treatise of Human Nature*, ed. L. A. Selby-Bigge (Oxford: Clarendon Press, 1888).

Hylton, Peter 'Logic in Russell's Logicism', in *Meaning, Thought and Knowledge*, eds. David Bell and Neil Cooper (Oxford: Blackwell, forthcoming).

—— 'The Nature of the Proposition and the Revolt Against Idealism', in *Philosophy in History*, eds. R. Rorty, J. Schneewind, and Q. Skinner (Cambridge: Cambridge University Press, 1984), pp. 375–97.

—— 'Russell's Substitutional Theory', *Synthese*, vol. 45, pp. 1–31.

Joachim, Harold H. *The Nature of Truth* (Oxford: Oxford University Press, 1906).

Kant, Immanuel, *Critique of Pure Reason*, trans. Norman Kemp Smith (London: Macmillan, 1968; 1st edn. 1929).

Kemp Smith, Norman *A Commentary to Kant's 'Critique of Pure Reason'*, 2nd edn. (London: Macmillan, 1927).

Kline, Morris *Mathematical Thought from Ancient to Modern Times* (Oxford: Oxford University Press, 1972).

Kuhn, Thomas S. *The Essential Tension* (Chicago: Chicago University Press, 1977).

—— *The Structure of Scientific Revolutions*, 2nd edn. (Chicago: Chicago University Press, 1970).

Kuklick, Bruce 'Seven Thinkers and How They Grew: Descartes, Leibniz, Spinoza; Locke, Berkeley, Hume; Kant', in *Philosophy in History*, eds. R. Rorty, J. B. Schneewind, and Q. Skinner, (Cambridge: Cambridge University Press, 1984), pp. 125–39.

Lackey, Douglas 'Russell's 1913 Map of the Mind', in *Midwest Studies in Philosophy, VI*, eds. Peter A. French, *et al.* (Minneapolis: University of Minnesota Press, 1981), pp. 125–42.

Leibniz, Gottfried Wilhelm 'On Newton's Mathematical Principles of Philosophy', trans. Samuel Clarke, in *Leibniz Selections*, ed. Philip P. Wiener (New York: Charles Scribner's Sons, 1951), pp. 216–80.

Levy, Paul *Moore: G. E. Moore and the Cambridge Apostles* (London: Weidenfeld & Nicholson, 1979).

Linsky, Leonard 'Russell's "No-Classes" Theory of Classes', in *On Being and Saying*, ed. J. J. Thomson (Cambridge, Mass.: MIT Press, 1987), pp. 21–39.

—— 'Terms and Propositions in Russell's *Principles of Mathematics*', *Journal of the History of Philosophy*, vol. 26 (1988), pp. 621–42.

Locke, John *An Essay Concerning Human Understanding*, ed. Peter H. Nidditch (Oxford: Oxford University Press, 1975).

McTaggart, John M. E. *A Commentary on Hegel's Logic* (Cambridge: Cambridge University Press, 1910).

——Review of Bradley's *Appearance and Reality*, *Revue de métaphysique et de morale* (1894), pp. 98–112.

—— *Studies in the Hegelian Dialectic*, 2nd edn. (Cambridge: Cambridge University Press, 1921).

Mill, John Stuart *A System of Logic*, 8th edn. (London: Longmans, Green, Reader, and Dyer, 1872).

Moore, G. E. Critical notice on Russell's *An Essay on the Foundations of Geometry*, *Mind* (1899), pp. 397–405.

—— 'Experience and Empiricism', *Proceedings of the Aristotelian Society* (1902–3), pp. 80–95.

—— 'Identity', *Proceedings of the Aristotelian Society* (1901–2), pp. 103–27.

—— 'Kant's Idealism', *Proceedings of the Aristotelian Society*, vol. 4 (1903–4), pp. 127–40.

—— 'Mr. McTaggart's *Studies in Hegelian Cosmology*', *Proceedings of the Aristotelian Society* (1901–2), pp. 177–214.

—— 'Nativism and Empiricism', in *Dictionary of Philosophy and Psychology*, 3 vols., ed. James M. Baldwin (New York: Macmillan, 1901–5), vol. 2, pp. 129–32.

—— 'The Nature and Reality of Objects of Perception', *Proceedings of the Aristotelian Society*, vol. 6. (1905–6), pp. 68–127, repr. in *Philosophical Studies* (London, 1922), pp. 31–96.

—— 'The Nature of Judgement', *Mind* (1898), pp. 176–93.

—— 'Necessity', *Mind* (1900), pp. 289–304.

—— *Philosophical Papers* (London: George Allen and Unwin, 1959).

—— *Principia Ethica* (Cambridge: Cambridge University Press, 1903).

—— 'The Refutation of Idealism', *Mind* (1903), pp. 433–53, repr. in *Philosophical Studies* (London, 1922), pp. 1–30.

—— *Some Main Problems of Philosophy* (London: George Allen and Unwin, 1953).

—— Letter to Desmond MacCarthy (August, 1898), unpubl.

—— Letter to Bertrand Russell (23 October, 1905), unpubl.

—— 'The Metaphysical Basis of Ethics', two versions of same title, both unpublished dissertations (1897 and 1898).

Muirhead, John H. *The Platonic Tradition in Anglo-Saxon Philosophy* (London: George Allen and Unwin, 1931).

Myhill, John 'The Undefinability of the Set of Natural Numbers in the Ramified *Principia*', in *Bertrand Russell's Philosophy*, ed. George Nakhnikian (New York: Barnes & Noble, 1974), pp. 19–27.

Parsons, Charles 'Infinity and Kant's Conception of "The Possibility of Experience"', repr. in *Mathematics in Philosophy* (Ithaca, NY: Cornell University Press, 1983), pp. 95–109.

—— 'Kant's Philosophy of Arithmetic', repr. in *Mathematics in Philosophy* (Ithaca, NY: Cornell University Press, 1983), pp. 110–49.

Passmore, John A. *A Hundred Years of Philosophy* (London: Duckworth, 1957).

Peano, Giuseppe *Selected Works*, trans. and ed. H. C. Kennedy (Toronto: University of Toronto Press, 1973).

Pears, D. F. *Bertrand Russell and the British Tradition in Philosophy* (London: Fontana, 1967).

—— 'Wittgenstein's Picture Theory and Russell's *Theory of Knowledge*', *Third International Wittgenstein Symposium* (Wien: Hölder-Pichler-Tempsky, 1978), pp. 101–7.

Pucelle, Jean *L'Idealisme en Angleterre* (Neuchatel: Editions de la Baconniere, Boudry, 1955).

Putnam, Hilary *Philosophical Papers, vol. 3* (New York: Cambridge University Press, 1983).

Quine, W. V. 'Carnap and Logical Truth', in *The Philosophy of Rudolf Carnap*, ed. P. A. Schilpp (LaSalle, Ill.: Open Court, 1963), pp. 385–406.

—— *From a Logical Point of View* (Cambridge, Mass.: Harvard University Press, 1953).

—— Introduction to Russell's 'Mathematical Logic as Based on the Theory of Types', in *From Frege to Gödel*, ed. Jean van Heijenoort (Cambridge, Mass.: Harvard University Press, 1967), pp. 150–2.

—— 'On Frege's Way Out', ch.XII of *Selected Logic Papers* (New York; Random House, 1966), pp. 146–58.

—— *Ontological Relativity and Other Essays* (New York: Columbia University Press, 1969).

—— *Philosophy of Logic* (Englewood Cliffs: Prentice-Hall Inc., 1970).

—— 'Quantifiers and Propositional Attitudes', in *Ways of Paradox* (New York: Random House, 1966), pp. 183–94.

—— 'Russell's Ontological Development', in *Bertrand Russell, Philosopher of the Century*, ed. R. Schoenman (London: George Allen and Unwin, 1967), pp. 304–14.

—— *Word and Object* (Cambridge, Mass.: MIT Press, 1960).

Ramsey, Frank P. 'The Foundations of Mathematics', *Proceedings of the London Mathematical Society*, series 2, vol. 25, part 5, pp. 338–84, repr. as ch. 1 of *The Foundations of Mathematics*, ed. R. B. Braithwaite (London: Routledge and Kegan Paul, 1931), pp. 1–61.

Richter, Melvin *The Politics of Conscience* (Cambridge, Mass.: Harvard University Press, 1964).

Ricketts, Thomas G. 'Objectivity and Objecthood: Frege's Metaphysics of Judgement', in *Frege Synthesized*, ed. L. Haaparanta, (Dordrecht: Reidel, 1986), pp. 65–95.

Robinson, Abraham *Non-Standard Analysis* (Amsterdam: North Holland Publishing Co., 1966).

Rorty, Richard 'The Historiography of Philosophy: Four Genres', in *Philosophy in History*, eds. Richard Rorty, J. B. Schneewind, and Quentin Skinner (Cambridge: Cambridge University Press, 1984).

—— *Philosophy and the Mirror of Nature* (Princeton: Princeton University Press, 1979).

Russell, Bertrand *Analysis of Matter* (London: Routledge, Kegan Paul, Trench, Trubner & Co., 1927).

—— *The Analysis of Mind* (London: George Allen and Unwin, 1921).

—— *Autobiography* (London: George Allen and Unwin, 1967).

—— *The Collected Papers of Bertrand Russell, vol. 1, Cambridge Essays*,

1888–99, eds. Kenneth Blackwell, *et al.* (London: George Allen and Unwin, 1983).

—— *The Collected Papers of Bertrand Russell, vol. 7, Theory of Knowledge: The 1913 Manuscript*, ed. Elizabeth Ramsden Eames, in collaboration with Kenneth Blackwell (1984).

—— 'De l'infini mathématique', *Mind* (1897), pp. 112–14.

—— *Essays in Analysis*, ed. D. Lackey (New York: Braziller, 1973).

—— *An Essay on the Foundations of Geometry* (Cambridge: Cambridge University Press, 1897).

—— *Introduction to Mathematical Philosophy* (London: George Allen and Unwin, 1919).

—— Letter to G. Frege, 12 December, 1904, in *Philosophical and Mathematical Correspondence*, trans. Hans Kaall, eds. Gottfried Gabriel, *et al.* (Oxford: Basil Blackwell, 1980), pp. 166–70. Orig. in G. Frege, *Wissenschaftlicher Briefwechsel*, eds. G. Gabriel, *et al.* (Hamburg: Meiner, 1976), pp. 250–1.

—— *Logic and Knowledge*, ed. R. Marsh (London: George Allen and Unwin, 1956).

—— *My Philosophical Development* (London: George Allen and Unwin, 1959).

—— *Mysticism and Logic* (New York: Longmans, Green & Co., 1918).

—— 'The Nature of Sense-Data — a Reply to Dr. Dawes Hicks', *Mind* (1913), pp. 76–81.

—— 'On the Relation of Number and Quantity', *Mind* (1897), pp. 326–41.

—— *Our Knowledge of the External World as a Field for Scientific Method in Philosophy*, 2nd edn. (London: George Allen and Unwin, 1926).

—— *Philosophical Essays* (London: George Allen and Unwin, 1966).

—— *Philosophy of Leibniz* (London: George Allen and Unwin, 1937).

—— *Principles of Mathematics* (London: George Allen and Unwin, 1937; first edn., Cambridge: Cambridge University Press, 1903).

—— *The Problems of Philosophy* (London: Oxford University Press, 1912).

—— Letter to G. E. Moore, 25 October 1905, unpubl.

—— 'On Fundamentals', (June 1905) unpubl.

—— 'On Matter', (1912) unpubl.

—— 'On Meaning and Denotation', (1904 or 1905) unpubl.

—— 'The Paradox of the Liar', (1906) unpubl.

—— 'Points About Denoting', (1904 or 1905) unpubl.

Sainsbury, Richard M. *Russell* (London: Routledge and Kegan Paul, 1979).

Schilpp, Paul Arthur (ed.), *The Philosophy of Rudolf Carnap* (LaSalle, Ill.: Open Court, 1963).

—— (ed.), *The Philosophy of G. E. Moore* (Evanston and Chicago: Northwestern University Press, 1942).

——(ed.), *The Philosophy of Bertrand Russell* (Evanston, Ill.: The Library of the Living Philosophers, 1946).

Sklar, Lawrence *Space, Time, and Spacetime* (Berkeley: University of California Press, 1976).

Somerville Stephen T. 'Wittgenstein to Russell (July 1913)', *Fourth International Wittgenstein Symposium*, (Wien: Hölder-Pichler-Tempsky, 1979), pp. 182–8.

de Spinoza, Benedictus *Ethics*, trans. Samuel Shirley, in *The Ethics and Selected Letters*, ed. Seymour Feldman (Indianapolis: Hackett, 1982).

Stace, Walter T. *The Philosophy of Hegel* (London: Macmillan, 1924).

Stirling, James Hutchison *The Secret of Hegel* (London: Longmans, Green, Longmans, Roberts, and Green, 1865).

Strawson, P. F. *Individuals* (London: Methuen, 1959).

Tarski, Alfred *Logic, Semantics and Metamathematics*, trans. J. H. Woodger (Indianapolis: Hackett, 1983).

Taylor, Charles *Hegel* (Cambridge: Cambridge University Press, 1975).

Urmson, J. O. *Philosophical Analysis* (Oxford: Clarendon Press, 1956).

van Heijenoort, Jean 'Logic as Language and Logic as Calculus', *Synthese*, vol. 17, pp. 324–330.

Whitehead, Alfred North Letter to the editor, *Mind* (1926), p. 130.

—— *Process and Reality* (London: Macmillan, 1929).

——and Bertrand Russell, *Principia Mathematica*, 3 vols., 2nd edn. (Cambridge: Cambridge University Press, 1925–7).

Wiener, Norbert 'A Simplification of the Logic of Relations', *Proceedings of the London Mathematical Society*, vol. 17, pp. 387–90, repr. in *From Frege to Gödel*, ed., Jean van Heijenoort (Cambridge, Mass.: Harvard University Press, 1967), pp. 224–7.

Williams, Bernard *Descartes, The Project of Pure Enquiry* (London: Pelican Books, 1978).

Wittgenstein, Ludwig *Notebooks 1914–16* (Oxford: Basil Blackwell, 1961)

—— *Tractatus Logico-Philosophicus* (New York: Harcourt, Brace & Co., 1922).

Wollheim, Richard *F. H. Bradley*, 2nd edn. (Harmondsworth: Penguin Books, 1969).

Index

Page numbers given in bold type indicate entire chapters or sections dedicated to the heading or subheading under which these page numbers appear.

In order to avoid especially long entries, when a heading has an entire chapter or section devoted to it, as, for example, chapter two is devoted to F. H. Bradley, references to page numbers within that chapter or section are for the most part excluded under that entry, except for the bold type designating the entire chapter or section.

Abbreviations used throughout the book, and which are to be found compiled at the beginning of the volume, have largely been adopted in the index. An exception is the abbreviation 'R-Leibniz', which denotes Russell's book *The Philosophy of Leibniz*, reserving 'Leibniz' to denote that philosopher's own work.

Many headings and subheadings have been followed by the name of an author or a book occurring in brackets. This is used to indicate that entries under that heading or subheading pertain specifically to that author or work. In some cases subheadings may be followed by more than one such bracketed entry, as under 'epistemology' one finds a subheading:

logic and: [Moore] 148–9; [R-Leibniz] 161

This indicates a discussion of logic and epistemology in the works of G. E. Moore may be found on pages 148–9, while discussion of the same subject, but in Russell's *The Philosophy of Leibniz*, may be found on page 161.

Dates of birth (and death, where applicable) have been given, except in the case of a few current writers, for whom such dates are not readily available. The names of people who are mentioned only in the Preface have not been included in the index.

and judgement [Russell] 334, 335,
336–8, 341, 343
in Platonic Atomism 108, 111
in relation to objects of knowledge:
[Moore] 127, 129, 133, 134 n., 136, 137;
[Russell] 273–4, 279, 370–5
and truth [Russell] 334, 337–8
which constitutes reality 34–5, 38–9,
41, 110, 111, 137
see also thought; Thought
intensions and extensions 222–3, 290, 297,
314
interpretations
of logical schemata 200–1, 202, 293
of philosophy texts 2, 3–5, 7, 8, 12, 13
introspection
and acquaintance 283, 331
as method of empiricism 23
see also reflection
intuition 87, 166, 177
of the Absolute [Bradley] 69
mathematical 169, 179, 180–1, 183,
184–5, 187, 191, 234
pure [Kant] 76–7
role of Kantian 36, 42, 77, 78, 180
of things in themselves 27, 33 n., 180

James, William (1842–1910) 331 n., 341
Judgement, Belief, and Knowledge: The
Emergence of a Method (Ch. 8)
328–91
judgements 281
abstraction and 132–3, 347
acts vs. objects of 109–11, 127, 137, 337,
338, 343
analytic 42, 74, 75–6, 80, 150
Bradley's attack on empiricist theory
of 59–64
experience comprising [FG] 73, 82
Frege's metaphysics and 223, 274
idealism and 106–7, 109–10, 113, 136,
137, 152, 177–8, 204, 338, 341
incompleteness of [Bradley] 64–8, 106,
134–5
knowledge, experience, and [Moore]
137
logical forms of 343–5, 346–8, 350,
352–4
Moore on Kantian categories in 118
multiple relation theory of 274 n., 282,
328, 331 n., **333–61**, 377–8
necessary and synthetic nature of all
[R-Leibniz] 161
ontological [McTaggart] 93–4
in Platonic Atomism 334–5, 357, 359–60
of perception 348
permutative [ThK] 349–50

presuppositions of: [FG] 82, 91, 94;
[Kant] 74–5, 91, 93, 110, 119, 128–9
propositions and 134–5, 137, 273,
274 n., 334–5, 342–5, 359, 366–7
relational character of: [Bradley] 69, 154;
[Principles] 343; [R-Leibniz] 153
subject–predicate view of: [Bradley]
61–2, 65, 68–9, 154; [Principles] 170;
[R-Leibniz] 154–8, 160, 162–4
synthetic, *see* analytic judgements;
synthesis
unity of 173 n., 177–8, 336, 338, 344–6
Wittgenstein on 358
see also Ideas, Judgement, and Truth;
propositions

Kant, Immanuel (1724–1804)
absolute truth in 115 n.
analytic judgements in 74, 75–6, 150
antinomies of 87, 93, 94, 181, 185, 194
a priori knowledge in 73, 76–7, 80,
191–2, 197 n., 378 n.
being and existence in Moore vs. 131
Bradley compared to 107 n.
experience as judgemental in 73, 136,
137 n., 172 n.
general, *see* formal logic, Kantian
geometry in Russell compared to 77, 81,
191–2
Green compared to 27
Green compares Hegel to 32
Green's reinterpretation of (Ch. 1.2)
31–9, 128–9
Hegel compared to 91, 92–5, 97 n.,
107 n.
Hegel on 78
Kemp Smith on 75
Moore's criticism of 118–20, 125–6
necessity in [Moore] 147 n.
possibility of knowledge in 24, 107 n.,
110, 197 n.
psychologism in 76–8, 106, 109, 110,
153, 378 n.
psychologism of empiricism attributed
by 76, 109
pure and applied geometry in 191 n.
refutation of empiricism and [Moore]
130
reinterpretation of [Green] (Ch. 1.2)
31–9, 128–9
relational judgements in 61 n., 158
Russell influenced by 72, 76, 80, 177
Russell's criticism of mathematics
in 168, 169, 179–82, 191–2
Russell on criticisms of empiricism in 80
space in 73, 76–8, 85, 124, 125, 130, 179,
183, 185

matrix, defined 302
matter 374, 384–9
  geometry and 88–9, 96, 99
  see also 'Ultimate Constituents of Matter,
    The'
meaning
  denotation and 241, 242, 247–8, 249–51,
    253–4, 255, 256, 257–9, 260, 261 n.,
    263, 264 *bis*
  denoting concepts occurring as being
    and as [*OF*] 253–4
  of descriptions 239, 241, 257–9
  Frege's context principle and 223, 274
  logic and 171
  ordinary language and [Moore] 144–5,
    151
  of propositional functions 239 n., 259 n.
  propositions and 263, 273, 341–3
Meinong, Alexius (1853–1920) 240, 242 n.,
    243, 244, 245
'Meinong's Theory of Complexes and
  Assumptions' (1904) 243–4
metageometry, *see* geometry, non-
  Euclidean
metalanguages 202–3, 313, 315, 316 n.
metaphysics
  absolute truth and: [Bradley] 53, 65, 66,
    67–8, 69; [*FG*] 99; [idealism] 107, 108,
    143, 180
  of change 194–5
  logic and 9, 79, 115–16, 168–9, 170, 179,
    205, 280–1, 285, 315, 325, 357
  in Moore 117, 130–43, 149
  in Platonic Atomism 279–81, 282, 337
  paradox of predication generated by
    Russell's 227–8
  presupposition in 300–1, 326–7
  psychologism and 78, 107, 110, 120
  Russell's: [after *OD*] 328, 337–9, 341,
    353, 364–6, 367 n.; [*OD*] 273–5;
    [*Principles*] 172–4, 178–9, 196, 235–6,
    see also metaphysics, theory of
    denoting and Russell's
  Russell's notion of classes shaped by his
    [*Principles*] 222, 223, 225
  theory of denoting and Russell's
    [*Principles*] 208–10, 211, 212, 251–2
  type theory conflicting with
    Russell's 231, 282, 326, 356
Metaphysics, The Underlying [Platonic
  Atomism] (Ch. 4) **117–66**
method
  constructional 281, 283, 328–9, 336,
    379 n., 385–9, 391
  dialectical 67
  empirical 23, 333
  general philosophical 14–15, 166, 167,

  328–9; *see also* 'On Scientific Method
    in Philosophy'
Mill, John Stuart (1806–73) 26 n., 63, 81,
    106, 388
mind, *see* intellect
moments 50–1
monads 162, 163–4
monism 331 n.
  in Bradley 56
  and subject–predicate theory 157–8, 164
Moore, George Edward (1873–1958)
    116 n., (Ch. 4.1) **117–52**
  act vs. object of judgement in 109–11
  being and existence in 160, 161, 171
  Bradley's influence on 44
  on *FG* 80 n., 108–9
  good and evil in 111 n., 144, 145
  holism and 113
  influence on Russell of 117, 152, 153,
    161–2, 166, 168–9, 245, 327, 362
  knowledge and truth in 109, 115
  notions of thought, mind, and
    experience in 108–9
  on 'On Denoting' 255–6
  propositions in 109–10, 114 n., 337
  on psychologism in idealism 107, 108,
    109
  psychology in 245
  realism in 172
  relative truth in 108 n., 112, 115
  rejection of idealism and 65, 105, 107,
    108, 112, 327, 339
  Russell's metaphysics in *Principles*
    compared to 173, 174
Morrell, Ottoline V. A., Lady (1873–1938)
    357, 361 n., 362
motion
  in Bradley 55
  and calculus [*Principles*] 184–5, 191, 194
    bis, 196
  in Moore 139–40
  and purely external relations 184
  in Russell 165
Murray, Gilbert (1866–1957) 362
Myhill, John (1423–87) 307 n.
mysticism 47 n., 59, 68, 69, 71

names
  logical 271 n.
  proper: [Bradley] 63; [*Principles*] 174
  theory of denoting and 272
necessity 144
  of Being 91–2
  in empiricism 42
  in Green 42–3
  in Hegelian dialectic 92
  and holism (Ch. 1.3) **39–43**

Index compiled by Bruce Johnsen